Uneven Roads

To the memories of Hanes, Linda, and Ron – Todd Shaw
To Janet, Chipotle, and Sisko – Louis DeSipio
To my sister Gayle – Dianne Pinderhughes
To my coauthors – Toni-Michelle C. Travis

Uneven Roads

An Introduction to U.S. Racial and Ethnic Politics

Todd Shaw
University of South Carolina, Columbia

Louis DeSipio
University of California, Irvine

Dianne Pinderhughes
University of Notre Dame

Toni-Michelle C. Travis
George Mason University

Los Angeles | London | New Delhi
Singapore | Washington DC

Los Angeles | London | New Delhi
Singapore | Washington DC

FOR INFORMATION:

CQ Press

An Imprint of SAGE Publications, Inc.

2455 Teller Road

Thousand Oaks, California 91320

E-mail: order@sagepub.com

SAGE Publications Ltd.

1 Oliver's Yard

55 City Road

London EC1Y 1SP

United Kingdom

SAGE Publications India Pvt. Ltd.

B 1/I 1 Mohan Cooperative Industrial Area

Mathura Road, New Delhi 110 044

India

SAGE Publications Asia-Pacific Pte. Ltd.

3 Church Street

#10-04 Samsung Hub

Singapore 049483

Acquisitions Editor: Sarah Calabi

Editorial Assistants: Raquel Christie and
                        Davia Grant

Senior Development Editor: Nancy Matuszak

Production Editor: Kelly DeRosa

Copy Editor: Talia Greenberg

Typesetter: C&M Digitals (P) Ltd.

Proofreaders: Kate Macomber Stern and
                Rae-Ann Goodwin

Indexer: Julie Grayson

Cover Designer: Anupama Krishnan

Marketing Manager: Amy Whitaker

Printed in the United States of America

Cataloging-in-publication data is available for this title from the Library of Congress.

ISBN: 978-1-6042-6544-6

This book is printed on acid-free paper.

14 15 16 17 18 10 9 8 7 6 5 4 3 2 1

Brief Table of Contents

Detailed Table of Contents

3 The African American Political Journey, 1500s–1965 69

Preface

Several years ago the road to this textbook began as a series of conversations among the authors and colleagues. Based on our experiences teaching courses on U.S. race and ethnic politics, we concluded it was time for a new introductory undergraduate text on the subject. Throughout our careers, we have researched and taught at large public and private universities in all regions of the country and have gathered a wealth of insights about the varying racial and ethnic identities and experiences of college undergraduates. Informed by real-world events as well as by our research and teaching, we realized that students needed a new framework to make sense of the so-called "postracial" twenty-first century. In addition to political science and public policy studies, students needed to broaden their analytical abilities by obtaining insights from other disciplines that have also studied the politics of race and ethnicity, including history, sociology, anthropology, psychology, and economics, as well as the various branches of ethnic studies.

Uneven Roads: An Introduction to U.S. Race and Ethnic Politics grew out of these realizations. We believe that race was and remains an uneven road in American politics. It has led some groups, specifically non-White groups, through winding and perilous journeys in search of citizenship and the ability to exercise rights and enjoy equal opportunities in U.S. society. We use the metaphor of the road because we borrow from path-dependence assumptions that where a group begins on its journey toward full citizenship and equal opportunity, with all of its attendant barriers and opportunities, strongly determines that group's eventual political location—though groups have widely different advantages and disadvantages in overcoming racial and ethnic barriers. The uneven road metaphor has been carefully integrated throughout the book's examination of the histories and current status of persons who fall within the five major racial/ethnic categories of the U.S. Census: American Indians or Native Americans, Blacks or African Americans, Hispanics or Latinos, Asian Americans, and White Americans.

ORGANIZATION AND APPROACH OF THE BOOK

Our discussion is organized into three parts. In Part I, Introduction, the first chapter defines race and racism and presents a racialization framework that explains *when*, *why*, and *how* race and ethnicity have mattered and still matter, as each of the groups pursues citizenship rights and equality opportunities through the political system. Within this framework, the "when" factors take into account the periods of time and the contexts in which the broader society and polity have racialized a group. The "why" factors consider the structural and ideological reasons and rationales for racialization. And the "how" factors include the mechanisms or processes by which a group has been racialized. These three factors provide the context from which to understand how, at different points in time and under widely varying circumstances, race has served as an absolute, decisive, inconsequential, or insufficient barrier for a group's progress. Through this framework and the chapters that follow, students will become equipped to think critically about the role of race and ethnicity in U.S. politics and society.

Part II, Historical Foundations, examines the political history of each group studied in the book. Students cannot understand the full import of today's racial and ethnic issues without also knowing the roots of these issues and the road each group has traveled to where it stands today. The histories of Native Americans, African Americans, Latinos, Asian Americans, and ethnic Whites are considered up to the Civil Rights Movement of the 1960s and 1970s. We end our histories there because the resultant landmark changes of this era had great legal, political, and social impacts, and dramatically changed the status of each group.

Part III, Policy and Social Issues, builds on the knowledge and experiences discussed in the political history chapters by providing a theoretical overview for explaining group identity. From controversies surrounding the enforcement of voting rights to the usefulness of affirmative action, there remains a large debate in American society about whether race, racism, and ethnicity present consequential barriers for racial and ethnic minorities. We seek to enhance students' understanding of why race and ethnicity continue to matter in contemporary civic engagement. Chapter 7 reviews voting rights and racial and ethnic minorities' continuing challenges in getting equal access to the polls. In Chapter 8, we show how political activism is also ethnically or racially based, and that it too is related to racial or ethnic attitudes and perceptions. Chapter 9 summarizes how minority communities use their numbers and organizations to influence U.S. electoral, civic, and political outcomes, and compares their civic and political activities with those of White communities. Chapter 10 addresses education and criminal justice because these policy domains may offer examples of policies that can provide opportunities versus policies that present barriers on the road to full citizenship.

Immigration policy and immigrant incorporation into U.S. society are detailed in Chapter 11, while Chapter 12 introduces the transnational spaces in which racial and ethnic groups express their interests from dual perspectives—that of the immigrants and that of their U.S.-born descendants. In Chapter 13, our final chapter, we consider how race is interrelated to or intersected by other forms of identity and discrimination, including sexism, classism, and homophobia or heterosexism. Ending our discussion with intersectionality will, we hope, show how many of the issues of today concern people of all backgrounds.

Our analysis will show that America is not yet "postracial"; instead, it is becoming a multi-racial, non-White-majority nation. We believe that there is a pressing need for undergraduates to understand the politics and political behavior of various racial and ethnic groups that currently are numerical minorities in the United States. But this is not a minority politics textbook, per se. Instead, it is a textbook on how race has shaped and continues to influence the political status of *all* racial and ethnic groups. Consequently, because we want students eventually to think about how the United States can genuinely get "beyond race," this text is organized according to four broad principles that make it unique in the small but growing market of textbooks on U.S. racial and ethnic politics. *Uneven Roads* is inclusive of all groups identified by the U.S. Census. It is instructive for students, through its carefully tailored learning aids; it is interdisciplinary, based on its incorporation of scholarship from multiple disciplines; and it is intersectional in its consideration of topics that go beyond race.

FEATURES

The features in *Uneven Roads* were constructed to help guide students' learning and present a layered, comprehensive introduction to U.S. race and ethnic politics. **Chapter Objectives** identify key takeaways. These objectives are reinforced by **Discussion Questions** at the end of each chapter that encourage students to develop their own opinions as they assess these topics in depth.

Crossroad boxes appear primarily in Part II's political history chapters and spotlight key moments in which pivotal decisions were made affecting minority rights and politics. Each of these boxes concludes with critical thinking questions that encourage closer analysis. **Road Sign** boxes highlight moments of historical and contemporary relevance that mark turning points for issues facing minority groups. **Coalitions in Action** boxes in Part III's policy and social issues chapters emphasize contemporary bridge-building measures concerning topics that affect U.S. racial and ethnic groups. Additionally, each chapter contains several **Stop and Think** marginal questions, identified by a stop sign icon, which encourage critical thinking and debate about the narrative and current events. These can be used as discussion-starters in class to generate dialogue and debate.

Key Terms at the end of each chapter call out important concepts and events and are defined in a **Glossary** at the back of the book. **Suggested Resources** at the end of each chapter lead the reader to further research in books, articles, film, and on the Web.

We do not want to leave students with the impression that all of the best solutions to questions of racial inequality or disparity can be found in between the covers of this textbook. The book is merely a point of departure in encouraging them to become examiners of U.S. racial and ethnic politics and to draw their own, informed conclusions. The critical thinking questions posed throughout these pages encourage students to think for themselves and to talk to one another as they further their investigations. In the end, our objective is not to tell students what conclusions to reach about racial and ethnic politics; instead, it is to help inform the differing conclusions they each decide to reach.

ACKNOWLEDGMENTS

We are thankful for the invaluable assistance and support we have received from many people on our journey of writing and publishing *Uneven Roads*. No text of this kind can be produced without the patience and encouragement of good editors. We thank CQ Press for agreeing that there is a great need for a text of this kind and for publishing our manuscript. We owe a special debt of gratitude to college editorial director Charisse Kiino and senior development editor Nancy Matuszak. Charisse first believed in our vision, got the ball rolling, and motivated us to hammer out a proposal that the Press would accept. Nancy soon took it from there and provided persistent encouragement through numerous deadlines (some of which we actually made) and extensive comments on numerous drafts. This all made the text the very good product we believe it is today. We thank editorial assistant Raquel Christie for pitching in to support Nancy at a key moment. We also thank our production editor, Kelly DeRosa, copy editor Talia Greenberg, and the production staff for guiding us through the final stages of getting the text properly copyedited, prepped, and in print. Our thanks also go to marketing communications manager Andrew Lee and the marketing staff for making audiences aware of the book.

Of course, we wrote *Uneven Roads* building on the scholarly insights of colleagues, and there are a number of political scientists and other students of U.S. racial politics who made invaluable contributions to our thinking. We thank Pei-te Lien, professor of political science at the University of California, Santa Barbara, for informing our initial discussion. We also thank the various people who served as CQ Press reviewers and gave us great recommendations for revision: Staci Beavers, California State University–San Marcos; Rodolfo O. de la Garza, Columbia University; Andra Gillespie, Emory University; Thomas Longoria, Texas State University; Clarissa Peterson, DePaw University; Anirudh V. S. Ruhil, Ohio University; Rob Scharr, University of Florida; Alvin Tillery, Rutgers University; and David E. Wilkins, University of Minnesota. We would like to extend special appreciation to David E. Wilkins for providing additional guidance on our Native American chapter.

Our thanks go to the American Political Science Association's Race, Ethnicity, and Politics Division, for accepting our paper for presentation at the 2013 Annual Meeting in Chicago. We also thank Christina Greer and Karthick Ramakrishnan for serving as discussants on the "Conceptualizing Race and Identity" panel, and, along with audience members, giving us excellent feedback. In addition, we are grateful for the insights of other colleagues who commented on parts of the draft or shaped our thinking, including Eduardo Bonilla-Silva, David Covin, Michael Dawson, Rudy de la Garza, John Garcia, Carol Hardy-Fanta, Claire Kim, Christine Sierra, Katherine Tate, Hanes Walton Jr., and David E. Wilkins. DeSipio, Pinderhughes, and Shaw taught together at the University of Illinois at Urbana-Champaign and worked with undergraduates on these topics; a number have since become faculty members in political science and other disciplines across the country and are now working in related research areas. They include Ruth Nicole Brown (University of Illinois at Urbana-Champaign), Lorrie Frasier (University of California at Los Angeles, or UCLA), Mark Sawyer (UCLA), and Dorian Warren (Columbia University).

As the authors, we invested innumerable hours of work into writing this book. But its completion would have been so much more difficult without the expert help that our research assistants provided us in flushing out bibliographies, locating data and figures, and performing several other necessary if sometimes tedious tasks. Our teaching assistants also fundamentally contributed to the process, helping us teach much of the material that would eventually find its way into the book.

Todd Shaw thanks his research assistant Athena King, then a student at the University of South Carolina, who assembled comprehensive bibliographies; and Kristin Bryant who served as a teaching assistant. He also thanks Tamela Grant, Bryan McBride, Eric McDaniel, Alcarcilus (Cil) Shelton-Boodram, and Vaughn Taylor, then students at the University of Illinois at Urbana-Champaign, who provided invaluable help as he taught an Introduction to U.S. Racial and Ethnic Politics course.

Louis DeSipio thanks the teaching assistants who have worked with him over the past decade in the Introduction to U.S. Race and Ethnic Politics class at the University of California, Irvine, and who served as the partial inspiration for this class, including Hannah Alarian, Matt Barreto, Kris Coulter, Archie Delshad, Charlene Engle, Danvy Le, Natalie Masuoka, Steven Nuño, Kim Shella, Chris Stout, and Victoria Wilson.

Dianne Pinderhughes thanks her U.S. Racial and Ethnic Politics teaching assistants at the University of Illinois at Urbana-Champaign, Nathaniel Sigger and Sergio Wals, and her research assistant at the University of Notre Dame, Garren Bryant, for their great assistance.

Toni-Michelle Travis thanks her research assistants at George Mason University, Gabriela Holdcroft and Melissa Clark, for all of their help.

Underlying our insights are numerous conversations we have had with students about the various difficult problems posed by race and ethnicity. We thank the students in our classes related to racial and ethnic politics for giving us feedback on broad concepts, and even some of the draft chapters when we assigned them as required readings.

And last but not least, we thank family and friends for their support during the time we spent away from them either writing or on myriad phone conferences. Todd Shaw thanks his parents, Jim and Ruby Shaw, as well as his other family members for all of their continued love and pride in his work. He gives a special thanks to Seneca Jackson for his loving support, as well his son, Deangelo Smith, for reading and commenting on the introductory chapter to determine whether it was "student friendly." Dianne Pinderhughes thanks her sister, Gayle Pinderhughes, for her patience, as Dianne's work took her way from their family over the years.

About the Authors

Todd Shaw has appointments in both the Department of Political Science and the African American Studies Program at the University of South Carolina. He was appointed the College of Arts and Sciences' Distinguished Associate Professor of Political Science and African American Studies by Dean Mary Anne Fitzpatrick in August 2012. For the 2014–2015 academic year, Shaw is interim director of the African American Studies Program. He researches and teaches in the areas of African American politics, urban politics, and public policy, as well as citizen activism and social movements.

Louis DeSipio is professor of political science and professor of Chicano/Latino studies at the University of California, Irvine (UCI). He also serves as director of the UCI Center for the Study of Democracy. His research interests include ethnic politics, Latino politics, immigration, naturalization, and U.S. electoral politics. He has designed and collected primary survey data that measure Latino political values, attitudes, and behaviors, and has designed and directed ethnographic research projects that added context and nuance to the survey data. DeSipio's research has expanded the boundaries of the race and ethnic politics scholarship to inform other subfields, particularly immigration and immigrant settlement policy studies.

Dianne Pinderhughes is Notre Dame Presidential Faculty Fellow at the University of Notre Dame, where she is professor of political science and of Africana studies. She is author of *Race and Ethnicity in Chicago Politics: A Reexamination of Pluralist Theory*. Pinderhughes's research addresses inequality, with a focus on racial, ethnic, and gender politics and public policy; explores the creation of American civil society institutions in the twentieth century; and analyzes their influence on the formation of voting rights policy. She served as president of the American Political Science Association from 2007 to 2008.

Toni-Michelle C. Travis is associate professor of government and politics at George Mason University and a former fellow of the Rothermere American Institute at the University of Oxford. She has taught and conducted research on urban, racial and ethnic, and Virginia politics, and is coauthor of *The Meaning of Difference*. Travis has served as a political analyst on Virginia and national politics.

CQ Press, an imprint of SAGE, is the leading publisher of books, periodicals, and electronic products on American government and international affairs. CQ Press consistently ranks among the top commercial publishers in terms of quality, as evidenced by the numerous awards its products have won over the years. CQ Press owes its existence to Nelson Poynter, former publisher of the *St. Petersburg Times,* and his wife Henrietta, with whom he founded Congressional Quarterly in 1945. Poynter established CQ with the mission of promoting democracy through education and in 1975 founded the Modern Media Institute, renamed The Poynter Institute for Media Studies after his death. The Poynter Institute (*www.poynter.org*) is a nonprofit organization dedicated to training journalists and media leaders.

In 2008, CQ Press was acquired by SAGE, a leading international publisher of journals, books, and electronic media for academic, educational, and professional markets. Since 1965, SAGE has helped inform and educate a global community of scholars, practitioners, researchers, and students spanning a wide range of subject areas, including business, humanities, social sciences, and science, technology, and medicine. A privately owned corporation, SAGE has offices in Los Angeles, London, New Delhi, and Singapore, in addition to the Washington DC office of CQ Press.

1 Introduction: Race as an Uneven Road

In order to get beyond racism, we must first take account of race.[1]

–U.S. Supreme Court Justice Harry Blackmun

On Tuesday, November 4, 2008, Senator Barack Obama (D-IL) became the first African American to be elected president of the United States. His electoral victory was stunning on many levels. A record sixty-six million people cast ballots for Obama, equating to 53 percent of the vote over his Republican challenger, Senator John McCain of Arizona. Obama garnered 365 electoral votes to McCain's 173. Four years later, nearly the same number of people voted for Obama over his challenger, former Massachusetts governor Mitt Romney. This time Obama received a slightly narrower 51.1 percent of the popular vote and 332 electoral votes. Both election nights were historic because Obama won states in all four regions of the country, including the Southern states of Virginia, Florida, and, in 2008, North Carolina, despite their legacies of Jim Crow racial segregation and Black voter disenfranchisement. But amidst the joyous celebration that erupted among many Americans, perhaps especially among African Americans, there remained one thorny question: Since an African American has been elected and reelected to the U.S. presidency, are race and racism still significant factors in American politics?

One answer is that Martin Luther King Jr.'s dream, in which people are judged by the "content of their character" and not the color of their skin, has finally been realized—race really does not matter anymore. Exit polls in 2008 indicated that candidate Obama garnered a larger share of the White vote (43 percent) than did Democrat John Kerry in 2004; and in 2012, Obama received the same share of the White vote as Kerry in 2004. In general, Obama has averaged a higher percentage of the White vote than many Democratic candidates who have run for president since 1972. The data in Table 1.1 illustrate these voting results, stemming from 1972 to the present.

A minority of voters polled in 2008 (19 percent) reported that race was an important factor in their voting decision; among them, 53 percent supported Obama. If race mattered in the 2008 election, it was because the record turnout of African

Box 1.1 Chapter Objectives

- Working definitions and theories of race, racism, and ethnicity.

- Describe how race developed as a social construct in Europe and the Americas.

- Interpret demographic and economic data on the racial status of various groups.

- Demonstrate the impact of racial and ethnic barriers on social and political equality.

- Summarize the approach and structure of this book.

Malia and Sasha Obama look on as their father, Barack Obama, is inaugurated for the second time as the U.S. president. While taking the oath of office, President Obama places his hand on a Bible held by Michelle Obama, a Bible which was used by President Abraham Lincoln and Dr. Martin Luther King Jr.

Americans, Latinos, and Asian Americans—who respectively gave Obama 95, 67, and 62 percent of their votes—were in part pleased to cast their ballot for another citizen of color. In 2012, with its many charged debates about the candidates' positions, Whites still comprised 66 percent of Obama's electoral coalition, with Blacks being the next largest group at 21 percent. From this perspective, neither election gave any explicit evidence for White anti-Black biases, with a few unimportant exceptions. Because of the diminished effects of race in these two elections, conservative commentators such as Tucker Carlson believe Obama's political successes should spell the end of affirmative action and programs that seek to actively recruit and hire underrepresented minorities into jobs and schools. In their view, such programs unfairly discriminate against Whites in a society that has already become color blind.[2] But have we become color blind, or is there more to be considered before eliminating measures intended to safeguard people against discrimination?

DOES RACE STILL MATTER?

Despite Obama's historic elections, we contend that race still matters in American politics. The central purpose of this book is to explain *when, why,* and *how* race has mattered in shaping the journeys of various racial and ethnic groups in the United States on the road toward full citizenship and equal opportunity. We do not presume, however, that race always has or always does matter.

Many in the news media and the academy debate whether we live in a postracial era of American politics. Many have and should attach enormous significance to Obama—a man born of a White mother from Kansas and a Black father from Kenya—breaking the highest racial barrier in American public office. A close look at Table 1.1, however, reminds us that Obama received a minority of the White vote, just as has every other Democratic candidate since 1972. This fact reinforces the conclusion that students of politics have reached: since the 1970s, there has emerged a persistent racial division in American political party support and identification, with Whites leaning Republican and minorities increasingly leaning Democratic. Obama was elected president because Blacks, Latinos, and Asian Americans

Table 1.1   Presidential Votes by Party Across Racial/Ethnic Groups, 1972-2012

		1972	1976	1980	1984	1988	1992	1996	2000	2004	2008	2012
White	Democrat	31	47	36	35	40	39	43	42	41	43	41
	Republican	67	52	56	64	59	40	46	54	58	55	59
	Independent	–	–	7	–	–	20	9	3	–	–	–
Black	Democrat	82	83	85	90	86	83	84	90	88	95	93
	Republican	18	16	11	9	12	10	12	8	11	4	6
	Independent	–	–	3	–	–	7	4	1	–	–	–
Hispanic	Democrat	63	–	56	62	69	61	72	62	53	67	71
	Republican	35	–	35	37	30	25	21	35	44	31	29
	Independent	–	–	8	–	–	14	6	2	–	–	–
Asian	Democrat	–	–	–	–	–	31	43	54	56	62	73
	Republican	–	–	–	–	–	55	48	41	44	35	27
	Independent	–	–	–	–	–	15	8	4	–	–	–

Source: "Election Results 2008" and "President Exit Polls," *New York Times,* November 5, 2012, http://elections.nytimes.com/2008/results/president/national-exit-polls.html; http://elections.nytimes.com/2012/results/president/exit-polls.

turned out to vote in greater numbers than they have in the past and were more solidly behind one of the candidates than were Whites. In this regard, minorities—most especially Blacks—played a pivotal role in a clear electoral balance of power. Seen from the flipside, close to a whopping 90 percent of Romney's electoral coalition was comprised of White voters.[3]

In a 2008 address to the National Association for the Advancement of Colored People (NAACP), candidate Obama readily concluded: "Just electing me president does not mean our work [against discrimination] is over." Due to what Obama in an earlier Philadelphia address labeled "the legacy of discrimination,"[4] he said that his election to the presidency would not automatically close the gaping racial disparities between Blacks and Whites. Once elected, he made an impassioned address at the NAACP's 100th Anniversary Convention and similarly stated: "I understand there may be a temptation among some to think that discrimination is no longer a problem in 2009. And I believe that overall, there probably has never been less discrimination in America than there is today. I think we can say that. But make no mistake: the pain of discrimination is still felt in America."[5]

Three years later, the fatal shooting of Trayvon Martin, an unarmed Black teenager in Florida, reopened a public debate about race and discrimination in the country. George Zimmerman, a self-identified White Hispanic man, shot Martin while on a neighborhood watch. Zimmerman considered Martin's walk through his residential neighborhood suspicious. The police did not initially charge Zimmerman, allowing that he may have needed to use lethal force. Both the shooting and the early lack of charges against Zimmerman generated outrage in Black communities and others across the country, exacerbated on July 19, 2013, after a jury found Zimmerman not guilty on all charges. President Obama made an informal but remarkable set of comments during a surprise appearance at a weekly press conference: "You know, when Trayvon Martin was first shot, I said that [he] could have been my son. Another way of saying that is Trayvon Martin could have been *me* 35 years ago. And when you think about why, in the African American community at least, there's a lot of pain around what happened here, I think it's important to recognize that the African American community is looking at this issue through a set of experiences and a history that—that doesn't go away." The fact that Obama used the language of "a history that . . . doesn't go away" asserts his belief that, for all of America's racial progress, race and racism still fundamentally matter in shaping the lives, rights, and opportunities of African Americans.[6]

We agree. Race still matters in *substantive* ways, meaning it can still structure opportunities and outcomes that determine the quality of life for U.S. citizens and residents alike—their education, housing, health, and so on. For instance, the criminal justice system has long produced discriminatory outcomes. Currently, African Americans are 13 percent of monthly drug users, but they represent 55 percent of all persons convicted on drug charges and 77 percent of all those who serve prison sentences related to drugs.[7] On the jobs front, Latinos and Blacks routinely have jobless and unemployment rates twice that of their White counterparts. In the summer of 2009, the height of the Great Recession, the jobless rate was 8.7 percent for White workers, while it was 12 percent for Latinos and almost 15 percent for Blacks. The above figures reflect the structural inequalities President Obama implied were the greatest barriers to full opportunity.[8]

Race also still matters in symbolic ways that involve words, ideas, and images that shape public attitudes and opinions. It shapes how persons and groups are influenced by and identify with various racial attitudes and what, if any, racial lens they use to "color" even their nonracial views. This was evident during the Obama administration's nomination of Sonia Sotomayor to the U.S. Supreme Court. She was a highly experienced federal judge and the first Latina and the third woman to be nominated to serve on the High Court. Sotomayor, however, was sharply criticized by several conservatives because she once remarked during a University of California, Berkeley, forum: "I would hope a wise Latina woman with the richness of her experience would more often than not reach a better conclusion [as a judge] than a White male

> U.S. Senate majority leader Harry Reid (D-NV) apologized for a comment he made during the 2008 presidential campaign about how Barack Obama was an attractive candidate to White Americans because he is a "light-skinned" African American with no discernible "Negro dialect." In a society where the color of one's skin still matters, were Reid's words racist or merely factual?

who hasn't lived that life."[9] Former Republican Speaker of the House Newt Gingrich said that her "new racism is no better than old racism."[10] Talk radio personality Rush Limbaugh charged that Obama's nomination of Sotomayor was a form of "reverse racism" akin to nominating Louisiana Ku Klux Klan leader David Duke. In other words, one symbol—*Sotomayor as an admirably hard-working and intelligent Latina*—was being countered by other symbols—*Sotomayor and Obama as racial/ethnic minorities who are racist and trying to unfairly guilt Whites into supporting her nomination*. Some Republican members of the U.S. Senate said that such comments by fellow conservatives went too far.[11]

Do we in the United States really reside in a postracial era where race, ethnicity, or racism play only minor, symbolic, or even no roles in our policy and political deliberations and outcomes? After all, if antiminority racism did not determine the outcome of whether an African American man (Obama) could be elected the forty-fourth U.S. president or if a woman of Puerto Rican descent (Sotomayor) could be confirmed a Supreme Court justice, then conceivably the postracial view is right and race's influence has greatly lessened across many if not all areas of American political life. To intelligently respond to this question, we need to understand when, why, and how race matters based on which groups, if any, it differently advantages and disadvantages.

When, Why, and How Race Matters

This book examines the four major groups that have experienced and endured sustained, multigenerational exclusion from the full rights and privileges of U.S. citizenship or residency based on their race, ethnicity, or ancestry—African Americans, Native Americans, Asian Americans, and Latinos. Each has traveled an uneven road toward U.S. citizenship and opportunity, especially when compared to the experiences of White/European Americans. While we use the metaphor of a road to describe the racial or ethnic status of various groups, this does not mean that groups have always experienced forward progress (some roads double back); and certainly different groups have experienced different rates of progress when they do move forward. This is the reason why we describe U.S. racial and ethnic politics as a series of uneven roads. The legacies of the group experiences we examine continue in today's society, providing a compelling reason for us to understand when, why, and how race and ethnicity matter, which in turn informs us about the contour, construction, and context of the uneven roads traveled.

- **When race and ethnicity matter** provides us with *context,* the time and place—the beginning, middle, or most current leg of its journey—that a group is most likely to experience advantages or disadvantages.
- **Why race and ethnicity matter** permits us to understand society's rationales behind the differing *contours* of various groups' experiences. For instance, think of a smooth decline as representing opportunities and advantages, and a bumpy and steep climb representing barriers and disadvantages.
- **How race and ethnicity matter** allows us to understand the specific *processes* that maintain a group's advantages or disadvantages, as well as government and group norms or laws, actions, and institutions responsible for the construction of a group's road.

Throughout our discussion we assume that the interactions between society, minority communities, and the polity (the broad governing framework within which political and economic interaction occurs)—what we label the factors of racialization—ultimately shape a group's destiny or the outcomes of racialization.

DEFINING RACE, ETHNICITY, AND RACISM

Before we analyze American racial and ethnic politics, we need to define what we mean by the terms *race, ethnicity,* and *racism*. We will present a broad definition of these terms as well as several theories to explain and provide contrasts to our definitions. Although the common U.S. conception is that race and ethnicity are fairly distinct, they have also been used interchangeably.

A Working Definition of Race

In the United States, **race** refers to the macro-categories society assigns and the significance it attaches to perceived groupings of human physical distinction such as skin color, hair color and texture, lips, nose, eyes, and body shapes (called phenotypes), as well as sometimes cultural differences including language, music, dancing, food, and family customs. We presume we can know how to classify individuals based on their appearance, which is a fallacy political scientist Melissa Nobles calls **racial essentialism**[12]—that one's racial essence is obvious from one's outer appearance. In reality, race is much more of an idea or a set of assumptions and practices that are rooted in our history rather than a physical reality that scientists can verify. (Race and science will be discussed later in the chapter.)

The contemporary macro-categories we most often use in the United States include Whites/European Americans, Blacks/African Americans, American Indians, Alaskan Natives, Asian Americans, and Pacific Islanders, though these categories have greatly changed over time.[13] When American society and individuals use these macro-categorizations to make assumptions about a person, a group, or a condition, they racialize this person, group, or condition, and the outcome of this process is **racialization**.[14] For example, if you presume a fellow student you have never met whose last name is pronounced *Lee* must be Chinese (as opposed to being of English or Korean ancestry), you have likely racialized this person.

It is important to understand, however, that race often overlaps with—but is not exactly the same as—racism or racial oppression. By this we mean that merely considering the importance and impact of race is not necessarily an act of racism. How we act on race matters. **Racism** uses race to not merely classify perceived differences but to use these perceptions to rank and order which group(s) enjoy full citizenship rights and opportunities according to where they fall within a system of racial classification. Social anthropologist Audrey Smedley explains that in the United States, Australia, South Africa, and other parts of the world, racism turns race into a hierarchal worldview "that divides the world's peoples into biologically discrete and exclusive groups. The racial worldview holds that these groups are by nature unequal and can be ranked along a gradient of superiority to inferiority."[15] For example, in 1882 California politicians helped to successfully pass a federal law, the Chinese Exclusion Act, that denied Chinese workers (and eventually other Asians) the ability to immigrate into the country. These workers were viewed as alien intruders—part of a Yellow Peril—that threatened the livelihoods of Whites. This use of race to exclude Asian immigrants directly contrasted with the experience of White immigrants at that same time, who were permitted to immigrate more freely. White immigrants were also the only group allowed to become citizens under the Naturalization Act of 1790. Alternately, race can be used to try to remedy past instances of racism, such as when Congress in 1988 issued an apology and paid $20,000 in reparations to Japanese American survivors of World War II internment camps.[16]

The Changing Concept of Race. The concept we in the United States have of race has not remained the same over time and is not perceived the same way everywhere in the world. The modern concept of race as understood in the United States stems from English thinking from the 1700s, emerging at the same time that the American institution of chattel slavery (slaves as a person's permanent property) was formalized. Political scientists Ali Mazrui, Audrey Smedley, and other scholars have speculated that during the evolution of the modern European nation-state and capitalism from the 1400s forward, the English Isles and other Teutonic groups like the Dutch and Germans of Northern Europe were more isolated from the multicultural conquest and exchange of the Mediterranean Sea when compared to Southern Europe. As a result of centuries of closer exposure with people of different skin colors, among other differences, Southern Europe, especially Spain and Portugal, came into more contact with others through exploration, military conflict, conquest, trade, scientific and cultural exchange, and even intermarriage. (See Map 1.1.) Thus Southern Europe more readily had firsthand knowledge of Africans, Arabs, the Chinese, Persians, and many other peoples whose cultures not only differed from theirs, but also, by our modern U.S. standards, differed in their physical features from those of Southern Europeans.[17]

By the mid–eighteenth century, when many European powers competed for colonies in the New World of North America, Latin America, and the Caribbean, many Europeans embraced notions of **racial superiority,** or the belief and practice that their race (however defined) was morally, culturally, and intellectually more advanced than others. This thinking justified their economic interests in the early conquest of Native American lands and the later enslavement

Map 1.1   The Multicultural Mediterranean

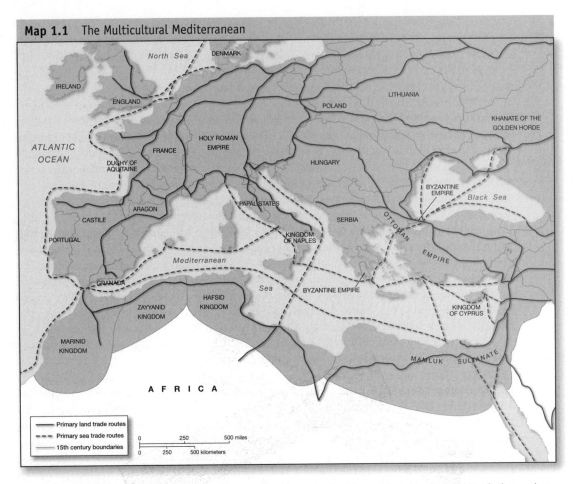

The more extensive trade routes through southern Europe, North Africa, and points East contributed to greater contact in these regions with different races and ethnicities and thus a different perception of human physical differences that was not shared by Europeans farther to the north, where trade routes were not as varied.

of Africans as a workforce. On the one hand, Southern Europeans like the Spanish and Portuguese extended the Old World, Mediterranean belief in cultural or **racial assimilation**—the practice of often intermarrying with "inferior races" but also demanding that they abandon their religions and cultures and assume those of the dominant group. On the other hand, Northern Europeans like the English and Dutch had developed a xenophobia, whereby they feared the outsider who was physically different. They saw racial superiority as a matter of maintaining **racial separation**—very strict lines of division between the dominant and subordinate races; thus they forbade intermarriage and various kinds of contact. The English first developed their notions of racial separation by racializing the Irish during their long conquest of Ireland from the twelfth century forward. They later racialized American Indians for the purposes of taking their lands and Africans for using their labor. (See Chapters 2 through 6.)[18]

Until recently, the U.S. Census treated race as an unchangeable category in which most often respondents were assigned, or selected, one racial identity, such as Black, White, or Asian. In contrast, the former Portuguese colony of Brazil recognizes race as a flexible, fluid color gradient—from *branco* (White) to *preto* (Black)—with a wide range of variants in between. Such differences between North American and Latin American views on race spring from the differing religious, political, and cultural values the former inherited from Northern Europeans and the latter inherited from Southern Europeans as the explorers, conquerors, and slave traders of both justified the subjugation of non-White populations.[19]

Race as a Social Construction

Many biologists, geneticists, and anthropologists have concluded that it is extremely difficult to isolate groupings of biological or genetic similarities that perfectly fit our U.S. Census categorizations of race (and the census admits this). In fact, Stanford University biologist Marcus Feldman concludes that for the purposes of scientific predictions like one's future likelihood of disease, the concept of ancestry groups, or where we geographically come from in the world, is more useful than race. Thus many scholars of race have concluded that race is a social construction; in other words, society believes that these categories are a result of birth, biology, and/or nature, and government acts upon them as though they were natural. Race has much more to do with the political, cultural, and social significance we assign to perceived physical differences than to any actual scientific basis for those differences. Whether or not race is a social construction, political leaders have acted as though it were very real. This is of paramount importance because often political rights and access to economic resources and opportunities have been allocated based on this concept.[20]

True to the U.S. assumptions of race outlined here, Whites, as the dominant group in the United States, have imposed the view that race has obvious boundaries or lines based on physical distinctions, such as Whites have variations of white skin and Blacks have variations of brown skin. The so-called **one-drop rule** emerged during the era of Jim Crow racial segregation in the South (1890–1960) and asserts that anyone with even the smallest traces of African ancestry or "Black blood" clearly falls on the Black side of a color line separating Whites and Blacks. Often, this rule was applied in ways that made racial distinctions appear arbitrary, as evident in the 1896 case of *Plessy v. Ferguson*.[21]

Homer Plessy was a thirty-eight-year-old shoemaker who claimed only one-eighth Black ancestry, what census takers labeled the racial category of "octoroon." For all intents and purposes, Plessy could have passed for or claimed to have been White because he had straight hair and a light complexion. Again, what matters is what Plessy *looked like*. As part of a test case to determine the status of mixed-race people, he boarded an East Louisiana Railroad passenger car in New Orleans reserved only for Whites rather than the train car reserved only for Blacks. The conductor called the police to eject Plessy from the train because he proudly claimed he was "colored" (had some Black blood). Plessy eventually appealed to the U.S. Supreme Court in a challenge of the Jim Crow law requiring the segregation of Whites and Blacks. He lost his appeal as the Court concluded that the Fourteenth Amendment, which requires "equal protection under the law" regardless of color, nonetheless permitted states and businesses to segregate all facilities and communities by race, what the Court termed a **separate but equal doctrine**.

Homer A. Plessy challenged Jim Crow segregation laws in 1896 when he boarded a train car for Whites and declared himself as having "colored" blood. The U.S. Supreme Court ruled against him when it concluded, "Legislation is powerless to eradicate racial instincts, or to abolish distinctions based upon physical differences."

Nearly one hundred years later, in 1982–1983, a woman named Susie Gillory Phipps sued the Louisiana Bureau of Vital Records because it claimed her one-thirty-second "Negro blood" made her Black when she had presumed all of her life that she was White. She lost the case even though a Tulane University professor found that most Whites in Louisiana had at least one-twentieth Black ancestry. Again, the presumption that physical markers indicate one's racial makeup—one's racial essence—is the fallacy of racial essentialism.[22]

Groups such as Hispanics or Latinos are highly diverse populations and, partly because of the complexities of race, class, and color in Latin America and the Caribbean, do not embrace American conceptions of being identified as either Black or White—the so-called Black/White paradigm. According to the U.S. Census, Hispanic or Latino is an ethnic identity and not a racial identity. Thus it is possible from an ethnic standpoint to identify as Cuban, for example, but consider oneself Black, White, or both from a racial standpoint. In fact, demographers Nancy Landale and R. S. Oropeca discovered that Puerto Rican respondents consider their Puerto Rican identity as a race, *la Raza,* when they are on the island of Puerto Rico, but think of their race as White and ethnic identity as Latino/Hispanic when on the American mainland. Sociologist Eduardo Bonilla-Silva speculates that this more fluid, Latin American view of race (grounded in racial assimilation) is influencing our U.S. racial essentialism (grounded in racial separation) and causing U.S. notions of race also to become more fluid. The old Black-White color lines are breaking down to create a new order according to color, class, *and* culture/ethnicity.[23]

A Working Definition of Ethnicity

While race in the United States is most often based on physical distinctions, **ethnicity** is the label we use to organize and distinguish peoples based primarily on their cultural practices or national or regional ancestries. The most common ethnic identities are based on national origins such as Italian American or Mexican American. When the ancestral connection is to a region, rather than to a specific nation, we consider this a **pan-ethnic identity.** The ethnic identity of American Jews is pan-ethnic because it is derived from the Middle Eastern region but has a worldwide dispersion. In contemporary America, Latino and Asian American are pan-ethnic identities because they are derived from the regions of Latin America/the Caribbean and Southeast, South, and East Asia/the Pacific Rim.

Differing systems of racial and ethnic categorization, however, are not mutually exclusive. For instance, if someone in the United States racially identifies as being Black or White based on physical appearance, she may also identify ethnically as Nigerian or Irish. There has often been significant overlap between definitions for race and those for ethnicity. For reasons we will discuss later, the U.S. government understands Hispanic/Latino to be an ethnic identity while it considers White, Black, Asian, American, and Native American to be racial identities. Consequently, the U.S. Census asks everyone to identify her race and whether or not she is Hispanic.[24]

Sociologists Stephen Cornell and Douglass Hartmann note that ethnicity has a long history as a concept dating back to the Greek word *ethnos,* meaning "nation," and assuming particular meaning among the fifteenth-century English whereby an "ethnic" was someone who was neither Christian nor Jew—in short, a heathen. But famed German sociologist Max Weber classically defined ethnic groups as "those human groups that entertain a subjective belief in the common descent because of similarities of physical type or of customs of both, or because of memories of colonialization and migration; this belief must be important for the propagation of group formation."[25] Thus, in Weber's view, ethnicity stems from the collective belief in a shared cultural origin. Political scientist John Hutchinson and sociologist Anthony D. Smith elaborated on Weber and identified common characteristics across ethnic groups:

- a common *proper name,* to identify and express the "essence" of the community;
- a myth of *common ancestry,* a myth rather than a fact, a myth that includes the idea of a common origin and place and that gives an [ethnic group] a sense of kinship;
- shared *historical memories* of a common past or pasts, including heroes, events, and their commemoration;
- one or more *elements of common culture,* which need not to be specified but normally include religion, customs, or language;
- a *link* with a *homeland,* not necessarily its physical occupation by the [ethnic group], only its symbolic attachment to the ancestral land, as with Diaspora peoples;
- *a sense of solidarity* on the part of at least some sections of the [ethnic group's] population. . . .[26]

There is little popular consensus in the United States about the definition of ethnicity. From the perspective of this book and its authors, the most important difference between ethnic groups and races is that while an ethnic group's identity tends to be constructed both by the individual and others, a racial group's identity is constructed only by others.[27] In other words, ethnic identity may be those identities that groups internally assume versus racial identities that are externally imposed.

From this perspective, American society might see some groups as more purely ethnic at various points in time (contemporary Latinos or Hispanics), some groups as more purely races (Negroes and Whites in the mid-1700s), and other groups as a mix of both (the post-1965 Asian American community). Today, it is quite conceivable that to be Black—meaning someone of African ancestry (whether one is African American, Nigerian, Jamaican, etc.)—is to have an ethnic identity, because it entails pride in one's cultural heritage, as well as a racial identity imposed by American/Western assumptions about race and the practices of racism. Likewise, to be Asian American can mean one embraces both an ethnic and racial identity; for, like Hispanics or Latinos, younger generations of Asian Americans embrace a pan-ethnic identity to approximate the U.S. macro-categories of race.

In the next U.S. Census in 2020, Latino and Hispanic leaders and interest groups may push to have their group classified as a racial rather than ethnic category. Do you think this is a good idea, or would it be best to have the category of "Latino or Hispanic" remain an ethnic category in the census?

A Working Definition of Racism

Like the concepts of race and ethnicity, the concepts and practices of racism have changed throughout U.S. history. There are a multitude of definitions and theories for the concept of racism. A vital feature of this chapter is that it familiarizes you with these theories—the debates of liberal and conservative thinkers—so that you can decide for yourself when, why, and how race matters in U.S. politics.

We argue that one of the ways present-day racism is detectable is when government and/or society use race to allocate benefits or sanctions and legitimacy or neglect to persons and groups in ways that reinforce a system of racial privilege or racial ordering. We borrow from the thinking of Beverly Daniel Tatum, current president of Spelman College in Atlanta, and others who argue that racism is "a 'system of advantage based upon race,'" that "Racism, like other forms of oppression, is not only a personal ideology based upon racial prejudice, but a system involving cultural messages and institutional policies and practices [especially those of government] as well as the beliefs and actions of individuals." She adds a controversial claim that we will unpack in this book: "In the context of the United States, this system clearly operates to the advantage of Whites to the disadvantage of people of color."[28] The concept of **White privilege** means a person is more likely to automatically have or inherit greater opportunities and more advantages—for example, longer life expectancy, higher median income, much greater wealth—than those afforded to racial and ethnic minorities (on average) simply if society perceives/classifies a person as White.[29]

Of course, this begs the question in this so-called postracial Obama era of whether Native Americans or Filipinos have the power to be racists because they can or cannot deny essential rights and privileges to Whites. In fact, this is precisely the point that conservative thinkers argue about contemporary aspects of civil rights policy and affirmative action. Such policies enforce reverse racism because, as stated in the Supreme Court decision of *Ricci v. DeStefano* (2008), Whites are denied job promotions if so-called racial preferences require Blacks to be better represented in certain job categories.[30] U.S. Supreme Court justice Clarence Thomas, as part of what conservatives consider victimology, once argued that such preferences lead to a dangerous pattern:

> The "We/They" mentality of calling oneself a victim of society breeds social conflict and calls into question the moral authority of society. The idea that whole groups or classes are victims robs individuals of an independent spirit—they are just moving along with the "herd" of other victims. Such individuals also lack any incentive to be independent, because they know that as part of an oppressed group they will neither be singled out for the life choices they make nor capable of distinguishing themselves by their own efforts.[31]

Thus Thomas advocates that any government intervention that takes steps to address disparities between racial groups (other than blatant discrimination) violates the spirit of

American self-help and free thought. Beverly Daniel Tatum's definition is a direct challenge to Thomas's perspective and akin to the classic liberal definition of racism that 1960s Black nationalist leader Stokely Carmichael and political scientist Charles Hamilton offered in their 1967 book *Black Power:* "By racism we mean the predication of [political, social, economic, and belief systems] on considerations of race for the purpose of *subordinating* a racial group and maintaining control over that group." Carmichael and Hamilton make a distinction between individual racism and institutional racism, whereby the latter is more destructive. In their view, only dominant groups have the capacity to be institutional racists, for only they have the power to reinforce and benefit from a racial order.

Racial theorists Michael Omni and Howard Winant slightly counter this view when they assert, "A racial project" or any effort to shape the use of race in society, "can be defined as racist if and only if it *creates or repro-

Protestors voice their opinions on the role of race in the 2013 George Zimmerman trial. Many allege that Zimmerman, self-described as a White Hispanic, would not have received the same verdict had he been Black and Trayvon Martin, White. Perceptions and definitions of race are often brought to the fore by events like this, indicating that it can still have an important role in parts of American society and government.

duces structures of domination based on essentialist categories of race."* They go on to say that "there is nothing inherently White about racism," though they add, "All racisms . . . are not the same" and cannot exert the same amount of political power.[32] For instance, even if one believes that all forms of racism are morally indefensible, the current number of White racial hate groups, such as the Ku Klux Klan and Neo-Nazi Skinheads, have a capacity for antiminority racial violence that far outweighs the number and capacity of Black and other non-White groups that observers also classify as hate groups. (See the Southern Poverty Law Center's "hate map" at http://www.splcenter.org/get-informed/hate-map.)[33]

Eduardo Bonilla-Silva notes that in this post-1965 period, overt, government-sanctioned racial discrimination has been outlawed through civil rights law. Yet the legacy of discrimination makes it possible for racial inequalities to exist even if there are fewer institutions and persons in power actively placing barriers in the path of minorities. He calls this "new racism," or a covert form of racial discrimination whereby a racial structure exists within American society and is supported by at least four forms of racial inequality. They include: (1) institutional racism, or "the maintenance of racial disparities through routine governmental practices" that claim race-neutrality, such as the achievement gap between Whites and some minorities on the Standardized Achievement Test (SAT); (2) latent racism, or "the more

BOX 1.2 ROAD SIGN

Race, Science Fiction, and Politics

The Road Sign boxes that appear in some chapters of this book highlight current events, developments, and debates. In this box, we consider how science fiction reflects race and racial issues. The genre of science fiction can imaginatively discuss (but just as often neglect) issues of race in politics as relevant to American society. By definition, science fiction is a form of storytelling that imagines possible futures and alternate realities. Its storylines of aliens, monsters, or talking apes, such as in the film series *Planet of the Apes* (1968, 1970, 1971, 1972, 1973, 2001, 2011, 2014), are often symbolic representations of human conflicts such as xenophobia (fear of outsiders) or racism.

The popular film trilogy *The Matrix* (1999, 2001, 2003) created a world in which all of those in authority within the machine-ruled, cyberreality of "the Matrix" appeared to be White and many of the human characters who resisted the machine's dominance were racial minorities, as shown in the multiracial human refuge-city, Zion. In the film *District 9* (2009), a world government segregates an alien race that has landed on Earth in one enormous quarantine zone called District 9. It makes contemporary references to South African apartheid, as well as to the war on terrorism and U.S. policies of racial segregation and anti-immigration. The film was praised for smartly showing that sometimes the "hostile aliens" are we humans, who apply our views of race to other beings; but it was also criticized for its not so subtle references to Africans (Nigerians, in particular) as gangsters and cannibals.

In another depiction of racial issues, the movie *Avatar* (2009) set its story more than a hundred years in the future on the world of Pandora, in which the blue, ten-foot-tall Na'vi, who live in complete harmony with nature, are attacked by a greedy human corporation and its mercenaries, who want to destroy these "savages" and their gigantic Home Tree in order to mine the Unobtanium deposits under the ground. Among many other themes, critics noted this film's reference to settler colonialism or the idea that, just like Europeans decimating Native Americans and taking their lands starting in the 1500s and 1600s, an Earth corporation in the future uses military mercenaries to violently take the land and resources of the Na'vi.[35]

In general, science fiction—through film, television programs, novels, and so on—provides an entertaining way to discuss serious issues like race and racial differences as they point to possible multiracial utopias (the *Star Trek* series), to racial apocalypse *(Planet of the Apes)*, or to visions of mixed futures in which hope is mingled with racism and social chaos (such as the novels of the award-winning science fiction author Octavia Butler). Such sci-fi stories provide us with opportunities to discuss race and racism now (and in the future) if we choose to have such discussions. But if most of us in the viewing public see these stories as only entertainment and nothing else, aren't we missing opportunities to think more deeply about racism? And therefore isn't racism subtly reinforcing a negative form of "color blindness"? You decide. For a discussion of how science fiction can be blind to race, see Adilifu Nama's *Black Space: Imagining Race in Science Fiction Film* (2008).

concealed and coded racism" often found in ordinary language and practices, including use of terms like *illegal aliens* or *welfare queens* as implicit references to all Mexican American workers or the African American poor; (3) residual Jim Crow racism, or the recognized practices and stereotypes that stem from America's past of sanctioned, racial segregation and

White supremacy, as illustrated by the state of South Carolina still officially flying the Confederate Flag; and (4) color-blind racism, or the assertion that any attention to race is inherently racist, as indicated in Supreme Court cases that have charged reverse racism when affirmative action programs call for the hiring or promotion of minorities over Whites.

In the end, Bonilla-Silva concludes that all of the above collude in creating an America in which it is possible to have "racism without racists." This means old opportunity gaps still persist between Whites and racial/ethnic minority groups, even though most White Americans have become more racially tolerant in their attitudes over the past forty years, and civil rights laws, such as the 1964 Civil Rights Act and the 1965 Voting Rights Act, prohibit blatant, anti-minority discrimination.[34] Later in this chapter we will explain how our Uneven Roads framework gives you the tools to sort out when, why, and how racism is operating to shape the status of a group.

RACIAL CLASSIFICATION, CITIZENSHIP, AND GROUP STATUS

 Does the requirement on a form to check just one box for racial or ethnic identity create an inaccurate picture of an increasingly diverse America? What would happen if we all checked more than one box?

Government can play a central role in determining the ways in which race, racism, and ethnicity matter within a society. No function is more important to that determination than a periodic census of the population. The census collects reams of data about the population and provides the logic and processes the state needs to categorize and classify individuals and groups according to many different characteristics, including perceived racial and ethnic ones. While conventional wisdom says that the census process in the United States is empirical (or objective), political and social biases have been and remain an inherent part of the process. Recall our earlier discussion of race and ethnicity as social constructions. Science, like religion, politics, culture, and other elements of society, has been pivotal in shaping the political uses of these concepts.

Scientific Racism: A Backdrop for Census Categories

The scientific Enlightenment that emerged in the late eighteenth century and throughout nineteenth-century America and Europe also birthed **scientific racism,** the incorrect use of empirical methods to justify assumptions of racial superiority and inferiority. Science is a voice of authority and, when used improperly, can badly mislead and give credence to the false, popular ideas of citizens and governments. In his 1735 work *Systemae Naturae,* Swedish botanist Carolous Linnaeus was among European scientists who first derived a system of racial classification not too different from the current Anglo-American scheme: Americanus (American Indian), Asiasticus (Asian), Africanus (Black/African), and Europeaeus (White/European). What made Linneaus's scheme problematic is that he used secondhand accounts riddled with racist stereotypes and assumed different human "species" had unique phenotypic and behavioral traits. Whereas Africanus had "hair—black, frizzled; skin—silky; nose—flat," he also reasoned that their "women [were] without shame" and this race was "crafty, indolent, negligent . . . and

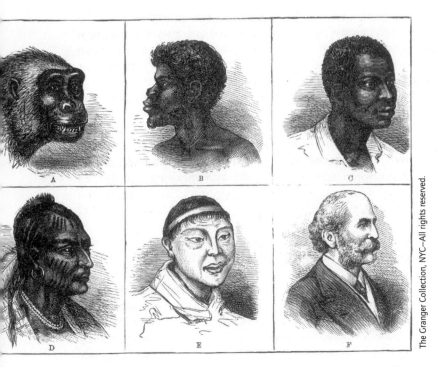

This late nineteenth-century chart on human evolution from ape implies that people of Aboriginal and African descent are most closely related to apes as part of the "missing link" theory of scientific racism.

governed by caprice." On the other hand, Europeaeus was "white, sanguine, muscular; hair—long; flowing; eyes—blue; gentle, acute, inventive; covers himself with close vestments; governed by laws."[36] The work of Linneaus was followed by that of German scientist Johann Friedrich Blumenbach and his *On the Natural Varieties of Mankind* (1776) and American scientist Samuel George Morton's *Crania Americana* (1839). To varying degrees, each extended upon the idea of scientifically discovering the natural divisions among human races.[37]

Scientific racism later shaped the thinking of the founders of the American Republic, most prominently Thomas Jefferson. Not only did Jefferson join others in believing in a myth of White Anglo-Saxon racial superiority, but he once reasoned in his famous *Notes on Virginia* (1787) that the orangutan sexually desired African women because Blacks belonged to a "missing link" race that was halfway between humans and apes. These conclusions are hypocritical, given Jefferson's long-time sexual relationship with his Black slave, Sally Hemmings. As explained further in Chapter 3, it is no wonder that the framers of the U.S. Constitution could strike a compromise in which enslaved African Americans were counted as three-fifths of a whole person if some of them believed Blacks were subhuman.

A multitude of similar rationales emerged over the next two centuries, from polygeny (a belief that the different races had entirely different origins), to Social Darwinism (the theory that Whites are the superior race because they are the most intelligent and adaptable), to eugenics (the science of breeding out racial contaminants to the White race). Again, such science was used in order to lend authority and credence to justifications for slavery and notions of a natural racial order. At its height in the 1930s, scientific racism justified the thinking of Adolf Hitler and the Nazi Party of Germany, which proclaimed Aryan racial supremacy and the necessity of annihilating the so-called Jewish race.[38]

Against this backdrop, the U.S. federal government first began to derive and constantly revise the categories it used to racially classify its population beginning in 1790. Article I of the U.S. Constitution requires a decennial (or every decade) census of the population.

Throughout its life, the census has involved a process of racialization to suit differing political as well as scientific and allocational purposes by which communities received public moneys for roads, schools, hospitals, and other services. Political scientist Melissa Nobles asserts that the census reflected each period's racial thinking, and thus we have gone through at least four, if not more, racial eras with the census and its racial categories. (See Table 1.2.)[39]

The first period was the Slaveocracy era (1790–1840), in which the primary consideration was demarcating Whites from enslaved Blacks and American Indians. Thus in 1790 the categories were: Free White Males, Free White Females, All Other Free Persons, and Slave. Later they included the category of Indians Not Taxed. By the 1840 census, the categories were Free White Persons, Free Colored Persons, and Slaves. As scientific racism took hold, two prominent Southern polygenists, Samuel George Morton and Josiah C. Nott—both medical doctors who believed in the scientific and moral validity of slavery—worked to demonstrate that miscegenation, or racial mixing, was problematic because it created a third "weaker race" of mulattoes.

The category of "mulatto" was officially added in the 1850 census, beginning the second racial era of the mulatto and race science (1850–1920). This was a period of great racial anxiety. Not only were slavery and, later, the postslavery emancipation period hotly debated with regard to the South, but out West the fates of American Indian tribes, Mexican American settlers, and Chinese and other workers were suppressed by claims of White land and economic entitlement. In the East and Midwest, a steady stream of Irish, German, and later Southern European immigrants made Anglo-Saxon proponents nervous about the character of their White racial republic because of the prejudicial views the latter had of these working-class immigrants. By becoming a rising power, the United States demonstrated to Europe in the late 1800s that it too believed in the White Man's Burden, or the civilizing of the so-called darker nations by assuming territory through conquest in Cuba, Puerto Rico, the Philippines, and Hawaii, among other places.[40]

Because of this internal and external racial turbulence and dramatic increases in immigration, census takers in 1880 and 1890 were asked (in quite arbitrary ways) to take note of new categories—Chinese and Japanese. Along with the category of mulatto, the strange gradations of quadroon (one-fourth Black) and octoroon (one-eighth Black) were added to the 1890 census, noting increasingly evident public unease with immigrant ethnicities. Prior to that change, the 1882 Chinese Exclusion Act was passed and Homer Plessy lost his 1896 appeal not to be shoved to the inferior side of the "separate but equal" color line.

The 1920s was a period of intense anti-immigration fervor and legislation; thus the "Americanization" movement emerged, calling for the submergence of non–Anglo Saxon ethnicity, and the census was directed to take note of the new racial categories of Mexican, Hindu or Asian Indian, Filipino, Korean, and Other. By the 1930s, the nation's racial and ethnic admixture was so diverse, segregationist thinking made it necessary to clearly demarcate White as the default category for all persons of European ancestry, beginning the third period, the One-Drop era (1930–1960).[41]

After the Civil Rights Movement challenged the 1930–1960 period of Jim Crow categories and both race and ethnicity came to be included in the census, the post–Civil Rights era (1980–present) began. In 1977 the Office of Management and Budget put forth Statistical Directive No. 15 to devise uniform racial and ethnic categories for the purposes of education, which in

Table 1.2 Racial Categories of the U.S. Census, 1790–2000

Racial Era	Decade	White	Negro/Black	Indian	Mixed Race	Mexican	Chinese	Japanese	Asian Indian	Filipino	Korean	Hawaiian	Alaskan	Vietnamese	Other Race
Slaveocracy Era →	1790	■	■												
	1800	■	■	■											
	1810	■	■	■											
	1820	■	■	■											
	1830	■	■	■											
	1840	■	■												
Mulatto & Race Science Era →	1850	■	■	■	■										
	1860	■	■		■										
	1870	■	■	■	■		■								
	1880	■	■	■	■		■								
	1890	■	■	■	■		■	■							
	1900	■	■	■			■	■							
One-Drop Rule Era →	1910	■	■	■	■		■	■							■
	1920	■	■	■			■	■	■	■	■				■
	1930	■	■	■		■	■	■	■	■	■				■
	1940	■	■	■			■	■	■	■	■				■
	1950	■	■	■			■	■		■					■
Post-Civil Rights Era →	1960	■	■	■			■	■		■		■	■		
	1970	■	■	■			■	■		■	■	■	■		■
	1980	■	■	■	■		■	■	■	■	■	■	■	■	■
	1990	■	■	■			■	■	■	■	■	■	■	■	■
	2000	■	■	■	■		■	■	■	■	■	■	■	■	■

Source: Melissa Nobles, *Shades of Citizenship: Race and the Census in Modern Politics* (Stanford, CA: Stanford University Press, 2000), 28, 44. Composite table created by authors based on Nobles's tables and text.

turn would be applied across all governmental functions. By this period, census takers were not to presume their definitions had scientific or social scientific validity as much as political legitimacy. The directive read that these racial and ethnic "classifications should not be interpreted as being scientific or anthropological in nature. . . . They have been developed in response to need by both the executive branch and the Congress."[42]

At approximately this same time, Hispanic leaders in Congress became concerned that government was inconsistent in the collection of data that allowed for measurement of the status of Latinos in the United States. Congress responded in 1976 with Public Law 94-311, requiring federal agencies to collect and publish statistics on the social, health, and economic conditions of Americans of Spanish origin or descent (the term used in the law). Most important among these federal agencies was the Department of Commerce, which is responsible for the collection of U.S. Census data. The implementation of this law led to the standardization of federal racial and ethnic data, with four recognized racial categories (American Indian or Alaskan Native, Asian or Pacific Islander, White, and Black) and two ethnic categories (of Hispanic origin and not of Hispanic origin). Latino leaders in the 1970s organized to ensure that "Hispanic" was categorized as an ethnic rather than a racial category, partly because race, color, and ethnic nationality are such fluid notions in Latin American identity.[43]

It is quite interesting that the notion of being mixed-race emerged again with the 2000 census, which permitted persons to identify themselves by more than one racial or ethnic category. In fact, there has been a vigorous debate about the use of multiracial categories within the census movement because of concern by some civil rights leaders that it would dilute the numbers counted as discrete, racial minorities. Figure 1.1, however, indicates that for most Americans, at least as of 2010, race is still a very fixed concept—the overwhelming majority of census respondents (about 98 percent) picked only one race; 74 percent selected White; 12 percent marked Black; and fewer than 5 percent chose all of the others. But there is a fairly significant percentage, 6 percent, who picked "Other" and thus refused to check the traditional boxes. In addition, the percentage of people who selected the ethnic category of "Hispanic" or "Latino" was 14 percent across all races. The vast majority of Hispanics or Latinos self-identify as White alone or some other race alone. Only 710,000 out of 50 million identify as Black/African American alone. This indicates the flexibility or permeability of the Latino category. Latinos are now the largest ethnic or racial minority in the United States, surpassing Blacks. But again, it is important to keep in mind that "Latino/Hispanic" is a pan-ethnic label comprised of many different ethnic-national and racial identities.[44]

Group Economic and Demographic Differences

One of this book's major objectives is to provide you with the ability to understand how government actions matter in the creation of persistent opportunity gaps. According to projections, by the year 2050 (and possibly sooner) immigration and demographic changes in the United States will result in there being no absolute racial majority. Whites will make up only 49 percent of the total population, just as they now do in California. In 2000 Whites (or Anglos—non-Hispanic Whites) were 75 percent of the U.S. population and generally speaking were doing much better economically and educationally than most other racial/ethnic groups. By 2010 this population figure dropped to just above 72 percent. Of all ethnic and racial groups, Latinos/Hispanics experienced the absolute largest increase in their percentage of the population—from just above 12 percent in 2000 to over 16 percent in 2010. Map 1.2 illustrates where minority populations are most concentrated in the nation. But a group's share of the

Figure 1.1 Race as a Percentage of Total Population, 2010

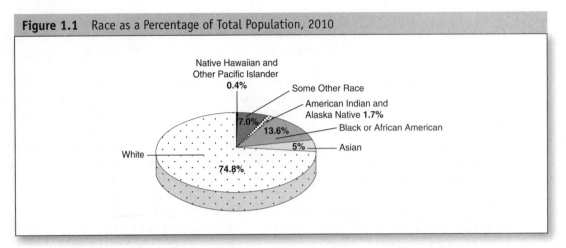

Source: U.S. Census Bureau, 2010 Census Redistricting Data (Public Law 94-171), Summary File, Table P1, p. 7.

total population is only one measure of its standing. Asian Americans, who were just under 5 percent of the total population, had a median family income in 2000 slightly higher than that of Whites ($59,000 versus $53,000) and twice as many college graduates. At no point in the early 2000s did African Americans, American Indians and Alaskan Natives, or Hispanics economically catch up with Whites, except with respect to high school graduation rates. The Asian-to-White income gap actually increased in the early 2000s, whereby in 2010 Whites had a median family income of $64,818 as compared to $76,736 for Asian Americans, who again had nearly twice as many college graduates.

Our larger point with this data is that government matters because it can determine when race and its opportunities are not experienced in exactly the same way across racial and ethnic minorities, despite important similarities. There is a general impression that asserts Native Americans economically benefit from land trust annuities, or payments the U.S. government makes to tribes in return for the use or taking of native lands and resources, as well as from the emergence of Indian-run casinos. Yet in 2010 Native Americans had the lowest median family income (on par with African Americans), the highest rate of individual poverty, and nearly the lowest rate of college graduation. While there are some positive benefits derived from the more than two hundred tribes who by state and/or federal agreement are permitted to run casinos, the effects are not equally beneficial in every locale and in a few cases, true to all casinos, there are negative effects, including increased "bankruptcy rates, violent crime, and auto thefts."[45]

Despite Latinos and Asian Americans being lumped into large, pan-ethnic groupings, there is enormous diversity between and within different pan-ethnic groups that also stems, in part, from government policy. Mexicans are by far the largest Hispanic group in the United States, with Puerto Ricans and Cubans a distant second and third. As we will explain in subsequent chapters, the economic differences between the groups, especially since Cubans had median family incomes nearly $10,000 higher than the other two groups in 2010, is partly explained by U.S. policy favoring Cuban immigrants in ways not true for Mexican immigrants or of

Map 1.2   Minority Population as a Percentage of County Population, 2010

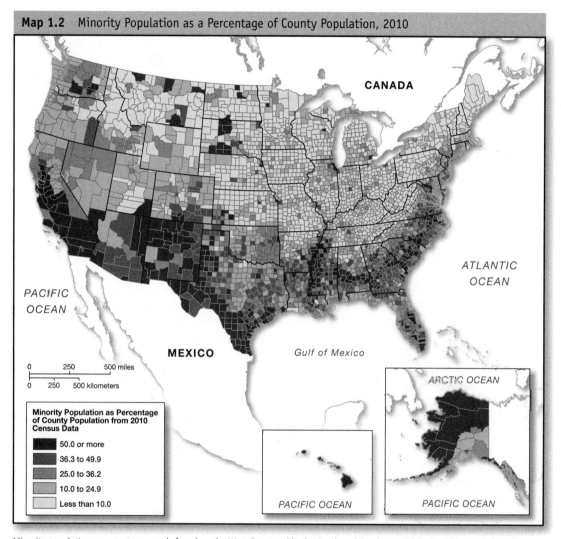

Minority populations are most commonly found on the West Coast and in the South and Southwest. While the Midwest and New England remain less diverse, demographics continue to shift from natural population growth and immigration. The U.S. government estimates that by 2050, there will be no true majority race or ethnicity in the United States.

Source: U.S. Census Bureau, 2010 Census Redistricting Data (Public Law 94-171), Summary File, Tables P1 and P2, as illustrated in U.S. Census Bureau, "Overview of Race and Hispanic Origin, 2010," *2010 Census Briefs,* p. 20.

domestic policies directed toward Puerto Ricans, who already are U.S. citizens. Large levels of stratification exist among Asian, Asian Indian, and Native Hawaiian (Pacific Islander) groups. On the high end of the economic ladder are Asian Indians and Japanese persons (whose median family incomes increased to a range between $85,000 and $100,000), with Vietnamese, Koreans, and Native Hawaiians making about $30,000 less in median family income across the decade. (See Figure 1.2 for demographic differences in social and economic characteristics.) In Chapter 5, we will address the greatly different resources and barriers each group has confronted as part of this larger story.

Overall, the emergent differences between these groups have led racial theorists to wonder if we now have a system of stratification that recognizes not only race/color but class as part of a system of advantages. Mindful of these very important variations, a 2013 report by a number of senior researchers concluded racial disparities actually impose costs on all of us by subtracting from the economy. If the average 30 percent gap between the income of Whites and racial/ethnic minorities did not exist, "total U.S. earnings [by all individuals] would increase by 12%, representing nearly $1 trillion today," and nearly $2 trillion more would be added to the gross domestic product, or the total output of the economy minus exports.[46]

Race and American Citizenship

Because the United States and its politics are becoming increasingly driven by racially and ethnically diverse constituencies, many have asked, What does it mean to be an American? And by paying attention to race and ethnicity, are we eroding the commonality we as U.S. residents should share? There are many answers that politicians and ordinary citizens have given to these questions, and two major opposing views in particular are highlighted here. By exploring these perspectives, our goal is to provide you with the objective tools and facts to reach your own conclusions about what role, if any, race does and should play in U.S. politics.

The multicultural view is argued by many scholars, including the prominent voice of historian Ronald Takaki. In his book *A Different Mirror,* Takaki asserts the belief that various cultural, racial, and ethnic groups in the United States should mutually coexist and maintain their distinct identities. In political science, this view somewhat approximates pluralist theory, or the belief that the American political system is fairly open and accessible; but current scholars of race and politics have greatly modified this theory. Like many other adherents of this view, Takaki believes that since America's founding it has been racially and ethnically diverse, though racist. He is critical of those who would argue that the United States should become one large melting pot in which all ethnic differences ultimately are submerged or assimilated into one larger American identity. Multiculturalists believe that to argue so in a society ordered by race only places racial and ethnic minorities at a distinct disadvantage in advocating for equality. Thus they support government policies along the lines of bilingual education (or initially teaching immigrant students in their native, non-English tongue), liberal immigration policies, affirmative action, or racial redistricting to achieve minority representation in legislative bodies.[47]

Do we foster greater unity and understanding in the United States by stressing a common American identity, or by embracing diverse American identities?

On the other hand, the transcendent view argues that American society represents universal values—individual liberty, equal opportunity, democracy—that shape American identity and transcend all differences.

Figure 1.2 Social and Economic Characteristics of Major U.S. Racial and Ethnic Groups, 2010

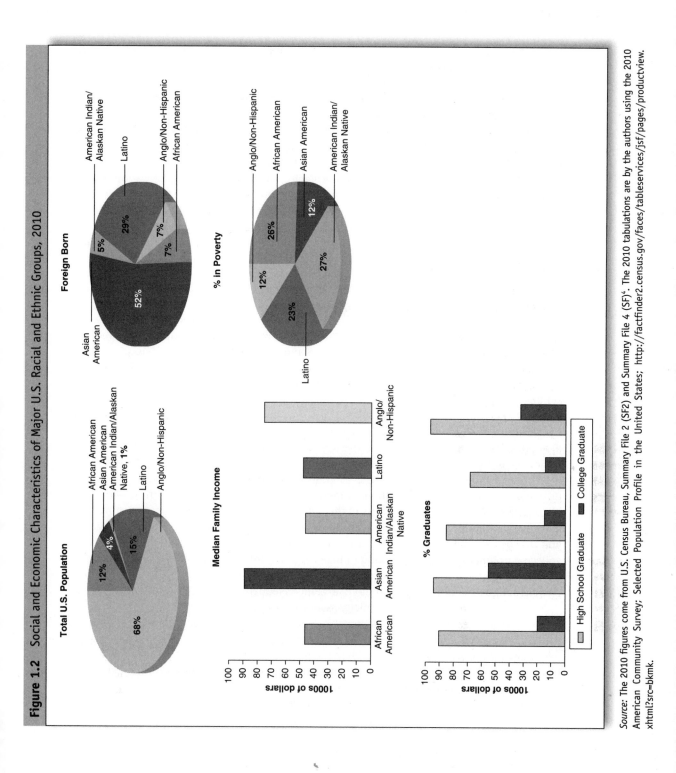

Source: The 2010 figures come from U.S. Census Bureau, Summary File 2 (SF2) and Summary File 4 (SF)[4]. The 2010 tabulations are by the authors using the 2010 American Community Survey; Selected Population Profile in the United States; http://factfinder2.census.gov/faces/tableservices/jsf/pages/productview.xhtml?src=bkmk.

It might otherwise be labeled the assimilationist approach. Historian Arthur Schlesinger once concluded in a book entitled *The Disuniting of America* that ethnic attachments to "hyphenated" identities, such as Italian American, African American, and Japanese American, are understandable at one level, but ultimately subtract from our common American identity. Schlesinger feared that ultimately emphasis on group differences would lead to chaos: "America in this new life is seen as preservative of diverse alien identities. Instead of a nation composed of individuals making their own unhampered choices, America increasingly sees itself as composed of groups more or less ineradicable in their ethnic character. The multiethnic dogma abandons historic purposes replacing assimilation by fragmentation, integration by separatism. It belittles *unum* [unity] and glorifies *pluribus* [diversity]."[48] Toward this end, the transcendent view approves of government policies of "English only" in schools, restrictive immigration policies, and the limiting or elimination of affirmative action (which it considers unfair racial quotas), and is more likely to oppose the use of race to achieve minority-majority legislative districts.

THE UNEVEN ROAD OF RACE: OUR FRAMEWORK

We began this chapter by posing the main questions of when, why, and how race has mattered as various groups pursued full citizenship rights and opportunities. We return to the image of the uneven road to fully demonstrate how our framework helps readers grasp why racial and ethnic minorities have had to travel different and often more difficult roads in comparison to Whites. Our answers to these when, why, and how questions inform readers of the relationships between three key factors of racialization—society, the polity (government), and minority communities—whose interactions result in a specific outcome (destiny). Figure 1.3 illustrates the relationship between these key factors and outcome.

Society in Figure 1.3 represents the dominant/majority group and its social as well as economic institutions, such as churches, neighborhood groups, and businesses. The Minority Community refers to a specific ethnic or racial minority at a certain point in time—for example, Blacks today or Italian Americans in the 1900s. The **Polity** stands for the government and its related institutions—for example, the U.S. Congress, the Federal Housing Administration, and U.S. political parties. Finally, Destiny signifies a specific status outcome, such as higher college enrollments, expanded voting rights, and lower infant mortality rates, which indicate what level of racialization a group currently experiences. These levels of racialization range from Absolute to Decisive, to Insufficient, and Inconsequential.

Remember that why race and ethnicity matter explains the specific reasons for or rationale behind a group's advantage or disadvantage. Answers to this question depend on the degree to which the dominant society perceives a minority community as a threat or as a benefit. It tells us why the dominant society believes the contour or the shape of a group's road should be bumpy versus smooth, a steep climb versus an easy roll downhill, twisted versus straight—especially as society and government place ramps (opportunities) or roadblocks (barriers) along a group's path. For example, were those who argued in 2013 that the Washington Redskins football team retain its name, despite its being a strong racial stereotype of Native Americans, subtly relying on past justifications for racial caricatures of Native Americans?

Figure 1.3   When, Why, and How Race Shapes a Group's Status

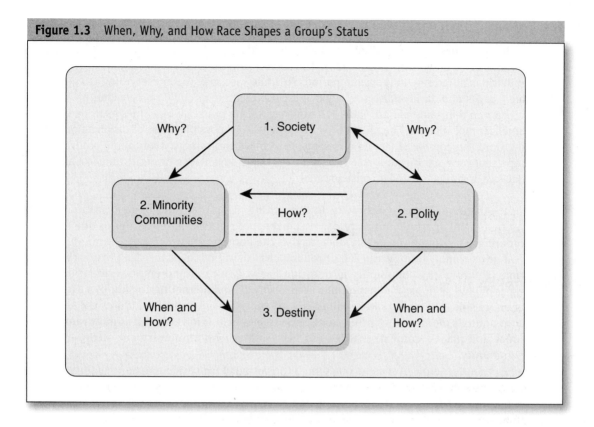

How race and ethnicity matter explains the specific processes that create or maintain a group's racial advantage or disadvantage. The answer to this question tells us how government creates and uses certain laws, actions, and institutions in the construction of a group's road partly as shaped by the laws, actions, and institutions a group has to use along its journey. For example, African Americans have lower rates of homeownership than do Whites today. This is at least partly due to the legacy of discriminatory federal government and private lender laws and practices that, until the early 1970s, denied many Black families subsidized loans that would have made home purchases much easier.

When race and ethnicity matter explains the specific periods in time or places in which a group's racial advantages or disadvantages are more likely to matter. The answer to this question provides us with the context of a group's road, meaning we can better identify when and where events occurred to gauge certain outcomes to determine how far along a group is on its journey. For instance, Italian immigrants in the early twentieth century arrived during a strong anti-immigrant period of American history and at times were racialized by Whites of English ancestry as dark-skinned and lacking a work ethic. The early twenty-first century is a different context, where ethnic barriers to Italian Americans have been replaced by ethnic barriers to Hispanic and Latino Americans.[49]

The Outcomes of Racialization

In our framework, we include ethnicity alongside race because it can overlap with but at times also be quite distinct from race. The society and the polity can treat racial and ethnic minorities differently in the same period. So while race may mean everything in the way of advantages and disadvantages in a specific period, ethnicity could be considerably less significant in that same period. Table 1.3 summarizes the potential outcomes as to when, why, and how race matters. The fourth column explains four possible levels of racialization resulting from the combined factors of society, the polity, and minority communities. The levels represent how significant a role race is in a group's advantages or disadvantages: absolute, decisive, insufficient, and inconsequential.

1. **Absolute: Race or Ethnicity Is Everything.** This first level of racialization occurs when a racial or ethnic minority has no citizenship rights and opportunities due to racial ordering. The dominant society decides that the contour of a minority community's road will be extremely bumpy and full of roadblocks, identified in Table 1.3 as very strong barriers. The minority community in question has very weak to no empowerment from the types of laws, actions, and institutions at its disposal; and neither timing nor place (context) is on its side. The polity likely colludes with society in the construction of the minority community's road and thus offers laws, actions, and institutions, as well as disadvantageous times and places (context) that lead to very weak or no empowerment of the minority community.

A perfect example of such an outcome is the period of African American enslavement from roughly the 1640s to the 1860s, when the vast majority of African Americans were enslaved and a tiny, mostly Northern freedmen class had few beneficial laws, actions, or institutions that they could use to promote their interests. One fundamental roadblock was that many Whites believed that African Americans were subhuman and indeed even fit for slavery; only a relatively small number of abolitionists within the dominant society believed otherwise. Until the 1850s, when tensions between slave states and free states boiled over, the federal government struck a series of compromises (laws) that perpetuated slavery, and thus very weak incentives for change existed.

2. **Decisive: Race or Ethnicity Matters.** This second level of racialization occurs when a racial or ethnic minority has very limited citizenship rights and opportunities as a result of racial ordering. Akin to, but not quite as bad as the "absolute" condition, the dominant society establishes many roadblocks, or strong barriers as identified in Table 1.3, that contour a minority community's road to equality with twists and turns. The minority community in question has weak empowerment from the types of laws, actions, and institutions available to it, and neither timing nor place (context) is on its side. Government or the polity likely colludes with society in the construction of a minority community's road and thus offers weak laws, actions, and institutions at disadvantageous times and places (context), which leads to the weak empowerment of the minority community.

Examples of this outcome include the period of Jim Crow segregation (the 1880s to the early 1960s) (timing or context), when only a minority of African Americans were permitted to register and to vote in the South (place) despite the Fifteenth Amendment. In the same

Table 1.3 Outcomes of the Uneven Roads Framework

The Questions/Factors of Racialization			The Outcomes of Racialization
Society (*Why this contour for the road?*): Does society believe/act as if a minority community should have racial/ethnic barriers (roadblocks, steep climbs, twists and turns) on its journey toward full citizenship rights and opportunities?	**Minority Community** (*How is the road constructed/when does context matter?*): Is a minority community empowered by strong laws, actions, and institutions (as well as advantageous times and places) to overcome any barriers on its journey toward full citizenship rights and opportunities?	**Polity** (*How is the road constructed/when does context matter?*): Does a polity empower a minority community with strong laws, actions, and institutions (as well as advantageous times and places) to overcome any barriers on its journey toward full citizenship rights and opportunities?	**Destiny:** What is the specific group status result of racialization based on the combined questions/factors of racialization?
Very Strong Barriers	Very Weak to No Empowerment	Very Weak to No Empowerment	1. **Absolute:** *Race or ethnicity is everything.* A racial/ethnic minority has no citizenship rights and opportunities due to racial/ethnic ordering (e.g., slavery, American Indian annihilation).
Strong Barriers	Weak Empowerment	Weak Empowerment	2. **Decisive:** *Race or ethnicity matters.* A racial/ethnic minority has very limited citizenship rights and opportunities due to racial/ethnic ordering (i.e., Jim Crow segregation, Japanese internment, anti-immigrant views against Hispanics).
Moderate to Weak Barriers	Strong Empowerment	Strong Empowerment	3. **Insufficient:** *Race or ethnicity is not enough.* A racial/ethnic minority has fundamental citizenship rights and opportunities though inequalities persist (i.e., Obama election, Asian American educational gains).
Very Weak to No Barriers	Very Strong Empowerment	Very Strong Empowerment	4. **Inconsequential:** *Race or ethnicity doesn't matter.* A racial/ethnic minority has equal citizenship rights and opportunities due to no racial/ethnic ordering or inequality (i.e., current status of the Irish and 'White' American Jews).

period, there also emerged a form of decisive exclusion that adversely affected the political and economic well-being of Hispanics, especially Mexican Americans. From the late nineteenth to twentieth centuries, Mexican Americans were often segregated by Anglos according to custom or law. They were frequently mistreated by law enforcement officials and the courts, often concentrated on the so-called Mexican side of towns and cities, isolated on small, impoverished farms, and faced dual systems of public education that segregated Mexican children from Anglo children. Many confronted perilous political and labor conditions as a result of ethnic and racial stereotypes that characterized them as illegal aliens, despite many families having several generations of U.S. citizenship. Some citizens faced the threat of mass deportation "back" to Mexico, as occurred in the 1930s. Beginning in the 1940s, immigrants could face difficult and unhealthy labor conditions as part of guest worker programs demanded by large growers. Not until after World War II were Mexican American and other "Spanish-speaking" labor, civic, religious, and civil rights groups able to effectively use their growing community resources and access to the ballot to challenge their relative exclusion from the political process.

3. Insufficient: Race or Ethnicity Is Not Enough. This third level of racialization is one in which race is one factor in a group's ability to exercise the rights and opportunities of American citizenship, but it is not significant enough to determine the final result. It occurs when a racial/ethnic minority has fundamental citizenship rights and opportunities although inequalities persist. In this instance, the dominant society has allowed the minority community's road to be flat and broad in many places; some roadblocks exist, but generally a group faces moderate to weak barriers, as noted in Table 1.3. The minority community in question enjoys strong empowerment from the types of laws, actions, and institutions at its disposal; and both timing and place (context) are often on its side. Government coordinates with society and offers moderate to strong laws, actions, and institutions at advantageous times and places. All of this leads to the strong empowerment of the minority community. To reiterate our earlier point, race and racial politics are present but do not determine the ultimate outcomes of a group, which may also be determined by other factors such as class/economics, gender, and religion.

We argue that this is precisely what occurred in the presidential election of Barack Obama, although arguably the early 2000s is a period of race as both decisive and insufficient. During the 2008 primary campaign, Obama had the strong community resources of solid African American and other minority voter support once he demonstrated his superior organizational, rhetorical, and financial prowess. Race presented his campaign with some roadblocks (such as when Obama's former pastor was accused of having made racially charged statements), but there were also opportunities in Obama's ability to use his biracial identity and his understanding of American racial dynamics to demonstrate his leadership abilities, as he did in his "More Perfect Union" speech in Philadelphia that we referred to earlier in the chapter. Clearly, there was also a climate of change within the polity (timing), for the Democratic Party had a unique opportunity to challenge the George W. Bush administration and the Republican Party as a result of policy failures and economic woes.

Race (or racism) was also not sufficient to determine the outcome of the U.S. Senate confirmation of Sonia Sotomayor as the first Latina justice of the U.S. Supreme Court, despite conservative objections to her perceived racial views. But precisely because the exercise of race and ethnicity are undergoing significant changes, some of the old barriers and problems that previously plagued minorities who enjoyed full citizenship and opportunities are likewise undergoing change.[50]

4. Inconsequential: Race or Ethnicity Does Not Matter. Last, there have been instances in which a racial or ethnic minority has equal citizenship and opportunities due to the absence of racial ordering or inequality. As scholars of American racial politics, we believe that U.S. society does not consider the impact of race often enough, although

ASSOCIATED PRESS

In 2013, immigrants from countries as diverse as Ghana, Venezuela, and the Philippines celebrate becoming U.S. citizens. Throughout U.S. history, race and ethnicity have mattered to varying degrees when it comes to the rights and opportunities that individuals receive.

we do not contend that race can explain every unequal outcome. There are groups (non-Hispanic Whites, in particular) that currently are not racialized in ways that greatly disadvantage them. In fact, we will later discuss how White privilege may still exist in U.S. society. In this sense, the dominant society's decision that a group will have very weak to no barriers on its road to equality may in fact be because the group is or is part of the dominant society. Specific communities in this case experience very strong empowerment from the types of laws, actions, and institutions at their disposal; and both timing and place (context) are on their side. The polity agrees with society and offers very strong laws, actions, and institutions at advantageous times and places that lead to the very strong empowerment of the community.

We will further discuss in Chapter 6 how, in the words of historian Stephen Erie, Irish Americans have been fully assimilated into American civic, economic, and political life. Another example of race or ethnicity becoming inconsequential is that of White American Jews. Despite the violent anti-Semitism Jews historically endured in Europe, many White American Jews enjoy civic, economic, and political inclusion in the American Dream. Although anti-Semitism can still fuel extremist rhetoric and actions in the United States, anthropologist Karen Brodkin attests to how in some cases groups can either submerge their ethnic identities to assimilate or how ideas of race, in this case Whiteness, can expand to include previously excluded groups.[51]

CONCLUSION: THE JOURNEY AHEAD

Going forward, we will use the framework laid out in this chapter to compare when, why, and how race has had an impact on a racial or ethnic group's status. The book is divided into three parts. Part I, comprised of this chapter, provides an introduction and a discussion of themes as well as theories of race, ethnicity, and racism in American life and politics. It provides the groundwork for understanding how the concepts of race and ethnicity developed in the United States.

Part II, Historical Foundations, presents in Chapters 2 through 6 the histories of the five major macro-categories of racial and ethnic groups in the United States: Native Americans, African Americans, Latinos, Asian Americans, and White Americans. This historical focus allows us to assess long-term processes and better identify how current issues may be influenced by the past. The historical coverage stops with the 1960s, which marks a turning point when civil rights and immigration began to change and liberalize, making the roads traveled very different from what they were before.

Understanding the past prepares you for Part III, Policy and Social Issues, in which Chapters 7 through 13 analyze the various ways that race, ethnicity, and racism matter relative to contemporary policy questions, political behavior, and ideology since 1965. Among its topics, Part III considers education and criminal justice because we believe that they are key policies that shape citizenship and opportunity. Chapter 13 also serves as a conclusion that brings together all of these roads and, we hope, leaves you with a framework for evaluating race, ethnicity, and politics in the future and an understanding of why race and ethnicity have and still do matter in U.S. politics. We hope you will learn a lot from your journey!

DISCUSSION QUESTIONS

1. How has the Anglo-American view of race led to race and ethnicity uniquely being defined in the United States as compared to elsewhere?

2. How did race as a social construct develop differently in North and South America?

3. How do the demographic data from the U.S. Census illustrate racial advantage or disadvantage and what role might the government have played in each group outcome?

4. Discuss the different degrees to which minority communities have experienced roadblocks to citizenship and equal opportunity because of race and ethnicity.

KEY TERMS

ethnicity (p. 10)
miscegenation (p. 17)
one-drop rule (p. 9)
pan-ethnic identity (p. 10)
polity (p. 24)
race (p. 6)

racial assimilation (p. 8)
racial essentialism (p. 6)
racialization (p. 6)
racial separation (p. 8)
racial superiority (p. 7)
racism (p. 7)

scientific racism (p. 15)
separate but equal
    doctrine (p. 10)
Statistical Directive
    No. 15 (p. 17)
White privilege (p. 12)

2 Native Americans: The Road from Majority to Minority, 1500s–1970s

Before any final solution to American history can occur, a Reconciliation must be effected between the spiritual owner of the land—American Indians—and the political owner of the land—American Whites. Guilt and accusations cannot continue to revolve in a vacuum without some effort at reaching a solution.

—Vine Deloria Jr.[1]

The journey of Native nations after the arrival of Europeans in the Americas has been long and arduous. Their road differs from that of other racial and ethnic groups discussed in this book because, unlike the others, they existed as distinct nations that farmed and hunted in communities across North America when Whites arrived. As European settlements expanded across the continent, the status of these original nations gradually changed from a majority culture of peoples living in sovereign nations to a disadvantaged minority living apart from mainstream U.S. culture and subordinate to U.S. law. This change stemmed in large part from Indian nations' loss of land, power, and independence, all of which had long-term repercussions still apparent in Indian communities today.

The arrival of Europeans to North American shores in the late fifteenth century signaled a decisive change in the Natives' way of life. Whites arrived with different conceptions of property, land use, culture, and spirituality. They brought with them firepower, disease, and a desire to conquer that eventually overwhelmed Native peoples, giving the

Box 2.1 Chapter Objectives

- Describe the fundamental differences in outlook between Native Americans and European settlers.

- Explain how White conceptions of race and desire for land disadvantaged Indians in the new United States.

- Explain how Supreme Court rulings helped the government justify Indians' forced removal and relocation.

- Assess how Indians' efforts to maintain their sovereignty and identity were challenged by U.S. federal policies.

- Evaluate to what extent race has mattered in twentieth century U.S.-Indian relations.

- Compare the accomplishments of the Native American rights movement with that of other groups.

© Bettmann/CORBIS

Native Americans gather on the steps of the Capitol in 1978 as part of a five-month cross-country walk to protest discrimination. Among their objections was what Indian leaders called a wave of anti-Indian legislation in Congress, challenges to which had made their way to the U.S. Supreme Court. Native Americans have faced a long and difficult road to retain and exercise their sovereignty, to protect treaty rights, and to be treated with respect as citizens entitled to equal rights and opportunity in the United States.

White population an advantage. As settlers arrived and sought land for homes and towns, Indians built relationships with the newcomers that often turned sour as the settlers' lust for land led to broken treaties and war. Yet the relationship between Native peoples and White colonists was not always completely adversarial. Many established trade relationships with merchants who were seeking furs and other goods to send back to Europe, and some fought alongside Whites in the French and Indian War (1754–1763), in which the French and British battled for control of land on the American "frontier."

As the White population grew and the nascent American government sought to expand its boundaries, it increasingly pushed against indigenous territories. The U.S. government's laws, actions, and institutions sometimes failed to recognize Indian nations as sovereign or Natives themselves as having any rights or say-so in who owned the land or how it should be distributed. This was in large part driven by the U.S. desire for land, but it was also driven by White perceptions of Indians as an inferior race—"savages" who needed to be civilized.

As the Native majority quickly shrank to a minority, with the rights and freedoms offered to other Americans in the United States not extended to them, Indians were left with limited resources with which to advocate for their rights. In fact, Native nations did not seek to become a part of the United States and its political process. They were sovereign nations demanding their rights first against colonial imposition and then against an expanding nation. With their resources diminished and their sovereignty only sporadically acknowledged, Native peoples later turned to the U.S. polity—its political system and institutions like the judiciary—for recourse. In this chapter, we explore when, why, and how these changes took place and seek to understand where Native nations and their citizens are on their road in the post–Civil Rights era.

Native nations, Tribes, American Indians, Native Americans, Natives, and *indigenous peoples* are all terms used to refer to the people living in North America at the time Christopher Columbus arrived in what Europeans called the New World. These terms will be used interchangeably in this chapter, but *Native nations, tribes,* and *Indians* will appear most often, as they are the terms preferred by most experts on American Indian studies. In another point of terminology, remnants of individual tribes sometimes were merged into a single tribal nation, and in some cases reservations are the home to more than a single tribal nation. For example, the Iroquois Confederacy is a political entity comprised of the Onondaga, Oneida, Seneca, Mohawk, Cayuga, and Tuscarora nations.

NATIVE COMMUNITIES IN NORTH AMERICA

Indigenous peoples in North America in the late fifteenth century were organized into a variety of diverse communities, as well as in sophisticated political confederacies across the continent, giving lie to the myth that all Native nations were either nomadic or sedentary. Although rivalries existed among Native peoples, they maintained an abiding respect for the land and the environment. Many lived in highly developed communities with irrigation systems for agriculture, religious traditions, and local governments. Three of the most prominent sets of indigenous peoples at the time of Europeans' arrival were the Pueblo communities of the Southwest, the so-called **Five Civilized Tribes** of the Southeast—Cherokee, Choctaw, Chickasaw, Creek, and Seminole—and the Iroquois Confederacy. The Pueblo peoples, actually twenty-one distinctive societies, comprised one of the most sophisticated indigenous populations, in part because they lived off of irrigated agriculture along the Rio Grande and Little Colorado Rivers.

The Choctaw, Creek, Chickasaw, Seminole, and Cherokee made their homes in the Mississippi Valley, where they operated along democratic principles and had efficient economies. These Indian nations adapted to the European culture by operating commercial ventures, creating governing systems that were loosely modeled after the U.S. Constitution, and operating large, plantation-type farms.

The Iroquois Confederacy, composed of the Mohawk, Oneida, Onondaga, Cayuga, and Seneca nations, was located in what are now the states of New York, Pennsylvania, and part of Canada. Later, in 1722 the Tuscarora joined the existing members. While most colonial Whites did not respect or understand Indian customs and views of government, the Iroquois were an exception because they had a significant military force that extended far west to the Great Lakes region of present-day Illinois. Indeed, between 1641 and 1779 the Iroquois Confederacy was a major player in the balance of power in northeastern North America because it was powerful enough to dominate rival tribes as well as the French, Dutch, and English.[2] The French and the British clearly respected the military power of the Iroquois, who were considered formidable opponents.

Some scholars believe that the Iroquois provided a model government for the colonists who wrote the Articles of Confederation (1777) and the U.S. Constitution (1787). The "Iroquois Influence Thesis" draws parallels between the Iroquois Great Law of Peace and the U.S. Constitution, which "adhered to balanced and limited political principles based upon the consent of the people." Both governing structures also utilized complex arrangements based upon "separation of powers, checks and balances, a veto power, ratification, and impeachment (or, for chiefs, 'dehorning')."[3]

Native peoples were spread across North America. In the east they were concentrated in New England; the eastern part of Virginia, known as the Tidewater; and the coastal area of the Carolinas. The Navajo and Apache peoples occupied what became Arizona. The Great Plains were home to dozens of Native nations, while in the Far West, a diverse array of indigenous peoples lived across Washington, Oregon, and California. Map 2.1 illustrates the location of major tribes prior to Europeans' arrival.

The Arrival of a New but Powerful Minority

Native peoples first encountered Europeans who were looking for gold, spices, and a route to India in the sixteenth century. The initial contacts were between explorers and indigenous Natives, and each culture was confident of its superiority. When Spanish and French explorers first arrived in North America they were surprised to encounter people who looked perceptibly different in skin color, language, lifestyle, religion, and cultural tradition. From the European perspective, Indians were heathen people who inhabited a wilderness that, to them, seemed unclaimed and largely underutilized.

Natives noticed that Europeans were different in physical appearance, style of dress, and a seeming lesser reverence for the land and natural environment. Because Indians relied primarily on oral tradition, they left scant written records; therefore little is known about their views of the first Europeans. Theda Perdue, a historian of Indian culture, says that Europeans were seen as merely foreigners. They were not viewed as enemies, but rather as potentially useful newcomers. These new arrivals were seen as being outside of a kin network and the indigenous political structure. Europeans were not seen in racial terms or as part of a racial hierarchy.[4]

Initially, many Whites had respect for Indians because they flourished in an environment that perplexed Europeans. For example, the leader Powhatan was considered the Great Emperor because he was the head of about thirty tribes in the Chesapeake area. His daughter, Pocahontas, who married English tobacco planter John Rolfe, was considered royalty in Europe.[5]

Settlers soon followed the traders to this New World to stake their claims and build new lives. As more Whites arrived, their relationship with the Indians also changed. Since European conceptions of race and civilization differed so radically from what they found in North America, they considered the Indians to be culturally, economically, and technologically inferior. Conflict over cultural values and ownership of the land followed when settlers wished to expand inland. The ensuing five centuries saw indigenous peoples and Whites contesting control of North America.

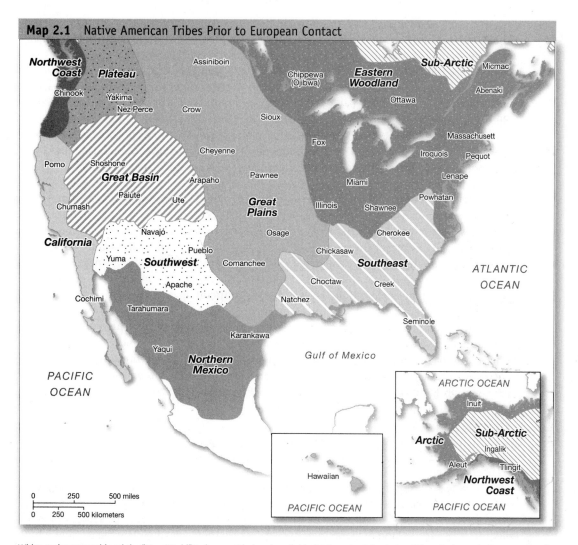

Map 2.1   Native American Tribes Prior to European Contact

White explorers considered the "New World" to be unsettled and available for them to claim, but as this map shows, Indians populated what is now the United States from coast to coast, with major tribes claiming large areas of land.

Europeans did not have a uniform view of the various Indian nations that they encountered, but they did see Indians in hierarchical terms, with Europeans being superior. Despite this, Indian tribes were initially treated as sovereign states. Historian Francis Parker simplistically summed up the perspectives of the English, Spanish, and French when he said, "Spanish civilization crushed the Indian; English civilization scorned and neglected him; French civilization embraced and cherished him."[6]

It is only possible to guess how many Natives populated the Americas before Europeans' arrived. Estimates range from five to eight million, far outnumbering early European settlers.

Europeans, however, brought with them disease and warfare, both of which contributed to a population decline. Native populations had no defenses against these diseases. In 1983 Henry F. Dobyns's study of Indian populations estimated that 3,800,000 had lived in the Great Lakes region; 5,250,000 in the Mississippi River Valley region; and 2,211,000 in the Florida to Massachusetts area.[7] The expansion of settlers became a twofold threat (disease and warfare) when Indians were trying to survive forty-one separate smallpox epidemics from 1520 to 1899, seventeen measles epidemics between 1531 and 1892, and ten major epidemics of influenza from 1559 to 1918. Plague, diphtheria, typhus, and cholera epidemics also struck.[8] The Indian population greatly declined as the Europeans now sought to establish permanent settlements versus the early exploratory ones along North America's east coast.

From the beginning, cultural and religious differences shaped the relationship between Native Americans, early European settlers, and later, the U.S. government. Native Americans traded with Europeans, made treaties, and even fought alongside them in wars. To the Indians, Europeans were strange because they destroyed forests, overharvested game, lived in settlements, and had a sense of individual ownership of land. Many who interacted with Whites on a regular basis learned their language, but most continued to adhere to their native language and preferred way of life. For their part, European understanding of the languages, histories, and religious beliefs of Indian nations was difficult, in part due to the lack of written records, but also because of the assumptions Europeans made based on the process of racialization. To them, Indians were uncivilized savages because the color of their skin, their religion, and their way of life did not conform to European values and preferences. The racialization of Indians in this way influenced Whites' interactions with Indians and, combined with the desire for land, resulted in hundreds of violated treaties, wars waged, and numerous programs to "civilize" Native peoples. From the start, race was one of the decisive barriers to Native-European relations.

Europeans and the Quest for Land in North America

When Europeans arrived in North America they began to create permanent settlements—clearing land, building homes, and establishing institutions such as schools and churches. They were the subjects of European monarchs who wished to claim the land, but who did not want to become involved in costly continental wars. As the monarchs and the settlers wrestled with the questions of land ownership in the New World they were aided by the papacy, which devised a new international law doctrine called the **doctrine of discovery**. Catholic countries such as Spain, Portugal, Italy, and France were interested in the potential riches of land in the New World. As head of the Catholic Church, the pope was the highest authority for Catholics. Under his leadership, rights to "unoccupied lands" were granted to Catholic sovereigns in the Western Hemisphere on the condition that the Natives became Christian, a policy established by the Church in the Middle Ages. Thus "European powers assumed they had a legal right to land discovered in the New World."[9] Natives were never consulted as to how this policy would be applied to them and their lands, but it was appealing to European monarchs because it kept disputes in the New World isolated from any possible European conflicts.

The French, Spanish, and British were the major powers claiming territory in North America. The British, as had the Spanish before them, wrestled over the extent of Indian property rights versus those of Europeans. The question was, if these Indian rights existed, how were they to be treated? Since the land was wilderness, with no cities or institutions that Europeans equated with ownership and civilization, they interpreted the land to be owner-less. Indians did not see land in terms of personal ownership. It was instead a sacred space that could also be used for hunting, fishing, gathering, and planting. The land was held collectively, not in ownership, but in stewardship.[10]

The Europeans' concept of community was based on an Old World model of civilization that valued Christianity, living in villages or cities, and the rights of individuals. These cultural values were in direct contrast with Native Americans, who were not Christian, viewed land as a part of their lives and spirituality, and did not operate under a governance structure premised on laws that were based on previous court decisions (known by the English as common law). In short, Indians were content with their lifestyle and uninterested in adopting the cultural norms, or the governing structure, of the newcomers. European relationships with Native Americans were thus primarily shaped by two forces—the European concept that Christianity was a superior religion of civilized people, and the doctrine of discovery. The cultural, religious, and property differences between the Whites and Indians helped to create a vastly uneven road in the ongoing relations between White settlers and Indians. Race was decisive, but not an absolute barrier in the beginning of the relationship between Indians and Whites.

In deciding who had title to the land on the American continent, the easiest way for Europeans to proceed was to make Native Americans fit into British concepts of law and individual property rights. Acquisition and ownership of land were of great importance to settlers, who in many cases had never owned land in their home country. When Europeans encountered the vast expanse of what they considered to be unclaimed and largely unoccupied land in North America, they relied on the historical pattern of acquiring it through purchase or conquest. President Thomas Jefferson followed this procedure when he bought land from France in what is called the Louisiana Purchase, land still inhabited by many Native nations. Jefferson and subsequent presidents faced a serious domestic problem with land-hungry settlers who pushed at the southern and western borders of the United States. The problem was that Indian nations had no interest in selling or moving westward.[11]

 How much did race matter in the doctrine of discovery used to justify White claims in America?

RISING TENSIONS: NATIVE AMERICANS AND THE NEW UNITED STATES, 1776–1830s

After the American Revolution in 1776, Indian nations were confronted by a new entity: the U.S. government. This government was based on a written document, the U.S. Constitution, which provided for a legal system based on English law. Consequently, all land disputes came under the authority of American jurisprudence. With the ratification of the Constitution (1789) a new relationship between the indigenous peoples and the United States had to be clarified because settlers wanted more land. Initially, Indians were treated as sovereign nations, as evidenced in the Commerce Clause, but were still considered inferior to Euro-Americans.

Race, culture, and property remained as decisive barriers to Natives receiving consistent respect as the U.S. drive for more land continued to push into the homelands of hundreds of Native nations. The roadblocks to Native sovereignty increased from the time of American independence, however, with the U.S. implementation of policies such as the civilization program, the diminished status of Indian tribes in the U.S. legal system, and the forced removal of many Natives from their lands to make way for more White settlements.

The Minority Threat: Westward Expansion Targets Indian Lands

Under President Jefferson's direction, the United States expanded its land holdings in 1803 by buying land ostensibly owned by the king of France and, before him, the king of Spain. While the westward expansion benefited the United States, Indian nations living in that territory faced an influx of settlers claiming their lands. (See Map 2.1.) President Jefferson expanded the borders of the United States by signing a treaty with France "to purchase rights to the Louisiana Territory," consisting of over eight hundred million acres west of the Mississippi. France was only giving the U.S. the right to be the sole purchaser *if* the Indian nations that owned and occupied the land decided to sell. Jefferson's initial reaction was to affirm the rights of the Indians "to hold the right to occupy their territory and maintain their political autonomy."[12]

While Jefferson observed that Indians were different from Europeans, he did respect their cultures enough to collect Indian vocabularies. The objective was ultimately to demonstrate "a common origin between the people of color of the two continents."[13] Refuting those who labeled the Indian inferior, Jefferson contended that Indians were "on a level with whites in the same uncultivated state."[14] Jefferson had such a keen interest in studying the Indians that he compiled notes on "their governments, numbers and their burial grounds," which he personally visited.[15] Race was very much on his mind because of slavery; however, he saw the Indian and slavery issues as being very different. Indians were seen as an immediate threat to the lives, property, and plans for westward expansion of White America, while slaves did not appear to be an immediate threat to the expansion of the United States.[16] President Jefferson clearly felt the burden of playing a major role in shaping and executing the United States' Indian policy. Even before acquiring the Louisiana territory, Jefferson had the land surveyed by Meriwether Lewis and William Clark. Their instructions were to inform the Indians that the United States had purchased France's rights to the territory. Lewis and Clark were reminded that the Indians still had the right to occupy the lands, but the U.S. government under Jefferson was now to act as their father. This marks the beginning of U.S. imposition over Indian nations.[17]

As president, Jefferson wanted the Indians to move west and become "civilized." He felt that the best route for achieving this objective was for the Native peoples to adopt the American-style agricultural lifestyle because hunting was perceived as an inadequate way of supplying clothing and subsistence.[18] His policy, called the **civilization program**, included the acquisition of huge tracts of land from tribal nations because more territory was needed as the White population inexorably expanded west. Jefferson felt that Indian removal would minimize the friction between the Whites and the Indians. Putting aside his scientific perspective, which showed a measure of respect for the Indian cultures, Jefferson requested $15,000 from

Congress in 1796 to civilize the Indians.[19] Jefferson's policies opened more land for settlers, as he initiated a removal policy that was in contradiction to his "openly stated goals to civilize, educate, and assimilate" Indians "into White society."[20]

Did Thomas Jefferson truly respect Native peoples and their culture, or was his perspective marred by expansionist ambitions?

Friction over land naturally arose between American settlers, who were defended by the U.S. Army, and Native nations that lived west of the Appalachian Mountains. Indians rejected Jefferson's perspective that abandoning their land and lifestyle would bring them one step closer to civilization.[21] Indians were content to remain on their own land and abide by the treaties that had been signed with the U.S. government.

In the nineteenth century, the United States began to expand across the North American continent and internationally through wars that increased its presence and prestige on the world stage. Americans increasingly believed that, as Anglo-Saxons, they had a "manifest destiny" to expand their civilization westward. Additional land was acquired through the annexation of Texas in 1845, the Oregon territory in 1848, and the Mexican Cession in 1848. Now, U.S. land extended to the Pacific Ocean. In winning the Spanish-American War in 1898, the United States acquired colonies such as Puerto Rico, the Philippines, and Guam. The fruits of war greatly increased the size of the United States, while simultaneously the population expanded to over seventy-five million with new immigrants. From the U.S. perspective, it needed land to satisfy its growing populace. From the Native perspective, U.S. expansion was an ever-growing threat to their remaining property, political rights, and their way of life as they became surrounded by the United States.

Native nations and individuals who had both worked with and fought against colonists in the Revolutionary War and French and Indian War now had to contend with an ambitious neighbor no longer burdened by foreign monarchs. As in past experiences with Europeans, Indians found that the United States frequently violated its treaties and other diplomatic agreements with Indian nations and failed to consistently recognize their sovereign rights. This lack of recognition would play out in the U.S. judicial system, as Native peoples felt compelled to use the laws and institutions of their aggressive neighbor to defend themselves.

U.S. FEDERAL POLICY ERODES INDIAN RIGHTS, 1830s

The nineteenth century was characterized by a struggle over Indian lands and an erosion of their rights that had been recognized in treaties. Settlers continued to encroach upon Indian lands, especially in the southern states, where the land was suitable for large plantations. This area of the United States was largely populated by the Five Civilized Tribes. The Cherokee, in particular, willingly engaged the U.S. economic and political systems and modified their legal and political society accordingly. The mixed-blood elite owned slaves, developed commercial enterprises, and built roads. By 1827 the Cherokee had developed a republican governmental structure with a bicameral legislature and a court system.[22] Between 1823 and 1832 three

Map 2.2   U.S. Westward Expansion

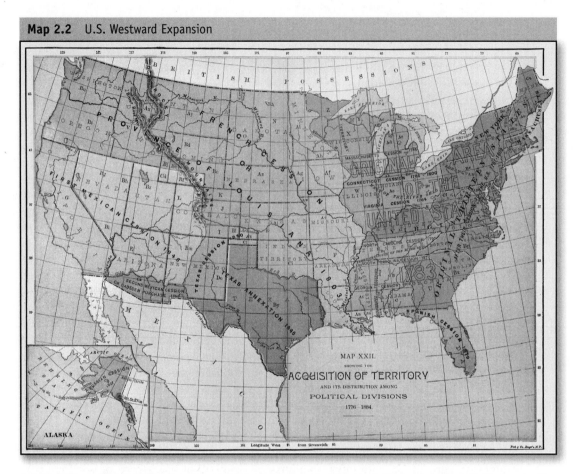

Between 1776 and 1884, the United States expanded its territory from the East Coast to the West, claiming lands that had previously been populated for millennia by Native nations. White settlers quickly became the dominant majority.

cases involving Native nations and issues came before the U.S. Supreme Court, with Chief Justice John Marshall presiding. These key Indian court cases—*Johnson v. M'Intosh* (1823), *Cherokee Nation v. Georgia* (1831), and *Worcester v. Georgia* (1832), commonly referred to as the **Marshall Trilogy of cases**[23]—determined, from the federal government's perspective, the political status of Native nations, their relationship with the United States and the states, and Native property rights.[24]

These cases involved conflicts between the states and the federal government whenever states did not wish to adhere to a federal law. The executive and judicial branches were still testing the scope of their powers prior to the Civil War. Could the president ignore a Supreme Court opinion that he did not like? Would Chief Justice Marshall's assertion that the Supreme Court could declare a state law unconstitutional be accepted by the states?

Undermining Indian Sovereignty:
Johnson v. M'Intosh and *Cherokee Nation v. Georgia*

Chief Justice Marshall's role was vitally important in all three cases. In *Johnson v. M'Intosh* (1823), the chief justice articulated a position that dramatically diminished property rights of Native nations. The dispute concerned property rights of American colonists who bought land from the Piankeshaw in contradiction of King George III's edict against individuals purchasing land west of the Appalachians without crown permission. The Piankeshaw owned the land, while simultaneously King George III of England claimed the land. After the Revolutionary War the United States acquired ownership and sold some tracts of land to William M'Intosh. Heirs of the colonists who purchased the land contested M'Intosh's ownership.[25]

The Marshall Court had to decide who owned the land if the Piankeshaw were a sovereign nation that could sell the land, or were they subordinate to the U.S. government? Chief Justice Marshall along with six other justices held that the doctrine of discovery granted first European countries and then the United States a superior title to Indian lands because, according to Marshall, the lands were "effectively vacant" when Europeans found them.[26] Marshall asserted that Indians "could not sell tribal lands without the consent of the United States because tribal sovereignty was 'limited' and 'impaired.'" Basing his opinion on the doctrine of discovery, Marshall held that the United States had "*paramount sovereignty* over all persons and lands within its borders." Justice Marshall's interpretation of the Doctrine of Discovery takes on a racial perspective in contrast to the original interpretation of relying on Christian principles. This case established that tribal **sovereignty** could be limited by Congress.[27] Prior to Marshall's ruling, Indians were understood as citizens of sovereign nations, which conducted foreign policy through diplomacy or warfare. This case effectively gave the U.S. government the power to limit the property rights of Native nations. The once sovereign Native nations that had wielded complete ownership of their own lands were now held to be territorially subordinate to the United States.

The Cherokee nation, which had a written language, national newspaper, political system based on laws and a constitution, and even slave labor, was involved in the next two cases—*Cherokee Nation v. Georgia* and *Worcester v. Georgia*.[28] As states saw increased conflict between settlers and Indians, they sought to remove Indians from the state. This was problematic because by treaty with the U.S. government, Indians owned their land but could sell it to the government. This situation led to multiple conflicts: between state and federal law; between President Andrew Jackson, a former Indian fighter, and the Supreme Court; and between the Cherokee and the state of Georgia. Boundary lines delineating the state of Georgia versus land to which the Cherokee and Creek had title were laid out in the Compact of 1802. Under the agreement Georgia obtained title and sovereignty to its present-day borders. However, the Cherokee and Creek did not relinquish their title to land within Georgia's new boundaries. Under this agreement the federal government was obligated to "extinguish all of the Indian titles within the new boundaries of the state of Georgia as soon as they could be 'peaceably obtained, and on reasonable terms.'" Ratification of the compact committed the federal government to the removal of the Indian nations.[29]

In the 1830s, in response to pressures from White settlers, Georgia attempted to move Indians out of the state by passing laws that abolished the Cherokee court and legislature. Georgia then extended its laws over Cherokee land while nullifying Cherokee laws and political institutions. The Cherokee chief John Ross sued Georgia to stop it from trespassing and intruding in Cherokee governance.[30] The outcome of the case was based on the technical issue of whether the Cherokee nation was a "foreign state." The Cherokee nation held that it was a foreign state whose citizens were not citizens of the United States. However, the majority of justices held that tribes were not states "foreign to the United States." Justice Marshall was caught between a position stated in treaties, which considered the various tribes as sovereign nations with title to their own land, and the reality of the increasing pressure of White settlers. Conflict arose when Georgia wanted the Indians to sell their lands to the U.S. government, but the Indians were content to remain on their own land. Therefore, Chief Justice Marshall created a new status for Indian tribes: "domestic, dependent nations." By his definition, tribal nations were within U.S. borders, and supposedly these Indian nations relied on "the protection and treaty promises of the federal government"; this made them dependent. Therefore, they did not constitute a foreign government, and they lacked any standing before the Court. Some scholars viewed this case as the source of the idea that "the United States had a trust responsibility to the Indian nations." Indian rights and freedoms had again been eroded, as they were now labeled domestics and dependents of the United States.[31]

Inconsistency in the Court: *Worcester v. Georgia*

In *Worcester v. Georgia* (1832) the issue was land within the state of Georgia—land that the Cherokee owned but were not interested in selling to the U.S. government. In 1828 Georgia passed a law that extended its jurisdiction over the territory of the Cherokee nation. Marshall also wrote the landmark decision in *Worcester v. Georgia* (1832), which was decided in favor of the Indians. Now that Indians were considered "domestic dependent nations," federal laws were to "Manifestly consider the several Indian nations as distinct political communities, having territorial boundaries, *within which their authority [was] exclusive,* and have a right to all the lands within those boundaries, which [was] not only acknowledged, but guaranteed by the United States."[32] This is significant because the Court upheld the territorial integrity of Indian lands and the rights of tribal authority, affirmed treaties, and reminded the states that they had no jurisdiction in Indian Country.

The *Worcester* decision, while creating lasting precedent, did not protect the Cherokee people from removal. In addition to public opinion, several factors worked against enforcement of the Supreme Court's *Worcester* ruling. In this case Georgia had an ally in President Jackson, who had "led negotiations in nine of the eleven treaties between the southern tribes and the United States." The Cherokee had well-known supporters in Daniel Webster, Henry Clay, and Davy Crockett. Congress had passed the Removal Act in 1830, which eventually forced the relocation of thousands of Indians from the southeastern United States to Indian Territory, in what is now Oklahoma. (The Removal Act is discussed in greater detail below.) Greed and racism were certainly factors in enforcing this policy, but most important was President Jackson's belief that Indians could not expect to sustain their land claims and their traditional customs with the increasing encroachment of White settlements.[33] Another problem was that enforcing the Court's decision would have required sending federal troops to Georgia to protect the Indians, instead of protecting settlers from the Indians. Although the Supreme Court's decision in *Worcester* was in favor of the Indians, the federal government had no compelling reason to enforce it and more of an advantage in ignoring it.

The Marshall Trilogy was followed by a number of cases with questionable reasoning and obvious contradictions, that collectively provided the underpinnings for a body of law that has come to be known as Federal Indian Law. In cases such as *Ex parte Crow Dog* (1883), *United States v. Kagama* (1886), *Lonewolf v. Hitchcock* (1903), *Tee-Hit-ton v. United States* (1955), and *Dann v. United States* (1985), the Supreme Court extended Marshall's concept that Native nations had a subordinate or limited sov-

An Oglala Sioux encampment in the 1830s has a new neighbor in a trading post that will soon become a fort. The United States ratified nearly four hundred treaties with Native peoples, only to break provisions in all of them as the United States expanded its borders. In response to several cases brought by Indians to the U.S. Supreme Court, the Court ruled inconsistently and established decisive barriers to Indian rights.

ereignty. In contrast, the U.S. Congress was granted **plenary**—that is, full and absolute—power over Indian nations by the Supreme Court.[34] The *Lonewolf* case, for example, gave Congress the prerogative to unilaterally break treaties with Indian nations without tribal consent. The impact was that the Court "removed tribal consent as a factor in federal efforts to acquire more Indian lands."[35]

The basis for many of the interethnic conflicts was land, which was the Indians' primary resource. Indigenous peoples, whose territory had originally extended from coast to coast, had been dramatically diminished by the continuous influx of settlers and the diseases they brought, such as smallpox. Indians tried to fight

> How did the U.S. system of government fail Indians after the *Worcester* ruling acknowledged their sovereignty?

for their rights by using U.S. laws and the courts to enforce treaties and federal statutes designed to protect Natives. The Supreme Court, however, generally ruled in favor of the federal government or the states after 1830. When the Court did rule in favor of the Indians, local, state, and federal authorities often did not choose to enforce the rights of Indians. By the end of the 1830s, it was clear that Native Americans had no reliable means to pursue their interests within the U.S. government. The Indian Removal Act of 1830 aligned the president and

Congress on what should be done about Indians, the main obstacle to White settlers who wanted to move west unencumbered. With only the Supreme Court occasionally supporting Indian rights, but having no formal means to enforce their rulings, it was obvious that maintaining sovereignty as independent nations or having access to equal opportunity under U.S. law would present additional barriers they would have to confront.

Removal and the Trail of Tears, 1838–1839

Westward expansion increased pressure on Congress and the president to remove the Indians from the Mississippi Valley. The pattern of interaction between Whites and the Indians was a familiar story. Settlers would encroach on the Indians' land. Their increasing numbers drove away the game that the Indians needed for food. If the Indians retaliated, the settlers as American citizens would seek federal, military protection. After hostilities, the victorious United States would have the Indians, often under duress, sign a treaty. The predictable result was that the Indians lost the vast bulk of their aboriginal homelands and were forced to relocate farther west.

This was a continuing cycle until President Jackson took drastic steps to remove Indians from all parts of the United States occupied by White settlers. Jackson, who had fought against the Indians as a general in the U.S. Army, did not place much stock in treaties. Instead, he believed that only military force would produce the desired results with Indians who were not adopting U.S. culture. With pressure from President Jackson, Congress passed the **Indian Removal Act of 1830,** which forced thousands of Native individuals in eastern states to move to what became present-day Oklahoma. Jackson used the military to enforce the act to remove most members of the Cherokee, Chickasaw, Choctaw, Creek, and Seminole from the southeastern states.[36] Numerous other Natives from many tribal nations were also forcibly relocated. Although they were assimilating to American social, educational, economic, and political customs, the Five Civilized Tribes, in particular, were physically in the way of White Americans who wanted their valuable land. This massive relocation sent Indians on an eight-hundred-mile journey known as the **Trail of Tears** to resettlement in western lands, called Indian Territory, in today's state of Oklahoma. The march resulted in the deaths of several thousand Indians due to illness and starvation during the harsh winter of 1838–1839. (See Map 2.2.)

Tribal nations were not monolithic, and there were divisions within some tribes over the issue of removal. Elias Boudinot was an assimilated Cherokee who had been educated in Connecticut and had married a White woman. However, he was ostracized and not accepted by Whites in Connecticut. As the editor of a Cherokee newspaper, he initially wrote articles in English that were pro–Cherokee nation and against the Indian Removal Act. He subsequently changed his opinion and advocated for removal because he thought it would be best for the Cherokee. However, Cherokee leaders who opposed removal ousted him as editor. He felt that for Cherokee "their only hope to continue as a people, to continue their nation, to preserve their sovereignty was to give up their land in the Southeast and move west." According to historian Theda Perdue, Boudinot "believed that it was more important to preserve the people than to preserve the land." Consequently, Boudinot, along with his cousin John Ridge, and his uncle Major Ridge, was instrumental in negotiating the Treaty of New Echota, which provided for the removal of most Cherokee.[37]

All Cherokee did not agree with Boudinot's position that moving west was good for the Cherokee nation. After the Cherokee arrived in the West, revenge was taken by those whose

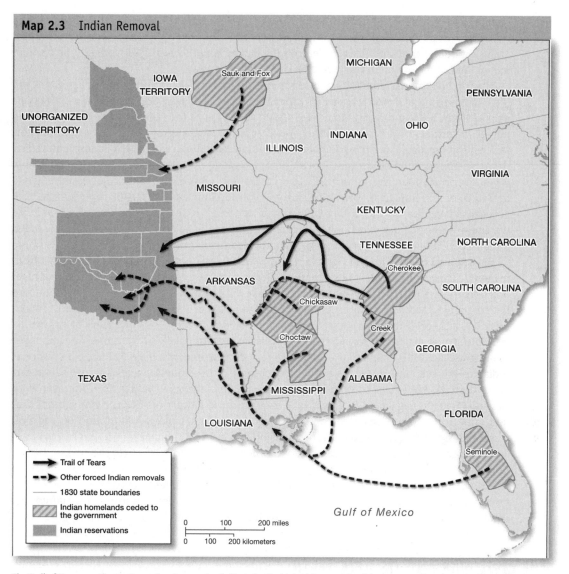

Map 2.3 Indian Removal

The Trail of Tears was the most prominent example of efforts by the United States to forcibly remove Indians from the land it wanted. Those removed during the Trail of Tears were settled in Indian Territory, which within a few decades was also desired by Whites, leading to additional property losses by those nations.

relatives had died on the arduous road from the Cherokee homeland. Elias Boudinot, his cousin, and his uncle were killed by fellow Cherokee.[38]

Indians who did not seek to assimilate were now quickly losing their battle to retain their land. The Trail of Tears set a pattern that would be repeated as Whites moved further west after the Civil War. Once the removal policy was implemented, the United States and Indians moved into a new phase of their relationship. Jackson's removal policy was the beginning of Indians coming under greater control of the U.S. government, with little autonomy and even fewer rights. Removal of the Indians was followed by confinement to reservations; assimilation programs that demeaned and disregarded tribal cultures; and the continued loss and breakup of Indian land, most of which was parceled out to White settlers.

The forced removal of Indians to reservations did not end the conflict between Indians and the U.S. government. Indians resisted further White intrusion and land grabs under the leadership of Red Cloud and Sitting Bull. Red Cloud, a leader of the Lakota, was an experienced fighter in territorial wars against other Indian nations. Starting in 1866, Red Cloud masterminded the most successful war between an Indian nation and the United States. Angered by the U.S. Army's building forts in Lakota territory along the Bozeman Trail, in what is now Wyoming to the Montana gold fields, Red Cloud began attacking the forts. He successfully defeated the U.S. forces at Fort Phil Kearny, Wyoming, in December 1866. By 1868 the U.S. government agreed to the Treaty of Laramie, whereby it relinquished its forts along the Bozeman Train and guaranteed the Lakota possession of the half of South Dakota that included the Black Hills, as well as parts of Montana and Wyoming.[39]

Indians had to continue to fight to retain their land to prevent miners and settlers from invading. This problem was taken on by the legendary Sitting Bull, a Hunkpapa Lakota chief and holy man. The U.S. Army sent George Armstrong Custer in 1874 to the Black Hills to confirm that gold had been discovered. This part of the Dakota Territory was considered a sacred area that was "off-limits to white settlement by the Fort Laramie Treaty of 1868." Despite this prohibition, prospectors stormed the Black Hills looking for gold. The U.S. government sought to buy the Black Hills area, but the Lakota were not interested in selling. The commissioner of Indian affairs responded to the Lakota by declaring all Lakota who were not on reservations by January 31, 1876, hostile to the United States. The battle of Little Big Horn followed with General Custer facing Sitting Bull and three thousand Native warriors from several nations that had joined him. The consolidated Native force won that historic battle, and Sitting Bull remained firmly defiant against White intrusion and cultural practices.[40]

The military loss compelled the U.S. government to send more troops to the area in dogged pursuit of Sitting Bull, whose combined forces had returned to their original nations. After spending several years in Canada he returned to the United States, where he lived on Indian reservations. In the end, he never accepted the rules of the reservation or Christianity, but instead lived in a cabin on the Grand River with two wives until his death in 1890.[41]

THE CIVIL WAR AND ITS AFTERMATH: SLAVEHOLDING AND THE FOURTEENTH AMENDMENT

The history and treatment of Native peoples is intertwined with that of Blacks. Indians and slaves were a problem for the U.S. government even when the Constitution was being written. Both are mentioned in Article I, Section 2, concerning Congress's power to levy taxes. In counting people in the states, the Constitution excluded "Indians, not taxed" and referred to slaves as "three-fifths of all other Persons." This officially codified the U.S. racialization of both Native Americans and Blacks as being inferior—and of lesser value—than Whites. There was Indian slavery in the colonies, but it became a divisive issue. By 1717 the Indian slave trade was waning because of the fear of future Indian rebellions. British colonists then concentrated their attention on African slavery, as they developed a racial ideology that sought to separate Africans from Indians and to keep them antagonistic toward one another.[42] Indians were far more difficult to control than slaves, who were neither organized nor armed. As racial policies evolved regarding Indians, the president and later Congress found it easier to advocate removal and separation of Indians from the U.S. population, while the more controllable African slave population could remain subordinate to all Whites. With the removal of most Indians from Georgia in 1830, the land in the lower South was available for White settlers to grow cotton on plantations with Black slave labor.

Slaves who were acquired through warfare were not uncommon within tribal nations in North America prior to European colonization. The Five Civilized Tribes were considered "civilized" by Whites in part because they had adopted the idea of private land ownership, plantation farming, and enslavement of Africans.[43] The Cherokee were notable because they retained slaves until 1866. Blacks were useful to Indians as workers, but also as middlemen in transactions with the White community. Racial identity as a result of slaveholding and intermarriage remains an ongoing issue in the twenty-first century, some Cherokee with African American and Indian ancestry—referred to as freedmen—acquired citizenship in that nation under the 1866 treaty and are entitled to tribal and federal benefits as Native citizens.[44]

In contrast, some Seminole in Florida refused to follow the U.S. dictate to move west of the Mississippi. In rejecting the policy of selling or owning slaves in the same manner as Whites, those who remained in Florida alongside free and runaway slaves became known as Black Seminoles. Blacks were treated as part of the community, rather than as a subordinate group in a racial hierarchy. They enjoyed personal freedom and owned property. In some cases, Seminole chiefs married Black women. However, Blacks were useful as translators in trading with the British or as military advisors. Black Seminoles still reside in Florida and in Oklahoma.[45]

Native American Exclusion, African American Inclusion

The Northern victory in the Civil War resulted in two different outcomes for Indians and Blacks, both of whom were outsiders of U.S. mainstream society and its political processes. Prior to the Civil War (1861), Blacks were either slaves, freedmen, or in some cases citizens of a state. After the Civil War, the Fourteenth Amendment was written expressly to incorporate Blacks into the political system by providing citizenship and granting Black men the right to vote. Blacks could now receive all of the rights and privileges of other U.S. citizens of European descent, at least theoretically. (See Chapter 3.) This was not the case for Indians, who did not seek political incorporation. The Union victory in the war did not restore their status as sovereign nations, nor did it bring them freedom from U.S. government intrusion.

Congress, in fact, hardly considered Indians at all when it drafted the Fourteenth Amendment. A congressional report stated that the status of Indians was based on numerous treaties, acts of Congress, and Supreme Court decisions. It concluded that Indians were members of separate nations, having treaty relations with the United States, which exempted them from U.S. laws. The Fourteenth Amendment was intended to address "the change in the status of the former slave which had been affected during the War, while it recognize[d] no change in the status of Indians."[46] Congress clearly wanted to follow the policy that had been estab-lished in Supreme Court cases such as *Johnson v. M'Intosh, Cherokee Nation v. Georgia,* and *Worcester v. Georgia,* that Indians were members of recognized tribes, had treaty relations with the United States, and were therefore exempt "from the operation of our laws, and the jurisdic-tion of our courts."[47]

The 1830s were a turbulent time during President Jackson's first term in office, as federal-ism was still evolving. Not only were there tensions between the federal government and the states, there also was no agreement on Indian policy between the Supreme Court and the president. Georgia and South Carolina were asserting states' rights in an attempt to override federal authority. South Carolina was opposed to a tariff act, and Georgia wanted to implement its own Indian policy. Consequently, there was no consistent Indian policy, although the Marshall Trilogy was beginning to set a federal policy regarding Indian rights.

As history prior to this point had shown, however, the United States frequently acted in a manner that did not respect the sovereignty of Indian nations and applied its laws and institu-tions to Native peoples when it was convenient to expand territorial, economic, and political interests. The decision not to include Indians in the Fourteenth Amendment, while broadly affirming tribal sovereignty, served to deny individual Natives who had abandoned their nations access to the laws and institutions that could grant them the same rights as other minority group members at this time and provide them with a path toward equal opportunity. Instead, Indian nations over time came to be dominated by the United States, and even indi-vidual Natives were deprived of any basic rights.

A Limited Solution: Reservations and the Bureau of Indian Affairs

By the 1880s Native nations no longer represented a military threat to the U.S. govern-ment. The process of forced removal, loss of land, and depopulation had significantly dam-aged the Indians' way of life. While some still fought against the Whites, many more were weary of battle and sought a resolution to their conflict with the United States. Indians and the U.S. government reached agreements whereby indigenous peoples now lived in reserved areas exclusively set aside for them, from which we get the term **reservation.** (Map 2.3 illus-trates reservations in the United States today.) Indians reluctantly agreed to cease military operations and to turn over their remaining lands to the U.S. government in exchange for guaranteed permanent protection from further incursion by White settlers.[48] They retained the right to self-governance within their diminished homelands. This federal policy offered transplanted or merely reduced Native peoples the possibility of rebuilding their communi-ties and attaining the self-sufficiency that had been slowly taken away from them over the preceding years.

With the establishment of reservations Native nations retained governing power, but over time they gradually became subject to U.S. and sometimes state law. U.S. citizenship for Native individuals was imposed in 1924 and tribal citizens remained marginalized and isolated from the mainstream society, with few resources available to them. Congress by then had largely assumed responsibility for managing Indian relations, and the long ago established **Bureau of Indian Affairs (BIA)** within the U.S. Department of the Interior was charged with the conflict-ing tasks of fulfilling the federal government's treaty and trust obligations to Native peoples,

Map 2.4   Indian Reservations in the Continental United States

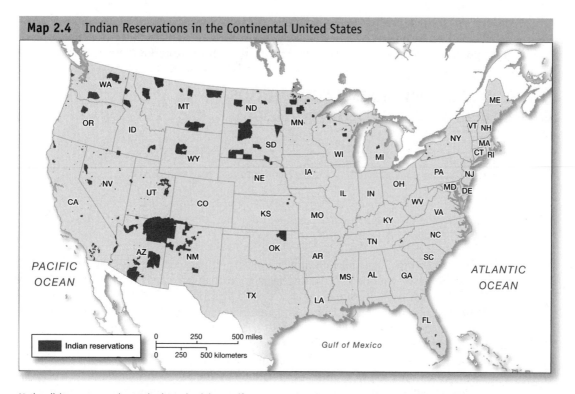

Natives living on reservations today have the right to self-governance, but the measures taken before the U.S. government agreed to their exclusive right to the land and honored that agreement frequently left Native peoples far from their original homes and greatly decimated in population and means.

Source: Indian Reservations in the Continental United States, National NAGPRA, National Park Service, U.S. Department of the Interior, http://www.nps.gov/nagpra/DOCUMENTS/ResMap.htm.

but also with forcing tribal individuals to assimilate into the larger society.

The confinement of Indians to reservations was one of the most stringent of government policies, since it permanently separated Native nations from American society. Indians had been the focus of federal attention since 1819, when

 What factors precluded the United States from bringing Native peoples and individuals and their concerns into its policymaking process?

Congress enacted "a permanent fund to 'civilize' tribal individuals." By 1824 John C. Calhoun had established an Office of Indian Affairs. In 1849 this agency was moved from the War Department to the newly created Interior Department. Later known as the Bureau of Indian Affairs, this often corrupt and inept agency became the hated source of unilateral government policies.

Representatives of the BIA made little effort to understand Indian culture, religious practices, or traditions. Native peoples, frequently confined to desolate reservation lands, were subjected to the paternalistic policies of members of Congress and the whims of bureaucrats. While Indians may have resided territorially within the United States, they remained outside of the political system and were not protected by the U.S. Constitution.

U.S. FEDERAL POLICY: ASSIMILATION VERSUS CULTURE AND SOVEREIGNTY, 1870s–1950s

The United States continued its practice of violating provisions of treaties with Native nations even after armed conflict ended. In 1871, as part of its ramped-up assimilation campaign, Congress decided that it would no longer conduct treaties with Indians:

> No Indian national or tribe, within the territory of the United States shall be acknowledged or recognized as an independent nation, tribe, or power, with whom the United States may contract by treaty. . . .[49]

In 1885 the United States began a policy whereby it usurped the sovereignty that it had recognized in Native nations by enacting legislation that effectively supplanted traditional tribal criminal and civil authority in Indian Country. The Major Crimes Act, which was part of the Indian Appropriations Act of 1885, "unilaterally extended [U.S.] jurisdiction over felonies occurring among Indians in Indian territories," stripping Indian tribes of jurisdiction in major criminal cases. This was only one act out of approximately five thousand federal statutes aimed at once more extending the U.S. reach into Indian affairs.[50]

A further blow was struck against tribal nations by the decision *United States v. Kagama* (1886), which challenged the assertion that Congress had jurisdiction over crimes between one Indian and another. In delivering the opinion of the Supreme Court, Justice Samuel F. Miller addressed the issue of sovereignty:

> . . . But these Indians are within the geographical limits of the United States. The soil and the people within these limits are under the political control of the United States. The soil and the people within these limits are under the political control of the Government of the United States. These Indian tribes are the wards of the nation. They are communities dependent on the United States. . . .[51]

These and other cases and statutes undermined the sovereignty, proprietary rights, and cultural distinctiveness that Native nations had struggled to protect, and their increasingly futile efforts faced another assault when the federal government increased pressure to incorporate Natives into the now-majority White mainstream. Indians' goal to preserve their cultural traditions and self-government was in stark contrast to the objectives of the waves of European immigrants seeking entry into the United States at the time. **Assimilation,** the process of becoming American, was desirable for immigrants who often observed special days or prepared ethnic foods, but simultaneously adopted American customs and language. Native peoples, for the most part, did not share this desire to assimilate. At the same time, Christian missionaries pushed for assimilation by converting Indians to Christianity and educating them in American customs.

Native indifference to Euro-American assimilation worried some Christian groups, which met at Lake Mohonk, New York, from 1883 to 1916 to discuss their concerns regarding Indian affairs. Assimilationist ideas from these conferences eventually became the core principles of the 1887 General Allotment Act as the government sought to territorially break down the remaining communal lands of tribal nations, believing that such a process would expedite the "Americanization" and "civilization" of individual tribal landowners. Coercive assimilation was the unilateral federal policy goal that aimed to destroy Indian cultural values such as the collective land system; respect for natural resources of land, water, and forests; and a society not stratified on the basis of racial distinctions.

The **General Allotment Act of 1887,** also known as the Dawes Act, became the major vehicle for assimilation. Federal legislation sought to assimilate Indians into American culture by unilaterally changing their lifestyle and relationship to the land. The plan was to shift Indians from their traditional collective land system to the White tradition of personal land use by granting (allotting) Indians a parcel of 40, 80, or 160 acres of land. The model for this land distribution policy was the 1862 Homestead Act, which allotted settlers 160 acres of land after the head of a family had cleared land, built a house, and lived on the land for five years. As we discuss in Chapter 6, most beneficiaries of the Homestead Act were White settlers. This plan had worked well with European immigrants who wanted to own their own land, but when it was applied to Native individuals, it disregarded their cultural values and lifestyle, territorial patterns, and sovereign rights.

The General Allotment Act was one more federal plan to civilize and Americanize Indians by eliminating collective landholdings, dismantling Indian governing institutions, and eradicating Indian cultural traditions. The allotment plan diminished remaining Native land holdings by approximately two-thirds. Tribes were coerced by the federal government to relinquish landholdings because of pressure from state and territorial leaders, Congress, the BIA, and White settlers who desired to settle in the West. The federal government supported the policy because it would "hasten the arrival of civilization and Christianity at the tribal doorstep."[52] Indian landholdings became fragmented, which in turn broke up tribal social structure. The result was that Indians and Whites gradually came to live side by side, creating a pattern of land ownership within reservations that, contrary to federal expectations, did not promote more amicable relations between Whites and Indians. What this policy did was dramatically undermine the structure of formerly cohesive tribal communities. By the 1920s, the government recognized that its plan had not worked. Indians had not warmly adopted the White occupational model of becoming farmers or ranchers, nor had most adopted American cultural or economic habits.

The Dawes Act marks an era—1887 to 1934—in which Indian nations and their citizens came to be treated as though they were wards of the federal government, which had formally adopted the role of guardian. Indians who were not adopting American cultural values and traditions were relegated to a subordinate status and deprived of the right to make decisions about their remaining lands, governments, and economies. Indians continued to meet and negotiate with representatives of the U.S. government, but they had little real influence and were unable to use the laws, tactics, or institutions available to the majority or other minority communities. For example, in this same period, many Mexican Americans had U.S. citizenship and could participate in the political process. They owned businesses alongside Whites, could buy land and build homes, and were able to use U.S. laws and institutions to promote their interests. (See Chapter 4.) In contrast, many Native individuals, while theoretically having the rights of U.S. citizenship, were largely denied actual benefits and protections as either Natives or Americans. Under the allotment program, the Department of the Interior acted as a trust agent for leasing Indian land allotments to the natural gas, oil, and timber industries, along with grazing and mining interests. Fees were paid to the U.S. Treasury that were held in trust for the Indians, but individual Natives rarely received all of the money due them, prompting a major class-action lawsuit in the 1990s that would finally be settled in 2010.

After enduring forced removal and U.S. assimilation efforts, Native peoples struggled to rebuild their communities and governing structures in order to maintain their way of life on reservations. The Dawes Act further reduced Indian resources and autonomy. These circumstances drastically limited their ability to act effectively to advance their interests. Native peoples are the only group subject to such focused legislative, executive, and judicial destruction of cultural values and confinement to reservations in peace time. The racist policies of the Jackson era were subsequently carried out under the guise of helping Indians assimilate by breaking up collective landholdings.

White Cultural Dominance and Indian Identity

The late nineteenth and early twentieth centuries were characterized by a dramatic loss of additional land, brought about by the Dawes Act, an imposition of U.S. cultural values, and a marginalization because of life confined to reservations. Natives were physically isolated from American society and marginalized politically because their sovereignty as Native nations was not being respected and they did not have the same rights of citizenship that European immigrants enjoyed. Consequently, Indians had very little influence on members of Congress who might have been supportive of their position. When it came to Indians, the United States continued to treat them as a special case.

Throughout the history of their interactions with Whites, Indians encountered significant barriers because Europeans, and then the U.S. government, firmly believed that White American culture was superior to the non-Christian Indian culture. Thus it seemed natural from this perspective that an assimilation policy would benefit all Indians. The federal government unilaterally decided to impose ethnocidal policies on Indians that were coercive, disrespectful of indigenous culture, and, in the long run, deeply harmful. While the government's objective was to reallocate the land, it also sought to influence cultural values in response to pressure from Christian groups that advocated assimilation.

By 1887 the government and Christian social reformers were anxious to assimilate Indians into American society. To speed up the process that would undermine tribal culture, they sought to replace the traditional communal economic base with a system of private property; send children to distant boarding schools that separated them from their families; and regulate every aspect of Indian social life, including marriage and religious beliefs. Indian tribes could only become self-governing by adopting constitutions that had been approved by the federal government.[53]

The Dawes Act was so antithetical to the values of Indian communities that it was considered by Indians to be part of a plan to destroy all of their culture.[54] As David Wilkins, a scholar of Native politics, notes, all of these policies "undermined the confidence, hopes, and self-respect of indigenous communities."[55] The allotment plan struck at the heart of tribal social structure, which was founded on a communal land policy. Indians did not have the perspective that property was private, belonging to only one person. Instead, land was a collective gift from the Creator for common usage, such as hunting, fishing, and planting. Land was to provide basic material needs and subsistence. Natives saw themselves as stewards, not as owners of the land.[56] In an effort to break up the reservations, the federal

Native American children stand before the Carlisle Indian School, where they will soon become students. The United States established boarding schools across the country to encourage Native children—sometimes forcibly—to assimilate to the dominant White culture. Students wore Whites' style of dress, were required to speak English, and were taught skills and trades that Whites deemed appropriate.

government offered Indians tracts of land—held in trust—with the hope and expectation that they would become "civilized," independent farmers within twenty-five years. The federal government retained control by prohibiting the sale of the land for twenty-five years without the permission of the secretary of the interior. This assimilation process was to make Indians conform to an American lifestyle by living on a parcel of land that was considered private property.

The government decided that any land that was not allotted to tribal members would be declared "surplus." This extra land could then be sold to non-Indians (Whites). The plan provided for non-Indians to reside among Indians to serve as appropriate models of White behavioral patterns.[57] Indians were powerless to contest the sale of the "surplus" land and, consequently, lost millions of acres. Not only was there a huge loss of land, but the land that was retained was often less desirable for farming.[58] The federal government purchased over 200,000 acres of the surplus land itself, which amounted to a more than 90 percent loss of Indian lands. In the case of the Cheyenne and Arapaho in Oklahoma, over 529,000 acres were retained, but over 3 million were declared surplus.[59] Between 1887 and 1934, the Indian land base dropped from about 138 million to only 48 million acres.[60]

The Five Civilized Tribes had been exempt from the Dawes Act because of previous treaties. They were placed under additional pressure by the Curtis Act of 1898, which provided for the allotment of their property. Interestingly, the original draft of the Curtis Act was authored by U.S. Representative Charles Curtis, who was of Kansa, Osage, Poawatami, and French descent. Curtis, however, was dissatisfied with the outcome because it contained little of the original draft. The Five Civilized Tribes had been running their own governments and schools, which "had produced more college graduates than were then living in either Texas or Oklahoma." Along with this, the federal government terminated the indigenous governance structure of the Five Civilized Tribes and replaced them with government officials appointed by the president.[61]

Theodore Roosevelt, a Spanish-American War (1898) hero, was president when the United States became an expansive colonial power by acquiring Puerto Rico, Guam, the Virgin Islands, and the Philippines. Acquiring land as a part of the peace treaty made the United States a powerful new member of the club of colonial powers. In the twentieth century, land acquisition remained a driving government interest, as did maintaining racial barriers against any group that was not White. President Roosevelt and the commissioner of Indian affairs, Francis E. Leupp, clearly stated that the goal of the forced assimilation policy, as expressed via allotment, was to act as "a mighty pulverizing engine to break up the tribal mass."[62] In 1921 Indian commissioner Charles Burke stated in unequivocal terms the real intent of the policy: "It is not desirable or consistent with the general welfare to promote [American Indian national] characteristics and organization."[63]

The Role of Blood Quantum in Indian Affairs

Racial classification had been an intractable problem for both the state and the federal government because of the introduction of Africans as slaves into the American population. Children resulting from unions between Whites and Blacks created a mixed-race population that Americans felt had to be classified. The category they developed was "mulatto." (See Chapter 1.) The federal government tended to classify persons with Native and any Black ancestry as Black because Southern planters found it easier to dominate a dual racial system of Blacks/Whites. It was simpler to classify everyone as either White, which gave you a privileged position no matter how poor you were, or Black, which usually meant you were a slave. This classification system facilitated capturing runaway slaves and maintaining order on plantations. Indians frequently identified as White to avoid the stigma of being Black. Not until after the Civil War in 1870 did a separate classification for Indians exist in the U.S. Census. Simultaneously, some people identified as Indians to reduce paying taxes to the federal government.

Not only did the Dawes Act attack Native American property and cultural values, it also set the stage for a new factor regarding indigenous identity. In 1917 the commissioner of Indian Affairs insisted that blood quantum be part of the calculation for determining whether a Native remained eligible for federal trust protection as a legally "incompetent" person. The presumption was that Natives with more than one-half Native blood were less "competent" to handle their own economic affairs, while individuals with less than one-half blood—the other half being White—were presumed to be more sophisticated because of the preponderance of White blood. This is similar to the ancestry rules devised for Blacks, discussed in Chapter 1, in which the federal government established categories like "octoroon" to represent those with one-eighth Black blood.

The **blood quantum** test was and remains a unique and arbitrary test, and many Native nations and federal agencies still rely on it to determine eligibility for services, benefits, and tribal citizenship. Certainly, European immigrants were never subjected to racial tests that determined their identity based on a percentage of blood. Yet there are similarities between Indians and African Americans on proving their identity based on the extent of their White ancestry. African Americans were subjected to the one-drop rule, which decreed that any ancestor of African descent, even one-sixteenth or one-thirty-second, made one Black. For Native people, an individual had to have a preponderance of Native blood to be deemed indigenous, and therefore eligible for tribal status. For both Indians and African Americans, being able to prove White ancestry was a way to elevate their status.

 Was blood quantum for Indians any less racialized a policy than the one-drop rule for African Americans?

Distinctions among Indians as to who was a full-blood, a half-blood, or simply a mixed-blood became important for many reasons. Membership in a tribal nation was determined on a nation-by-nation basis. Being a member depended on a number of factors: "social, cultural, linguistic, territorial, socio-psychological, and ceremonial."[64]

Through the blood quantum policy the federal government heavily influenced tribal membership and Native identity itself. This sometimes pitted Natives against one another based on how assimilated they allegedly appeared to be. But defining who is an *Indian* is a substantial problem because there are both ethnographic and legal definitions of the term. Felix Cohen, a leading attorney on federal Indian law in the 1930s and 1940s, explained it this way:

> Ethnologically, the Indian race may be distinguished from the Caucasian, Negro, Mongolian, and other races. If a person is three-fourths Caucasian and one-fourth Indian, it is absurd, from the ethnological standpoint, to assign him to the Indian race. Yet, legally such a person may be an Indian. From a legal standpoint, then, the biological question of race is generally pertinent, but not conclusive. Legal status depends not only upon biological, but also upon social factors, such as the relation of the individual concerned to a white or Indian community. . . .
>
> We may nevertheless find some practical value in a definition of "Indian" as a person meeting two qualifications: (a) That some of his ancestors lived in America before its discovery by the white race, and (b) That the individual is considered an "Indian" by the community in which he lives.[65]

Once the blood quantum was introduced as a qualifier for Indian benefits to property and continued federal trust protection, the government decided that it could also be used as a major "eligibility factor" for any federal benefit program for Native nations and individuals. Indians found themselves subject to the blood quantum standard in order to obtain health care, education, and annuity payments.[66] Tribal reservations, often located far from urban centers, have sometimes struggled to secure quality medical care, education programs, and economic development because of their remoteness. Other minority groups in urban areas have more accessible benefits to government programs such as Head Start and health clinics.

In the late nineteenth century, aside from the government, private individuals undertook assimilation efforts to bring Indians into American culture, so they would cut their hair, learn English, and wear suits and dresses. A prominent spokesman on Indian policy was General Richard Henry Pratt, who had served in the 10th Cavalry Buffalo Soldiers. As a former Indian fighter and an ardent proponent of assimilation, he was presumed to be an expert on what policy role the government should assume toward Indians. To promote his ideas, he founded and served as superintendent of the **Carlisle Indian School,** established in 1879. He emphasized learning English and becoming Christian as he endeavored to promote the philosophy of "kill the Indian, save the man." The culturally destructive plan forced young Natives into boarding schools run by Whites who sought to erase indigenous cultural identity. The boarding schools were designed so that members of the same tribe did not live together, in the hopes of breaking down tribal ties and fostering the learning of English. In order to socialize Indians into American habits and cultural values, they were placed in White homes in the summer to increase contact with American culture. The boarding school plan was only partially successful, however; Indian children who had spent years learning "civilized ways" often devised plans to retain their languages and values even while in school. Many of these individuals also decided to return to their reservations, which disappointed federal bureaucrats.

U.S. Citizenship Is Extended to Native Americans, 1924

By 1920 all U.S. citizens—men and women, Whites, Blacks, Latinos, Asians, and other groups—had the right to vote, even though serious issues remained for minority members, who frequently faced daunting obstacles to exercising the franchise. Still, they, in theory, could engage in the U.S. political process. Some Native individuals, however, still lacked U.S. citizenship and therefore could not vote in state or federal elections. In the 1920s, extending American citizenship to Indians remained an unresolved issue. Were Indians citizens or foreigners? Although nearly two-thirds of Native individuals had acquired federal and state citizenship by 1920 through allotment, treaties, or specific congressional acts, the other one-third remained citizens solely of their Native nation.

After World War I, however, the issue of extending U.S. citizenship to remaining Native individuals was raised again because Natives who had volunteered to fight for the United States in Europe felt that they were entitled to voting rights in light of their service. Congressional proponents were the Progressive senators Burton K. Wheeler, Bob La Follette Jr., and Lynn Frazier. "Friends of the Indian" Whites, who were concerned about the condition and status of Indians, were advocates for assimilation and citizenship. These "friends" asserted, "The sad uniformity of savage tribal life must be broken up! Individuality must be cultivated."[67]

Native individuals had their own perspective. Anthropologist Arthur C. Parker, a Seneca, was active with the Society of American Indians (SAI), a group of college-educated men who had integrated into American society. They were the most pro-citizenship, assimilationist group. A founding member of SAI and a Santee Sioux, Charles Eastman, summed up the SAI position: "We do not ask for a territorial grant of separate government. We ask only to enjoy with Europe's sons the full privileges of American citizenship."[68]

After several bills were considered that tried to tie Indian lands to the granting of voting rights, Congress unilaterally extended citizenship to those remaining Native individuals in 1924 who had not yet acquired it. This made Native individuals, the original peoples of the land, the last category of individuals to acquire American citizenship. Importantly, it was understood that the grant of U.S. citizenship would not affect existing tribal property rights. Consequently, Native individuals remained simultaneously under the jurisdiction of tribal governments, state governments, and the federal government.[69]

Not all Native nations or individuals welcomed the imposition of U.S. citizenship. The Iroquois Confederacy responded to this political incorporation with a note to the federal government stating that they were not, had never been, and did not intend to become U.S. citizens.[70] As Wilkins notes, the Iroquois and members of other tribal nations refused to accept federal citizenship, arguing that their preexisting national status was sufficient. Since they had neither requested American citizenship nor gone through the normal procedures to attain it, they questioned how the United States could unilaterally extend its citizenship to their peoples, who constituted separate governmental bodies previously recognized in ratified treaties. Many Iroquois nationals today maintain the position that the congressional act that extended them U.S. citizenship has no effect on them. Moreover, a number of tribal nations continue to seek recognition before the United Nations as separate nations. Some Hopi and Iroquois citizens "travel abroad on passports issued by their own governments."[71] (See Box 2.2.)

Assimilation's End: The Indian Reorganization Act of 1934

Despite this backdrop of a struggling Indian identity in the face of a determined dominant culture, it was clear by the 1920s that the government's assimilation policies and allotment provisions were not having the desired effects. Boarding schools did not ease the paths of Natives into American society, while the allotment policy had only pauperized and made landless thousands of Natives. In some cases fraud was so rampant that some Indians lost all of their land, an integral part of their cultural fabric. With so many broken agreements, Indians were also less trusting of American motives. The federal government was searching for a new Indian policy, so it commissioned the Brookings Institution, an independent, non-government organization, to examine the conditions of Natives throughout the United States. The 1928 study, popularly known as the Meriam Report, was critical of past policies that had not adequately addressed the health, economic, educational, land, or legal status of Indians, who generally lived in dire poverty. The criticism of the BIA showed that federal administrators had not taken into account Indian cultural or property values. The report recommended the following:

> The fundamental requirement is that . . . [the Indian Service] be made an efficient educational agency, devoting its main energies to the social and economic advancement of the Indians, so that they may be absorbed into the prevailing civilizations. . . .
> The effort to substitute educational leadership for the more dictatorial methods now used in some places will necessitate more understanding of and sympathy for the Indian point of view.[72]

BOX 2.2 ROAD SIGN

Sovereignty Controversy: Indians Denied Travel with Tribal Passports

While newcomers to the United States often sought citizenship, a majority of Native individuals were never strong advocates for it. They were proud citizens of their own sovereign nations, and the United States sporadically acknowledged tribal sovereignty. Yet in 1924 the United States thrust citizenship upon tribal citizens, and consequently Natives now possessed dual and later treble citizenship, when states extended the franchise. Supporters of federal citizenship had various motives—from a desire to applaud Natives' military service in World War I, to diminish the oppressive regulatory powers of the Bureau of Indian Affairs over individual Indians, and to spur Indians to accept American culture. At its heart, Indian citizenship was a further effort by the U.S. government to absorb Indians into mainstream American life.

The issue of citizenship gained contemporary media attention in 2010, when a lacrosse team from the Iroquois Confederacy (the Iroquois invented the sport) sought to enter the United Kingdom for an international competition. They traveled with Haudenosaunee (Iroquois Confederacy) passports

but were denied entry. The British first required the United States to confirm that the athletes would be allowed reentry, which it initially refused to do. Once confirmed, the British again denied the team, claiming members would only be allowed entry with a passport from the United States or Canada. Changes in passport standards since 2001 established more stringent requirements and technology, and the Haudenosaunee passports did not meet these standards. Although the Iroquois Confederacy and its athletes lobbied hard for the British to allow them to travel with their documents, the conflict ended in a stalemate.

The altercation raised an enduring issue over recognition of Indian nations' sovereignty. The lacrosse team members had the option of using a U.S. or Canadian passport, but as part of the sovereign member nations of the Iroquois Confederacy, using the Haudenosaunee passport became an important matter of principle and, for a time, garnered national and international attention to barriers that Native peoples continue to face when they are exercising their national sovereignty.

It, along with other analyses, culminated in the federal government developing a modified statutory and policy approach to Indian affairs—the **Indian Reorganization Act (IRA).** The IRA was also known as the Wheeler-Howard Act, named after its sponsors, Senator Burton K. Wheeler and Representative Edgar Howard. This powerful law dramatically rejected the allotment policy, which had been in effect since 1887 and provided for the return of some Indian landholdings. Reservations were now to be considered important cultural units where Indians could govern themselves, writing their own constitutions and establishing elected tribal councils. Under the IRA, tribal governments would have a greater degree of self-governing authority, though still subject to the approval of the secretary of the interior.

This new perspective was driven in part by evaluating federal costs and by the belated realization that the unilateral imposition of non-Indian policies on Native peoples without any regard for their own distinctive institutions, languages, and cultures was fundamentally wrong and antidemocratic. With the collapse of the stock market in 1929 and the Great Depression, the federal government reconsidered the costs of running Indian affairs compared to allowing a measure of indigenous self-governance. New policies were crafted to show respect for the cultural and political traditions of Native nations.

The incoming Franklin D. Roosevelt administration proved to be favorable to the Indian community. The appointment of John Collier as head of the BIA was key to implementing the new policy because he was not a traditional bureaucrat. Formerly a social worker, Collier had respect for and knowledge of tribal cultures. When he accepted the position he felt optimistic that he could garner sufficient federal support for implementing the needed reforms. The IRA, which he helped draft, sought to reverse policy not only by stopping the allotment of Indian lands, but also by instituting educational reforms. And for the first time the federal government asked Native nations for their opinion about the bill and gave them an opportunity to choose their own governing arrangements. Indigenous support for the IRA was far from unanimous. Collier's greatest achievement, however, was giving the tribes an opportunity to express their views on the IRA.

A key player who facilitated getting Indian support was a Chippewa-Cree anthropologist and writer, D'Arcy McNickle, who worked hard to gain the trust of Natives wary of such a dramatic shift in federal policy. With considerable effort by both Collier and McNickle, 189 Indian nations—a total of 130,000 people—agreed to reorganization, while approximately 90,000 rejected the proposal.[73] This new government policy, which gave Indians a direct vote in accepting or rejecting a government proposal, was a substantial departure from previous unilateral federal decisions regarding Indian governance.

The IRA was a landmark law. Although it left the newly created tribal constitutions and bylaws subject to the approval of the secretary of the interior, for those tribes that accepted the provisions of the act, the allotment policy was terminated, a $10 million revolving credit fund was created to spur economic development, and tribal governing bodies were enabled to negotiate with non-Indian governments. This plan was to promote joint ventures with non-Indian businesses in order to improve the economic condition of Indians living on reservations. However, this effort to make the IRA acceptable met swift and strong resistance.[74]

In addition, the IRA provided for the regulation of resources and the establishment of an affirmative action policy for Indians within the BIA. This preferential hiring program, which favored Indians who worked at the BIA, was challenged in *Morton v. Mancari* (1974).[75] The Supreme Court held that affirmative action for Indians was a political, not a racial, classification that would be "upheld if rationally related to Congress's unique obligation to Indian tribes."

As was typical with Indian affairs, there was a contradiction in the IRA. The tribal constitutions rarely coincided with traditional White understandings of political authority and governance. In some cases, the IRA sometimes supplanted those indigenous institutions, which increased internal tribal differences.[76]

TERMINATION OF FEDERAL SUPPORT OF TRIBES, 1945–1950s

John Collier resigned from the BIA in 1945. His departure and the onset of World War II resulted in another period of upheaval in U.S.-Indian affairs because World War II took priority in government spending. Despite government reports documenting Indians' economic conditions and the extent of poverty among the tribes, and the mismanagement of the BIA, congressional policy preference continued to be for assimilation over tribal cultural autonomy.

In the 1940s most Indians were organized on reservations, but not all tribes had accepted reorganization. Indians were not confined to reservations, but they were still viewed as "problems" because often land on the reservations contained coal or uranium that the private sector wanted to mine. This question was part of the debate between the "assimilators" and "terminators," who wished absorption of Indians in order to create internal territorial integrity, and the "IRA liberals," who advocated maintaining Indian nations as colonized enclaves.[77] Indians were offered the choice between endorsing the IRA liberal position of colonization or finding ways to quietly express their discontent.

By 1952 the Bureau of Indian Affairs had submitted a list to Congress of various Indian tribes that it deemed "ready to undergo . . . complete termination of all federal services." This would effectively end the federal government's trust responsibility over "terminated" tribal communities.

ASSOCIATED PRESS

George Gillette (left), chair of the Fort Berthold Indian Tribal Business Council, covers his face and weeps as J. A. Krug, secretary of the interior, signs a contract accepting the tribe's sale of 155,000 acres of its reservation for a federal dam project in 1948. The termination of federal support for impoverished tribes left them with few resources to support themselves beyond what comparatively little land was left to them.

The proposal culminated in House Concurrent Resolution 108, known as the Termination Act, passed in 1953. Abruptly removing 2.5 million acres of land from Indian control only further destroyed links among tribal communities. This measure established the policy that would culminate by 1960 in the processing of some 109 cases of termination "affecting a minimum of 1,362 acres and 11,466 individuals."[78]

Besides termination, the federal government also spent about $1 million attempting to relocate thousands of Natives from rural or reservation areas to cities. Relocation was appealing to some Indians because the government provided moving expenses and job training if they went voluntarily. Approximately thirty-five thousand were resettled in Los Angeles, San Francisco, Denver, Phoenix, Minneapolis, Seattle, Boston, and Chicago, in the hope that they would abandon their ties to their tribal communities and join American society.[79]

Termination and relocation were two related policies that aimed to end tribal sovereign status. The negative consequences of termination were disastrous and utterly predictable. Wilkins notes how in two cases the Menominee of Wisconsin and the Klamath of Oregon found that their conditions declined precipitously after they had been terminated. Previously, both tribes were sustaining their peoples on reservations with more than adequate natural resources. After termination, conditions declined as tribal lands moved into private ownership and the trust relationship ended, which now placed Indians under state laws and subjected them to state taxes. In addition, federal services were ended and their status as legal and political sovereigns was effectively concluded.[80]

In what ways did the termination policy continue to erode indigenous sovereignty, treaty rights, and access to equal opportunity?

Native nations and individuals around the country began to openly protest and resist both termination and relocation. The Blackfeet of Montana, with the help of attorney Felix S. Cohen, physically occupied tribal buildings in the face of BIA impoundment of them. Another standoff was carried out by the Oglala Lakota of Pine Ridge, South Dakota. Spokespersons for the Association of American Indian Affairs used lobbying and public relations to defend Indians. They even endorsed IRA colonialism as their defense against termination. It was not until 1959 that the Eisenhower administration shifted the policy, announcing that it would no longer "terminate tribes without their consent."[81] The relocation policy continued until 1980, when the urban employment centers were closed.[82]

CIVIL RIGHTS AND SELF-DETERMINATION, 1960s–1970s

From the early days of their relationship with Whites, when that group was itself a minority, Native peoples have persistently resisted efforts to integrate into White society. Although just as persistently at a disadvantage when it came to combating such policies, the advent of the Civil Rights Movement in the 1960s and 1970s heightened public attention to the inequities in American social, economic, and political life. From Rosa Parks's defiance of Southern segregation in 1954 to D'Arcy McNickle's drafting of the Declaration of Indian Purpose in 1961, and through the 1960s, minority groups—Indians, African Americans, Latinos, and others— demanded their rights and equality. For Indians, who had long tried to promote their interests from both outside and within the U.S. system, the founding of the American Indian Movement (AIM) in Minnesota in 1968 ushered in a new wave of militant activism. Native rejection of federal mandates became more visible and insistent in 1969, when scholar and activist Vine Deloria Jr. published *Custer Died for Your Sins: An Indian Manifesto,* often viewed as the seminal work in Native resistance literature. This was quickly followed by *We Talk, You Listen,* which has been described as "an American Indian Declaration of Independence."[83]

Heightened Native activism took place in an era when other marginalized groups—Blacks, students against the Vietnam War, and the women's and Chicano movement for rights—were gaining momentum. While some Indian activists in the 1960s and 1970s adopted some strategies and rhetoric from the Civil Rights Movement, many others found the movement's call for equality and integration incompatible with their own vision of a separate, sovereign indigenous identity, rooted in their having their own governments, their own homelands, and their own unique cultural identities. Nevertheless, the goal of equal rights had widespread appeal and received support from across racial and ethnic groups, including that of some prominent Native leaders.

Dennis Banks, cofounder of AIM, contended that inequality and injustice for Indians had never abated. He described the conditions under which many Native Americans were living at the time:

> [T]he living conditions we found ourselves in were deplorable. It wasn't that we didn't know there was racism in the cities. It was how racism forced us into squalid slum tenement buildings, closed doors to job opportunities, and fostered racist laws, jails, and prisons. . . .[84]

Indians' use of interest group politics moved them closer to their goal of **self-determination,** which meant respect and support of tribal sovereignty, especially regarding a tribe's authority to decide on actions to support its people and the right to control how those needs were met. They wanted to end the **termination policy,** and stop the relocation program that fractured Native communities. There was a new attitude under Presidents John F. Kennedy and Lyndon B. Johnson, who were sympathetic as Indians began to press the government for "restoration of lands, federal recognition of government-to-government relations, legal and political participation, and inclusion enough to negotiate their interests and rights."[85]

After a meeting in Chicago in 1961, delegates from over one hundred tribal nations agreed on a **Declaration of Indian Purpose,** drafted in part by activist D'Arcy McNickle. This document, which was presented to President John F. Kennedy, "called for an end to termination, major educational reforms, and tribal control of resource management and social services." Kennedy's interior secretary, Stewart Udall, subsequently submitted a report in 1961that supported ending termination.[86]

In 1963 President Johnson's War on Poverty legislation attempted to address tribal issues through the Economic Opportunity Act. Indians could now benefit from access to private and public organizations (community action programs), which were focused on empowering the poor, without having to go through the BIA. This allowed tribes to match federal programs with their particular needs. The policy, however, was a minor reform that did not address the larger issues of sovereignty or the need for federal compliance with treaty obligations.

When Native activists seized Alcatraz Island in 1969, this proved a pivotal event that received broad media coverage as Indians from many tribal nations asserted their right to self-determination. First, some history to this crucial event. After the federal prison on Alcatraz was shut down in 1963, a group of Native Americans filed an unsuccessful lawsuit claiming the island under a Sioux treaty that gave them the right to unused federal land. On March 9, 1964, Allen Cottier, president of the American Indian Council, led Sioux Indians in a brief occupation of the island and demanded that Alcatraz be used for a Native American cultural center and university. The U.S. Coast Guard established a blockade around the island, but the federal government did not interfere because the protest was nonviolent. In June 1971, as the number of occupiers waned, a small federal force peacefully retook the island. The event marked the beginning of the **Red Power movement** of 1969–1978, which focused on holding the federal government to "account for its past and present misdeeds and omissions." Deloria was forthright when he noted that "the criteria for protest and the idea was to play directly on whatever reservoir or cumulative guilt lay hidden in the public psyche."[87]

In 1968 Congress passed the **Indian Civil Rights Act (ICRA),** extending the protections of most of the Bill of Rights to all persons in Indian Country. The act appears to directly contradict an 1896 Supreme Court decision, *Talton v. Mayes,* that held that the U.S. Constitution's Fifth Amendment did not apply to Indian tribes. Passage of the ICRA was not without controversy, as this represented the first time that portions of U.S. constitutional law were made applicable to Native governments. The act legitimized tribal dispute resolution forums and expedited the evolution of tribal courts and tribal laws. The act also required states wishing to assume civil and criminal jurisdiction in Indian Country to first obtain tribal consent, which they not previously had to do.

As laws slowly changed, Indians continued to fight for their rights through interest groups such as the **American Indian Movement (AIM)** and a myriad of others that focused on law, treaties, education, economic development, health, and other concerns. Considered the most militant of the Indian rights groups, AIM found it difficult to reverse years of federal policy. The seventy-one-day occupation at Wounded Knee, South Dakota, in 1973 gave the protesters from sixty-four tribes—as well as Black, Chicano, and White activists—national

> How have Native nations' and individuals' collective activism affected the political, legal, and cultural status of indigenous peoples?

press coverage. (See Box 2.3.) The standoff did little to bring about positive, long-term change, however, and AIM began to unravel as the federal government essentially bankrupted the organization through lengthy court battles.[89] The Alcatraz and Wounded Knee occupations garnered press coverage when the United States was still fighting the Vietnam War, which caused some people to see similarities in the two situations. American imperialism in Southeast Asia and the colonial status of Indians within the United States drew the attention of activists who were opposed to federal policies in both cases.

The reservation system was essentially a colonial policy that resulted in abysmal living conditions comparable to those in a poor, developing nation. As of 2008, 40 percent of a total 4.9 million Indians lived on reservations; of these, 38 percent were below the federal poverty level. Although the federal government remains the largest employer on reservations, unemployment is a major problem because of the lack of jobs and job skills. Housing remains inadequate, and "90,000 are homeless or under-housed" on the reservations. Existing housing is overcrowded, with "less than 50 percent connected to a public sewer."[90] Currently, 55 percent of Indians are relying on the Indian Health Service for medical care as they battle diseases such as diabetes, heart disease, tuberculosis, and cancer.[91] One factor that significantly impacts health and employment is the high rate of alcoholism. The Indian Health Service notes that "the rate of alcoholism among Native Americans is six times the U.S. average." It is important to note that medical research has shown that there are two genes that protect against alcoholism, and Native Americans do not have them.[92]

✝ BOX 2.3 CROSS ROAD

The Occupation of Wounded Knee

In 1890 a final clash between the U.S. military and the Lakota Sioux took place at Wounded Knee, South Dakota. Up to three hundred Indians were killed, many of them women and children. The Wounded Knee Massacre became one of the worst stains in U.S.-Indian relations and, with the deaths of so many women and children, an illustration of the extreme force the United States exercised against Indians.

In 1973 Wounded Knee once again became a focal point for indigenous activity. Allegations of corruption on nearby Pine Ridge reservation prompted some residents to try to impeach tribal chair Richard "Dick" Wilson. When the effort failed and Wilson called in federal troops, the residents sought outside help. On February 27 the Oglala Sioux Civil Rights Organization and the American Indian Movement (AIM) led an occupation of Wounded Knee village in an effort to publicly force change at Pine Ridge. Representatives from sixty-four tribes participated, along with African American, Chicano, and White activists. AIM leaders Russell Means and Dennis Banks also played key roles.

Among the occupiers' demands were Wilson's removal as chair and Senate hearings to review treaty violations and government abuses. The 1890 massacre was deliberately referenced to raise the profile of their efforts. More than three hundred National Guard troops, U.S. marshals, tribal police, and others surrounded Wounded Knee and cut off supplies going into the village. AIM supporters attempted to deliver food, but much of it was confiscated. Eventually, phone lines, electricity, and water were also shut off.

Following the lead of other Native American demonstrations, the protesters focused on more than just the troubles at Pine Ridge. On March 11, the Oglala demanded that the tribal council be abolished, announced a new Independent Oglala Nation, and demanded recognition from the United Nations. To support their claim, they pointed to the 1868 Treaty of Fort Laramie, which acknowledged Sioux ownership of portions of the Dakotas, Montana, Nebraska, and Wyoming. Negotiations were ongoing throughout the siege but broke down several times.

On April 26–27, federal agents opened fire and launched tear gas into the encampment. Many protesters were injured and two were killed. On May 8, after seventy-one days, the protesters peacefully ended their occupation, largely because of the efforts of Hank Adams, an Assiniboine Sioux, who brokered the deal allowing both sides to step away without further bloodshed. In his autobiography, Russell Means reflected that "what Wounded Knee told the world was that John Wayne hadn't killed us all . . . Suddenly billions of people knew we were still alive, still resisting."[88]

While the Wounded Knee occupation heightened Americans' awareness of government actions against Native Americans and their current struggles, it did not accomplish much for the long term. More than two hundred occupiers were arrested, AIM leaders were prosecuted, and Wilson remained tribal chair at Pine Ridge. He retaliated forcefully against those who had acted against him, and national attention waned.

Considering This Crossroad

- Do you agree with the federal government's handling of the Wounded Knee occupation? Why or why not?

- Native American rights activists adopted strategies and rhetoric from the Civil Rights Movement, but instead of integration, they called for recognition of their sovereign status as tribal governments. How did the Wounded Knee occupation attempt to achieve this, and how successful was the occupation in achieving its goals?

- Consider the context of the time, with protests and demonstrations across the nation against discrimination, and minority groups advocating for equal rights. Did the federal government respond appropriately to the protesters at Wounded Knee?

Most Indian tribes are located in remote areas with no ready tax base, and tribal governments must develop what business opportunities are available. This has historically included negotiating with corporations that have sought to extract increasingly valuable natural resources (e.g., coal, natural gas, uranium, etc.) from Indian lands. In addition, Congress passed several measures to help spur tribal economic development, including tribal gaming. Although Indian gaming generates billions of dollars, its benefits are poorly distributed, and most Native Americans on reservations continue to struggle to meet basic needs.

Getty Images

In 1972 members of the American Indian Movement and numerous allies marched on Washington DC during the Trail of Broken Treaties, temporarily over-taking the Bureau of Indian Affairs to gain attention for their concerns. AIM was a militant group established to ensure and protect the rights of Native Americans. The formation of AIM and similar groups allowed Native Americans to organize collectively as they sought to address their grievances with the U.S. government, including treaty rights, the reclamation of tribal land, and high unemployment and poverty.

CONCLUSION: A CONTINUING STRUGGLE FOR EQUAL RIGHTS

The grievances of Native nations and Native individuals, who have not been as visible as other racial or ethnic groups in American society, have frequently been ignored by the U.S. government. It was not until Indians followed the twentieth-century model of civil rights organization used by the Black and Latino communities that media attention briefly focused on the Indian Rights Movement in the late 1960s and the 1970s. This new visibility, however, was temporary, and in stark contrast to what had been an often invisible struggle for the past five hundred years.

Without the attention of national news, the internal and external problems that continue to plague Indians went unnoticed by the majority. Unlike other minority groups in the United States today, Indians remain trapped in a colonial relationship because the U.S. government has never disavowed the plenary power (full and absolute) doctrine. Treaties signed by the U.S. government and Native nations are only sporadically enforced by the federal government. American citizenship thrust upon Indians in 1924 extended the franchise to individuals, but failed to address the issue of restoring or protecting the sovereignty rights of Indian nations;

Table 2.1   Indians' Road of Racialization

When Barriers Arose	Why Barriers Arose	How Barriers Were Overcome	Outcome
Colonization, 1400–1776	• White conceptions of race and civilization marked Indians as inferior • Whites' quest for land dominated their agenda	• Indians allied with French or British forces against the English colonists	Insufficient Barriers
U.S. founding– Pre–Civil War, 1777–1830s	• Forced removal of Indians damaged tribal social structure as America pushed beyond the thirteen colonies	• U.S. Supreme Court rulings recognized Indian sovereignty but were ignored (no barriers overcome)	Insufficient → Decisive
Post–Civil War, 1840–1886	• Assimilation programs aimed to "civilize" Indians and incorporate them into White mainstream society	• Indians agreed to relocate to reservations, where they were promised self-governance (no barriers overcome)	Decisive → Absolute
Assimilation, 1887–1950s	• General Allotment Act (1887) divided Indians' communal land into individual plots, damaging Indian social structure • Policy of blood quantum raised debate over who is Indian • Termination Act (1953) resulted in reservations struggling after federal support ended	• Indian Reorganization Act (1934) ended the allotment policy • Indians began to collectively organize for the right of self-determination	Absolute
Self-determination, 1960–2014	• Federal policies created unequal rights and opportunities	• Indian Rights Movement (1960s–1970s) drew media attention to federal treatment of Indians	Absolute → Decisive

in fact, as this chapter has shown, it failed even to extend the full protection of the Bill of Rights to individual Indians until 1968.[93]

The intent behind the 1988 Indian Gaming Regulatory Act (IGRA) was to help tribal governments become more financially self-sufficient. Today, tribes are fragmented and conflicted over the issue of who is legally an enrolled Indian (a problem created by blood quantum) because only enrolled Indians can share in gaming revenues. This has led to the disenrollment of several thousand Native citizens from numerous tribal nations. While mainstream media emphasize the potential income from tribal casinos, this income is primarily derived from casinos near urban areas. And despite increased money coming into tribal coffers, problems caused by long-term poverty remain intractable. Federal aid to tribes since 2008 has risen to over $4.5 million. These funds, which are used for health care services, road repair, and environmental preservation, do not have to be repaid because they are for the support of tribal governments.[94]

Land continues to remain Indians' most valuable resource. The question of claiming tribal membership endures as Indians face perennial conflicts over governance as well as use and reclamation of their land, especially when the value of that land is enhanced by natural resources such as oil, gas, and minerals. Numerous treaty issues and Indian claims to sovereignty have never been resolved.

Federal policy has gone through periods of annihilation, annexation, and assimilation, only to find that its measures failed to completely destroy Indian culture and identity. Members of Indian nations are neither silent nor invisible, and they challenge those laws deemed unjust or intrusive. While Indian rights activists have continued to stage protests, their most significant victories have been won via sophisticated legal challenges launched by tribes and individual Indians. Their successes include the 1973 Menominee Restoration Act, the 1978 American Indian Religious Freedom Act, the 1990 Native American Graves Protection and Repatriation Act, and the 2010 Cobell claims settlement act. Through these efforts and interest groups such as the National Indian Education Association and American Indian Business Leaders, Indians continue to assert their identity and shape their own future.

DISCUSSION QUESTIONS

1. Why did White explorers and settlers not always act honestly and respectfully in their dealings with Native peoples? Explain your answer.

2. What mattered more in the history of U.S.-Indian relations—race or land? Identify three moments in which each played a significant factor in Whites' treatment of Indians.

3. How did Whites' perceptions of race influence their dealings with Native peoples? Have these views changed over time?

4. How were Indians' efforts against the U.S. government's policies and actions limited by their lack of access to laws and institutions that Whites recognized and understood?

5. To what extent did the granting of U.S. citizenship to Native individuals help them to achieve more equal rights and opportunities? How did this affect their tribal relationship?

6. Did Indians benefit from their civil rights activism as much as other groups? Explain your answer.

KEY TERMS

American Indian
  Movement (AIM) (p. 63)

assimilation (p. 50)
blood quantum (p. 55)

Bureau of Indian Affairs
  (BIA) (p. 48)

Carlisle Indian School (p. 56)

civilization program (p. 38)

Declaration of Indian Purpose (p. 62)

doctrine of discovery (p. 36)

Five Civilized Tribes (p. 33)

General Allotment Act of 1887 (Dawes Act) (p. 51)

Indian Civil Rights Act (ICRA) (p. 63)

Indian Removal Act of 1830 (p. 44)

Indian Reorganization Act (IRA) (p. 58)

Marshall Trilogy of Cases (p. 40)

plenary (p. 43)

Red Power movement (p. 63)

reservation (p. 48)

self-determination (p. 62)

sovereignty (p. 41)

termination policy (p. 62)

Trail of Tears (p. 44)

Treaty of Fort Laramie (1868) (p. 64)

3 The African American Political Journey, 1500s–1965

It is obvious today that America has defaulted on [its] promissory note insofar as her citizens of color are concerned. Instead of honoring [its] sacred obligations, America has given Negro people a bad check; a check which has come back marked "insufficient funds." But we refuse to believe the bank of justice is bankrupt. We refuse to believe that there are insufficient funds in the great vaults of opportunity of this nation.

—Martin Luther King Jr., "I Have a Dream,"
March on Washington, August 28, 1963

No part of the American story better captures how the contradictions and complexities of race have mattered in shaping U.S. politics than the African American story. From the eloquent but, for African Americans, false promises of American liberty written by Thomas Jefferson in the Declaration of Independence to the important but often forgotten metaphor about false promises in Dr. Martin Luther King Jr.'s "I Have a Dream" speech, Black Americans have had to contend with an American Dilemma of lofty ideals but cold racial realities in their journey toward greater freedom. This is not to suggest in any way that African Americans are the only racial or ethnic minority that has been adversely racialized. The purpose of this chapter, however, is to detail the unique

Box 3.1 Chapter Objectives

- Explain how racial ideas and institutions transformed Africans into a shared community as African Americans.

- Describe the process of racialization that Blacks endured from the late 1600s to the mid-1860s.

- Demonstrate how U.S. society struggled with issues of Black citizenship, equality, and racial status in the antebellum period.

- Identify the ways in which social institutions and political organizations helped to develop African American political identity.

- Explain how Blacks at times used race as a resource for community building and collective action.

- Discuss how the African American political journey paralleled civil rights organizing by other groups in the United States.

Blacks struggled for equal rights and opportunity in America from its earliest days as a colony, when they were forcibly transported to serve as slave labor. Through the creation of a strong African American identity and collective organizing, they challenged laws and social practices to overcome racial barriers. These are participants in the 1963 March on Washington on August 28, 1963.

reasons why, when, and how race has shaped the journey of African Americans toward first-class citizenship, opportunity, and self-determination.

Our understanding the African American journey provides us with an important background narrative as we seek to understand when, why, and how race and ethnicity still matter in American politics. First, from the founding of the U.S. government through the end of the twentieth century, African Americans have been the largest non-European group in the population; today, they are second only to Hispanics or Latinos of all races. Second, they have also been a group, somewhat akin to Native Americans, that has a very long and continuing history of challenging the imposition of race, racism, and White supremacy that at times has contributed to the creation and definition of U.S. social norms, laws, and citizenship rights. Third, and somewhat true of the early Chinese American experience, if different in severity, African Americans were used as a supply of free labor (in the slavery era) or cheap labor (in the post-slavery era). This enabled affluent and middle-class Whites who exploited their labor to amass great and disproportionate wealth that, for varying reasons, persists in some form today.

Fourth, biological myths and perceived differences of color, body type, and cultural customs have led many Whites to view African Americans as racially distinct from other groups. Some of these false presumptions linger to this day. And fifth, the practice of Whites perceiving the greatest racial differences between themselves and African Americans placed African Americans near or at the lowest rung of an American racial hierarchy. When it has been perceived as an absolute political boundary, it has been called the **color line.** Where precisely other non-White races ranked along this hierarchy—whether they were more or less included or excluded as members of the dominant polity and the society—depended on how closely Whites morally or intellectually associated them with Blacks. Even with the expanding racial and ethnic national diversity of American citizens, this Black/White polarity remains an important determinant of our politics and of citizen opportunities.[1]

The interaction between the development of the United States and the presence of Africans as slaves is complicated and central to American politics. The American nation's political and economic development was related to the central notions of democracy, freedom, and, in the words of Thomas Jefferson and the Declaration of Independence, self-evident truths "that all men are created equal." By the 1800s, the ability to sustain that notion of freedom and equality while simultaneously enslaving roughly 13 percent of the population was a fundamental contradiction within early American politics. Eventually, as we will explain, the political tensions between slavery and freedom became too great to sustain the existing arrangements within the polity and the American Civil War ensued, although it failed to fully resolve the tension or the contradiction. Constitutional amendments and laws addressed the status that the Black population would have in the post–Civil War era by ending slavery and creating citizenship and the right of Blacks to vote. But the persistent tensions between the powers held by the states and the federal government as they defined citizenship and the responsibilities for addressing the status of Blacks sparked continued clashes. The lingering vestiges of slavery left the nation unable to fully overturn past patterns of discrimination, and the powers associated with state-level politics prevailed and dominated national patterns for almost a century.

However, this is not simply a story of when, why, and how race has been a barrier to fundamentally impede or slow the progress of Blacks. It is also one of Blacks politically responding to the barriers imposed by race to debate and define their group interests, as well as to meet their needs. We call this broader process "African American politics." Africans arrived in North America as many ethnically and culturally diverse groups. But their racialization and enslavement in the American colonies and states compelled these many groups to define themselves as one common group. In this chapter, we trace the most significant periods of Black political history—before, during, and after the ending of slavery and through the era of **Jim Crow** segregation—in order to understand the breadth if not the depth of how race has affected the African American and thus the larger American political experience.[2]

RACE, SLAVERY, AND THE ORIGINS OF AFRICAN AMERICANS, 1500s–1790s

We first turn to an exploration of the origins and arrival of Africans into the Americas, the basis for their presence in the British North American colonies, and how they were racialized from noticeably distinct populations used for labor into a hard and permanent legal status of slaves seen as property in an institution called chattel slavery. We will examine the importance of race and slavery in the founding of the American republic and thus spend most of the chapter examining race as an absolute and/or decisive factor in American and African American politics.

African Origins and the Transatlantic Slave Trade

The group identity of African Americans evolved over centuries. For nearly three hundred years between the 1500s up to the mid-1800s, Africans were captured by Europeans or sold into slavery from populations spread over many different West and Central African linguistic and ethnic groups, including what are now the modern nations of Ghana, Sierra Leone, Senegal, and Angola. They arrived in the Americas first as **indentured servants** and later were enslaved—possessing no citizenship and no rights, and with no agreed-upon notion of their common political identity and interests. From the colonial era to the 1800s, imposed processes of race and racialization compelled Blacks to blend their cultural differences into a broad, shared culture and recognize themselves as a single group. Their common ethnic name varied over eras, in popular usage as well as in the census—for example, Africans, Ethiopians, Negroes, Coloreds/Colored People, Blacks, Afro-Americans, African Americans. They gradually developed vernaculars of American English, and they recognized that they had broad similar interests despite their persistent diversity.[3]

Slavery in the American context has often been framed as if it were a singular experience. In reality, the basic practices and patterns of the slave trade and slavery conducted by European nations evolved over the centuries and varied widely. The practices and patterns in the North American British colonies and the American nation differed from those of the Portuguese, French, and Spanish American colonies in how the former embraced notions of racial superiority rooted in separation (the Anglo-American view) versus notions of racial superiority rooted in assimilation (the Latin view of Portuguese, French, and Spanish). (See Chapter 1.)

The best estimates of the slave trade show that the arrival of slaves into British North America began on a regular basis in the 1650s and continued until shortly after the United States legally ended the international (but not domestic) slave trade between 1810 and 1820. The peak decades were the 1730s, 1750s, and 1760s, with 1800 to 1810 being the highest decade, as the slave trade was about to conclude. (See Figure 3.1.) Roughly 500,000 slaves were brought into the geographic area of British North America and the United States—5 percent of the total number of ten million persons brought to the Americas as slaves. The Atlantic slave trade had operated for a century and a half before the trade accelerated in North America, and it was active at a much higher volume in Portuguese, French, and Spanish colonies and in the British Caribbean, as compared to its height in British North America.[4]

The enslaved populations transported to the United States were brought through a variety of methods. They were captured from a wide swath of the African continent, along the west coast from the countries now known as Senegal and Sierra Leone, through Benin, Ghana, Nigeria, and Angola, and a portion of South East Africa, as shown on Map 3.1. There were a large number of national and language groupings in these areas, and these regions stretched along three thousand miles of the West African coast, reaching inland for hundreds of miles. As previously mentioned, African Americans originated from culturally, linguistically, socially,

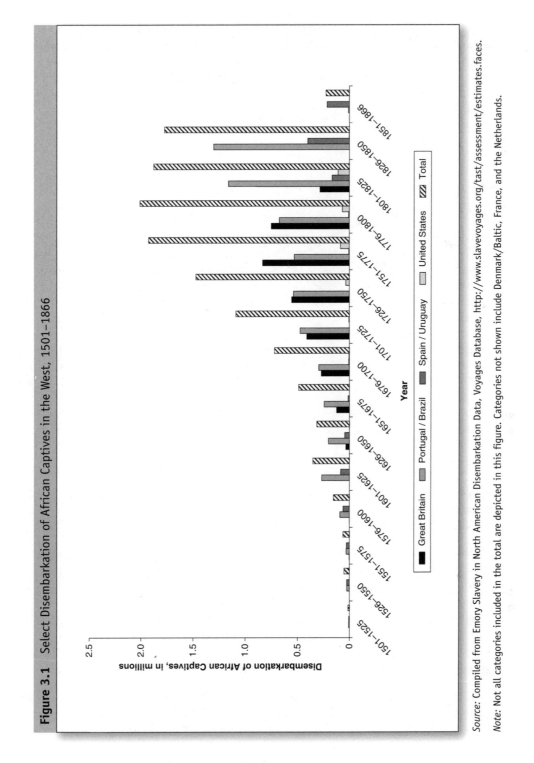

Figure 3.1 Select Disembarkation of African Captives in the West, 1501–1866

Source: Compiled from Emory Slavery in North American Disembarkation Data, Voyages Database, http://www.slavevoyages.org/tast/assessment/estimates.faces.

Note: Not all categories included in the total are depicted in this figure. Categories not shown include Denmark/Baltic, France, and the Netherlands.

73

Map 3.1   The Slave Trade and the American Colonies

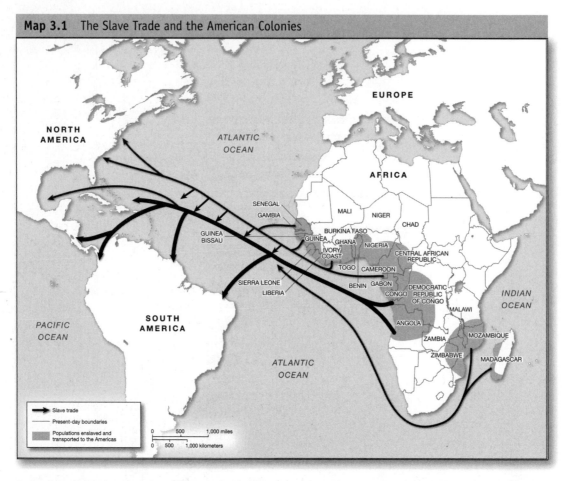

Enslaved populations from throughout Africa embarked on a long journey from Africa's western coast to America, where they were denied the rights of other residents.

and ethnically distinct populations. Figure 3.1 shows the distribution of the population transported to the Americas from 1501 until 1860. There was no single dominant region from which ancestors of contemporary African Americans were drawn. Captured Africans often were not transported directly from Africa to North America, but were first sent to locations in the Caribbean, where traders subjected them to "seasoning," or forced adjustment to their new status as docile, enslaved property.

Race and the North American Evolution of Slavery

The evolution of slavery in North America is integrally connected to evolving notions of race among the English. In order to exploit the economic resources of their North American and Caribbean colonies and to supply laborers, capital, and goods to British companies and the British Empire, the English justified the creation of a New World, racialized form of permanent, hereditary slavery. It was different from Old World or classic conceptions rooted in the possibility of slaves earning their freedom and partly assimilating into the master class. This new form of enslavement, however, was long in development.

The first Africans brought to the English Jamestown colony of Virginia in 1619 were more often **indentured servants** bound to a time-limited period of service rather than permanent slaves. Race had not been cemented along lines of absolute separation even as late as the mid-1600s. Slavery was first recognized as an institution by the Puritan Massachusetts Bay colony in 1641, but no mention was made of race. In fact, non-English White workers, especially the Irish, were also indentured servants alongside Africans, and as many as 10 to 20 percent of Whites who were in servitude were slaves. Likewise, a handful of African Americans owned property and hired servants to work their lands.

The turning point, or what has been dubbed the terrible transformation, was the racialization of slavery—the creation of an absolute color line—confined to Blacks. By the late 1660s, colonial law slowly began to redefine the status of slaves from a temporary status into one of heredity based on the status of the mother. Gender mattered, since slaves were property and the law allowed the owner to use his property as he willed. Women were used not only for labor, but also for reproduction, leading to an increase in slaves and therefore in the wealth of their owner. In order to protect that property, English laws governing slaves came to emphasize legal status or descent through the bloodline of the enslaved mother, or **hypodescent**. Any offspring of women who were slaves thus held the status of slaves, regardless of the legal or racial status of the father.

BOX 3.2 ROAD SIGN

Contradictions between American Ideals and American Slavery

"We hold these truths to be self-evident, that all men are created equal, that they are endowed by their Creator with certain unalienable Rights, that among these are Life, Liberty and the pursuit of Happiness."[5] Despite these words, by the nineteenth-century Thomas Jefferson, founding father and author of the Declaration of Independence, there are clearly noted differences in slaves' legal status. He discussed the biological and legal status of African slaves through interracial reproduction in an 1815 letter to Francis Gray, an attorney who visited Monticello. Following a previous exchange with Gray, Jefferson addressed the

legal definition of mulatto or mixed-race persons; traced the consequences of interracial reproduction over several generations; and used mathematical formulae to the point where the descendant, he argued, is no longer biologically a "Negro." Jefferson cautioned, however "But observe, that this does not re-establish freedom, which depends on the condition of the mother." He continued: "But if he be emancipated, he becomes a free white man and a citizen of the United States to all intents and purposes."

Jefferson, who owned more than two hundred slaves whom he never freed and had children from

(Continued)

(Continued)

a relationship with a fifteen-year-old slave girl named Sally Hemings, also embraced views about the racial superiority of Whites in comparison to Blacks grounded in "scientific racism." As stated in Chapter 1, scientific racism is the misuse of science to justify beliefs of racial superiority. In a passage in his 1781 scientific treatise, *Notes on the State of Virginia,* Jefferson drew several curious conclusions about the characteristics and abilities of African Americans in comparison to Whites. Note how Jefferson assumed physical markers—skin color, hair texture, facial features—determine group characteristics and abilities:

> The first difference [between Whites and Blacks] which strikes us is that of color. . . . The difference is fixed in nature, and is as real as if its seat and cause were better known to us. And is this difference of no importance? Is it not the foundation of a greater or less share of beauty in the two races? Are not the fine mixtures of red and white, the expressions of every passion by greater or less suffusions of color in the one, preferable to that eternal monotony, which reigns in the countenances, that immoveable veil of black which covers all the emotions of the other race? Add to these, flowing hair, a more elegant symmetry of form, their own judgment in favor of the whites, declared by their preference of them, *as uniformly as is the preference of the orangutan for the black women over those of his own species.*[6] [Emphasis added.]

There has long been a debate among students of U.S. political history as to what currents of political thought most influenced the nation's founding fathers. This is the *why* question of race and slavery. When Thomas Jefferson in 1776 penned in the Declaration of Independence the words, "all men are created equal" and had the right to pursue "Life, Liberty, and the pursuit of Happiness," how could he and they believe it when they also owned enslaved Blacks? More broadly, political scientists Desmond King and Rogers Smith ask how America's racial order or its original arrangement of ideas and institutions emerged to create a ruling or governing coalition of interests and how and why this order changed over time. Did most of the founders believe in what Smith calls ascriptivism, or the belief that classes and races of human beings had inherent, biologically determined (and/or God-determined) attributes and thus naturally assumed a place in a hierarchy of characteristics, such as intelligence, physical ability, morality, and creativity? Then how do we also account for what political theorist Louis Hartz calls the liberal tradition, or many framers' strong embrace of republicanism? This was the belief that individual citizens had inherent rights, and foremost among them was the right to a representative government, limited in its authority. Clearly, there is an expression of egalitarianism in Jefferson's words, or the belief that all human beings are inherently equal, with God-given, "self-evident" rights; thus the reason why even Jefferson, who never freed his own slaves, still occasionally worried about the contradiction of a "free society" embracing slavery. King and Smith explain that the framers and their White descendants were often unevenly influenced by these multiple traditions.

In their most basic formulation, views of White racial superiority, or what social anthropologist Audrey Smedley considers an Anglo-American racial worldview, were fused with justifications for slavery in order to solve a labor shortage problem in the English colonies and the new

Republic. Beyond its economic rationale, race also became a system of social and intellectual norms and mores to govern society. The hypodescent rule was first passed into law in Virginia in 1662, followed by a 1667 law prohibiting slaves from being freed even if they were baptized as Christians. Maryland followed suit with similar laws in 1664 and 1681, respectively, and these examples were copied in other states. At the heart of these new regulations were White colonial fears of more labor uprisings similar to a series of multiracial worker rebellions like Bacon's rebellion of 1676. Nathaniel Bacon, an Englishman, wanted all Native Americans eliminated from the Virginia colony; Governor William Berkeley feared such an effort would risk loss of support from "friendly" tribes. In the resulting conflict, Bacon generated support from White indentured servants, Black slaves, and Native Americans, threatening English colonial control.[7]

Colonial authorities slowly increased the legal, racial distinctions they had already begun to make between workers and codified stricter dividing lines of race. Smedley notes of this period, "the political leaders of the colonies, all great planters, began to homogenize all Europeans regardless of ethnicity, status, or class, into a new category. The first time the term 'white' rather than 'Christian' was used for Europeans appeared in a 1691 law prohibiting the marriage of any 'Englishman or other *white* man or woman' to any 'negro, mulatto, or Indian man or woman.'"[8] By the early 1700s, when various colonies—from New York to South Carolina—worried over the threat of slave rebellions, they were equipped with a concept of race and a new form of racialized slavery to use to make distinctions and mete out punishments in the interests of social control.[9]

In the colonial era, Africans were present in all of the thirteen colonies, but from the 1660s through the Revolutionary era, Africans remained less than 10 percent of the population in the colonies of the Mid-Atlantic and New England. In the Chesapeake and Lower South, the proportion of the African population

> How did Whites' conceptions of race contribute to their creation of legal, economic, and social controls that excluded Blacks from the polity's resources?

diverged sharply from that of the more northern colonies. It rose from under 10 percent in the 1660s and 1670s, to above 20 percent by 1690, and continued to climb in the eighteenth century to above 40 percent of the population. Ninety percent of the population in coastal regions around Charleston, South Carolina, was composed of African slaves. At the beginning of the American republic, the first census showed free Blacks comprised roughly 8 percent of the total Black population in the United States, and 20 percent overall. Their numbers and proportions continued to increase until about the 1830s, when Nat Turner's rebellion in Virginia resulted in the deaths of fifty-seven Whites in 1831, and other slave uprisings precipitated more extensive controls on the growth of the free Black population and on the activities of the slave population.[10] (See Figure 3.2.)

THE EARLY AMERICAN REPUBLIC AND BLACK POLITICAL RESISTANCE, 1770s–1865

The United States was formed in the context of the economic and military struggles the British Empire waged with its competitors, the Spanish and the French. With harassed

Figure 3.2 U.S. Population by Race, 1790–1830

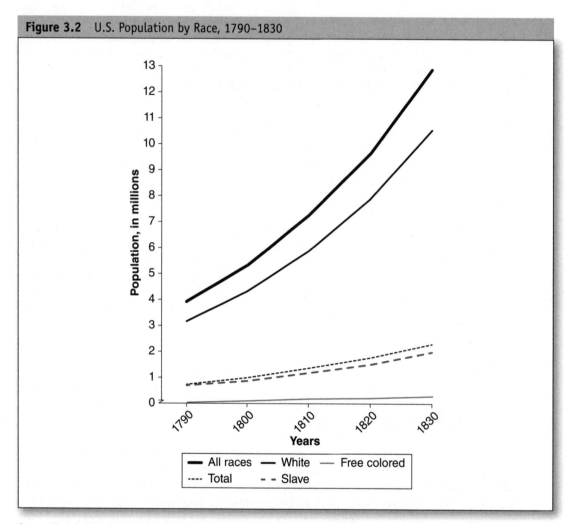

Source: Historical Statistics of the United States Millennial Edition Online, ed. Susan B. Carter, Scott Sigmund Gartner, Michael R. Haines, Alan L. Olmstead, Richard Sutch, and Gavin Wright. Available at http://hsus.cambridge.org/HSUSWeb/HSUSEntryServlet. ©Cambridge University Press, 2012. Reprinted with the permission of Cambridge University Press.

British troops firing on a Boston crowd in 1770 and killing the first American patriot, a Black man named Crispus Attucks, the American war for independence was partly instigated by an earlier series of laws the British Parliament passed to extract more taxes from the colonies to fund the armies and other infrastructure needed to maintain the empire. It was also an age of European Enlightenment, a time when innovations in science and technology as well as revolutionary sentiments about liberty, individual rights, and republican or representative government inspired educated American colonialists to press for greater rights as British subjects, and then for complete independence. African Americans contributed to this revolutionary fervor in the hope of arguing for their freedom from slavery. For example, in 1775 five groups of African Americans petitioned the Massachusetts legislature for the emancipation of the slaves, and one noted the hypocrisy of the age when he asked the Sons of Liberty pro-independence leaders, "Are not

 Did the American war for independence include the goal of freedom for all residents of the American colonies?

your hearts also hard, when you hold [Blacks] in slavery who are entitled to liberty, by the law of nature, equal as yourselves? If it be so, pray, sir, pull the beam out of thine eyes."[11]

Although initially prohibited by General George Washington from serving in the army that the Continental Congress authorized in 1775, as many as five thousand Blacks may have served in a 300,000-man army, many in the hopes of being granted freedom. Thousands more African Americans fled from slavery when British armies arrived and often promised emancipation to those who fought with King George's troops.[12] The early Black resistance to their enslavement was one of many ways in which Blacks sought to change their status within the dominant White society. The absolute barriers they faced as a result of racialization, however, were embedded into the nation's founding documents. Only White male property owners could vote in the early decades of the republic; in contrast, free Black men had access to the franchise in only a few states, such as Rhode Island, Massachusetts, and Vermont—and even those rights eroded over time.

Slavery and the Founding Documents

Ratified in 1781 as the United States won its independence, the Articles of Confederation was the first U.S. Constitution, but it proved weak and ineffectual. The subsequent constitution that fifty-five White men vigorously debated and drafted in Philadelphia in the summer of 1787 contained several political compromises to form "a more perfect Union" among the thirteen states. Unlike the Declaration of Independence, which was egalitarian and revolutionary in its language— including a rejected draft in which Jefferson admonished King George's government for abetting the slave trade—the second U.S. Constitution was an extremely pragmatic document that upheld the institution of slavery so that the Southern slaveholding states would remain partners in the Union. South Carolina delegate John Rutledge bluntly stated that the Convention's decision on the slavery issue would determine "whether the southern states shall or shall not be parties to the Union." Fellow South Carolina delegate Charles Pinckney reiterated what he and other slaveholders saw as their interests: "South Carolina and Georgia cannot do without slaves."[13] Most notable among the many provisions that upheld slavery in the Constitution were the Three-Fifths Clause, the Fugitive Slave Clause, and the **1808 Prohibition**. (See Figure 3.3.)

Since the framers agreed that representation in the lower chamber of Congress would be based on population, the **Three-Fifths Clause** of Article I counted each enslaved person as three-fifths of a free (White) person for the purposes of determining how many seats each state would be apportioned in the U.S. House of Representatives. This formula also determined the number of electors each state had in the Electoral College that officially elected the president. Until the Thirteenth Amendment in 1865, when this provision was officially voided, Southern states had a political advantage over Northern states in that the former had just over 40 percent of the total

UNITED STATES SLAVE TRADE.

1850.

Library of Congress

While the Declaration of Independence announced that "all men are created equal," the slave trade continued in America after it fought and won the Revolutionary War for freedom. Men, women, and children continued to be bought, sold, and forced to labor under difficult conditions by those who wanted unpaid labor and who believed that Blacks' skin color meant that they were less intelligent and less civilized than Whites.

U.S. population but nearly 45 percent of all seats in the House. They also enjoyed an economic advantage in the national government in that this provision (and others) prohibited a direct head tax on each slave, as well interstate taxation on slave-made products.

The Fugitive Slave Clause of Article IV required government authorities and presumably civilians of each state and locale to aid federal officials and the representatives of slave owners in returning runaway slaves to their masters. This meant Northern locales that had many fewer slaves or had abolished slavery still had to directly support the institution. In 1793 and in 1850 Congress passed laws to stipulate the legal sanctions that slave owners had in retrieving their "property" and the requirements for returning slaves from other states. These laws prompted fierce opposition from Northern abolitionists, especially since the 1850 act required civilians found in violation of the law to be fined or jailed. As we will explain, this 1850 act was at the heart of one of the most important and infamous Supreme Court cases of the nineteenth century—the *Dred Scott v. Sandford* decision.

 Can you identify contemporary instances of racism that link back to these original constitutional barriers?

Last, Article I contained a clause that prohibited Congress from passing any law that ended the importation of slaves from Africa into the United States until twenty years after the Constitution was ratified. This **1808 Prohibition**, however, did not prevent what came to be an even more dynamic form of slave trading—the domestic slave trade, in which enslaved African Americans and their descendants were sold between various states. Overall, this measure was extraordinary in that it was one of the few original measures that barred congressional legislation over an arena of international commerce.[14]

Sectional Tensions over Proslavery Compromises

Sectional divisions between North and South made not only for wide variation in the treatment of free Blacks but intense and frequently violent disagreements over the entire issue of

Figure 3.3   Constitutional Provisions Upholding Slavery

Three-Fifths Clause Article I, Sec. 2 (clause 3)	• Counted "those bound to service for a term of years", or enslaved, Africans as three-fifths (3/5s) of a person for the purposes of determining federal "direct taxes" and the number of seats a state held in the House according to population size
Slave Trade Abolition Article I, Section 9 (clause 1)	• Prohibited Congress from abolishing the slave trade until 1808
Head Tax Article I, Section 9 (clause 4)	• Interpreted as discouraging a "direct tax" or head tax upon each slave (supposed to be counted as only three-fifths of a person)
Slave Product Taxation Article I, Section 9 (clause 5) and Section 10 (clause 2)	• Came to be interpreted as prohibiting federal and state taxation on the exports of other states, including slave products
Fugitive Slaves Article IV, Section 2 (clause 3)	• Required the return of fugitive slaves to their masters; later reinforced by the 1793 Fugitive Slave Act and 1850 Fugitive Slave Act
Slave Rebellions Article IV, Sec. 4 (clause 3)	• Guaranteed federal military assistance to states in the event of "domestic violence" or internal rebellions, including slave revolts
The Southern Veto Article V	• Prohibited the amendment of slave trade and tax provisions until 1808, essentially giving Southern slaveholding states a veto over any constitutional changes

slavery. The Northwest Ordinance of 1787 first opened up Western lands for White settlement and the creation of territorial government. While stipulating that slavery would be permitted south but not north of the Ohio Valley region, the ordinance established a "free North" versus "slave South" precedent along what was later called the Mason-Dixon line.[15] Cotton was rapidly becoming the king crop of the South, and with the technological innovation of the cotton gin, its cultivation rapidly spread westward across the Deep South. Whereas in 1800, 76 percent of all Southern slaves were in the Upper South (states like Virginia and Maryland), by 1860 nearly 60 percent were in the Deep South (states like Mississippi and Georgia). They were most heavily concentrated in areas in the South where the soil was richest and where cotton was grown in huge volume for commercial production in the United States as well as overseas, along the east side of the river known as the Mississippi Delta. These regions in the South were therefore alternately named the Black Belt or the Cotton Belt.

Slave labor produced enormous wealth—likely the greatest capital investment in the United States outside of real estate—and slavery's westward expansion was inevitable. A series of compromises were struck in Congress to intricately delineate free and slave states, such as the 1820 Missouri Compromise, the 1850 Compromise, and the 1854 Kansas-Nebraska Act. Still, these efforts could not contain political enmities between North and South or between abolitionists and proslavery interests. Thus the decade of the 1850s was marked not only by policy and electoral struggles, including the formation of an antislavery Republican Party, but real violence. Opposing sides physically attacked or "caned" one another in the halls of Congress while bloody struggles ensued elsewhere, from a civil war in the Kansas Territory, to John Brown's failed raid on Harper's Ferry, in 1858, to arm and free slaves.[16]

What helped to fuel this incendiary period was the 1850 Fugitive Slave Act and the subsequent U.S. Supreme Court's verdict in the 1857 *Dred Scott v. Sandford* case. The **Fugitive Slave Act** was part of the 1850 Compromise. It authorized and monetarily compensated federal marshals and bounty hunters to forcibly return escaped slaves to their masters, holding not only state and local governments but individual civilians liable if they did not comply with the law. It created resentment among various constituencies in the North, for it made Southern slave laws valid in the North even if a state had outlawed slavery. In response, abolitionists convened and formed vigilance committees to look out for and resist slave hunters. Black civil rights champion Frederick Douglass, often an advocate for peaceful moral suasion, uncharacteristically proposed one method for countering the act: "The only way to make the Fugitive Slave Law a dead letter is to make half a dozen or more dead kidnappers."[17] Famed abolitionist William Lloyd Garrison eventually called for the dissolution of the Union given the irreconcilable Southern position on slavery. Roughly four hundred slaves were returned into (or taken into) bondage under the Fugitive Slave Act, but many thousands remained in the North fearful of capture.

The Supreme Court's decision in *Dred Scott v. Sandford* further stoked the fires of anger that blazed around slavery. John Emerson was a white man who served as a U.S. Army surgeon. He traveled with his enslaved servant, Dred Scott, from Missouri (a slave state) to Illinois and then to the Wisconsin Territory (free jurisdictions). Scott eventually turned to the institutions of the White majority—the courts—to sue for his freedom because he resided in a free jurisdiction. While a circuit court ruled in his favor, the Missouri Supreme Court reversed the decision. Scott appealed his case to the U.S. Supreme Court, and in a now infamous ruling Chief Justice Roger Taney, joined by six other justices (all proslavery Democrats), declared that the U.S. Constitution did not apply to Black people because they "had no rights which the white man was bound to respect." Furthermore, the Court declared the Missouri Compromise of 1820 unconstitutional because Congress violated the Fifth Amendment in prohibiting slavery in some territories. Race was clearly an absolute barrier to Blacks at this time.

THE ANTEBELLUM BLACK COMMUNITY AND POLITICAL RESISTANCE

Not only are race and slavery fundamental to understanding the broad details of African American political history, but they inform us of why certain ideas, issues, institutions, and interests emerged to formulate Black politics in the antebellum period—that is, before the Civil War. Historian Steven Hahn asserts, "slavery was not mere background or prologue [to Black politics]; it was *formative and foundational*. In countless ways, freed people built and drew on relations, institutions, infrastructures, and aspirations that they and their ancestors struggled for and constructed as slaves." He concludes, "Without this legacy, activism and mobilization could not have taken place so rapidly after slavery had been abolished; and without consideration of this legacy, we cannot begin to understand how activism and mobilization did take place, and around what sorts of issues."[18] Key to this mobilization and these politics was the tiny minority of free Blacks.

The Status of Free Blacks

Because the United States took the path of being, in the words of Abraham Lincoln, a nation "half slave and half free," free Blacks experienced a very precarious, in-between class of citizenship and opportunities. The *Dred Scott* decision confirmed that slavery was an omnipresent threat to all Blacks, so free Blacks frequently had to carry some form of documentation with them to prove they were free and permitted to travel. Under the shadow of the 1850 Fugitive Slave Act and well before it, some free Blacks, including New York–born Solomon Northup, author of *Twelve Years a Slave,* were actually kidnapped and taken into slavery. Others in the South often were perceived as provocateurs or possible instigators for slave rebellions within slave communities. Charleston, South Carolina, provided grounds after the rumored Denmark Vesey slave rebellion plot, for the state of South Carolina to pass the 1822 Negro Seaman Act, as well as other measures. The laws permitted the summary jailing of all Black sailors who came to port, and imposed significant constraints on all Blacks, whether slave or free. But all were extremely valuable because the institution of racial slavery permitted the confiscation of Black men and women and the use of their labor without compensation.[19]

In the North, free Blacks were seen by many as an economic threat to the White working class, especially as increasing numbers of Irish and German workers immigrated into large cities like Boston, Philadelphia, and New York. Thus these African Americans often had to do the dirtiest and most unhealthy work, such as running bath houses, working in stables, and other menial jobs. In attempts to reduce racial and economic tensions by allaying White concerns, some Northern and later Western states outlawed free Blacks from entering their states and attempted to expel those present. Often, free Blacks paid taxes for public schools their children could not attend, and when all-Black schools existed, they may have had to pay fees and taxes that were redistributed to White schools.

The citizenship rights and opportunities of free Blacks partly depended on individual attributes such as skills, family background, and color, or whether they were mixed-race mulatto and possibly the progeny of slave masters. For example, up until the Civil War in states such as Louisiana and South Carolina, there was a very tiny minority of free Blacks who were affluent, often of mixed-race ancestry, and a few even owned slaves. They were the rare exceptions, however, for overwhelmingly slaveholders were White and slavery was a practice and economy that undergirded White supremacy. Thus much more important determinants of the status of free Blacks were contextual or geographical factors, including variations in local laws and customs, residence in the North or South, and residence in the Upper or Lower South. For example, African Americans in Upper South regions such as Maryland and Virginia or Chesapeake cities like Baltimore, Washington DC, Richmond, and Norfolk shared great commonalities with their Northern counterparts, but they also were much more at risk for enslavement, as they still resided in slave states. A handful of Northern states permitted Black men to vote for a period of time, but this was not the case in any Southern state; this illustrates the unevenness of the road African Americans traveled to equal rights.[20] Despite the precarious state of free Blacks, they were indispensable leaders and allies in the processes of building African American communities that rallied together to resist slavery in favor of their collective freedom.

Black Community-Building and Civil Society

Both free and enslaved African Americans created institutions prior to the Civil War that subsequently contributed to the formation of Black politics. But since the overwhelming majority of Black Americans were enslaved, experiences with slavery and racism were foremost in shaping Black political resistance. Despite the chains of slavery, these communities laid the foundations for ordinary folk institutions and politics through various connections like strong friendship and family ties, as well as master-sanctioned and secretive social gatherings. By the mid-1800s, slaves who lived in the Upper South or in districts with White majorities likely lived on very small farms—fewer than ten slaves—and not on large plantations. Thus there was considerable exchange between these communities as they formed or struggled to maintain families; labored on other farms or were permitted to sell or barter their products; celebrated holidays; and formed religious communities, including hush arbors (secret gatherings in the wilderness), praise houses (communal and religious gathering sites), or full-blown churches with preachers.[21] Not only were these important sites for the religious life of the community, they were also places to gather to initiate persons into the community, to judge persons found guilty of violating community norms, or to whisper to one another and share rumors about freedom. The Black church became such a strong symbol of Black resistance that, for example, Whites disbanded and destroyed the African Church in Charleston, South Carolina, for fear that it would incite rebellion after the dissolution of a planned rebellion led by Denmark Vesey.[22]

The formation of the free, Black, independent church in the late 1700s was indispensable to the development of Black resistance to slavery. More important, these African Americans wanted to foster their own Black religious culture and worship traditions. Congregations sprang up in cities like Petersburg, Virginia; Charleston, South Carolina; and Savannah, Georgia, in the

1770s. Between the 1790s and 1820s, a number of Black denominations or all-Black churches within White denominations were founded, including the African Methodist Episcopal (AME) Church founded by Richard Allen (its first bishop) and Absalom Jones in Philadelphia; the African Methodist Episcopal Zion Church of New York founded by Jones as he broke away from the former; and various all-Black Baptist, Presbyterian, and Episcopalian churches. These churches not only produced a class of preachers and other leaders like Richard Allen, Henry Highland Garnett, and Henry McNeal Turner, who exhorted against the evils of slavery; they also served as key resource sites for antislavery efforts throughout the 1800s. The churches were part of a budding, antebellum Black civil society of communal organizations necessary for fostering a collective identity and collective action. For example, by the early 1800s mutual aid societies emerged such as the Free African Society founded by Richard Allen and others, fraternal lodges like Prince Hall's African Masonic Lodge, and schools like the African School of Boston. Despite the politics of some of these institutions depending on White philanthropy, they nevertheless laid the groundwork for periods of vibrant Black civic, associational, and intellectual life that would follow after the Civil War and into the twentieth century.[23]

Black Politics and Forms of Antislavery Resistance

African American communities deployed a range of strategies in their determined opposition to slavery and hoped for its abolition, spanning the gamut from violent to peaceful resistance, or moral suasion; but they all demonstrated the ways in which, prior to the Civil War, African Americans developed a Black politics that strongly resisted racialization and racial oppression. Among the leading Black abolitionists of the mid-1800s, who mostly advocated the peaceful overthrow of slavery, were civil rights spokespersons and newspaper publishers such as Frederick Douglass and Mary Ann Shad Cary; escaped slaves turned brilliant orators, such as Sojourner Truth; and activists who escaped slavery and helped scores of others to escape to freedom, such as Harriet Tubman. They joined White allies in various Northern antislavery societies. Most prominent among these groups was the American Anti-Slavery Society (AAS), cofounded in 1833 by newspaper editor Theodore Dwight Weld, philanthropist Arthur Tappan, and staunch antislavery spokesman William Lloyd Garrison. Many White abolitionists disagreed with the American Colonization Society (ACS) and its belief that Blacks must be shipped out of the United States and back to Africa or to the Caribbean for there ever to be racial peace (a view long held by Abraham Lincoln). Abolitionists believed Black Americans must not be enslaved in the United States; this did not mean, however, that they all saw Blacks as their social equals worthy of full civil rights and full leadership in the abolition movement.

Partly due to the interracial politics of cooperation, between the 1830s and 1850s free Blacks sought ways to independently articulate their opposition to slavery through a multitude of petitions to governments, often directed at state legislatures and Congress, as well as through a series of all-Black national conventions. With the conventions, delegates from various Upper South and Northern states met in Rochester, New York; Cleveland, Ohio; Philadelphia, Pennsylvania; and many other

 Why would Blacks work with White allies who racialized them and considered them undeserving of equal rights and opportunities?

locales with their broad mantra to "devise ways and means of bettering our condition." More than one hundred delegates met in Rochester in 1853 and founded the National Council of Colored People, the precursor to many other antebellum national and local Black-led civil rights organizations and efforts. Blacks joined in the propaganda campaign or efforts to directly move public opinion and make Whites more sympathetic to Black freedom through slave narratives, speeches, pamphlets, newspapers, public displays, and direct mass mailings, to name some of the tactics. Most effective of all was the **Underground Railroad,** called so in the 1830s to describe the extensive formal and informal network of agents and allies who led and assisted enslaved Blacks in their flight to Northern states, and especially to the free nation of Canada. Estimates are that forty thousand fugitives fled through Ohio alone by the mid-1800s. Harriet Tubman is among the most famous conductors of this "Underground" Railroad.[24]

In this period up to the Civil War and especially the 1850s, Black political ideology—the range of ideals that determined the goals and strategies of African Americans—has been described as existing along the main poles of liberal integrationism, or those who wanted full American citizenship, versus Black nationalism, or those who believed Blacks should become a separate nation. Instead, it is fair to say that there was no absolute Black opposition to a plan for emigration back to Africa despite concerns that the ACS was a racist organization. In fact, a number of Black leaders—from sailor and businessman Paul Cuffee to physician and later Civil War hero Martin Delaney—argued for the creation of an African nation(s) to become the new (or renewed) home of African Americans, thus escaping White racism. Delaney's ideas of "Africa for the Africans" influenced one of the largest Black social movements of the twentieth century—Marcus M. Garvey's United Negro Improvement Association.[25] It is also clear from the powerful leadership and activism of Black women such as AME evangelist preacher Jarena Lee or abolitionists Sojourner Truth, Harriett Tubman, and Frances Ellen Watkins Harper that what came to be known as Black feminism (the belief of freedom from racism, sexism, and related oppressions) was critically important to Black America's well-being.

It may have been nationalist visions of freedom that in 1829 partly inspired David Walker, a North Carolina–born free person, when he wrote his famous *Appeal in Four Articles* that called on the use of violent resistance if necessary to attack slavery. Published and distributed widely, it caused a panic in the South because slavery interests were constantly fearful of the threat—sometimes manufactured—of violent slave uprisings. From 1712 to 1838, several dozen uprisings were attempted or occurred—the most famous being those of Gabriel Prosser, Denmark Vesey, and Nat Turner. By one estimate, all of these uprisings involved more than 2,500 enslaved participants and the deaths of more than 500 Whites. But the true impact of these rebellions cannot be captured in whether they were successful or thwarted or whether they were measured in bloodshed. Among their real effects is that they challenged the racist beliefs and caricatures that slave owners projected of African Americans as a largely docile, compliant, and ignorant people who were happy in slavery. Abetted by federal laws of the 1850s, slave states substantially tightened their restrictions on the lives of free persons and slaves after these rebellions. This only exacerbated the dissidence of Black and White abolitionists and led to one of the most famous armed rebellions against slavery—John Brown's raid on Harpers Ferry in 1858, which is credited as one of the many sparks of the Civil War. To be sure, slave uprisings were simply the most visible signs of the unrest and often invisible resistance that millions of slaves demonstrated toward their oppression, from sabotage to suicide.[26]

THE CIVIL WAR AND ITS AFTERMATH, 1860–1877

One of the most extraordinary periods in American and African American political history is the period during and after the Civil War, when the U.S. government made a reluctant but radical departure from its tacit support of the institution of slavery and came closer to a multiracial democracy than ever before. As explained previously, the tensions that sparked the war grew out of the uneasy relationship between the North and South that became more untenable with each successive compromise. While the war divided White Americans by region, most African Americans saw it as a war for their freedom, the anticipated moment that they referred to as the Day of Jubilee.

While Abraham Lincoln won only 40 percent of the popular vote, his election and that of his nominally antislavery Republican Party in 1860 prompted Southern rebellion. South Carolina seceded from the Union in December of that year, and more states followed to form the Confederate States of America. The Confederacy was ultimately comprised of eleven states: Alabama, Arkansas, Florida, Georgia, Louisiana, Mississippi, North Carolina, South Carolina, Tennessee, Texas, and Virginia. Historian Darlene Clark Hine notes, "Slavery caused the War. Yet when the war began in 1861, neither the Union nor the Confederacy entered the conflict with any intention or desire to change the status of black Americans. It was supposed to be a white man's war."[27] Lincoln was compelled and reluctantly agreed to enlist Black troops into the fight in April 1862. More than 40,000 Black men answered his call, fought, and died as Union soldiers by the time the conflict ended in April 1865, and all together more than 600,000 died on both sides. Among the 180,000 Black Union soldiers who enlisted were men such as those in the 54th Massachusetts Colored Regiment, whose bravery is partly immortalized, despite some historical inaccuracies, in the 1989 film *Glory*.

© Lee Snider/Photo Images/Corbis

Union Army colonel Robert Gould Shaw led the 54th Massachusetts Colored Regiment into battle during the Civil War. Although President Lincoln only reluctantly agreed to enlist Black troops, about 180,000 Blacks signed up to fight for their rights. The Robert Gould Shaw Memorial, pictured, is located at Beacon and Park Streets in Boston, Massachusetts. The memorial was created by the artist Augustus Saint-Gaudens.

Lincoln was eventually immortalized as the Great Emancipator for finally agreeing that this White man's fight to preserve the Union was ultimately a fight about slavery, but the Emancipation Proclamation for which he is credited, which took effect January 1, 1863, only freed slaves who resided behind Confederate lines that did not recognize his authority as U.S. president. Not until after Lincoln's assassination and the passing of the **Thirteenth Amendment** in 1865 were all slaves freed, and then the fight for full citizenship began.[28]

The Reforms of the First Reconstruction

The program of Southern Reconstruction was one in which the U.S. federal government formulated policies and programs to reintegrate the South into the Union and grant citizenship rights to Blacks. In place from roughly 1867 to 1877, Reconstruction was a complex, tumultuous, often violent, but also progressive period of American history. For the first time since Africans were brought to North America, they were freed, granted citizenship and universal male suffrage, and elected to public office. Yet White scholarship and attitudes in the years following Reconstruction often portrayed it as a period of mob rule in which corrupt, lazy, and ignorant Black politicians subjected innocent White Southerners to destructive legislation. In one example of such attitudes, the 1915 film *The Birth of a Nation* portrayed the Ku Klux Klan as the savior of the South, as well as protectors of the virtue of White womanhood against attacks from arrogant Black men. (This was a lie long perpetuated by White Southerners to justify anti-Black violence.) In his seminal work *Black Reconstruction in America, 1860–1880*, scholar and civil rights leader W. E. B. Du Bois argued against this persistently negative attitude toward African Americans. Du Bois conceded that there was some corruption during Reconstruction, but that the tragedy in these race-driven interpretations is that "there is no room for the real plot of the story, for the clear mistake and guilt of rebuilding a new slavery of the [Black] working class in the midst of a fateful experiment in democracy; for the triumph of sheer moral courage and sacrifice in the abolition crusade; and for the hurt and struggle of degraded black millions in their fight for freedom and their attempt to enter democracy."[29] In this section, we briefly summarize this real story.

Political sociologist Manning Marable refers to this period from 1867 to 1877 as the First Reconstruction because he saw great similarities between it and Civil Rights Movement of the mid-1950s to late 1960s. That is how we will refer to it here.[30] (See Box 3.3 for more details.)

A series of political and military acts were passed under the First Reconstruction to govern the reincorporated Southern states and provide institutional support for the transition of Blacks from slavery to freedom. The **Thirteenth Amendment,** passed in 1865, officially outlawed slavery everywhere in the United States. The **Freedmen's Bureau,** established under the War Department, was an all-purpose but temporary agency charged with helping newly emancipated African Americans in their transition to freedom. It also provided aid to White Southerners affected by the devastation of the Civil War, which was extensive. The Freedmen's Bureau's enormous responsibilities were carried out by its roughly one thousand nearly all-White Army officers and agents, who were empowered to establish freedmen schools; settle land, labor, and other legal disputes; provide direct

✟ BOX 3.3 CROSS ROAD

Persistent Struggles of the First and Second Reconstructions

Major parallels exist between what political sociologist Manning Marable calls the First Reconstruction, the period from 1867 to 1877 that saw the nation struggling and adapting to the new rights granted to now-freed Blacks, and the Civil Rights Movement of the 1950s and 1960s, which Marable calls the Second Reconstruction. The parallels include the following:

- The involvement of states' rights debates and the federal government as a reluctant ally to African Americans

- Public pressure on the federal courts and Congress to act

- The role of each in fundamentally shaping Black politics through their involvement in public debates and mobilizations around Black citizenship status

- Subsequent growth of significant Black voter empowerment and the election of Black officials

- Expansion of the Black middle class and the creation of a new leadership

- Collapse or constraint on the movements' efforts by Northern collusion with renewed White Southern opposition[31]

Similarities also exist in the civil rights laws passed under the First and Second Reconstructions. For instance, the Civil Rights Act of 1875 anticipated the 1964 Civil Rights Act by declaring discrimination in public accommodations—such as hotels and street cars—a federal crime. Although the Supreme Court declared it unconstitutional in 1883, Congress, enacting the Civil Rights Act of 1964, took the matter up again, barring racial and gender discrimination in public facilities and accommodations and forbidding job discrimination by employers or unions. The Fifteenth Amendment (1870) declared it unconstitutional for any state to deny an adult male the right to vote due to "race, color, or previous condition of servitude," but nearly ninety years later, voting rights remained an issue. The Civil Rights Act of 1957 created a division within the Department of Justice to oversee their protection, and the Voting Rights Act of 1965 (VRA) provided much more powerful federal authority over the states' control of voting. Significantly, the VRA included triggering provisions to determine those counties and locales eligible for federal scrutiny, and preclearance provisions required these states to clear any changes in their election laws and boundaries through the federal courts.

Considering This Crossroad

- What do the similarities between the First and Second Reconstructions, despite the nearly one hundred years separating them, say about the persistence of racialization and the barriers that existed for African Americans?

- Based on what you've read in this chapter, what constraints in the dominant society and polity are present in both Reconstruction eras, and how were they perpetuated?

- Why was it so difficult for the South and Southern Whites to recognize Blacks' rights as citizens—civil rights, the right to vote, to own property, and to earn a living—and for Northern political interests to protect those rights?

food, medical, and other social aid; monitor elections and the right for Blacks to register and vote; and assist in the transportation needs of Black and White refugees. The bureau, operating for only four years, with a budget based on receipts from rental of lands to former slaves, was unable to address the complex range of problems included in its charge.[32] The **Civil Rights Act of 1866** was the first law of its kind and stated that all persons born in the United States were citizens of their state and of the nation. It also outlawed the Black Codes, which many Southern governments enacted in an effort to control and possibly re-enslave freed African Americans by fundamentally curtailing their economic and political rights. This law preceded the **Fourteenth Amendment** (1868) that enshrined the above standard of citizenship within the Constitution, extended equal protection of the laws to all, and provided sanctions against state governments that did not comply with new civil rights standards in their constitutions and laws. A few years later, the **Fifteenth Amendment** (1870) prohibited state governments from denying a citizen the right to vote based on race or former enslavement. These legislative changes helped, at least institutionally, to remove significant barriers from African Americans obtaining the same rights and opportunities as the White majority.

Much of this legislation stemmed in part from the efforts of the Radical Republicans in Congress, a wing of the Republican Party that believed in full Black equality. They fought Lincoln's successor, Andrew Johnson—a strongly anti-Black, Tennessee Democrat—on the scale and breadth of Reconstruction. Johnson was not particularly concerned about repairing the economic, social, and political status of former slaves. In the Senate, the radical faction was led by Charles Sumner of Massachusetts, and in the House of Representatives by Thaddeus Stevens of Pennsylvania.

From 1867 to 1877, the Radical Republicans enacted their vision of civil and social reforms by overriding President Johnson's objections, authorizing military governments to rule Southern states until they reformed their constitutions, and passing a bevy of new laws. Political scientist Linda Williams notes that "White skin privilege" still fundamentally mattered in how benefits were bestowed on Black and White war veterans, as well as the Black and White poor, and there was extensive anti-Black violence as White Southerners continued to rebel. But in a very short period of time, Reconstruction transformed Black politics to such an extent that even after its decline and fall in the late 1870s, generations of African American leaders and organizations remembered how they or their ancestors were empowered under it and continuously mobilized for greater self-determination and reform.[33]

Black Politics and the First Reconstruction

Reconstruction aimed at racial democratization of Southern society and politics by passing voter and other citizenship laws that were race neutral. In a number of ways, it involved or mobilized large numbers of African Americans in processes that permitted them to deliberate and to make decisions about their futures at levels not previously possible. Union leagues were social and civic organizations partly comprised of veterans who recruited Blacks to support the Republican Party and to use their newly won right to vote. Black political conventions and assemblies were held in a number of states and locales before and after the Civil War. They often included men and women and both formally and informally debated prospective state constitutional revisions and other measures. A small protest movement even emerged during this period in which Blacks held labor strikes, called **sit-ins**, in opposition to discriminatory employment practices and laws condoned by White-controlled Southern governments and White-owned businesses.

Because of widespread Black mobilization, the size of Reconstruction-era Black populations (in three states Blacks comprised a majority of eligible voters) and

© Bettmann/CORBIS

The first Black members of Congress elected during the First Reconstruction of the 1870s set an example that inspired generations of African American leaders. From left to right, U.S. Senator Hiram Revels of Mississippi and U.S. Representatives Benjamin Turner of Alabama, Robert DeLarge of South Carolina, Josiah Walls of Florida, Jefferson Long of Georgia, Joseph Rainey of South Carolina, and Robert Elliott of South Carolina. All were Republican.

the temporary denial of the vote to White ex-Confederates who had not yet sworn loyalty to the Union, an unprecedented 1,465 Black men were elected to public office between 1867 and 1877. True to our assertion that the journey of African American political freedom has many twists and turns, more Blacks held office in the United States in 1873 than did ninety years later, in 1963. The range of offices held under Reconstruction is impressive. Fourteen Blacks were elected to Congress, and one—Hiram Revels of Mississippi—served as a U.S. senator. In addition, P. B. S. Pinchback served briefly as governor of Louisiana, and 6 Blacks served as lieutenant governors. In Mississippi and South Carolina a majority of the state legislatures were Black for a time, including 112 senators and 683 representatives. Four Blacks served as state superintendents of education, and at least one—Jonathan Wright of South Carolina—sat upon a state supreme court. There were 41 Black sheriffs, 5 Black mayors, 31 Black coroners, and even 4 Black police chiefs. Black state legislators discussed and attempted to enact a number of reforms in these states, including compulsory public education for the first time, land reforms that would redistribute former plantation properties, and civil rights laws. More often than not their proposals and actions were blocked or reversed by White lawmakers who regained state political control, as well as by federal officials who did not enforce fairness, illustrating that despite changes in federal policy, discrimination and racialization continued.[34] For this period, race was no longer an absolute barrier to equal opportunity, but it did remain decisive. As Chapter 4 will show, there were important parallels and contrasts to Latinos in the Southwest. They were citizens and landholders in Texas, New Mexico, and California just after the 1848 Treaty of Guadalupe Hidalgo that ended the Mexican-American War that began in 1845. Despite the treaty's recognition of natives' citizenship and economic rights, Anglo migrants rapidly disenfranchised Mexican Americans in the Southwest, as well as Chinese in California. The native Mexican American elite in the Southwest held high political office at the outset, but this declined rapidly, so by the late 1870s their political participation was inconsequential. In this respect, the experiences of Blacks in the South, Mexicans in the Southwest, and Chinese in California were very similar.

The Fall of Reconstruction and the Rise of Jim Crow

What Du Bois called this "experiment in democracy" was derailed in the early 1870s and entirely reversed by the end of the decade. Though the federal administration of President Ulysses Grant applied pressures for reform, White Southerners vehemently resisted and White Northerners never fully supported the full equality of Black citizens. After nearly five years of the painful Civil War, the end of slavery, and the creation of African American citizenship and voting, the North was unwilling to continue to struggle to sustain these changes of Black over White. "White redemption" became the mantra of the conservative, Southern wing of the Democratic Party, with the explicit intention of returning Southern state governments to the control of White men. One newspaper declared, "Mississippi is a white man's country, and by the eternal God we'll rule it!" By the mid-1870s, White Democrats and their allies successfully carried out a campaign of mass intimidation and violence through a number of methods. They ignored federal laws and mandates; organized vigilante organizations like the White League; and threatened, beat, and in several cases murdered Black voters, jurors, and officials, as well as sympathetic White Republicans. They also refused to seat duly elected Black officials or charged them with misconduct and removed them from office. From 1870 to 1877, White Democrats regained control of Southern state legislatures and governorships from Blacks. All of this set the context for the 1876 presidential election. Republican Rutherford B. Hayes and Democrat Samuel Tilden negotiated a compromise in the U.S. House of Representatives that permitted Hayes, who won fewer popular votes, to assume the presidency if he agreed to withdraw all federal troops from the South. The Republicans in the House and Hayes did agree and thus, with the end of federally enforced martial law, Reconstruction collapsed.

By the turn of the twentieth century, Black political, economic, and social gains nearly evaporated with the emergence of **Jim Crow** politics—the official government sanction of anti-Black racial discrimination, racial separation, and violence. Historian Rayford Logan called this era the lowest point of postbellum Black history. In the political realm, state constitutions and electoral laws were rewritten with the expressed intent of reasserting a "White man's government." New methods of disenfranchisement, such as the Grandfather Clause or the literacy test, were put in place to circumvent the Fifteenth Amendment. Older ones, such as the poll tax, were also effective in constraining the vote by the new citizens. As a result, one million Black voters were removed from the voting rolls by the turn of the century. The few Black voters who were still permitted to vote were severely harassed, or their votes were nullified by White electoral fraud. In 1901 North Carolina representative George White became the last African American to serve in Congress for a generation. White segregationists openly gloated over their victory, with South Carolina governor Ben "Pitchfork" Tillman stating, "We have done our level best [to prevent Blacks from voting] . . . we have scratched our heads to find out how we could eliminate the last one of them. We stuffed ballot boxes. We shot them. We are not ashamed of it."[35]

With such words giving an official impunity to the mob violence of White vigilante groups, it is no wonder that the late nineteenth century witnessed the highest rates of anti-Black lynching of any era. **Lynching** was the extralegal use of torture and murder, including hanging, burning, castration, and dismemberment of victims, most often Black, who were accused of alleged and most often false crimes. (See Figure 3.2.) The ultimate motive was to use fear to exert social control over the victim's group.

The Ku Klux Klan, founded in 1866, was among the leading White supremacist vigilante organizations using methods of racial terror like lynching. It was suppressed during Reconstruction, but it was reconstituted around 1915 and grew greatly in strength by the 1920s. (Note a great spike in lynchings around 1918 in Figure 3.4.) Courageous journalist and tireless civil rights leader Ida B. Wells investigated many of these lynchings in her report *A Red Record*, and found the charges against victims were invariably doubtful. White mobs frequently accused Black men of raping White women, when in actuality these mobs were fearful of consensual, interracial relationships, or of Black economic success. Between 1882 and 1925, more than 3,200 African Americans, mostly men but also some women and children, were lynched. It is important to note, however, that this period was a high point of American xenophobia overall, and 1,266 White persons also were lynched. These victims often were ethnics like Catholics and Jews who were "guilty" of being immigrants or of not being White, Anglo-Saxon Protestants.[36]

In the economic realm, Jim Crow criminal justice and employment practices devised a convict lease system through which millions of Black inmates (many arrested on false charges or even kidnapped) were deliberately given extraordinarily long and harsh sentences. In turn, local sheriffs and state prison departments leased the labor of these convicts to industrial firms and planters—an effort at reenslavement—with no regard for the inhumane exploitation and treatment these men experienced inside mines or out in fields. Black farmers were exploited under a system of sharecropping. Landless Blacks farmed land owned by Whites and earned their pay from a proportion of the crop—hence "sharecropping"—and those who participated were called sharecroppers. This system, like a form of feudalism, tied them to the land and cheated them out of a fair share of the crop revenues they produced while sometimes renting land and tools from White owners. In the North and South, other Black workers had little recourse against blatant discrimination and everyday racial indignities, whether they were domestics, stevedores, or factory workers.

In the social realm, Southern racial customs as well as state and local laws eventually dictated the separation of Blacks and Whites in public facilities such as railroad cars, schools, theaters, libraries, parks, water fountains, and sometimes in places of employment. The

Did racialization of African Americans increase in the Jim Crow era? If not, what accounted for the rise in violence against them?

Figure 3.4 Total Lynchings by Race and Year, 1882–1968

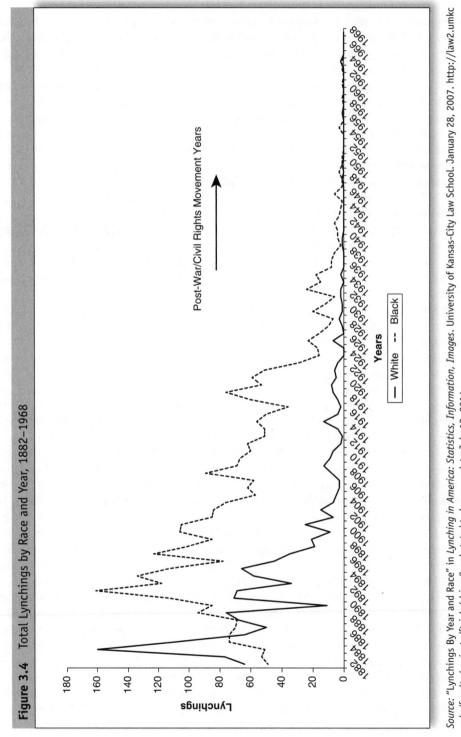

Source: "Lynchings By Year and Race" in *Lynching in America: Statistics, Information, Images.* University of Kansas-City Law School. January 28, 2007. http://law2.umkc .edu/faculty/projects/ftrials/shipp/lynchstats.html, access date July 18, 2014.

popular term for this collection of informal practices and formalized law was *Jim Crow*. The origins of Jim Crow—both the name and the language for laws and politics—can be traced to the 1820s, when Thomas Dartmouth Rice, a White performer with artificially darkened skin, portrayed a stereotypical Black man onstage; the response was highly favorable and brought him fame. The name of the character "Jim Crow" then began to be used after the Civil War and Reconstruction as the informal name for the complex array of racial caste systems and laws and policies that stigmatized and controlled the status of Black Americans. Jim Crow laws and politics therefore symbolized the uneven roads to which Blacks were restricted.[37] One Jim Crow law went so far as to require Black and White jurors to use separate Bibles when being sworn to give truthful testimony in court.

The federal government turned a blind eye to many of these violations of the Fourteenth and Fifteenth Amendments. As we explained in Chapter 1, the U.S. Supreme Court rendered the infamous 1896 ***Plessy v. Ferguson*** decision, which declared the practice of "separate but equal" or segregation of public facilities—constitutional. Despite Homer Plessy's charge that the Fourteenth Amendment's Equal Protection Clause had been violated when he, a mixed-race man, was forced to sit in the Colored section of a railway car, the Court's majority disagreed with Plessy. It concluded that the Fourteenth Amendment "could not have been intended to abolish distinctions based upon color, or to enforce social, as distinguished from political, equality, or a commingling of the two races upon terms unsatisfactory to either." For more than two generations, this precedent solidified the walls of segregation in many respects before a Second Reconstruction tore them down.[38]

BLACK POLITICS IN THE JIM CROW ERA, 1880–1940

Because of the reconfiguration of White supremacy in the South and continued discrimination in the North, African American communities refocused their attention on Black self-help and the development of Black civil society to press for greater citizenship rights and opportunities. Leaders and organizations enumerated wide-ranging strategies for Black progress, including the political accommodation and economic self-help model promulgated by the conservative race leader and head of the Tuskegee Institute, Booker T. Washington; the conservative newspaper writer George Schuyler; and the civil rights protest and direct agitation model advanced by scholars and civil rights leaders like W. E. B. Du Bois and Mary McLeod Bethune. Other strategies included a separatist model that encouraged movement to all-Black towns, advocated by Benjamin "Pap" Singleton and his forty thousand Exodusters, and emigration from the United States and the building of an independent Black nation, advanced by Black Nationalist leader Marcus Garvey and later Elijah Muhammad of the Nation of Islam.

This was a period of expansive growth for Black civil society, including groups and institutions with varied educational, religious, economic, and political purposes, all of whom played key roles in the shaping of Black politics. Despite class and other differences among African Americans, segregation fostered a strong racial group consciousness because the system of separation, somewhat akin to slavery, made many Blacks painfully and intensely aware of their second-class citizenship. In the context of our framework, however, Black racialization during this period was not an absolute bar against Black citizenship rights and opportunities. Race mattered—significantly so—and Blacks had only weak empowerment to advance their interests. They possessed limited citizenship rights and opportunities, and the barriers they faced remained decisive.

Black Civil Society

Throughout Black political history, Black teachers played a pivotal role in the development of Black communities and political leadership. During Reconstruction a number of all-Black colleges and universities, such as Howard University, Fisk University, Morehouse College, and Spelman College, were founded because various Christian denominations sent missionaries South or Congress authorized land grants. Out of these institutions came leaders who would shape the course of Black America.

The most intense political debate of the early 1900s was over the role that education should play in the racial uplift of African Americans. On one side was the Tuskegee Model of Booker T. Washington, a brilliant former slave who amassed enormous contributions from White philanthropists. In public, Washington advocated for Black industrial and mechanical education so that Black workers could compliantly assume their place in the racial order of the New South. In private, he supported civil rights lawsuits. On the other side was W. E. B. Du Bois, who received his doctorate from Harvard and advocated for a classical liberal arts education for Blacks that could in part develop a Talented Tenth, a leadership class to guide others. Several scholarly and activist conferences were created and helped to debate the way forward, from 1898 through 1945, in charting Black self-determination in the United States and abroad.[39]

Along the other lines of civic life, various Black Protestant denominations greatly expanded—Methodist (AME and AME-Zion) and Baptist; or took root—Holiness and Pentecostal churches during this era. AME, Baptist, and Holiness and Pentecostal churches became the three dominant churches of Black America by the end of the twentieth century. Methodist and Baptist ministers in particular were among the leaders of the Civil Rights Movement of the 1950s and 1960s, although there was considerable disagreement among some ministers and churches about supporting this movement. Added to this educational and religious basis for Black politics was the founding of various Black fraternal organizations on college campuses (such as Alpha Phi Alpha and Alpha Kappa Alpha) and Black professional associations, like those for Black physicians (the National Medical Association) and lawyers (the National Bar Association).

One set of civic affiliations easily overlapped with others to create broadening networks of Black leadership. Business associations and labor unions were equally important in shaping elite and grassroots agendas. Booker T. Washington encouraged the spread of Black entrepreneurship in founding the Negro Business League in 1900. Madame C. J. Walker, formerly Sarah Breedlove, founded a cosmetics empire that employed thousands of Black women and made her a millionaire, and she used her enormous wealth to support civil rights and other political causes. Black workers struggled to defend their right to fair wages and working conditions. When they were unable to receive fair treatment and were relegated to segregated locals, as was the case with the American Federation of Labor, they created their own powerful unions, such as A. Philip Randolph's Brotherhood of Sleeping Car Porters, or they joined unions that had made more concerted efforts (or that they could compel to make such efforts) at nondiscrimination, such as the United Autoworkers or the Congress of Industrial Organizations.[40]

The Early to Mid–Twentieth Century Civil Rights Movement

Black civil society undergirded the efforts that African American leaders and groups made to pursue Black self-determination strategies, especially the Du Bois civil rights approach of pressing against the strictures of Jim Crow segregation in the South and *de facto* segregation in the North. Domestic tensions and two unique global conflicts in the early twentieth century affected African Americans and contributed to these strategies.

The domestic tensions partly stemmed from burgeoning economic and demographic shifts when, between 1910 and 1930, nearly two million African Americans migrated out of the rural South during the first **Great Migration.** These migrants underwent urbanization as they created or expanded new communities in Northeastern and Midwestern cities such as New York, Chicago, Philadelphia, Detroit, St. Louis, Cleveland, and Pittsburgh, while others moved to Southern cities like Atlanta and Birmingham to gain greater opportunities within industrial and commercial labor forces. Given continued White racial animus toward African Americans, as evidenced by the continuance of lynching, a wave of race riots ignited in cities ranging from Atlanta (1906) to Chicago (1919), followed by even bloodier riots in the 1920s. These conflicts were mostly driven by persistent racist stereotypes of Blacks as well as White/White ethnic resentment of the changing civic and economic status of Black Americans.

One particularly bloody riot in Springfield, Illinois, in 1908 prompted the formation of the **National Association for the Advancement of Colored (NAACP),** created to advance the status of the Black population. The NAACP was preceded by W. E. B. Du Bois's 1905 Niagara Movement. Du Bois predicted, "The problem of the twentieth century is the problem of the color-line—the relation of the darker to the lighter races of men in Asia and Africa, in America and the islands of the sea."[41] To challenge this divide and the conservative approach of Booker T. Washington, Du Bois invited twenty-eight other delegates to a conference in upstate New York. They decried the indignities of segregation and called for a number of reforms, including improved housing, health care, and schools for African Americans, as they challenged White racial prejudice. Although this conference and its subsequent meetings garnered the support of hundreds of people, the internal disagreements among its Black leaders, combined with the attacks of Washington and his powerful allies, led to its demise. As the Niagara Movement dissipated and race riots continued, a group of forty White philanthropists, moderates, and leftists, as well as Du Bois, met and established the NAACP four years later.

Over the next four decades, African Americans increasingly assumed the leadership of the NAACP, built an organizational membership of roughly 300,000, and established hundreds of state and local chapters. It became a leading, if not *the* leading, organization in the Black Civil Rights Movement up to the 1950s. Some of the many ways it challenged racial discrimination and Jim Crow segregation included confronting anti-Black racial stereotypes in art and popular culture in the early 1900s and 1920s, such as when it protested D. W. Griffith's 1915, pro–Ku Klux Klan film *The Birth of a Nation,* waging a long period of public protests and demonstrations over the film, and lobbying Congress to have lynching declared a federal crime. The NAACP also assembled a brilliant legal team through its affiliate, the NAACP Legal Defense Fund, and from 1915 to the 1950s waged an incremental but eventually successful battle to overturn segregation and discriminatory laws with regard to voting, housing, public accommodations, and education. (See Figure 3.5.) It investigated and pursued hundreds

> Consider the early twentieth-century organization efforts by African Americans. Are they still relevant and meaningful today?

of cases of anti-Black racial violence and discrimination through the work of its state and local chapters, often helping to provide legal counsel and support for victims. The NAACP also worked with other civil rights groups during the Great Depression of the 1930s and, during President Franklin D. Roosevelt's administration, it objected to the exclusion of Black farm workers and domestics from the social and employment insurance portions of the 1935 Social Security Act. Additionally, the NAACP used scholarly research, the arts, and literary avenues to keep Black America and its allies informed about the advances and barriers to racial progress through the publication of its national magazine *The Crisis*, founded and edited by W. E. B. Du Bois.[42]

BOX 3.4 ROAD SIGN

African American Women Organize for Civil Rights

While the NAACP is properly credited as the first major national civil rights organization of the twentieth century, the deep roots of the early Civil Rights Movement are connected to the leaders of the national Black Women's Club Movement. In 1896 two rival organizations merged and formed the National Association of Colored Women (NACW) in Washington DC, with influential spokesperson Mary Church Terrell as its first president. In 1914, this association had approximately one thousand affiliates (clubs) under its umbrella and fifty thousand members. At times, ideological tensions existed among the women regarding endorsing Washington's approach to Black progress, and the clubs also faced issues over class and skin-color politics associated with the "racial uplift" philosophy of some of the lighter-complexioned, elite women who founded the association. The group called for a host of social reforms, such as kindergarten and daycare facilities, better working conditions and employment services for urban women, and better health services and community clinics, that preceded the agenda of a second great civil rights organization, the National Urban League, founded in 1910.[43]

Black Politics from the Great Depression to World War II

While Black civil rights leaders pressed for expanded citizenship rights and opportunities through the courts, a handful of African Americans who retained or held elected or appointed office helped to advance these concerns. In 1929 U.S. representative Oscar DePriest of Chicago became the first African American elected to Congress in nearly thirty years. In addition, a group of African Americans such as educator Mary Mcleod Bethune and an economist with a Harvard PhD, Robert Weaver, held limited and sometimes advisory posts in President Franklin D. Roosevelt's administration. They became known as Roosevelt's Black Cabinet. Roosevelt assumed office in 1932 during the Great Depression, when national income dropped by half and 25 percent of all Americans were unemployed. As many as 50 to 60 percent of African Americans were unemployed in certain cities, and Blacks were particularly

Figure 3.5   Select Civil Rights Legal Victories of the NAACP/ NAACP-LDF, 1915–1954

Guinn v. United States
(1915)

- The grandfather clause exception in state constitutions (those with grandfathers who were permitted to vote prior to 1867 had been exempt from a literacy test before voting) was declared unconstitutional under the Fifteenth Amendment.

Missouri ex. rel Gaines v. Canada
(1938)

- Under the separate but equal precedent, Missouri was found to be in violation of the equal protection clause of the Fourteenth Amendment and was required to establish a separate law school that African Americans could attend; other states soon followed this model.

Smith v. Allwright
(1944)

- The Democratic Party of Texas could not consider itself a private institution—and thus allowed to hold all-White primaries—since it was the dominant party of the South, and being barred from voting in a primary would bar one from casting a meaningful vote.

Shelley v. Kraemer
(1948)

- Private neighborhood associations could make—but could not sue in court to legally enforce—restrictive covenants (contracts among White homeowners that prohibited selling their homes or property to prospective Black and in some cases Latino or Jewish buyers).

Sweatt v. Painter
(1950)

- The condition of segregated Texas law schools and the resources made available to Black students were poor and not equal, thus failing to meet the separate but equal standard, helping to lay the groundwork for *Brown v. Board of Education*.

Brown v. Board of Education
(1954)

- Unanimous ruling that the separate but equal precedent established in *Plessy v. Ferguson* (1896) was unconstitutional under the Fourteenth Amendment; desegregation "with all deliberate speed" was called for a year later.

hard-hit as agricultural workers, given the economic and climate devastation that farms endured in the 1930s.

While Roosevelt proposed and Congress launched numerous new federal agencies and programs to rescue the economy, Blacks faced intense discrimination in New Deal programs. Title I of the 1933 National Industrial Recovery Act, which was later ruled unconstitutional by the Supreme Court, set minimum wage standards and hours, but it exempted domestic workers and farmers—which made up 70 percent of the Black workforce. Southern Democrats in Congress deemed this provision necessary to protect planter interests and the White middle and upper classes affluent enough to hire Black domestics. Title II of the Public Works Administration was important to U.S. economic recovery but initially only provided a handful of jobs to African Americans because of local, discriminatory hiring practices. Black recipients of federal poverty relief were likewise shortchanged because of discrimination in local county offices.[44]

The NAACP and the National Urban League engaged in intense lobbying for Black workers to be included under the provisions of the Social Security Act, finally winning modest gains in the 1950s. With regard to economic rights, the New Deal was a period of militant left and labor activism in which White communists and other leftist organizers briefly made in-roads among African American communities, from Harlem, to Birmingham, Alabama. Some African Americans perceived these White radical organizers as advocates for the poor and unemployed, and as antiracist in their practices and beliefs. The famous Scottsboro Boys case was a touchstone for this activist period. In this case, nine young Black men from Alabama were falsely accused of raping two White women. Court proceedings continued from 1931 to 1937, even though the women had admitted the story was not true.

Grassroots leaders like Alabama coalminer Angelo Herndon or intellectuals and labor rights leaders including W. E. B. Du Bois and A. Philip Randolph for a time embraced or at least admired communist or socialist thought for its calls for racial egalitarianism and economic redistribution. Such radicalism influenced efforts to set a national Black political agenda in the 1930s and 1940s, which included labor organizing by the National Negro Congress and full citizenship rights and an end to Jim Crow by the National Council of Negro Labor. This was a period of enormous growth for the American labor movement, and Black leaders argued for African Americans to be included as full participants.[45]

On the political front, Roosevelt's economic reform agenda began the transformation of the Democratic Party from its base in the conservative, anti–civil rights South to a more liberal, national coalition comprised of labor and the White working class, Catholics and Jews (or some White immigrants), the elderly, women, and minority voters, including African Americans. It became known as the **New Deal (or Democratic) Coalition.** African Americans slowly began to switch loyalties from the Republican Party (formerly the "Party of Lincoln") to the Democratic Party between 1932, when Roosevelt beat incumbent Republican president Herbert Hoover, and 1964, when incumbent Democratic presidential candidate Lyndon B. Johnson roundly beat Republican candidate Barry Goldwater. Despite the strong objections of White Southern Democrats, especially in Congress, Roosevelt, influenced by Black civil rights leaders and First Lady Eleanor Roosevelt, also embraced more Black policy interests. Between 1935 and 1941, Roosevelt made small but important strides to appeal to Black voters: he openly denounced the practice of lynching and announced support for a federal antilynching bill, hired forty-five African Americans to federal posts, and conceded to some Black demands of nondiscrimination directives in New Deal as well as war production agencies.

This was especially true in 1941, when civil rights leader A. Philip Randolph protested that Blacks were not being hired in those industries that received federal contracts and subsidies for producing World War II armaments and supplies. Randolph threatened to have as many as 100,000 marchers converge on Washington, DC, to press the point. Roosevelt ultimately issued **Executive Order 8802** in July 1941, establishing broad antidiscrimination guidelines as well as a Fair Employment Practices Committee (FEPC) that had limited powers to monitor hiring practices in war industries. It was a modest effort, but it was the first successful, federal civil rights initiative since Reconstruction; and, arguably, it was the beginning of what became affirmative action.

From the time the United States entered World War II in 1941 until the end of the conflict in 1945, more than 500,000 African Americans enlisted and served, supposedly in a war for freedom and democracy against the Axis powers of Nazi Germany, Italy, and Japan. The great irony is that similar to the generations that preceded them, African Americans served loyally in segregated military units despite intense racial discrimination. Units such as the Tuskegee Airmen and the 99th Fighter Pursuit Squadron illustrate that as in the past, African Americans fought with valor. Black leaders and groups supported the fight to defeat fascism abroad, but they also demanded racial justice at home.

Other groups, such as Japanese Americans, served in similar group-based units in the military. The 442nd Combat Team included men from the internment camps, Hawaii, and men already in the army at the start of the war; the 100th Infantry Battalion based in Hawaii was also composed of Japanese Americans. Both served in the European theater of war, and fought in five major battle campaigns. The late senator Daniel Inouye of Hawaii served in the 442nd, which was "the most decorated unit in American history," winning the Distinguished Service Cross, and eventually the Medal of Honor in 2000 bestowed by President Bill Clinton.[46]

The demands for racial reform bore fruit when, in 1948, Roosevelt's successor, Harry Truman, issued Executive Order 9981, which desegregated the armed forces. While this won wide acclaim from the African American community, it intensified the fight within the Democratic Party with anti–civil rights Southern Democrats like Strom Thurmond, otherwise known as Dixiecrats.[47]

THE SECOND RECONSTRUCTION: POSTWAR AND CIVIL RIGHTS MOVEMENT ERA, 1950s–1960s

Among other scholars, sociologist Charles Payne concludes that when African American World War II veterans, like Amzie Moore of Mississippi, returned to the United States having fought to preserve democracy abroad, their expectations helped fuel Black hopes for greater rights and opportunities at home. It was veterans like Moore who rolled up their sleeves and helped to revive the grassroots activist tradition of Black politics that had persisted long before and after the First Reconstruction. They joined younger generations of Black activists to help develop a mass protest wing to what political sociologist Manning Marable labels the beginning of the Second Reconstruction—the 1950s and 1960s Civil Rights Movement. Prior to this grassroots mass mobilization movement, groups like the NAACP had mainly (but not exclusively) conducted the movement in the courts and inside the normal channels of government.

The postwar 1950s was a period of both prosperity and prejudice. The prosperity was evident from the American middle class growing in leaps and bounds. The economy during the war years had resulted in tight savings that were unleashed in the 1950s and greatly expanded the consumer economy, while federal subsidies and loans rewarded the service of veterans and their families, who in turn sought homeownership and higher education. But the Black middle and working classes experienced intense prejudice and racial discrimination when, for example, they sought to move into White suburban neighborhoods made accessible by the construction of the federal highway system, or when they applied for federally subsidized home loans and college scholarships. Scholars have framed these publicly supported programs as "White affirmative action."[48]

Moreover, the 1950s was a period of mainstream political conservatism partly due to the anticommunist fervor that emerged in the United States with the onset of the Cold War, the global competition between the communist Soviet Union and its allies versus the democratic, capitalist nations of the United States and the West. Senator Joseph McCarthy (R-WI) led an anticommunist, moral panic, dubbed McCarthyism, that led to a series of public and private investigations. Like others, it pressured some mainstream Black leaders to prove their **patriotism** by red-baiting, denouncing communist or socialist sympathizers in their ranks. The legendary civil rights attorney and first Black U.S. Supreme Court justice, Thurgood Marshall, felt compelled to hand over a list of potential sympathizers within the ranks of the NAACP-LDF to the Federal Bureau of Investigation. Famed baseball player Jackie Robinson publicly denounced world-renowned singer and activist Paul Robeson before McCarthy's House Un-American Activities Committee for the latter's pro-Soviet comments.[49]

Despite this political upheaval, the 1950s and 1960s were an opportune time for a Black-led mass movement. This was for several reasons. First, African American activists and their allies witnessed a new political consciousness and benefited from new leaders, resources, and networks. Second, Southern governments and civil societies remained racially oppressive but did not have (or could not as frequently use) the same tools of suppression and violent retaliation that were available decades earlier. Third, the federal government and Northern public opinion were compelled to give greater scrutiny to the actions of Southern governments as they attempted to hide behind states' rights justifications in the postwar period. Finally, activists were able to form coalitions with or be the beneficiaries of actions by powerful external allies, including the courts. The high period of the Civil Rights Movement, which was complex and vibrant, was roughly between 1955 and 1965. For the purposes of this chapter we will briefly summarize a few of its key events to illustrate the unique ways that these activists challenged mid–twentieth century barriers to African Americans enjoying full citizenship and expanded opportunities.

One way in which scholars have categorized the high and low points of social movements is through a concept that sociologist William Gamson calls protest cycles, the dynamic peaks and valleys of a movement's actions. If we break the 1950s and 1960s Civil Rights Movement into broad but unique periods, one would be roughly from 1955 to 1960, beginning with the Montgomery bus boycott and ending with the new student protest movement. The next is from 1960 to 1965, from the new student protest movement to the passage of the 1965 Voting Rights Act. This precedes the beginning of the competing **Black Power** Movement in 1966.[50]

The Montgomery Bus Boycott and Rise of
Student Protest: The First Major Protest Cycle, 1955–1960

The U.S. Supreme Court's 1954–1955 decisions with the ***Brown v. Board of Education*** case illustrate how external influences mattered. The Court's unanimous decision in *Brown* that separate but equal accommodations in public schools are unconstitutional gave the budding protest movement enormous leverage. The ruling disrupted the normal flow of business in the South, which was arranged around keeping Whites and Blacks separate, and firmly placed the U.S. Constitution and the Court on the side of the Black protesters. Although Southern governments strongly reacted to the ruling and to subsequent federal actions by appointing commissions to introduce measures to resist the decision and intimidate protesters, a substantive victory had been won.

The *Brown* ruling was one of several high-profile events providing momentum to the Civil Rights Movement. The new consciousness, resources and networks, and external pressures necessary to begin a successful movement are illustrated in the events surrounding the murder of Emmett Till and the Montgomery, Alabama, bus boycott. Emmett Till was a fourteen-year-old boy from Chicago, Illinois, who in the summer of 1955 went to visit relatives in the rural town of Money, Mississippi. Unaware of the racial mores of the deep Jim Crow South, he boyishly flirted with a White woman. In retaliation, at least three men took him from his uncle's house and murdered him. They shot Till, mutilated his body, and threw it in the Tallahatchie River with a cotton gin fan tied around his neck with barbed wire. Till's murder received extraordinary public attention, particularly within the Black press, precisely because it occurred in this post–World War II period when Black expectations for fairness had markedly increased **(new consciousness)**. The United States was also attempting to win a propaganda war with the Soviet Union by projecting itself as a bastion of equality and democracy (external pressures), and the Civil Rights Movement's decades-long antilynching campaign had helped to significantly reduce the number of reported lynchings by this time (resources and networks). Additionally, technological changes in the production of agriculture connected to the second Great Migration of African Americans who moved from the South to the North—roughly five million people from 1940 to 1970—put pressures on Southern planters, employers, and law enforcers to shift their tactics lest they increase the number of Blacks fleeing to Northern opportunities and lose access to that labor. While the men were tried for Till's murder, they were found not guilty by an all-White jury after an hour of deliberation. Later, in a *Look* magazine article, the men revealed to journalist William Bradford Huie that they had killed Till.[51]

In the wake of the Till murder, the Montgomery bus boycott illustrated many possibilities, but especially the prospect for the rise of new leaders, **networks, and resources.** When Rosa Parks, a professional seamstress, decided in December 1955 not to move to the back, Colored section of a city bus, an entire movement sat down with her. Parks was strongly connected to the networks and resources of Black civil society, civil rights leadership, and the Black church in Montgomery, Alabama. She was a leader in the Women's Political Council, which became an indispensable group in conceiving, advertising, and promoting the bus boycott. Parks was also an officer in the local NAACP, which connected her to a larger local, state, and national network of activism; and she was a colleague of E. D. Nixon, the president of the local chapter of the NAACP and the Brotherhood of Sleeping Car Porters, an influential and national African American labor group.

Parks's act helped to move the agenda of and provide a protest opportunity for the newly formed Montgomery Improvement Association (MIA), an activist coalition of church, labor, and other civil society leaders and groups dedicated to using an African American economic boycott of riding city buses as a tactic to challenge segregation. During the boycott tens of thousands of Blacks in Montgomery either walked or carpooled to their destinations. It was Nixon who in turn recruited a young Reverend Dr. Martin Luther King Jr. to become the president of the MIA, and King's leadership became an undeniable source of charisma for the movement as it was joined by many other pivotal leaders. A discouraging, year-long stalemate between the MIA and White city leaders and Alabama courts that refused to desegregate buses was broken by an external development. The U.S. Supreme Court ruled in the 1956 *Gayle v. Browder* decision that segregation in transportation (as sanctioned by the *Plessy* decision) was unconstitutional. As a result, the bus company hired many Black drivers and pledged to treat, as well as seat, all passengers with dignity on an equal, first-come, first-served basis.

The period of the late 1950s witnessed more victories: the founding of a leading civil rights organization, the **Southern Christian Leadership Conference (SCLC),** headed by Dr. King; the Eisenhower administration enforcing the *Brown* decision and, in 1957, sending in the National Guard to help nine Black students desegregate the all-White Little Rock High School in Arkansas; and the passage of the historic but modest 1957 Civil Rights Act. It also witnessed significant setbacks stemming from a White backlash against these changes: Southern White retribution, including the rise of White Citizens Councils—middle-class-oriented, White supremacist organizations; and the state prosecution and persecution of the NAACP and other civil rights groups, especially Black school teachers. But the movement moved farther down the road of greater equality due to the second cycle of protests.[52]

Civil Rights Demonstrations and Mass Protest in the South: The Second Major Protest Cycle, 1960–1964

It is not an exaggeration to say that without the development of the second protest cycle of the Civil Rights Movement, the major laws that resulted from it—the 1964 Civil Rights Act and the 1965 Voting Rights Act—may have not have been as strong in content and may have been passed much later. After the Southern segregationist backlash of the late 1950s, the Civil Rights Movement was revived in part by the efforts of thousands of Black and some White youth and young adults, who brought new energy and innovations to the movement. When four Black male students from North Carolina Agricultural & Technical (A&T) College sat down at a Woolworth lunch counter in Greensboro, North Carolina, in February 1960 to protest segregation in public and private facilities, they ignited a new form of protest—the sit-in—and sparked a new wing of the movement. Shortly thereafter a new student organization, advised by veteran activist Ella Baker, formed at Shaw University. The Student Nonviolent

Would African American efforts to attain greater equality have been as successful if it had engaged in more violent protest?

Coordinating Committee (SNCC) helped spark the hundreds of sit-ins that spread explosively across the South, and leaders such as Robert "Bob" Moses, Diane Nash, Ruby Bates, and later John Lewis and Stokely Carmichael, along with hundreds of others, became the new foot soldiers of civil rights activism in the Deep South. They often challenged the older generations and more established organizations like the NAACP and SCLC to understand the need for more grassroots organizing.

President John F. Kennedy and his brother Attorney General Robert Kennedy urged SNCC and the Council of Federated Organizations (COFO) to invest their energies in voter registration drives in the Deep South. They believed this was a less dangerous activity than nonviolent protests and would lessen federal involvement, especially of the Federal Bureau of Investigation (FBI), in local affairs with prosegregationist interests. But the 1964 murder of three civil rights workers engaged in voter registration activity in Freedom Summer in Philadelphia, Mississippi, combined with the enormous FBI resources required to find their bodies and apprehend the murderers, proved this assumption unfounded.

Despite the threats and realities of violence, younger and older civil rights activists used **external pressures** like the U.S. Justice Department to enforce new court decisions against segregation, public scrutiny of Southern state-sanctioned violence, and the weight of Northern White public opinion to force reforms. For instance, the Congress of Racial Equality (CORE) and its 1961 Freedom Rides campaign tested the limits of the federal government's readiness to enforce antisegregation rulings regarding interstate bus transportation. And in a 1963 Birmingham campaign, young Black people protesting the city's segregation ordinances were met with police dogs and fire hoses by the city's infamous Public Safety Commissioner Eugene T. "Bull" Connor and his officers. Along with King's passionate criticism of White indifference with his "Letter from a Birmingham Jail" and the mediation of a U.S. Justice Department official, it was the adverse publicity garnered from nightly newscasts of such state-sanctioned brutality against innocent young Black people that helped turn the tide of events and made modest reforms possible. These images in national magazines, showing Southern resistance to African American efforts to exercise routine citizenship rights, spread across the nation and the entire world.

The historic 1963 March on Washington, attended by over 200,000 marchers and where King delivered his iconic "I Have a Dream" speech, created broad-based, public pressure for the passage of the 1964 Civil Rights Act in July. Activists also directly confronted political inequalities and drew others into their fight during the whole year. During the SNCC Freedom Summer, hundreds of young people went South to register disenfranchised African Americans to vote and confronted intransigent local authorities. And, at the 1964 Democratic National Convention in August, Fannie Lou Hamer and the Mississippi Freedom Democratic Party's protest of the seating of an all-White delegation drew President Johnson, Dr. King, and the party leadership into a fight about fairness. By the time the Selma to Montgomery, Alabama, march took place in the spring of 1965—after a bloody episode in which police bludgeoned and initially turned back marchers on the Edmund Pettis Bridge—the movement had nearly perfected the use of an expanded consciousness, new resources and networks, regime constraints, and external influences to marshal effective protests. It was clear that this march and the movement swayed a very powerful ally when President Johnson introduced the 1965 Voting Rights bill to Congress and used the Civil Rights Movement's own anthem, "We *Shall*

Martin Luther King Jr.'s "I Have a Dream" speech, delivered on the steps of the Lincoln Memorial before over 200,000 demonstrators during the 1963 March on Washington, created public pressure that led to passage of the 1964 Civil Rights Act.

Overcome," to demonstrate the intensity of his support. After the successful passage of the Voting Rights Act in August 1965, as soon as 1966 these advantages had shifted toward another set of activists. These people, inspired by the example of Black nationalism, revolutionary violence, and Pan-Africanism as preached by Malcolm X, called for **Black Power** as opposed to racial integration. The term, used by Stokely Carmichael in a march in which Martin Luther King and other, more traditional, protest stalwarts walked and debated goals and tactics, was very different from previous efforts. The event marked the end of the integrationist stage of civil rights, and the beginning of a focus on Black nationalism by SNCC. It also heralded the growth of new groups, including the Black Panthers, and awareness of others such as the Nation of Islam.[53]

Table 3.1 provides a snapshot of how the 1950s and 1960s Civil Rights Movement—both its legal and mass mobilization wings—influenced the percentage of Black Southerners registered to vote. In the early 1950s, only 20 percent of Black Southerners were registered to vote, but that number more than doubled by the mid-1960s. These are voters who by the early 1970s elected record numbers of Blacks to public office, much in the same way newly emancipated Black voters did a hundred years earlier. The 1944 *Smith v. Allwright* decision by the U.S. Supreme Court appreciably increased the percentage of registered Black voters in states like South Carolina, Arkansas, Tennessee, Louisiana, and Georgia. But not until the registration efforts of SNCC and its allies, as well as the passage of the 1965 Voting Rights Act, were large majorities of eligible African Americans registered and able to cast votes.

By this point in 1965, racialization had reached the third level: Insufficient—"Race Is Not Enough" in our framework. Fundamental citizenship rights, particularly the right to vote, and protections against discrimination in the public sector were agreed upon during the 1964, 1965, and 1968 Civil Rights, Voting Rights, and Fair Housing legislation. Despite these rights and opportunities, many inequalities persisted and persist to this day. Economic status based on income, unemployment, and wealth remains of considerable concern. Yet the road to participation and

Table 3.1   Percentage of Registered Black Voters in the South, 1940-1970

State	1940	1947	1952	1960	1962	1964	1970
Alabama	0.4	1.2	5.0	13.7	13.4	23.0	65.0
Arkansas	1.5	17.3	27.0	37.3	37.3	49.3	71.6
Florida	5.7	15.4	33.0	38.9	36.8	63.8	67.0
Georgia	3.0	18.8	23.0	29.3	26.7	44.0	63.6
Louisiana	0.5	2.6	25.0	30.9	27.8	32.0	61.8
Mississippi	0.4	0.9	4.0	5.2	5.3	6.7	67.5
North Carolina	7.1	15.2	18.0	38.1	35.8	46.8	54.8
South Carolina	0.8	13.0	20.0	15.6	22.9	38.7	57.3
Tennessee	6.5	25.8	27.0	58.9	49.8	69.2	76.5
Texas	5.6	18.5	31.0	34.0	37.3	57.7	84.7
Virginia	4.1	13.2	16.0	22.8	24.0	45.7	60.7
Total	*3.0*	*12.0*	*20.0*	*29.1*	*28.4*	*43.1*	*64.0*

Smith v. Allwright, 1944	Early registration campaigns, pre-SNCC registration	SNCC-COFO voter registration (initial)

		Selma, AL, March and 1965 Voting Rights Act

political empowerment has been significantly upgraded, smoothed, and broadened from previous eras of slavery and *de jure* segregation. We've also noted the growing interest in similar tactics and strategies of other groups traveling other roads, such as Native Americans, Latinos, and Asian Americans. They began to use similar strategies and tactics, including protest, legal campaigns, group identity, and the legal protections provided by the 1960s legislation. While the civil rights protest grew out of Southern and slavery-based patterns of discrimination, the legislation rapidly was implemented to provide protections to the other groups as well. In other instances—for example Native Americans—sovereignty issues provided them with distinctive and very different legal foundations for their journey.

CONCLUSION: THE ROAD TO BLACK POLITICS UP TO 1965

Central to the main framework of this book, this chapter has argued that the Black political journey from roughly 1619 to 1965 was one of frequent attempts by African Americans and their allies to develop a free Black civil society. At the same time, they challenged or reformed the polity in the hopes that African Americans would become less subject to the stark dividing lines of race and racialization. Table 3.2 summarizes how African Americans confronted a particular racialization journey from the period prior to the 1600s and the emergence of chattel

Table 3.2 African Americans' Road of Racialization

When Barriers Arose	Why Barriers Arose	How Barriers Were Overcome	Outcome
Slavery, 1600s–1860	• White conceptions of race mark Blacks as inferior • Blacks enslaved for cheap labor • Laws draw strict racial lines • Economy increases demand for slave-made goods	• African communities merge to form common identity • Local-level civic infrastructure and institutions by free Blacks resist slavery • Slavery abolition movement emerges • Enslaved Blacks rebel	Absolute Barriers → Decisive
Civil War and Reconstruction, 1861–1880s	• White resistance to Reconstruction reforms • Uneven federal enforcement of Black citizenship rights	• Government reforms improve the status of Blacks • Black elected officials and new leadership class emerge	Decisive → Insufficient
Jim Crow, 1880s–1940s	• Disenfranchisement of Black voters and racial segregation • Violence against Blacks used as social control	• Black social, religious, and civil rights organizations enable political mobilization • U.S. Supreme Court decides civil rights cases that weaken Jim Crow	Insufficient → Decisive
Civil Rights Movement, 1950s–1960s	• Continued racial discrimination • Southern resistance to civil rights reforms • Class and ideological divisions among Black leaders	• *Brown v. Board of Education* struck down segregation • New generation of activists and civil rights coalitions challenge Jim Crow	Decisive → Insufficient

slavery, past the Civil War and its abolition of slavery, through *de jure* segregation, and to the end of the Civil Rights Movement era of the 1950s and 1960s.

The toppling of segregation became the chief political goal framed by Black civil rights groups during the first decades of the twentieth century. They were successful in overcoming the legal structures of segregation and barriers to political participation by the latter half of the century, especially with the long antisegregation campaign that ended with the 1954 *Brown* decision, and triumphed in the 1950s and 1960s Civil Rights Movement. But despite these successes, figuring out how to reframe their goals and deciding how to use their enhanced political resources while living in an increasingly complex racial and ethnic polity have become most difficult issues in recent decades.

DISCUSSION QUESTIONS

1. How did economic concerns contribute to the creation of racial distinctions in colonial America?

2. In what ways did the barriers in the U.S. Constitution contribute to long-term institutionalized racism against African Americans?

3. Compare the perspectives of the North and South in their treatment of Blacks. How did they contribute to Blacks' differing access to equal rights and opportunities?

4. How are the barriers that existed at the time of Reconstruction and during the Civil Rights Movement similar, and how are they different? What are the reasons for these similarities and differences?

5. To what degree did social institutions and political organizations focused on race contribute to the creation of an African American political identity?

6. How did African Americans' long-standing collective identity and institutions benefit other racial and ethnic groups during the Civil Rights Movement?

KEY TERMS

1808 Prohibition (p. 80)
Black Power (p. 106)
Brown v. Board of Education (1954–1955) (p. 103)
Civil Rights Act of 1866 (p. 90)
color line (p. 71)
Dred Scott v. Sandford (p. 82)
Executive Order 8802 (p. 101)
External Pressures (p. 105)
Fifteenth Amendment (p. 90)
Fourteenth Amendment (p. 90)

Freedmen's Bureau (p. 88)
Fugitive Slave Act (p. 82)
Great Migration (p. 97)
hypodescent (p. 75)
indentured servant (p. 75)
Jim Crow (p. 92)
lynching (p. 93)
National Association for the Advancement of Colored People (NAACP) (p. 97)
New Consciousness (p. 103)

New Deal (or Democratic) Coalition (p. 100)
Networks and Resources (p. 103)
Plessy v. Ferguson (1896) (p. 95)
sit-in (p. 91)
Southern Christian Leadership Conference (SCLC) (p. 104)
Thirteenth Amendment (p. 88)
Three-Fifths Clause (p. 79)
Underground Railroad (p. 86)

4   The Road toward Contemporary Latino Politics, 1500s–1970s

Society is made up of groups, and as long as the smaller groups do not have the same rights and the same protection as others . . . it is not going to work. Somehow, the guys in power have to be reached by counterpower, or through a change in their hearts and minds, or change will not come.

—César Chavez[1]

This chapter explains when, why, and how ethnicity mattered, prior to the 1970s, in shaping the citizenship and political opportunities of persons in the United States who trace their origin or ancestry to the Spanish-speaking nations of Latin America or the Caribbean, what we would today call Hispanics or Latinos. Latinos are a **pan-ethnic group** comprised of many ethnic-national communities—Mexicans, Puerto Ricans, and Cubans, among others. Like other racial and ethnic minorities, each of these populations endured a process of racialization whereby Whites, or Anglos, created social, economic, and political roadblocks because Latinos were assumed to be inferior or a threat to Whites. As is evident from our discussions so far, assumptions about ethnicity vary from those we apply to race, so our task is to explain the unique history of the racialization of Latinos as well as the emergence of Latino politics. Recall from Chapter 1 that the concept of race—*La Raza*—in Latin America is more fluid because it involved the European (Spanish, Portuguese) assimilation of non-Europeans rather than the English concept of racial separation.

Box 4.1 Chapter Objectives

- Describe the origins of Latino diversity and how cultural differences were used to their disadvantage.

- Identify how social and economic factors combined with demographic shifts to limit Mexican Americans' options.

- Illustrate how the emergence of civic infrastructure led to the creation of a new Latino ethnic identity prior to the Civil Rights Movement.

- Demonstrate how Latino communities were able to organize and build political alliances to overcome their disadvantages.

- Compare the advantages and disadvantages faced by Puerto Ricans and Cubans in the United States.

- Assess how the Latino demands for civil rights paralleled civil rights organizing by other groups in the United States.

Demands for equal education galvanized Latino communities from their earliest days. In this photo, Puerto Rican demonstrators walk in silence from City Hall in Manhattan to the New York Board of Education offices in Brooklyn.

The origins of today's Latino community can be traced to the colonial expansion of the Spanish empire in the sixteenth century. Spanish colonists, in what is now the Southwestern United States and Florida, predated the U.S. Revolutionary War and the ratification of the Constitution. These Spanish émigrés and migrants acted collectively to achieve common goals and established governing structures to allocate resources; in other words, they engaged in politics.

It would be a serious misreading of history and of the creation of U.S. ethnic identities, however, to say that this means that Latino politics began in the sixteenth century—or, for that matter, in the early nineteenth century. Instead, the construction of a Latino politics is a twentieth-century phenomenon resulting from shared experiences of exclusion and a collective effort to build a political identity based on those experiences.

How was a shared Latino identity created that was understood both by the White majority and by Latinos to be ethnically/racially distinct from the (non-Hispanic) White majority? U.S. society tapped the cultural distinctiveness of Latinos, the racial biases of the majority, and the economic resources or tools of Latinos, particularly their labor. Latinos used their cultural connections, first to others of the same national origin and then to Latinos of different national origins, to overcome exclusion by society and demand equal rights and full citizenship in the United States. Latino politics in this formative period focused on the national-origin, rather than pan-ethnic, politics.

As we explore the evolution of Latino politics across this period, we see several outcomes of racialization based on the interaction of society, the polity, and Latino communities. (See Table 1.3 for the uneven roads framework.) Anglos increasingly used ethnicity to define limits on Latino political and economic progress until Latinos could effectively harness their own resources and overcome these barriers. Prior to the U.S. conquest of the Southwest in 1848, ethnicity was largely inconsequential for the descendants of Spanish colonists; rather, it was class status that determined most rights in a largely feudal system. By 1900, however, ethnicity proved to be a nearly absolute barrier to those seeking to exercise political and economic rights despite a formal grant of U.S. citizenship in 1848. The Latino population grew when the United States added Puerto Rico as a colony in 1898. Puerto Ricans on the mainland faced a decisive barrier to political incorporation based on their ancestry and use of Spanish. As we will show, the early decades of the twentieth century through the dawn of the Latino era in the early 1970s was a period of transition, from ethnicity playing a nearly absolute barrier to one in which it was decisive in galvanizing Latinos to organize, make political demands, and ultimately to shape some aspects of governance. These initial efforts to overcome the barriers of ethnicity laid the foundation for leaders from Mexican American, Puerto Rican, Cuban American, and other Latino communities to create a pan-ethnic U.S. Latino politics.

Today's Latino politics cannot be understood without first reviewing the distinct civic and political evolution of the three Latino populations that dominated the U.S. Hispanic experience prior to the modern era—Mexican Americans, Puerto Ricans, and Cuban Americans. We will examine how their distinct though overlapping experiences united into a collective pan-ethnic politics by the late 1960s. We will also identify comparable experiences to other racial and ethnic populations in the United States so that the Latino experience can be understood broadly as part of the story of the uneven roads of today's racial/ethnic communities.

THE ROAD'S COLONIAL BEGINNINGS, 1493–1850

Ethnicity emerged slowly as a barrier to Latino populations in the United States. Like race, ethnicity was not a fully formed concept several centuries ago. The initial contacts between Anglos and what would today be understood as Latinos saw both cooperation and conquest. Quickly, however, a structure of inequality emerged in which Latinos had little opportunity to exercise political or economic rights. Cultural differences—ethnicity—came to be used by Anglos to explain and justify Latino disadvantage.

Spanish Exploration and Conquest

The Spanish presence in what became the United States predated colonization by Northern Europeans, and Spanish colonists created the first permanent European settlement in the continental United States in St. Augustine, Florida, in 1565. Santa Fe, New Mexico, represented the first Spanish settlement in the Western United States when it was incorporated in 1608. Unlike the Northeastern settlements by Northern European colonists, Spanish settlements had small populations. Their residents were primarily focused on agricultural and religious pursuits rather than on mercantile endeavors. Estimates of the European-origin population at the time of the Southwest's transfer to the United States in 1848 place it between 75,000 and 100,000 (the population of this territory now exceeds 72,000,000). These settlements had a small governing elite made up of large landholders and clerics. The Spanish crown provided large landholdings to elite migrants; the rest of the population (including many Native Americans) worked for these landholders in a form of indentured labor that extended across generations. The landholdings did not produce crops for export, but were instead primarily used for residents and the small towns in the region.

These sixteenth- and seventeenth-century Spanish colonists did establish early forms of governance. New Mexicans created institutions to regulate irrigation that remain today. In Texas, local Mexican leaders allowed Anglo colonists to migrate and buy land so as to build the territory's population and provide a buffer against raids by Native Americans upon whose lands they had encroached. These migrants from the United States quickly outnumbered the Mexicans. By 1835, the Anglo population in Texas was approximately thirty thousand, compared to just six thousand Mexicans.

With Mexican independence in 1821, the territories became part of a new and weak Mexican government. The internal political struggles of the new Mexican state quickly led to efforts by the northern territories to separate from Mexican rule.

In 1819, a few years prior to Mexican independence, the United States purchased Florida from Spain. Its population remained small until the U.S. Army subdued Native American populations in the 1830s, opening Florida to migration from the North. As was the case in the Southwest, the Spanish presence in Florida was quickly overwhelmed by the in-migration of White settlers and Black slaves from the North.

Latinos and the Western Expansion of the United States

So how did ethnicity initially emerge as a line of division? Puerto Ricans and Mexican Americans became part of the United States through conquest.[2] The largest example of this was the 1848 **Treaty of Guadalupe Hidalgo,** which ended the war between the United States and Mexico begun in 1845.[3] The treaty significantly changed the border between the two nations, transferring to the United States approximately half of what had been the prewar territory of Mexico, which included what today are the states of Texas (which had been in dispute before the war), California, New Mexico, Arizona, Colorado, Nevada, Utah, and part of Wyoming. The treaty guaranteed the former Mexican subjects U.S. citizenship and the protection of their rights as landholders. With the grant of citizenship, these new citizens became subject to U.S. and state/territorial laws, including a new responsibility to pay taxes

Map 4.1   U.S. Territory Gained from Mexico

The United States acquired extensive territory from Mexico under the Treaty of Guadalupe Hidalgo (1848) and the Gadsden Purchase National Archives.

on their land. Slavery was extended to these territories, where it had previously been formally prohibited by the Mexican government. Native American residents of the newly acquired U.S. territories were not accorded these same rights and protections and, in most cases, did not become U.S. citizens until 1924.

The treaty established rights for the new U.S. subjects and responsibilities for the new sovereign. U.S. states, however, often failed to live up these responsibilities. This failure to abide by treaty responsibilities is a central example of the uneven road for Mexican Americans. The polity (often state and local governments) used their power to advantage White settlers over Latino populations despite promises by the federal government in the treaty negotiations to do otherwise. The consequence of these violations was to eliminate the small pre–U.S.-Mexican War landed elite, removing the one group in society that could challenge the broader denial of political rights of the new Mexican American subjects.

BOX 4.2 CROSS ROAD

In re Ricardo Rodríguez and Mexican American Citizenship

While the Treaty of Guadalupe Hidalgo provided U.S. citizenship to former Mexican subjects who resided in the Southwest at the end of the U.S.-Mexican War, it did not guarantee citizenship to future immigrants. It also did not address the meaning and exercise of citizenship—would it resemble that of White migrants from Europe (see Chapter 6) or African Americans in the post–Civil War era (see Chapter 3)? The case of *In re Ricardo Rodríguez* (1897) brought this question before the courts for a landmark ruling that provided for a citizenship with substantive meaning and the foundation for civil rights organizing in Latino communities in the twentieth century.

In 1896 Ricardo Rodríguez applied for naturalization in San Antonio, Texas. Rodríguez had lived in the United States for ten years at the time of his application and met other statutory requirements for naturalization. His application was challenged by San Antonio politician T. J. McMinn on the grounds that he was racially ineligible, being neither White nor of African descent.[4] (Only White and Black males were eligible for naturalization at the time.) Rodríguez chose to pursue the application, moving the case into federal court.

Rodríguez proudly recognized his cultural heritage as "pure-blooded Mexican."[5] Mexican ancestries included a mix of indigenous populations, Europeans, and Blacks, and did not fit cleanly into U.S. notions of racial categories. The question the court faced was whether Mexicans were White or Black (and thus eligible to naturalize). Although Rodríguez did not know of any indigenous ancestors, he also made no claim of being the descendant of European or African migrants. The judge described Rodríguez's appearance as "copper-colored or red." The court, however, chose to look at the question of race more deeply than simple physical appearance.

The court instead turned to the history of U.S.-Mexican relations and the grant of citizenship to the former Mexican subjects in the Treaty of Guadalupe Hidalgo. It reasoned that when the treaty was ratified only Whites could become naturalized citizens. As a result, Congress must have either understood Mexicans to be White or as eligible for citizenship as Mexicans regardless of race. The court held that Rodríguez and Mexicans more generally were eligible for naturalization. While Mexicans were not necessarily considered White, they were to be treated as if they were for purposes of naturalization.[6]

Not all naturalization officers or state courts followed the ruling in *In re Rodríguez*, but the holding in the case remained the law of the land. This laid the foundation for Mexicans and, later, other Latinos to make claims as Whites in the pre–Civil Rights era. Yet the ability to claim White status did not guarantee equal outcomes with Whites of (more direct) European ancestry. A ruling that Mexicans were not White or entitled to be treated as White would undoubtedly have led to an even more absolute barrier between Mexicans/Latinos and European Whites.

Considering This Crossroad

- Do you agree with the Court's reasoning in *In re Rodríguez*? Why or why not?

- How would the emergence of Mexican American civic life around 1900 have changed if the court had ruled that Ricardo Rodríguez was not eligible to naturalize based on his race?

- Mexican American leaders in the early twentieth century used the ruling in *In re Rodríguez* to assert that Mexicans were White. An example of this was their objection to the inclusion of "Mexican" as a racial category in the 1930 census. Why did these leaders see it as important to link Mexican American identity to the White community?

Independence and the Mexican Elite

Considering the outcome of the U.S.-Mexican war, it is easy to view this period simply as an example of **Manifest Destiny,** the notion popular at the time that the United States was destined to dominate the North American continent from Atlantic to Pacific. Certainly, this guided much of the popular rhetoric in the United States, but it is important to look at the roots of the war to understand another story: some of the Mexican subjects *and* Anglos worked collectively and cooperatively to separate from Mexico.

Texas governed itself as an independent nation from 1835 to 1845, while leaders in the United States debated its admission to the Union. Its likely entrance as a slave state, in an era where the slave and nonslave states were evenly balanced, gave many in the United States pause while Texas's leaders espoused sometimes conflicting desires for independence. Mexico's effort to reassert control over Texas led, in large part, to the U.S.-Mexican War.

In the period of Texas independence, and in the years just after the war, Texas's leadership included both former Mexican subjects (what we would today identify as Latinos) and former U.S. subjects, many of whom had become Mexican citizens in the 1820s and early 1830s as a condition for receiving land grants from the Mexican government. These "new" citizens of Mexico were non-Hispanic Whites of Northern European ancestry, or Anglos in our contemporary understanding. At the elite level, then, race and ethnicity were inconsequential. Anglos dominated government, but the former Mexican elite maintained a minority hand. The first vice president of the Republic of Texas was Lorenzo de Zavala. Several *Tejanos* (Texans of Mexican or Spanish ancestry) were signatories to the Constitution of the Republic of Texas.

Although California did not go through a period of independence prior to joining the United States as a state, it too saw a brief period after statehood in which former Mexican elites maintained a role in state politics. The 1849 constitution that preceded California's admission as a state recognized Spanish language rights. Ten of the forty-nine delegates to this state constitutional convention were of Mexican/Spanish ancestry, as were two early lieutenant governors.

The presence of this prewar Mexican elite explains in part the strong focus in the Treaty of Guadalupe Hidalgo on protections for land rights (Articles VIII of the treaty provided, "In the said territories, property of every kind now belonging to Mexicans . . . shall be inviolably respected"). The treaty's negotiators realized that a guarantee of U.S. citizenship alone was not enough to protect the rights of these new subjects; they would also need to ensure protection of their economic status. Economic rights such as ownership of large tracts of land ensured that some of the Mexican elite took an early place in the postwar governments, ensuring their status. As such, class—not race/ethnicity—shaped the political and economic opportunities of Mexican Americans.

These opportunities to share in the governance of the new states and territories soon declined, but later generations of Latino leaders were able to tap this history to organize Mexican American communities, a resource that was not available to African American or Asian American leaders in the early Civil Rights era. Of greater importance, they were able to use the

Although they were subject to discriminatory policies, what advantages did Mexican Americans possess that other minority groups of the time did not?

guarantees of the Treaty of Guadalupe Hidalgo—negotiated in an environment of accommodation between Mexican and Anglo elites—to make legal claims on the United States and the states of the Southwest.

DESTRUCTION OF MEXICAN AMERICAN POLITICS, LATE 1800s

Ethnicity became a more decisive roadblock for Mexican Americans in the late nineteenth century because portions of the Mexican elite assimilated into the Anglo population, and other Mexicans, especially the laboring classes, were marked by Anglos as non-White and as a threat. As a result, the brief period of political voice by the small Mexican American elite quickly evaporated, with Mexican-origin elected officials and political leaders all but gone by the late 1870s. As the White population grew and Mexican American economic power diminished, fewer Mexican Americans were elected to state office. Race/ethnicity in the late nineteenth century then shifts from inconsequential to nearly absolute (with some exceptions that we will note).

The decline of Mexican American political fortunes in the late nineteenth century echoes in some ways those of freed slaves in the Reconstruction era. Political and economic rights offered by the federal government were undermined by state and local elites. What distinguished the Mexican American experience was that a Mexican elite existed that controlled resources (mostly land) in 1848 and expected that they would have a political voice commensurate with the social and economic status they had before Texas independence and the U.S.-Mexican War. It was this elite that participated—as minority partners—in the political births of the states of Texas and California, as well as in other new territories in the Southwest.

At its core, the decline reflected a widespread perception among Anglos that the former Mexican subjects were simply not a part of the polity. The majoritarian institutions of the Southwestern states offered these White populations a resource to disenfranchise Mexican Americans and other racial minorities. Electoral rules were written to exclude Mexicans and other racial minorities from using the franchise.

Political Losses and Economic Disempowerment

The second half of the nineteenth century was also a period of severe economic disempowerment for Mexican Americans, particularly the small landholding elite who had dominated prewar society. Although some of this land was simply stolen (mobs of gold prospectors in northern California would occupy land that they perceived to be vacant), most was taken more insidiously. The protections of Mexican American land rights in the Treaty of Guadalupe Hidalgo failed to anticipate the actions of state and local governments in the Southwest.

Anglo-dominated governments frequently seized Mexican-held lands on the claim that the landholder could not prove his ownership. Ownership was based on royal land grants issued in Spain many generations before and less-than-specific demarcations of where a landholding began or ended. The grants were often very expansive, conflicting with Anglo notions of smaller and more economically productive plots that would annually produce a cash crop. Legal ownership or "title" could be proven in the courts, but this was very expensive. Frequently, the only asset the landholder had to fund a legal battle was the land itself, so while he might win in court, he would subsequently lose the land to creditors.

Landholders also faced another new challenge—property taxes. In many cases, these lands had not been used to produce cash crops for market. The Spanish notion was that a large tract of land, under the control of a resident landholder, would provide for the needs of people who lived on the land. This included the laborers and their families and, often, members of the clergy. These large tracts rarely produced significant revenue, or at least revenue that reflected the large size of the landholdings, since most of the production was for internal use. The new yearly property tax necessitated changes to the land's use so that the tax could be paid. Very large landholders were the most politically and socially powerful in the prewar era, and over time, many lost their land to taxes or the inability to change the mode of production to make land more economically productive.

A Demographic and Social Shift in Influence

A final source of declining economic power among the prewar Mexican elites speaks to the fluidity of race/ethnic differences for some of the former Mexican subjects in the face of class similarities. Over the period from 1850 to approximately 1900, many of the landholding prewar Mexican families intermarried with Anglos of a similar class background. By the early twentieth century, these blended families tended to focus more on their Whiteness and did not offer political or economic leadership in Mexican American communities.

Other demographic and economic reasons also contributed to the decline of Mexican American influence. The small prewar population was almost immediately swamped by massive in-migration of Anglos from the East (and to some degree by Chinese migrants). Within days of the signing of the Treaty of Guadalupe Hidalgo, gold was discovered in California, leading to a migration of over 300,000 from the eastern United States and China, increasing the population of the region by a factor of three. Over the next twenty years, the United States incorporated its new territories into its growing national economy in a way that Spain and Mexico never did.

This Anglo population surge occurred in all of the newly obtained states and territories. The population of Texas, for example, increased from 213,000 in 1850 to 819,000 in 1870. California's population grew from 93,000 to 560,000 in this same period. White migrants from the eastern United States predominantly fueled this growth, while the small Mexican population that had been present in the Southwest at the end of the war remained relatively unchanged. New migration from Mexico did not begin until the 1890s. (See Table 4.1.)

During this period of transition, Mexican Americans began to experience increasing levels of discrimination. Certainly, they were always subject to some discrimination, though arguably it was as much class-based as racial/ethnic at the end of the war. Late in the nineteenth century, Anglos imposed both de jure and de facto segregation that mirrored the discrimination experienced by African Americans in the eastern United States.

At the end of the U.S.-Mexican War, the small Mexican population was concentrated on Mexican-owned agricultural lands. Population was low, so Mexican Americans and Anglos had little contact. By the turn of the twentieth century, the Anglo population had grown dramatically and the Mexican American population increasingly lived in small towns. Many of the Anglo migrants came from the South and the border states, bringing with them a system of racial ordering driven by relations between Whites and Blacks. In both Texas and California, dual (segregated) education systems emerged. The educational opportunities available to

Table 4.1 Migration to Permanent Residence from the Americas, 1821–1969

Country/Region of Migration	1821–1899	1900–1919	1920–1939	1940–1959	1960–1969
Mexico	27,766	308,401	531,654	330,005	433,128
Central America	2,131	23,033	23,351	60,336	98,560
Caribbean	120,942	221,820	101,534	161,855	427,235
Cuba	—	—	23,410	275,251	256,497
South America	11,981	55,191	53,015	98,080	250,754

Source: Authors' calculations based on U.S. Department of Homeland Security, 2012, 2011 Yearbook of Immigration Statistics, Table 2, www.dhs.gov/immigration-statistics.

Notes: The data, particularly in the period before 1917, underestimate the levels of legal immigration from the Americas. These data exclude unauthorized immigrants and migrants who entered the United States legally as part of programs to recruit labor migrants on short-term visas. Based on their residence status after 1898 and citizenship status after 1917, migrants from Puerto Rico are not counted as immigrants.

Mexican Americans were considerably poorer than those available to Anglo children, ended much earlier, and frequently failed to teach English. Anti-Mexican violence also became more common; in fact, lynching of Mexican Americans became more common than lynching of African Americans in Texas. Dual societies appeared in many small towns where Anglos and Mexicans resided, with Mexicans often literally living on a different side of the tracks than Anglos.

The parallels to the African American experience under Jim Crow racial segregation are notable, but there were differences that need to be acknowledged. Mexican Americans could frequently vote, but their votes were manipulated by political machines. (In South Texas and New Mexico, these political machines were sometimes controlled at the local level by Mexican Americans and allowed for the election of Mexican Americans to office.)[7] Manipulation ranged from telling Mexican Americans how to vote (providing a string with knots to match up to the ballot to show illiterate voters where to vote) to simply voting on their behalf. Thus, in the late nineteenth and early twentieth centuries, Mexican Americans continued to exercise the franchise and, at the beginning of the Civil Rights era, voted in large numbers.

Exceptions to this pattern of rapidly declining Latino social, economic, and political fortunes did exist in the Southwest. Prewar Mexican elites and their descendants continued to dominate politics and society along the U.S.-Mexican border in Texas and in New Mexico into the early twentieth century, in large part because Mexican Americans remained a numerical majority in this region and Mexican elites continued to own the land. This Latino dominance of territorial politics in New Mexico, however, slowed its admission to statehood. Unlike Texas, which became a state in 1845, and California, which followed quickly in 1850, New Mexico did not gain statehood until 1912, in large part out of fears over having a state with a Latino majority and rights for Spanish speakers. Here, race served as an advantage for statehood. Territories in which Anglos dominated politics had an easier path to statehood.

By the turn of the twentieth century, fifty years after the end of the U.S.-Mexican War, Mexican American political and economic influence was at its nadir. Despite the citizenship and land rights guarantees in the Treaty of Guadalupe Hidalgo, there were few Mexican American officeholders or other influentials outside of South Texas and New Mexico. The prewar elite invested little in establishing a civic infrastructure such as building local governments (outside of New Mexico), so it too was absent. Since there was little risk that Mexican Americans would elect candidates

The early twentieth century saw the emergence of "dual societies" in the small towns of the Southwest. In this case, the dual society created an entrepreneurial opportunity for a Mexican American pharmacy, but also included separate schools and residential segregation that limited social and educational opportunities for Mexican Americans.

of their choice because they were an increasingly small share of the population and lacked local leaders who could become political leaders (again, with some exceptions in New Mexico), they did not regularly face the violent exclusion from the polls that African Americans in the South did at this time.

Mexican Americans did begin to face class-based restricted voting rights, similar to what poor Whites faced at the turn of the century.[8] This potential for class-based exclusion was tempered in Texas and New Mexico by the fact that Mexican American votes were often important to political machines, so leaders made accommodations for them. The steady loss of Mexican-owned landholdings and the slower conversion of the economy away from agriculture (the sector of the economy in which most Mexican Americans worked) to extraction and agricultural processing reduced the immediate opportunities for Mexican Americans to build economic power. Finally, this approximate point of the lowest Mexican American influence also reflected its population nadir. Estimates suggest that the Latino population nationally in 1900 made up just 0.9 percent of the national population. (See Table 4.2.) Most of these Mexican Americans lived in a world in which ethnicity served as a nearly absolute bar to the free exercise of the citizenship rights guaranteed in the Treaty of Guadalupe Hidalgo.

Do class-based restrictions present lower barriers to equal rights and opportunity than race-based restrictions?

Table 4.2   U.S. Latino Population, by Decade, 1900–2010

Decade	Latino Population	Percent of National Population
1900 (est.)	656,000	0.9
1910 (est.)	999,000	1.1
1920 (est.)	1,632,000	1.5
1930 (est.)	2,435,000	1.9
1940 (est.)	2,814,000	2.1
1950 (est.)	4,039,000	2.6
1960 (est.)	6,346,000	3.5
1970	9,616,000	4.7
1980	14,604,000	6.4
1990	22,354,000	9.0
2000	35,305,818	12.5
2010	50,477,594	16.3

Source: Latino population estimates for 1900–1960 are from Jeffrey Passel and Barry Edmonston, "Immigration and Race: Recent Trends in Immigration to the United States," in Barry Edmonston and Jeffrey S. Passel, eds., *Immigration and Ethnicity: The Integration of America's Newest Arrivals,* (Washington, DC: Urban Institute Press, 1994), 31–72, Table 2.3; 1970–2010 data are from the U.S. Census Bureau.

Note: The Census Bureau did not collect data on Hispanics prior to 1970. The estimates of the Hispanic population from 1900 to 1960 are calculated by Passel and Edmonston (1994). The census excludes Puerto Ricans resident in Puerto Rico from its counts of the Latino population. In 2010 the population of Puerto Rico was 3,725,789. Most would be Latino were they residing on the U.S. mainland.

THE REBIRTH OF MEXICAN AMERICAN POLITICS, 1900–1960

By roughly 1900, Mexican Americans were at their political, as well as social and economic, low. They lacked political and civic leadership, had few economic resources or tools, faced increasing discrimination, and made up a declining share of the population in areas that they formerly dominated. What had been a powerful economic resource for some in the community and a potential resource for political influence and leadership at the end of the war—land-holdings—had largely disappeared by the turn of the century. Despite these barriers, Mexican Americans were able to build a political community in the twentieth century and lay the foundations for the Latino politics that emerged in the 1960s and 1970s.

The origins of the rebirth of Mexican American politics appear in the destruction of the prewar society. With the end of the prewar elite, new local-level leaders emerged who slowly created civic infrastructure such as civic organizations and, ultimately, political groups that could support the election of Mexican Americans to political office. Unlike what had preceded the war, this nascent structure for action existed at the mass level. Such groups initially emerged to overcome the roadblocks and economic exclusion created in the late nineteenth century. Importantly, they found a tool for organizing in the promises—particularly the guarantee of U.S. citizenship—in the Treaty of Guadalupe Hidalgo. Demographics also began to work to their advantage. Migration began to build in the 1890s and surged in the first decades of the twentieth century, as the United States restricted migration from Europe. (See Table 4.1.)

While ethnicity continued to be a significant bar to Mexican American exercise of political and economic rights in the early twentieth century, community organization slowly emerged to challenge racial restrictions. White leaders saw the emergence of Mexican American civic and political organization and in some areas, particularly those where new White populations migrated from the U.S. South, began to implement racial restrictions against them comparable to those imposed on African Americans in the South. Even with these changes, however, the outcome of racialization slowly shifted from absolute to decisive because Mexican Americans were able to organize over time to assert their rights in U.S. society.

The first mass organizations to focus on serving the immediate needs of Mexican American communities took three forms: mutualist, trade union, and religious. **Mutualist organizations** were designed to meet specific collective needs that could not or would not be met by Anglo organizations, such as providing for the burial of the poor. As early as the 1890s, there is evidence of local organizations offering a form of life insurance. Mutualist organizing also focused on celebrating shared holidays and challenging overt discrimination in the schools.

In this same period, unions began to organize some Mexican American workers. As is true today, agricultural workers have not traditionally been the focus of successful trade union organizing, and most Mexican Americans worked in agriculture. The unions that did organize focused on Mexican Americans in mining, particularly in Arizona. These were not Mexican American unions. Instead, they were national unions, particularly the International Workers of the World (IWW). The rhetoric and ideology of the IWW was nondiscriminatory; unlike the skilled trade unions, the IWW organized all workers, regardless of ancestry.

The third early form of mass organizations serving Mexican Americans was via religious organization through the Catholic Church. The church has long been an important presence in Mexican American and other Latino communities, but its political role has often been secondary to its spiritual and social role. In this era, most Catholic priests were not themselves Mexican American, and they limited the use of the church as a locus for political organizing. The priests often accepted the larger society's view that Mexican Americans were second-class citizens.[9] The church nevertheless offered a safe center for civic organizing.

Migration Spurs a New Ethnic Identity

Throughout the late 1800s, few people emigrated from Mexico. Before railroads crossed it in the 1880s, the Northern Mexican desert provided an effective barrier to migration, and the Mexican government used its national police force to restrict emigration in order to keep labor plentiful and exploitable in Mexico. By the early 1900s, the Mexican government's ability to control emigration declined and U.S. employers began to actively recruit Mexican labor. Official figures, which probably underestimate the true levels of migration, indicate that

31,188 Mexicans migrated to the United States between 1900 and 1909; 185,334 migrated between 1910 and 1919; and 498,945 migrated in the 1920s. (See Table 4.2.)

These new migrants brought with them a new ethnic identity. Beyond simply being immigrants, they carried with them a rising recognition of the racial composition of Mexico that played a significant role in the early ideology of the Mexican Revolution of the 1910s. The revolutionary racial ideology valorized the Mexican blending of indigenous populations with European and African peoples to build Mexican national identity.[10] Although this ideology often overlooked the dominance of lighter-skinned Mexicans in that country's governance and economic leadership, it placed Mexican Americans (and, by extension, Latinos) outside of U.S. racial categories (White, Black, Asian, and Native American), seeing the Americas as the amalgam of all the other races. For this reason, Mexican American and Mexican leaders feared the U.S. Census Bureau decision to add "Mexican" as a racial category in the 1930 census (see Table 1.1); they successfully organized to have this category removed in 1940.

The large numbers of Mexican émigrés—people who leave their native country for another—spurred another form of local civic organizing in the 1920s: the Mexican government sought to organize some of its nationals within the United States.[11] These efforts ultimately collapsed because Mexico attempted to control émigré civic organizing rather than allowing the émigrés to set the agenda for their organizing. This transnational organizing, however, offered another path to Mexican American collective action that had not been available prior to the rebirth of Mexican American civic organizing in this era. Although its utility was limited in the 1920s, future generations of Mexican Americans would organize in the United States to address the needs of friends and family in Mexico.

The League of United Latin American Citizens and *El Congreso*

Mutualist civic organizing was local and reflected the efforts of friends, neighbors, and coworkers to meet collective needs, such as providing insurance to cover the costs of burial. These early community-level efforts provided the foundation for regional civic organizing. The **League of United Latin American Citizens (LULAC)** formed in Corpus Christi in 1929 as the first regional civic organization for Mexican Americans. Its early members reflected a small, newly emerging group within the Mexican American community in the Southwest, a middle class made up of small-business owners and professionals who provided services, such as small shops, hair cutting, and mortuary services, that Whites hesitated to provide to Mexican Americans. A very small professional class of Mexican Americans had emerged, including some teachers in the Mexican schools. This small professional class grew as a result of World War I, as the military offered some Mexican Americans opportunities to move out of their small towns, receive advanced training or college degrees, and return at the end of the war with a willingness—and the skills—to challenge the local status quo.

LULAC's approach to civic organizing reflected its membership, but not the larger Mexican American community. It was open only to male U.S. citizens and conducted its meetings in English. It saw the ultimate advancement of Mexican Americans through the adoption of the values of the larger American society.[12] Fundamental to LULAC's organizing principles was the full and equal exercise of U.S. citizenship.

In these organizing principles, LULAC reflected the civic organizing patterns of White ethnics of European ancestry in this period and an expectation on the part of this new small Mexican American middle class that Mexican Americans would have the same political and economic opportunities in U.S. society that White ethnics were beginning to exercise. By the end of the 1930s, LULAC had chapters throughout the Southwest and focused its resources on using the courts to challenge educational and employment discrimination. As was the case in African American communities, this first generation of Mexican American civic leaders saw the courts as the branch of government most responsive to constitutional equal protection guarantees.

LULAC was not the only example of regional Mexican American civic organizing in this period. *El Congreso de Pueblos Que Hablan Español* (the Congress of Spanish-Speaking Peoples), formed in 1939, organized the "Spanish speaking" regardless of nativity, and called for an end to discrimination against the foreign born and an end to the large-scale deportations of as many as one million Mexican Americans that had taken place throughout the Great Depression. *El Congreso* opposed the denial of labor rights to immigrants, recognizing that the demand for immigrant labor by U.S. employers is one of the causes of migration. *El Congreso*'s ranks included Latinos of non-Mexican origin/ancestry, making it in some sense the first national Latino organization.[13]

Although these organizations represented different segments of the Mexican American community and had somewhat different visions for the path to Mexican American civic, political, and social incorporation, they signify the emergence of a Mexican American/Latino political voice in the Southwest and nationally. Such a voice was hard to imagine in 1900 but grew from local roots over the subsequent forty years. These organizations also reflect that race/ethnicity was no longer an absolute barrier to civic organizing.

They by no means replaced the community-level organizing that had preceded their formation. Local organizations continued to grow increasingly diverse. Beginning in the 1920s, Mexican Americans became much more urban and more likely to work in manufacturing. Their expanded employment opportunities included public employment as well as union efforts to mobilize Mexican Americans and other Latinos. National and state political leaders and the parties—particularly the Democrats—began to look to Mexican Americans for their votes and, more slowly, for new leaders.[14]

> How do the historical examples of Latino organizing and influence relate to today's struggles for Latino political incorporation?

FROM CIVIC ACTIVISM TO POLITICAL ENGAGEMENT

While the political and economic incorporation of Mexican Americans into the wider American polity accelerated after World War II, this period also saw an increasing focus on electoral politics, including the election of the first generation of twentieth-century Mexican American leaders.[15] Organizing to elect Mexican American candidates was not always well received by Anglo leaders, who were loath to give up power, particularly to those they felt were less capable of leadership. Generally, however, Anglo political racialization of Mexican Americans was less severe than of African Americans in the South in this same period. Part of the reason why is that Mexican American voting had been tolerated (if not encouraged) in most of the Southwest since the end of the U.S.-Mexican War. Mexican Americans often provided votes for Anglo candidates, including Lyndon Johnson, who owed his initial election to the U.S. Senate and later to the vice presidency to manipulated Mexican American votes.[16]

In the period after World War II, Mexican Americans challenged local electoral power structures and won local and, ultimately, congressional offices in areas of high population concentration. They did so by organizing at the community level around issues critical to Mexican Americans such as education and limiting abuse by the police. This first generation of Mexican American elected leaders included Edward Roybal (Los Angeles city councilperson, 1949–1962; member of Congress, 1962–1993), Henry B. Gonzalez (San Antonio city councilperson, 1953–1956; Texas state senator, 1957–1961; member of Congress, 1961–1999), and Raymond Telles (mayor of El Paso, 1957–1961; U.S. ambassador to Costa Rica, 1961–1967).

Victory for this first generation of Mexican American officeholders usually required multiracial support and, often, support from trade unions and civic organizations. Mexican American leaders needed to build a new type of community political organization to make voters of citizens. Unlike the civic organizations that preceded them, these organizations focused specifically on mobilizing voters and running candidates for office. Political organizations such as the Mexican American Political Association (MAPA) in California and the Political Association of Spanish-Speaking Organizations (PASSO) in Texas formed to register and turn out voters.

Finally, in this period, Mexican American candidates needed to run from electoral districts with high concentrations of Mexican Americans. Efforts by the first wave of Mexican American officeholders to move on to higher offices with non–Mexican American electorates resulted in defeat. Edward Roybal, for example, relied on the Community Service Organization to win election to the Los Angeles city council in 1949, but lost campaigns for California's

ASSOCIATED PRESS

President John F. Kennedy and First Lady Jacqueline Kennedy greet Latino activists at a LULAC gala in 1963. The 1960 presidential election was the first in which the Latino vote became influential, and Kennedy actively sought Latino support.

lieutenant governorship in 1954 and the Los Angeles County Commission in 1958. Roybal moved onto the U.S. House of Representatives in 1962 (the second Latino in the modern era to serve in the House).

 Are demographics the most important element in Latino electoral influence?

The growing size of the Mexican American electorate and its concentration in a few states ensured that it would ultimately become important in national electoral politics. In the 1960 presidential race, Richard Nixon and John F. Kennedy faced a nearly evenly divided electorate. (See Box 4.3.) A few states, including Texas, would determine the outcome. Recognizing the importance of Mexican Americans to the Texas race, the Kennedy campaign invested in building an organization to target the Latino vote. *Viva Kennedy!* was the first national partisan organization targeting Latinos by registering new voters, informing potential voters, and turning them out on Election Day. Kennedy's investment in Latino voters paid off, and he narrowly won the Electoral College.[17]

The opportunity to elect Mexican American candidates to local and national office came more easily in Mexican American and other Latino communities than it did in Black communities. The barriers that Mexican Americans faced were, nevertheless, considerable. Registration rates were lower than in Anglo communities, and the organizational infrastructure was weaker. Incumbent Anglo officeholders used the power of their offices, particularly in the design of electoral rules and districting strategies, to block the emergence of Mexican American leaders. This first wave of officeholders, however, is a critical piece of the story of political (re)building of Mexican American influence. These leaders, and the organizations that ensured their election, guaranteed that Latino voices were also heard when African American and Latino activists organized to demand federal action to protect minority civil rights. These officeholders at times disagreed with the civil rights activists, but ultimately they were its voices in Congress and in state legislatures.

DIFFERING PATHS: PUERTO RICANS AND CUBANS, 1890s–1950s

At about the same time that Mexican Americans in the Southwest began to build the road toward the rebirth of their politics, the United States added new Latino populations to the nation through the conquest of new territories, such as the colony of Puerto Rico in 1898. (Puerto Rico remains a colony today.) Unlike the end of the U.S.-Mexico War, this expansion accorded the new residents few treaty-based or statutory protections, resulting in their increased racialization. Cuba, briefly a U.S. colony and now a sovereign nation, has a contentious relationship with the United States, partly because of Cuban American émigrés who strongly oppose the island's communist regime. Though the nature of their arrival in the United States differs from that of Mexican Americans and Puerto Ricans, Cuban American émigrés also found themselves facing social and political barriers.

The reason why Puerto Ricans and Cubans encountered differing ethnic barriers from Mexican Americans stems from a perspective popular at that time. The late 1800s was a period of Western empire–building guided by a racial worldview—the **White Man's**

BOX 4.3 ROAD SIGN

Viva Kennedy! and Latino Electoral Influence

The Latino vote was arguably more influential in the 1960 presidential election than in any subsequent presidential election, helping John F. Kennedy win the presidency.[18] Kennedy earned his victory in part by seeking Latino votes more skillfully and more energetically than had most of his successors in what was the first targeted outreach campaign to win Latino votes in a presidential campaign—*Viva Kennedy!* His campaign efforts also reflected the fact that the influence of Latino or, more generally, minority voters is often out of minorities' control.

The Kennedy campaign invested in Latinos for three reasons: the closeness of the election, the near-equal division of non-Hispanic votes in Texas, and the importance the campaign placed on winning Latino votes there. Kennedy beat Nixon by just 119,000 votes in the national popular vote, and victory in the Electoral College depended on two states—Illinois and Texas. Illinois's vote for Kennedy was subject to intense media scrutiny and probable fraud. Had Texas given its Electoral College votes to Nixon, the Nixon campaign would have been able to win with Illinois's votes and would have been much more likely to contest the outcome.

In addition to the organizing funds dedicated to the *Viva Kennedy!* clubs across the country, it assigned a national campaign staff member—Carlos McCormick—to coordinate *Viva Kennedy!* efforts and, more important, sent John and Jacqueline Kennedy to campaign in heavily Mexican American areas. John Kennedy spoke of his immigrant and Catholic roots to establish a bond with Mexican Americans and made a specific promise: the appointment of a Mexican American to an ambassadorial post in Latin America. Jacqueline Kennedy spoke Spanish at rallies targeting Mexican Americans and cut what is probably the first Spanish-language television commercial dedicated to winning Latino votes.

Did *Viva Kennedy!* make the difference in Texas? Without opinion polling, it is not possible to say conclusively. A more interesting question, which can never be answered, is whether it was the *newly mobilized* Mexican American voters—those registered or mobilized by *Viva Kennedy!*—or the general excitement of the Kennedy candidacy that gave Texas and the presidency to Kennedy. In other words, did the campaign's efforts pay off, or would Kennedy have won regardless, based on the "normal" Mexican American vote?

This is a question that the Democrats asked again in the 2012. The sizeable Obama victory in 2008 included votes from many *new* minority voters who were caught up in the excitement and energy of the Obama campaign. In 2012 Barack Obama was able to mobilize minority voters at rates comparable to 2008. Two states did, however, shift in the Electoral College— North Carolina and Indiana—in large part because of declines in minority voting relative to 2008.

Burden—the belief that White America and Europe should "civilize" less developed nations while extracting their mineral resources and agricultural product. The result was that the United States racialized the residents of Puerto Rico and Cuba, who became U.S. subjects due to colonial expansion.[19]

The United States acquired Puerto Rico, Cuba, the Philippines, and Guam after Spain's defeat in the 1898 Spanish-American War. The territories became U.S. colonies, without any expectation that they would eventually move toward statehood. The United States had sole determination of the future of these lands and their peoples.[20]

Cuba was granted a quick, though limited, independence, and the 1902 Cuban constitution granted the U.S. military the

Library of Congress

Efforts to industrialize in the years after World War II pushed many of Puerto Rico's rural residents to the cities and into the migration stream. With opportunities limited in Puerto Rico, many instead migrated to New York and the cities of the northeastern United States.

authority to intervene in Cuban affairs. The Philippines was put on a slower path to independence (to be achieved in 1946). Puerto Rico remains a colony of the United States, though a 1950s agreement between the two has changed the name of this relationship to "commonwealth" (a status in which Puerto Rico has some autonomy over local governance). None of the peoples of these conquered territories were guaranteed U.S. citizenship as a result of the **Treaty of Paris (1898)** that ended the war.

The end of the war sped what in the late nineteenth century had been a slow migration from the Spanish-speaking Caribbean to the United States. Migrants from Cuba moved primarily to Florida and New York. Migrants from Puerto Rico began to move to New York in the 1880s. These migration streams were small and did not organize around distinct national or ethnic identities. They were instead part of the massive migration of this era that was dominated by migrants from Europe. The small Cuban, Puerto Rican, and other Latino populations of New York worked largely in manufacturing and were less likely to be unionized. Caribbean migrants formed *mutualistas* and worked as part of civic organizing efforts. As was the case with Mexican Americans, these initial efforts focused mostly on meeting collective needs and did not initially seek to influence electoral politics. Labor organizing offered a more explicitly political outlet for some of these migrants, but this political activity was distinctly multi-ethnic, and the leadership of the unions was European in origin or ancestry. The Latinos of this era in the East were not able to gain entry into public employment as a path to political and economic advancement. As was the case with White ethnics in New York at the same time, Puerto Ricans and Cubans faced exclusion on a variety of dimensions, including ethnicity. As such, ethnicity was insufficient to explain group status.

In 1917 Congress passed the **Jones Act,** which granted U.S. citizenship to Puerto Ricans and established Puerto Rico as a "self-governing unincorporated territory" of the United States, a legal status that formalized the differences between Puerto Rico and the states of the Southwest after the Treaty of Guadalupe Hidalgo.[21] Debates among Puerto Rican political elites spurred the Jones Act, but neither these elites nor mass opinion in Puerto Rico influenced congressional action. Unlike the treaty-based guarantee of U.S. citizenship for former Mexican subjects, Puerto Ricans' U.S. citizenship is statutory and could, in principle, be reversed by Congress (subject to the Fourteenth Amendment's guarantee of citizenship to all persons born or naturalized in the United States).

The small U.S. Puerto Rican and Cuban populations grew rapidly in the first decades of the twentieth century and also began to migrate to areas other than Florida and New York. The expansion of this migration reflected two structural changes in U.S. policy. First, the war and subsequent American political domination of Puerto Rico and Cuba ensured that these nations and their economies were increasingly linked to the U.S. economy. This created information for potential migrants about opportunities in the United States, and disruptions in the domestic economies of Cuba and Puerto Rico ensured that more people would migrate. Second, Puerto Rican and Cuban migration, like Mexican migration in this era, was spurred by the steady restrictions imposed by Congress on migration from Europe, which we discuss in more detail in Chapter 6. Many of the restrictions on European migrants implemented beginning in the 1910s, and particularly in the 1920s, excluded Western Hemisphere migrants. Consequently, Puerto Rican and Cuban migration increased dramatically. (See Table 4.1.)

Puerto Rican Politics in the Pre-Latino Era

The growth in Latino populations in the East, and particularly of Puerto Ricans in New York, led to a change in the manifestations of Latino politics. Between the 1920s and the dawn of the Latino political era, New York Hispanic politics was dominated by Puerto Ricans despite the presence of Latinos from other Latin American and the Caribbean nations. Like Mexican Americans in the Southwest, Puerto Ricans needed to build a politics largely out of whole cloth.[22] They were relatively advantaged, however, in that the fluid, politically liberal, and competitive nature of New York electoral politics ensured that they had the opportunity to compete for and win electoral offices and to make demands on city resources. In this, Puerto Ricans were more like other, mostly European, migrant populations in New York than they were like Mexican Americans. As a result, Puerto Rican politics more quickly included an electoral dimension than did Mexican American politics.

Beginning in the 1930s, Puerto Ricans ran for and, less often, won local and state offices in New York. These candidates, interestingly, are found across the partisan spectrum, from Republican to Socialist, reflecting the fluidity of partisan boundaries in the New York of this era. Because of these occasional electoral successes, some New York Puerto Rican civic organizations were able to tap municipal and state resources for their operations and become part of political machines. These favored organizations grew much more rapidly than did comparable groups in the Southwest. From the outside, this may have appeared to be a form of political power, but that was not the case. New York Puerto Ricans were very much the junior partner to other racial and ethnic groups in the city, including African Americans,[23] who dominated the city's racial politics and were more numerous, better organized, and had a cadre of leaders in civic organizations, churches, municipal employment, and elective office.

The New York political leadership sought intermittently to disenfranchise Puerto Ricans along racial/ethnic lines. Since their citizenship was uncontested, this disenfranchisement used literacy tests to make Puerto Rican voting more difficult and districting strategies to make it less likely that they would be able to elect the candidate of their choice. Between the 1920s and the 1960s, these periods when political leaders sought to exclude Puerto Ricans were the exception, but the fact that they existed gave many in the Puerto Rican community doubts about whether they were full members of New York's multi-ethnic tapestry. Puerto Ricans were slower to achieve electoral positions than were White European ethnics, and they were not elected to major citywide offices in this period.

Although Puerto Ricans were often at a disadvantage in asserting their political rights, they had one resource that was unique to their status—mobilization by the government of Puerto Rico. Beginning in the 1950s, these efforts included the promotion of cultural connections to Puerto Rico, such as celebrations of national holidays and cultural performance; assistance for Puerto Rican residents on the mainland with municipal and state social service agencies; and support for electoral participation, including voter registration and get-out-the-vote in some elections. The promotion of U.S. electoral participation is usually the responsibility of civic and political organizations, not the government, so Puerto Rico's efforts were notable (and controversial).

These organizational and electoral gains in Puerto Rican communities at midcentury were not matched by economic and social advances. Migration from the island surged after World War II as part of a conscious effort by the U.S. and Puerto Rican governments to develop Puerto Rico's economy by moving Puerto Ricans off rural lands. The island's industrial economy could not absorb them all, so many moved to the mainland. Puerto Rican labor was initially in great demand, particularly in New York and other U.S. cities. But as urban industrial economies decreased, opportunities for Puerto Rican migrants declined commensurately. In addition to limited economic opportunities, group advancement was stymied by the failure of Northeastern cities to invest in education and housing, and by residential discrimination that limited Puerto Ricans' ability to join White ethnics in the mass move to the suburbs. Over time, and certainly by the dawn of the Latino era, Puerto Ricans had social and economic characteristics closer to those of urban African Americans than to the descendants of European immigrants.

At the beginning of the period of Hispanic pan-ethnicity, Puerto Rican politics was much more institutionalized than was Mexican American politics. Puerto Ricans were routinely part of the elective officeholder landscape of New York, and several Puerto Rican organizations were large and had reliable sources of state support. The government of Puerto Rico added to this organizational infrastructure. Puerto Ricans, nevertheless, found themselves to be increasingly economically and residentially disadvantaged, so these institutional successes contradicted their daily lives.

Puerto Ricans outside of New York experienced a political and civic world much more like that of Mexican Americans in the Southwest. Outside of New York, Puerto Rican leaders had not been co-opted into partisan politics and local political machines, so they were nearly all political outsiders. Interestingly, it was in Chicago—a northern city with sizeable Puerto Rican and Mexican American populations—that some of the earliest efforts to build a pan-ethnic Latino politics emerged.[24]

The Cuban Revolution and Rise of Cuban American Politics

A final Latino political force appeared in the years just before the emergence of pan-ethnic Latino politics in the late 1960s and early 1970s. The Cuban Revolution (1953–1959) and the victory of Fidel Castro spurred unprecedented levels of migration from Cuba. These postrevolutionary Cuban émigrés arrived in the United States with clear organizational and political objectives, somewhat higher levels of human capital—education, skills, training, and professional connections—and more political experience than did other migrants from the Americas (or than those who came from Cuba later). They joined what had been a small prerevolution Cuban immigrant population, though the post-1959 migrants quickly came to dominate the civic life and politics of the community. Between 1959 and 1980, ethnicity moved from inconsequential at the national level and insignificant at the state and local level to more decisive, particularly in electoral politics and in meeting the policy needs of Cuban Americans.

The first wave of postrevolution Cuban migrants included many who did not expect to stay in the United States for long. These were largely self-identified **political refugees,** who left Cuba because they did not feel they would be safe there, but expected to return soon. Most expected the Cuban Revolution to follow the pattern of previous regime changes in Cuba, particularly as the Castro regime moved closer to the Soviet Union. As a result, they initially focused their political energies on working to destabilize the new regime, a goal they shared with policymakers of both parties in Washington, and were able to gain influence in national policymaking over U.S.-Cuba relations very quickly, particularly with those for whom ethnicity was largely inconsequential. This national political influence, however, was not initially matched by local- and state-level political influence.

Because of their shared goal, the U.S. government aided the initial incorporation of the Cuban émigrés, investing considerably in efforts both in building the internal resources of the Cuban American community and in enterprises that would undermine the Castro regime.[25] Many of these resources went directly to activities to destabilize the regime, including support for paramilitary activities and the creation of front businesses for Central Intelligence Agency activities. This investment benefited the Cuban American community by providing jobs, leadership opportunities, and an outlet for the anger felt for the Castro regime. The U.S. government also invested more directly in the Cuban American community to use it as an example of the benefits of the American ideal. These policies included such programs as direct financial assistance for migrants, employment programs, resettlement assistance, aid to local education, funding for community-based organizations and religious groups assisting with migration and resettlement, and training programs to convert professional credentials. No other large migrant population from the Americas has received such an extensive set of government resources for such an extended period of time.

This direct investment served as an unintentional **settlement policy** (a policy designed to assist in the incorporation of immigrants). As part of the U.S. effort to destabilize the Castro regime, it spent freely in Cuban American communities—estimated between $2 and $4 billion between 1959 and 1980—particularly in South Florida. These resources ensured that Cuban Americans were able to adapt more rapidly to life in the United States than were other immigrant groups who lacked comparable resources. U.S. funds provided seed capital for the development of a vibrant Cuban American business community. The long-term consequences of these measures, particularly after it became evident that the Castro regime was not going to fall, added to the political and social capital, business acumen, and collective identity of the Cuban émigré community as it began to build a Cuban *immigrant* (as opposed to refugee) community. Unlike refugees, immigrants anticipate a much longer—if not permanent—residence in the country of destination and migrate for a combination of familial, economic, and political reasons.

The growth of a Cuban American politics, rather than Cuban émigré politics, was slow and remains contested by some in the Cuban American community, particularly those who arrived soon after the Cuban Revolution. As the duration of the Cuban stay in South Florida lengthened and the numbers of immigrants grew, however, Cuban Americans began to organize to meet community needs in the United States and to shape domestic politics.[26] They were quicker to achieve these goals than were other immigrant groups because of the strong sense of collective identity that grew from the community's émigré origins, the level of human capital possessed by many early postrevolutionary émigrés, and the leadership that had emerged to oppose the Castro regime, as well as U.S. investment in the Cuban American community. Organization and resources aside, however, Cuban Americans faced many of the same challenges as other racial/ethnic groups.

The origins of collective political action were quite similar in many ways to other immigrant populations. Cuban Americans found themselves subject to discrimination based on language and culture and were initially unable to use electoral politics to achieve community goals because of low rates of U.S. citizenship. Local political institutions denied Cuban American leaders access to positions of power and influence, a denial that was particularly galling because many had greater access in Washington than they did in Miami or Tallahassee. Discrimination in the housing sector and in schools were of particular concern.

As the Cuban presence grew and the likelihood that they would soon return to Cuba diminished, however, tensions with native populations surfaced. For example, Miami, which had initially been tolerant of the Cubans (and appreciative of the massive federal funding that accompanied them), reversed course and barred the use of Spanish by city agencies. Local governments in South Florida continued to be under the control of native White populations and used their institutional powers to slow Cuban political empowerment.

These tensions came to a head in 1980, when the Castro regime seized an opportunity and opened the port of Mariel to Cubans seeking to flee the country. It became known as the **Mariel boatlift.** Castro's decision was initially viewed positively in the United States, and particularly in the Cuban American community. The Cuban regime had barred emigration for a long period prior to this. It soon became evident, however,

Are Cuban Americans at more of an advantage today because they were recipients of early, favored policies by the U.S. government?

ASSOCIATED PRESS

The rapid migration of more than 100,000 Cubans from the port of Mariel in 1980 changed the dynamics of Cuban American politics. Community leaders quickly realized that they needed to develop local political influence in South Florida to match their influence with national policymakers.

that some of the tens of thousands of migrants fleeing Cuba were being forced to leave and had come from prisons. The forced émigrés were a significant minority of the Mariel immigrants, but in the popular racial imagination, violent criminals made up the majority of *Marielitos.*

This sudden influx of more than 100,000 émigrés created concern in Miami and unleashed vitriol in the Anglo community that had been below the surface for years. The fact that some of the émigrés were violent criminals inflamed the situation. Concerns that the United States could not control migration and had simply responded to the whims of Fidel Castro added to these fears. The excitement felt in the Cuban American community and their willingness to charter boats to go to Mariel and pick up migrants was seen in Anglo communities as an open flouting of U.S. immigration law. The political and economic establishment of Miami—and particularly the *Miami Herald*—turned against the Miami Cuban community in a way that the community had not experienced in the twenty years since the Cuban Revolution, and in a way that it did not expect, based on its increasingly important (and positive) role in South Florida's economy and society.[27]

Until this point, Cuban Americans had seen themselves broadly as part of the American mainstream. With the public reaction to Mariel and the ability of (non-Hispanic) White Miami and Florida to quickly turn against them (and to reduce the settlement resources that previous waves of Cuban migrants had experienced), Cuban Americans began to see themselves as an ethnic minority in a (non-Hispanic) White-dominated society.

Although their origins and initial experiences were somewhat different from those of Mexican and Puerto Rican migrants, the Cuban American response to the native U.S. population's reaction to Mariel was similar. They organized and used the resources at their disposal (which were somewhat greater than those of early Mexican or Puerto Rican migrants) to ensure that they would have a voice in the Miami and U.S. electoral politics commensurate with their influence over U.S. policy toward Cuba. Over the next four years, in anticipation of the next presidential election, Cuban immigrants naturalized at unprecedented levels, using the connections their community had developed with policymakers in Washington to expedite the process. Cuban American leaders also looked for local- and state-level elective offices that would be likely to elect Cuban Americans to office. By the end of the 1980s, Cuban Americans had been elected to a wide range of offices, including the Dade County Commission and the U.S. Congress.

In their organization around U.S. domestic politics, Cuban Americans' early political socialization is similar to that of early Mexican and Puerto Rican migrants. They were aided by the legacy of the civil rights battles of the 1960s and 1970s in African American, Mexican American, and Puerto Rican communities. It is those battles, and a major policy outcome—the Voting Rights Act—with which we conclude our discussion in this chapter.

CIVIL RIGHTS AND ETHNIC NATIONALISM IN LATINO COMMUNITIES, 1960s–1970s

By the late 1950s and early 1960s, Mexican American and Puerto Rican communities had built small civic organizational infrastructures and used these bases to begin to get some co-ethnics elected to office. By any standard, these communities were underrepresented in elective office (and in every other elite sector, such as business owners, college graduates, and the professions), but the opportunities that each community seized offered some hope for the future. This (re)building of Mexican American and Puerto Rican politics throughout the early twentieth century was comparable to processes in White ethnic communities in this same period, but the outcomes were becoming increasingly different. By 1960, White ethnics (the descendants of the late-nineteenth and early-twentieth-century migrants from Southern and Eastern Europe) were also underrepresented in elective office and elite positions, but they had been able to use the economic growth of the post–World War II era to dramatically improve their opportunities at the mass level and position themselves for further political, economic, and social advance. They had been considerably aided by government programs that benefited White ethnics but did not offer the same opportunities to Blacks and Latinos (see Chapter 6).[28] Local and state policies in this era also reduced levels of discrimination against White ethnics, particularly in housing and schools, but were not as quick to reduce discrimination against Latinos and, particularly, Blacks. Certainly, the expanding gap between White ethnics and Latinos cannot entirely be placed in the hands of government social policies. New migration continued in Mexican American and Puerto Rican communities throughout the twentieth century, while it slowed after the mid-1920s in White ethnic communities.

Continued discrimination and disparate outcomes spurred organizing in Black and Latino communities, the roots of which are perhaps somewhat deeper in African American communities than in Latino communities. (See Chapter 3.) Latino civil rights organizing is important to understand not only for its positive outcomes for the community, but also for its critical role in demonstrating the shared civic and political needs of Latinos of different national origins. Thus contemporary Latino identity needs to be understood not simply in terms of creating an umbrella for people who share a regional ancestry/origin, roots in a common non-English language, and (at least in the era under study here) religion. Latino identity is also a political identity forged to overcome a common set of barriers and exclusion that distinguished these populations from the majority.[29] All of these factors—ancestral, cultural, experiential, and political—came together in the 1960s to begin the process of cementing the Hispanic pan-ethnic identity.

Latino civil rights organizing began when the first Mexican American mutualist organizations recognized that they could only meet collective needs by challenging authorities in their local communities who treated Mexican Americans differently from Anglos. These groups showed their members the value of collective action and offered a forum to discuss differential treatment of Mexican Americans. LULAC, *El Congreso*, MAPA, and PASSO reflected organizational efforts to challenge discrimination and denial of Latino citizenship rights. Each of these efforts was critical, but they were not in any sense a movement. Latinos in one state knew little of and had little connection to Latino civic or political organizing in other states. The 1960s and 1970s saw the emergence of regional civil rights movements that spoke to the nation and a national representation of Hispanic demands for inclusion.

Not surprisingly, the 1960s Latino civil rights efforts began locally. Their demands—modest by today's standards—were fundamentally revolutionary in that they sought for Mexican Americans' and Puerto Ricans' treatment as equal citizens, as guaranteed by the Treaty of Guadalupe Hidalgo, the Jones Act, and the Fourteenth Amendment to the U.S. Constitution. Anglo power structures recognized that if these changes were implemented, the racial hierarchy that had emerged over the previous century would disintegrate and Latinos would be able to compete as equals in U.S. society. Anglo resistance, particularly in rural areas of the Southwest, grew. Furthermore, as they had for the past century when facing serious challenges from Mexican Americans and Puerto Ricans, local political leaders sought to limit Mexican American and Puerto Rican political gains—particularly by restricting voting rights in areas where historically they had been manipulated, and by limiting educational access.

Latino civil rights organizing in the 1960s took a variety of forms: voter mobilization and challenges to discriminatory registration and districting rules, labor organizing in the agricultural sector, anti–Vietnam War organizing, land rights claims resulting from the loss of Mexican-owned lands after the U.S.-Mexican War, youth organizing focused on high schools and colleges demanding access to educational opportunities equivalent to White students, and challenges to the legacies of colonialism such as the failure to teach Mexican American history. The rhetoric of these new civil rights organizations, particularly those organized by young adults, was confrontational and sometimes violent, but the demands, at their core, were for full inclusion—for ethnicity to be inconsequential. The mobilizing activities focused on community improvement. For example, the Young Lords, an ethnic nationalist civil rights organization, swept up trash in New York City, forcing the city to haul away large piles of trash, and delivered vaccinations and checkups at community sites.[30] This and other Latino civil rights organizations mobilized a new generation to involvement in politics (and political activism) while making alliances with non-Hispanic civil rights and antiwar organizing by African Americans, women, Native Americans, and others seeking change in the United States. Mexican Americans, and to a limited degree, Latinos, formed a political party in 1970—La Raza Unida—that held a national convention, elected candidates at the local level, and challenged incumbents for statewide offices.

It is not possible here to examine each of these efforts individually, but several patterns emerge that link them, including the Fourteenth Amendment principle of equal protection of the law and the national civil rights rhetoric that grew in African American communities in the 1950s and early 1960s. The membership and leaders of these organizations were more likely than not to be young adults who were U.S.-born and raised. Relative to the mass of the Latino population, they were better educated. Latino civil rights organizational efforts emerged out of alliances, particularly with unions and other grassroots organizations in the localities.[31] Almost to a one, these organizations rejected the incremental change that had characterized the civic and political gains in Latino communities between 1900 and 1960 and sought a more rapid democratization of U.S. political life. The rhetorical demand for dramatic change, such as the creation of a Mexican American political party or independence for Puerto Rico, however, was often tempered by a willingness of many Latino civil rights leaders to accept more incremental change that allowed for an increased Latino political voice.

The movement's organizations also dramatized for the national population, Latino and non-Latino alike, that there was a national Latino, rather than Mexican American, Puerto Rican, or Cuban American, political identity. To encourage this perception, Latino organizations spoke of a shared set of needs that distinguished Latinos as a group from Anglos: educational access; nondiscrimination in the schools, housing, and job market; language rights; redress for past discrimination; bilingual education; culturally relevant K–12 and college curricula; labor rights in agriculture; and job training. None of these demands individually was revolutionary, but taken as a whole, they reflected an expectation of equal citizenship that had not been made so forcefully or so articulately before. Out of these Latino civil rights demands came both contemporary Latino politics and a growing recognition by the government of the need to design programs to overcome past discrimination and ensure Latinos' full incorporation into U.S. politics. We explore the outcomes of these movements in subsequent chapters.

The Beginning of the Latino Political Era

As we will show in the discussion of political behavior and participation (Chapter 9), Latino politics has never been as cohesive as African American politics, and this was all the more the case at the dawn of the Latino era. By the late 1960s, Mexican Americans and Puerto Ricans organized to influence local and, in some cases, state-level politics. Cuban Americans would follow a decade later. Latinos were largely unrepresented at the national level in this era and had little influence on national policymaking. Why, then, can this era be seen as the beginning of a pan-ethnic Latino politics?

The answers focus on the development of a collective identity within Latino communities and on efforts by the national government to measure the relative status of different groups in U.S. society as a tool to understand the pervasiveness and consequences of discrimination, on an increasing recognition by Latinos of different ancestries that they shared experiences with language and national origin–based discrimination, and on efforts to craft legislation to redress these collectively experienced barriers.

Latino civil rights organizing highlighted the policy dimensions of this collective identity but did not immediately translate to the mass level. That would be a process of the 1970s and 1980s. Instead, their efforts forced government to recognize and measure the relative social and economic status of Latinos as a group. In 1976 Congress passed PL 94-311, the Americans of Spanish Origin–Social Statistics law (note that Congress really did not yet have a name for this population). PL 94-311 required that the U.S. Census and other government agencies collect data on Latinos as it long had for African Americans and Whites. With this law, and the implementation of *Hispanic* as a collective ethnic identity term to categorize this group, advocates and leaders would have concrete data with which to show where Latinos stood in U.S. society. It would also allow them to make reasoned social science inferences about how government policies and social practices led to these outcomes. Finally, discrimination and opportunity could be measured and Latinos, regardless of national origin or ancestry, could see what they shared.

With evidence of a shared status and increasing contact across Latino groups, Hispanic leaders were able to make the case at the mass level that there was a Latino political identity built upon the national origin identities, which had been the experiences of most Latinos up until that time. It is also important to observe that Latino leaders and Congress ensured that the pan-ethnic term *Hispanic* (and *Latino*) was not a racial identification. PL 94-311 mandated that *Hispanic* was an ethnic identity and that all Hispanics could identify separately in racial terms. Hispanic leaders sought to ensure that this pan-ethnic identity would not place Latinos into the racial hierarchy, with Whites at the top and other racial groups, of which they would be one, subordinate.

The discoveries of shared experiences and similar policy needs across Latino communities were reinforced by government efforts to homogenize the Latino experience. Government policies, such as PL 94-311, would henceforth focus on Hispanics as a single population and not on national origin–based identities.

Identify two modern-day examples that inhibit the rights of Latinos. How and why do they present roadblocks?

A notable example of government steps to combat discrimination against Latinos was the 1975 extension of the Voting Rights Act to include "language minorities," one of which was the "Spanish-origin" population (Latinos).[32] When the Voting Rights Act, enacted in 1965 to prevent discrimination in voting on the basis of race or color, came up for renewal in 1975, Latino leaders seized the opportunity to explore whether Latinos should be similarly protected. Extensive hearings in both the House and Senate documented cases of voter exclusion and intimidation targeting Latinos in the Southwest and in New York. Beginning in 1975, the Voting Rights Act extended its protections to Latinos, and some jurisdictions, in California and New York, were added to the preclearance provisions of Section V of the Voting Rights Act (discussed in Chapter 7; preclearance required that all electoral rule changes be reviewed by the U.S. Justice Department to ensure that the change did not diminish minority electoral participation or the ability of minority communities to elect the candidate of their choice). Texas had been included in 1965.

Congress also identified a form of discrimination experienced not just by Latinos, but also by the other populations added to the protections of the Voting Rights Act in 1975—Asian Americans, Alaskan Natives, and Native Americans. Congress determined that one cause of lower than average Latino participation was the inability to read or speak English. Many Latinos and the other covered language minorities could not understand the voter registration materials and ballots. Congress discovered that many U.S.-born Latinos experienced this linguistic disadvantage even after attending schools in the United States. Many had been sent to

Table 4.3   Latinos' Road of Racialization

Group	Why Barriers Arose	How Barriers Were Overcome	Outcome
Mexican Americans	• Grabs for territory and rising discrimination (nineteenth century) • Decline of prewar elite • A sense among Whites that Mexican Americans are not part of the polity	• Local-level civic infrastructure and organized interests, rising political power	Nearly Absolute Barrier → Insufficient
Puerto Ricans	• Migration after Spanish-American War • Attempts at disenfranchisement due to race/ethnicity	• Multi-ethnic organizations allowed for political mobilization • Puerto Rican links to U.S. economy influenced politics	Decisive → Insufficient
Cubans	• Cuban Revolution refugees stayed longer than anticipated • Language and culture discrimination • Public backlash over influx of *Marielitos* (1980s)	• U.S. government support for anti-Castro émigrés • Strong leadership and economic capital	Inconsequential → Insufficient

segregated schools, in which the language of instruction was Spanish. Therefore, the inability to participate in elections was the result of state inaction. As a result, Congress added a specific set of protections in the 1975 amendments to the Voting Rights Act that mandated bilingual election materials in areas with concentrations of any of the covered populations.

CONCLUSION: LATINOS AS A PAN-ETHNIC GROUP

With the passage of the 1975 amendments to the Voting Rights Act and other civil rights legislation, Hispanics became a political community, at least in the eyes of the government. This political community resulted from the steady growth of Mexican American, Puerto Rican, and Cuban American civic and political organizing throughout the first six decades of the twentieth century.

This new status saw a tangible manifestation in the 1980 census. For the first time, the Census Bureau added a specific question on Hispanic ethnicity. Although the census likely undercounted Latinos, the 1980 census offers the first definitive measure of this population. It found 14.6 million Latinos in the United States, who made up approximately 6.4 percent of the national population.

Over the next three decades, the Latino population grew dramatically, and diversified in terms of national origin, nativity, and place of residence in the United States. It became a national population and the nation's largest minority in a way that simply could not have been imagined within the community or without at the dawn of the Latino era. The contours of the community and its politics, however, emerged from the organizing and politics of this earlier era; today's politics cannot be understood without a recognition of how the Latino political pasts built to today's pan-ethnic whole.

DISCUSSION QUESTIONS

1. How did Mexican American cultural differences with the majority in the Southwest contribute to their disadvantage in the U.S. political and social system?

2. Can distinctions be made between the application of race- and class-based discrimination against Mexican Americans in the late 1800s?

3. Has the creation of a pan-ethnic Latino identity helped to minimize the racialization of people of Spanish origin or ancestry? Why or why not?

4. In what ways did Latino social and political opportunities change in the Civil Rights era?

5. Compare the role of social and class factors in the racialization of Cuban Americans and Mexican Americans. How did U.S. policy speed the incorporation of Cuban refugees and slow it for Puerto Ricans?

6. How do contemporary Latino civil rights concerns continue to mirror those of other groups, such as African Americans? Do you think there are more similarities now or in the past?

KEY TERMS

El Congreso de Pueblos
Que Hablan Español (p. 125)
Jones Act (p. 130)
League of United Latin
American Citizens
(LULAC) (p. 124)

Manifest Destiny (p. 117)
Mariel boatlift (p. 133)
mutualist organizations (p. 123)
pan-ethnic group (p. 111)
political refugees (p. 132)
settlement policy (p. 133)

Treaty of Guadalupe
Hidalgo (p. 114)
Treaty of Paris (1898) (p. 129)
White Man's Burden (p. 128)

5 Different and Common Asian American Roads, 1800s-1960s

We who came to the United States as immigrants are Americans too. All of us were immigrants—all the way down the line. We are Americans all who have toiled for this land, who have made it rich and free. But [we were told] we must not demand from America, because she is still our unfinished dream. . . .

— Carlos Bulosan, Filipino American activist and writer[1]

While Chapter 4 traces the distinct histories of individual Latino groups, this chapter will discuss the history of Asian Americans in a way that demonstrates both the commonalities and differences of their experiences. From the nineteenth through much of the twentieth century, various Asian or South Asian communities in the United States witnessed extremely uneven, winding, and often dead-end roads in their quests for equal opportunity and citizenship rights. To state it according to the terms of Chapter 1, for much of Asian American political history up until the mid-1960s, race was an absolute or decisive barrier because they were treated as alien others unequal to Whites. For example, in *People v. Hall* (1854) the California Supreme Court ruled that a White man had been falsely convicted of murdering a Chinese person due to the testimony of Chinese witnesses. The state did not recognize the Chinese and other

Box 5.1 Chapter Objectives

- Explain how and why Whites racialized Asian immigrants along a shifting range from a model minority to a racial threat.
- Describe the domestic and international impetus for Asian migration to the United States.
- Discuss how the economic opportunities that drew Asians to migrate also set the stage for their exclusion.
- Identify how Asian institutions and organizations formed and at times embraced pan-ethnic identities like "Asian American" to resist their racialization.
- Contrast the moments in history when Asian immigrants and Asian Americans were most vulnerable to discrimination and exclusion.
- Explain the factors leading to Japanese internment during World War II and the shifting status of other Asian Americans.
- Evaluate how the Asian American political journey paralleled civil rights organizing by other groups in the United States.

A Japanese American man and his grandsons await relocation to an internment camp during World War II. The tags they wear on their clothing indicate that they are required to relocate. More than 100,000 Japanese Americans, deemed a security threat after the attack on Pearl Harbor, were forced to abandon their homes and move to internment camps in remote areas of the country.

Time & Life Pictures/Getty Images

Asians as full persons whose testimonies were admissible in court. The majority opinion concluded that the Chinese were among "a race of people whom nature has marked as inferior, and who are incapable of progress or intellectual development beyond a certain point . . . differing in language, opinions, color, and physical conformation; between whom and ourselves nature has placed an impassable difference."[2] During the nineteenth century, Chinese were permitted to immigrate to California and some other states or U.S. territories because many nineteenth-century industrialists, manufacturers, and planters viewed the labor of so-called "Heathen Chinee" as absolutely necessary to vital activities such as mining, railroad construction, and agricultural harvesting. In many instances, Whites even cited them as model workers, more industrious than other ethnic/racial groups. But like "Negroes," "Indians," and "Mulattos," the *Hall* case stated the Chinese were also clearly "non-White" or non-Caucasian. Thus as racial inferiors they naturally could not claim any citizenship rights, especially the right to testify against White defendants in court. Recall that in this same period the U.S. Supreme Court concluded in the *Dred Scott* case (1857) that a Black person had "no rights a white man is bound to respect."

Almost seventy years later, with the case of *United States v. Bhagat Singh Thind* (1923), an Asian Indian man named Bhagat Singh Thind demonstrated that even when some Asian immigrants were considered Caucasian, their road toward citizenship and opportunity could still wind toward a dead end. The U.S. Supreme Court denied Thind's application for citizenship on the eve of the 1924 Immigration Act—the most restrictive immigration law in U.S. history, which prohibited nearly all Asians and South Asians from immigrating into the United States or naturalizing as citizens. Although anthropologists who constructed racial classifications had concluded that Indians were "Aryans" and thus Caucasians, the Court concluded that Thind was not "White" simply because most Whites would not consider him as White. This seemingly arbitrary drawing of a White/non-White color line so fundamentally upset Thind that he declared, "And now they say I am not an American" in a final note, and then committed suicide.[3]

The history of how the United States has racialized Asian immigrants and Asian Americans is one, to paraphrase political scientist Claire Kim, of "jurisprudential" or legal and political "contortions" in which the dominant society was "determined to use whatever arguments [that] proved useful in maintaining the boundary between Whites and Asian immigrants, regardless of how inconsistent or illogical their decision may have appeared."[4] Less than twenty years after the *Thind* case, this line shifted again. At the beginning of the U.S. entry into World War II, in the 1940s, an absolute line was drawn against the Japanese. Due to Japan's attack on Pearl Harbor, Japanese in the United States were deemed the greatest threat out of all Asian Americans; and President Franklin D. Roosevelt authorized confining (i.e., racially segregating) more than 100,000 of them—citizens and noncitizens alike—in internment or concentration camps.[5]

Our chief purpose in this chapter is to explain when, why, and how Asian Americans confronted differing absolute or decisive roadblocks and barriers up to the mid-1960s, and to present the often untold stories of their ability to create diverse ethnic communities, economies, and organizations in spite of (and precisely because of) these barriers. We focus on those groups that have the longest histories and the largest numbers among Asian Americans, especially the Chinese, Japanese, Filipinos, Koreans, and Asian Indians. Because the Pacific Coast of the United States has been the major zone of entry for Asian immigration, some of the history of the Hawaiian Islands and those groups identified as Native Hawaiian or Pacific Islander are also included.

U.S. society and its polity rapidly changed the racial conclusions and racial lines it drew to separate itself from different Asian American communities. Between the hundred-year period of 1830 (when a small group of Chinese sugar makers arrived in Hawaii) to 1930 (at the height of immigration exclusion and the occupation of the Philippines), there were two broad poles as to how Whites treated Asian Americans. At times Whites considered Asians "model minorities," and thus desirable if still alien workers. At other times Whites considered them racial threats—elements of a so-called Yellow Peril—and thus excluded them and/or denied them citizenship, land, and livelihoods. U.S. racial views and thus foreign and domestic policy displayed a dizzying, zigzag pattern of "divide and conquer," of changing in-groups and out-groups. For example, by the 1890s, U.S. treaty relations with China had dissolved, the Chinese were feared as competitors to White labor, and most Chinese immigrants were excluded. And due to favorable treaties with Japan, Japanese laborers briefly became "noble" alternatives to the Chinese. By the 1940s, Japan and the United States were at war, and the Japanese were viewed as an enemy within and literally were confined. However, because China had become a U.S. ally during World War II, some restrictions on Chinese immigration, as well as barriers on the wartime employment of Chinese Americans, were relaxed.[6]

Although Asians/Asian Americans comprised only about 5 percent of the U.S. population in 2010, they have been among the fastest-growing immigrant populations since the 1965 Immigration and Nationality Act abolished the national origin quotas of 1921 and 1924. We stress, however, that the broader story we are telling is not that we understand a group's importance within American politics according to its size.[7] Moreover, we can only fully appreciate the twists and turns of how race, ethnicity, and racism have affected various facets of the United States and its politics—that is, modern American trade and military policies, the operations of multinational corporations and the global economy, U.S. immigration policy, citizenship and naturalization laws, civil rights policy, or unionization and labor rights—if we better understand the political history of Asian Americans.

THE RACIALIZATION OF ASIAN AMERICANS

In order to grasp the complex history of Asian Americans, let us first define who currently belongs to this group. According to the 2010 U.S. Census, "The term 'Asian' refers to a person having origins in any of the original peoples of the Far East, Southeast Asian, or Indian subcontinent, including, for example, Cambodia, China, India, Japan, Korea, Malaysia, Pakistan, The Philippine Islands, Thailand, and Vietnam." The classification of this so-called minority group includes roughly 60 percent of the world's population. We will use *Asian American* throughout this chapter as a shorthand term that encompasses Asian immigrants and Asian citizens; for, as political scientists Pei-te Lien, Margaret Conway, and Janelle Wong reason, "In a general sense, an Asian American is any Asian who resides in the United States on a permanent or long-term basis, regardless of citizenship or other legal status."[8]

The term *Asian American* is a pan-ethnic identity precisely because it clusters a diversity of ethnic/national identities under one broad (racial) identifier. The term is a fairly recent creation that emanated out of the Asian American empowerment movement of the late 1960s and early 1970s. But the U.S. government has long both conceived of Asian Americans as a group—e.g., "Orientals"—and as distinct ethnic communities—e.g., "Hindus," which was a stereotypical mislabeling, since most early Asian Indian immigrants in the U.S. community identified with the Sikh religion.[9] As a consequence of the shifting attitudes of White Americans toward Asian Americans beginning in the nineteenth century, the racial classification of Asian American populations dramatically changed in each decennial census. (Refer back to Chapter 1.) Precisely because Chinese Americans are the largest Asian American community and the one with the longest presence in the United States, there has been a "Chinese" category in the census since 1870.

Although there is great ethnic/national and cultural diversity among Asian Americans, one element of their shared historical experience is that they collectively have been racialized between the poles of two broad, racial myths—a model minority versus a foreign threat. On one side, Asian immigrants and Asian Americans are distinguished as a **model minority** who are highly intelligent, industrious, and politically passive or apolitical, and thus by implication ideal workers in comparison to many other racial and ethnic minorities. Ethnic studies scholar Paul Wong and his colleagues summarize this myth as, "Asian Americans are believed to enjoy extraordinary achievements in education, occupational upward mobility, rising income, and are problem-free in mental health and crime."[10] This myth stems in part from the misinterpretation of differences attributed to culture. For instance, Asian American families inherently value education more than most other groups. The myth also stems from the failure to understand the following:

Table 5.1   The Growth of Asian American Populations, 2000–2010

Group	2000 Population	2010 Population	Percent Change
Total	10,242,998	14,675,252	43.3
Chinese	2,564,190	3,535,382	37.9
Asian Indian	1,718,778	2,914,807	69.8
Filipino	1,908,125	2,649,973	38.9
Vietnamese	1,169,672	1,632,717	39.6
Korean	1,099,422	1,463,474	33.1
Japanese	852,237	841,824	−1.2
Pakistani	164,628	382,994	132.6

Source: U.S. Census Bureau, "The Asian Population: 2010," in 2010 Census Briefs, vols. 1–23 (Washington, DC: U.S. Department of Commerce, Economics and Statistics Administration, 2012).

1. Some Asian Americans' relatively higher rates of income, skill, and education in comparison to other groups are due to post-1965 immigration policies that favored immigrants with higher rates of income and education.

2. There is a wide span of achievement levels across Asian American groups—e.g., Asian Indian households had 2010 median incomes of $90,528 versus the median household income of Vietnamese Americans was $55,667.

3. Asian Americans work longer hours on average, have larger families than their White counterparts (and thus enjoy smaller amounts of per capita income), and (along with racial stereotypes) can still suffer from discrimination because they are underrepresented in some educational and occupational fields.[11]

On the other side of the continuum, Asian Americans have been stereotyped as racial threats, at one point called a **Yellow Peril**. The term is based on a racist depiction from the late nineteenth and early twentieth centuries that portrayed Asian Americans as contaminating America with their foreign influences. Also described as the Oriental Problem—akin to Blacks as the Negro Problem in the Jim Crow South, who could not fully integrate into White society—the so-called Yellow Peril projects Asian citizens and immigrants as being secretive, unable and/or unwilling to fully assimilate into American society, and possessing destructive, alien attachments to their homelands as well as to alien beliefs and customs. Historian Ronald Takaki explained that nineteenth-century newspapers and labor union depictions of the Chinese give us prime examples of this Yellow Peril fear: "White workers referred to the Chinese as 'naguars' [a variation on a racist term used against Blacks] and a magazine cartoon depicted the Chinese as a bloodsucking vampire with slanted eyes, a pigtail, dark skin, and thick lips. Like blacks, the Chinese were described as heathen, morally inferior, savage, childlike, and lustful."[12] The *New York Times* and other newspapers presented racist and sexist accounts that raised White fears of attacks upon White women. One story it shared in the 1870s was of "a handsome but squalidly dressed young white girl" who was entrapped in a Chinese opium den, with a Chinese man supposedly boasting, "Oh, hard time in New York. Young girl hungry. Plenty come here. Chinaman always have something to eat, and he like you white girl! He! He!" Historian Gordon Chang concludes that such racist caricatures have lingered throughout American history, rendering Asian Americans "eternally foreign" and not fully trustworthy, no matter how long they have been U.S. citizens or residents.[13]

Claire Kim, an Asian American politics scholar, states that these two contrasting myths have led to the placement of Asian Americans within a **racial triangle.** This is a process in which Whites view Asian Americans as not fully equal to Whites (because they are foreign), or what she calls "civic ostracism," but also as racially and ethnically superior to other minority groups, or what she calls "relative valorization." Back in the late 1960s, sociologist Hubert Blalock coined the term *middleman minority* to mean a process in which a dominant racial group uses the small economic or political progress of one ethnic or racial minority as leverage against other racial and ethnic minorities the dominant group wishes to replace or suppress. For instance, during the post–Civil War Reconstruction era of the late 1860s to the 1870s, Chinese laborers were used to replace freed Blacks who were once enslaved in the South.

How might both the "model minority" and "racial threat" concepts work against Asian Americans as college applicants, job applicants, or citizens running for elected office?

Kim's "civic ostracism" concept correlates with the racial threat myth and, as stated, is the belief that Asian Americans are marked as perpetual or eternal "foreigners" and thus should be ostracized or set apart from civic and economic life. Here again, Asian Americans are at times lumped together with other "racially inferior" non-White groups, as the aforementioned *Hall* case indicates. There are, however, many contemporary examples of civic ostracism. One anecdotal but poignant example of this concept comes from a former colleague of some of the authors of this text. Our colleague, who is Chinese American, recounted a puzzling story. Each time he went to vote he first was invariably asked the question, "Are you an American citizen?" even though he had voted at the same polling place year after year. He was automatically presumed to be foreign. Kim's "relative valorization" concept correlates with the model minority myth and White beliefs that Asian Americans are racially superior to other minorities, such as Blacks. For example, Asian Americans can score nearly two dozen points higher on standard undergraduate and graduate admission exams than do Blacks and Latinos (although such tests are not indicators of ultimate academic or career achievement); therefore, some may presume that Asian Americans are inherently more academically gifted.[14]

With the understanding of how Asian Americans have been subject to historic and contemporary racialization, we next examine the geopolitical and historical reasons, or "whys," that Asian Americans emigrated from their homelands to the United States up until the early 1900s. This history serves as a precursor to understanding the economic and political processes and periods in which the dominant White majority used its laws and institutions to enact measures that excluded various Asian American groups from the resources, protections, and rights offered by the polity.

EUROPEAN IMPERIALISM AND ASIAN EMIGRATION

The first age of Europeans creating colonies or colonialization in the seventeenth and eighteenth centuries occurred when European powers such as Portugal, Spain, the Netherlands, and England sought raw goods and trade routes to Asia. This period combined the economic expansion of merchant businesses and budding capitalist economies with the political and territorial expansion of the nation-state, often backed by the use of military power. Historical sociologist Immanuel Wallerstein referred to this empire-building process as the emergence of the "world-system" and its international market economy, in which the United States became intricately involved. For example, the British East India Company, founded in 1600, was granted a monopoly on British trade with Asia by the Crown. In 1773 it was precisely this company's monopoly pricing with the trade in tea from the East that angered some American merchants and colonists, sparking the Boston Tea Party as part of a larger set of grievances that became the American Revolution. Along with the British, the Portuguese, Dutch, and Spanish actively plied trade routes to Asia (which helped enrich nations on both ends of these routes). Europeans used Asians as well as African slaves as ship laborers and transported small groups of craftsmen to colonial possessions to serve as part of a budding class of workers. Historian Gary Okhiro notes that the lucrative trade between Spain and its eventual colony of the Philippines resulted in a group of "Filipino 'Manila men'"—Manila is the Filipino capital—reaching the shores of Louisiana and establishing small "fishing and shrimping villages in the bayous of New Orleans as possibly as early as 1765. These were probably the first permanent settlement[s] of Asians in North America."[15] We know that the early contact between Europeans and Asians shaped the racial worldview of Europeans, for in 1735 a Swedish botanist, Carolous Linnaeus, derived what he thought was a scientific, racial classification system that was based on reports from sailors and merchants. It described Asians, or *Asiaticus,* as "severe [or hostile], haughty [or arrogant], avaricious [or greedy] . . . and ruled by opinions."[16] Below, we focus on the particular role that the English and, later, Americans played in this power struggle for the material resources and human labor of what was then called the Far East, or the Orient.

Reasons for Asian Emigration to the United States

A number of factors help to explain "why" by the late 1800s persons entered the United States and the Hawaiian Islands from the nations of China, Japan, Korea, the Philippines, and India; they had no opportunities to become citizens in this period, since citizenship was exclusively reserved for Whites. The first factor is that of traditional, self-motivated, "push" and "pull" factors such as economic or political turmoil in one's home country, and the lure of economic opportunity in the foreign land. In large part, the story of the Chinese follows this traditional pattern. A second factor is that of manufacturing interests—most especially in Hawaii—actively recruiting Asian workers in order to cheaply fill pressing labor shortages. Such is the story of how Hawaiian sugar plantation owners employed labor agents to locate Japanese, Korean, and some Asian Indian contract laborers. A third factor is that of laborers or entrepreneurs leaving their homeland precisely because they are a global servant class, and taking indirect or circuitous paths to North America (and the United States) by way of Canada.

This is the story of a majority of early Asian Indian immigrants. Below, we discuss each main route of Asian emigration to the United States.

U.S. Imperialism and the Hawaiian Gateway. The West Coast of the United States is a natural gateway to the Pacific region; thus various Asian immigrants used it as a port of entry. Of course, the islands of Hawaii are even closer to Asia than to the West Coast. Therefore, the immigration and recruitment of Asians to work in the Hawaiian Islands were due to the islands' proximity or closeness to Asia as well as to the labor needs of the White settlers and business interests that eventually dominated Hawaii. Through warfare King Kamehameha I united the Hawaiian Islands into a single kingdom in 1795. But Western contact actually preceded and aided the founding of the kingdom due to the weapons European traders provided the king's army. By the 1840s, the West had become so politically and economically dominant upon the islands that Native Hawaiians petitioned Kamehameha III to resist further incursions by the Russians, the French, the British, and later the Americans, as each sought to exploit Hawaii's land and resources. By the 1870s, American sugarcane planters reaped such enormous wealth from sugar production that the island kingdom was viewed as a great economic prize by the United States. The story of Native Hawaiians parallels that of Native Americans, because Hawaiians also are an indigenous people who have made territorial claims against American settler colonialists. (See Chapter 2.) Also like Native Americans, Native Hawaiians lost ground to American settlers. In fact, even decades prior to annexation, land was a serious issue. When a group of Native Hawaiians petitioned King Kamehameha III for land in the 1840s, a whopping 75 percent of the lands of the island of Oahu were in the hands of foreigners.

White American missionaries, sugar manufacturers, and other business owners greatly outnumbered Native Hawaiians by the 1870s, and a coalition of sugar and other manufacturing interests eventually forced Hawaii's last monarch, Queen Lilluokalani, to abdicate her throne and turn over her government under what was called the 1898 Bayonet Constitution, instituted by an American military occupation. This marked the end of Native Hawaiians having control over their islands. The Hawaiian context is most relevant to this chapter because it became the vital Pacific gateway to the United States, through which many Asian American immigrant groups—from the Chinese to Asian Indians—passed.[17]

Imperialism Forces Chinese Emigration. The Chinese story of emigration to the United States is one of where economic and political turmoil in their homeland, as partly created by Western incursions, prompted the need for emigrants to look for opportunities elsewhere. Of the nearly million Asian/South Asian emigrants, the largest group, or roughly 370,000 persons, between 1840 and 1880 were Chinese. Most Chinese emigrants were from two provinces and its subregions within the southeastern region of mainland China—Fujian and Guandong. The city of Canton (or Guanzhou) became a springboard for this emigration because it became the center for Chinese trade and commerce with the West by the 1760s. In short, "Canton became a funnel through which Western influence penetrated the country."[18]

The Empire of China attempted to tightly control the trade between itself and the West so as to maintain an economic advantage. When it tried to curtail the importation of the drug opium (as smoked in tobacco), the British navy forced it to open five of its ports to the West in order to (among other things) trade in tea and opium. The British won the First Opium War of 1839–1842, and this resulted in the so-called "opening" of China and the Chinese having to make deep concessions, including the ceding of Hong Kong to Great Britain. The economic turmoil caused by the adverse Treaty of Nanking, which required the Chinese government to greatly increase taxes so to pay tribute, upended ordinary workers—especially porters as well as dockhands—and thus Canton city was no longer the center for all trade. These workers had strong incentives to search for work that would support their families across the seas.

This emigration stream was further swollen by the Second Opium War, or Anglo-Chinese War of 1856–1860 (which included the French), and its resulting Treaty of Tianjin that opened additional ports, legalized opium, permitted in Christian missionaries, and exacted more tribute and land from China. When combined with internal strife including a terribly bloody civil war—the Taiping Rebellion of 1850–1864, whereby a whopping ten million deaths resulted from a zealous Christian movement that the central government violently repressed—the stage was set for inner-land farmers, villagers, and other ordinary laborers to ignore the central government's prohibitions and to join the fisher and dockworker stream leaving to find a means of support in the West. We later discuss how the American West and the discovery of gold in California in the 1840s propelled this process.[19]

Military and Economic Interests Spur Japanese Emigration. American military and economic interests had an even more direct hand in the so-called "opening" of Japan to the West. But Japanese emigration was driven more by business relationships and labor recruitment than by individuals and families suffering economic hardship. The greatest number of early Japanese emigrants to the United States and Hawaii, who numbered about 400,000 by the twentieth century, came from the southwestern prefectures of the islands that comprise Japan. During the Tokugawa period of 1600 to 1868, Japan encountered much less European incursion than did China, as a ruling elite of very powerful Japanese military leaders, or *shoguns,* consolidated power over weaker feudal lords to eventually crown an emperor. But in 1853 U.S. Commodore Matthew Perry, on a mission to compel Japan to open to the West, disturbed its seclusion by a show of naval force in Tokyo Bay. Bothered by the example of European conquest over China, a group of Tokugawa leaders conceded to negotiations with the United States. Unfortunately, not only did this result in a treaty unfavorable to Japan, it opened the floodgates for other unequal arrangements with European powers. Various political, social, and economic changes within Japan set the stage for a significant number of Japanese looking outside their homeland for their fortunes. Among these changes was the 1868 Meiji Restoration, an elite movement that sought to Westernize Japan—supposedly to restore a figurehead emperor to the throne. The movement imposed new, heavy taxes on small landowners and farmers, and it instituted a military draft law that exempted students studying abroad and other emigrants.

Because of the relationship between American businessman Robert Irwin Walker, Japanese foreign minister Inoue Kaoru, and Masuda Takshi, the president of an import-export company, the Japanese government lifted a long-standing ban and permitted nearly 30,000 Japanese citizens to work as contract laborers on Hawaiian sugar plantations from 1885 to 1894. These circumstances differed from those of African American agricultural laborers in the South around the same time, in that American growers had to appeal to a foreign power, at least initially, and were not completely free in exploiting these workers. With very attractive wages (despite labor abuses, as some 7 percent of these immigrants died), about 44 percent of these laborers settled on the island, another 46 percent returned home to Japan, and a tiny 3 percent were allowed into the mainland United States. After this period, a number of private companies took up this recruitment trade.[20]

Koreans and Filipinos Recruited for U.S. Labor. Korean and Filipino emigrants had incentives similar to those of Japanese emigrants. For both, the West created the lure of economic opportunities to fill its labor needs. By the beginning of the twentieth century, about 7,000 Koreans emigrated to the United States or Hawaii. Unlike the Chinese and Japanese, they came from diverse regions within their country. From roughly 1592 until well into the twentieth century, Korea fought against domination by Japan and other imperial nations that frequently considered it a subject and certainly a battleground for their military conflicts—e.g., the 1894–1895 Sino-Japanese War; the 1904–1905 Russo-Japanese War; and the 1950–1953 Sino-Korean War, known in the United States as the Korean War. Thus the Koreans attempted to close their ports to Japan and all other would-be intruders. They were successful until they lost to Japan in 1875 and had to sign a treaty modeled after those the West compelled China and Japan to sign. The United States entered into such a treaty in 1882, as negotiated by U.S. Admiral Robert Shufeldt; this further opened the door to the British, the Germans, the Russians, the Italians, and the French. Such incursions created economic hardship for ordinary Koreans, including famine. Furthermore, these incursions stoked internal unrest and calls for a return to traditional Korean beliefs, as exhorted by the religious group the *Tonghak* (or those who favored Eastern learning over Western learning).

Horace N. Allen, an American missionary and later a U.S. diplomat, emerged during this tumultuous period to facilitate a labor relationship between Korea and the **Hawaiian Sugar Planters' Association (HSPA)**. Due to Allen's personal friendship with King Kojong, the Korean monarch granted a labor-recruitment franchise to David W. Deshler's HSPA-related firm. This permitted Korean subjects to emigrate in order to relieve some of the economic pressures felt at home and as a means to counterbalance Japanese workers on Hawaiian plantations who had begun to strike for higher wages.[21]

Based on your readings in other chapters, what commonalities are there in the reasons why Asians migrated to the United States and their initial reception?

Many more Filipinos than Koreans—or 180,000— entered the Hawaiian Islands and the U.S. mainland around this same period. A great majority of them came from the northern provinces, where there were populations concentrated in mountainous regions with little room for farming. Thus there were people with long traditions of migrating in search of work. Similar to Puerto Ricans (see Chapter 4), Filipinos endured a complicated and unique relationship with the United States because the Philippines (named after King Philip of Spain in the 1560s) became a possession of the United States after the Spanish-American War of 1898. Preeminent Filipino studies scholar E. San Juan Jr. concludes: "The reality of U.S. colonial subjugation and its profoundly enduring effects—something most people cannot even begin to fathom, let alone acknowledge—distinguish Filipinos from the Chinese, Japanese, Koreans, and others from the Asian continent."[22]

Prior to American occupation, Spain ruled the Philippines as a prosperous colony and created an educated, mixed-race elite called the *illustrados*. The *illustrados* were a middleman class, and they mobilized a reform movement that called for greater political freedom and other opportunities, such as the ordaining of more Filipinos as Catholic priests. This percolated into a broader revolt in which Spanish authorities arrested, exiled, and in some cases executed the leaders of the reform movement and its militant counterparts. When the United States won the Spanish-American War in 1898, it added Spain's colonies of the Philippines and Cuba to the American imperial empire. The U.S. military encountered the same stiff, anticolonial, guerilla resistance that had challenged Spanish rule. In retaliation, U.S. forces conducted a brutal pacification campaign that inflicted hundreds of thousands of Filipino deaths from disease, starvation, and combat.

In the early 1900s, Filipino workers became the triangulated other, if you recall Kim's theory, because they were exploited as the "middlemen" Whites used against Japanese workers, who after 1907 were seen as too rebellious and less desirable by Hawaiian plantation owners. As we will see later, the irony is that Filipino workers became among the most outspoken Asian American labor leaders. But in 1901 American diplomat William Haywood helped foster an agreement whereby the HSPA could actively benefit from the recruitment of Filipinos, who, as U.S. "nationals" with American passports but not citizens, were not subject to the same restrictions placed on the vast majority of other emigrants from Asia and Southeast Asia.

The Indirect Immigration of Asian Indians. Asian Indian emigrants into the United States came mostly from the Sikh-majority, Punjab districts of northern India; they found their way to Hawaii but mostly to the American mainland. Roughly the same number of Asian Indians, or 7,000, entered the United States at the turn of the twentieth century as had Koreans. But, as mentioned earlier, the unique immigration experience of Asian Indians is that they or their predecessors often entered circuitously, through other British colonies such as Hong Kong, Shanghai, South Africa, or Canada; this also meant that their fares to the United States were more expensive than those of other Asian Americans. In particular, Sikh men, who wore distinguishing beards and turbans, were soldiers in the British army, and along with some Hindus became part of a British servant/solider class that was exported to work in various outposts. They expected that service in the military would permit them to enjoy at least a modest level of respect and opportunity in these outposts, but the Asiatic Exclusion League emerged as one organization of White workers that spanned Canada and America and coordinated a fierce opposition to Asian labor immigration across these countries. While immigration laws tightened in Canada in the wake of racist, "anti-Oriental" violence, Asian Indians applied to directly immigrate to the United States, where they also encountered hostile receptions from White workers and outright exclusion from the 1917 Immigration Act.[23]

IMMIGRATION AND ECONOMICS BEFORE THE ANTI-ASIAN ZENITH, UP TO THE 1870s

It is important to understand the early immigrant experience of Asian Americans as ordinary laborers, merchants, and landowners prior to the onerous immigration and civil rights restrictions of the late 1800s forward. A common thread that runs through the experience of all Asian American groups—and that of many other immigrants—is their desire to benefit from the job and other economic opportunities provided by an industrializing American economy. In fact, Chinese immigrants were so enthusiastic about their prospects for wealth during the California gold rush (beginning in 1849) that they referred to themselves as *gam saan haak,* or "travelers to the Gold Mountain." But it is also very important to understand the developments that set the stage for the racial rationales, processes, and contexts that delayed or detoured these and other Asian American travelers on their journeys toward citizenship and opportunity by the early twentieth century.

Chinese Labor and Early Economic Competition

The discovery of gold at Sutter's Mill in California in 1848 started a population trickle into California and the American West that by the end of the rush in 1855 was a swelling tide of some 300,000 new persons, both citizens and immigrants. The Chinese comprised only 325 of the initial "forty-niners" but by 1870 numbered 63,000. The vast majority of them, 77 percent, were in the state of California, where they comprised 25 percent of the workforce. But Chinese immigrants could also be found in other parts of the West and Southwest, New England, and the South. The concentration of Chinese in California, however, was highest and is part of a broader story of race and U.S. immigration policy: one in which a group that is initially welcomed can, with increased numbers, be quickly viewed as a racial threat to White economic interests and political stability.[24]

In 1850 the Chinese and other foreigners were initially welcomed in California, seen by the White majority as a small but hardworking and diligent workforce that would help mine the newly discovered gold and contribute to the new state's economy in many other ways. California Supreme Court justice Nathaniel Bennett, who was asked to speak at a ceremony celebrating statehood, declared, "Born and reared under different Governments and speaking different tongues, we nevertheless meet here today as brothers. . . . You stand among us in all respects as equals. . . . Henceforth we have one country, one hope, one destiny." In San Francisco, Chinese residents demonstrated their appreciation to then-mayor John Geary for inviting them to join in a memorial to the late president Zachary Taylor: "The China Boys feel proud of the distinction you have shown them."[25]

Unfortunately, this mutual regard was short-lived. By 1852 state lawmakers viewed Chinese miners and Chinese laborers more broadly as potential economic menaces that had to be contained. The shift in attitude was the result of growing concern that Chinese laborers were taking away jobs from and undercutting the wages of Whites miners, among other workers. With Governor John Bigler newly elected, a committee of the state assembly issued a report warning against the supposed miner threat to White interests, and elements of this report became law. A special foreign miner's tax singled out the Chinese when it demanded a monthly $3 tax be paid by each miner who was not a citizen. The Naturalization Act of 1790 was a federal law declaring that unless a person was "White" he could not become a U.S. citizen. By the time the 1870 Civil Rights Act made the miner's tax illegal, California had collected some $5 million in fines. Likewise, in 1855 the legislature "Discourage[d] the Immigration to this State of Persons Who Cannot Become Citizens Thereof" by imposing a whopping fifty dollar docking tax on each ship's passenger who was ineligible for citizenship, to be paid by the ship owner. And in 1862 the state imposed a monthly "police tax" of $2.50 on each Chinese noncitizen (with some exceptions) in order to—and they were explicit in their intent—"protect Free White Labor against competition with Chinese Coolie Labor, and to Discourage the Immigration of the Chinese into the state of California."[26] *Coolie* was a term used to imply that these laborers were not being paid a wage but essentially were indentured servants.

Despite these growing restrictions to limit their economic opportunities in California and other states, Chinese laborers and merchants were vital economic contributors to the manufacturing and industrialization workforce throughout the nation. On the eastern seaboard, Chinese immigrants by the 1870s were pivotal to the emerging mill industry of towns like Lowell, Massachusetts—often labeled the cradle of the American industrial revolution—and the Chinese assumed various occupations in New York City and other urban centers. But they also found themselves increasingly economically segregated into restaurant and laundry businesses. A much touted contribution by Chinese laborers was the building of the **transcontinental railroad.** As one of the nineteenth century's technological marvels, the railroad ran the width of the continental United States and was the product of the Union Pacific Railroad that built east to west and the Central Pacific Railroad Company that built west to east. By 1865, some three thousand Chinese workers were employed in extremely tough and hazardous work. Although they did the same and often more difficult work than their White coworkers, they were paid less. Examples of this work included being lowered into the crevices of giant boulders in order to place explosives (many died because they were not pulled to safety in time) or to grade roads and lay track in scorching heat or subzero temperatures. These harsh conditions for unequal pay prompted two thousand Chinese workers to go on strike in 1867, although their demands were not met. When in 1869 at Promontory Point, Utah, the final spike was laid to connect the western and eastern tracks, no Chinese worker was invited to attend the ceremony.

Afterward, all ten thousand of them immediately had no job, and the company charged fares, despite meager wages, for them to ride the railroad they had just built to find new work. The alternate work they found included only a small range of occupations: restaurant operators, laundry and store owners, and more often as agricultural works or tenant farmers in areas like California's Central Valley. Such work segregated the Chinese, and eventually local ordinances were passed to further separate them from Whites, who perceived them as unsanitary, racial aliens with heathen ways.[27] This rapidly shifting process of Chinese workers being perceived by Whites as welcomed laborers and then as intruding aliens—i.e., as model minorities versus real threats—was not unique to the Chinese. As we stress throughout this chapter, this is a common set of roadblocks Asian American groups, at different times, have had to confront throughout their journeys in the United States.

Japanese, Filipino, and Korean Labor and the Hawaiian Plantation System

Unlike Asian laborers—e.g., Chinese railroad workers—who lived on the U.S. mainland, those who settled in Hawaii became such a large majority of the island's population and workforce that they had a greater ability to resist the mistreatment by employers against them. As Whites stiffened their opposition to Chinese labor in the mid–nineteenth century, this island kingdom, which was greatly influenced by White business and clerical interests, began to host much larger

Chinese workers were instrumental in the construction of the transcontinental railroad in the nineteenth century. Despite working alongside Whites and doing the same work, they were paid less and were excluded from the formal celebration of the railroad's completion.

numbers of Japanese, Korean, and Filipino workers. To provide a suitable "cognate" or proxy race to the Chinese, Hawaii's King Kalakau (1836–1891) made an agreement with the government of Japan in 1881. Between 1850 and 1920, some 300,000 Asians entered Hawaii, with the Japanese constituting about 43 percent of the total; Filipinos were 8 percent; and Koreans were a much smaller 2 percent. An obvious imbalance existed: whereas Asians became 62 percent of the island's population—e.g., the Japanese were 70 percent of the workforce—the proportion of Native Hawaiians was reduced to a mere 16 percent.

The conditions these immigrant workers confronted were often quite harsh. The plantation system of the island, like elsewhere in the world, was one of racial hierarchy—White managers, clerks, and foremen were at the top, with Asian workers at the bottom. One typical laborer job was to chop and gather huge, twelve-foot-high stalks of sugarcane all day in blazing heat for processing into molasses or sugar. Asian workers suffered many indignities, including drivers and foremen depersonalizing them by calling them by their assigned identification numbers (which hung by chains around their necks) and not by their names; or whipping them (among other forms of severe physical punishment), even though the kingdom had outlawed such practices by the 1860s.

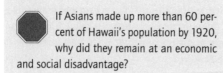

If Asians made up more than 60 percent of Hawaii's population by 1920, why did they remain at an economic and social disadvantage?

The contract labor system under which these early workers entered meant that they had to work essentially without wages until they could repay the recruitment company's costs for transporting them. After Hawaii was forcibly annexed as a territory and the 1900 Organic Law extended all U.S. laws to Hawaii, the contract labor system was abolished. In response, White planters formed the Hawaiian Sugar Planters Association (HSPA) in order to keep wages low. As we will detail below, these conditions and wages fomented an increasing number of strikes among Asian American workers, and many of these strikes were pan-ethnic, or across different groups.[28]

EARLY COMMUNITY FORMATION AMONG ASIAN AMERICANS

Despite the increasing level of hostility Asian immigrants faced in the late nineteenth and early twentieth centuries, and partly because of it, various Asian American groups formed strong ethnic communities. This process gave these groups specific resources—e.g., mutual aid or capital to form businesses, or the social cohesion to withstand anti-Asian regulations—thus shaping the roads of opportunity they would travel. For example, the rise of what came to be known as **Chinatowns** in San Francisco, New York, and elsewhere were essentially the Chinese adapting to the increasing racial strictures placed upon their businesses and often their residential communities, as Whites viewed them as alien and threatening.

Such communities not only compensated for the broader society's hostility toward an Asian American group by cultivating strong family, business, and social ties grounded in the specific needs and ethnic-national cultures of each group, they also formed **Asian American ethnic associations** or organizations that at times politically advocated on behalf of the group. When the 1882 Chinese Exclusion Law was enacted and began to place high restrictions on the number of Chinese laborers who were permitted to immigrate into the United States, a confederation of Chinese associations, facilitated in part by the Chinese consul in the United States, created a unified front—the *Zhonghua Huiguan* (Chinese Consolidated Benevolent Association)—to fight this legislation through litigation. The Japanese Association of America, formed in 1908, played a similar role in challenging anti-Japanese laws as they emerged.

This was also a time when African Americans and Mexican Americans were challenging their racial/ethnic exclusion from the rights and opportunities of being residents or citizens of the United States. In 1915 the National Association for the Advancement of Colored People (NAACP) filed its first civil rights brief in the U.S. Supreme Court with *Guinn v. United States,* which successfully struck down one unconstitutional attempt to disenfranchise Black voters. In 1931 *Alvarez v. the Board of Lemon Grove School District*, the first case to successfully challenge in a U.S. state court the racial/ethnic segregation of school children, was brought by a group of Mexican American parents, assisted by the Mexican government.[29]

In-Group Unity and Cross-Ethnic Challenges

The creation of Chinatowns and similar ethnic enclaves certainly did not mean that all Chinese or all Japanese shared similar interests. Many early Asian American associations were formed by groupings of immigrants who came from specific regions or villages of their homelands. It was only later that they organized across region-specific identities. Thus, in the words of Asian American historian Suecheng Chan, these organizations eventually helped transform persons into being "Chinese, instead of Toisanese or Heugsanese; Japanese, instead of Hiroshima or Kumamoto kenjin; Koreans, instead of Pyongyang or Inchon residents," and so on. In 1913 various Asian Indians in the United States submerged their sectarian differences to form a united Ghadar Party, or revolution party, that pushed for Indian independence from British rule. They actively attempted to stir rebellions against the British back home in the central Punjab region. To further understand how immigrant groups can maintain meaningful connections between themselves and their homelands, see Chapter 12.[30] A growing in-group unity allowed Asian American associations to generate wider memberships and effect more change through the strength of their supporters.

Often, unity between different ethnic-national groups, however, was complicated by the dynamics of homeland politics. For example, a cross-ethnic unity between Koreans and Japanese was very difficult precisely because of Japan's historic treatment of Korea as a political subject/colony, which fomented groups in the United States like the Korean Independence League and Korean National Brigade to protest this relationship. With the array of early Asian political, fraternal, civic, religious, cultural, and business groups that formed, some groups such as the so-called Chinese Six Companies served as vital intermediaries or even "power brokers"; although this was more true with some groups than with others. Some groups could be power broker elites because Asian American immigrant communities were often small and isolated.

These organizations, often supported by tradition, could direct the community's limited resources toward individuals and decide which persons and causes were legitimate and thus worthy of broad community support. Fairly sizable ethnic communities with thriving businesses such as Chinese "laundry men" or Japanese farmers could develop "ethnic economies" in which they created mutually beneficial business relationships that would circulate dollars among members. This process of group self-help in spite of (and often because of) racial exclusion was also fundamental to African Americans and Latinos. In contrast, smaller groups, such as Koreans and Asian Indians, had greater difficulty creating such communities.[31]

The Role of Women in Community Formation

It is worth noting that gender also fundamentally mattered in the early formation of Asian American communities. While there were differences among various Asian groups regarding the treatment of women within their communities and by White Americans, gender beliefs and norms that privileged the standing of men affected the well-being of Chinese and Japanese women, among others.

For all groups, there was the great difficulty of transporting and supporting a family on meager wages. But both the often male-dominant gender norms of these women's homelands and the racist and gendered assumptions of White state and federal government officials impacted the treatment of these women as immigrants. For example, the nature of the work that had American companies demand large numbers of Chinese male workers—mining and building railroads—was reinforced by homeland norms that disallowed women from traveling and doing manual labor assigned to men. As historian Sucheng Chan explains, "In societies where girls were reared to serve men and to procreate, respectable women did not travel far from home. The only females who left their ancestral villages were girls from destitute families sold as servants or prostitutes."[32] The handful of Chinese women who did immigrate prior to the 1880s were presumed, by many White officials, to be sex workers, and thus a series of local ordinances and then state and federal laws were enacted. These included the 1875 federal Page Act, which closed the immigration doors to a host of persons Congress presumed "undesirable."

The aim of these restrictions on the immigration of Asian women was to stem a perceived tide of prostitution. For all of these reasons, Asian men were in turn much more likely to be recruited by American and other companies than were women and especially children. The exact proportion of each, however, depended upon the group and the circumstances under which they immigrated. Among the Chinese who arrived in the United States between the late

1840s and 1880s, a mere 2 percent of them were women for precisely the reasons we have discussed. Among the Japanese, about 16 percent of those who arrived by the turn of the twentieth century were women. The Japanese example differs primarily because the U.S. government suddenly cut off the flow of Chinese

 How did the gender discrimination against Asian women discourage the establishment of strong community formation in the United States?

immigration, as opposed to the more gradual barriers erected against the Japanese. Thus formation of Japanese families inside the United States was still possible, as Japanese men unable to bring their wives initially to Hawaiian plantations could send for "picture brides," or women they married through mail correspondence. Wedding ceremonies literally occurred in two places; then these "picture brides" gained passports as tightly regulated by the Japanese and U.S. governments.[33] Overall, racial and gender discrimination impacted the growth of Asian American communities and their ability to grow in numbers large enough to lobby for equal opportunities and, eventually, citizenship rights.

RACE, REGION, AND THE ANTI-ASIAN ERA, 1870s–1940s

Because the majority White, Anglo-Saxon Protestants feared that new immigrants in general might change the "racial" composition of the United States, the period of the late nineteenth and early twentieth centuries was especially one of dead-end roads for the Chinese and of increasing roadblocks for the Japanese, Koreans, and Asian Indians. The 1924 **Immigration Act** completely closed off the entryway for all of these groups. In the case of Filipinos and others who were colonial wards of the United States, such as Puerto Ricans, it was a period of narrowing, uneven roads. Recall that the factors that determine a group's specific course and destiny, discussed in Chapter 1 and Table 1.3, include *why* it is perceived as a threat to the larger White society; *how* barriers are erected to its progress by those in government in certain contexts and periods; and *when* this occurs, given the resources the group could use as it presses for equity and opportunity. To explain these differences between how the major groups were treated, we stress the *when* part of this story in exploring how the racialization of groups differed according to region (such as Hawaii versus California) and timing (who was the out-group at each point in time).

The Anti-Asian Movement and the Chinese Exclusion Act

In 1868 the United States and China signed the **Burlingame-Seward Treaty,** which prohibited Chinese from naturalizing as U.S. citizens. This treaty established the right of citizens to mutually emigrate between both nations to fulfill the increasing labor demands of the United States. However, the economic and racial tensions of the 1870s, including an 1873 economic depression, brought increased White resentment of the Chinese and eventual anti-Chinese violence in California and elsewhere in what is termed the **Anti-Asian Movement.** Earlier perceptions shifted from the Chinese as noble and conscientious laborers to racial threats to White economic security.

In Los Angeles, almost twenty Chinese men were murdered—hanged or shot. In Chico, California, four Chinese workers were murdered by White men. The Knights of Labor, a union with a reputation for greater racial tolerance, passed in 1880 a bitterly anti-Chinese resolution that justified Chinese exclusion given "their bad moral habits, their low grades of development, their filth, their race differences with the Caucasian, and their status as willing slaves."[34] Dennis Kearney of the Workingmen's Party was an infamous leader of the Anti-Chinese Movement who was among those who demanded that the Chinese leave. By 1886, White miners complied at Rock Springs of the Wyoming Territory, and thus chased 550 Chinese coal miners and their families as they fled for their lives; 28 Chinese were killed and all of their homes were destroyed. By 1905, many of these labor unions had formed an alliance we referred to earlier as the Asiatic Exclusion League.[35]

It was in the midst of this labor turbulence and partly because of it that the 1882 **Chinese Exclusion Act (CEA)** was passed by the U.S. Congress as an answer to the so-called "Chinese problem." The 1875 **Page Act**, a federal statute, set the stage by prohibiting the entry of female prostitutes, contract laborers, and felons, but when interpreted liberally had the effect of excluding all Chinese women. The 1882 CEA prohibited the reentry of "Chinese laborers . . . both skilled and unskilled and [those] employed in mining" for ten years after they departed the United States, exempting students, diplomats, merchants, and teachers. Those who desired reentry had to get a certificate authorized by the Chinese and American governments. This certificate soon became the only document accepted for reentry. By 1888, to further tighten the screws after Congress was angered by China's refusal to sign a new treaty, the Scott Act, which prohibited all Chinese laborers from returning to the United States, cut off some 20,000 Chinese residents who had left property and family in the States. After the 1892 Geary Act and the 1902 extension of these measures, the exclusion was made permanent in 1904.

The United States tightened its Asian immigration restrictions for both domestic and international reasons. What motivated foreign countries to go along with the U.S. racialization of Asians?

As a result of the CEA, a series of agreements and laws then began to slowly shut off the flow of immigration from Japan, Korea, and India, but international politics played a role in this process. On the one hand, Japan wanted to ensure that its citizens were not treated as pariahs like the Chinese; on the other hand, the United States did not want to provoke a rising military power. Therefore, in 1907 a **Gentlemen's Agreement** was signed between the United States and Japan whereby Japan imposed restraints on the numbers of Japanese who could apply for emigration to the United States. Later, Japan did not object to President Theodore Roosevelt's Executive Order 596 that further limited the passports of Japanese laborers, and by 1920 Japan prohibited the practice of "picture brides."

Koreans comprised such a small percentage of the U.S. foreign-born, and their emigration was already so tightly regulated by Japanese colonial officials, that U.S. officials had no need to put specific restrictions in place. Asian Indians were excluded by an extremely broad net that the anti-Asian advocates cast in the 1917 Immigration Act, or what was later labeled the **Barred Zone**. This zone included most of the Middle East, Central Asia, South Asia, and Southeast Asia. (See Map 5.1.) There was a specific racial rationale for this exclusionary perimeter, which we explore in detail below. As colonial subjects of the United States, Filipinos had

Map 5.1 Asiatic Barred Zones, 1917

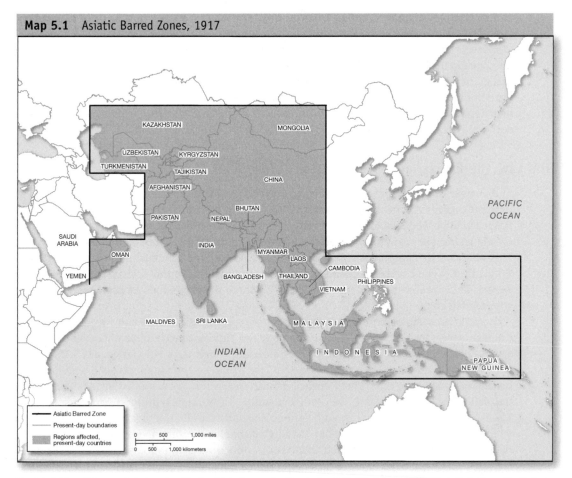

The Asiatic Barred Zone excluded most residents of Asia from emigrating to the United States. It was one of many measures the United States undertook to control immigration and the diversity of those coming into the country. The Philippines was exempt because of its status as a U.S. colony, but Filipinos were subject to strict immigration limitations.

a different status from all other Asian Americans; they were neither citizens nor immigrants, and were not subject to the same kinds of restrictions as other Asian groups. However, the 1934 Tydings-McDuffie Act that laid out the process of Filipino independence fundamentally limited Filipinos to a quota of no more than fifty new U.S. immigrants per year.[36]

Overall, it is important to note that residents of such U.S. colonies did not enjoy citizenship rights and opportunities on par with those of U.S. citizens, most especially White citizens. Even the handful of Asian immigrants and their children who became naturalized citizens, prior to immigration reforms in the 1950s and 1960s, did so through an extremely confusing patchwork of often contradictory court rulings that were influenced by White racial perceptions of a group as a model minority (i.e., a deserving immigrant) or a racial threat (i.e., an undeserving immigrant). Some rulings granted limited citizenship in a few cases—e.g., the Supreme Court ruling in *United States v. Wong Kim* (1898) that permitted the children of Chinese immigrants born in the United States to become naturalized citizens despite the Chinese Exclusion Act—while other rulings denied it—e.g., the 1923 *Thind* case discussed earlier, in which Asian Indian immigrants were denied naturalized citizenship because they were not considered White. It is only through their ethnic associations and civil rights groups that Asian Americans were able to mobilize challenges to the severe restrictions that the dominant society placed on them.[37]

The Law, the Courts, and Whiteness as a Roadblock to Citizenship

As was done with many other racial and ethnic minorities, one of the chief arenas used to limit the progress of Asian Americans who resided in the United States was the courts. Those Whites who viewed Asian Americans as racial threats used legal processes to prevent the foreign-born from being naturalized as citizens and from retaining rights such as landownership. This was done by demarcating persons who were considered White from those deemed non-White. Even if the courts conceded that those of Asian background born in the United States were in fact citizens, they did not consistently uphold the rights these Asian Americans were supposed to enjoy.

Recall that at the beginning of this chapter we explained how in *People v. Hall* (1854) the Chinese were considered too much of a non-White "inferior race" to have the right to testify against Whites in California courts. A generation later, in *In re Ah Yup* (1878), a U.S. California circuit court ruled that Ah Yup, who was Chinese, could not be a naturalized citizen because racially he was "Mongolian," not Caucasian; furthermore, as was validated by racial scientists, the plaintiff did not satisfy the "well settled meaning [of White] in common popular speech."[38] The U.S. Supreme Court supported a softened legal discrimination against Asian Americans when in *Yo Wick v. Hopkins* (1886) it concluded that local ordinances that racially discriminate against people, whether aimed at citizens or noncitizens (in this case, immigrant Chinese laundrymen), violate the Fourteenth Amendment's Equal Protection Clause. In the 1894 *In re Saito* case, however, a Massachusetts U.S. circuit court similarly upheld the bar against Japanese being eligible to naturalize as citizens.

Recall from Chapter 1 that in the late nineteenth and early twentieth centuries courts embraced the assumptions of scientific racism. For example, various races were presumed to be Aryan or descended from Indo-European language groups—i.e., Spanish, English, Hindi, Punjabi—but not all Aryans were White. This is why, as discussed at the beginning of this chapter, the U.S. Supreme Court arrived at two highly contradictory conclusions. In *Takao Ozawa v. United States* (1922), it stated that this Japanese man who wanted to be a naturalized citizen was "yellow" and thus not Caucasian or White according to the 1790 legal requirements. But just a year later the same Court stated in *United States v. Bhagat Singh Thind* (1923) that Thind, according to science, was in fact Caucasian because he was Aryan (i.e., Indian) but clearly not White as commonly understood. The underlying motive was one of racial distinction because from 1880 to the 1920s a series of laws were instituted in California, Arizona, and other western states barring Asian Americans as well as Blacks and sometimes Hispanics from intermarrying with Whites or Anglos.

Similarly there were a series of "Alien Land" acts in various states that forbade the Japanese, among others who were foreign-born, from owning property. It was not uncommon in California to see signs in the early twentieth century that read, "Japs Keep Moving! This Is a White Man's Neighborhood." Asian Indians so acutely feared the repercussions of the *Thind* case that many of them put their property in the names of their American-born wives, some of whom were Mexican. Generally, the 1920s was a period of heightened racial xenophobia or separatism— thus the reason why the 1922 **Cable Act** mandated that any White female citizen who married a noncitizen who was ineligible to naturalize would be stripped of her citizenship.[39]

Hawaii and the Spread of Pan-Ethnic Coalition-Building

Asian American communities resisted the tightening of U.S. immigration and citizenship requirements and other anti-Asian measures. Between 1882 and 1943, Asian American citizens and immigrants filed over 1,100 legal challenges to laws and court rulings. On the political and labor-organizing front, there was political conflict and competition among various Asian American groups. But there also were instances of political solidarity across different ethnic-national communities, as well as pan-ethnic coalition-building. Hawaii served as an incubator of pan-ethnic solidarity because Asian immigrants constituted a majority of the workforce on the islands, there was close contact among their communities, and they shared common grievances as workers. At the turn of the century, the Japanese were among the first to protest the wages and working conditions of Hawaiian plantations. In 1904 about 1,200 Japanese men who were field hands and skilled workers refused to resume work, despite police intimidation, until many of their demands were satisfied; this preceded an even larger strike of 7,000 workers in 1909 that was significant but sputtered to an end because of divisions among Japanese leaders. All the same, this incident demonstrated that workers were able to build solidarity strong enough to protest their conditions.

In an example of pan-ethnic coordination, Japanese and Filipino workers banded together ten years later in 1919 and cofounded the efforts of the Federation of Japanese Labor of Hawaii, led by Noboru Tsutsumi, and the Filipino Higher Wages Association, led by Pablo Manlapit, though Manlapit was a respected leader among both groups for a while. Although there was a lack of coordination due to Manlapit's erratic leadership, some 8,000 workers joined the action in February 1920. When Manlapit tried to end the strike, his Filipino comrades refused, and the plantation owners evicted 12,000 people from their homes (including children) in the middle of an influenza epidemic. This harsh punishment did not dissuade the workers, and 3,000 Japanese and Filipino workers held "77-cent flag parades" to protest wage inequities. Their six-month-long strike, which produced hardship due to lost wages, cost the HSPA some $12 million. Eventually, the planters made significant improvements in the areas of housing, sanitation, and pay. Such pan-ethnic coordination also occurred in California, where in 1903 a group formed the Japanese–Mexican American Labor Association (JMLA) that pushed for, but never convinced, the American Labor Federation to accept them as an affiliate.

When the Japanese became the targets of anti-Asian fervor both in Hawaii and on the West Coast, Filipinos in both locales emerged as the most militant group and provided leadership over a series of worker actions in the 1920s and 1930s, especially during the Great Depression.

Hawaii's sugar and pineapple plantations obtained cheap labor from Asian migrants. The harsh working conditions and low pay gave the migrants a set of shared grievances, and they banded together to protest conditions and advocate for greater equality.

Their militancy spread from Hawaii to the mainland of California, and while forming co-ethnic unions such as the Filipino Labor Union, they also formed the Field Workers Union, which included Filipino and Mexican workers.[40] These stories are part of an often unrecognized history of activism and multiracial, multi-ethnic coalition-building within Asian American communities. It's a history that is similar to twentieth century calls for fair wages and working conditions made by African Africans—e.g., the 1930s Brotherhood of Sleeping Car Porters led by A. Philip Randolph—and by Hispanics—e.g., the 1960s United Farm Workers Union led by Cesar Chavez.[41]

SHIFTS AND DECLINES IN THE ANTI-ASIAN ERA, 1940S–1960S

World War II brought a host of changes to American society, and Asian American communities were swept up in these changes. True to the often contradictory, divide-and-conquer approach that American policymakers took to questions of Asian American citizenship and opportunity during the early 1900s, the 1940s witnessed one of the most egregious examples of anti-Asian discrimination in American history—Japanese internment—as well as a relaxing of the 1920s immigration and civil rights restrictions placed on many of the other groups. For example, a 1942 Gallup Poll revealed the following: whereas most Americans had very negative attitudes toward the Japanese, they had positive feelings toward the Chinese because they were allies of the United States during World War II. A perfect example of the racial distrust of and animus toward the Japanese is given in the comment of a U.S. congressman, John Rankin of Mississippi: "Once a Jap, always a Jap. You can't any more regenerate a Jap than you can reverse the laws of nature."[42] At the conclusion of the war, international relationships had shifted; the Cold War between the Soviet Union and the United States created new geopolitical alliances; and the Civil Rights Movement—among other momentous, postwar changes—laid the groundwork for eventual Asian American political empowerment, as well as the end of the immigration quotas and restrictions of the 1920s.

World War II and Japanese Internment

On December 7, 1941, what President Franklin D. Roosevelt famously described as "a date which will live in infamy," the Empire of Japan launched a devastating air attack upon the U.S. military base of Pearl Harbor—killing more than 2,400 American personnel as well as destroying more than two dozen war vessels. The Roosevelt administration and the U.S. military declared virtually all persons of Japanese ancestry in the United States (citizen and noncitizen, no matter how strong their loyalty) as potential enemies of the state. Because the U.S. Congress declared war on the Axis Powers of Nazi Germany, fascist Italy, and imperial Japan, at first all foreign-born Germans, Italians, and Japanese were treated alike by the State Department. Shortly thereafter, however, the Japanese were racially singled out by the government in ways that were not done for Germans and Italians.

General John L. DeWitt, in charge of the U.S. Army's Western Defense Command, strenuously argued that the Japanese were a unique threat—they were likely internal spies—and eventually convinced the Roosevelt administration to issue Executive Order 9066. It and the subsequent Public Law 503 prohibited all persons of Japanese ancestry from living in areas and regions designated as vital to national security and authorized the U.S. Army and other agencies (especially the War Relocation Authority) to provide for the evacuation of such persons to in-land concentration camps. Quite notably, no evacuation orders were issued for Japanese Americans in the Hawaiian Islands. Once again, race and region mattered. After all, the Japanese comprised nearly 40 percent of the islands' workforce, and this was cited as the reason why "Different histories were coming home to roost in Hawaii [versus] California."[43]

Given that White ethnics also faced discrimination at this time, what were the biggest factors contributing to Asians' more extensive racialization during World War II?

As mentioned earlier, more than 110,000 Japanese American internees were processed and had to suffer relocation under this order, including 2,000 civic leaders who were first incarcerated on nothing more than racial suspicions. The forced relocation of so many persons and families exacted enormous psychological and personal costs—leaving their jobs, homes, and most of their possessions and wealth—and only taking some of their clothes and other bare necessities. Among the nearly dozen major internment centers that were established, three were the largest—Tule Lake, California (18,700 persons); Poston, Arizona (17,800 persons); and Gila River, Arizona (13,300 persons.) Often, these centers had been hastily constructed, were cramped, and provided spartan housing conditions against desert heat and harsh winters. In fact, Tule Lake had an excess of 6,000 more persons than it was built to accommodate. Likewise, the personal treatment of internees depended on whether the White administration of a camp was racially intolerant. Tule Lake was a racially hostile camp, and during one protest more than 2,500 persons demanded their immediate release. Likewise, at the camp of Manazar, California, 3,000 persons held a protest and tried to form a Kitchen Workers' Union. Army guards shot and killed two internees and wounded many others. It is very important to keep in mind that the overwhelming majority of these internees were American citizens who endured the great insult of being asked to reject their presumed allegiances to the "emperor of Japan," when, as *Nisei*—or second-generation Japanese Americans—many neither spoke Japanese nor had ever visited Japan.[44]

Copyright Bettmann/Corbis/AP Images

After the attack on Pearl Harbor, the U.S. government passed legislation that restricted Japanese Americans from living in certain areas and forced their relocation in-land. Anti-Japanese sentiment was high across the country, and Japanese Americans faced overt discrimination as they lost their jobs and homes, and had their families uprooted to internment camps.

Although there was only modest organized resistance to the order to evacuate (especially from the conservative Japanese American Citizens League), there clearly was great resentment after the evacuation process took effect. Along with numerous protests within the campus, some 4,000 *Nisei* refused to register for the army draft. More than 5,000 internees were so disgusted with these infringements upon their civil liberties by their own government that they eventually renounced their American citizenship. There were also several legal challenges to internment, which enjoyed little to no success. Among these challenges were four cases including those of three men—Minoru Yasui, Gordon Hirabayashi, and Fred Korematsu—and one woman, Mitsuye Endo.

These cases were eventually appealed to the U.S. Supreme Court. Yasui was a Japanese American citizen who worked for the Japanese consulate; he challenged the military's authority to nullify his citizenship, to arrest him, and to detain him under a curfew that only applied to noncitizens. The U.S. Supreme Court decided that a district court could not strip him of his citizenship under the Fourteenth Amendment, but Executive Order 9066 and Public Law 503 were still constitutional in giving General DeWitt wartime authority to order the evacuation of Japanese Americans. Hirabyashi was a college student who also challenged the curfew and the order to evacuate to an internment center; he was not vindicated in his claim of unconstitutional detention until 1987. Korematsu was a navy shipyard worker who also evaded the evacuation order until finally he was arrested by the military police outside a courtroom. Endo was a California state clerical worker who was a Methodist, had a brother in the U.S. Army, and had never been to Japan when she was fired and eventually relocated to Tule Lake. While the justices split over the *Korematsu* case and upheld the legality of DeWitt's evacuation orders, one small victory is that with the *Endo* case the Court unanimously agreed that President Roosevelt and the military had exceeded

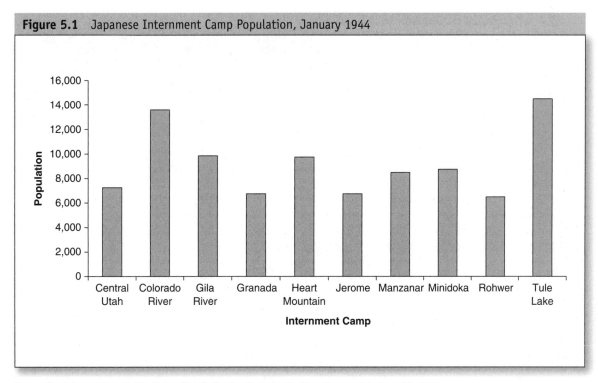

Figure 5.1   Japanese Internment Camp Population, January 1944

Source: Semi-Annual Report, War Relocation Authority, Statistics Section, January 1 to June 30, 1944.

their constitutional authority in detaining citizens who had never demonstrated any disloyalty to the United States.[45]

The Shifting Statuses of the Chinese, Filipinos, Koreans, and Indians

While the rights and opportunities of Japanese Americans were fundamentally narrowed during World War II, most other Asian American groups witnessed modest improvements in the areas of wartime employment, service in the American armed forces, and the relaxation of immigration quotas. For example, the ranks of Chinese Americans, especially Chinese American women employed in professional and clerical posts, tripled during the early 1940s. Well over a third of Filipino and Chinese servicemen and women were foreign-born; likely, some 20,000 Chinese Americans served during the war years—of course, in racially segregated units. As U.S. "nationals," Filipinos and their military service proved indispensable, especially in espionage efforts against the Japanese military.

It is ironic that given the treatment of Japanese Americans during the war, one of the most decorated battalions in the U.S. Army was the 442nd Regional Combat Team, or the military regiment whose tremendous valor won it seven Presidential Distinguished Unit Citations, 18,000 individual decorations, and a Congressional Medal of Honor. Due to manpower

BOX 5.2 CROSS ROAD

Still "Racial Threats"? From Japanese Internment to Post-9/11 Attacks on Arab and Asian Americans

The devastating attack by the Empire of Japan on the Pearl Harbor U.S. naval base was roughly seventy-five years ago. President Franklin Roosevelt's Executive Order 9066, which required the immediate relocation and internment of Japanese Americans into guarded camps, as well as the laws passed by Congress and verdicts rendered by the U.S. Supreme Court upholding internment, are also about eight decades old. And it has been many generations since a solid majority of Americans supported (or turned a blind eye toward) the blanket incarceration of 110,000 fellow American citizens—in this case, Japanese Americans—simply because it was presumed that their ethnic heritage made them inherently disloyal and a foreign threat during wartime. We may be tempted to argue that all of this happened so long ago that it has no bearing on the early twenty-first century and the current treatment of Asian Americans. After all, by 1999 the U.S. government had issued an official apology and paid $1.6 billion in reparations to more than 82,000 Japanese American families and their descendants. We might also reason that the U.S. government's internment of Japanese Americans and its turning a blind eye toward anti-Japanese racial violence after the Pearl Harbor attack differed from the U.S. government and specifically the George W. Bush and, later, Obama administrations' cautioning against anti-Arab and anti-Muslim violence after the September 11, 2001, attacks, perpetrated by about twenty men of Middle Eastern descent. But we do not need to argue that race played little to no role in the post-9/11 treatment of Arab Americans, Asian Americans, and Muslims to recognize that race and thus racial reactions have changed since the 1940s.[46] They still matter in the twenty-first century, especially as Asian Americans can still at times be perceived as racial threats.

The administration of George W. Bush and certain state and local law enforcement agencies were accused by civil rights and civil liberties groups of instituting national security and public safety policies that subtly encouraged the racial profiling of thousands of Arab Americans, South Asians, and Muslims, especially as Congress, through the 2001 Patriot Act and subsequent laws, granted the executive branch extraordinary powers to watch, arrest, question, and deport immigrants and detain citizens suspected of terrorism. By 2011, the Justice Department under President Barack Obama reported that anti-Muslim hate crimes, complaints of anti-Muslim job discrimination, and the harassment of children from Muslim families were on the rise. By 2007, the Justice Department had investigated nearly one thousand complaints of violence or discrimination directed at "Arab, Muslim, Sikh, and South Asian Americans." And in 2011, whereas 56 percent of Muslims polled by the Pew Research Center stated that Muslims who immigrated seek to adopt the customs and culture of Americans, only a third of the general public believed this to be the case.[47] In the end, race still shapes the lives of Asian Americans precisely because they and others who are perceived as foreigners can, at times of national crisis, be placed outside the boundaries of mainstream citizenship and political life.

Considering This Crossroad

- How did the U.S. response to the 9/11 attacks differ from its reaction to the bombing of Pearl Harbor? Consider both government and societal responses.

- More than a decade after the 9/11 attacks and the death of Osama bin Laden in 2012, why might Arab Americans and immigrants continue to be racialized?

- Can a nation ever respond to a surprise attack like Pearl Harbor or 9/11 without profiling or otherwise discriminating against those who share the perpetrators' descent? How?

requirements and the need to smooth over relations with allies like China, in 1943 the United States rescinded the Chinese Exclusion Act as well as elements of the 1924 immigration restrictions, therefore permitting 105 Chinese immigrants to enter each year. By 1952, particularly under the anticommunist McCarren-Walter Act, naturalization rights were expanded for all Asian immigrants, especially the Japanese.[48]

ASIAN AMERICAN POLITICAL EMPOWERMENT IN THE CIVIL RIGHTS ERA

The postwar years of the 1950s and 1960s witnessed the African American–led Civil Rights Movement and the Cold War ideological contest between the United States and Communist Russia. Both events pressured the U.S. government to rethink the paradox of projecting America as a bastion for democracy if its government sanctioned racial discrimination. Thus small gateways were opened for Asian Americans to be elected to public office, opportunities that had not existed prior to then. Akin to Latinos, as described in Chapter 4, these gateways were due to increasing numbers of Asian Americans forming communities that numerically could create effective electoral coalitions, as well as their being able to overcome race as a determinative or decisive barrier. In 1956, the same year that California finally repealed its law prohibiting "aliens" from owning land, Asian Indian American Dalip Singh Saund was elected to the U.S. Congress, representing the Imperial Valley area.

Along with this very important breakthrough, Hawaii, with its large population of Japanese Americans and other Asian Americans, also witnessed the election of Asian American officials. When it officially became a state in 1959, it elected Daniel K. Inouye and Hiram Fong to Congress. In 1962 Inouye, who was a decorated World War II veteran and Japanese American, was elected to represent Hawaii in the U.S. Senate and was the first Asian American to hold such a post. That same year Spark Matsunaga succeeded Inouye and was elected to the U.S. House. In 1964, a year prior to the landmark Immigration and Nationality Act that repealed the 1924 quotas, among other provisions (see Chapter 11), Patsy Takemoto Mink became the first Asian American woman elected to the U.S. House, again representing Hawaii. Mink served a total of twelve terms, or twenty-four years, in the U.S. House, and Inouye served forty-nine years, or eight terms, in the U.S. Senate before his death in 2012. Each of these people paved the way for the record election of Asian Americans (including three state governors) by the early twenty-first century.[49]

The "Model Minority" and "Racial Threat" Myths Today

While history is important because it tells us how a group's journey began, it is vital that you understand how past perceptions affect the well-being of Asian Americans today. The "model minority" myth and the "racial threat" myth are two such perceptions, but they take us in the wrong direction of understanding how the group can enjoy full citizenship rights and equal opportunities. Both of these myths racially degrade Asian Americans as alien "outsiders" to the dominant White society and polity or government and related political groups.

On the one hand, the model minority myth is wrong for it discounts the racial discrimination and prejudice Asian Americans face in contemporary society and misinterprets their progress. The model minority myth believes Asian Americans have overcome all racial barriers and are *such* highly successful non-White imitators of White values and norms that they are exemplary

ASSOCIATED PRESS

Senator Daniel Inouye (left), Representative Patsy Mink, and Representative Spark Matsunaga (right), all of Hawaii, talk with a visiting official (center) on the steps of the U.S. Capitol in June 1966. Hawaii's large Asian American population helped it to elect several Asian American candidates to Congress to represent their interests.

role models for other minorities. In 2013 Yale law professor and commentator Amy Chua, who is of Chinese ancestry, wrote a book with her husband, Jed Rubenfeld, who is of Jewish background, entitled *The Triple Package: How Three Unlikely Traits Explain the Rise and Fall of Cultural Groups in America*. The book stirred controversy because the authors claimed, similarly to the model minority argument, that there are eight cultural groups in the United States—including the Asian American groups of Asian Indians, Chinese, Iranians, and Lebanese Americans— that succeed above other groups because they have three key cultural traits: a superiority complex (belief that they are equipped to excel above others); inferiority complex (anxiety about falling behind other groups); and impulse control (ability to exert self-control over their actions and resources). The issue is whether Chua and Rubenfeld placed so much emphasis on the cultural strengths of these groups that they underestimated just how much the larger society and government does or does not erect racial or ethnic barriers to the progress of various groups.

If we only focus upon the educational and economic progress Asian Americans have made over the last several generations—e.g., high median incomes among Asian Indians—not only will we likely misinterpret the real reasons for this relative progress—e.g., higher numbers of household earners among Asian American families—we will miss instances when Asian Americans still confront barriers and prejudice. Only a few days after the 9/11 terrorist attack, a White man, Frank Roque, shot and killed an Asian Indian gas station owner in Arizona, Balbir Singh Sodhi, because Roque wanted to retaliate against the "Arabs" he saw as responsible for the attack; Sodhi was a member of Sikh religion, and thus he and his turban where taken as a foreign threat. Likewise, a Sikh Temple in Oak Tree, Wisconsin, was attacked in 2012 and six persons (not including the gunman) were killed when a man saw them as dangerous outsiders. And these were only two of a possible thousand threats or attacks that have occurred since 2001.[50]

On the other hand, the "racial threat" myth is wrong for it ostracizes or alienates Asian Americans. It presumes them to be too different from Whites, too foreign to American society, and/or too dangerous to the polity or the state to be given rights or access to opportunities. As was clear from the Japanese internment camps during World War II, at its extremes, this myth sees the only solution as one of alienating the person or group, containing them, and/or possibly violently attacking them. More recent

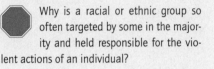

Why is a racial or ethnic group so often targeted by some in the majority and held responsible for the violent actions of an individual?

examples of racially motivated containment or violence against Asian Americans include the hate crimes of the 1982 murder of Vincent Chin; the 1989 murder of Ming Hai Loo; and the 2006 attacks upon Chinese teens in Queens, New York. When South Carolina governor Nikki Haley, who is of Asian Indian background, ran as a candidate for the Republican nomination in 2010, she was attacked as a foreign "turban" wearer and "raghead" (as was President Obama) by a member of her own party, state senator Jake Knotts, who is White. He considered her a foreigner and outsider that Republican voters and others would not accept as a legitimate leader. In all such instances Whites attack Asian Americans because they are feared and stereotyped as alien intruders or foreign threats.[51] Because Asian Americans are at times perceived as outsiders despite their educational and economic progress, race ranges from being a sometimes decisive to sometimes insufficient barrier to their having full citizenship rights and equal opportunities.

CONCLUSION: THE UNEVEN ROADS OF ASIAN AMERICAN OPPORTUNITY

Similar to the experiences of other racialized minorities, Asian Americans were racialized in ways that relegated their status and well-being to that of Whites, especially when they were viewed as threats versus contributors to the economic and political interests of Whites. Unlike the experiences of other racialized minorities who had resided in the United States for much longer periods, Asian Americans experienced fairly radical shifts in their rights and opportunities in short periods of time; furthermore, they were sometimes exploited (then as now) as "in-between" groups that Whites could project as hard workers but also as perpetual foreigners. Asian American political history greatly informs us as to how the process of racialization from the mid-1800s to the mid-1960s led Whites sometimes to perceive and act upon the broad racial category of "Asian" on the basis of group differences—e.g., the Chinese versus the Japanese in the early 1900s—or on the basis of this category as one undifferentiated group—e.g., the bar against all Asian immigration by the 1930s. In this respect, race and racism changed to suit the particular political and economic ends of Whites who were in power—i.e., politicians, industrialists and manufacturers, some union leaders, and so on. In the previous era of the late 1800s there was a great need for new workers while in the latter era of the 1930s there was a need for "racial stability" to create a broad White/non-White "color line."

Table 5.2   Asian American Roads of Racialization

When Barriers Arose	Why Barriers Arose	How Barriers Were Overcome	Outcome
Initial Recruitment of Asian Laborers, 1860–1882	• American empire-building leads to the political and economic domination of the Pacific (especially Hawaii) and the "Orient." • Chinese initially recruited as laborers but increasingly perceived as racial threat to White workers.	• The nations of Japan, Korea, and the Philippines had differing relationships with the United States as compared to China.	Insufficient → Decisive
Chinese Exclusion Act and Beyond, 1882–1940	• A series of anti-Asian acts and Supreme Court rulings result in the racialization and exclusion of Asian American populations.	• Asian American workers who were a majority in Hawaii had a different experience from Asian American workers who were a minority on the mainland. • Asian Americans very slowly formed communities and multi-ethnic labor groups to challenge their status.	Decisive → Absolute
Japanese Internment of World War II, 1940s	• World War II executive orders and laws forced Japanese Americans into internment camps while racializing them as automatic enemies of the state.	• Various Asian Americans legally challenged their being denied citizenship rights as part of an ongoing movement.	Decisive → Absolute
Cold War to Immigration Reform, 1950s–1960s	• Immigration and citizenship barriers persisted.	• Cold War tensions that resulted in the relaxing of barriers against the Chinese. • Passage of the 1965 Immigration and Nationality Act. • The initial election of Asian Americans to office.	Decisive → Insufficient
Race Matters with Opportunities, 1960s–2014	• Whites sometimes still perceive Asian Americans as a racial threat.	• Post-Immigration Reform gains in the economic and educational standing of Asian Americans.	Decisive → Inconsequential

The stories of the *Ozawa* and *Thind* Court cases are examples of how Asian American identity and citizenship claims sought to blur that color line.

While this chapter tells a story about when, why, and how race mattered most in shaping Asian American citizenship and opportunity, the factor of "when" entails both the times and locales race mattered most. We have stressed throughout this chapter that the experience, for instance, of Japanese and Filipino Americans in Hawaii somewhat differed from their counterparts on the mainland precisely because in Hawaii Asian Americans comprised a multiracial plurality. Although Asian Americans in Hawaii still suffered from racial discrimination, they also occasionally witnessed their interests being incorporated as part of the economic and social interests of the islands. Historian Gail Nomura is correct in stating that many Americans know far too little about the political history of Asian Americans. We have demonstrated just how integral this group has been in our understanding of race and ethnicity as a rapidly changing but still uneven road.[52]

DISCUSSION QUESTIONS

1. How have U.S. economic needs and foreign involvement encouraged the perception of Asian immigrants as model workers? In what ways is this perception evident today?

2. To what extent did foreign affairs play a role in the Asian migrant experience in the United States?

3. How and why did the experiences and racial treatment of Asian immigrants on the West Coast of the U.S. mainland differ from those on the islands of Hawaii?

4. Asian Americans established a pan-ethnic identity, as did Latinos (see Chapter 4). Comparing the histories of these two groups, what factors account for the opportunities and barriers for each forming such an identity?

5. How did the United States erect barriers to Asian inclusion from the 1870s to 1940s, and how successful were Asian Americans in challenging these roadblocks?

6. In what ways did Japanese internment during World War II encourage a continued policy of racialization—formal or informal—that may still resonate today?

7. Consider the history of Asian American ethnic and labor associations and civil rights groups. What are the commonalities and differences between the paths that Asian Americans took to lobby for civil rights compared with those of African Americans, Latinos, or Native Americans?

KEY TERMS

Asian American ethnic
  associations (p. 155)
Anti-Asian Movement (p. 157)

Barred Zone (p. 158)
Burlingame-Seward Treaty
  (1868) (p. 157)

Cable Act (1922)
  (p. 161)
Chinatown (p. 155)

6 Whiteness and the Shifting Roads of Immigrant America, 1780s–1960s

Instead of learning our language, we must learn theirs, or live as in a foreign country. Already, the English begin to quit particular neighborhoods surrounded by Dutch, being made uneasy by the disagreeableness of dissonant manners. . . .

—Benjamin Franklin (1751)[1]

The position in U.S. society held by racial and ethnic minorities, as well as their access to the rights and privileges of residents or citizens of the United States, can only be understood by assessing their position relative to that of White Americans. Throughout the nation's history, Whites have been at the top of the nation's racial hierarchy and have set the bar for measuring minority populations' relative advantage or disadvantage. We use the term *White* cautiously, however, because the popularly accepted definition of who is White and who holds the position at the top of the nation's racial hierarchy—let alone who controls government policies that define who is White and who is not—has changed considerably over time and will never be resolved. In 1751 founding father Benjamin Franklin feared the influx of Dutch immigrants to Pennsylvania, as noted in the quotation that introduces this chapter. In Franklin's view, the Dutch were lower on his racial hierarchy than the English and Scottish. A century and a half later, prominent scientist and social critic

> ## Box 6.1 Chapter Objectives
>
> - Explain the racial considerations incorporated into the nation's founding documents and the motivations behind them.
> - Identify how societal factors and government practices shaped options for new populations arriving from Europe and challenged the conception of Whiteness.
> - Explain how White identity expanded to include White ethnics by the dawn of the Civil Rights era.
> - Discuss the ways in which government created long-term advantages for Whites not available to other races in U.S. society.

The late nineteenth century saw a diversification of the origins of immigrants to the United States and, particularly, the migration of many Southern and Eastern Europeans who passed through Ellis Island and other immigrant inspection stations. When these "new" migrants arrived, some in the dominant society challenged whether they could assimilate, participate in the democracy, and, ultimately, whether they were White.

Madison Grant wrote a bestselling book on the changing ethnic composition of the United States. He identified similar racial gaps to Franklin, but his comparison was to the new immigrants of his era, migrants from Mediterranean and Baltic countries. Grant observed that the new immigration "contained a large and increasing number of the weak, the broken and the mentally crippled of all races drawn from the lowest stratum of the Mediterranean basin and the Balkans. . . . Our jails, insane asylums and almshouses filled with this human flotsam and the whole tone of American life. social, moral and political has been lowered by them."[2] The ethnic groups feared by Franklin and Grant traced their origins to Europe, and today would be understood as White. This chapter explores how, at various points in U.S. political history, nationality groups previously thought to be racially different from Whites came to be understood as such both in popular discourse and, more important, in terms of rights and privileges. As should be evident in our discussion so far in *Uneven Roads*, this ability to move from a status of "other" and lower on the nation's racial hierarchy to being understood as equal to the White majority has not been universal.

In this chapter, we examine the historical building blocks of White racial identity in the pre–Civil Rights era and offer some preliminary assessments of its legacies for today's society. First, we analyze the constitutional and statutory roots of White identity in the United States and how these changed from 1787 to the 1960s. We show that from the nation's first days, U.S. society sought to privilege Whites relative to non-Whites. Although policymakers were not always clear on who was White and who wasn't, the nation created powerful incentives to be seen as White and introduced roadblocks for those who were not. Next, we assess specific policies that created opportunities and advantages for Whites relative to others in U.S. society. This is not a recap of policies that disadvantaged Native Americans, African Americans, Latinos, and Asian Americans (see Chapters 2 through 5). Instead, we identify specific policies that gave Whites added resources and advantages—including wealth in land, other property, financial assets, education, and social networks—that put them on a highway that skipped over many parts of the uneven roads that non-Whites had to travel.

WHO IS WHITE? RACIAL CONSIDERATIONS AT THE TIME OF THE FOUNDING

The nation's concerns with allocating state benefits based on race are evident in some of its earliest documents, including the Constitution and some of the first legislation passed by Congress. This practice continued through the Civil Rights era of the 1960s. Yet despite this desire to allocate state benefits based on race, federal and state governments proved less able to define who was "White" and, consequently, should receive the benefits. As immigrants in the nineteenth century began to arrive in the United States from parts of Europe other than the north and west, conflict arose over who was White. This was particularly evident in the port cities of the East Coast such as Boston, New York, and Philadelphia, and the industrial cities of the Midwest such as Chicago and Detroit, where both **native stock** (U.S.-born adults of U.S.-born parents) and new European immigrants resided. Courts tried to sort out this question, using an amalgam of the judges' perceptions of common sense and, beginning in the twentieth century, efforts to interpret genetics, biology, and social science. Ultimately, these efforts failed.[3] Courts and policymakers found it much easier to define who was *not* White and, consequently, not entitled to the full benefits of U.S. citizenship.[4] Changes in legal interpretations of White identity, then, were more often the result of an individual or group's battle for inclusion than a consensus over what it meant to be White. In this sort of environment, varying popular perceptions meant that an individual could be White in some places or some social settings and not White in others.

Legal Foundations of Racial Difference in Early America

Although explicit mentions of race were largely absent in the debates that surrounded the founding of the United States, race and racial hierarchy were central to the compromises that allowed for the nation's founding. Quite simply, the United States would not have been able to establish the Constitution that has served as its governing document without a willingness to treat African American slaves as three-fifths of a person. For reasons that we have discussed in Chapter 2, Native Americans were also constitutionally distinct. In contrast, indentured servants—European immigrants, often of a lower social class than the U.S. natives—were offered constitutional protections equivalent to the native (White) stock, although these were guaranteed somewhat ambiguously. Early U.S. law, specifically the first **naturalization** law, established privileges that were available to Whites—White males, to be more specific—that were not available to residents of other races. As a result, White males had a presumption of citizenship throughout the nation's history; their political organization could focus on ensuring that they could exercise the rights and privileges of citizenship fully, regardless of their ancestry or ethnicity.

Native Americans and Blacks in the Constitution

Under the nation's first governing document, the Articles of Confederation, the power of state governments was dominant. Governance under the Articles of Confederation, however, was unstable, and a new document was drafted to succeed it. The U.S. Constitution established prerogatives for the federal government that limited state powers. It concentrated power over relations with Indian tribes with the national government. Article I, Section 8, of the Constitution provided that Congress held the exclusive power "To regulate Commerce with foreign Nations, and among the several States, and with the Indian Tribes."

After the United States was founded, a formal structure of treaties helped to shape U.S.–Native American relations. Under this approach, vesting the federal government with the power to negotiate with Indians made a great deal of sense. Yet, as the U.S. treatment of Native populations worsened in the nineteenth century, federal regulatory powers enforced over Indian nations ensured that Native Americans had little voice in their governance and little ability to improve their position in U.S. society. Indians were not viewed as U.S. citizens at the time of the Constitution's ratification, and it wasn't until 1924 that U.S. law recognized all Indians as U.S. citizens. Without citizenship, Native American resources to advocate for their interests were limited. They could not use the vote or democratic institutions to protect their interests, or legislatures to protect their economic interests.[5] (See Chapter 2.) At least, early in the nation's history—had they been granted the same rights as Whites—their large numbers and population concentration would have ensured substantial representation in Congress and the state legislatures.

The Constitution also failed to speak of slaves, though it did create protections for slavery as an institution. This absence of discussion should not be read to mean that slavery was not an active part of the debates over the Constitution in 1787. The framers understood that slavery was too contentious an issue to leave regulation solely to the states. In fact, the Constitution would not have been ratified without a series of compromises that further entrenched slavery and diminished the rights of Blacks in U.S. society relative to White Americans. Perhaps the most controversial of these was the **Enumeration Clause,** or Three-Fifths Clause (Article I, Section 2), which states: "Representatives and direct Taxes shall be apportioned among the several States which may be included within this Union, according to their respective Numbers, which shall be determined by adding to the whole Number of free Persons, including those bound to Service for a Term of Years, and excluding Indians not taxed, three fifths of all other Persons." In this clause, "three fifths of all other Persons" refers to Black slaves.

Neither side was particularly concerned about African American rights in this debate over representation. Instead, the Enumeration Clause pitted slave against nonslave states. Slave states wanted slaves counted as individuals for the purpose of "enumeration," the allocation of seats in the U.S. House of Representatives, which was based on population for all but the smallest of states (each state is guaranteed one seat in the House regardless of population), but not counted as persons for the purposes of taxation. States with few slaves did not want them counted at all for purposes of enumeration, recognizing that the bodies of the slaves would add to Southern representation in Congress and that slaves would not have any voice in the selection of their congressional representatives. They did, however, want slaves counted for the purposes of taxation. The resolution of this controversy—the three-fifths compromise—counted each slave as three-fifths of a person for the allocation of congressional representation and for taxes. (At the time of the Constitution's ratification, the only tax the national government could charge was a "head tax," a tax of equal amount on each individual.)

A further protection of slavery was needed to ensure ratification of the Constitution. Slave states wanted to ensure that the new Congress would not halt the slave trade. Although there was little opposition to slavery as an institution at the time, there was a growing international movement opposing the slave trade. Article I, Section 9, of the Constitution prohibited Congress from prohibiting the importation of slaves before 1808, while avoiding a mention of slaves or immigrants destined for slavery: "The migration or importation of such persons as any of the states now existing shall think proper to admit, shall not be prohibited by the Congress prior to the year one thousand eight hundred and eight. . . ." When this prohibition expired in 1808, Congress immediately passed such legislation.

The final recognition of slavery in the U.S. Constitution required that all states enforce the rights of slaveholders to exercise their right to hold slaves as property. Article IV, Section 2, of the Constitution, popularly known as the Fugitive Slave Clause, added to the responsibility of all states under the Constitution the following: "No Person held to Service or Labor in one State, under the Laws thereof, escaping into another, shall, in Consequence of any Law or Regulation therein, be discharged from such Service or Labor, but shall be delivered up on Claim of the Party to whom such Service or Labor may be due." (See Chapter 3.) This remains a part of the Constitution to this day in Article IV, the section that focuses on the responsibilities of the states to the other states and to the federal government. An effort to explicitly repeal it as part of the post–Civil War constitutional amendments failed in the U.S. House of Representatives.

Immigrants and Naturalization: White Inclusiveness

The limits placed on non-Whites in the exercise of citizenship extended beyond Native Americans and African Americans during the nation's founding. Among its first acts, the new U.S. Congress passed the Naturalization Act of 1790, which limited immigrants' ability to naturalize (to become voluntary U.S. citizens) to "free white persons" who had lived in the United States for two years. This legislation is important both for what it does and does not say. It explicitly limits voluntary citizenship to Whites (and, more narrowly, to White males; until the 1920s, only men could naturalize). For the era, the legislation was largely a recognition of immigration patterns, as almost all voluntary immigrants to the

Can the nation ever overcome the racialization incorporated into America's founding documents?

United States were from Europe. Although not so obvious, the Naturalization Act of 1790 is also important to Whites for its inclusiveness. Other than "free," it establishes no other limits within Whiteness, such as Benjamin Franklin's observations quoted earlier in the chapter might suggest would have appeared in law. Europeans were granted largely unfettered access to immigration and to citizenship in 1790, which remained the legal norm until racial restrictions on immigration were removed from U.S. immigration law in 1950.[6]

The founding of the United States included the establishment of a racial hierarchy in which Whites, however defined in policymakers' minds, had rights not available to other races. From its first days, this notion of Whiteness included Europeans who were not from Northern and Western Europe and those of a lower social class (those "bound to service for a term of years"), although these groups faced discrimination as well. For these non–native stock Whites, then, race was insufficient to explain differences in rights and social mobility. As the previous chapters have shown, this racial hierarchy established specific limits—roadblocks—to other races. For non-White populations, race was decisive at the time of the American founding and for many years afterward. At the time of the founding, there was little need to define who was White. Instead, the law (and practice) identified racial groups—particularly Native Americans and Blacks—to whom the rights and protections of citizenship would not apply. As we will see, states were more explicit in their definition of Whiteness—and, more important, non-Whiteness—though their definitions varied from state to state.

LARGE-SCALE IMMIGRATION AND OVERCOMING ETHNIC EXCLUSION

The meaning of White identity in the United States faced its first significant challenge in the mid–nineteenth century as the origins of European immigrants in the United States diversified. These new immigrants—who began migrating in large numbers in the 1830s—were diverse on two dimensions. First, their countries of origin widened the sources of newcomers to the United States, adding Ireland and Germany in particular. Second, many were Roman Catholic and Jewish. Immigrants prior to this period were overwhelmingly Protestant. (We discuss the history of U.S. immigration policy in Chapter 11.) Here, it is important to note that these new arrivals (whose numbers continued to grow and diversify for nearly one hundred years) were initially viewed as non-White by many. White, in this sense, was synonymous with origin in countries that sent the original immigrants to the United States, particularly England, Scotland, and perhaps France and the Netherlands.

Over time, and certainly by the dawn of the Civil Rights era, immigrants and their descendants from other parts of Europe were more commonly viewed as part of the White mainstream. Although there are many signs of this acceptance, perhaps the most dramatic was the election of John F. Kennedy—a descendant of Irish immigrants and a Roman Catholic—as president of the United States in 1960. To the modern eye, this electoral outcome was no great accomplishment in racial/ethnic inclusion. In its time, however, it reflected almost as dramatic a change in intergroup relations and acceptance as did the election of Barack Obama to the presidency in 2008.[7]

State and Local Tolerance: The First Step in Acceptance

Immigrants from throughout Europe made the transition from racial outsiders to widespread acceptance as White in two stages. The first phase appeared at the local and state levels, emerging slowly in the late nineteenth and early twentieth centuries. European immigrants from "new" parts of Europe or who were not Protestant—such as those from Ireland and Germany in the mid–nineteenth century and from Southern and Eastern Europe late in the nineteenth century—were initially met with contempt and discrimination. In some cases, though not universally, this took on a racial dimension, with immigrants from new parts of Europe understood to be non-White (the sign "No Irish or Blacks Need Apply" appeared in different iterations for most subsequent European immigrant groups). Although these new immigrants were not understood to be White, they also were not subject to the same restrictions in the law that African Americans faced. David Roediger, a historian of U.S. race, immigration, and labor, characterizes their racialization from the time of their immigration to the mid–twentieth century as racially "in-between" peoples.[8] It was this in-between status that we argue allowed White ethnics to become White by the Civil Rights era.

Immigrants in this racial middle ground were able to overcome their initial exclusion with two resources—numbers and federalism.[9] The numbers story is relatively straightforward. In the nineteenth century, the United States increasingly urbanized and industrialized. The engine of this national change was the massive migration from the "new" immigrant-sending countries. In other words, economic leaders in the United States needed labor and sought immigrants to fill that need. European immigrants in the nineteenth and early twentieth centuries provided the labor to fuel the massive national economic growth of this period. Although White ethnic workers were preferred by most employers to free Blacks (before the Civil War) and Black workers (after the War), the African American labor force was not large enough to meet national economic demands. This gave White ethnic workers the potential to influence how they were treated, not just in the workplace, but also in the larger society. New immigrants saw how Blacks were treated in society and organized to ensure that they were seen differently (and in a better light), despite the fact that free Blacks and recent immigrants shared a class position at the bottom of the economic ladder in many cities.[10] As unions grew in the period after the Civil War, industrial workers organized to distinguish themselves from slaves and, later, from agricultural labor that they argued was less than free.[11]

> Could White ethnic immigrants have improved their position in society without engaging in the racialization of Blacks?

The unionized workers (and industrial workers, more generally) made the claim that they were in control of their labor where slaves and, later, agricultural workers were dependent on their masters or the landowners and, consequently, not free. In this racialized behavior, White ethnic immigrants reinforced the U.S. racial hierarchy and further ensured that African Americans remained at its bottom rung.

Throughout this period, White ethnics were more likely to come into routine contact with African Americans than were the native stock population. Their similar class positions meant that they were more likely to live around each other and to compete for nonskilled employment.

Copyright Bettmann/Corbis/AP Images

The Civil War draft placed a heavy military burden on White ethnics and free Blacks. As the two groups often competed for the same jobs, the tensions increased with the war. Draft riots like this one in New York City in 1863 often resulted in casualties.

This labor market competition and residential segregation led to open and frequent racism and often violence against Blacks in northern cities. Violence flared when Blacks were perceived to encroach on White prerogatives. A notorious example was the Civil War–era draft riots. Rich Whites could buy their way out of the draft, leaving much of the military service burden on free Blacks (who were more than willing to join the Union Army) and White ethnics, some of whom objected to risking their lives to free Southern slaves. The draft riots resulted in at least one hundred Black deaths, many by lynching, and over two thousand injuries. Ultimately, the Union Army had to be called in to restore the peace.

The role of federalism in structuring White advantage is a bit more complicated, but equally important to the steady transition of European immigrants into White racial identity. **Federalism** is a system of government in which both the national government and subnational governments—the states, in the case of the United States—have independent powers and responsibilities to their citizens. The concentration of significant political power at the local and state levels and the concentration of many European immigrants in the nation's major cities ensured that White ethnics were able to gain political power relatively quickly. They developed institutions—such as urban political machines and trade unions—that mobilized the ethnic vote, educated new immigrants to American citizenship, and rewarded ethnic leaders. This local political power ensured that, despite the discrimination that White ethnics experienced based on native stock perceptions that they were less than equal ("in-between peoples" in the Roediger model), their newcomer status, and their class position, neither national, state, nor local governments created laws or policies that excluded *all* Irish or Italians or Poles as a racial group from citizenship rights. In other words, the state never formally racialized these populations. The children and grandchildren of immigrants from new parts of Europe undoubtedly faced more exclusion and fewer opportunities than did the native stock population, but this exclusion was primarily class-based (although certainly ethnic discrimination remained) and could, over time, be overcome. Thinking back to the framework discussed in Chapter 1, ethnicity was an insufficient barrier for White ethnics.

✚ BOX 6.2 CROSS ROAD

General Grant's Expulsion of Jews "as a Class"

The Jews, as a class violating every regulation of trade established by the Treasury Department and also department orders, are hereby expelled from the department [of Tennessee] within twenty-four hours from the receipt of this order.

—Excerpted from General Orders No. 11,
Military District of Tennessee,
December 17, 1862

Just two weeks before President Abraham Lincoln issued the Emancipation Proclamation, one of Lincoln's generals in the field, and future president, Ulysses S. Grant issued an order that, had it stood, would have taken U.S. race relations in a very different direction. Grant used his authority as general of the district of Tennessee (extending from southern Illinois through Mississippi to the Gulf of Mexico) to issue General Orders No. 11, which called for the expulsion of all Jews from the district. Neither the order itself nor the historical record offers explanation for why Jews were targeted for this punishment. The order may have taken as fact discriminatory sentiments of Jews as profiteers in wartime.[12] Such a belief taps millennia of anti-Semitic bias evident in Europe in this era, but much less prevalent in the United States.

Jews in the district quickly mobilized to have the order reversed. One resident traveled to Washington and, with the intervention of a Republican member of Congress, spoke with President Lincoln, who immediately commanded General Grant to reverse the order. Many newspapers also editorialized against it. That orders such as these would be issued, even in wartime, raises troubling questions about religion and the boundaries of White ethnicity. Although the Fourteenth Amendment was still a few years in the future, the principle of individual liberty was one that was understood to extend to all Whites (or, perhaps, to all White males). Thus a group punishment such as that called for in General Orders No. 11 indicated a perception that Jews were substantively different from other Whites and did not share the same constitutional protections. It also raised fears in Jewish communities that the United States could move toward policies that treated Jews not as individuals, but as members of a suspect class. Were this to have happened, the treatment of Jews in the United States would have more closely paralleled their treatment in Europe, an ominous trajectory for the small U.S. Jewish community.

The historical record indicates that General and later President Grant strongly regretted issuing General Orders No. 11. His administration was noted for appointing more Jews to public office than had previous administrations, and appointments of Jews to posts they had not previously held.[13] Grant won great admiration from Jewish leaders and earned a high share of the Jewish vote in his 1872 reelection campaign. His administration also shared the major policy concern of the era's Jewish leaders. Both opposed a proposed constitutional amendment to "declare the nation's allegiance to Jesus Christ and its acceptance of the moral laws of the Christian religion, and to so indicate this as a Christian nation." Ultimately, the proposed religious amendment failed.[14]

Though the order ultimately had little effect, it may have sensitized Grant to the plight of Jews in the United States, and it offers an example of the constant negotiation over the boundaries and limits of White ethnicity in the United States. Just as Germans in the pre-Revolutionary era or southern and eastern

(Continued)

(Continued)

European immigrants in the early twentieth century found, Jews in this era had to fight to maintain what had previously been widely accepted about their status in the United States.

Considering This Crossroad

- As White ethnics, how were Jews able to use the institutions and resources of the government to promote their concerns and interests on the expulsion order?

- Had President Lincoln chosen to defer to General Grant on General Orders No. 11, how might the racialization of Jews in the United States have paralleled that of Blacks, Latinos, and/or Asian Americans?

- Based on your readings in this chapter and others, why are individual liberties, particularly of minority groups, under greater threat in wartime?

Scientific Racism and National Policy: The Second Step in Acceptance

The second stage of this transition from a potential path as racial outsiders to White racial identity for new European migrants and their descendants occurred around the turn of the twentieth century. Newly emerging scholarship in the social sciences in this period began to add a scientific veneer to what had long been group biases against the new European migrants.[15] Madison Grant, quoted earlier in this chapter, was among the best known proponents of this scientific racism. (See Chapter 1 for a more detailed discussion of scientific racism.) Southern and Eastern Europeans, who made up the vast majority of new immigrants in the early 1900s, were viewed in this scholarship as a lower race than Northern Europeans—not as low as Blacks, but also not the highest example of White. Scientific racism led to efforts to shape national policy, an area of politics in which the new European immigrants and their descendants had little influence. One tangible effort to restrict their rights included **Prohibition,** the nationwide ban on the sale, production, importation, and transportation of alcoholic beverages that was enacted in the U.S. Constitution from 1920 to 1933. In the popular understanding, the new immigrants consumed more alcohol and society needed to control their excesses. In reality, of course, alcohol consumption was not limited to Southern and Eastern Europeans, but advocates of Prohibition were able to tap native stock resentment against the new immigrants and their children to amend the Constitution and create a massive new law enforcement bureaucracy.

Other initiatives that appeared in this period that privileged descendants of Northern and Eastern European migrants over other Whites included new class-based limits on voting (such as poll taxes, secret ballots, and voter registration requirements) that disproportionately lowered urban and White ethnic voting, new restrictions on immigration (national origin quota laws, discussed later), and restrictions on union organizing. In addition, Congress refused to pass a reapportionment act after the 1920 census, the only decade in which Congress waited until the end of the decade to reapportion Congress as required by the Constitution to reflect the changed population found in the decennial census. This was in part because of the recent rapid growth of the new White populations; Congress recognized that a reapportionment early in the decade would speed the political transition that the nation was experiencing by increasing legislative representation of Southern and Eastern European migrants and their U.S.-born children. Nongovernmental actors also sought to slow the opportunities of this era's new immigrants and their children. Elite universities sought to establish maximum quotas, particularly for Jews. Racial covenants were added to the titles of new residential communities to prevent the sale of the property to Jews (or to Blacks).

The scientific racism of this era had the potential to divide what would today be viewed as Whites along racial lines. Yet, by the time scientific racism began to shape political debates on European immigrants and their status in society, White ethnics had expanded their political resources so that they could mobilize to challenge and overcome efforts to limit their rights. The repeal of Prohibition, for example, became a political reality when White ethnics moved into the Democratic Party and voted at unprecedented levels in the 1932 election.

WHITE IDENTITY AT THE DAWN OF THE CIVIL RIGHTS ERA

The steady expansion of White identity to encompass all immigrants from Europe and their descendants was largely complete when civil rights organizing became a mass movement after World War II. This is not to suggest that significant differences had disappeared among "White" Americans. On the contrary, significant class, religious, regional, educational, and attitudinal differences remained, but these differences no longer served as an effective barrier to Euro-American racial identification as White.[16]

Why did White identity coalesce in the mid–twentieth century? We offer five overlapping explanations, all of which were necessary preconditions for the expansion of White identity. First, Congress enacted the national origin quota laws in the early 1920s. This immigration legislation sought to limit the migration of Southern and Eastern Europeans by allocating immigration visas based on the nation's ethnic composition in 1890, the last census before Southern and Eastern European migration surged. (For a more complete discussion of this legislation, see Chapter 11.) These laws slowed immigration from Europe. They were followed over the next two decades by the Great Depression, and World War II, which slowed migration from Europe further. As a result, the number of new immigrants to the United States was at a historic low. New immigrants are more likely than longer-term immigrants or their children to be culturally and linguistically different from majority populations. Given the low levels of new immigrants, majority populations were less likely to focus on the differences among European migrants (and, hence, differences among Whites).

For some populations, the boundaries of race and ethnicity have been fluid, while others are more rigid. Will racial boundaries continue to be in flux in the future? Why or why not?

Second, European-descent populations had continued to use the political process to progressively improve their ability to defend their rights in the United States. As we have shown, this ability to use politics has first appeared at the local level—in cities with large numbers of immigrants—in the mid–nineteenth century, but increasingly their political influence spread to the state and national level in the twentieth century. This new political influence appeared most dramatically beginning in the late 1920s. In 1928 the Democratic Party nominated a Catholic New Yorker of Irish descent, Al Smith, to serve as the party's candidate for the presidency. Smith was easily defeated by Republican Herbert Hoover, but his successful nomination demonstrated the new centrality of the urban, ethnic vote for the Democratic Party. (See Box 6.3.) Smith's candidacy also began a steady process of the naturalization and political mobilization of large numbers of turn-of-the-century immigrants (many Southern and Eastern Europeans) and their children, as well as their increasing Democratic partisanship.[17] Their votes ensured the election of Franklin D. Roosevelt in 1932 and the ethnic diversity of the leadership of the New Deal. The newly central role of White ethnic Democratic voters ensured the repeal of Prohibition in 1933. By the early 1930s, these new immigrants and their children had attained sufficient political power through naturalization, mobilization, and electoral participation to advocate for themselves, assert their right to drink, and elect candidates of their choice, including many co-ethnics.

Third, the Great Depression in the 1930s and then World War II in the early 1940s served in different ways to equalize European-descent Americans. Class differences between native stock and new immigrant Whites diminished considerably during the economic hardships of the Great Depression. World War II showed the bravery and collective spirit of Americans of all racial and ethnic backgrounds (including non-Whites). The rhetoric of the war amplified this shared struggle against the racial/ethnic triumphalism of the German and Japanese regimes. The popular fiction that appeared soon after the war, frequently authored by the sons of Southern and Eastern European migrants, showed a military in which White soldiers of varied ancestries ensured the American victory.[20] (These novels were less concerned with presenting Native American, African American, Latino, and Asian American soldiers as heroes.)

Fourth, with the decline of new immigration, the descendants of earlier waves of European migrants came into more contact with one another and intermarried in larger numbers. Although this was a slow process at first, intermarriage sped the recasting of White identity away from a purely ethnic identity.[21] As national origin identities began a slow decline, differences between European-ancestry populations in the larger population also diminished. This process reduced the salience of claims that some European immigrants or ancestries were not racially White.

Finally, the economy of the postwar period allowed for what sociologist Richard Alba has called non-zero-sum mobility for White ethnics.[22] In other words, second- and third-generation migrants from Southern and Eastern Europe, whose ancestors' Whiteness had been challenged in earlier eras, could make economic and social gains in the 1940s and 1950s without taking away from the economic or social positions of Whites whose roots in the United States went back further in the nation's history. The postwar economy grew sufficiently rapidly, and the need for skilled workers so outstripped the labor pool that White ethnics were welcomed into the economic and social benefits of Whiteness and not seen as challengers to the status quo. Blacks, Latinos, and Asian Americans, on the other hand, were not welcomed into new sectors of the economy as readily, and a much lower share had the educational credentials and personal contacts to enter the skilled professions. Employers in this era sought to change immigration law to expand immigration opportunities from Europe rather than to train and employ U.S. minorities.

BOX 6.3 ROAD SIGN

Not White Enough for the White House? Al Smith's 1928 Presidential Candidacy

In 2012, three of the four candidates for the U.S. presidency and vice presidency were not mainstream Protestants—a first in U.S. history. Each of the vice presidential candidates was Roman Catholic, and the Republican presidential nominee—Mitt Romney—was a Mormon. Governor Romney's religion was not a central theme of the general election, nor was the Catholicism of the vice presidential candidates. This tolerance of candidates' religious beliefs did not always characterize American politics. The nomination by a major party of the first non-Protestant for the presidency—New York governor Al Smith by the Democrats in 1928—spurred a national debate on whether Catholics were qualified to be president.

Prior to the 1928 presidential campaign, all nominees of the major parties for the presidency had been Protestants who traced their ancestries primarily to Great Britain (with a few candidates of Dutch ancestry thrown in). Smith's candidacy reflected the growing political influence of and alliances between the descendants of Irish immigrants who migrated in large numbers between the 1820s and 1840s; the "new" immigrants and their children who arrived in growing numbers in the 1880s; southern Whites who had been solidly in the Democratic camp since the Civil War; and some rural voters in the rest of the country. Although these communities did not agree on all issues, they opposed Republican policies and saw Smith as the party's best chance to beat Republican nominee Herbert Hoover.

Smith's greatest advantage in his pursuit of the Democratic nomination was his strong opposition to Prohibition. White ethnics had opposed Prohibition from the start, but their political voice was limited. By 1928, the costs of Prohibition, particularly the rise of organized crime and the increase in overall consumption of hard liquor, had become evident.[18] Thus Smith could support the repeal of Prohibition in terms of good government policy and not simply as ethnic pandering. Equally important, the new immigrant populations, many of whom came from cultures where alcohol was not shunned, had become increasingly mobilized in politics. They saw Prohibition as a challenge to their status as Americans equal to those whose ancestors had migrated in earlier eras. They sought a candidate who would advocate the repeal of Prohibition and found one in Smith.

Although Prohibition worked to Smith's advantage in the Democratic primary, it did not in the general election. Republican constituencies, as well as some rural and Southern Democrats, continued to support temperance. They used Smith's opposition to Prohibition as evidence that his policies would empower the newer White ethnic populations, who could challenge the political power of the segments of the White population traditionally dominating U.S. politics. Smith also faced outright prejudice based on his religion. Popular rhetoric asserted that, as a Catholic, Smith would govern at the behest of the pope. Smith's only response was the he had served as governor of New York and in other offices without any favoritism to the Catholic Church.[19] He lost the 1928 election.

The charges that a Catholic could not serve as president resurfaced during John Kennedy's 1960 campaign—a race that he won, making him the first (and only) Catholic U.S. president. Doubts about Mitt Romney's ability to serve as president based on his religious beliefs appeared in a more muted form (and with a different church) in 2012.

Despite the fact that President Barack Obama was the only mainstream Protestant among the 2012 party nominees for president and vice president, he is unique on another dimension, one that connects him more to Al Smith than to Herbert Hoover. Obama is only person to become president who traces his ancestry to post–Civil War migration. Obama's father migrated to the United States in 1959 as a student , though Obama's mother's family had early roots in the U.S. John Kennedy, like Al Smith before him, traced his immigrant roots to Irish migration before the Civil War. Al Smith, then, broke a glass ceiling of presidential nomination for White ethnics, but the great wave of post–Civil War White ethnic migrants has yet to see one of its descendants in the Oval Office.

Thus by 1965 White identity and European ancestry were largely contiguous in the American popular consciousness and, as a result, among Whites, ethnicity became largely inconsequential in terms of educational or economic opportunity. Doubts about Southern and Eastern European migrants' assimilability or ability to adapt to American constitutional values, which had been widely accepted in the early twentieth century, had largely disappeared by the dawn of the Civil Rights Movement. Undeniably, the remnants of ethnic distinctions between the descendants of immigrants from different parts of Europe remained, particularly in cities where ties to ancestral identities remained strongest, such as Boston or Philadelphia.[23] Even in areas where European-descent ethnic groups competed, however, this competition did not focus on whether European-ancestry populations were White.

Since Whiteness is a social construction shaped by mass views and elite institutions, the boundaries of Whiteness will continually be debated. In today's society, for example, migrants from the Middle East may categorize themselves on the census in a significantly different way (as White) than would the majority of U.S. citizens (as non-White). But as debates about the scope and extent of civil rights policies emerged in the 1960s, the White population included not just the descendants of the immigrants who arrived on the *Mayflower,* but also the descendants of those who fled the Irish Potato Famine of the 1840s, those who passed through Ellis Island from Southern and Eastern Europe in the 1890s and early 1900s, and all others whose ancestors left Europe for the New World.

THE STATE AND WHITE ADVANTAGE

From their earliest days, the colonies and territories that would become the United States devalued and, for a time, destroyed the assets of non-Whites to the advantage of European settlers. Land, the primary asset of indigenous populations in North America, was expropriated for use by the new arrivals. (See Chapter 2.) Early Black settlers, like many early White settlers, were recruited to the new colonies under terms of indentured servitude. The period of indenture could be a lifetime but did not extend to the next generation. By the late 1600s, the periods of White indentureship diminished considerably to five to seven years (and often could not be enforced, as White indentured servants could simply migrate to newly settled lands in the West). At the same time, states established slavery as the norm for Black labor. (See Chapter 3.) Non-Whites who became part of the United States, such as the former Mexican subjects of the Southwest or Native Hawaiians, also lost many of the assets that they had prior to colonization, particularly landholdings. (See Chapters 4 and 5.) Each of these non-White populations—Native Americans, African Americans, and colonized Americans—lacked the political resources and, in some cases, citizenship to challenge these initial efforts to limit their status in U.S. society and devalue or steal the value of their labor.

The exercise of state power to entrench **White advantage**—the social, economic, and legal privileges that Whites could exercise or exercise more freely than non-Whites—did not simply appear early in the relationship between Whites and non-Whites. On the contrary, the state played an ongoing role in advantaging Whites—however defined in a specific period of U.S. history—relative to others. Instead of retelling U.S. history through this lens, we will explore this phenomenon in several periods of U.S. national history. We examine how state policies structured White advantage in the Revolutionary era, in the period of westward expansion of the nineteenth century, in the post–Civil War era, in the period of mass migration at the turn of the twentieth century, and in the emergence of the national welfare state with the New Deal. Our goal is not to offer a complete chronicle, a task that would require a book in itself. Instead, it is to demonstrate what we believe is a pattern in American governance—at least in the period leading up to the Civil Rights Movement of the 1960s—that explains significant racial disparities in a wide variety of measures of group attainment. These include wealth, income, educational attainment, health outcomes, and residential patterns apparent as civil rights legislation was being debated in the 1960s and still evident today.[24]

The Revolutionary and Early Constitutional Era: Structuring White Advantage

As we discussed earlier in the chapter, the ratification of the U.S. Constitution entrenched a racial hierarchy in law that had developed in practice over the previous two hundred years. Although the Constitution limited its mention of race to Indian tribes (rather than Indians as individuals), it established a system whereby Native Americans were outside of the protections of the Constitution and where relations between the United States and Indian governments were concentrated in the federal government rather than with the states. The Constitution also established protections for the institution of slavery and a recognition of the slaves as less than full human beings. Laws passed by the new Congress soon after the ratification of the Constitution also established rights for Whites that were not extended to other groups, most notably the right to naturalization (the ability for immigrants to become U.S. citizens). These national laws mirrored steadily increasing restrictions on voting rights and economic liberties being imposed on free Blacks by the states.

At the time of the Constitution's ratification, most immigrants to the United States were from Northern and Western Europe. There was no discussion of immigration in the Constitution, reflecting the popular understanding of the era that immigration could not be regulated by governments (except, perhaps, for involuntary migrants destined for slavery after 1808). The framers did vest in Congress the power to "establish a uniform rule of naturalization" (Article I, Section 8) in order to ensure that all states would welcome immigrants at equal levels (with a low population density, national leaders recognized that the new nation needed immigrants; some states were more resistant). The constitutional grant of authority over naturalization to the federal government ensured that it, rather than the states, had the authority to regulate immigration, and over the next century the nation came to see the regulation of immigration as being within the federal government's authority.

Congress quickly used the powers granted it in the Constitution to place race into national law. Among its first acts was the first U.S. immigration law—the Naturalization Act of 1790—that established the standards for naturalization, the legal process by which an immigrant becomes a U.S. citizen. The standards were few in the first naturalization law. Immigrants had to reside in the United States for just two years and be of "good moral character." The opportunity to naturalize was limited in the law to "free white persons," an exclusion that prohibited free Black immigrants, slaves, and indentured servants from naturalizing. Certainly, the final category included some Whites, though by 1790, when this legislation was passed, the number of indentured servants was low. For White immigrants, this legislation was inclusive—ethnicity was inconsequential. Not only was the required period of residence between immigration and naturalization quite brief (it was expanded to five years in 1795), the law allowed naturalization for populations that had not yet established a firm hold on Whiteness, such as European Catholics and Jews.

Fears about the beliefs and political intentions of some immigrants led to a brief change in naturalization law as part of the Alien and Sedition Acts in 1798. These laws, which were repealed in 1802 after the election of Thomas Jefferson, extended the period of residence prior to naturalization to fourteen years out of a fear that some immigrants were insufficiently loyal to American values and might bring the radicalism of the French Revolution to the United States. It is important to note that this change was short-lived (the period of residence prior to naturalization was returned to five years, where it has remained since), and that even with this fear, White immigrants were not denied access to U.S. citizenship as were non-White immigrants. The right of immigration was not limited by the Alien and Sedition Acts (though the wars in Europe in this era made trans-Atlantic migration difficult).

This national effort to entrench White advantage in the national law paralleled state efforts to restrict key rights of citizenship to Whites. Most important among these was voting. At the time of the Constitution's ratification, most states limited voting rights to landholding males (some states allowed Black landholders to vote early in the nation's history, though new restrictions on Black voting appeared in the early 1800s). By the 1830s, property restrictions on the franchise largely disappeared and most White men could vote.[25] In this pre–Civil War era, some Northern states also extended the franchise to Black men, though their numbers were sufficiently small that Black voters had little influence on electoral outcomes. The steady expansion in the franchise for White males extended to immigrants, who in this era were almost all from Europe. States saw the extension of the franchise to "intending citizens" (immigrants with at least two years of residence in the United States) as a tool to attract new residents. In urban areas, political machines also encouraged voting by some immigrants. Here, perhaps, the motivations were less noble. The votes of new immigrants (often not yet naturalized) could often be managed to the advantage of the leaders of political machines to maintain power.[26] This expansion of the franchise to immigrants and their descendants ensured that the steadily increasing numbers of European immigrants, including those from new parts of Europe, would be able to organize at the local level and influence local government. This local power base, made possible by the rights granted to them in the Constitution and in law, ensured that these White immigrants were able to establish the foundations of their position in U.S. society, an opportunity that non-White immigrants did not have in this era or for many years afterward.

White Privilege as Part of U.S. Westward Expansion

As the United States expanded westward, it faced a question that would in many ways shape the future of the nation: How would lands newly acquired by the United States be transferred to private ownership? One model used early in the nation's history was to use the lands (most formerly controlled by Native American populations) to be sold as large tracts to raise revenue for the government. A second model, which existed in some form from the nation's first days and became the dominant model in the mid–nineteenth century, was to sell the land in small plots so that families could afford it. In this way, settler families would colonize the West. Although the first model was more profitable, it led to speculation and frequent booms and busts in the credit market. The second model allowed for the steady westward migration of millions and the "closing of the American frontier" by the 1890s.

The federal government's promise of land in the West was primarily a resource for White Americans and for European immigrants who had declared their intention to become U.S. citizens (an assertion that they could make after two years of residence). Of the federal legislation that made Western lands available to small holders (individuals who owned small plots of land), the most important was the **Homestead Act of 1862.** Over the next century, this law allowed for the transfer of 285 million acres—nearly 10 percent of the land mass of the United States—to individual landholders who were able to purchase 160 acres of public land for modest sums after occupying the land for five years.[27] Almost all American-citizen adult heads of households, as well as immigrants who had declared their intention to naturalize, were eligible to take advantage of the Homestead Act. The exceptions weren't explicitly racial, but instead concerned those who had "borne arms against the United States Government or given aid and comfort to its enemies"—in other words, Whites who had participated in the Confederacy. Although the land only cost a small amount, families seeking to homestead needed money for transportation to the land, for seed, and to support themselves until the crop came in. Ownership only transferred after the homesteader had occupied the land for five years. Few non-Whites in the late nineteenth century had sufficient resources to take advantage of this massive government land transfer. After the end of slavery and the Civil War, free Southern Blacks (the vast majority in this period) faced the added burden of vagrancy laws that criminalized refusal to work on White-held lands; therefore, by law, they had less opportunity to move to the lands where they could assert their right to homestead.

Congress also passed a Southern Homestead Act at the end of the Civil War that made public lands in Southern states available to homesteading.[28] This legislation was more likely to create opportunities for Southern Blacks, as well as poor Whites in the region, because the land was closer to where they lived, yet these lands were also less productive than the Western lands provided through the 1862 Act. Consequently, it was more difficult for lands allotted under the Southern Homestead Act to meet the purchase requirement that they be occupied for five years.

ASSOCIATED PRESS

Farm homesteaders get off a train in 1893 to stake their claim on newly opened lands in Oklahoma. As Native populations lost control of Western lands, the United States sought to populate them. The Homestead Act of 1862 made available 160-acre plots to Americans (including immigrants) who committed to living on the land and farming it for five years.

Land-Grant Colleges Expand Higher Education. This era immediately after the Civil War also saw the emergence of another institution that had the potential to ensure that the children in poor families could obtain the training necessary to move out of poverty: public higher education. Beginning with the passage of the **Morrill Land-Grant College Act of 1862,** the federal government made large tracts of public lands available to each state in exchange for the establishment of state colleges devoted to the "agricultural and mechanical arts." This legislation sought to ensure that higher education was not just available to the rich and that the curriculum of higher education not only included classical studies and philosophy but also science, engineering, and agriculture.[29] With the passage of the Morrill Land-Grant College Act, public colleges opened in every state and, over the next half-century, many grew to be among the best universities in the world, including the University of California at Berkeley and the University of Illinois at Urbana-Champaign.

Black Americans (and later Mexican Americans and Asian Americans) were not able to take advantage of this resource for democracy to the same degree as were White citizens, particularly in the late nineteenth and early twentieth centuries. When Congress extended land-grant universities to Southern states in 1890, it did not require that these new public universities admit qualified Black students. Instead, in those states that refused to admit Blacks to the state land-grant university, the law required that the state establish a separate institution for Black students.[30] This congressional acquiescence to racial discrimination in education anticipated the Supreme Court's ruling in *Plessy v. Ferguson* (1896), which made "separate but equal" legal for the delivery of all government services. The Black-serving institutions of higher learning that states created in response never had access to resources or networks comparable to the White land-grant universities. Thus they reinforced rather than diminished White advantage.

While in principle these new land resources—for homesteading and public higher education—were available to all Americans, Black citizens (and the small number of Mexican Americans and Asian Americans resident in the United States at the time) were not able to take advantage of these opportunities. The long-term legacy of these denied opportunities remains today in the significant gaps in wealth between Whites and non-Whites.[31] Land transfers resulting from the Homestead Act ensured that many White families today have greater wealth than do descendants of non-White families who did not benefit from a similar discounted gift of federal (originally Native American) land, even if their ancestors long ago moved off the land. Similarly, some of the White working class and agricultural labor force of the late nineteenth century were able to begin to acquire the training and skills necessary to move into skilled professions as a result of the new state colleges and universities that opened after the Civil War. Having a parent (or grandparent) with higher education is a strong predictor of going to college. Thus these early beneficiaries of public higher education have spurred now-several generations of offspring who have a higher likelihood of joining the nation's educated and skilled elite.

White Advantage in the Newly Urbanizing America

By the end of the nineteenth century, the United States became increasingly urban. With the growth of cities, a new form of White privilege emerged—the racial covenant in real estate titles. These covenants, or agreements, were included in the ownership title to land and prevented the person who bought the house on the land from subsequently selling it to a person of the race or ethnicity listed in the covenant. Initially, covenants focused on African Americans. By the 1920s, however, they frequently also precluded sale to Jews, Asian Americans, and (in the Southwest) Mexican Americans. The Supreme Court ratified the constitutionality of racially restrictive real estate covenants in 1926 in the case of *Corrigan v. Buckley,* reasoning that real estate transactions were private actions and, consequently, not subject to the Due Process Clause of the Fourteenth Amendment. It was not until 1948, in *Shelley v. Kraemer*, that the Court reversed itself and held that racially restrictive real estate covenants are unconstitutional under the Fourteenth Amendment. From the 1890s to 1948, several generations of African Americans, Asian Americans, Jews, and others precluded from owning property in many neighborhoods lost opportunities for social integration and for the appreciation in the value of homes in many neighborhoods. Meanwhile, White homeowners were able to purchase housing with less competition and, presumably, at lower prices than if all Americans were able to purchase property equally. Although the property that had restrictive covenants may have been sold long ago, the wealth that this land ownership generated undoubtedly also contributes to today's wealth gap between Whites and non-Whites (recognizing that Jews were victimized by covenants as well).

Immigration Law's Role in Maintaining White Privilege

The rapid expansion of immigration after the Civil War created a new venue in which federal law (and state implementation of it) ensured opportunities for Whites in U.S. society that were denied to non-Whites. The period from the end of the Civil War to the 1920s saw increasing restriction on immigration and the beginning of a regulatory structure to implement these policies. Ultimately, the restriction extended to most of the world. The road to these limitations began with restrictions on non-Whites and ultimately extended to Southern and Eastern Europeans, whose Whiteness was more contested. Chapter 11 explores immigration policy in depth. Here, we further consider how U.S. and state law structured White advantage. By privileging some immigrants over others (White immigrants over non-White immigrants) in this period, federal law increasingly defined the racial and ethnic composition of the nation.

Prior to 1875, immigration to the United States was a near-universal privilege. Slaves could not be imported to the United States after 1808, but in principle, migrants from Africa or Black migrants from the Caribbean could immigrate regardless of race. Certainly, few Africans or African-ancestry peoples would migrate because they would risk enslavement, but migrants from Africa, like migrants from anywhere else in the world, were eligible to immigrate freely throughout the nineteenth century. Immigrants prior to 1870 were entitled to permanent residence and, if White (or of African descent, after 1870), they could naturalize as U.S. citizens. This open-door policy changed for the first time with the passage of the Page Act in 1875, which racialized Asians. The Page Act prohibited the migration of criminals, prostitutes, and "Oriental persons" (Asians, particularly Chinese) "without their consent." (See Chapter 5.) This final—racial—category reflected a concern in Congress and in the general public that Chinese immigrants were under the control of the fellow Chinese who paid for their passage to the United States. In the rhetoric of the day, the "coolie" laborers, as they were called, were all but new slaves. There was little bureaucracy to enforce the Page Act, so its effect should be seen as largely symbolic (and empowering to advocates of further immigration restriction).

The principle that the United States could restrict immigration led to further popular organizing against immigrants and expanded racial exclusion. The motivations for this increased demand for immigration restriction were several and included economic fears (the labor market competition of the new immigrants) and cultural concerns (differences in language, customs, and practices of the new immigrants). The Page Act was limited to Chinese immigrants who migrated "without their consent," a standard that could not be measured and that could be abused and used against all Chinese laborers. Congress expanded the exclusion of potential Chinese migrants in 1882 with the Chinese Exclusion Act, which explicitly excluded all Chinese labor migrants, skilled or unskilled. Over the next thirty years, Congress extended these restrictions to all of Asia, applying them to all nations east of Iran, and to all migrants from these countries, regardless of their class status. The standard Congress used in 1917 to decide which countries were barred from sending immigrants to the United States was that there could be no immigrants from countries whose nationals could not naturalize as U.S. citizens. That being the case, since Asians could not naturalize because they were not White, they also could not immigrate. Thus the 1790 standard of "free white persons" came to be used a hundred years later to limit immigration by race—another instance in which race was inconsequential for White ethnics and decisive for other racial/ethnic groups.

The restriction on immigration in this era did not simply focus on race, but the racial restriction increasingly was not limited to Asians. In the early 1920s, Congress enacted the national origin quota laws, which sought to freeze the ethnic composition of the United States as it was in 1890. This legislation allocated visas (a legal document issued abroad and necessary to immigrate to the United States) based on the percentage of a nation's émigrés resident in the United States at the time of the 1890 census. Congress selected 1890 because it was the last year when Northern and Western Europeans (those from the United Kingdom, Germany, Scandinavia, France, and Holland) dominated the migration flow. Although the national origin quota laws were designed to slow the growing migration of Southern and Eastern Europeans (particularly Italians, Poles, and Jewish immigrants from throughout Eastern Europe and Russia), the consequence was practically to eliminate immigration from Africa or the Middle East, parts of the world that had sent few migrants to the United States in 1890. After passage of the 1924 immigration law, the continent of Africa (with the exception of Egypt) had an annual quota of just 1,100 immigrants.

As we will discuss in Chapter 11, the national origin quota laws did not discriminate against all non-White potential immigrants. The law exempted the Western Hemisphere in order to ensure that the U.S. economy would continue to have access to a large source of labor migration. With the resultant severe reductions in labor immigration from Southern and Eastern Europe, demand for eligible migrants from the parts of the world that continued to be eligible to send migrants increased dramatically. As a result, immigration from the Caribbean and Mexico grew dramatically.

Emergence of the National Welfare State

The twentieth century saw a steady expansion in the federal government's role in ensuring wider competition in U.S. society and a safety net for those in distress. As this set of federal protections emerged, however, it consciously excluded non-White populations who were arguably most in need. The exclusion of African Americans, Native Americans, and, to a lesser degree, Mexican Americans and Puerto Ricans from the full protection of the New Deal and post–World War II programs added to the relative disadvantage of minority populations relative to Whites at the dawn of the Civil Rights era.

New Deal Programs. The collection of federal programs implemented by President Franklin D. Roosevelt in the 1930s to assist the citizenry and move the nation out of the Great Depression—systematically excluded Blacks and, when they were included, offered them less access to resources and jobs than Whites. As political scientist Linda Faye Williams has observed, "there is ample evidence to support the view that the New Deal, in some critical instances, did little or nothing to shake up the system of white privilege and in some others bolstered it."[32] The reason was not necessarily racial animus on the part of President Roosevelt, but instead a political calculus. To pass these programs through Congress, Roosevelt needed the votes of Southern Democrats and the support of key committee chairs in Congress, many of whom were from the South. As a result, the New Deal programs consistently short-changed Blacks, regardless of the evidence of their need.

The National Recovery Administration, designed to put people to work early in the New Deal, gave White workers the first opportunity to be assigned to jobs and authorized lower pay scales for Blacks. The Civilian Conservation Corps, which put the unemployed to work in public works projects, maintained separate residential camps for White and Black workers. The Federal Housing Administration, which was designed to guarantee home loans and spur the mortgage market, would not guarantee loans to Black borrowers who were seeking mortgages in White

Initially, some of the residential camps of New Deal–era Civilian Conservation Corps (CCC) were racially integrated. In response to local complaints, however, CCC administrators segregated all camps by 1935.

neighborhoods. Additionally, federal encouragement to let agricultural land lie fallow under the provisions of the Agricultural Adjustment Act provided financial incentives to White landowners to evict their largely Black tenant farmers. Each of these forms of discrimination ensured that Whites would feel the effects of the Depression less than Blacks. They also laid the foundation for Whites to gain resources that could be tapped to allow for economic gain after the end of the Depression and earlier than other groups.

Some of the racial bias built into New Deal legislation had longer-term effects on resources in African American and other minority communities. In order to ensure the passage of the Social Security Act, the Roosevelt administration had to exclude two industries that overwhelmingly employed Black and Mexican American workers—farmworkers and domestics. The exclusion of these workers in Social Security's early years meant that many minority workers received lower benefits when they retired (both industries were later brought into Social Security coverage, though employers of domestic workers continue to fail to pay into the system for their household labor). The National Labor Relations Act required that employers recognize the demands of their workers for unions. Initially, this legislation included an antidiscrimination provision forbidding discrimination by federally recognized unions, but it was removed from the bill prior to passage.

Benefits of the G.I. Bill. The racial preferences in early U.S. social welfare legislation continued after World War II (at the beginning of the Civil Rights era). Government programs to reward veterans, in particular, advantaged White veterans more than they did non-White veterans.[33] Educational benefits were one of the primary components of the **G.I. Bill of Rights**—legislation passed near the end of World War II that sought to assist veterans in adapting to civilian life through low-cost mortgages, low-interest loans to start a business, and cash payments of tuition and living expenses to attend college or vocational school. Most important, the G.I. Bill provided for veterans to attend school for up to four years at government expense. This resource spurred the move of many formerly working-class young men (and some women) into the middle class. Discrimination in admission to institutions of higher education, as well as bias in the implementation of the law by the staff at the Veterans Administration, tracked many African American veterans into trade and vocational programs and discouraged their enrollment in colleges and universities. Black veterans were much less likely than White veterans to use the G.I. Bill to earn a college degree after World War II or the Korean War. Thus, despite their service to their country, Black and other non-White veterans were less well positioned to seize the new economic opportunities in the 1950s and 1960s, as the economy moved from industrial to knowledge-based. While race continued to be inconsequential to Whites, legislation continued to set up roadblocks to other races and ethnicities seeking equal opportunity.

Non-White veterans were also less likely to benefit from a second key component of the G.I. Bill—housing loans. Residential discrimination called **redlining,** sanctioned by mortgage

Consider how the definition of Whiteness as a category expanded after World War II. What lessons might this period offer for diminishing contemporary racial and ethnic inequalities?

lenders through policies that denied mortgages in some areas—particularly areas with high concentrations of African Americans and other minorities—limited the opportunities of non-White veterans to move outside U.S. cities (particularly to the newly emerging suburbs). So, as was the case with educational benefits, access to a specific benefit in the law was not sufficient to ensure equality. Instead, discrimination ensured that Whites were better able to use state resources to position themselves to seize economic opportunities.

Nonveterans also saw differential opportunities to purchase housing in the post–New Deal era. The Federal Housing Administration (FHA) mandated that racial homogeneity be a consideration in the decision to award a mortgage, and in the size of mortgages awarded. Less than 2 percent of houses financed by FHA prior to 1960 were purchased by African Americans. (Blacks made up approximately 11 percent of the national population in 1960.)[34] The long-term consequence of redlining ensured that Whites in the 1950s and after were able to amass

Table 6.1   White Ethnics' Road of Racialization

Period	Why Barriers Arose	How Barriers Were Overcome	Outcome
Colonial Era	• Indentured servitude structured class differences among Whites • Origins of White colonists diversified to include non-Protestants	• Whites fled indenture • Demand for labor overcame objections to non-Protestant newcomers	Insufficient Barriers → Inconsequential
U.S. Constitution	• States received authority to set voting rules • First naturalization law limited naturalization to Whites	• Courts became the venue for arbitrating Whiteness until the 1950s	Decisive (for Whites, Decisively Advantageous)
Civil War—1800	• Proposals made to extend the period prior to naturalization for White immigrants	• Parties mobilized men regardless of class and ethnicity to expand their base • Debate over naturalization interrupted by the Civil War	Insufficient Barriers
Post–Civil War—1920s	• Selective immigration restrictions presented barriers to migrants from Southern and Eastern Europe • Political and economic limits placed on White ethnics	• Political influence of White ethnics grew • Post–World War II economic changes and "non-zero-sum mobility"	Insufficient → Inconsequential

more wealth from the appreciation of homes, often with federal mortgage subsidies, than were African Americans and other minorities.

The federal government's new role in promoting social change in the Civil Rights era had the perhaps unintended effect of reinvigorating the ethnic identities of White Americans by reminding them of their own ancestries and allocating some state resources by race. For the most part, these newly ethnically aware Americans were the children or grandchildren of immigrants who had, in many cases, seen their ethnic identities become largely symbolic as White ethnics were incorporated into the White mainstream beginning in the 1930s. Although this phenomenon manifested itself as a rediscovery of national origin–based identities (e.g., Italian American or Irish American), it reflected how White ethnic identity had become largely symbolic by the 1960s. The rhetoric of this newly discovered White ethnic identity focused primarily on asserting the rights of White ethnics relative to African Americans. These reinvigorated ethnic identities didn't reflect a hierarchy within the White identities, or at least not one that was reinforced through government policies and social exclusion.[35] Instead, they valorized the histories of their ethnic ancestors and selectively tapped their cultures to offer a way to present a newly reinvigorated culture in an increasingly diverse U.S. society.

CONCLUSION: LEGACIES OF RACIAL HIERARCHY AND THE ROOTS OF CONTEMPORARY POLITICS

The legacy of these post–World War II policies was part of the national political discourse during the Civil Rights era. In 1965 President Lyndon B. Johnson received an honorary doctorate at Howard University and used the opportunity to comment on the "facts of this American failure," referring to the United States' racial inequalities. Johnson observed that in 1930, White and Black unemployment rates were comparable but that by 1965 the Black rate was twice that of Whites. In 1948 Black teenage males had lower unemployment rates than did White teens; by 1964 Black male teens had an unemployment rate of 23 percent, compared to 13 percent for White male teens. Also in the post–World War II period, the gap in incomes and opportunities between Whites and Blacks increased, while infant mortality rates decreased more precipitously for Whites than for African Americans. Reviewing these and other measures of White and Black life in the United States, Johnson observed: "You do not wipe away scars of centuries by saying: Now you are free to go where you want, and do as you desire, and choose the leaders as you please. You do not take a person who, for years, has been hobbled by chains and liberate him, bring him up to the starting line of a race and then say, 'you are free to compete with all the others,' and still justly believe that you have been completely fair."[36]

To remedy the legacies and material consequences of racial exclusion and racial hierarchy in the allocation of state resources and services, Johnson proposed both legislation that provided for equal protection of the laws, such as the Civil Rights Act of 1964 and the Voting Rights Act of 1965, and also **affirmative action** programs that ensured African Americans—and, later, other racial/ethnic minorities—would be able to gain greater access to social resources, particularly higher education, government jobs, and government contracts.

Affirmative action programs have been controversial since their first days; at this stage, it is important to understand that such programs were designed to increase the probability that over time racial and ethnic minorities would be able to compete from an equal starting place with White Americans—that the uneven road that characterized minority access to state resources and government services since the nation's founding would be evened over time. In other words, affirmative action programs were designed so that the state would partially remedy the long-term legacy of state programs that existed in some form since 1787 to advantage Whites.

As we have shown in this chapter, the consistent pattern over the course of U.S. history was for racial difference within the White population to be insufficient or inconsequential for Whites to exercise the rights and privileges of citizenship under law (see Table 6.1). Instead, as we have discussed in Chapters 2 through 5, the fundamental division in law and in social practice from the nation's earliest days through the 1960s—the perpetually uneven road—was between Whites and non-Whites. While the boundaries of Whiteness certainly changed between the colonial era and the 1960s, the nation's laws made few distinctions between Whites based on race. New White migrants clearly faced discrimination, particularly at the local level, but the discrimination declined and, ultimately, disappeared as White immigrants—and, particularly, their children and grandchildren—adopted the cultural practices of descendants of earlier immigrants and, often, married Whites of other ancestries. Regardless of the recency of migration, White migrants benefitted from the nation's racial hierarchy that allocated national resources to Whites more than to other racial/ethnic groups in U.S. society. Thus the social changes inspired by the Civil Rights Movement and the legislation and court rulings that followed fundamentally changed race relations and racial politics in the United States. In the chapters that follow, we examine several policy areas to assess how the legacies of past discrimination and the post–Civil Rights era policy interventions create the foundation for a nation of more even, if not the same, roads.

DISCUSSION QUESTIONS

1. How did the racial differences established in law at the time of the nation's founding serve as a foundation for constructing White advantage?

2. Compared to other racial and ethnic groups, how were White ethnics advantaged from the start, and how did those advantages help them to overcome the discrimination they faced from the "native stock" Whites?

3. What elements were most beneficial in eliminating barriers for White ethnics and contributing to a coalesced White identity?

4. Consider the impact of programs like the Homestead Act, the New Deal, and the G.I. Bill, for Whites and other racial groups. What conclusions can you draw, based on the information presented, about the possible long-term impact of these programs on racial inequalities?

KEY TERMS

affirmative action (p. 196)

Enumeration Clause (p. 176)

federalism (p. 180)

G.I. Bill of Rights (p. 194)

Homestead Act
of 1862 (p. 189)

Morrill Land-Grant
College Act of 1862 (p. 190)

native stock (p. 175)

naturalization (p. 176)

Naturalization Act
of 1790 (p. 177)

New Deal (p. 193)

Prohibition (p. 182)

redlining (p. 195)

White advantage (p. 186)

7 Voting Rights in American Life

The voting rights bill will be the latest, and among the most important, in a long series of victories. . . . But freedom is not enough. You do not wipe away the scars of centuries by saying: Now you are free to go where you want, and do as you desire, and choose the leaders you please.

You do not take a person who, for years, has been hobbled by chains and liberate him, bring him up to the starting line of a race and then say, 'you are free to compete with all the others,' and still justly believe that you have been completely fair. Thus it is not enough just to open the gates of opportunity. All our citizens must have the ability to walk through those gates.

– President Lyndon B. Johnson[1]

This chapter marks the transition in *Uneven Roads* from our presentation of individual groups' journeys before 1965 to their efforts to enhance their respective standing in different policy arenas. Here, the metaphor of an uneven road takes on new meaning and new language as Native Americans, African Americans, Latinos, Asian Americans, and Whites undertake various means to traverse the public policy arena. Though the routes and means vary considerably in these public policy areas, common threads persist. Beginning with this chapter, we build on comparisons in the first half of the book and provide a view to understanding why race and ethnicity continue to matter in contemporary civic engagement.

The Civil Rights Movement ushered in landmark changes legally, politically, and socially, but it did not end discrimination. Racialization of individuals and groups continues, and is evident in the areas of public policy we study in this and succeeding chapters. This chapter provides an overview of when, why, and how race has mattered for voting rights issues in American politics. We recognize the right to

Box 7.1 Chapter Objectives

- Explain the importance of voting rights to minority groups and efforts at disenfranchisement.

- Identify the ways in which the Civil Rights Movement contributed to voter expansion.

- Summarize the purpose of the Voting Rights Act and the needs addressed by its major provisions.

- Describe how redistricting works and how the Supreme Court districts drawn has responded to on racial considerations.

- Compare the politics behind the 2006 renewal of the Voting Rights Act with previous instances.

- Assess continuing challenges to voting rights and the long-term outlook for the Voting Rights Act.

The road to equal voting rights in the United States has long been uneven, with challenges arising regularly. In 2013 the Supreme Court ruling in *Shelby County v. Holder* struck down a provision of the 1965 Voting Rights Act that required federal approval for any proposed voting changes in several states. The provision, originally intended to prevent the disenfranchisement of African Americans, is still held by many to be necessary.

vote—to select officeholders, and in some cases to vote directly on issues—as a central component of citizenship. This is a complicated area that unites the experiences of all minority groups in their efforts to assert citizenship, but differentiates them in the ways in which that right was denied. The goal of voting rights itself is a convoluted effort for the United States, and its story is not linear. As with each group's road to citizenship, voting rights have progressed unevenly toward equal participation.[2] While voting is emphasized as a core element of the democratic process, much of the population—divided prominently by gender, as well as by race and ethnicity—has been excluded from the franchise for much of the nation's history. African Americans, Latinos, Asian Americans, Native Americans, and women of all groups have struggled to establish the right to vote. Even after their access to the franchise was established, at various times these citizens have still had to struggle to maintain their right to cast the ballot.

In an illustration of this book's uneven roads metaphor, the accomplishments frequently emphasized in the aftermath of the Civil Rights Movement and rapid increases in voting pre-cipitated by the passage and implementation of the 1965 Voting Rights Act (VRA) have often been followed by the rise of new local and state policies and practices that challenge routine exercise of the franchise.[3] Successive extensions and expansions of the VRA in the late twen-tieth century quickly broadened coverage and addressed enfranchisement issues identified by other groups. For instance, electoral constraints originally defined as based on race came to include minority language protection. Disenfranchisement efforts also came to be incorpo-rated into voting rights policy areas through means such as felony disenfranchisement, voter/photo identification requirements, and registration requirements. The nation's ethnic and racial groups were affected by each of these green lights, potholes, and wrong turns on their way to equal participation, although the extent of the influence varies, given the different roads traveled by each. Knowledge of each group's political history, taken from Chapters 2 through 6, provides an essential component to understanding the need for and impact of vot-ing rights in the United States from the 1960s to today.

MINORITY GROUPS AND VOTING RIGHTS

Native Americans, African Americans, Asian Americans, Latinos, and Whites have had group-specific experiences in establishing their respective rights to the franchise. All have faced significant challenges in their pathways to voting, although they vary considerably. In this section, you'll come to understand the differing bases that limited access to the franchise, and how those limitations had to be attacked at different points in time. You will learn how decades of litigation, followed by protests and demonstrations, were succeeded by decades of congressional legislation, and how these enhanced the voting rights of the other groups on the road.

Efforts at enhancing **enfranchisement**, or opening up access to voting, were often followed by new efforts at voter **disenfranchisement** based on the commission of crimes (felony dis-enfranchisement), changing voting requirements by inventing new policies such as requiring voter identification at the polls, or increasing the frequency and complexity of voter registra-tion. The groups' differing geographical locations, legal status, languages spoken, and socio-economic dependence generated an array of opportunities for voting barriers. While there might have been group-specific barriers, the most consistent pattern has been and remains the efforts to control racial and ethnic groups' access to the polls. The following section pro-vides detailed introduction to the reasons why race has mattered in gaining electoral access for the groups on our uneven roads.

Native Americans: Still Struggling for Recognition

Although citizenship for Native Americans was recognized nationally with passage of the Indian Citizenship Act of 1924, Indians' exercise of the franchise was controlled by the states, some of which denied it to them. Political scientists Daniel McCool, Susan Olson, and Jennifer

Robinson note that in 1938, seven states "still refused to let Indians go to the polls." A Mississippi Choctaw chief questioned President Franklin D. Roosevelt about the contradiction between not being allowed to vote and being drafted to fight in World War II. Fred Daiker, assistant to the Bureau of Indian Affairs commissioner John Collier, drafted Roosevelt's response, stating aggressively, "Choctaws were indeed citizens and subject to the draft . . . [but] the matter of voting is governed by the laws of each state." Almost 25,000 Indians fought in World War II, and Navajo "code talkers" used their language to establish an unbreakable code vital to advancing the war in the Pacific.[4]

Native American veterans, like African American veterans discussed in Chapter 3, came home from the war willing to fight for their rights to the franchise. These veterans, and others they helped to mobilize, faced a complex array of legal elements used to limit their access to the polls. Among them were state constitutions, which prescribed voting procedures; tribal status, which determined whether the tribe had reached sovereignty; and federal guardianship, cultural identity, taxation status, and literacy, which could be used by the states to circumscribe access to registration. Voting was by no means guaranteed, and access to the ballot, even after passage of the Voting Rights Act, remains a challenge even in the early twenty-first century.

States sometimes argue, for example, that "reservation Indians . . . do not share the same interest in county government as the residents of the organized counties," and therefore should not be permitted to vote. The Voting Rights Act has not been enforced as consistently among Native Americans as it has been for other groups. Only one lawsuit challenging at-large electoral systems was brought between 1974 and 1990 in Montana, while African Americans sued ninety-seven Georgia counties and cities during these years. Native Americans speak a significant variety of languages, and voting materials aren't always provided in their languages. Additionally, felony disenfranchisement has a devastating impact on Native American populations, who frequently are subject to arrest and prosecution. These are only some of the voting constraints that continue to challenge Native American voters today.[5]

African Americans: Roadblocks in the South

The abolition of the institution of slavery began over 150 years ago, when President Abraham Lincoln issued the Emancipation Proclamation in 1863. It was confirmed for the nation with the Thirteenth Amendment in 1865. African Americans' status as citizens was established by the Fourteenth Amendment to the Constitution in 1868, followed in 1870 by the Fifteenth Amendment's establishment of their right to vote. Because the vast majority of the population of African descent in the United States was enslaved during the colonial era, as well as after the Revolutionary War, citizenship and the exercise of its privileges, such as voting, were largely inaccessible to Blacks as a group, even among free men. A few states permitted voting under state law, including Delaware, New Hampshire, New York, Massachusetts, and Pennsylvania, but this was not upheld by federal law until the passage of the Fifteenth Amendment. Yet even then voting was not stabilized in the South, where the bulk of the Black population lived, until almost a century afterward, when Congress passed the 1965 Voting Rights Act and supported federal enforcement of voter protection. It designed the legislation to give federal authorities the right to intervene in voting and election procedures in Southern states and counties in specific circumstances. If discriminatory state voter registration laws resulted in voting and registration levels that were less than 50 percent of a state's voting-age population in 1964, that state or county was designated a "covered jurisdiction." Covered jurisdictions received distinctive attention and observation by the national government. Election and registration procedures had previously only been the domain of the states. Passage of the 1965 act was therefore powerful acknowledgement by Congress, by the president, and later when the legislation was upheld, by the Supreme Court in *South Carolina v. Katzenbach* (1966), that state-level, race-based discrimination deeply constrained the exercise of African American voting rights.

Although the Voting Rights Act has been reaffirmed, expanded, and strengthened in law over the last sixty years (we explore these points in greater detail later in the chapter), challenges continue to arise. In late February 2013, the Supreme Court heard oral arguments on the voting rights case *Shelby County v. Holder*, which challenged the standing of Section 5 of the act, allowing for preclearance (the review of any new voting law changes) by the Department of Justice or the U.S. federal courts in specific covered jurisdictions before they are implemented. Examples of new voting laws include changes in the location of polling places away from Black neighborhoods and the creation of electoral districts that reduced the possibility of Blacks winning election to office. When the proposed new legislation was found to have a discriminatory impact, thereby reducing the effectiveness of the VRA, the Department of Justice had the right to deny the state the right to implement it.

The creation and implementation of the Voting Rights Act has significantly enhanced African American political participation, measured both in voting and in the election of Black officials. Because of the partisan concentration of Black voters within the Democratic Party, their increased participation has been followed by efforts by Republicans in states such as Ohio, Texas, and Florida to disenfranchise Black voters. The Supreme Court's 2013 decision in *Shelby County v. Holder*, discussed in more detail later in the chapter, has significantly changed the African American voting rights agenda.

Latinos: Leveraging Political Influence

Latinos, particularly those original residents in the American Southwest, were subject to considerable legal constraints—a failure to uphold their full citizenship as had been promised after the Mexican American War. They even suffered disenfranchisement after California, Arizona, and Texas became states and other territories in the region were integrated into the United States. As we discussed in Chapter 4, Mexican Americans in the new U.S. territories and states were granted U.S. citizenship, but the dominant White majority quickly implemented measures to exclude them from voting and other forms of politics. Despite their ability to exercise the franchise (barring restrictions), Mexican Americans faced political discrimination, and their vote was often manipulated to minimize any electoral influence they might have. There was some variation in these patterns, primarily because of the geographic dominance of Mexican Americans along the Texas southern border, where they voted in large numbers and in fact were influential in giving Texas to John F. Kennedy in the 1960 presidential election.

Puerto Ricans—citizens of the United States, and at least early on, concentrated in New York City—had been relatively easily co-opted into partisan politics and had somewhat easier access to the electorate. But even with access, efforts existed to minimize their political participation in New York City. The Puerto Rican Legal Defense and Education Fund, founded in 1972 (now Latino Justice PRLDEF), modeled on the National Association for the Advancement of Colored People Legal Defense and Education Fund and Mexican-American Legal Defense and Education Fund, sued and won the right to have access to bilingual ballots and interpreters for school board elections and, later, in all New York City elections.[6] Outside of New York City, Puerto Ricans' status more closely resembled that of Mexican Americans, as they were subject to electoral discrimination based on language and cultural identity.

Cubans were uniquely welcomed into the American mainland as refugees and opponents of Fidel Castro's communist regime and had settled into the United States on a short-term basis. That changed dramatically, however, after the 1980 Mariel Boatlift, and Florida's state and local political interests turned strongly hostile. Once Cubans saw themselves as immigrants, as an ethnic minority no longer welcomed and facing opposition from state and local officials based on their language and culture, they worked to become citizens and to influence electoral politics. In Florida, in particular, that effort has had significant electoral payoffs.

Mexican Americans, Puerto Ricans, and Cuban Americans thus have made significant inroads into electoral participation, but even after these changes, they face continued challenges. Increased hostility toward immigrants and non-English-speaking populations has been apparent in efforts in a variety of states to constrain electoral participation through the use of voter ID laws, to reduce the use of bilingual ballots, and to limit access to voter registration and flexible voting hours.

While U.S. citizens have the right to vote, there is no right to proportionate minority representation in Congress. Should there be? Why or why not?

Asian Americans: Growing Representation

Asian Americans previously faced complex and confusing detours in their efforts to achieve full citizenship or to sustain it in others. Arrival in the United States in the late nineteenth century led to the passage of numerous laws barring subsequent immigration of Chinese, Japanese, and other Asian groups. (See Chapter 5.) The Supreme Court offered contradictory rulings denying Asian Americans the right to immigrate or to naturalize as citizens. While the Court did not hold unconstitutional the right of the U.S. government to subject Japanese American citizens to internment during World War II, it conceded in one case that President Franklin D. Roosevelt and the military exceeded their constitutional authority in doing so.

Asian Americans live in thinly concentrated numbers in most regions of the United States, with the largest and densest concentrations in the western states, Hawaii, or in a few urban areas. Even after immigration reform in 1965, they comprised only a small portion of the U.S. population outside of these regions, but their ability to participate electorally was recognized in locations where they constituted a significant portion of the population or were protected under the Minority Language provisions after the 1975 extension of the VRA. Three-quarters of the Asian Americans elected to the 109th Congress were in districts covered by a portion of the VRA.[7] Their success at electoral participation was also demonstrated by the regional origins of Asian American elected officials. As discussed later, Hawaii has had significant Asian representation in Congress since it became a state. The only Asian American governor, Gary Locke of the state of Washington, served from 1997 to 2005, subsequently serving as Secretary of Commerce and Ambassador to China.

Asian Americans' relatively small—although growing—numbers, combined with their high levels of education and occupation, mean they are rarely denied access to the polls based on the types of barriers Blacks have faced. The fact that more than a majority of Asian Americans speak a language other than English does mean that language barriers similar to those faced by Latinos often become a strategy for those seeking to limit their electoral access.

When he died in 2012, Senator Daniel Inouye was the longest-serving Asian American in Congress. Mazie Hirono, elected the same year that Inouye died, is the first Asian American woman to serve in the U.S. Senate.

U.S. Senate Historical Office

White Americans: Greater Privilege

In our framework of uneven roads, Whites might be presumed to have the smoothest pathway to political power and authority, but as Chapter 6 has shown, the story of White ethnics, although certainly different from the other groups, has not been without its own roadblocks. From the limitation of voting rights only to landholding males after the Revolutionary War, to their erosion by the 1830s, most White men—and in a very few instances in Northern states, Black men—could vote. The expansion of post–Civil War immigration to Europeans but not to non-Europeans in the late nineteenth and early twentieth centuries, and the increasing emphasis on restrictions based on race in immigration policy during this period, provided greater privileges for Europeans in economic and political life for most of the first two hundred years of the nation's history.

Women as a group were incorporated into the electorate with the passage of the Nineteenth Amendment in 1920. Women of color, however, were denied the ballot until their respective racial and ethnic groups gained access. While immigrant voting was by no means rapid, there were no barriers to electoral participation specifically organized to limit the Irish, Italians, Germans, Poles, or others based on their ethnic or national origins. Race mattered among Whites, but in general their electoral participation was facilitated rather than impeded. In the South, voting restrictions, the poll tax, and literacy tests were in place, but were applied lightly or not at all to Whites. In the north, European immigrants were encouraged to vote by machine-based organizational structures.

BOX 7.2 ROAD SIGN

Minority Representation in Congress

The U.S. population continues to become more diverse. With Latinos poised to become 29 percent of the population by 2050, followed by African Americans at 13 percent (about what they are now), the U.S. Congress remains less representative of this national diversity.[8] The reasons why range from the gerrymandering of electoral districts to minority populations' geographic concentrations; minority politicians are more likely to be elected from districts with a majority of minority voters. Hawaii is a case in point. Since its early years of statehood, Hawaii has had a majority or near-majority Asian population, with Native Hawaiian residents and those of Asian descent comprising an estimated 48 percent of the state population in 2012.

Five of the seven U.S. senators Hawaiians have elected since statehood in 1959 have been of Asian descent. Hiram Fong (R, 1959–1977), Spark Matsunaga (D, 1977–1990), Daniel Akaka (D, 1990–2013), and Mazie Hirono (D, 2013–present) each served in one of Hawaii's two Senate seats in Congress, and Daniel Inouye (D, 1963–2012) in the other. Inouye, a World War II veteran, war hero, and Congressional Medal of Honor winner, served the longest, at forty-nine years, followed by Daniel Akaka, who served in the Senate for twenty-three years after a twenty-three-year stint in the U.S. House of Representatives. The first Asian American woman U.S. senator, Mazie Hirono, was elected in 2012. She had served previously in the House for six years (D, 2007–2012). Hawaii has also sent nine Asian Americans to the U.S. House of Representatives, including Representative Patricia Mink, the first woman from Hawaii, the first minority woman elected to Congress. Among their contributions while in Congress, Fong challenged the

long-established national origins policy and contributed to reframing policy in passage of the 1965 Hart-Cellar Immigration and Nationality Act; Inouye played a major role during his service on the Watergate Committee; and Mink led in the passage of Lyndon Johnson's War on Poverty legislation, the 1974 Women's Education Equity Act, and decades of other legislation addressing social welfare policy.[9]

This level of state minority representation in Congress is unprecedented in American political life. In comparison, the other forty-nine U.S. states have sent a total of one Asian American to the Senate in all of American history: Samuel Ichiye Hayakawa of California (R, 1977–1983). The representation numbers for other minority groups are similar. Senator Edward Brooke, an African American and a Republican, represented Massachusetts, a state with a relatively small Black population, from 1967 to 1979. Although African Americans comprise 12.6 percent of the population, only forty-two Black House members and two Black U.S. senators serve in the 113th Congress. Table 7.1 shows the distribution of House members by minority group, including nonvoting delegates and Senate members in proportion to the total U.S. population in 2010.

Minority populations have struggled and fought for equal rights and opportunities, but what does it mean when their representation in government is so disproportionate with their populations? How effectively does a majority White, male Congress support those in the minority? The legislation and renewal of the Voting Rights Act from 1965 through 2006 is a prominent example of Congress legislating to protect and promote minority rights. At the same time, as this chapter notes, state legislative efforts have since been passed that seek to undermine those protections. Partisan and other legally critical interpretations of the Voting Rights Act have gradually reached all the way to the Supreme Court, based on the 2013 decision in *Shelby v. Holder* that substantially weakened its standing. Yet minority voters today do indeed have considerably greater access to the polls, and elected representation at all federal levels, than they did in 1965.

Table 7.1   The Minority Road to Congress

| Racial/Ethnic Group | 113th Congress | | | | % of U.S. Population, 2010 |
| | House | | Senate | % of Congress | |
	Representative	Delegate			
African American	42	2	2	8.1	12.6
Latino	33	0	4	6.9	16.3
Asian American	11	2	1	2.4	4.8
Native American	2	0	0	<1	0.9

Sources: Jennifer E. Manning, "Membership of the 113th Congress: A Profile," Congressional Research Service, January 13, 2014, http://www.fas.org/sgp/crs/misc/R42964.pdf; Karen R. Humes, Nicholas A. Jones, and Roberto R. Ramirez, "Overview of Race and Hispanic Origin: 2010," 2010 Census Briefs, C2010BR-02, March 2011, 4, http://www.census.gov/prod/cen2010/briefs/c2010br-02.pdf.

THE CIVIL RIGHTS MOVEMENT AS A FOUNDATION FOR VOTING EXPANSION

There are important core elements of resistance to any American political participation by non-Whites, such as the poll tax, literacy tests, and complicated voting registration procedures, that the Black Civil Rights Movement of the 1950s and 1960s began to break open. While there were distinctive, group-specific actions that opened the franchise and electoral participation for Asian Americans, Latinos, and Native Americans, the Black **Civil Rights Movement** moved all three branches of government toward making the political system more accessible to all minority groups. Presidents John F. Kennedy and especially Lyndon B. Johnson helped spur decisive support for change, and Congress passed the 1964 Civil Rights Act and the 1965 Voting Rights Act (discussed in more detail later) with bipartisan majorities. By creating a framework for attacking discrimination against Blacks, the 1960s legislation also opened the way to attacking other forms and types of discrimination, such as direct race-based discrimination and minority language discrimination that affected Latinos,

Asian Americans, Native Americans, and Alaska Natives. And while Blacks, Asian Americans, Latinos, and Native Americans trod different paths, all were significantly organized and advanced by the successes of the Civil Rights Movement.

The significant size of the Black population, its concentration in Southern states, and its centuries of engagement with the American colonial and national governments provided African Americans with a network of social, religious, and political resources that served as a foundation for political change and culminated in the Civil Rights Movement. (See Chapter 3.) Founded in 1909, the National Association for the Advancement of Colored People (NAACP) worked on a legal strategy for attacking *de jure* and *de facto* segregation after 1915, and the strategy began to demonstrate considerable success in the 1940s and 1950s in areas such as voting rights, education, housing, and employment. The NAACP Legal Defense and Education Fund (NAACP LDEF) won a string of civil rights cases in the U.S. Supreme Court in the mid–twentieth century. The NAACP's lawyers successfully tackled the constitutionality of the Texas **White primary** (in which only White Democrats were allowed to participate) in *Smith v. Allwright*, in 1944. The Court struck down **restrictive covenants**, ending the ability of property owners to prohibit the sale of property based on race or ethnicity (*Sweatt v. Painter* [1947]). And in the 1954 *Brown v. or Oliver Brown, et al. v. Board of Education of Topeka, et al. Board of Education* decision (including cases drawn from several states), the Court ruled that separate but equal segregation in education was unconstitutional.

On another front, the development of larger numbers of African American college students attending historically Black colleges and universities (HBCUs; most were founded in the wake of the U.S. Civil War) provided the foot soldiers for protest in the 1950s and early 1960s, thereby bringing racial discrimination into the public arena and making discrimination visible to the nation. Many of the members of the Student Nonviolent Coordinating Committee (SNCC) drawn from HBCUs, acted because they felt that segregation was unjust, immoral, and discriminatory. They felt that the time had come for society to change, and they were willing to sit-in at lunch counters, to ride buses to integrate public way stations, and to work in many locations to encourage people to register and vote. This occurred at the same time that the United States was positioned as the beacon of freedom in competition with the Soviet Union in the Cold War, and as such attracted the attention of developing-world African and Asian nations recently decolonized from European control. The student protests by African Americans, which were covered on television evening news programs and in the national media for the first time, helped to push the U.S. national leadership into realizing that past patterns of racial discrimination were no longer acceptable.[10] In addition to the student protesters and older leaders who had been participants in the military during World War II, new generations of organizations were also helping to lay foundations for voting participation. Beginning in 1962, the Voter Education Project coordinated the voter registration campaigns of five civil rights groups, including the NAACP, the Southern Christian Leadership Conference, the Student Nonviolent Coordinating Committee, the

> How important was civil rights activists' access to U.S. laws, institutions, and resources in their advancement of voting rights protections?

Congress of Racial Equality, and the National Urban League.[11] These voter registration efforts focused on African Americans. (See Table 3.1 on p. 107.)

African American protests during the Civil Rights Movement drew public attention to racial inequities in the American system and society by generating direct action and confrontation in some of the most difficult locations in the South. Sit-ins, in which protesters peacefully occupied seats in diners and other locations to highlight the business's discriminatory practices, began in the 1960s and led to integration of a number of lunch counters; but they also laid the groundwork for the 1964 Civil Rights Act, which outlawed discrimination in public accommodations. The Freedom Rides took civil rights activists on interstate buses into the South to challenge segregation in public restrooms. In 1962, one of the first groups that made this effort was violently attacked and beaten, and the bus was burned. The 1964 Freedom Summer, organized by the Student Nonviolent Coordinating Committee, intended to draw public attention to the violent oppression directed against Blacks in Mississippi. The day after they arrived, three of the workers—Andrew Goodman, James Chaney, and Michael Schwerner—disappeared, and their bodies were later found buried in an earthen dam. New Yorkers Goodman and Schwerner were shot, and Mississippian Chaney had been beaten to death. The murders demonstrated the challenges African Americans faced more brutally and vividly than any of the organizers had expected.[12]

These measures, while mobilizing activists, also rapidly publicized the willingness of Southern public officials to engage in considerable violence, most prominently using fire hoses and police dogs against school children in Birmingham in 1963. The August 1963 March on Washington brought over 200,000 people from all over the United States to petition the national government to provide legislation to advance legal protection for basic civil rights as well as economic resources, including jobs. (See Box 7.3 for examples of modern student activism.)

The peaceful actions of the demonstrators served as a stark contrast to the violence they often faced. For instance, in Selma, Alabama, on a Palm Sunday march in 1965, many neatly dressed adults were beaten bloody and senseless by state police trying to prevent their protest to win the right to vote. While the Fifteenth Amendment affirming the right of former slaves to vote was constitutional, an array of laws created in the late nineteenth century by the Southern states after the national commitment to reform waned, effectively prohibited Black electoral participation. Literacy tests, poll taxes, complicated voter registration procedures, and racial violence were just a few of the strategies Southern Whites used to control the political environment. These public displays of violence against African Americans peacefully seeking the right to participate in electoral politics moved the Kennedy and Johnson administrations, as well as members of the House and Senate, toward support for the 1964 Civil Rights Act and the 1965 Voting Rights Act.

CIVIL RIGHTS AND VOTING RIGHTS LEGISLATION AFTER 1965

Although voting rights legislation during the Civil Rights era had a powerful impact on Black voter participation, it also served as a foundation for advancing the electoral participation of Latinos and Asian Americans and provided protections to other minority groups. In particular,

BOX 7.3 COALITIONS IN ACTION

Students Speak Out

Students at colleges and universities across the United States, and even abroad, have begun to create new ways of bringing to light the daily, discriminatory slights and "microaggressions"* they face on campus. In 2012 students at the University of Notre Dame created performance events, called *Show Some Skin*, in which performers recited poetry or small essays written by other students to express examples of racial, gender, and other types of hostilities. Harvard students in 2014 began the #*I Too Am Harvard* campaign, using Twitter, Tumblr, and other social media to call out other students, faculty, and administrators about their exclusionary behavior and to claim their space within the university. The campaign has received national media attention, including from the *Washington Post*, *Boston Globe*, NPR, and *The Nation*.

Minority law students at UCLA created a video exploring the anxieties they experienced in reaction to the very small numbers of students in their classes in the wake of California's policies, which have amended affirmative action in admissions policies. The student campaign *Being Black at the University of Michigan* emphasized many of these issues, but also pointed to declining Black student enrollment and the lack of university response to address these problems in the past. Black, African, and Asian students at Oxford and Cambridge Universities in England also began to point out the challenges they've faced in their *I Too Am Oxford* and *I Too Am Cambridge* protests.

All of these student measures have drawn public attention to the small ways that discrimination persists in society and highlight how, even today, race matters. While the contemporary barriers faced by racial and ethnic groups are no longer absolute, they do persist and present roadblocks that must be overcome.

*Derald, Wing Sue, Christina M. Capodilupo, Gina C. Torino, Jennifer M. Bucceri, Aisha M. B. Holder, Kevin L. Nadal and Marta Esquilin. "Racial Microaggressions in Everyday Life, Implications for Clinical Practice." *American Psychologist*, Vol. 62, No. 4, May-June 2007, 271-286.

The *I, Too, Am Harvard* Production and Campaign Team

the Civil Rights Acts of 1957 and 1964 established a framework for protecting voting rights. With the expansion of these rights and, subsequently, the growth in electoral participation (see Figure 7.1), minority groups had a growing influence on the election of officials of color and better access to the institutions and resources of the polity.

The **Civil Rights Act of 1957** created basic civil rights administrative infrastructure in the federal government, including a bipartisan Commission on Civil Rights, and a Civil Rights Division within the Department of Justice. **Civil rights** are the enforceable rights or privileges of citizens to political and social freedoms, such as free speech, assembly, and free press. Although the law also provided for jury trials for civil rights cases, this point had been a matter of considerable debate during the legislative process, and it substantially weakened the law. Under this provision, any White defendant charged with discriminating against a Black citizen would be tried by a jury selected from an overwhelmingly White electorate. The racial hostility in the environment made the likelihood of a finding of discrimination highly improbable. The trial by jury provision in the 1957 Civil Rights Act substantially weakened the legislation.

Seven years later, Congress passed the **Civil Rights Act of 1964**, legislation that addressed a variety of concerns, including voting rights, relief against discrimination in places of public accommodation, desegregation of public facilities and public education, equal employment opportunity, and registration and voting statistics, among other things.[13] Voting protections addressed the right to vote in federal elections, and prohibitions of differential standards and

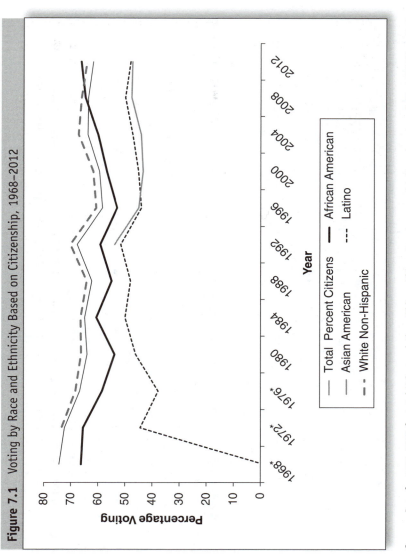

Figure 7.1   Voting by Race and Ethnicity Based on Citizenship, 1968–2012

Sources: Data for 1968–1976 for total U.S. population, Whites, African Americans, and Latinos based on Table A-10, "Reported Registration Rates in Presidential Election Years, by Selected Characteristics: November 1968 to 2012." Total U.S. population is based on percent registered of total voting-age population, from the same table, http://www.census.gov/hhes/www/socdemo/voting/publications/historical/index.html. These are *not* data based on citizenship.

*Data for 1980–2012 based on Table A-1, "Reported Voting and Registration by Race, Hispanic Origin, Sex and Age Groups: November 1964–2012," http://www.census.gov/hhes/www/socdemo/voting/publications/historical/index.html. These data are based on citizenship.

literacy tests. But as had been the case in previous legislation, prosecution of violations continued to be conducted on a case-by-case basis. Any litigation was thus a long, slow, and often unsuccessful process. More important, even when a case was successful, it was just that—a single case—and of significance only in a single jurisdiction.[14]

The **Voting Rights Act of 1965** was framed to address voting discrimination and voting rights in a more strategic and more administrative fashion. Under the 1957 and 1964 legislation, each violation was handled as an individual court case, requiring lengthy periods for the collection of evidence, investigation, and prosecution. Although the Fifteenth Amendment (1870) included the right to vote and prohibited denial of that right on the basis of "race, color, or previous condition of servitude," it had not been enforced consistently after the end of Reconstruction in 1876. (See Chapter 3.) The text of the VRA thus begins: "An Act to enforce the Fifteenth Amendment to the Constitution of the United States, and for other purposes." Section 2 of the act limited the ability of "any State or political subdivision to deny or abridge the right of any citizen of the United States to vote on account of race or color." Section 3 allowed for the appointment of federal examiners in order "to enforce the guarantees of the Fifteenth Amendment."

Sections 4 and 5 are the most significant, and even today remain controversial provisions. **Section 4** identified tests or devices by which states or subdivisions in any federal, state, or local election discouraged electoral participation. It also specified that citizens could not be denied the right to vote. States or political subdivisions that the attorney general found using such tests, *and* where the census determined that less than 50 percent of voting-age persons were registered on November 1, 1964, or had voted in the November 1964 presidential election, were subject to the VRA's Section 5. **Section 5** required that any state or political jurisdiction that met the tests of Section 4(a) had to seek agreement from the U.S. District Court for the District of Columbia (and later the Civil Rights Division of the Department of Justice) when it tried to administer new voting laws different from those in effect in November 1964, to ensure that the new law "will not have the effect of denying or abridging the right to vote on account of race or color."[15]

Unlike the civil rights legislation of 1957 and 1964, the VRA was not based on a requirement of trial by jury. It transformed the effort to prove discrimination from a case-by-case judicial procedure in Southern courts into administrative judgments made outside of the Southern jurisdictions in which voting occurred. National officials had the responsibility for investigating and verifying a series of facts. The federal courts and the civil rights divisions determined whether a city, town, or state was covered by Section 4 based on whether less than 50 percent of the voting-age population was registered to vote in the 1964 presidential elections (and then again in later elections, as the Voting Rights Act was extended), and the attorney general judged whether tests or devices were used by political jurisdictions. These tests or devices might have included the requirement for a voter to do the following:

1. demonstrate the ability to read, write, understand, or interpret any matter,

2. demonstrate any educational achievement or his knowledge of any particular subject,

3. possess good moral character, or

ASSOCIATED PRESS

In 1966, the first major election year after passage of the 1965 Voting Rights Act, an estimated 1,000 African Americans lined up to vote in Birmingham, Alabama. The VRA was designed to address voting discrimination, particularly against African Americans, and soon expanded to include protections for other minority groups.

4. prove his qualifications by the voucher of registered voters or members of any other class.[16]

The director of the census evaluated the voter registration evidence, and appeals were handled by federal courts outside of the region in which the practices were most frequently in place. While the process was still not simple, the changes had a genuine impact on Black voter registration and, within a few years, Black electoral participation. Law professor Nathaniel Persily explains the power incorporated into Section 5 of the VRA:

That measure stands alone in American history in its alteration of authority between the federal government and the states and the unique procedures it requires of states and localities that want to change their laws. [Emphasis added.] No other statute applies only to a subset of the country and requires covered states and localities to get permission from the federal government before implementing a certain type of law. Such a remedy was necessary because case-by-case adjudication of voting rights lawsuits proved incapable of reining in crafty Dixiecrat legislatures determined to deprive African Americans of their right to vote, regardless of what a federal court might order.[17]

The Voting Rights Act laid the framework for and was explicitly designed to enhance African American political participation. Its effectiveness attracted the attention of other racial and ethnic groups, including non-Mexican and Asian immigrant groups, who argued that the discriminatory group–based patterns they faced, such as ballots and electoral materials available only in English, deserved legislative attention as well. After the 1965 Immigration and Nationality Act was passed, significant numbers of non-English speaking Mexican and Asian immigrant groups immigrated to the United States for the first time in its history.[18] It is important to think about the implications of voting rights for the United States not only as a democracy but also as an immigrant nation, with increasingly complex electoral sectors that include distinctive racial/ethnic and/or language groups with lower voting and turnout rates.[19] In subsequent years, beginning in the 1975 extension with the addition of clauses attending to minority language issues, Latinos and other "language minorities" (such as Asian Americans and Native Americans) that met specific criteria were also brought under the protection of the Voting Rights Act. The minority language protections were renewed in 1982, 1992, and 2006. (See Box 7.4, on legal challenges to the VRA.)

BOX 7.4 CROSS ROAD

Contesting the Constitutionality of the Voting Rights Act

The passage of the Voting Rights Act in 1965 was revolutionary. It ensured that Blacks and, after 1975, Latinos, Asian Americans, Native Americans, and Alaskan Natives had federal protections for registration and voting. The VRA also ensured, particularly after 1982, that jurisdictions with high concentrations of minority voters would draw electoral districts in which minority voters could elect the candidates of their choice, often candidates of the same race or ethnicity as the constituency.

The act has been controversial since its passage, and it remains so today. Contemporary critics often concede that the act's protections were necessary in 1965, when racially exclusionary policies in Southern states justified federal intervention. They note, however, that Congress initially passed the most contentious parts of the VRA for five years and later extended them. To critics, these serial extensions represent an overreaching federal power. Their objections are exacerbated by an observation that the most overt forms of electoral discrimination originally used to justify the VRA, such as barriers to voter registration, have largely disappeared according to Abigail Thernstrom.[20] VRA critics also contend that there is no continued constitutional justification for holding parts of the country, mostly in the South, to a higher standard of federal oversight—the mandate to preclear changes to registration and voting rules—than the rest of the country under the act's Section V. Those making this criticism observe that while electoral discrimination may remain,

it is not concentrated in the states that had the worst records in 1965.

In 1966, when the Supreme Court first reviewed the act's constitutionality in *South Carolina v. Katzenbach* (1966),[21] it found it to be constitutional. The Court held in *Katzenbach* that the Fifteenth Amendment, which prohibited denying a citizen's right to vote based on "race, color, or previous condition of servitude," provided authority to the federal government to intervene in what had traditionally been the states' responsibility to manage elections. VRA advocates saw this shift from state to federal power as necessary to implement the Fifteenth Amendment. Subsequent extensions of the act reflect recognition that minorities continue to participate at lower rates than do non-Hispanic Whites, and that some of this gap can be attributed to the discriminatory effects of state and local voting practices. The expansions grow from a realization that simply equalizing rules will not overcome the legacies of past discrimination, and that voting alone will not ensure a minority political voice. Instead, the act must ensure minority representation as well as participation.

The Supreme Court's most recent review of the VRA's constitutionality was in *Shelby County, Alabama v. Holder* (2013). It ruled that the criteria for added federal monitoring of registration procedures and voting practices found in the VRA's Section

IV were unconstitutional because they had been established in the 1960s and 1970s and not updated. It left to Congress the responsibility to establish new standards. Until Congress does so, jurisdictions that had been subject to preclearance requirements under Section V are free to make changes without Justice Department or federal court review. Many voting rights advocates feared that without preclearance, states and localities will be able to implement new restrictions on minority voting.

Considering This Crossroad

- When the VRA was initially passed in 1965, there were fewer than 1,500 African American

elected officials.[22] Today, there are more than 9,000, and one has occupied the presidency. How might these numbers be used both to justify ending VRA protections and to extend them?

- Opposition to the VRA focuses, in part, on state authority to regulate voting. Is the VRA's creation of voting rules at the federal level an appropriate solution to the problems of voting discrimination if it occurs at the local level?

- After reading this chapter, in what ways do you think legislation like the VRA falls short of addressing the problems of minority participation and representation?

Extending VRA Protections, 1970 and 1975

The Voting Rights Act was passed with a five-year time limit. If it was to be extended, Congress needed to reconsider, amend, and reauthorize it in 1970. (See Figure 7.2 for a summary of all VRA-related legislation.) On June 22, 1970, the Ninety-first Congress extended the legislation for another five years and lowered the voting age to eighteen.[23] The 1970 extension also reduced residency requirements to thirty days before a presidential election and suspended the literacy test for an additional five years. The trigger that had originally applied Section 4 to states of the former Confederacy was expanded to cover jurisdictions "with a literacy test in which less than 50 per cent of the voting-age residents were registered on Nov. 1, 1968, or voted in the 1968 presidential election."[24] This resulted in new districts or counties in Alaska, Arizona, California, Idaho, New York, and Oregon becoming subject to Section 4.

When the VRA was next considered, in 1975, the debate around it brought new challenges to civil rights groups that had been supporting voting rights legislation for decades. The Leadership Conference on Civil Rights (LCCR) was first founded in 1950 as a broad coalition of fifty labor, civil rights, religious, and racial/ethnic organizations to promote and protect civil rights. Its three founders included A. Philip Randolph, founder of the Brotherhood of Sleeping Car Porters, a union of the Black men who worked on the Pullman Company's sleeping cars; Roy Wilkins, executive director of the NAACP; and Arnold Aronson, a leader of Jewish labor and social welfare organizations who was also president of the Leadership Conference's Education Fund.[25] Clarence Mitchell, director of the NAACP's Washington Bureau, and Joseph Rauh, attorney for the LCCR, had successfully worked together as LCCR representatives on civil rights legislative campaigns in 1957, 1964, 1965, and 1970, and they faced another VRA extension in 1975.

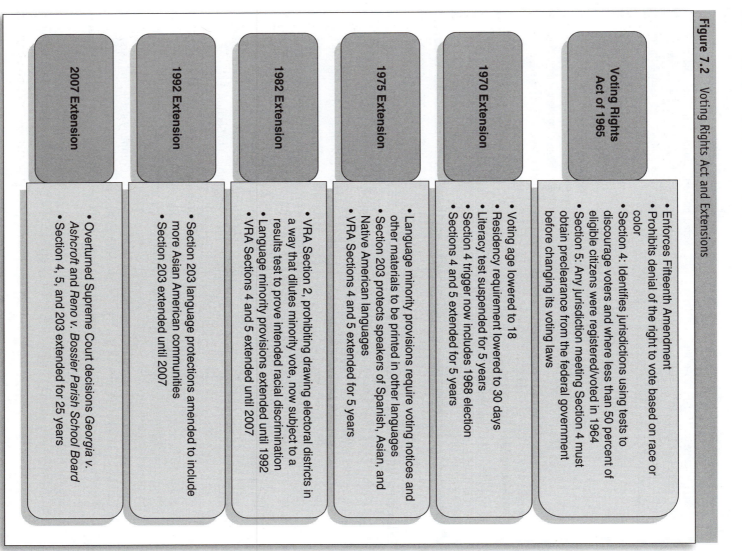

Figure 7.2   Voting Rights Act and Extensions

Voting Rights Act of 1965

- Enforces Fifteenth Amendment
- Prohibits denial of the right to vote based on race or color
- Section 4: Identifies jurisdictions using tests to discourage voters and where less than 50 percent of eligible citizens were registered/voted in 1964
- Section 5: Any jurisdiction meeting Section 4 must obtain preclearance from the federal government before changing its voting laws

1970 Extension

- Voting age lowered to 18
- Residency requirement lowered to 30 days
- Literacy test suspended for 5 years
- Section 4 trigger now includes 1968 election
- Sections 4 and 5 extended for 5 years

1975 Extension

- Language minority provisions require voting notices and other materials to be printed in other languages
- Section 203 protects speakers of Spanish, Asian, and Native American languages
- VRA Sections 4 and 5 extended for 5 years

1982 Extension

- VRA Section 2, prohibiting drawing electoral districts in a way that dilutes minority vote, now subject to a results test to prove intended racial discrimination
- Language minority provisions extended until 1992
- VRA Sections 4 and 5 extended until 2007

1992 Extension

- Section 203 language protections amended to include more Asian American communities
- Section 203 extended until 2007

2007 Extension

- Overturned Supreme Court decisions *Georgia v. Ashcroft* and *Reno v. Bossier Parish School Board*
- Section 4, 5, and 203 extended for 25 years

While earlier legislative efforts had focused on African Americans, the 1975 effort was different. Recognizing how valuable a resource the 1965 VRA had become, representatives from Mexican American organizations such as the Mexican American Legal Defense and Educational Fund (MALDEF) pressed to achieve recognition of Latinos as a group also subject to discrimination. Rauh and Mitchell struggled with each other as to whether this expansion of protections to other minority groups was an appropriate move. Mitchell feared that incorporation of Latinos within civil rights legal protections might lead to the legislation's rejection by the Supreme Court, therefore weakening protections for Blacks. This concern generated considerable conflict within the LCCR, which had previously been organized around the concept of racial discrimination as a problem specifically facing African Americans. Political scientist Dianne Pinderhughes noted, "Mitchell and the NAACP were opposed and vetoed the LCCR's support for including them. Because of the NAACP veto, LCCR members who favored the inclusion of Latinos in the 1975 legislation worked as individuals to achieve this result."[26]

But despite this internal challenge, the LCCR reached agreement and eventually supported the 1975 extension. Congress passed legislation with expanded protection for Mexican Americans, as well as for Asian Americans, Native Americans, and Alaskan Natives. The specific legislation was broadened to characterize a type of discrimination against "language minorities," and **Section 203** of the 1975 extension provides, "Whenever any State or political subdivision [covered by the section] provides registration or voting notices, forms, instructions, assistance, or other materials or information relating to the electoral process, including ballots, *it shall provide them in the language of the applicable minority group as well as in the English language.*"[27] (Emphasis added.) Jurisdictions in which more than 5 percent of voting-age citizens were members of a covered language group and where literacy rates were lower than the national average were required to comply with Section 203's requirement.

As originally specified in Section 4, the Bureau of the Census received responsibility for calculating which jurisdictions should be subject to the minority language provisions of Section 203.[28] Because this was defined by generic legal language, voters who spoke Spanish, Asian languages, and Native American languages, and who met the other requirements, were also protected by Section 203, rather than just Mexican American Spanish speakers. Congress, however, did not extend these protections to all non-English-speakers. It limited protections to groups that had experienced multigenerational political exclusion based, at least in part, on language discrimination. In addition to the minority language provisions, the protections provided by Sections 4 and 5 were extended for a slightly longer period of time, seven years, until 1982.

With the minority language provisions amended to the Voting Rights Act, more eligible voters received access to the information they needed to participate in U.S. democracy. While English-only movements exist in the United States, the Constitution and legislation like the VRA help to ensure that citizens who do not yet speak English or whose comprehension is better in another language are not barred from participating in the electoral process. Thus they are better able to use the laws, institutions, and resources of the polity to advance their interests. Just as the 1960s civil rights legislation eliminated the use of the literacy test as a barrier to Black voting, the minority language provisions removed English literacy as a requirement for voting participation among citizens who were natives from non-English-speaking countries.

Minority Vote Dilution and the 1982 VRA Extension

The legislative issues discussed when the Voting Rights Act was considered for renewal in 1982 were considerably more complicated than they had been for any previous period. The minority language provisions remained a source of debate between African American and Mexican American interest groups, but by 1981 civil rights lobbyists were joined in Washington by a group of civil and voting rights attorneys who had previously worked in Southern states to implement the civil and voting rights legislation of the 1960s and 1970s. They had extensive grassroots experience, and in addition to monitoring the implementation and pre-clearance provisions of the VRA, were involved in desegregating public accommodations, schools, state agencies, and a host of other areas.[29] Frank Parker and Barbara Phillips of the Mississippi Lawyers for Civil Rights Under Law's Voting Rights Project, Lani Guinier of the NAACP LDEF, Joachin Avila of MALDEF and Laughlin MacDonald of the American Civil Liberties Union's Voting Rights Project were just a few of the attorneys involved.[30] They brought with them a commitment to convince Congress to amend the 1982 legislation to respond to a recent Supreme Court decision.

Voting rights advocates such as Wiley Bolden challenged the electoral system used in the city of Mobile, Alabama, which had been using at-large systems for selecting members since 1911. An **at-large election** is conducted on a citywide basis; even if a numerical "minority" of the city's population votes for a single candidate from the same minority group, it is unlikely to be able to elect that individual. If the election is based on a system of smaller districts, the minority has a greater chance of selecting an individual representing the minority population. By 1980, Mobile had a population of 200,452—36.2 percent of which was Black.[31] The city's three commissioners were elected by at-large elections. The city's Black population was too small to prevail under that system at a time when voting was usually **racially polarized.** In other words, when Whites voted for Whites and Blacks voted for Blacks in locations in which Blacks were in the minority, Black candidates were defeated. With an at-large electoral system in Mobile, Blacks were always in the minority. The voting rights attorneys argued that in locations like these with at-large systems, even when Blacks were successful in registering and voting, they were subject to **minority vote dilution.** This meant that even though Blacks' votes were counted, they were considerably less likely to result in the election of officials of their choosing, or that those elected met the standard of descriptive representation of the Black population.

The Supreme Court had ruled in *City of Mobile v. Bolden* (1980) that **discriminatory intent** or purpose had to be proven in order to overturn an at-large system, meaning one had to prove that the electoral system in place was intended to disadvantage Blacks or another minority population.[32] The decision held that the Fifteenth Amendment, reaffirmed in Section 2 of the Voting Rights Act, did not protect against vote dilution, even when it reduced the collective voice of minority voters. The challengers were successful in the retrial, which had been ordered by the Court to take the intent standard into account. They proved the original law *was intended* to be discriminatory, but the voting rights attorneys argued that the length of time, and the financial costs required to reach a finding of intentional discrimination, was too high and too complicated. Some of the laws had first been passed in the dawn of the twentieth century, and it took several historians months of research to investigate the history of the legislative process.[33]

Having not achieved the result they desired from the Supreme Court, the voting rights attorneys took their case to Congress. They convinced Washington-based civil rights lobbyists in the NAACP and the Leadership Conference on Civil Rights to ask Congress to include a discriminatory results standard for Section 2 of the VRA to the extension due in 1982. This discriminatory results standard would make it possible to prove discrimination in the use of at-large electoral systems, and allow for a remedy in the creation of a number of legislative districts for city councils and/or state legislatures; creating smaller districts would increase the possibility of the election of officials from groups not in the majority population. Crafted by Senator Robert Dole (R-KA), the so-called Dole Compromise allowed for a results, rather than an intent, test for Section 2 cases. Plaintiffs challenging an electoral system only had to prove that the outcome of a districting system discriminated against a VRA-covered minority. This was accomplished more readily than the previous intent standard, which had required evidence of intentional discrimination. The 1982 extension also extended the Section 5 preclearance provision, this time for twenty-five years, until 2007.[34] The Supreme Court upheld the basic components of the Dole Compromise in the *Thornburg v. Gingles* case decided in 1986.

The content of the 1982 extension shifted the center of attention back toward African Americans in the South and away from the growing language minorities, whose populations had begun growing exponentially in the 1980s and would continue to grow in the 1990s. While the minority language provisions were extended in 1982, they were scheduled for reconsideration after only ten years, in 1992, rather than twenty-five years, in 2007, along with the rest of the renewal.[35]

Minority Language Provisions in the 1992 Extension

The Voting Rights Act was first passed in the same year as the 1965 Immigration Act, which produced unexpectedly significant increases in non-European immigration. The Immigration Act of 1965 changed U.S. immigration policy, which had previously been structured around race and quotas, by completely eliminating those racial restrictions. (See Chapter 11.) This led to an explosion in immigration from non-Western countries. By 1992, the size of the Latino population had reached 22.3 million, or 9 percent of the national population, and the Asian American population had climbed to 6.9 million (2.9 percent). Among the 31.5 million Latinos five years of age and older in 2000, about 20 percent spoke only English, 78.6 percent spoke Spanish and some English, and around 40 percent spoke English less than well.

The growth of Asian immigration introduced many more languages to those already in use. Ten distinctive national language groups existed among Asian Americans at the time of the 1965 Immigration Act, with the largest groups being Chinese, Filipino, Japanese, Asian Indian, Korean, and Vietnamese—each comprising 8.9 percent or more of the Asian American population. After 1965, 2 percent or less of Asian populations in the United States spoke Laotian, Cambodian, Thai, and Hmong, followed by Burmese, Sri Lankan, and Bangladeshi. Based on the 1990 census, 66 percent of Asians had been born in foreign countries, with 38 percent having entered between 1980 and 1990. The census reported in 1993, "Of the 4.1 million

Asians 5 years old and over, 56 percent did not speak English 'very well' and 35 percent were linguistically isolated."[36] The least isolated were Filipinos and Asian Indians, with the lowest portions of the population that did not speak English very well. The highest proportion included the Hmong (from Cambodia) and Laotians, but even those groups with longer histories in the United States, such as the Japanese and Chinese, had relatively high proportions that did not speak English very well, at around 60 percent.[37]

The first minority language provisions had been enacted in the mid-1970s, when the Asian American population was much smaller. Political scientist Pei-te Lien notes that most of the Asian American population groups on the mainland were relatively small (or at least too small to reach the Section 203 criteria requiring 5 percent of the voting-age population). Consequently, "no one outside of Hawaii could receive coverage under the 1975 law."[38] As the Southern voting rights attorneys had done in 1982, Lien reports that community advocacy and other civil rights groups worked to expand coverage in time for the 1992 extension of the minority language provisions: "[S]ection 203 was amended to include large Asian American communities that either met the 5 percent test or had at least 10,000 voting-age citizens" in minority languages and lower levels of English literacy. Specifically, this applied to Chinese Americans in California and New York; Japanese in Los Angeles, California, and Honolulu, Hawaii; Vietnamese in Southern California counties; Tagalog in Los Angeles; and Ilocano in Hawaii.[39] Under the 1992 extension, jurisdictions were required to provide assistance to voters in these languages, including electoral materials, bilingual registrars, interpreters for oral assistance, and other means.

The extremely rapid growth of the Asian American population in the 1980s meant that jurisdictions in California, New York, and Hawaii had to address the complex challenges associated with incorporating a population from across a large range of nations with very distinctive languages, histories, and abilities. These states had Asian populations from different nations, speaking multiple languages. There were sufficient numbers to require election and voting materials in a number of languages. However, producing voting information on candidates and referenda before elections, making sure that ballots were correctly printed in multiple languages, and properly distributing election officials with appropriate language skills across numerous polling places demanded very careful planning. Some jurisdictions lacked full compliance with the 1992 standards, and they experienced a variety of problems providing workers with appropriate language abilities.[40]

Successful extension of the minority language provisions required collaborative work and political mobilization by a variety of minority interest and advocacy organizations. The Mexican American Legal Defense and Education Fund, the NAACP LDEF, the Lawyers Committee for Civil Rights Under Law, and the Asian American Legal Defense and Education Fund collaborated in lawsuits, voter mobilization, redistricting, and lobbying for and implementation of the 1992 legislation. Through their efforts, the roads to equal voting rights converged under a common cause that effectively expanded electoral access for these language minorities.

> How does resistance to minority language provisions reflect the persistence of racialization?

REDISTRICTING AND MINORITY REPRESENTATION

The Supreme Court issued two rulings in the mid-1960s that changed the way redistricting was handled, from an unregulated process to one focused on creating legislative districts relatively equal in population. In *Baker v. Carr* (1962) the Court ruled that requiring consistent procedures in the reapportionment of legislative districts in Tennessee by the courts was appropriate. These were considered equal protection issues, as specified by the Fourteenth Amendment. In *Reynolds v. Sims* (1964), the Court coined the phrase "one person, one vote." The Court reviewed a number of cases, including one involving the Alabama legislature, which had not revised district boundaries since 1900 even though the state's population distribution had shifted significantly from rural to urban centers. Rural districts with far fewer voters were represented at the same rate as large cities such as Mobile, Montgomery, and Birmingham. The Court held that the Fourteenth Amendment guaranteed relative equality of voting power; meaning districts should reflect the principle of "one person, one vote" and that state electoral systems which failed to allocate voting power on the basis of population were unconstitutional.[41]

The minority language provisions included in the 1992 extension of the Voting Rights Act ensured that American citizens who were more comfortable speaking and understanding a language other than English would now be ensured equal access to voter information and ballots in that language.

While these cases didn't explicitly address race, they had important racial implications, since many of Alabama's large cities had significant African American populations.

For every year in which the census is held, the U.S. Bureau of the Census provides population data that states, counties, and local jurisdictions use to draw legislative districts of relatively equal size. With the passage of the Voting Rights Act, the creation of equally sized legislative districts as required by *Baker v. Carr* and *Reynolds v. Sims* also added distinct racial implications into the redistricting process. Congressional, state legislative, city council, school board, county, and other types of districts are redrawn every ten years to account for changing populations, but this has also become a major opportunity for partisan as well as racial competition. Districts can be redrawn in many different ways. Drawing district lines to reach into an urban area, or to swing outside of a city, can have very significant partisan implications by adding more Democrats to create a majority-Democratic or majority-Republican legislative district. State legislatures, city councils, and county commissions often engage in lengthy battles over the shape, urban-rural distribution, or racial balance of their legislative districts to give their political party an advantage. Drawing district lines skillfully by taking all these factors into account can frame the balance of political power in the state legislature for a whole decade. In some cases the state legislature may draw congressional or state legislative districts, while in others nonpartisan state redistricting commissions have the responsibility for this task.[42]

By the 1990s, redistricting to attend to the issues of relative equity in the size of legislative districts intersected in hard-fought battles with policies related to voting rights, such as issues of minority vote dilution, racially polarized voting, and the creation of majority-minority districts. The battle over population equity and minority voting rights began to occur with regularity after the 1990, 2000, and 2010 censuses, and will occur again after the 2020 census.[43]

One example of redistricting is evident in North Carolina's Twelfth Congressional District, which was redrawn after the 1990 census. At the direction of the U.S. Department of Justice, the North Carolina legislature was required to take into account the size of the state's Black population by drawing a second majority-Black district. The Department of Justice's ruling required North Carolina to create the Twelfth District. The shape and character of that district became the subject of the federal voting rights case *Shaw v. Reno* (1993), which raised multiple issues before the Supreme Court, including the constitutionality of majority-minority districts. The Court ruled the Twelfth Congressional District unconstitutional in 1993. The district was redrawn and reconsidered at the district court level, and the Supreme Court reviewed it several times as late as 2001. Yet by that time the North Carolina legislature needed to redraw districts based on the new 2000 census. Map 7.1 shows the first version of the district in 1992, and the district as it was drawn in 2000. The Court eventually judged a version of the district drawn in 2000 as constitutional based on the close relationship between race and political behavior in the state. In other words, the North Carolina legislature had drawn a district in which Blacks were the majority, and the Court reasoned, since most Blacks were Democrats, drawing a Democratic district was acceptable. In other words, the Supreme Court used African American partisanship to explain its acceptance of the constitutionality of the majority-Black Twelfth District that the district had not "proved to be an unconstitutional racial gerrymander . . . where race correlates highly with political affiliation."[44]

At the time of this writing, the Twelfth District's congressional seat is vacant. Congressman Mel Watt was nominated by President Barack Obama to serve as head of the Federal Housing Finance Agency. Watt was confirmed late in the fall of 2013 after the Senate changed its rules to eliminate use of the filibuster.[45] North Carolina Republican governor Pat McCrory has ruled that the seat will be filled in a primary and general election following the existing election schedule for the 2014 election year and has appointed no one to fill the seat for the duration.[46]

Table 7.2 provides basic information on the actual numbers of officials of color elected in recent decades. The data highlight the impact of the civil and voting rights legislation discussed in this chapter. The U.S. Census Bureau has collected information infrequently on

Map 7.1   North Carolina's Twelfth Congressional District, 1991 and 2010

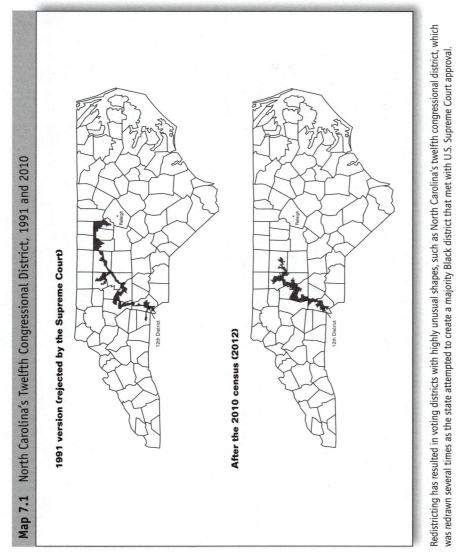

1991 version (rejected by the Supreme Court)

Raleigh

12th District

After the 2010 census (2012)

Raleigh

12th District

Redistricting has resulted in voting districts with highly unusual shapes, such as North Carolina's twelfth congressional district, which was redrawn several times as the state attempted to create a majority Black district that met with U.S. Supreme Court approval.

Source: Congressional Districts in the 1990s: A Portrait of America (Washington, DC: Congressional Quarterly, 1993), 548; "Congressional Districts," National Atlas.gov.

the total numbers of elected officials in the United States, with 513,200 reported in 1990,[47] but we can use this total number as a frame of reference when looking at the minority representation numbers in Table 7.2. In 1970 there were fewer than 1,500 African American elected officials. By 1990, there were over 7,000, with about 4,000 Latino and 362 Asian American elected officials. The numbers have continued to rise, with 77 Native American state representatives by 2010, and the number of Asian American elected officials doubling. While these are significant increases, based on their total number of elected officials in 1990, Asian Americans remain a relatively small proportion of U.S. elected officials as a whole. By 2010, African American legislators numbered over 10,500, and Latinos have reached over 5,850.

After nearly fifty years of protection under the Voting Rights Act, all the citizens on America's uneven roads vote routinely and elect representatives from Black, Latino, Native,

Table 7.2   Elected Officials by Race and Ethnicity, 1970–2010

Racial/Ethnic Groups	1970	1990	2000	2010
Native Americans	N/A	N/A	N/A	77[1]
African Americans	1,469[2]	7,370	9,001	10,500[3]
Latinos	N/A	4,004	5,019	5,850[4]
Asian Americans	N/A	362[5]	587[6]	892[7]

Note: Only limited information exists on these numbers by specific groups, especially before 1990.

1. The 2009 data are from the National Conference of State Legislatures, http://www.ncsl.org/legislatures-elections/legisdata/native-american-legislators-2009.aspx. The most frequently elected officials among Native Americans are state legislators.

2. U.S. Census Bureau, *Statistical Abstract of the United States: 2007*, 126th ed. (Washington, DC: 2006). "Black Elected Officials: 1970–2000, " Table 403, p. 255; "Latino Elected Officials: 1990 and 2000," Table 404, p. 255.

3. *National Roster of Black Elected Officials: Fact Sheet*, Joint Center for Political and Economic Studies, November 2011, http://jointcenter.org/sites/default/files/upload/research/files/National%20Roster%20of%20Black%20Elected%20Officials%20Fact%20Sheet.pdf.

4. *2011 Directory of Latino Elected Officials*, National Association of Latino Elected Officials, http://www.naleo.org/directory.html.

5. *National Asian Pacific American Political Almanac, 1994* (Los Angeles: UCLA Asian American Studies Center, 1994).

6. Don T. Nakanishi and James S. Lai, eds., *National Asian Pacific American Political Almanac 2003–04*, 11th ed. (Los Angeles: UCLA Asian American Studies Center, 2003), 52.

7. Don T. Nakanishi and James S. Lai, eds., *2007–08 National Asian Pacific American Political Almanac* (Los Angeles: UCLA: Asian American Studies Center, 2007).

and Asian American groups in greater numbers than they did in 1965. Political contests at the state level continue over important elements of participation such as voter ID, felony disenfranchisement, and same-day voter registration, but congressional support for voting rights legislation increased over the decades through the early years of the twenty-first century.

The presence of elected representatives from all of these groups at the national level in Congress, in state legislatures, and in state governments has gradually created a political environment in which it's been possible to have Asian Americans elected to the Senate in Hawaii, and to the governor's office in the state of Washington. They provide opportunity for day-to-day service to all the constituents of their respective states, but they also participate in the evolution of political crises such as Watergate in the 1970s, debate over educational and social welfare policy, and make important contributions to the process of dismantling the long-term immigration policies that limited access to U.S. citizenship for

Latinos, Asians, and Africans. Mexican Americans, Cuban Americans, and Puerto Ricans are elected in even far larger numbers to national and state legislative posts than Asian Americans because of their strong settlement patterns in the West and Southwest, but they have also increased their presence throughout the country in recent decades. With voting rights protections based on language, they have been able to increase their participation in electoral politics and legislative policymaking. Some have served as senators, such as Ted Cruz from Texas, and Marco Rubio as senator from Florida. Others have served as governors, such as Susannah Martinez of New Mexico, or mayors of major cities, such as Antonio Villaraigosa of Los Angeles. African Americans have been elected governors and senators, but not as frequently. On the other hand, their total number of elected officials—10,500—significantly outpaces all of the other groups, as Table 7.2 shows.

The year 1965 marked a profound change in America's uneven roads. Voting rights protection, combined with the impact of the Immigration Act, have changed the composition of the American nation, and provided protections for the routine civil and voting rights citizens' exercise, even when they are African American, Latino, Asian, and Native American. Voting and the election of representatives for policy are no longer unusual or infrequent. Public officials are drawn from throughout the geographic and demographic national rainbow. Nonminority officials, such as Texas governor and later U.S. president George W. Bush, approached their political campaigns at the state and national level, as well as their voting and immigration policies, by taking these facts into account. We now turn to a discussion of the most recent consideration of voting rights, in 2006–2007.

THE POLITICS BEHIND THE 2006 EARLY RENEWAL OF THE VOTING RIGHTS ACT

Congress took on the next renewal of the Voting Rights Act a year before the 1992 extension was set to expire. The Fannie Lou Hamer, Rosa Parks, and Coretta Scott King Voting Rights Act Reauthorization and Amendments Act of 2006 was passed with relatively little difficulty, receiving votes of 390–33 in the House and 98–0 in the Senate. Political scientist Katherine Tate explains that President George W. Bush did not play "a race card style of politics that [fed] on Whites' racial resentment of Blacks and [helped] the party's candidates win elections."[48] Instead, she argues that Black officials chose not to mobilize, and that President Bush and the Republicans chose not to oppose renewal in order to avoid encouraging the concerns of African Americans.

A number of amendments, all proposed by Republicans, were debated on the House floor and ultimately rejected, but they are significant in highlighting the persistence of efforts to restrict voter participation by minority groups through the introduction of roadblocks. The first amendment to the 2006 VRA extension fought to revise the preclearance requirement from Section 5, to subject a jurisdiction "to the pre-clearance requirement if it had had a discriminatory test in place or voter turnout of less than 50 percent in any of the three most recent presidential elections."[49] It was rejected, 318–96, in the House. The next amendment would have facilitated covered jurisdictions' removal from the preclearance requirement if they met the standards of current law. It was rejected, 302–118. The third amendment proposed eliminating bilingual ballots and gained the most support, but was defeated, 238–185. Republicans sup-

BOX 7.5 CROSS ROAD

Congressional Votes on Voting Rights

It is interesting to track congressional support for voting rights legislation over time. Congressional support for the Voting Rights Act in 1965 showed about three-quarters of each house of Congress supported the legislation, with support crossing partisan lines, but noticeably greater proportions of Republicans than Democrats voting *aye*. Overall support fell in 1970, and then increased on an ongoing basis afterward, in 1975, and again in 1982. The 1992 minority language provisions were voted upon apart from the original elements of the legislation; the House was considerably more divided, and the Senate less supportive than the chambers had been ten years before. By 2006 both the House (90 percent) and the Senate (98 percent) voted overwhelmingly for the legislation.

As Figure 7.3 shows, there was considerable change in the overall support for voting rights legislation, for its extension, and for the broadened coverage that was created for minority language provisions, and other types of access after 1980. There were, however, important shifts in partisan support for the legislation as well. While Democratic president Lyndon B. Johnson of Texas played the definitive role in moving Congress and the nation toward a national political reaffirmation of the Fifteenth Amendment in order to end Southern states' barriers toward electoral participation, the Southern Democratic Party was less supportive than the Republican Party when the legislation passed in 1965.

But the president also understood that the Democratic Party supported strong enforcement. He offered a prediction as he signed the legislation: that the South would be lost to his own party for a generation. Johnson was an astute political observer, and his prediction proved accurate. Previously Democratic, White Southern voters shifted their allegiance from the Democratic to the Republican Party rapidly. Although opposition to the legislation was small,

Why does minority representation in government matter if these groups now have civil and voting rights protections under the law?

southerners moved away from Democratic members of the House and Senate, and toward Republican Party members over the years. But even with that partisan shift, the legislation won increasing support in both houses and across the parties, to the point that Supreme Court justice Antonin Scalia commented critically in the *Shelby County v. Holder* oral arguments on February 27, 2013: "originally [in 1965] the vote in the Senate, for example was something like 79 to 18, and in the 2006 extension, it was 98 to nothing . . . decided that perhaps they'd better not vote against it, that there's nothing, that there's no–none of their interests in voting against it."*

*U.S. Supreme Court oral arguments, Shelby County, Alabama v. Eric H. Holder, Jr., Attorney General, et al., February 27, 2013, http://www.supremecourt.gov/oral_arguments/argument_transcripts/12-96.pdf.

Figure 7.3   Congressional Votes on Voting Rights

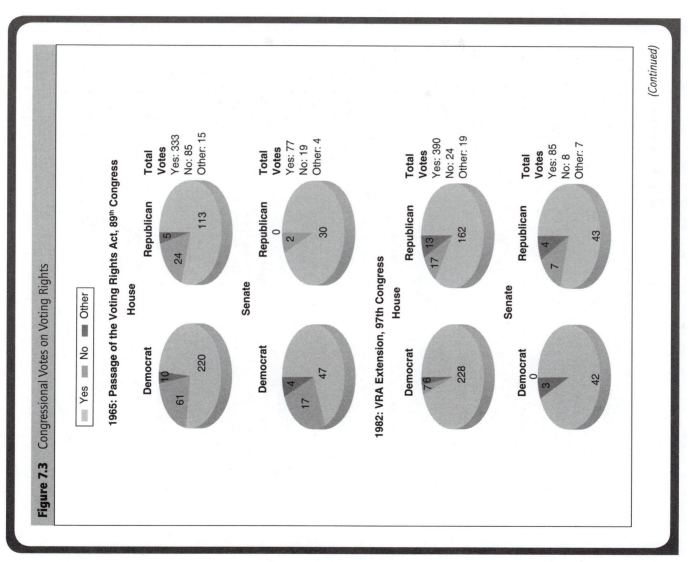

Yes   No   Other

1965: Passage of the Voting Rights Act, 89th Congress

House

Democrat
10
61
220

Republican
5
24
113

Total Votes
Yes: 333
No: 85
Other: 15

Senate

Democrat
4
17
47

Republican
0
2
30

Total Votes
Yes: 77
No: 19
Other: 4

1982: VRA Extension, 97th Congress

House

Democrat
76
228

Republican
17   13
162

Total Votes
Yes: 390
No: 24
Other: 19

Senate

Democrat
0
3
42

Republican
4
7
43

Total Votes
Yes: 85
No: 8
Other: 7

(Continued)

(Continued)

2006: VRA Extension, 109th Congress

Yes   No   Other

House

Democrat	Independent	Republican	Total Votes
197 4 0	1	192 33 6	Yes: 390 No: 33 Other: 10

Senate

Democrat	Independent	Republican	Total Votes
44	1	53 2	Yes: 98 No: 0 Other: 0

U.S. House Vote, July 13, 2006

Democrat	Independent	Republican	Total Votes
197 4 0	1	192 33 6	Yes: 390 No: 33 Other: 10

U.S. Senate Vote, July 20, 2006

Democrat	Independent	Republican	Total Votes
44	1	53 2 0	Yes: 98 No: 0 Other: 2

Source: CQ Press Congress Collection, http://library.cqpress.com/congress.

ported the amendment, 181–44, with Democrats opposing it, 193–4. The final amendment proposed a ten-year reauthorization rather than twenty-five, but this was also rejected, 288–134.[50] Given these strong rejections of amendments in the House, no amendments were offered in the Senate. Yet the nature of these amendments highlights the continuation of efforts to rescind voter protections for African Americans begun during the Civil Rights Movement.

These Republican-proposed amendments were intended to weaken voting rights protection in several ways. They tried to make it harder to continue monitoring cities' and towns' creation of new voting laws; to shorten the extension of coverage; and to eliminate bilingual ballots, thereby introducing a form of literacy test. All of these factors would have enhanced limitation on electoral participation by "language minorities." Most of the groups that have been protected have become more strongly identified with the Democratic Party, as have Blacks since initial passage of the 1965 Voting Rights Act. As the Republican Party has racialized Latinos and Asian Americans over immigration and language issues in the last decade, Latino and Asian American voters, provided with minority language protection, have also moved much more strongly toward the Democratic Party. Even though President George W. Bush supported VRA renewal, members of his party made efforts to weaken the act and to eliminate language protections. The amendments thus reflected complex racialization arising from partisan opposition to more racially heterogeneous electorates, which have consequently moved toward the Democratic Party.

In general, the 2006 extension reaffirmed the overall framework of the legislation that preceded it, including covering the same jurisdictions, requiring preclearance by the Department of Justice, and reauthorizing provisions such as Section 203 for another twenty-five years.[51] The legislation also addressed two Supreme Court decisions that impacted voting rights, *Georgia v. Ashcroft* (2003) and *Reno v. Bossier Parish School Board* (1997), which had reduced racial or language minorities' ability to "elect their preferred candidates of choice."[52] This discussion concentrates only on the *Georgia v. Ashcroft* case. See Figure 7.4 for a brief summary of both cases.

Georgia v. Ashcroft (2003) adjusted the standards for minority voters as the "effective exercise of the franchise." Law professor David Becker explains that those standards had previously been based on "minority voters' ability to elect candidates of their choice." This had resulted in a significant increase in the number of Black elected officials after 1965.[53] (See Table 7.2 on p. 224.) Voting rights lawyers had been uncertain about whether the new standards would assist in the continued election of minority voters' chosen candidates. The 2006 VRA extension clarified these questions when the congressional legislation stated that the Court's interpretation in *Georgia v. Ashcroft* was incorrect. The 2006 law specified that the basis for judging whether new state and county laws were limiting Blacks, others of color, or any citizen was the "'ability to elect'" "their preferred candidates of choice," rather than the overall circumstances.[54]

THE LONG-TERM STABILITY OF THE VOTING RIGHTS ACT

Despite the seeming ease with which the Voting Rights Act was extended in 2006 and the continuation of its existing framework, there are important challenges to the policy in the national environment. Although all four of the Republican-backed amendments failed in the House in 2006, the size of the Republican Party's majority increased in 2008, and again after the 2010 midterm elections with the rise of the Tea Party.[55] In the midterm elections that followed in 2010, the Republicans' congressional votes shrank to 234 from 242.[56] Republi-

How much did race matter in the relatively easy passage of the 2006 VRA extension, as compared with the 2013 Supreme Court decisions that struck down some VRA protections?

can House members have grown increasingly conservative in recent decades. This has been apparent in the growth of the Tea Party, beginning in the 2010 elections. Many of those elected in 2010 and 2012 would have been strong opponents of the 2006 VRA renewal. The case *Shelby County v. Holder* (2013), involving a challenge to the constitutionality of Section 5 of the Voting Rights Act, was heard by the U.S. Supreme Court in February 2013, and observers have raised grave concerns about its likely outcome. Chief Justice John Roberts inquired in oral arguments whether "the citizens in the South are more racist than citizens in the North."[57] The Court failed to directly invalidate the preclearance permitted by Section 5. Rather, in June 2013 Chief Justice Roberts, along with Justices Antonin Scalia, Anthony Kennedy, Clarence Thomas, and Samuel Alito, ruled that the formula contained in Section 4 of the VRA had not been updated since 1965 to take into account the geographic areas covered by the legislation, and that Section 4 was therefore unconstitutional. Congress can, the Court argued, pass legislation specifying a new formula under which Section 5 can be applied. Because of Republican dominance of the U.S. House of Representatives, and the strong Tea Party influence, this will not be an easy task. Congress, often stymied by partisan conflict, has not yet passed new legislation, although Representatives Jim Sensenbrenner of Wisconsin and John Conyers of Michigan, and Senator Patrick Leahy of Vermont have introduced the Voting Rights Amendment Act of 2014 (HR 3899).[58] (See Figure 7.4 for a summary of major rulings on voting rights.)

Recall that the Voting Rights Act had been renewed regularly since 1970, and most recently in 2006, with little debate. On its surface, this would seem to signal a certain level of acceptance that the VRA's protections are recognized as necessary. Indeed, as recently as 2007 Nathaniel Persily noted that "even Justice [Antonin] Scalia has suggested that he would allow stare decisis [standing law] to apply to congressional actions under section 5 . . . and has recognized compliance with the VRA as a compelling state interest."[59] But in the 2013 oral arguments, several of the justices expressed outright skepticism about the law. Justice Scalia said the VRA "now amounted to a 'perpetuation of racial entitlement.'" The same news analysis suggested that Justice Sonia Sotomayor, the first Latina appointed to the bench, was responding to Chief Justice Roberts when she asked, "Do you think that the right to vote is a racial entitlement?"[60]

CONCLUSION: THE ROLE OF RACE IN CONTEMPORARY VOTING RIGHTS

The Civil Rights Movement of the 1960s and 1970s prompted legislation to aid African Americans in accessing equal rights and opportunities in the polity. Over time, these protections

Figure 7.4   Major Supreme Court Rulings on Voting Rights

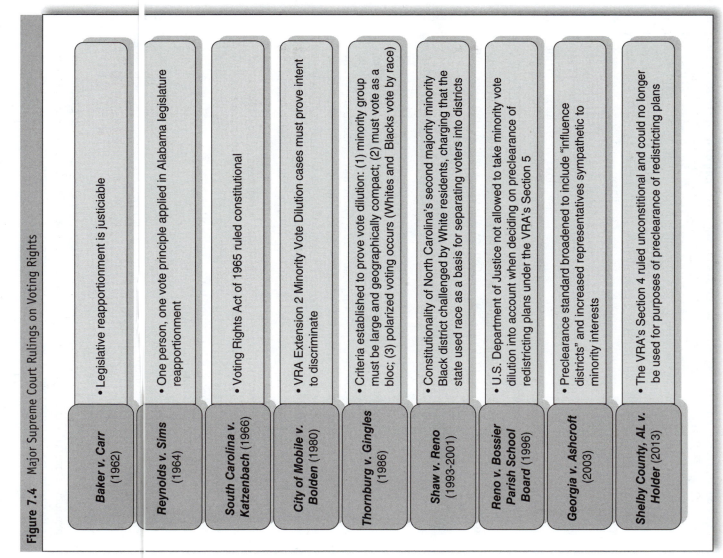

Baker v. Carr (1962)	• Legislative reapportionment is justiciable
Reynolds v. Sims (1964)	• One person, one vote principle applied in Alabama legislature reapportionment
South Carolina v. Katzenbach (1966)	• Voting Rights Act of 1965 ruled constitutional
City of Mobile v. Bolden (1980)	• VRA Extension 2 Minority Vote Dilution cases must prove intent to discriminate
Thornburg v. Gingles (1986)	• Criteria established to prove vote dilution: (1) minority group must be large and geographically compact; (2) must vote as a bloc; (3) polarized voting occurs (Whites and Blacks vote by race)
Shaw v. Reno (1993-2001)	• Constitutionality of North Carolina's second majority minority Black district challenged by White residents, charging that the state used race as a basis for separating voters into districts
Reno v. Bossier Parish School Board (1996)	• U.S. Department of Justice not allowed to take minority vote dilution into account when deciding on preclearance of redistricting plans under the VRA's Section 5
Georgia v. Ashcroft (2003)	• Preclearance standard broadened to include "influence districts" and increased representatives sympathetic to minority interests
Shelby County, AL v. Holder (2013)	• The VRA's Section 4 ruled unconstitional and could no longer be used for purposes of preclearance of redistricting plans

were extended to other minority groups, helping to ensure that all citizens—regardless of race, ethnicity, or spoken language—could exercise their rights at the polls. And yet, as this chapter has shown, minorities' representation in government—at all levels—remains significantly disproportionate to their numbers in the overall population.

Representation and participation in governance through the election of public officials is an essential element in the democratic process. Without racial and ethnic integration of the electorate and of the legislative process, the core political and economic interests of the increasingly diverse American population remain outside the daily competition of the polity. Polity refers to the broad governing framework within which political and economic interaction occurs. Contemporary hostility to broader electoral representation of racial and ethnic populations seems to arise from a combination of partisan suspicion and group hostility to non-Europeans. The Republican Party's association with portions of the Tea Party has usually made its efforts to reach out to the groups on our uneven roads ineffective and, more often, disastrous.

The Voting Rights Act, although renewed as recently as 2006 with the full support of Congress and the president, is now in political limbo after the Supreme Court's 2013 *Shelby County v. Holder* ruling. With the strong impact of Tea Party Republicans within the U.S. House of Representatives, the likelihood of an updated recalculation of requirements for Section 4 of the VRA is difficult to envision. With most of the African American population identified with the Democratic Party, and majorities of Latinos and Asians moving in that direction, the Republican Party's opposition to civil and voting rights reform demonstrates how race continues to matter in the twenty-first century.

Do minority groups still need the protections provided by the Voting Rights Act, particularly Section 5?

DISCUSSION QUESTIONS

1. In what ways did the major civil and voting rights legislation of the 1960s begin to remedy prior limitations in minority groups' access to the polls? Where did it fall short?

2. How did African American civic organizing during the Civil Rights Movement provide a foundation from which other minority groups could advance their rights? Refer to your readings from previous chapters to compare and contrast.

3. In what ways did racial and ethnic groups organize to expand the protections of the Voting Rights Act, particularly minority language provisions?

4. To what degree does redistricting for racial balance address the long-term legacies of racialization? What advantages do racial and ethnic groups within these districts have that they might not have otherwise?

5. Did the early renewal of the Voting Rights Act in 2006 mark a substantive shift in attitudes toward the need to protect voting rights? Explain your answer.

6. Given repeated efforts to limit the protections of the Voting Rights Act, how much does race matter in contemporary voting rights?

KEY TERMS

at-large election (p. 218)

civil rights (p. 207)

Civil Rights Act of 1957 (p. 210)

Civil Rights Act of 1964 (p. 211)

Civil Rights Movement (p. 207)

discriminatory intent (p. 218)

disenfranchisement (p. 201)

enfranchisement (p. 201)

minority vote dilution (p. 218)

racially polarized (p. 218)

restrictive covenants (p. 208)

Section 4 (p. 212)

Section 5 (p. 212)

Section 203 (p. 217)

Shelby County, Alabama v. Holder (p. 214)

South Carolina v. Katzenbach (1966) (p. 214)

Voting Rights Act of 1965 (p. 212)

White primary (p. 208)

8 Group Identity, Ideology, and Activism

We can think of ideologies as representing every day, commonsense knowledge of the political world—as lenses through which political information is focused. The ideological lenses of opposing groups often lead them to understand the same political event from two (or more) stunningly different perspectives.

—Michael Dawson, author of
*Black Visions: The Roots of Contemporary
African-American Political Ideologies*

I t is difficult to gauge whether a racial or ethnic group has made progress on the American road of citizenship and opportunity if it does not conceive of itself as a group—with some common or shared interests—and does not take collective action to promote its shared interests. **Collective action** is the process of individuals coming together and agreeing to act in ways they consider mutually beneficial—i.e., forming a neighborhood crime watch or signing a petition to city hall demanding improved neighborhood trash pickup. In Chapters 2 through 6, we demonstrated how political history up to 1965 fostered racial and ethnic group consciousness—and often political solidarity—among those who self-identified as White, Black, Latino, Asian/Asian Pacific Islander, or Native American. This chapter will link contemporary public opinion, group identity, and political ideology with activism to demonstrate when various groups—from ethnicity-based labor unions like the United Farm Workers to contemporary social justice groups like Black-led community development organizations—act upon group consciousness or a community identity.

The central, although not only, method political scientists and other social scientists use to examine these concepts is the survey, which is a public opinion poll of scientific, random samples of selected individuals. The process of random samples merely means that the laws of statistics inform us that we can make valid estimations of what a large community, such as a city, a state, or the nation, believes if we systematically sample a selection of individuals. At the same time,

235

ASSOCIATED PRESS

In February 2013, Native Americans came together for a shared cause, marching on Washington DC and calling on President Barack Obama to reject the Keystone XL oil pipeline from Canada and to act on other issues of their concern. A shared group identity and set of beliefs can form the foundation for advancing collective interests.

we must be careful about how we interpret survey findings and avoid the presumption that we can fully understand group dynamics and political participation simply by studying the attitudes of individuals. Likewise, we cannot assume that we understand collective action by asking individuals to self-report their political actions, absent some understanding of the communities and identities that inform their views. With these caveats in mind, however, we examine when, why, and how race and ethnicity shape public opinion, group identity, and political ideology within U.S. politics. The broader question of ideas and beliefs leading to political action is vitally important because we presume, as we do in Chapter 9, with political behavior, that absent an engaged and mobilized citizenry, a democracy is not likely to be as representative, responsive, or accountable.[1]

The above questions are not merely intellectual or academic debates. They are vital considerations in understanding the host of reasons why race and ethnicity matter in encouraging collective action. For example, public opinion matters when we observe Whites being less racially prejudicial toward Blacks and Hispanics—although anti-Black and anti-Hispanic attitudes persist. Such attitudinal shifts make not only multiracial electoral coalitions possible, but also small but significant multiracial grassroots coalitions on issues such as schools in Baltimore, Maryland; economic justice in Oakland, California; and environmental justice in Augusta, Georgia.

Group identity mattered when college students with Mexican American, Puerto Rican, and Cuban American ancestry banded together under the pan-ethnic identity of "Latino" to organize opposition to anti–affirmative action state amendments in the 1990s and 2000s. Political ideology mattered when some supporters of the Tea Party movement expressed racial and conceivably racist attitudes in their conservative, small-government opposition to national health care reform, and when Native American activists and supporters opposed conservative anti-abortion image campaigns. In each of these instances, these citizens engaged in forms of political participation—protest and demonstrations, gathering petitions, involvement in ballot initiatives—whose costs are heavier than more routine forms, such as voting. In this respect, the activism we discuss in this chapter references contemporary social movements at the grassroots level that, like their predecessors, are motivated or framed by ideals, values, and systems of belief about the interests or "group interests" of a racial or ethnic group.[2] The discussion of ideology and activism in this chapter serves as a primer for the discussion of political ideology and political behavior found in Chapter 9. But whereas that chapter focuses on how the conventional political participation of minority communities (such as voting and working on campaigns) leads to the election of persons to positions in government, this chapter addresses how nonconventional political participation like activism and protest pressure those in government and business to be more accountable to the varying needs of minority communities.

WHY GROUP IDENTITY, IDEOLOGY, AND ACTIVISM MATTER

Group identity is the social or cultural commonality an individual recognizes he or she shares with others so as to claim membership in a specific community—i.e., race, ethnicity, gender. Political psychologists and sociologists such as Henri Tajfel, John Turner, and Michael Hogg inform us that "social identity" or "group identity" is fundamental to building a sense of community. As Tajfel explains, it is "the individual's knowledge that he/she belongs to certain social groups together with some emotional and value significance [to] his/her group membership."[3] On the one hand, social or group identity matters with regard to race because persons are racialized by society and placed into groups (thus membership is externally imposed), as was the case of Southeast Asians following the Sikh religion, who were violently attacked in 2001 for being "foreigners." On the other hand, persons may also reinforce their personal attachments to these groups, as is the case with contemporary Irish Americans who have at least a symbolic attachment to being Irish, especially around St. Patrick's Day. Again, the specific linkages persons make are shaped by history or the path they took to reach this current point.[4]

A better understanding of how race, ethnicity, and racism affect identities and ideologies can tell us when and why racial and ethnic groups believe they share common views and interests with other groups and thus perceive these groups as allies as opposed to adversaries.

What, if any, racial or ethnic groups do you self-identify with? What perceptions do you believe other racial or ethnic groups have of your group, and why do you hold that belief?

For example, research by a number of racial and ethnic politics scholars, including Lawrence Bobo, Vincent Hutchings, Paula McClain, Albert Karnig, Claire Kim, and others, reveals that in certain economic and social arenas there can be strong multi-ethnic competition and sometimes even conflict among racial and ethnic minorities. African Americans, Hispanics, and Asian Americans can subtly perceive each other as mutual economic threats because of the belief (often a misperception) that they are competitors in tight labor markets. This competition is frequently framed by local economic development decisions that constrain opportunities for all. For example, in the early 1990s, in New York, there were a number of highly publicized clashes between Korean American convenience store owners and African American customers—sparked by interracial misperceptions and perceived slights—though both groups were at least somewhat disadvantaged in the area's tight labor market.[5] However, in political and electoral arenas, African Americans, Hispanics, and Asian Americans can form very effective, multiracial coalitions and share perceptions of a relative, intergroup "closeness," especially when individuals are guided by the belief that communities of color confront forms of racial and economic discrimination that make them distinct from their White counterparts.[6]

The authors of this text consider ethnicity-based activism to be a reaction to various racial and ethnic attitudes and perceptions. Ideology is very important when it comes to understanding what motivates persons to engage in collective political actions. It provides lenses one can use to see and politically interpret the world. For example, ethnic nationalism is an ideology that asserts that a racially oppressed group has the right to be politically and economically independent and form (at least symbolically) a "separate nation" or "nation within a nation." Variants of this ideology, as rooted in different group experiences, guided the militant activism of groups such as the (Chicano/Latino) Brown Berets, the Black Panther Party, and the Japanese "East Wind" organizations of the 1960s and early 1970s in Los Angeles. One very contentious debate is whether ideologies of White nationalism, which have guided White supremacist groups like the Aryan Nation or Ku Klux Klan, are simply any other forms of ethnic nationalism. Our aim in this chapter is to draw upon the work of various scholars to equip you with the ability to reach your own conclusions about the similarities and differences of how identity, ideology, and activism operate with different racial and ethnic groups and within different political settings.[7]

RACE, ETHNICITY, AND PUBLIC OPINION

In order to explain how individuals politically think about as well as react toward group memberships, we must define several terms important to understanding political attitudes. **Public opinion** represents the various attitudes or views large communities of people hold about politics and the actions of government. It thus inherently establishes the range of views most likely expressed when a population is polled or surveyed. It then represents the arrangement of political attitudes into specific or systematic schemes that justify specific interpretations of what is in a community's best interests.[11] For example, economic conservatives such

⚠ BOX 8.2 COALITIONS IN ACTION

Reducing White Racial Stereotypes through College Clubs

At the beginning of this book, we gave several reasons for you as a student to doubt whether the election of Barack Obama, the first African American to serve as president of the United States, had ushered in a "postracial" era of American politics where race, ethnicity, and racism do not matter nearly as much as before. In fact, there is strong evidence that racial politics have worsened in some ways. The Southern Poverty Law Center, a civil rights group dedicated to monitoring and challenging racial supremacist groups, counted a record increase in the number of "Patriot" extremist/vigilante groups that often use racially charged rhetoric in their criticism of Obama and the federal government. They nearly doubled, from 519 in 2009, to 1,007 by 2012. And two Associated Press polls found that White racial attitudes have not improved with Obama's presidency, and in some cases have worsened.[8]

But countering these rather gloomy findings are studies that show the attitudes of White college-age students who are part of the "Obama generation" are more racially liberal than were their predecessors under particular conditions. Political psychologists Tatishe Nteta and Jill Greene found that "members of the Obama generation not only hold more liberal racial attitudes than older generations, but they

harbor less racial resentment than cohorts who are closer in age to them."[9] Social psychologist Mary Fisher likewise found that White college-age students potentially were less likely to harbor anti-Black stereotypes.

What all three scholars found made the difference was the greater degree of interracial contact these younger Whites were likely to have with Blacks and other racial minorities. In particular, White student participation in extracurricular activities that involved significant numbers of Blacks, Hispanics, or Asian Americans in many cases was the strongest determinant in liberalizing the racial views of White students. As Fisher explains, "extracurricular activities represent contact in which participants are clearly cooperating in some shared goal,"[10] and shared goals lead to or may be due to sentiments of camaraderie and friendship. Given what we conclude in this chapter about the importance of groups and group identities, it makes sense that the more broadly we define our social and civic worlds relative to race and ethnicity, the more likely we are to see others who are racially or ethnically "different" from us as similar to ourselves, our families, and our communities.

as 2012 Republican presidential candidate Mitt Romney likely believe that when it comes to economic markets, government should be relatively restrained in its regulation of businesses. Economic liberals such as President Obama believe that government should be relatively active in its regulation of businesses in order to promote fair markets. Survey researchers who have examined race and American political ideology continue to debate whether racial and ethnic politics correlate with political ideology. In other words, do political and economic conservatism strongly correlate with or predict support for racial conservatism, and do political and economic liberalism strongly correlate with or predict support for racial liberalism?[12] We will explore this debate at greater length below.

Figure 8.4   Group Differences for Increased Government Spending by Policy Area, 2004

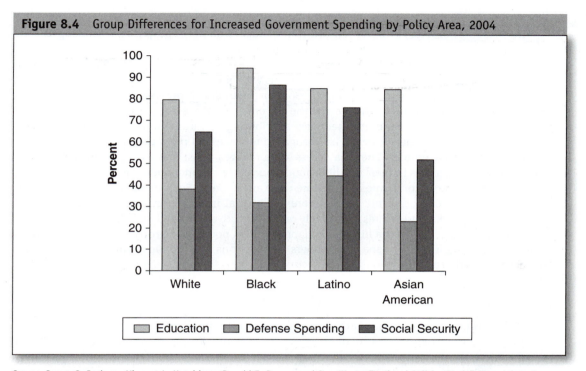

Source: James S. Jackson, Vincent L. Hutchings, Ronald E. Brown, and Cara Wong, "National Politics Study" (Ann Arbor: Program for Research on Black Americans, Center for Political Studies; University of Michigan's Institute for Social Research, 2004).

Note: 2004 is the most recent year for which data are available.

experiences of each of these groups may shape or "color" their views in each policy domain. For instance, Blacks and Hispanics lag behind Whites in their educational attainment and income or retirement resources; therefore, these minorities tend to support greater government spending on education and Social Security. In Chapter 13, on intersectionality, we will discuss how racial and ethnic minorities are not uniformly liberal in their policy views, especially regarding social policies like same-sex marriage that involve conceptions of morality and religion—though even this may slowly be changing.[32]

ACTIVIST PATHWAYS TO EMPOWERMENT

Strongly held beliefs that coalesce through group identity and ideology may prompt individuals—either singly or collectively—to act to advance their interests in the public arena. Chapter 9, on political behavior, will survey the broad range of political participation activities individuals and groups have used to advance their interests. The specific range of political actions or forms of involvement discussed in this chapter fall under the broad labels of civic involvement and/or grassroots activism. Racial and ethnic politics scholar Todd Shaw, one of the authors of this text, has previously defined **grassroots activism,** or "community organizing," as "a form of political action that assumes ordinary citizens can confront maldistributions of power by organizing as communities of geographic or ascriptive identity (race, class, and gender) and thus use their indigenous creativity, leadership, and resources." Shaw goes on to qualify this statement: "While protest has often been mistaken as synonymous with grassroots activism, it is only one strategy within this activism's dynamic range."[33] So along with public protests or demonstrations like rallies, sit-ins, and pickets, which are at the extreme end of the range, there are other forms of activism—such as community meetings, distributing literature, and contacting public officials—in which ordinary citizens have engaged to voice and press their demands on government and private entities. They may press for fair wages, insist that young people have quality recreational facilities in their neighborhoods, pursue fair home-lending practices from banks, or insist that large companies not pollute their air or water. Such demands are not unique to any specific racial or ethnic group; there are several instances in which Asian Americans, Hispanics, Blacks, and Whites have singly or collaboratively worked to address such needs. But as we can discern from the historical chapters of this book, each group has a particular set of circumstances that help shape members' perceptions and political opportunities as they respond to these needs.

Volunteerism: Influencing Government Action

One broad way to think of activism is to consider patterns of American volunteerism, or the many ways persons get involved in groups and activities to meaningfully participate in the life of their communities. This may include activities such as participation in church groups, bowling leagues, and neighborhood associations. Political participation scholars Sidney Verba, Kay Lehman Schlozman, and Henry Brady define what they call **civic voluntarism** or "voluntary political activity," as "activity that has the intent or effect of influencing government action—either directly by affecting the making or implementation of public policy or indirectly by influencing the selection of people who make those policies." They clarify that, "By *voluntary* activity we mean participation that is not obligatory—no one is forced to volunteer—and that receives no pay or only token financial compensation."[34] Between 2007 and 2011, only a little more than a quarter of people in any racial groups reported volunteering with a group in the previous year. Whites were the most likely to report having volunteered, as compared to Blacks, Asians, and Hispanics (in order of declining participation). Yet over this four-year period increased numbers of people reported volunteering across all groups, and the rate of increase is larger for racial and ethnic minorities than it is for Whites. (See Table 8.4.) There are many factors that may explain these increases, including more Americans being asked to be altruistic during the tough times of the Great Recession. But it is also possible that the political mobilization of these groups, certainly during the 2008 and later the 2012 elections, which witnessed significant increases in voter turnout, had a bearing on participation across the board.

Religious or faith-based organizations are important outlets for volunteerism across all racial and ethnic groups. They are also among the few arenas of voluntary activity in which Blacks, Asians, and Hispanics report higher total percentages of participation than do Whites. (See Table 8.5.) The African American Protestant Church and the Hispanic Roman Catholic

Table 8.4   Volunteerism in the United States by Race, 2007–2011

	2007 %	2008 %	2011 %
White	27.9	27.9	28.2
Black	18.2	19.1	20.3
Asian	17.7	18.7	20.0
Hispanic or Latino	13.5	14.4	14.9

Source: Bureau of Labor Statistics, "Volunteering in the United States" (Washington, DC: U.S. Department of Labor, Bureau of Labor Statistics, 2012).

Church, just as two examples, remain important centers for the cultural identities and civic lives of these respective groups. In differing ways, both institutions can assume a wide array of spiritual, social, cultural, and political functions—from traditional worship services to providing assistance to needy families (food pantries or housing assistance), to observing special celebrations and festivals (Kwanzaa or Cinco de Mayo), to registering people to vote. Recent scholarship has also revealed that while there has been a decline in religious affiliation among younger Whites, this is not true or not as pronounced for Blacks and Hispanics.[35] It follows the data shown in Table 8.5 that for the category of educational or youth service groups, Whites, Blacks, and Asians are roughly on par with one another in their rates of reported volunteering; for Hispanics, the rates are even higher than those of the other groups.

Why are these rates rising? One reason may be that access to quality public schools has long been a central focus of Latino grassroots activism and social justice movements—from Los Angeles to New York—and education quite logically remains a central concern to Latinos because of the ways in which it provides a means for social mobility and greater opportunity for this community with a strong immigrant heritage.[36] Social or community service groups are the only other category in which all four racial and ethnic groups report relatively equal levels of volunteerism. Such groups are especially important in the civic life of Asian American communities. Recall that in Chapter 5 we discussed the early experiences of Chinese and other Asian American communities, in which mutual aid, business, and cultural organizations were very important to their group identities and processes of community formation. Such organizations, in varying ways, have remained important in the civic lives of these groups.[37]

Low- and High-Cost Civic Activism

While broad indicators of voluntary activity inform our understanding of the civic well-being of a community, Verba, Scholzman, and Brady remind us that an important distinction must be made between nonpolitical activity and political activity—or, rather, activities that are not explicitly concerned about the allocation of resources, government, and public policy, and

Table 8.5   Volunteerism by Type of Main Organization and by Race, 2011

Organization Type	White %	Black %	Asian %	Hispanic %
Civic, political, professional, or international	5.7	3.2	5.5	3.8
Educational or youth service	25.7	23.9	29	36.6
Environmental or animal care	2.6	0.2	0.5	1.2
Hospital or other health	8.0	6.4	6.5	6.0
Public safety	1.4	0.8	0.2	0.5
Religious	31.9	44.5	35.5	32.9
Social or community service	14.4	13.1	14.7	10.4
Sport, hobby, cultural, or arts	4.1	1.5	3.9	2.7
Other/Not determined	6.3	6.5	3.9	5.8

Source: Bureau of Labor Statistics, "Volunteering in the United States" (Washington, DC: U.S. Department of Labor, Bureau of Labor Statistics, 2012).

those that are. When examining political activity, scholars have drawn further distinctions between activities that exact low versus high "costs" from their participants. For instance, there are activities that may require significant commitments of time, money, and willingness to be fully informed, and/or may carry risks like police arrest, losing one's job, or being a subject of press scrutiny. For several weeks in the summer of 2013, some seven hundred North Carolina participants of the Moral Mondays Movement—a liberal, civil rights–led coalition that has objected to, among other things, a conservative governor and legislature enacting voter ID laws and not enacting health care reform—peacefully got arrested when they conducted a civil disobedience, sit-in campaign inside the state house. Another prominent example of a group that in 2013 also conducted a peaceful state house sit-in is the Dream Defenders. It is a multi-racial but Black- and Latino-led group of young Florida activists partly inspired by the example of the Student Non-Violent Coordinating Committee (SNCC), the leading student and youth organization of the 1960s Civil Rights Movement. The Dream Defenders attempted coura-geously (if not successfully) to pressure Florida governor Rick Scott and the state legislature to repeal the controversial "stand your ground" law, which they and others believe unjustly ratio-nalized George Zimmerman's racially profiling and killing Trayvon Martin. In both instances, these peaceful protests entail the time and expense of activists being processed through the court system.[38]

There are also activities that are directly related to electing people to office—talking about candidates, donating money, working on a campaign—and others that are more broadly related to affecting public or private policy outcomes, such as protesting, meeting on an issue, and working with a group. Table 8.6 broadly follows the logic of what Harris,

Sinclair-Chapman, and McKenzie call "civic activism," or the combination of traditional political activity (as in election participation) and organizational work (as in public/private policy participation). For example, in the 1990s, Black and other activists in Detroit, who cared about affordable housing, ran candidates for the city council and lobbied city council for equitable funding.[39] Each column in this table indicates the "yes" answers respondents in that group gave to various participation activities. At the bottom of the table are various summary averages.

 Have racial and ethnic groups gained greater equality more from low- or high-cost activism such as protest?

Table 8.6 reveals that Black and Hispanic respondents were more likely than their White counterparts to state that they engaged in forms of civic activism like protest or attending meetings than in more traditional forms of political participation such as voting or raising money for a candidate. A number of political participation and social movement scholars have corroborated that racial and ethnic minorities are more likely to participate in forms

Table 8.6 Percentage Who Answered "Yes" to Participation versus Civic Activism Questions by Race, 2004				
Political Participation Questions	**White**	**Black**	**Hispanic**	**Asian**
Talk to persuade vote choice	55.0	44.9	39.9	50.0
Work on campaign for party candidate	27.2	24.4	12.4	11.8
Attend meeting to support candidate	18.8	19.0	13.0	13.1
Raise money for candidate	26.5	18.0	8.6	14.1
Civic Activism Questions				
Protest on an issue	10.4	6.9	6.1	7.6
Attend meeting about issue	36.3	43.1	27.0	34.0
Work with others to deal with issue	39.0	45.9	23.1	32.5
Work together to improve racial/ethnic group's position	71.5	84.3	73.9	71.8
Summary Percentages				
Average political participation %	31.9	26.6	18.5	22.3
Average civic activism %	39.3	45.1	32.5	36.5
Gap = Participation % - Activism %	7.4	18.5	14.1	14.2

Source: James S. Jackson, Vincent L. Hutchings, Ronald E. Brown, and Cara Wong, "National Politics Study" (Ann Arbor: Program for Research on Black Americans, Center for Political Studies; University of Michigan's Institute for Social Research, 2004).

of political activity that are rooted in civic and social organizations, as opposed to explicitly political groups. Compared to traditional political organizations like political parties or campaigns, minority civil society groups, such as church auxiliaries, fraternal groups, or racial or ethnic identity groups, create greater levels of **social capital** or stronger relationships of trust and reciprocity; these, in turn, provide many more opportunities for participation, with fewer "costs."[40]

The very last row of the summary averages displays the gap or difference between the average percentages of each group that engages in civic activism versus traditional political participation. Although there is a gap for every group, the gap is twice as large for Hispanics and Asian Americans as compared to Whites, and more than twice as large for Blacks as compared to Whites. This reemphasizes the point that racial and ethnic minorities are more likely than their White counterparts to engage in civic activism as compared to traditional arenas of political participation. We conclude this chapter with several examples of how civic or grassroots activism, as inspired by racial/ethnic group identity and ideology, has pressured public and private institutions to be responsive to the economic and quality of life needs of various communities.

THE LEGACY OF GRASSROOTS AND CIVIL RIGHTS ACTIVISM

Not all forms of civic activism or grassroots activism effectively pressure those in power to be accountable to the concerns of ordinary communities. Borrowing from the literature on social movements, Shaw has argued that it is necessary to understand the existence of "political opportunities." By **political opportunities,** he and others mean those methods, periods, and contexts that can take advantage of a power structure's political vulnerabilities or weaknesses and make it attentive to the concerns of activists—such as a sit-in that disrupts business as usual; an incumbent who during a reelection campaign event is cornered by a group to account for his or her record; a city where there is a strong tradition of grassroots involvement and strong grassroots alliances. Shaw says this is when activism, broadly, and protest, in particular, is "the right tool [utility], at the time [timing], in the right place [context]." To make a real difference, activists must be concerned about whether they have "strong allies, advantages, and adaptive tactics" or powerful insiders and outsiders who favor their cause; beneficial policies or rules on their side such as a court injunction or a new law; as well as tactics that are the most appropriate for the target. With the latter factor, protest in a court room will not faze a judge but simply have him or her rule protesters in contempt of court. Shaw's framework is broadly useful in explaining when, why, and how grassroots activism that involves race and ethnicity can positively affect various White, Black, Hispanic, Asian American, and Native American communities.[41]

It is important to recall from the historical chapters (2–6) that each of these racial and ethnic communities in the United States have their unique social movement legacies in the twentieth century. For example, African Americans have the legacy of the 1950s and 1960s Civil Rights Movement, rooted in activist Black churches and affiliated groups. Students of this movement vary regarding its precise beginning, but it was at least in June of 1953, after the period of return for Black and other World War II veterans, that a bus boycott occurred in Baton Rouge, Louisiana, that helped set the stage for the 1955 Montgomery, Alabama, bus boycott. The Baton Rouge campaign sought to end the practice of segregated seating on city buses where Whites were given priority for seats at the front and thus Blacks were successively pushed toward the back. The United Defense League (UDL), led by the Reverend T. J. Jemison of Mt. Zion Baptist Church and many other Black ministers and civic leaders, mobilized this effort by serving as an umbrella movement organization. They organized a carpool and security force to give rides to and protect protesters, drew in influential allies, regularly held mass meetings that drew thousands of attendees, and pooled resources. The boycott ended with a compromise between the UDL and the city of Baton Rouge, which permitted on each bus limited, reserved seating for Whites and then open-occupancy for all other seats. This campaign served as a role model to the more highly publicized Montgomery bus boycott led in 1955 by Dr. Martin Luther King Jr. and the Montgomery Improvement Association. It demonstrated the use of an effective tactic—an economic boycott, at an advantageous time—when the fed-

> Do the tactics of civil rights activists from the 1950s and 1960s still work today?

eral government and especially courts were being drawn into legal challenges to racial segregation. It also garnered powerful allies from within and outside the African American community, including fellow Black churches and media coverage.[42]

Another example of unique movement legacies is the multifaceted Chicano or Mexican American Movement of the 1960s and its basis in grassroots labor organizing as well as electoral and educational activism. The United Farm Workers (UFW), as led by Arizona-born Cesar Chavez and accompanied by Dolores Huerta and Gil Padilla, made significant gains in organizing and improving the wage and working conditions of Chicano as well as Filipino agricultural field workers in California's San Joaquin and Salinas Valleys, among other locales—especially those who worked in grape orchards and lettuce fields. UFW was a 1966 merger of the Filipino-led Agricultural Workers Organizing Committee (AWOC) and Chavez's earlier National Farm Workers Association (NFWA). However, Chavez and the UFW faced considerable opposition to their efforts, including from the Teamsters Union as a rival. Yet they won a number of wage, right-to-organize, and collective bargaining concessions from wineries and large farms because of the effective use of economic boycotts. NFWA and UFW called on sympathetic consumers not to buy the targeted products such as table grapes and lettuce; thus they greatly affected demand.

To reiterate, this movement demonstrated the use of an effective tactic—an economic boycott, at an advantageous time; brought about the end of the *Bracero* program, which lessened pressure on workers fearful of organizing due to the ability of growers to retaliate; and garnered powerful allies from within and outside of the Chicano community, including most certainly fellow Filipino workers, civil rights activists, union activists, activist Catholic parishes, and sympathetic consumers.[43] Similar patterns of alliances, advantages, and pressure tactics are clear in the efforts of 1960s political and educational activism. In 1963 the Crystal City Revolt of Crystal City, Texas, occurred when the Political Association of Spanish Speaking Organizations (PASSO) led a successful effort to unseat a White and conservative city council with Chicano officials. The East Los Angeles school movement of the late 1960s,

E.LA walkout

which was centered around Lincoln High School, used school walkouts to demand greater attention to the heritage and educational needs of Chicano students.[44]

Despite the unique histories and demands that motivated various communities, there is also a shared starting point for the use of community organizing and grassroots activism in the United States. Starting in the 1930s, a Chicago-based community organizer named Saul Alinsky, with his Back of the Yards campaign, developed an approach to community organizing that at first mobilized White ethnic neighborhoods and Catholic parishes in Chicago concerned about the terrible wages and working conditions of stockyard and slaughterhouse workers. Later, Alinsky founded the pivotal Industrial Areas Foundation and expanded his work to directly consult with many other communities, including working-class African American neighborhoods in the Midwest and Northwest as well as Hispanic communities in the Southeast. Mentored by Civil Rights icon and Congressman John Lewis, Alinsky was certainly not the only American to devise a philosophy of activism or community organizing, but Alinsky's contribution is that he purported to be a radical pragmatist who was nonideological in his approach. He cultivated grassroots leadership and attempted (not always successfully) to build bridges across ethnic and racial, as well as class, divides to achieve tangible if still modest outcomes. These included increased public welfare rolls, improvements in substandard housing, and increased public safety in a community. The impact of his community organizing philosophy has likely waxed and waned over a number of years. It is notable that Barack Obama's earliest involvement in politics in the 1980s used the same community organizing philosophy and tactics that Alinsky helped to pioneer—and was based in some of the same southside of Chicago neighborhoods—so this type of activism appears still to matter today.[45]

Labor and Community Development Activism

Those who engaged in activism in the 1980s, 1990s, and 2000s in issues relating to economic or racial justice often were motivated by the examples provided by earlier civil rights activism. We began this chapter by examining how race and ethnicity impact political ideology and group identities. While these relationships are intrinsically interesting, a fuller understanding requires an examination of how these relationships also motivate collective political or economic action. Each of the grassroots movements we briefly discuss in this section have successfully mobilized at some level by taking the needs or grievances of ordinary people, such as workers, the unemployed or underemployed, renters or homeowners, and organized them around powerful broad causes or "frames"—livable wages, quality and affordable housing. These groups also created new collective identities—for example, all building services workers, those who care about the well-being of young people—and acted upon meaningful, preexisting identities—we who are Filipino, African American, or people of color. Other than race and ethnicity, issues and identities relevant to class and/or gender have certainly motivated people to join such movements, although the creation of coalitions across different identities remains a difficult problem. Thus we remind you to refer to Chapter 13, on intersectionality, to more fully understand the multiple identities that often are necessary to mobilize successful grassroots movements, even as they pose interesting tensions.

The New Labor Movement: Latino Women Advance Workers' Rights

There have been contentious ideological debates in American politics about whether or not labor unions unfairly demand that all workers join them, when employers and employees should have the right to decide whether or not they associate with them, versus the view that unions use collective bargaining to positively affect the working conditions and wage levels of their members. Today, just 8 percent of the private-sector workforce and 12 percent of the combined public and private workforces in the United States belong to a union. Union membership in the United States has undergone drastic declines in the last several decades, due in part to changing demographics. Latino immigrants as well as other immigrant workers are a rapidly expanding but difficult to organize part of the American workforce, often because they must work in sectors and states that discourage unionization. Large firms do not permit it, and in turn many of the smaller subcontractors they work with also discourage unionization. However, in the last two decades a multiracial pool of workers in the health care and building (janitorial) services industries have not only joined unions in increasing numbers but have enjoyed significant wage increases as well.

In 1987 the Service Employees' International Union (SEIU) of the AFL-CIO (American Federation of Labor and Congress of Industrial Organizations) launched the Justice for Janitors campaign with the goal of organizing low-wage-level health care and janitorial workers, especially given the racial and ethnic changes of this workforce. Of all janitors employed in metropolitan Los Angeles between the 1970s and 1990s, African Americans went from 31 to 12 percent of the total, and White Anglos went from 24 to 11 percent of the total. Hispanic immigrants, particularly from Mexico and Central America, comprised some 61 percent of the total, and more than 60 percent of these Hispanic workers were women. SEIU focused upon the Los Angeles Local 399, as it was connected to the Kaiser Health Maintenance Organization (HMO). After direct appeals and effective appeals to public sentiments—instrumental efforts at consciousness raising within the communities of these workers—the rate of unionization among Los Angeles janitors went from a mere 10 percent in the late 1980s to a whopping 90 percent by the mid-1990s. Early rounds of contract negotiations, as propelled by boycotts and the use of other creative protest tactics, resulted in these workers winning small but important increases of 20 to 45 cents per hour in their meager average wage of $4.50 per hour.

After this and other very important advances, however, ethnic fissures developed in Local 399 between a veteran Anglo leadership and an emergent, Hispanic and woman-led, multiracial leadership coalition—the *Reformitas*—that demanded greater worker democracy and won an overwhelming majority of positions on the Local's executive committee. Although this resulted in a trusteeship takeover of the Local by SEIU and the eventual splitting of the health care versus janitorial wings of the Local 399, SEIU's Justice for Janitors campaign made many gains. It was effective in building a broad coalition and soliciting public sympathy, including a 1996 "voter-mandated increase in the state minimum wage"; it also sparked various local living wage ordinances, encouraging unions to mobilize against other anti-union measures and for pro-union state and local candidates for office, and highlighting the leverage workers of color could have in the broader union movement when effectively organized.[46]

The Community and Economic Development Movement: Grassroots Revitalization

A man holds a photo of Cesar Chavez, the founder of the United Farm Workers, during an immigration rights rally. Chavez's activism and community organizing efforts helped to improve the wages and working conditions for many agricultural workers in California and laid the foundation for contemporary collective action in the advancement of minority rights.

© JEFF TOPPING/Reuters/Corbis

One area of grassroots advocacy that Alinsky's philosophy clearly influenced was that of community and economic development. In cities like Detroit, Michigan, with its West Central Organization (WCO), Alinsky and his lieutenants established grassroots community organizing coalitions that eventually partnered with or helped to found other organizations, like the United Tenants for Collective Action (UTCA), which focused upon housing and community development.[47] The overall community development movement began in the late 1960s and early 1970s, but Avis Vidal, a scholar of urban policy and community development, explains that Alinsky was just one of this movement's ideological or programmatic influences: "Spawned amid the activism of the War on Poverty in the 1960s, some early [community development groups] got their start with federal funding under the Equal Opportunity Act's Special Impact Program. Others are deeply rooted in the civil rights movement, often linked (at least initially) to a church with an activist ministry." She goes on to explain that groups formed in the 1970s were often influenced by Alinsky-style community organizing and "neighborhood-based advocacy and protest activities" due to urban renewal or government efforts to redevelop distressed communities through the demolition of blighted properties and reconstruction that attracted higher-income tenants.[48]

The purpose of this movement was the human, economic, physical, and environmental revitalization of low-income and working-class neighborhoods by cultivating their indigenous values, leadership, and resources—now often termed *capacity building*—and effectively partnering these assets with significant external resources and allied institutions such as government, banks, or philanthropic foundations in ways that empower and materially benefit these neighborhoods. Community Development Corporations (CDCs) or Community Development Organizations (CDOs) are the not-for-profit groups or vehicles that carry on this work and often, under the direction of a board of directors (representative of the community) and an executive director, pursue a range of goals and programs, including youth job training, small-business and commercial development, the clearance of abandoned lots/ creation of community gardens, housing rehabilitation and the development of affordable rental units, and technical assistance to prospective homebuyers as well as existing home-owners. Currently in the United States there are some four thousand CDCs, and more often than not, affordable housing is a central program of these organizations.[49]

Race and ethnicity matter in community and economic development because often there is a politics of whether the distressed communities that are being served, which frequently include significant numbers of persons of color, are reflected in the leadership of various CDCs. One 1990s survey discovered, "Whereas 81 percent of target areas serving white communities had white executive directors, nearly 40 percent of all target areas serving blacks had white executive directors, and the percentage was 67 percent for black/white areas." Over the past several decades there have been a number of groups rooted in predominantly African American, Hispanic, or non-Hispanic White communities, including BUILD (Baltimoreans United in Leadership Development) or the East Brooklyn Nehemiah Project. Still others have emerged that are multiracial in their composition or that promote "cross-cultural, pluralistic community building" like the Sherman Park Community Association in Milwaukee or the Dudley Street Neighborhood Initiative (DSNI) in Boston.[50] Founded in 1985 in the ethnically diverse and low-income Boston community of Roxbury/North Dorchester, this broad community development collaboration explicitly requires parity representation of the constituent groups that comprise its neighborhood on its board of directors—African American, Cape Verdean (East African), Latino, and Non-Hispanic White. It is a unique organization, for under the liberal city administration of Mayor Kevin Flynn, it was one of the few CDOs to acquire the power of eminent domain in the nation, gaining the limited legal author-

 How is economic fairness linked to racial equity?

ity to compel landlords to sell their vacant and/or tax-delinquent properties to the DSNI. Among its breakthroughs are the rehabilitation of some 1,300 vacant lots; the building of 400 units of affordable housing; and the construction of "community centers, new schools, Dudley Town Common, a community greenhouse, parks, playgrounds, gardens, an orchard, and other public spaces."[51]

CONCLUSION: MOBILIZING FOR A CHANGED FUTURE

In this chapter, we have explained that in order to more fully understand U.S. racial and ethnic politics, it is vital for us to analyze why and how people see themselves as connected to racial/ethnic groups. Group identity, or one's identification with a group, in turn affects or shapes political attitudes and, more broadly, ideology, or the lenses—from liberal to conservative—we use to interpret various political actions and outcomes. Racial and ethnic attitudes often congeal into assumptions and sometimes racial stereotypes the society uses to assess the motives and behaviors of specific groups. Because racial and ethnic minorities, like Hispanics or African Americans, have frequently confronted negative stereotypes about their groups or discrimination toward their groups, they may feel they share a "linked" or "common" fate that in turn leads to conclusions about their "group interests" in the political system. Such interests often are the basis for politics and political mobilization. From a handful of Tea Party extremists on the conservative right who liberals believed wildly claimed Obama's health care plan intended to promote "White slavery," to Black activist groups like the "New Panther Party" on the militant left who conservatives believe stridently called for violent retaliation against George Zimmerman's jury acquittal after he killed Trayvon Martin, there is a wide range of examples of how group identities and perceptions of group interests can powerfully mobilize assertions about justice, freedom, and equality in the United States.[52]

Much of American politics resides in between and not at such extremes, but even in a wide middle area there are often strong disagreements about which policy, law, or candidate best serves the interests of a group or the wider public. In 2012 there were a number of groups, some of which had racial or ethnic identities that aligned behind President Barack Obama as a Democrat (i.e., American Indians for Obama) or Governor Mitt Romney as a Republican (i.e., Latinos for Romney).[53] With the stark racial divide that persists in presidential elections, with a majority of Whites supporting Republican candidates and racial/ethnic minorities supporting Democratic candidates, these types of ethnic/racial political groups and the mobilization they inspire are only likely to proliferate. Beyond perceived racial and ethnic group interests, however, there are a range of other concerns around which these and other groups might mobilize—from affirmative action to abortion. Our chapter on intersectionality addresses some of these other concerns that involve gender, religion, class, sexual orientation, and a host of other factors.

DISCUSSION QUESTIONS

1. To what extent does group identity influence racial attitudes for those inside the group and outside the group?

2. Why might different racial and ethnic groups consistently divide over particular issues, such as education and Social Security?

3. Why is political ideology—from liberal to conservative identifications—sometimes unable to accurately characterize a racial/ethnic group's policy stances?

4. What similarities and differences are there between the activism of the Civil Rights era and that of today? Why might these differences exist?

5. In what ways can a person engage in political activism, both individually and as part of a group? How can these actions contribute to collective political empowerment?

KEY TERMS

Bradley effect (p. 242)
civic voluntarism (p. 252)
Classical Prejudice
    Model (p. 246)
collective action (p. 235)
collective memory (p. 240)
explicit racial attitudes (p. 240)
grassroots activism (p. 252)
group identity (p. 237)

group interests (p. 243)
Group Position/Group Threat
    Theory (p. 243)
Implicit Association Test (p. 242)
implicit racial attitudes (p. 242)
linked or common fate (p. 243)
political culture (p. 240)
political ideology (p. 238)
political opportunities (p. 256)

political socialization (p. 240)
Principled Objection
    Model (p. 246)
public opinion (p. 238)
Simple Self-interest
    Model (p. 246)
social capital (p. 256)
social desirability
    effect (p. 242)

9 Political Behavior and Representation: Minorities' Growing Voice

Our ways of handling power differences and diverse points of view and cultures should be models of the civic life we wish to engender in our communities. Encouraging the articulation of differences, and then finding areas for collaboration, should be the norm rather than the exception.

Zelda F. Gamson[1]

As we stressed in Chapter 1, Barack Obama's victories in the 2008 and 2012 presidential elections reflect many firsts for U.S. society. Obama's race and his father's immigrant roots make him unique among U.S. presidents. Although it is too early to assess the long-term meanings of his election for U.S. race relations, it is safe to say that few who participated in the Black, Latino, Asian American, or Native American civil rights movements or advocated for the Voting Rights Act anticipated that the United States would elect an African American or other minority to the presidency within a generation of the act's passage. Although the long-term significance of the Obama victories will not be clear for many years, the changes in the minority electorate and its potential to influence national and state elections that appeared in 2008 and 2012 will undoubtedly be a continuing part of U.S. politics.

Obama's electoral coalition—and his narrow victories in several states that he surprised observers by winning in the **Electoral College** (which formally elects the president)—included a higher share of

---

Box 9.1 Chapter Objectives

- Compare the impact of the minority vote in elections from 2000 to 2012.

- Discuss the reasons for different levels of civic engagement between racial and ethnic populations.

- Identify characteristics of minority ideologies and how they differ from White populations on partisanship.

- Discuss the barriers that continue to dampen minority participation and what resources exist to overcome them.

- Assess the consequences of minority civic and political engagement in representing minority political interests in representative bodies.

Getty Images

In the 2008 and 2012 elections, Barack Obama made history as the first African American to become president. In 2012, despite 59 percent of the White electorate supporting his opponent, strong minority support and a growing minority electorate ensured Obama's reelection victory.

minority voters and stronger support for Obama than for recent Democratic nominees. His victory was certainly also built on White votes, but his opponents, John McCain and Mitt Romney, carried the majority of White votes (55 percent to 43 percent in 2008, and 59 percent to 39 percent in 2012). Obama's 2008 and 2012 victories, and the size of his majorities in the Electoral College, would not have been possible without his strong support by minority voters and the steadily increasing mobilization of new minority voters.

In this chapter we will explore when, why, and how race matters in civic life and in electoral participation. In the context of this discussion, the "why" question often focuses on how laws, electoral rules, and practices differentially shape the likelihood of minority participation and White participation. In the current era, laws and electoral rules do not absolutely preclude participation on the basis of race or ethnicity, as they often did in the pre–Civil Rights era. Instead—and this gets to the "how" question—laws and electoral rules intersect with race/ethnicity or with demographic characteristics more likely to be found in Black, Latino, Asian American, or Native American populations to reduce the likelihood of minority civic or electoral participation. The practice of politics also plays a role. Campaigns and parties are less likely to reach out to newer participants and to irregular participants in politics, again groups more likely to be found in minority populations. As a result, minority communities have less of a voice in the nation's civic and political life than their raw population numbers would predict.

We also look at a different "how" question. We analyze how minority communities use the laws, institutions, and resources of the polity to influence U.S. civic and political outcomes through their numbers and organization. We will look at minority civic and political activity in relationship to White communities and show how individuals can express their political interests in a variety of settings. These include efforts within communities, workplaces, or houses of worship, or among people with whom one identifies to shape one's community and life. Such activities have often been understood to be the backbone of American democracy, but they have been atrophying in recent years, as the society has invested less in mobilizing its members to civic and political engagement, and individuals have found less time for civic engagement.[2]

If civic engagement is going to grow, minority communities have to be a central part of the rebirth. As we will soon explore, the minority vote played an important role in the 2008 and 2012 presidential elections, signaling how minority civic engagement can be influential. We also examine minority electoral participation and the ideological and partisan foundations that undergird voting. Finally, we consider the representational outcomes of minority participation, with particular attention to the election of minority candidates to elective offices.

WHY IS THE MINORITY VOTE IMPORTANT?

While the role of minority voters grew in importance during the 2008 and 2012 presidential elections, they were considerably less important in shaping the outcomes of the 2000 and 2004 elections. By briefly highlighting some key differences in these two elections as compared with the 2008 and 2012 races, we can begin to realize the opportunities and limits of contemporary minority electoral behavior and representation. In 2000 and 2004, minority electorates more evenly divided their votes between the two parties' candidates, which limited their ability to shape the outcomes of the elections; in 2008 and 2012, minority support for the Democrats grew, allowing for a more distinctive minority voice in the election outcomes. Over the course of the decade, the minority share of the electorate also increased, and this increase was more dramatic in the highly contested "battleground" states that shaped victory in the Electoral College. Finally, issues important to minority communities were more central to the national debate in 2008 and 2012 than in 2000 and 2004. We will discuss how these three sets of factors explain increased minority influence in 2008 and 2012 relative to 2000 and 2004.

Each of these elections saw a gap in the candidate preferences between White and minority voters. Whites supported candidate George W. Bush in 2000 by a margin of 54 to 42, and in 2004 by a margin of 58 to 41. They supported McCain in 2008 with a margin of 55 to 43, and in 2012 White support for Romney was 59 to 39.[3] (See Figure 9.1 for a breakdown of support for presidential candidates by race and ethnicity.) In each of these elections, Blacks, Latinos, and Asian Americans preferred the Democratic candidates (Al Gore, John Kerry, and Barack Obama). What's notable about 2008 and 2012 is that the margin that each group offered the Democrats grew. By 2008, Blacks offered 95 percent of their votes to the Democrats, Latinos 67 percent, and Asian Americans 62 percent. Although there are no estimates of Native American presidential candidate preference before 2008 or 2012, a 2008 preelection poll of Native American and Alaskan Native voters in thirty states found that Obama led McCain by a margin of more than 9 to 1.[4] Black voters have long been reliable members of the Democratic coalition and to a lesser degree, so have Latinos; Asian Americans have more recently moved into the Democratic camp (a theme to which we return later). Influence is undoubtedly more likely to be felt when the majority of any community is allied with the winning candidate and contributes to his or her victory. This alliance raises the likelihood that the issue preferences of the community will be a part of the administration's agenda, and that leaders from the community will be appointed to positions in the administration.

The importance of the slow but steady movement of minority voters into the Democratic coalition was reinforced in 2008 and 2012 by the increasing share that non-Whites made up

Figure 9.1 Candidate Vote in Presidential Elections by Race and Ethnicity, 2000–2012

Presidential Election and Candidates	Percent of Vote by Race and Ethnicity			
	Whites	Blacks	Hispanics	Asian Americans
2000				
George W. Bush (R)	54	8	31	41
Al Gore (D)	42	90	67	54
Ralph Nader (I)	3	1	2	4
2004				
George W. Bush (R)	58	11	43	44
John Kerry (D)	41	88	56	58
2008				
Barack Obama (D)	43	95	67	62
John McCain (R)	55	4	31	35
2012				
Barack Obama (D)	39	93	71	73
Mitt Romney (R)	59	6	27	26

Source: Election Results 2008, *New York Times,* November 5, 2008, http://elections.nytimes.com/2008/results/president/national-exit-polls.html; Election Results 2012, *New York Times,* November 5, 2012, http://elections.nytimes.com/2012/results/president/exit-polls.

Note: There are no reliable exit polls of Native American preferences across election years. A 2008 preelection poll of Native American and Alaskan Native voters in thirty states found that Obama led McCain by a margin of more than 9 to 1.[5]

of the electorate relative to earlier elections. The non-White share of voters nationally grew from 19 percent in 2000 to 26 percent in 2012.

This steady growth in the minority share of the electorate should not obscure the fact that minorities continue to have a larger gap than do Whites between their share of the adult population and their share of voters. For instance, in 2000 Whites made up 73 percent of the adult population and were a slightly larger percentage of the electorate, at nearly 81 percent, meaning that a higher share of White adults went to the polls to vote. In comparison, African Americans comprised about the same percentage of the adult population and electorate, at around 11.5 percent, and Latinos were nearly 8 percent of the adult population but less than 4 percent of those who voted. Asian Americans made up 4 percent of the adult population but less than 2 percent of all voters.

By 2012, Whites continued to make up a higher percentage of the electorate than they did the adult population, at 74 and nearly 66 percent, respectively. African American participation increased, with over 13 percent of the electorate compared to 12 percent of the adult population. In a notable increase, Latinos in 2012 now comprised 15 percent of the adult population and more than 8 percent of all voters. Asian American participation increased to nearly 3 percent, with just over 5 percent of the adult population. Later in the chapter we'll discuss the gap between minority voters and their share of the adult population in greater detail. For now, it's important to note that a higher share of Latino and Asian American adults turned out to vote in 2008 than they did in 2000 or 2004, and that in 2012 African Americans turned out in rates higher than non-Hispanic Whites.

The increase in minority voting in 2008 and 2012 reflected a response to incentives and encouragement to participate, called **voter mobilization,** which was much higher for minority communities in the Obama elections than it had been in 2000 or 2004. In part, this mobilization was made easier because of the excitement that surrounded the Obama candidacy in the November general election and, in 2008, because of a series of highly competitive Democratic primaries that also energized minority communities. In the 2008 Democratic primary, the candidacies of New York senator Hillary Clinton, New Mexico governor Bill Richardson, and Illinois senator Barack Obama all staked their primary victories and potential for electability in the general election in part on minority votes. Clinton was the first woman to lead the race for her party's presidential nomination and ran highly targeted campaigns in several of the early primary and caucus states to win Latino votes. Richardson was the first Latino to make a serious run for the presidency, and he expected to use the Latino community as a foundation for building a winning coalition. Equally as important was the recognition that minority votes would potentially be critical in 2008 both in the Democratic primary and in the general election, both because there was competition for them (leading to higher levels of mobilization) and because there were likely to be a higher share of minority voters than in earlier elections. Consequently, candidates, campaigns, and political parties invested unprecedented amounts in voter registration and get-out-the-vote (GOTV) efforts, which included significant efforts to win minority votes, particularly by the Democrats. Nonpartisan efforts also sought to increase the minority vote.[6] In Latino and Asian American communities, community-based organizations such as the We Are America Alliance focused their energies on encouraging naturalization-eligible immigrants to obtain U.S. citizenship and, then, to vote.[7] While mobilization of minority communities was not new to the 2008 and 2012 elections, the excitement many Blacks, Latinos, and Asian Americans felt about the Obama candidacy ensured a more receptive audience than in previous elections. Obama campaign and Democratic Party leaders and organizations seized this opportunity.

Finally, 2008 and 2012 were unique in that minority mobilization can be said to have had a tangible effect on the outcome of the election, though this impact was a result of the institutional design of U.S. presidential elections. U.S. presidents are elected indirectly through the **Electoral College,** which is made up of delegates from each state. The number of electors for each state is the number of members of Congress for the state (allocated by population every ten years after the census) plus two (based on each state's Senate representation). Since 1961, the District of Columbia has been represented in the Electoral College, but it can have no more electors than the least populous state (three in the 2008 election).[8] All states but Maine and Nebraska allocated their Electoral College delegates in 2008 and 2012 on a winner-take-all basis, meaning that the candidate who receives the most votes wins all of the states' electors. In the 2008 election,

Why did Latinos and Asian Americans vote at higher rates in 2008 and 2012, and why did they give a higher share of their votes to the Democrats?

Black, Latino, Asian American, and Native American voters provided the margin that allowed Obama and the Democrats to win five states that had voted for Bush and the Republicans in 2004—Florida, New Mexico, Indiana, Virginia, and North Carolina. In 2012 minority voters provided the margin for Obama's victories in Florida, Nevada, Colorado, New Mexico, and Virginia.

Though tangible, the consequence of this new minority influence was limited. Race and ethnicity mattered at the polls, though as a sign of minority groups' increasing influence. Obama would have carried the Electoral College even if he had lost these states in each election. By winning them, however, his symbolic mandate was greater than it otherwise would have been. In 2008 he received the highest number of electors since President Bill Clinton's reelection in 1996 (Obama received the highest share of the popular vote since President George H. W. Bush's election in 1988). Also, the Obama victory in these states would not have been felt without movement among the White electorates among these states, who divided their votes in such a way that the more cohesive, though smaller minority vote could prove decisive.

The lessons of the 2008 and 2012 presidential elections relative to 2000 and 2004 are that minority influence on electoral outcomes is far from guaranteed. The number of minority votes is increasing, as is their share of the electorate, both nationally and in most states. That alone, however, isn't enough to guarantee routine minority influence in national elections. Instead, influence will be felt, as it was in 2008 and 2012, when White electorates are more evenly divided than are minority communities, and when extensive efforts are made—both from within minority communities and without—to increase minority participation. In the discussion that follows, we will analyze rates of minority engagement in civic life and in electoral politics; the underpinnings of minority engagement, such as ideology and partisanship; differences between minority and White engagement and differences between minority communities; and the share of minority representatives in elective office.

MINORITY CIVIC ENGAGEMENT: PATTERNS IN PARTICIPATION

People seek to influence government and public policy in a variety of ways, from individual to collective efforts. Individual efforts can include activities such as writing, calling, or e-mailing officeholders, or writing letters to the editor of newspapers. Collective efforts, which are the more common mode of seeking to influence government, include activities such as attending meetings; joining organizations; volunteering with community groups; serving on boards or commissions; protesting; and, among immigrants and their children, engaging in the civic or political life of their country of origin or ancestry (discussed in Chapter 12). Clearly, this list is not exhaustive, and the complexity of civic life and politics ensures that there are many ways that people seek to exert their influence. Here, we look at patterns that appear in who participates and why. We will also assess whether minority communities engage in civic life differently from non-Hispanic Whites.

One form of seeking to influence government—voting—will be discussed later in the chapter. This is for two reasons. First, voting is the most common form of political participation and sees the most effort by political institutions to mobilize individuals and groups. As such, it deserves more focused attention. Second, minority communities have tended to vote at lower rates than Whites and have seen the greatest restrictions on their participation. Most of these formal restrictions were prohibited by the 1965 Voting Rights Act (see Chapter 7), but some of their legacies remain among today's voters. Restrictions on voting remain today—specifically the prohibitions on voting; by U.S. citizens under the age of eighteen; and, in many states, by most convicted felons. Minority communities are more likely to include members in both of these categories than does the White community. For the most part, these restrictions do not apply to civic participation, the topic to which we turn first.[9]

Means of Engagement

Although there is variation in the types of civic engagement in different racial/ethnic communities, non-Hispanic Whites tend to be somewhat more civically engaged than are minority communities. Likewise, African Americans are somewhat more likely than Latinos or Asian Americans to engage in the civic life of their communities.[10] (See Table 9.1.) For instance, Whites are more likely to make campaign contributions or to contact officials than are Blacks or Latinos. Blacks, however, are more likely to volunteer in a campaign than are Whites or Latinos. There is also variation by gender, with White women, Black women, and Latinas less likely to participate than males in their communities; this gender gap is particularly wide in Latino communities.[11] It should be noted that participation rates in many of these activities are low for all groups. The activities that see the highest rates are voting and passive activities such as discussing politics. Within minority communities, there is undoubtedly variation. Table 9.1 shows that, among Latinos, U.S. citizens are more likely to be civically engaged than are non-U.S. citizens. This pattern is likely true in all racial and ethnic groups.[12]

Although not necessarily political, religiosity offers another tool for people in the United States to engage in politics. Religious institutions provide a venue to meet others and to discuss secular as well as spiritual concerns. Houses of worship are more protected than other public spaces, so individuals who distance themselves from politics or civic life may be more comfortable in engaging in the political world from the safety of a church, mosque, or temple. Religious texts and leaders also frequently offer guidance on political issues and civic behaviors, though they need to take care to frame this potentially political advice in spiritual or textual terms to ensure that they remain nonpartisan (so as not to endanger the protections religious institutions have under the tax code). As with other forms of civic life, there are variations in religiosity. African Americans are much more likely to attend religious services regularly and to report that religion is "very" or "extremely" important to them than are Whites, Latinos, or Asians. Nearly 60 percent of Blacks report attending religious services "nearly every week," compared to 39 percent of Whites.[13] Latinos also have somewhat higher levels of religiosity than do Whites, though their patterns are much closer to those of Whites than of African Americans. Asian Americans show considerably lower levels of church attendance and report religion to be less important to their political decision making than do Blacks, Latinos, or Whites.

Participation in organized religion is not primarily a political activity for many churchgoers, yet religion offers the opportunity to engage in civic life from a different starting point. Group-based differences in religiosity add to the complexity of minorities' civic worlds. For instance, as discussed in Chapter 3, much of the African American civil rights organizing of the 1950s and 1960s emerged from Black churches. In addition, many of the movement's leaders were

Table 9.1   Political Activities by Race and Ethnicity*

Political Activity	Percent of Participants by Race and Ethnicity				
	Whites	Blacks	Latinos	Latino U.S. Citizens	Asian Americans
Vote	73	65	41	52	**
Campaign work	8	12	7	8	4
Campaign contributions	25	22	11	12	12
Contact local officials	37	24	14	17	9
Protest	5	9	4	4	4
Informal community activity	17	19	12	14	21
Board membership	4	2	4	5	**
Affiliated with a political organization	52	38	24	27	**

Source: Compiled from Sidney Verba, Kay Lehman Schlozman, and Henry E. Brady, *Voice and Equality: Civic Voluntarism in American Politics* (Cambridge, MA: Harvard University Press, 1995), Table 8.1; Hane Junn, Karthick Ramakrishnan, Taeku Lee, and Janelle Wong, *2008 National Asian American Survey* (community presentation in New York, July 2009), http://www.naasurvey.com/presentations_assets/NAAS-nyc-presentation.pdf.,

* Data for Asian Americans are from 2008. Data in all other categories are from 1989.

** Data not available in the categories of voting, board membership, and affiliation with a political organization.

pastors, like the Reverend Dr. Martin Luther King Jr. Likewise, early leaders of the Mexican American civil rights movement tapped the Catholicism of many Mexican Americans in their organizations and in the iconography of the movement. In the period since, churches have been a particular locus for turning out the Black vote. These resources also exist for Latinos and Asian Americans, certainly; however, lower rates of church attendance mean that churches will be less central to political outreach and organizing in these communities.

Reasons for Lower Levels of Engagement

There are various explanations for why minority communities have lower levels of civic activity. Some explanations focus on minority communities themselves and attribute the differences to community characteristics, such as the composition of minority populations and their assessment of the degree to which they believe that they or minority communities in general can affect political outcomes—what political scientists call **political efficacy**. Relative levels of trust in government may also play a role. Other explanations focus on political institutions and their failure to reach out to minority communities or to encourage minority participation as compared to non-Hispanic White participation.

On average, Blacks, Latinos, and Asian Americans are younger than non-Hispanic Whites, and with the exception of Asian Americans, they have lower levels of formal education and lower incomes. Across the board, civic engagement is generally more common among older people and those with higher education and incomes, so minority communities are disadvantaged, at least for now, by the composition of their populations. Some of these compositional disadvantages—par-

ASSOCIATED PRESS

Religion and labor organizing offer alternative paths to politics for people in society who are either formally excluded from electoral participation or do not feel welcome in U.S. electoral politics. In this rally, religious leaders and organized labor join to advocate for immigrant rights.

ticularly differences in the average age of different populations—should diminish over time. Latinos and Asian Americans face an added barrier in that a high share of their adult populations are not U.S. citizens (33.7 and 33.9 percent, respectively).[14] Although non-U.S. citizens can certainly participate in many civic activities, they are, at least during their early years in the United States, less connected to U.S. politics and have less socialization into how civic institutions work in the United States. These barriers do not apply to religious institutions, which is among the reasons it is important to include religiosity as part of a study of civic engagement. Religious institutions are more open to people who share a belief system. Consequently, they take all comers, regardless of their demographic characteristics or immigration/citizenship status.

A second set of possible explanations for lower levels of minority participation has to do with differences in political efficacy and political trust in minority communities relative to that in White communities. Here, minority communities have an advantage when compared with Whites, at least in terms of political efficacy. Minority communities are generally more likely to report that they are able to shape government outcomes than are White communities. They are also slightly more likely to report that public officials care about what "people like me" think. When it comes to trust in government, the story is a bit more mixed. Latinos are somewhat more trusting of government than are Whites and other minority communities. African Americans are less trusting of government than are Whites.[15]

Are the gaps that remain between minority and White civic and electoral participation an example of racialization or other factors? Does the government have a role in reducing these gaps?

Any gap between minority and nonminority participation, however, should not be attributed entirely to minority communities themselves. Research into minority civic engagement shows a consistent pattern of lower levels of recruitment or outreach to Blacks, Latinos, and Asian Americans. Participation often results from being asked to participate; to the extent that minorities are less likely to be asked, they are less likely to participate.[16] This is a particular problem in communities where immigrants make up the majority of the population. These communities are less likely to have a rich infrastructure of civic organizations and, consequently, fewer lessons about how to participate.

Today's minority communities have come of political age at a particularly poor moment in American political history. Previous waves of immigrants and politically excluded populations have had a resource that is much rarer in today's politics—institutions that spur incorporation and mobilization among the politically marginalized. In the past, political parties, trade unions, civic organizations, and national and local political movements have been agents of incorporation. (See Chapters 2 through 6.) Some of these organizations, such as the NAACP and the League of United Latin American Citizens, certainly still exist, but they no longer fill a mass mobilization role except under narrow circumstances (such as during the 2008 and 2012 presidential elections).[17] Minority organizations and leaders can fill this role over time; in previous eras, however, it was not the sole responsibility of minority communities to ensure that all participated in democratic institutions.

The causes of these gaps between majority and minority participation vary by types of activity and specific communities but have consistently serious consequences. Lower levels of community organizing in minority communities means that minority communities are less able to advocate in order to meet their own needs. Race/ethnicity, then, predicts lower participation even in the post–Civil Rights era.

MINORITY IDEOLOGY AND PARTISANSHIP: FINDING A PLACE IN THE U.S. POLITICAL SYSTEM

Partisanship (preference for one political party over another) and **ideology** (the groups of fundamental beliefs and ideas that shape an individual's understanding of the political system) offer predictable tools for individuals to interpret the political world. All people, regardless of race/ethnicity use these tools to synthesize the information they receive and to process that information in predictable ways to make decisions about how they will act politically. Not surprisingly, immigrants are somewhat less connected to American understandings of ideology or to the U.S. political parties. Even among immigrants, however, policy interests quickly shape understandings of where one fits in the American political system.

Characteristics of Minority Ideologies

Minority communities tend to see themselves as somewhat more liberal than non-Hispanic Whites. (See Table 9.2.) Approximately 14 percent of Whites identified as liberal or very liberal in 2008, and 23 percent as conservative or very conservative.[18] The comparable rates for Blacks were 16 percent liberal and 13 percent conservative; for Latino U.S. citizens (in 2006), 15 and 22 percent; and for Asian American U.S. citizens (in 2008), 21 percent liberal and 18 percent conservative.[19]

For immigrant ethnic communities, ideological positions are less defined. As Table 9.2 shows, significant portions of Latino and Asian non-U.S. citizens are more likely to place themselves off of the ideological scale than are U.S. citizen Latinos and Asian Americans. For new immigrants, then, ideology is learned; consequently, U.S. minority communities will not so easily fit into U.S. ideologies for the foreseeable future.

We offer a caution in interpreting these data. Ideology may mean different things in different communities, particularly immigrant communities. Surveys of Latinos, for example, have often found a high share of conservatives, a characteristic that often gives Republican leaders hope Latinos can be recruited to their party. In the Latino case, however, some of the self-identified conservatism does not fit so easily on the contemporary ideological frame of American politics. Many self-identified Latino conservatives also seek an expanded role for government and express a willingness to pay additional taxes for these added government services. These are not positions that would be shared by many Anglo conservatives.[20]

Partisanship in Minority Communities

One of the key dimensions on which minority communities differ from non-Hispanic White populations is partisanship. The majority of Blacks, Latinos, Asian Americans, and Native Americans routinely vote for Democratic candidates; the majority of non-Hispanic Whites vote for Republicans, a difference that is of particular importance because Whites make up a much larger share of the electorate (people who vote) than they do of the population as a whole. Democrats maintain a sizeable advantage among African Americans: 86 percent to 8 percent among African Americans who either identify with one of the parties or who report that they are independent but lean toward one of the parties. (See Table 9.3.) The Democratic advantage among Latinos and Asian Americans is smaller—64 to 22 and 61 to 28, respectively—but quite substantial nevertheless. Republicans have a 52 to 39 advantage among Whites, who either identify with one of the parties or who report that they are independent but lean toward one of the parties.

Approximately one-third of the electorate, including many minorities, understand themselves to be independent. Of these independents, however, 70 percent report that they routinely lean toward either the Democrats or the Republicans and we count these leaners with the partisans. Latinos and Asian Americans are somewhat more likely than Whites and African Americans to include independents who report that they do not lean toward one party or the other. These true independents number approximately 6 percent of Blacks, 9 percent of Whites, 11 percent of Asian Americans, and 14 percent of Latinos. There are no reliable measures of Native American partisanship; even if there were, we would anticipate variation across tribes. Two measures, however, suggest a strong preference for Democrats among Native Americans. First, the vast majority of Native Americans elected to state legislatures are Democrats. Second, a 2008 preelection poll of Native Americans and Alaskan Natives nationwide showed strong preference for Obama over McCain.[21]

Table 9.2   Ideology by Race/Ethnicity and Citizenship Status

Ideology	Percent of Respondents by Race and Ethnicity					
	Whites	Blacks	Latinos	Latino U.S. Citizens	Asian American	Asian American U.S. Citizen
Very Liberal	2.5%	4.6%	6.8%	8.2%	9.0%	10.2%
Liberal	11.2	11.8	6.3	6.7	11.8	11.3
Slightly Liberal	9.5	16.5	2.4	3.2	23.1	21.7
Moderate	37.3	46.3	12.1	13.9	–	–
Slightly Conservative	16.9	8	2.3	2.1	15.5	16.2
Conservative	18.8	7.2	9.4	8.9	9	10.6
Very Conservative	3.7	5.7	11.6	13.1	5.9	7.2
Don't think of self in these terms/haven't thought about/other			49	44	25.6	22.9

Sources: Data on Whites and Blacks from the 2008 General Social Survey. Data on Latinos from the 2006 Latino National Survey. Data on Asian Americans from the 2008 National Asian American Survey. Tom Smith, Peter V. Marsden, and Michael Hout. 2011. *General Social Survey, 1972–2010* [Cumulative File] [Computer file]. ICPSR31521-v1. Storrs, CT: Roper Center for Public Opinion Research, University of Connecticut/Ann Arbor, MI: Inter-university Consortium for Political and Social Research [distributors], 2011-08-05. doi:10.3886/ICPSR31521.v1. John A. Garcia, Rodney Hero, Michael Jones-Correa, Valerie Martinez-Ebers, and Gary M. Segura. 2008. *Latino National Survey (LNS),* 2006 [Computer file]. ICPSR20862-v4. Ann Arbor, MI: Inter-university Consortium for Political and Social Research [distributor], 2010-05-26. doi:10.3886/ICPSR20862.v4. Karthick, Ramakrishnan, Jane Junn, Taeku Lee, and Janelle Wong. 2011. *National Asian American Survey, 2008* [Computer file]. ICPSR31481-v1. Ann Arbor, MI: Inter-university Consortium for Political and Social Research [distributor], 2011-08-12. doi:10.3886/ICPSR31481.v1. National weight used for National Asian American Survey.

Notes: These data were collected by different organizations, using slightly different questions. The surveys of Asian Americans and Latinos provided the opportunity to define oneself as being off of the seven-point ideological scale; the Asian American data do not offer a direct measure of being in the middle of the of the scale ("moderate"). Some share of the "don't think of self in these terms/haven't thought about/other" responses for Latinos and Asian Americans should be understood as respondents who understand themselves to be broadly in the middle of the scale.

The Latino data were collected in 2006, and the data on Whites, Blacks, and Asian Americans were collected in 2008.

Partisan loyalties do shift modestly in election cycles when particularly strong or weak candidates are nominated by one party or the other. Table 9.3 illustrates shifts in partisan identification for African Americans, Latinos, and non-Hispanic Whites between 2008 (an election year with a strong Democratic candidate) and 2011 (a nonelection year in which many voters were judging Democrat Obama against the Republican Party as a whole and not a specific opponent). For African Americans and Latinos, the likelihood of voting for Democratic candidates has remained largely constant over the past twenty years; Asian Americans have become more reliable

Table 9.3   Party Identification by Race/Ethnicity, 2011

Race/Ethnicity	Democrat	Republican	Republican Gain 2008–2011
Black (non-Hispanic)	86	8	2
Latino	64	22	–6
White (non-Hispanic)	39	52	6
Asian American (2008)	61	28	N/A

Sources: Pew Research Center for the People and the Press, "GOP Makes Big Gains among White Voters: Especially among the Young and the Poor" (Washington, DC: Pew Research Center, 2011), http://people-press.org/files/legacy-pdf/7-22-11%20Party%20ID%20 commentary.pdf. Data on Asian Americans: Jane Junn, Taeku Lee, S. Karthick Ramakrishnan, and Janelle Wong, "Asian American Public Opinion," in Robert Shapiro and Lawrence Jacobs, eds., *The Oxford Handbook of American Public Opinion and the Media* (New York: Oxford University Press, 2011), 520–534, http://www.naasurvey.com/publications_assets/OUP-Junnetal-chapter.pdf.

Notes: The Democrat and Republican categories include people who identify with each party and who initially indicate that they are Independents, but who say that they lean toward one party or the other in a follow-up question.

There are few reliable measures of Asian American partisan identification. The data reported here are from a national survey of Asian Americans conducted in 2008. We do not have estimates of changes in Asian American partisanship between 2008 and 2011.

There are no reliable measures of Native American partisanship.

Democratic voters.[22] Non-Hispanic Whites have also become more reliably Republican in national elections, although the share of Anglos voting for each party does vary by state. The early years of the Obama administration saw even more movement along these lines.

Is it possible for these minority partisan loyalties to shift, significantly, in the *near* future? The answer is probably not. Partisan attachments remain relatively consistent over time. The roots of these attachments reflect linkages between the issues that each party organizes around and advocates and the interests of party members and voters who routinely vote for the party. The Democrats, for example, are more likely to advocate for enforcement of civil rights laws, which wins support from many African Americans, and for opportunities for unauthorized immigrants to attain legal status, which wins support from many in the Latino and Asian American communities. Democrats also tend to be more supportive of increasing funding for education, an issue that speaks to minority communities more generally. In order to ensure that they retain support from conservative voters, Republicans in today's political order are less likely to advocate positions on issues that are held by African Americans, Latinos, Asian Americans, or Native Americans.

These issue-based connections between voters and parties are reinforced by party recruitment and leadership. The recruitment often begins when voters are very young. Young adults coming of voting age often follow the partisan leanings of their parents. In immigrant communities, where partisanship cannot so easily be learned from parents, the racial and ethnic face of the party often serves to recruit new members. So in Latino communities, for example, almost all Latino locally elected officials and party leaders are Democrats (outside of South Florida). Therefore, Democrats have a natural advantage in making connections to young Latinos entering the electorate and to the newly naturalized, regardless of age. Asian American

What factors would change the distribution of minority votes for each of the parties?

and African American officeholders are also overwhelmingly Democrats and put a face on the party. The connection, however, only works when the party is also advocating issues of concern to this community.

In the longer run, partisan loyalties can change. Between the end of the Civil War and the 1930s, African Americans were solidly Republican. Republican leadership during the Civil War and Reconstruction cemented this connection. Black Republican partisanship began to atrophy, however, as Republicans sacrificed African American interests in the post-Reconstruction period. Black loyalty to the Republicans shifted when Democrats began to speak to Black economic needs in the 1930s, and northern urban political leaders—largely Democrats—began to include some African Americans as candidates for local office. Democrats cemented this relationship in the 1960s, with President Lyndon B. Johnson's advocacy of civil rights legislation and policies, and with the election of most Black officeholders as Democrats.

African Americans appear to be solidly in the Democratic camp for the foreseeable future, a connection made even stronger by Barack Obama's election to the presidency.[23] Republicans express hope that they will be able to make greater inroads with Latinos and Asian Americans, groups with which they have a stronger foundation for future growth. In the case of Latinos, Republicans observe that many are more socially conservative than is the Democratic Party; they believe that Latinos are patriotic, have a higher share of small-business owners, and (as we have noted) identify as conservative. Each of these characteristics, Republican leaders believe, makes Latinos a prime target for Republican recruitment. While possible in the long run, these hopes are diminished by the issues that are of most importance to Latinos—immigrant incorporation and support for resources to ensure that immigrants and others who are disadvantaged in U.S. society can improve themselves. Republicans' opposition to comprehensive immigration reform (see Chapter 11) and, particularly, their unwillingness to consider any path to legal status for unauthorized immigrants, limits their abilities to make inroads with Latino and Asian American electorates. Their disadvantage is compounded by their resistance to expanding social safety net programs that provide opportunities for all newcomers in U.S. society. This incorporation agenda that serves as a glue in Latino and Asian American politics is much closer to today's Democrats than to today's Republicans.

Equally problematic for Republicans seeking to recruit Latinos is that they must maintain the support they receive from their current voters. Consequently, Republicans cannot moderate positions on key issues of importance to Latinos—for example, on comprehensive immigration reform (see Chapter 11)—without alienating voters who routinely support the party. Contemporary Republican voters are more conservative and more White than are Democratic voters.[24] Equally important, the parties don't so much set their agendas as do the parties' candidates and officeholders. These candidates need to win support from the party's core voters in order to win nomination, and, consequently, they may take positions that make it difficult to win over moderates in the general election. This is particularly the case when the nomination for a specific office is contested. So, for example, in 2012 Republican Party leaders spoke of the need to reach out to Latinos and Asian Americans in order to ensure that the Republican Party would be successful in the future, but the candidates for the Republican presidential nomination (and many Republican candidates at the state and local level) took stridently anti-immigrant positions in order to win the support of the primary voters who select the party candidates for office. As a result, it is safe to say that party coalitions will undoubtedly change in the long run. In the short run, however, the position of minority voters in the Democratic coalition is likely to remain stable (just as the majority of White votes are solidly in the Republican camp).

MINORITY ELECTORAL PARTICIPATION: UNREALIZED POTENTIAL TO INFLUENCE POLITICS

As is the case with civic engagement, minority communities generally vote at lower rates than do non-Hispanic Whites. (See Figure 9.2.) In both the 2000 and 2004 elections, Blacks voted at rates 5 to 6 percent lower than did Whites.[25] Latino and Asian American adult citizens voted at rates approximately 20 percent below those of Whites. These gaps narrowed in 2008 and 2012. In 2008—the first election with an African American as the nominee of a major political party—Whites continued to vote at higher rates than did Blacks, Latinos, or Asian Americans. In 2012 African Americans turned out at higher rates than Whites, a first in American political history. Latino and Asian American voting continued to trail behind White voting.

As these examples indicate, our discussion on electoral participation will primarily focus on voting in national elections. In state and local elections, the gap between White and minority voting is often larger. Local races are often less well known to registered voters who do not vote regularly, are often held on a different schedule from national elections, and in many states do not allow candidates to run as members of a party. Each of these factors reduces voting overall in state and local elections and dampens minority turnout relative to White turnout. In this section, we discuss why minorities vote at lower rates, what can be done to increase minority participation, and how minority electoral influence can be felt.

Barriers to Minority Voting

Minority adults face many of the same barriers to voting that they do in engaging civic life. Sociodemographic characteristics such as age, education, and income dampen participation. Minority communities are more likely to have younger adults and individuals with lower incomes or low levels of formal education than do non-Hispanic Whites. Minority communities also have higher shares of immigrants than does the White population. Noncitizenship, including noncitizenship among legal permanent residents who are eligible to naturalize, reduce the number of people who are eligible to participate at the polls.

As was the case with civic engagement, however, it is inappropriate to place the responsibility for low rates of voting entirely in minority communities themselves. Voting is extensively regulated, and the rules enacted by local jurisdictions often disproportionately disadvantage minority communities. The Voting Rights Act (VRA) reduced, but did not eliminate, these barriers. (See Chapter 7.) Requirements that people register in advance of the election in order to be eligible to vote offer a particular burden for potential voters who are less engaged in the electoral process. The election often becomes most heated in the weeks just before Election Day. In most states, however, it is too late to register during this period. Finally, people vote in response to being asked. In most elections, the campaigns, candidates, community-based organizations, and parties focus their mobilization efforts on people who have voted in the past and in communities

Figure 9.2   Registration and Turnout as a Percentage of Citizen Adults by Race and Ethnicity, 2000–2012

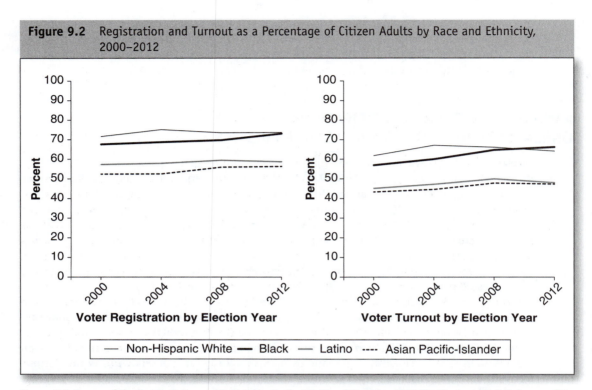

Source: U.S. Bureau of the Census, *Voting and Registration in the Election of November 2012* (Washington, DC: U.S. Bureau of the Census, 2013), Table 4b. Data are available at http://www.census.gov/hhes/www/socdemo/voting/publications/p20/index.html.

Note: These percentages are calculated based on registration and turnout among U.S. citizen adults. Media accounts often present registration and voting as a share of all adults, including non-U. S. citizens. These rates are lower, particularly for Asian Americans and Latinos.

where voter turnout is high. Not surprisingly, perhaps, minority voters and the communities where they reside are less likely to be targets of mobilization efforts, except in the closest of elections. The two Obama campaigns challenged this norm and did more outreach to irregular and new voters, at least in the highly contested "battleground" states. This outreach—which included unprecedented use of social media, rallies, door-to-door canvassing, and in-person follow-up with potential voters identified in the weeks before the election—undoubtedly increased the youth vote and the minority vote (as well as the overall vote) for Obama.

Overcoming Barriers to Minority Voting

There are three areas to consider for increasing minority electoral participation: the changing composition of minority populations; voter registration requirements; and more minority candidates and issues in campaigns. We first consider that some of the barriers that minorities face are compositional. In other words, they are the results of the makeup or composition of U.S. minority populations. On average, minority populations are younger, poorer, and less formally educated than White adults. These compositional differences have narrowed and will likely continue to narrow further, but not disappear in the future. Another compositional characteristic—low

 To what extent are the barriers to minority voting a result of the legacies of racialization versus a reflection of individual responsibility?

rates of naturalization among U.S. citizenship–eligible immigrants—requires different remedies in a period, such as the current one, in which immigration continues at high levels and will for the foreseeable future.

Although immigrants become eligible to naturalize after five years of legal residence, many wait much longer, and some eligible immigrants never become U.S. citizens. The most straightforward solution to high rates of immigrant non-U.S. citizenship is mobilization and education in immigrant-ethnic communities to promote naturalization and offer assistance to those seeking to complete the application. Such efforts have proved very successful during periods in which U.S. immigration policy has been a point of contention during a campaign.[26] Such efforts, however, are expensive, so they require support from the philanthropic sector and/or from political institutions.

Non-U.S. citizenship, of course, does not have to be a barrier to voting. Through much of the nineteenth century, many states allowed noncitizens to vote. Groups seeking greater opportunities for immigrant-ethnic participation could advocate for a return to noncitizen voting.

We think it unlikely, however, that many states will move to large-scale, non-U.S. citizen voting, so the remedy for compositional gaps between the non-Hispanic White population, on the one hand, and Latinos and Asian Americans, on the other, is to ensure that eligible immigrants naturalize. This, unfortunately, is only the first step. Their move to becoming voters, however, will not be automatic; the newly naturalized will need the same mobilization and encouragement to participate as all newly eligible voters.

Equalizing voter participation rates between Whites and minority populations is more than a matter of allowing time to close the gap in minority compositional characteristics. Electoral rules also need to change to increase minority voting rates. One key barrier to participation—both for minorities and in general—is **voter registration requirements.** These rules—requiring potential voters to certify their eligibility to vote with the state in the weeks or months before the election—were implemented around the turn of the twentieth century to control what was perceived to be widespread voter fraud. In the current era, however, there are many other techniques available to control fraud, such as monitoring data collected by voter registrars to ensure that individuals do not vote when they are ineligible and to prosecute those who violate the law, but the barriers established by registration remain. Minorities (and adults newer to the electorate in general) are less likely to be registered and, consequently, unable to participate in elections if they develop an interest in the weeks immediately before an election. People who move regularly (which disproportionately includes young adults and people who rent rather than own their homes) are also more likely to fall out of registration by failing to reregister at their new address.

Ten states plus the District of Columbia permit **Election-Day registration,** a system in which voter registration continues to be required but allows for registration up to and including Election Day. They include Maine, Minnesota, Idaho, New Hampshire, Wisconsin, Wyoming,

Opponents of strict voter identification requirements considered by many states since 2008 see a racial as well as partisan motive in the passage of such laws. The groups in U.S. society least likely to have the required forms of identification are racial and ethnic minorities, young voters, and elderly voters. Supporters note that requiring identification to vote is no different from requiring it to drive.

and Oregon.[27] Almost all of these states have relatively low percentages of minorities; while there is no direct correlation between racial diversity and legislative openness to Election-Day registration, more homogeneous states manifest a greater trust in the honesty of electoral behaviors. A study of registration and turnout in California finds that turnout would increase by 4.8 percent if California were to shift to a system of Election-Day voter registration. Latino and naturalized citizen voter turnout would increase by an even higher rate.[28] California offers an interesting test of the future of Election Day registration. In 2012 the California legislature authorized Election Day registration in the year following the year that the California secretary of state certified the state had established a statewide database of adults eligible to vote which complied with the Help America Vote Act of 2002. California has not yet developed this database but will in the near future.

Voter registration requirements are just one example of electoral rules that disproportionately dampen minority participation and turnout. Many states, however, are going in the opposite direction and increasing rather than decreasing voting barriers. Like voter registration, rules requiring voters to show photo identification or reductions in the provision of early voting (the opportunity to vote in weeks leading up to the election) tend to dampen the minority vote more than the White vote. (See Box 9.2 as an example and Map 9.1 to see where these new rules are being implemented.)

A final resource available to narrow the gap between White and minority voting is more election-specific. As the 2008 and 2012 elections showed, minority-focused get-out-the-vote efforts can be very effective in mobilizing new voters. The election, however, has to offer compelling reasons for irregular and new voters to go to the polls, and campaigns and candidates have to have the resources and make the decisions to invest in minority outreach. In most elections, issues central to minority communities—such as expanding the role of government in assisting the disadvantaged or adding resources for public education—are not central to the campaign rhetoric, and candidates/campaigns do not make targeted efforts to reach out to minority voters. On the contrary, it is much more common to concentrate mobilization efforts on segments of the White electorate, such as Christian conservatives (most of whom are White) in the 2004 election or Tea Party activists (most of whom are White) in the 2010 election.

Map 9.1   States with Voter ID Requirements, 2014

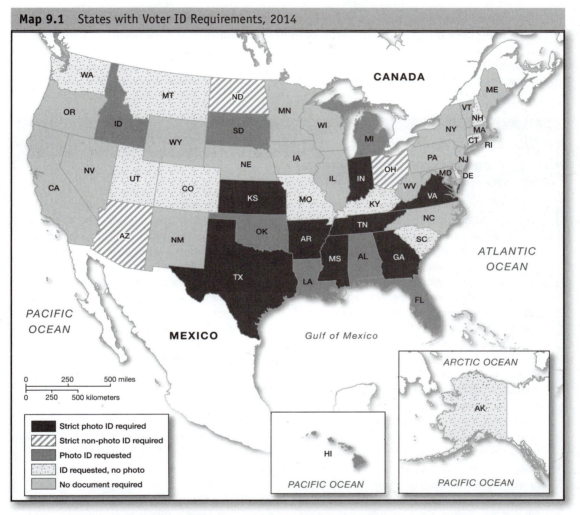

New voter identification laws are being enacted across the United States, from the more strict provisions that require a government issued photo ID (which excludes student IDs and includes drivers' licenses and passports, documentation less likely to be held by lower income people) or some other documentation to those that request but do not require an ID. Concerns have been raised that these requirements unfairly restrict minorities from access to the polls.

Source: © National Conference of State Legislatures.

Source: Voter Identification Requirements 2014, National Council of State Legislatures, http://www.ncsl.org/research/elections-and-campaigns/voter-id.aspx#map.

Note: A state court struck down Arkansas's strict photo voter ID law in April 2014, and the Arkansas Supreme Court has put the ruling on hold while it considers the case.

Minority candidates and issues central to minority communities increase the salience of the election in those communities. Minority candidates do not have to be as prominent as Barack Obama. State candidates—such as Marco Rubio, who won one of Florida's U.S. Senate seats in 2010, or candidates for local office such as Antonio Villaraigosa, who was elected Los Angeles's first Latino mayor in the modern era in 2005—can energize minority voters and increase their turnout. The presence of minority candidates and the discussion of issues relevant to minority communities increase both the likelihood that there will be widespread mobilization of minority voters by parties, candidates, and political institutions, and that the message of mobilization will be heard by new or irregular voters.[29]

BOX 9.2 ROAD SIGN

Changing Voter Requirements

In early October 2012, a federal court upheld a controversial South Carolina law that required voters to show one of a limited number of state-issued identification documents in order to vote. The court ruled that the law did not discriminate against minorities but that South Carolina could not enforce the law until after the 2012 election because, without reasonable exemptions, the law could potentially discriminate.

Since the passage of the Voting Rights Act (VRA) in 1965, many states eased voter registration requirements and provided more opportunities for voters to vote early. This liberalization in access to the polls spurred an increase in registration by groups in the population such as minorities, who register at lower rates,[30] and expanded the number of voters through early voting opportunities. Many states, however, are now passing legislation to narrow access to the polls by reducing or eliminating early voting and by requiring voter identification at the polling place on Election Day. Each of these restrictions reduces the likelihood of voting, and minority voters will pay the highest price.

By 2013, thirty-four states required some form of identification to vote; fourteen of these states required a photo ID at the polling place.[31] In 2014 the states with the most restrictive identification requirements were Texas, Georgia, Tennessee, Indiana, Kansas, Arizona, Ohio, and Virginia. Many states have also reduced the opportunities for early voting.

Reducing opportunities for early voting cuts costs on the staffing and rental of early polling locations—financial cuts that may be attractive to states trying to reduce spending. The impetus for state efforts to require identification at the polls, however, is more complicated. Advocates of voter ID requirements are concerned that people ineligible to vote were flouting the law and voting despite their ineligibility. Though little evidence is available to substantiate this concern, advocates of these restrictions note that some elections are determined by small margins, so even a few ineligible voters are too many.[32] Such efforts expanded considerably after Republicans won state legislative majorities in states where they had traditionally been in the minority in the 2010 elections.[33] These Republican legislators focused on concerns about fraud rather than on the effects on minority voting.

Opponents of identification requirements, however, express concern that the requirement itself could discourage eligible voters from voting, which could also influence election outcomes. The dampening effect of such laws, they say, would not be equally felt across the electorate. Approximately 12 percent of eligible voters do not have a government-issued photo ID, such as a driver's license. The rates are higher for the elderly and urban populations (who are less likely to drive). Minorities are less likely than non-Hispanic Whites to have IDs that would meet state requirements.[34] Some estimates suggest that as many as 25 percent of eligible African American voters do not have the required identification.

Each of these newly emerging sets of restrictions will likely dampen minority voting in future elections, and may well shape the outcome in close races. As the laws have steadily become more restrictive, courts may find they do violate the VRA because the effects will be felt most strongly by Blacks, Latinos, Asian Americans, and Native Americans—the populations the VRA was designed to protect. These legislative changes offer an important lesson that challenges to minority electoral gains will continue and may well be masked in more universalistic principles, such as the high cost of providing electoral access or the risk that some will take advantage of lax regulation.

Minority Political Influence

Lower than average rates of minority voting obscure the growing importance of minority votes, as does the number of elective offices in the United States. More than 600,000 public offices are filled through elections. As the minority population grows and coalesces in its support for Democratic candidates, minority votes increasingly shape the structure of campaigns and their outcomes. This phenomenon has not just appeared in the last two presidential races. Steadily increasing mobilization of minority voters, for example, has dramatically increased the share of Democrats in California's legislature;[35] Democrats now routinely dominate this institution and often elect two-thirds of the members, allowing them to pass the state budget with ease.

There is no consensus on how to measure group electoral influence. The 2008 election discussed at the beginning of this chapter shows the dilemma. Were minorities influential? At the simplest level, yes, they were. Had no minority voter gone to the polls, John McCain would have easily won the presidency, with 55 percent of the White vote. This is, of course, a silly standard. Minority voters have been part of the electorate since the nation's first days, and the 1965 Voting Rights Act prohibits race-based exclusion from the polls. There will not be an election with no minority voters. Yet the example shows how, as a bloc, the minority vote has power in the U.S. electoral system. The question, then, is what share of the electorate will be made up of minority voters and whether minority electorates will continue to vote more cohesively than nonminority voters.

Any definition of influence—for any electoral group—needs to account for the routine level of participation for that group. As we have suggested, California now routinely elects Democrats in statewide elections in part because of the steady growth of the Latino and Asian American electorates and their overwhelming support for the Democrats. This is critically important to national elections, where it makes the Democrats more competitive, but it does not lead to a specific claim of minority or Latino influence in 2008 or 2012. Why is that? In both 2008 and

2012, Latino and Asian American voters in California voted in predictable ways, so it is harder to make a claim of group influence in a specific election. That routine influence in 2008 and 2012 should not mask the long-term importance of minority electorates to reshaping California's partisan balance.[36]

The 2008 and 2012 elections offer several possible examples of minority influence over and above what could be considered their routine contributions to electoral outcomes. Among the more surprising states that Obama carried in the 2008 Electoral College were Indiana, North Carolina, and Virginia. In each case, these Democratic victories resulted from very high levels of minority turnout and their support for Obama. Thus, higher than expected turnout among minorities, combined with the fact that these votes tipped the votes in states that otherwise had very divided electorates, leads to a reasonable—though contestable— claim of influence at the state level. One other state in the 2008 and 2012 elections offers a clearer claim of minority influence: Florida saw a dramatic increase in its African American vote, most of which went to Obama. These added Democratic votes were supplemented by increasing turnout and division in the Latino electorate. Unlike Latinos in the rest of the country, many Florida Latino voters are Republicans. This pattern has been slowly changing, though, and it did so more dramatically in 2008 and 2012. Thus these two changes in Florida's minority voting patterns lead to a claim of minority influence. More Blacks and Latinos voted in these two elections than in previous elections, and they voted more Democratic than they had in the past. Although these states did not determine the outcome of the race in the Electoral College in either 2008 or 2012—arguably the ultimate measure of influence in the presidential race—they did add to the Obama mandate in both elections.

Indiana, North Carolina, Virginia, and Florida also offer a lesson in claims of electoral influence. Influence is more easily asserted when minorities—or any other electoral group— change political behavior, either by changing the number of votes or their candidate or party preference. In 2008 and 2012, minorities had more of an incentive to vote, saw more efforts to ask for their votes, and responded by voting in higher numbers and at higher rates for the Democrats. As the sizes of minority electorates grow and candidates and parties learn more about how to ask for their votes, we are likely to see more elections in which minority electorates determine the outcome and see the candidate of their choice elected despite opposition from the frequently larger White electorate.

REPRESENTATION: ELECTING A VOICE FOR MINORITY INTERESTS

Political engagement has value in itself. The opinions and energy of those who participate are much more likely to influence leaders and governance than are the opinions and values of those who do not participate. Participation, however, is often only part of the story. People who have opinions that are never part of the majority (and who, consequently, don't select the winners in elections) are likely to become frustrated, and, over time, to disengage from a political system that never works to their advantage. The founders of the United States recognized this risk and built a system in which numerical minorities could overcome the power of majorities. The allocation of U.S. Senate seats by state rather than by population, the Electoral College, lifetime appointment of members of the federal judiciary, and the practice of the **filibuster** (the procedural rule in the U.S. Senate that ending debate requires the votes of sixty of the one hundred senators) by the U.S. Senate are all examples of rules and practices that grant cohesive minorities powers or influence over numerical majorities. We should be clear here: the "cohesive minorities" that are protected by the rules are rarely racial or ethnic minorities. Instead, the Electoral College protects the smaller states. Filibuster protects the interests of the smaller of the two political parties and, again, the small states that are overrepresented in the allocation of seats in the U.S. Senate.

The drafters of the Voting Rights Act (and the courts that interpreted its provisions, at least until 2013) also recognized that simply ensuring that minority communities had access to registration and voting was insufficient to guarantee that they would become active and equal members of the polity. The VRA provided that local jurisdictions could not change electoral rules in a way that would diminish the likelihood that minorities would be able to register and vote. It also required that changes in electoral rules in the states that had the highest levels of racial/ethnic discrimination in the pre–Civil Rights era be reviewed (precleared) by either the U.S. Justice Department or the federal district court in Washington DC, where it was assumed that the judges would less likely be swayed by local passions. This was so that jurisdictions couldn't use their rule-making authority to diminish minority influence. (See Chapter 7.) In a 2013 ruling (***Shelby County, Alabama v. Holder***), the Supreme Court ended this preclearance review of state and local changes to electoral rules by the states that had had the highest levels of racial/ethnic discrimination.[37]

Majority-Minority Districts: Increasing Minority Influence

As we have discussed in Chapter 7, the Voting Rights Act gave the federal government the tools to implement the Fifteenth Amendment to the U.S. Constitution and established national standards for nondiscrimination in voting. In this, the VRA was fundamentally revolutionary and had an immediate and positive effect on Black (and, later, Latino, Asian, American, and Native American) registration and voting. States and localities, however, quickly adapted to the new political environment and identified new strategies—such as shifting from district-based elections to at-large elections to minimize the influence of geographically cohesive racial or ethnic minority populations—to dampen minority political influence. As a result, many minority communities were still not able to elect the candidates of their choice. To address this concern, Congress added a further protection for minority representation in the 1982 amendments to the VRA. Congress stipulated that where minority populations resided in sufficient concentration to allow for the drawing of a **majority-minority district,** the body doing the redistricting had a responsibility to draw a district with a majority made up of minority voters. In the redistricting that followed the 2010 census, state legislatures drew twenty-seven congressional districts with African American majorities, thirty districts with Latino majorities, and one district with an Asian American majority. An additional four districts had Black pluralities (in which Blacks made up the largest racial/ethnic group, but not a majority) and Latinos made up the plurality in eight districts. Most Black and Latino members of Congress have been elected from these districts; some have been represented by White or Asian American officeholders.

The majority-minority districting requirements have been controversial since their passage. By increasing the responsibility to draw districts in which minority communities can elect the candidate of their choice, White communities or other communities of interest are less likely to be able to elect candidates of their choosing; some see this as a violation of the Constitution's guarantee of equal protection of the laws. The federal courts have not shared this position. The Supreme Court has held that the VRA's majority-minority districting provisions are constitutional but are subject to the highest form of judicial review—strict scrutiny.[38] To come to this ruling, the Supreme Court looked to the history of antiminority electoral discrimination included in the congressional testimony on the VRA and its amendments. It is likely that the constitutionality of these provisions will again come before the Supreme Court in the near future.

A Growing Diversity in Elected Officials

As should be evident by the fact that some majority-Black or majority-Latino congressional districts are represented by White or Asian American officeholders, the VRA does not guarantee **descriptive representation,** which is representation by a person of the same racial or ethnic group as the majority of voters in the district. In other words, the VRA did not guarantee the election of Blacks, Latinos, Asian Americans, Native Americans, or Alaskan Natives to offices. Quite the contrary, the principle that guided Congress in its debates over the VRA was the principle that minority communities should be able to elect the candidates of their choice to office in areas where minority populations are concentrated. Congress documented a long history not just of denial of minority voting rights, but also of majorities that diminished the power of minority votes by limiting minority communities' ability to elect the candidates of their choice. (See Chapters 2 through 5.) Congress's goal, then, was to ensure that minority voters, at least in areas where they are concentrated and where they could agree on a candidate, would be able to elect people who would represent their interests—what is called **substantive representation.**

There are many examples of minority communities electing White officeholders or of a community made up of one minority population electing an officeholder from another racial or ethnic community. Partisanship and the shared policy interests of Democrats or Republicans often trump shared racial or ethnic identity when a minority candidate runs under a party opposed by the district's minority community (Republicans, for the most part, though with some exceptions, such as Cuban American Democrats in South Florida or Vietnamese American Democrats in Southern California). What is much less common, however, is White communities electing minority officeholders in White-majority districts. There certainly are examples—including the 2004 election of Barack Obama to the U.S. Senate from Illinois, the 2010 election of Marco Rubio to the U.S. Senate from Florida, and the 2012 election of Ted Cruz to the U.S. Senate from Texas—but there are fewer examples of Whites electing minorities than of minorities electing Whites or minority officeholders of other races and ethnicities. The fact that minority candidates face difficulties in winning party nominations or election to office in White-majority districts demonstrates that despite the VRA, race and ethnicity continue to matter for some White voters.

VRA protections have ensured a dramatic increase in the number of minority officeholders. Although there are few reliable estimates of minority officeholding before the VRA's passage, the best estimates suggest that there were fewer than 100 African Americans elected to office at all levels in the early 1960s. The first count of Latino officeholders, completed in 1974, found 3,128 in the six states with the largest Latino populations. These numbers have grown. Although an exact count is not available, the best estimate suggests that there are approximately 10,000 Black elected officials.[39] The National Association of Latino Elected Officials, which counts the number of Latino officeholders annually, identified more than 6,000 Hispanic officeholders in 2014. A UCLA project documented approximately 3,000 Asian American elected officials in 2011. There are no enumerations of Native American officeholders nationally.

© Tristan Spinski/Corbis

Marco Rubio was elected to the U.S. Senate from Florida in 2010. A Republican, Rubio is seen by many as a potential bridge builder between his party and many moderate and conservative Latinos.

These numbers certainly reflect a dramatic growth in minority officeholders in the VRA era. Yet it should also be noted that minorities continue to be dramatically underrepresented. There are approximately 600,000 elective offices in the United States. Blacks hold just 1.6 percent of elective offices; Latinos less than 1 percent; and Asian Americans approximately 0.5 percent, well less than their shares of the U.S. population. The dramatic increases in minority representation in the VRA era have only begun to compensate for the fact that there were so few minority officeholders prior to the passage of the act. This pattern will likely not change until majority communities more regularly vote minority candidates into office.

 Why is it important for minorities to be represented at all levels of government?

CONCLUSION: HAVE MINORITIES OVERCOME POLITICAL EXCLUSION?

To some observers, the 2008 and 2012 elections of Barack Obama to the presidency were a signal that minorities, or at least African Americans, had overcome the history of political exclusion that spurred the passage of the Voting Rights Act. A minority candidate was elected to the highest office in the land, based in part on the votes of minority voters and with a majority of White voters preferring the other candidate. The discussion presented here, however, should challenge such a conclusion. Blacks, Latinos, Asian Americans, and Native Americans continue to participate in civic activities and in electoral politics at rates lower than non-Hispanic Whites. These participation gaps result, in part, from differences between minority and White communities, but such compositional differences are only part of the explanation for the "why" question. Electoral rules and the decline in resources to mobilize nonparticipants into politics explain a great deal of the gap. Two elections for a single office, no matter how important the office, will be unlikely to change this long-term pattern in U.S. politics. The rules that shaped these racial/ethnic differences—that created the "how" of participatory differences—remain and have, arguably, expanded in the years since President Obama was first elected.

Group-based gaps in civic and electoral participation, however, can be overcome. The Obama elections offer some insights into how this can be achieved. Nonparticipants and irregular participants need to be encouraged to participate. Racial, ethnic, and mass organizations need to increase in number, and those that already exist need to operate more effectively to conduct this mobilization and to translate the importance of political engagement to those who feel distant from politics or confused about how to translate their beliefs into political outcomes. Legal barriers to participation need to be scrutinized to ensure that the barriers they create meet a substantial need and not simply serve as a tool to maintain the power of those currently in power.

To ensure that the gaps between White and minority participation diminish and, eventually, disappear, however, the Obama elections must be replicated at all levels of government. Our discussion of minority representation should offer some serious notes of caution about the likelihood of this sort of candidate-driven political mobilization in state and, particularly, local elections. Minorities are severely underrepresented in elective offices relative to their share of the population. This underrepresentation results from the fact that few minority officeholders are elected in White-majority districts. The VRA has been successful in creating more opportunities for concentrated minority populations to have districts in which they can elect the candidates of their choice. It will take more significant changes in White attitudes and political behaviors to extend the opportunities for minority officeholding to areas where White populations dominate electoral districts.

Race, then, continues to matter in determining who participates and what influence will come from that participation. As we have shown, the playing field is in constant flux. Legislative action—such as the passage and implementation of the VRA—can and has have dramatic and positive effects on minority participation. New legislation—such as changes to districting practices or new requirements that voters have specific forms of state-issued photo identification in order to vote—can reverse some of these gains. The lesson here is that the battle for equal access to the polls, initially guaranteed in the Fifteenth Amendment (1870), will likely be an ongoing one in U.S. politics. The road to equal participation based on race and ethnicity was leveled in 1965, but more barriers continue to be found in the lanes used by most Blacks, Latinos, Asian Americans, and Native Americans than in those used by most Whites in U.S. society.

DISCUSSION QUESTIONS

1. What factors will be most important in increasing the influence of the minority vote in future midterm and presidential elections, and why will they be important?

2. Which is the most influential reason for lower levels of minority engagement—minority community characteristics, or the failure of political institutions to reach out to these communities? Explain your answer.

3. Compare how the ideologies of minority communities and the issues that guide their politics conflict with each of the major political parties. How might these differences affect minority partisanship? How might they change the two political parties' agendas and coalitions in the future?

4. How is racialization a component of continued barriers to civic engagement and political participation? How is it not?

5. If minorities' electoral participation remains lower than that of Whites, what challenges might they face by a government that continues to be dominated by non-Hispanic Whites?

KEY TERMS

descriptive
  representation (p. 288)
Electoral College (p. 265)
Election-Day
  registration (p. 281)
filibuster (p. 287)
ideology (p. 274)

majority-minority
  district (p. 288)
partisanship (p. 274)
political efficacy
  (p. 273)
*Shelby County, Alabama v.
  Holder* (2013) (p. 287)

substantive
  representation (p. 288)
voter mobilization (p. 269)
voter registration
  requirements (p. 281)

10 Education and Criminal Justice Policies: Opportunity and Alienation

From public educational institutions where students of color are too often confined to racially isolated, underfunded and inferior schools, to a criminal justice system that disproportionately targets and incarcerates people of color. . . . The dream of full equality remains an elusive one.

–American Civil Liberties Union, Racial Justice Program[1]

Racial and ethnic politics shape the outcomes of public policy. Public policy includes those governmental decisions and actions that address social problems, which in turn affect various public interests. We focus on the issues of education and criminal justice in this chapter because they exemplify or are best examples of the types of opportunities versus the types of barriers—the smooth upward slopes versus the roadblocks—that determine the well-being of racial and ethnic minorities. There are a host of other public policies that capture either the opportunities or the barriers imposed by racial and ethnic inequalities, depending on how they are implemented by government or the polity. One example is homeownership policy, where there are debates over whether the federal Community Reinvestment Act, passed in 1977, encourages banks and other lenders to treat potential, minority homebuyers fairly when they apply for home loans, versus unregulated practices that permit some lenders to target minorities for risky subprime loans they cannot afford and cause them to lose their homes. A second example is public health policy, where there are debates about minorities possibly benefiting from signing up for health insurance

Box 10.1 Chapter Objectives

- Identify conservative and liberal perspectives that inform and motivate public policy.
- Discuss the legacies of segregation in the public education system.
- Assess how education policy has disadvantaged or continues to disadvantage minorities.
- Identify the factors that contribute to the mass incarceration and profiling of minorities.
- Evaluate how criminal justice policy disadvantages minorities.

ASSOCIATED PRESS

Education opens up a wealth of opportunities, but U.S. policy historically has not been focused on equal access to quality education for minorities. The legacies of education inequality, combined with a contemporary criminal justice system that disproportionately punishes minorities, creates an uneven road of public policy that puts many at a disadvantage.

under the Affordable Care Act (so-called "Obamacare") and reducing the high rates of those who are uninsured versus their being more likely than Whites to live in communities with more environmental hazards and unregulated "brownfields."[2]

When we look at education we can see that increasing educational attainment has been fundamental to the social mobility of all Americans, especially those suffering from racial and ethnic discrimination. In 1960 only about 4 percent of African Americans and Latinos had college degrees, as compared to about 12 percent of Whites. In 2009, after doors were opened by affirmative action and civil rights laws, those percentages were, respectively, 19 percent, 13 percent, and 29 percent, and there were much larger middle classes among all groups. Education conveys what sociologists call "cumulative advantages," such as enabling people to secure more prestigious and higher-paying jobs. These, in turn, give them a higher earning potential over the course of their lives, and thus more wealth to pass on to future generations.[3]

In contrast, criminal justice or criminal prosecution and incarceration inflict what legal scholar Gabriel Chin calls "collateral consequences." These include the "penalties, disabilities, or disadvantages that occur automatically because of a criminal conviction, other than the sentence itself."[4] For example, ex-felons cannot vote in some states; nor can they hold a wide range of jobs, receive government benefits like public assistance, or live in public housing. Thus they face many barriers to providing viable sources of income for themselves and their families. These disadvantages only worsen their plight and, according to some studies, promote recidivism (the likelihood of repeat offenses and reconviction).[5]

Thousands of Latino, African American, Native American, and some Asian American young people come from families and communities in which the lingering effects of racial and ethnic segregation are partly to blame for the lower quality of schools, greater levels of poverty, and more intense policing they endure. Absent such youth being given educational opportunities that counter these problems, they are more at risk for being entangled in the criminal justice system. As one result of the increasing penalties given to nonviolent drug offenses, Blacks and Hispanics, ages eighteen to twenty-nine, have incarceration rates nearly five and two times higher, respectively, than those for Whites of the same age. An oft-quoted set of disparities powerfully conveys the polar extremes confronting some minority communities: whereas in 2008 African Americans comprised 12 percent of the U.S. population and 13.5 percent of students enrolled in institutions of higher learning, they constituted a whopping 42 percent (nearly three times the amount) of all persons incarcerated in federal and state prisons, as well as local jails. Latinos are now the largest racial/ethnic minority in the United States, comprising 13 percent of the total, but in 2011 they constituted the majority of all persons sentenced to serve time in federal prisons. At the same time, Latinos have historic and significant population concentrations in states like California, but because of diminished commitments to affirmative action and educational opportunity, there have been drastic decreases in the enrollment of both Latino and Black students in these states' most prestigious private and public institutions, such as the University of California at Berkeley (UC-Berkeley), the University of California at Los Angeles (UCLA), and Stanford University.[6] These examples are important because they illustrate what we emphasize throughout this book—that on the road to full citizenship and equal opportunity, where one begins greatly influences where one ends up.

This chapter will illustrate that race, ethnicity, and racism have been and still can be decisive factors in determining how far different U.S. ethnic and racial groups have progressed down the roads toward full citizenship and equal opportunity. Our examination continues to scrutinize when, why, and how race and ethnicity matter, taking careful consideration of the public policies of education and criminal justice. We will pay attention to specific periods and places most likely to shape policy outcomes and impact racial and ethnic inequalities ("when"). We will examine public policy as an arena of criminal justice that is greatly influenced by public opinion and societal norms, and where minorities may, to some extent, be perceived as a threat ("why"). And throughout the chapter, as we explore the education and criminal justice policies, we will consider the interactions and mechanisms through which public policy is formed and administered—such as affirmative action referenda and judicial decisions on sentencing disparities—that directly or indirectly impact existing racial and ethnic inequalities ("how").

RACE, ETHNICITY, AND PUBLIC POLICY

Public policy fundamentally matters because it determines what political scientist Harold Lasswell describes as the most important "outputs" of the government and the political process. An output is an outcome of the system such as a law, an executive order, or a constitutional amendment. **Public policy,** then, is not simply the formal outcome of governmental actions, such as regulations, laws, and court orders. It also includes the political processes through which these outcomes are shaped, such as citizen and lobbyist interactions with bureaucracies, legislative processes, and judicial proceedings. There are many factors that affect and determine policy outcomes, including race, ethnicity, and the lingering vestiges of racial discrimination. We are mindful, however, not to presume that these factors are always the main culprits responsible for creating inequalities. Indeed, there are many other possible causes, including gender/sexism, class bias, and homophobia, which we consider at length in Chapter 13. For our purposes in this chapter, however, we will first explain when, why, and how race, ethnicity, and racial discrimination matter with regard to public policy before detailing the racial and ethnic politics of U.S. education and criminal justice policies.

Conservative and Liberal Perspectives on Race, Ethnicity, and Public Policy

Whether an individual believes the processes and outputs of U.S. public policy are affected by race, ethnicity, and racism depends on the interpretation he or she draws from observable differences among the status of groups, and this interpretation is partly filtered through ideology. Ideology is defined as the organization of attitudes into belief systems that provide persons with broad lenses or filters that they can use to simplify, explain, and judge the motives and behaviors of individuals, groups, and institutions.[7] It helps persons to determine when certain political actions benefit or disadvantage a group in which they claim membership, whether they identify as, for example, middle class, Republican, American Indian, or homosexual. On the one hand, a person who is a **racial conservative** (who may self-describe as a racial realist) does not believe that race, ethnicity, and racism have a significant impact on the current outcomes of public policy. Thus these constructs are insufficient or inconsequential explanations for any political or economic differences we observe between racial and ethnic groups. A racial conservative may believe race, ethnicity, and racism had strong effects prior to the civil rights reforms of the 1960s, but that the political and economic differences we now observe are more due to differences in individual behavior and group cultures than to any systematic, institutional discrimination or its aftereffects. Scholars and commentators like Thomas Sowell, Abigail and Stephen Thernstrom, Linda Chavez, and Dinesh D'Souza have argued that American society has nearly witnessed, in D'Souza's words, "the end of racism," especially given Barack Obama's election as the first self-identified African American to serve as U.S. president. Thus, in their view, racial and ethnic minorities who on average are able to succeed educationally and economically in comparison to Whites—such as Asian Americans—or in comparison to native-born populations—such as Afro-Jamaicans compared to African Americans—do so because of the norms and behaviors of their ethnic cultures that promote educational excellence, hard work, and responsibility.[8]

On the other hand, a person who is a **racial liberal** (who may self-describe as a racial progressive) believes that race, ethnicity, and racism have a significant impact on current public policy outcomes and that these factors are decisive, if not absolute, explanations for key political or economic differences we observe between racial and ethnic groups. A racial liberal likely believes that race, ethnicity, and racism not only strongly influenced group status prior to the civil rights reforms of the 1960s, but that lingering institutional discrimination still advantages many White citizens to the detriment of many racial and ethnic minorities. Scholars such as Cornel West, Claire Kim, Rogers Smith, Audrey Smedley, and Eduardo Bonilla-Silva have in various ways argued that race, ethnicity, and racism still fundamentally matter in shaping the quality of life in America. They believe American society has been forced to adapt and change its uses of these constructs over time because civil rights reforms in theory outlawed many elements of ***de jure* racial discrimination,** or discrimination sanctioned by law.

But discrimination is often more difficult to recognize because it is ***de facto*** (in fact), meaning a permissible inequality that persists without explicit references to race and ethnicity. Examples would be ethnic and racial disparities in college graduation rates or Black and Latino youth still suffering job discrimination because employers secretively use a person's name or accent to screen prospective job recruits. Racial liberals recognize the importance of personal responsibility in individuals succeeding in society. Yet because race, ethnicity, and racism affect groups, they believe that institutions and structures such as schools, the courts, and corporations are among the main factors contributing to the advantages and disadvantages that individuals experience in their journeys toward full citizenship and equal opportunity.[9]

Quite logically, racial conservatives, racial liberals, and persons situated in between these poles can disagree about whether and to what degree race, ethnicity, and racism impact public policy. Stephen Colbert, the Comedy Central comedian anchor of the *Colbert Report,* has a satirical, running pun about this point. For instance, "Now, I don't see race. . . . People tell me I'm white, and I believe them, because I own a lot of Jimmy Buffet albums."[10] This pun illustrates a concept that political scientist Michael Brown and his colleagues label the **color-blind society,** which is an ideological debate as to whether—across a host of public policy arenas such as voting and election laws, education, criminal justice, housing and mortgage lending, job hiring, and college admissions—we should not pay attention, or be *blind* to, the racial and ethnic background of individuals. Does taking note of race and ethnicity in formulating public policy violate an important principle of fairness, or does it ensure equal opportunity by rooting out any lasting effects of past discrimination?[11]

This argument about a color-blind society undergirds various legal challenges to affirmative action laws across the country, most especially the 1996 California Civil Rights Initiative, or Proposition 209, a referendum proposed and passed by California voters that effectively outlaws any consideration of race and gender in state employment and admission to state colleges and universities. It is a debate about the best interpretation of Dr. Martin Luther King Jr.'s admonition that people should "not be judged by the color of their skin, but by the content of their character."[12] Keep in mind, a racial liberal assumes that since racial inequality is still fairly widespread, in order to observe King's vision, government policy needs to balance this inequality by directly extending opportunities to minorities. A racial conservative assumes that King's vision has pretty much come true, and since racial inequality is largely nonexistent, any government policy that extends opportunities to minorities is racially discriminating against Whites. Given the different ideologies of racial conservatives and racial liberals, it is easy to understand how the policy process can be subject to competing aims and result in incon-

> Is it useful to understand whether a public policy comes from the standpoint of a racial liberal or a racial conservative? Do you think some assume one is more "racist" than the other?

sistent or contradictory outcomes. As we stress, is it fair to ask whether race, ethnicity, and racism can explain in whole or in part a specific inequality or disparity? We believe that they cannot explain, or are not the sole determinants of, all group differences. But we likewise seek to equip you with concepts that indicate when, why, and how race, ethnicity, and racism continue to impact public policy to enable you to become wise observers of and participants within the American political process.[13]

When, Why, and How Race Affects Public Policy

As previous chapters have shown, there are many similarities prior to 1965 about when, why, and how race matters for the groups examined in this book. This continues to be the case when it comes to public policy. We can understand when it may matter through observation of specific periods (such as during the Obama administration) and places (like in the state of Michigan) that are most likely to shape policy outcomes and thus impact existing racial and ethnic inequalities. The 2008 election was a period in which a majority of American voters elected then-senator Barack Obama (D-IL) as the first African American to serve as president of the United States. As a U.S. Senate candidate, Obama criticized the practice of racial profiling, and as president he not only appointed Eric Holder, the first African American to serve as U.S. attorney general, but also signed into law a reduction in the crack cocaine to powder cocaine sentencing disparity from 100:1 to 18:1. What this meant was that the administration equalized the sentencing for conviction of two drugs that are chemically equivalent, but one of which was more likely to be abused by African Americans and the other by Whites—with radically different consequences.[14] In another example of when race matters, the American Civil Rights Institute, led by conservative businessman Ward Connerly, in 1996 helped to pass Proposition 209, California's anti–affirmative action amendment. The institute then went on to identify other states, including Washington and Michigan, where demographic changes prompted racial and ethnic anxieties that contributed to the passage of similar state constitutional amendments.[15]

Why race, ethnicity, and racism may matter in public policy can most clearly be understood in areas greatly influenced by public opinion and societal norms—such as criminal justice policy—and ones where at least some racial or ethnic minorities are consistently perceived as a problem or threat to public well-being disproportionate to the actual behavior of the group. For example, criminologist Michael Tonry, sociologist Lawrence Bobo, and their respective coauthors discovered that there are strong correlations between the degree to which White survey respondents support conscious or unconscious anti-Black racial stereotypes and exhibit racial resentment toward Blacks, and White support for highly punitive criminal sanctions such as the death penalty. Such respondents fundamentally overestimate the extent and breadth of Black criminality, and such overexaggerated public threats can be used to advocate public policies that only reinforce racial and ethnic inequalities in the society.[16]

How race, ethnicity, and racism may matter in instances of public policy can be understood through observation of specific policy arenas, interactions, and mechanisms through which public policy is formulated and administered—such as affirmative action voter referenda and court decisions on sentencing disparities—that involve and have a direct or indirect impact on existing racial and ethnic inequalities, even when these processes intend to produce race-neutral outcomes. The stated intention of the advocates of California's Proposition 209, which prohibited the use of race and gender in state employment and college admissions, was to uphold their interpretation of the Fourteenth Amendment's Equal Protection Clause and promote color-blind and gender-blind results. One report from the University of California system concluded seven years after 209's passage that "implementing race-neutral policy [has led] to a substantial decline in the proportion of entering students who are African American, American Indian, and Latino." Some California colleges and universities recovered from these declines in minority undergraduate enrollment due to alternate recruitment methods that relied on need-based criteria.

On the criminal justice front, the U.S. Supreme Court's stated intention in recent sentencing disparity cases was to confirm the discretion of federal judges to interpret the criminal sentencing guidelines enacted by Congress, especially when judges conclude that strictly following the guidelines will not result in evenhanded outcomes. In the case of *Kimbrough v. United States* (2007), the justices by a 7–2 vote confirmed that lower courts may see these sentencing guidelines as advisory. The result in this specific case was that Derrick Kimbrough, a Persian Gulf War veteran and African American arrested for distributing fifty grams of crack cocaine, received a fifteen-year as opposed to a twenty-two-year sentence. The broader result was that the Court modestly improved the chances of African Americans and others sentenced under the 100:1 crack cocaine versus powder cocaine disparity created after passage of the 1986 Anti–Drug Abuse law. African Americans comprised 80 percent of all those convicted.[17]

Today, overt antiminority discrimination is in many instances unconstitutional, and we should expect the effects of race, ethnicity, and any lingering racism to provide for complex, often mixed group outcomes. For instance, considering employment in the education and legal/law enforcement fields by racial and ethnic background provides us with one set of indicators on whether current hiring policies are equitable. Figure 10.1 shows that in 2010, possibly as an indirect result of the *Brown v. Board of Education* decision and as a direct result of

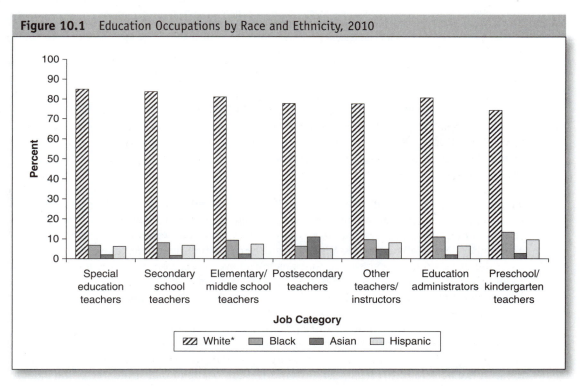

Figure 10.1   Education Occupations by Race and Ethnicity, 2010

Source: U.S. Census Bureau, *Statistical Abstract of the United States: 2012,* Table 616, "Employed Civilians by Occupation, Sex, Race, and Hispanic Origins: 2010," 393, 394.

*White includes Non-Hispanic Whites and others.

Figure 10.2 Legal and Law Enforcement Occupations by Race and Ethnicity, 2010

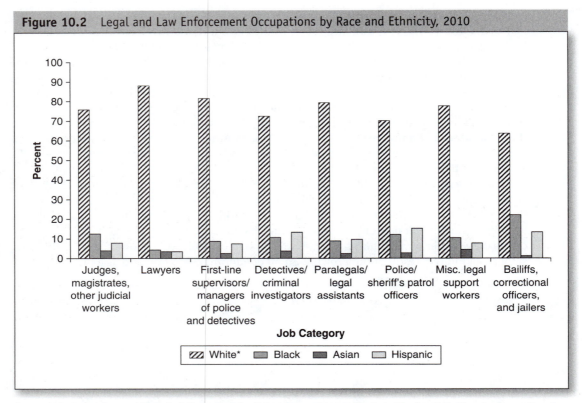

Source: U.S. Census Bureau, *Statistical Abstract of the United States: 2012,* Table 616, "Employed Civilians by Occupation, Sex, Race, and Hispanic Origins: 2010," 393, 394.

*White includes Non-Hispanic Whites and others.

affirmative action, minorities were fairly well represented among the ranks of America's teachers and education administrators. Interestingly, Blacks and Hispanics were well represented among administrators, and Asian Americans were best represented among postsecondary teachers. Yet in all categories, Whites comprised the majority of educators by far.

In the criminal justice sphere, minorities are unevenly represented among the top legal ranks of judges, magistrates, lawyers, and judicial workers. Figure 10.2 illustrates that Asian Americans, who comprised 4 percent of the U.S. population in 2010, were somewhat evenly represented among the ranks of lawyers and judges, or just below 4 percent of each. But Hispanics, who comprised more than 12 percent of the U.S. population in 2010, made up only 7.8 percent of the judges, magistrates, and judicial workers, and a mere 3.4 percent of the lawyers. Overall, minorities comprised a third—their largest percentage in this arena—of all those at the bottom of the legal and law enforcement occupational strata, including bailiffs, correctional officers, and jailers. True to our claim that we should expect complex patterns, however, it is notable that the largest percentage of African Americans held jobs as police and sheriff patrol officers, with the next largest percentage, for Hispanics and Asian Americans, in legal support positions. As with educators, Whites made up the vast majority of all legal and law enforcement workers. These data illustrate the central point of this chapter, that our educational and criminal justice systems provide uneven opportunities for racial/ethnic minorities; and this is true even from the vantage point of those in authority.

PUBLIC EDUCATION: OPPORTUNITIES AND DETOURS

Today, public education is accessible to all, but this was not always the case. Here, we explore when, why, and how race and ethnicity have mattered in obtaining access to education, and we examine how minority groups used the laws, institutions, and resources available to them to push for equal access. At the same time, attaining access to public education is only half of the challenge, because the quality of education, then and now, varies across the nation. Lower-income neighborhoods tend to have poorer performing schools, and while the U.S. Supreme Court ruled during the Civil Rights era that schools should be desegregated, our public schools often look much less like the melting pot our society is often described as being.

These matters are important because we presume that access to public education for all Americans provides a road toward a better life, but the roads through education for African Americans, Asian Americans, Latinos, and Native Americans are not quite so well paved. Prior to the 1960s, the dominant society decided that education for anyone who was not of European ancestry was not a primary public policy concern. The 1896 U.S. Supreme Court decision in *Plessy v. Ferguson* legitimated the doctrine of separate but equal facilities for African Americans and hardened the lines of segregation. As we discussed in Chapter 1, *Plessy* was a case in which Homer Plessy, a mixed-race man, sued a railroad company in Louisiana for contravening the Fourteenth Amendment's Equal Protection Clause by maintaining separate cars for Whites and Blacks. In upholding the segregation, the Supreme Court moved racial practices from custom to law by creating a biracial society that identified a person as either White or non-White, though European ethnicity still mattered in places. This decision created a color line that confronted not only African Americans, but also Mexican Americans in the Southwest and Chinese in the West.

Public school systems were traditionally administered by counties, which varied in the quality of education that they provided to minorities in observing the "separate but equal" ruling. Some provided African Americans with education up to the secondary or high school level, and others only provided elementary education with impoverished, one-room school houses. *Plessy* reinforced that Native Americans, Mexicans, and Asians were not considered White, and therefore were not entitled to the privileges of the public education provided to White Americans. The lack of equal access to education meant fewer employment advancement opportunities for minorities and lower overall earnings, which resulted in fewer overall opportunities and greater inequalities between minorities and Whites. Because of racial discrimination in the electoral system at this time (see Chapter 7), minority groups lacked sufficient members elected to their state house or the U.S. Congress to change laws and ensure their inclusion. Instead, they had to fight their battles for equity through the court system.[18]

Early Legal Challenges for Equality in Education

Until recently, the history of the fight for equal education has primarily been framed as an issue of courts recognizing the right of African Americans to attend racially integrated schools. Yet equal education concerned more than just Blacks, and African American legal challenges in the early twentieth century were greatly assisted by the efforts of other racial and ethnic minorities, such as Asian Americans and Latinos. The Supreme Court's landmark ruling in *Brown v. Board of Education* (1954–1955), which declared racial segregation in schools unconstitutional, was preceded by numerous other cases brought by minorities that challenged the "separate but equal" doctrine and laid the groundwork for *Brown*.

In a series of cases between 1900 and 1954, the National Association for the Advancement of Colored People (NAACP) and its Legal Defense Fund chipped away at the rationale for the racial segregation of African Americans. At the same time, Asian Americans and Latinos also brought suits that challenged the educational color line. In 1927 a Chinese father sued on behalf of his daughter, who wanted to attend a local White high school in Mississippi. In *Gong Lum v. Rice* (278 U.S. 78), the U.S. Supreme Court held that Gong Lum was not White, which barred her from attending the school. In an era when race was rigidly construed as White or non-White, the Court said that she was free to attend an all-Black school. About twenty years later in California, Mexican Americans brought the suit of *Mendez v. Westminster,* which preceded and also made the case for *Brown*.

In 1946 Gonzalo Mendez and four other parents brought suit against the school district of Orange County, California, because it arbitrarily placed their and other children into "Mexican" public schools (*Mendez v. Westminister,* 64 Supp. 544 (S.D.Cal. 1946). Orange County had separate schools for Mexicans, even if they were American citizens and had European (as in Spanish) ancestry. The criteria used to assign students to a school were "simple observation," ability to speak English, and the quality of the school. The superintendent claimed that segregation was beneficial for the Mexican American children, for they were primarily suitable for manual labor and low-paying jobs. In deciding the case, U.S. district judge Paul J. McCormick stated a fundamental principle of public school education in the United States: the general commingling of children of all ancestries and descents is part of the Americanization role of public school instruction. He held that California law required public schools to admit all children over age six, regardless of whether their parents were American citizens, and that "education was mandatory for both citizens and noncitizens."[19]

The issues in *Mendez* remain relevant, with today's debate of whether or not to provide an education for both citizens and noncitizens, including children whose parents have migrated illegally to the United States. Although *Mendez* was not brought on the grounds of race, NAACP lawyers submitted an *amicus curiae* brief supporting the plaintiffs and closely watched the outcome. As a forerunner to the *Brown* decision, this case paved the way for challenging pupil assignments that violated the Fourteenth Amendment by segregating a group of students.[20]

The *Brown* Decision and Desegregation

As we explained in Chapter 3, the 1954–1955 ***Brown v. Board of Education of Topeka*** case was named after a lawsuit brought by the father of a little girl named Linda Brown, who attended a segregated Kansas school; but it was, in fact, a compilation of five cases. *Brown* was a landmark decision in which a unanimous U.S. Supreme Court declared "separate but equal" school accommodations unconstitutional, although it provided the contradictory directive of desegregation "with all deliberate speed." How is it possible to "deliberate," or to proceed slowly, and to proceed quickly, with "speed," at the same time? The *Brown* decision concerned education and did not explicitly overturn the *Plessy* decision in all of its facets—public accommodations, interstate transportation, and business interactions. It did, however, mark the beginning of the end of Jim Crow racial segregation and had a significant impact on American society. For education policy, it meant that schools needed to desegregate "with all deliberate speed" so that they served all students, not just White students or Black students. Implementing the *Brown* decision, however, was complicated by the fact that the Supreme Court has no enforcement powers. The U.S. system of separation of powers left it to Congress and the executive branch to carry out the ruling. Initially, this made it relatively easy for any school district, especially those in the South, not to comply with the *Brown* decision. Southern states interpreted the Court's order to desegregate "with all deliberate speed" as open to interpretation, and in some instances took up to twenty years to desegregate their public schools.[21]

In 1957 the federal government responded to the *Brown* ruling in at least two ways. Congress passed the 1957 Civil Rights Act, a weak but important law that among other things authorized a civil rights commission to propose measures to strengthen civil rights laws. And that same year President Dwight Eisenhower enforced *Brown* over the objections of segregationist Arkansas governor Orville Faubus by authorizing National Guard troops to protect the right of nine Black students to enroll in Central High School of Little Rock, Arkansas. Additionally, the Supreme Court continued to hear cases and make rulings about desegregation in public schools. In the 1971 *Swann v. Charlotte-Mecklenburg Board of Education* case, the Court approved court-ordered busing as one of several approaches to ending the dual-school system. This controversial approach bused students away from their neighborhood schools to attend those that were sometimes across city and county school district boundaries, so that the schools would achieve racial balance between predominantly Black and White students. The policy, however, actually increased racial tensions; did not achieve integration; and was objected to by both Black and White parents who did not want their children bused to districts away from their neighborhoods, or who feared perceived outside intruders. White objections resulted in sometimes violent clashes in both Southern and Northern communities, like Boston, in the early 1970s.

Party politics fueled these tensions. With federal policy turning against discrimination of minority groups, it became less acceptable for political parties and their candidates to overtly support it. So when the Republican Party made a concerted effort to attract White voters in the 1970s, it changed the way it used language—from language that was more to less racially overt. Lee Atwater, a chief campaign adviser to Republican president George H. W. Bush, bluntly explained: "You start out in 1954 stating, 'Nigger, nigger, nigger.' By 1968 you can't say 'nigger'—that hurts you. Backfires. So you say stuff like forced busing, states' rights, and all that stuff."[22] The result for party politics was that Whites who supported continued discriminatory practices sought to align themselves with the party or candidate promoting policies that would encourage or maintain that result. Today, the Republican Party is less likely to support affirmative action policies than is the Democratic Party. Remember when considering contemporary policy positions, however, that racialization is not always a contributing factor, and that ideologies such as racial conservatism and racial liberalism help to shape them.

Other underlying racial shifts contributed to conditions that made integration difficult. In the 1950s, a massive highway construction, subsidized by federal housing and urban renewal grants, made it easier in the following decades for White middle-class families to buy new housing in suburban areas. As a result, many Whites left central city neighborhoods in places like Detroit, Chicago, and Atlanta, and established new, often all-White neighborhoods in the suburbs. The consequence was that children from low-income, minority families became the majority population in inner cities and their public schools. This movement of Whites away from city centers has been called **White flight.** Another consequence of White flight was that public schools in the suburbs remained largely White, and inner-city schools were by and large populated by African Americans and other minorities. This has changed to an extent in the twenty-first century, with minorities also moving out into the suburbs, but fully integrated public schools continue to be a road much less traveled.

Today, American public schools remain highly segregated by race, especially between Black and White students. Between the 1990 and 2000 census, urban studies scholar John Logan and his fellow researchers discovered that among the top twenty-five metropolitan school districts with the highest rates of Black-to-White school segregation—where Black students were most likely to attend schools that were nearly all-Black, with few to no White students—rates of segregation declined very little over the course of the decade. Likewise, policy analyst Richard Rothstein discovered that majority-Black schools enrolled smaller percentages of White students by 2010 than they did in 1980. (See Figure 10.3.) A major reason for these outcomes is that the neighborhoods from which school assignments are drawn remain relatively segregated. In short, if students live with their families in racially segregated neighborhoods, then school enrollments drawn from these neighborhoods will be racially segregated as well. Interestingly, although Southern states were initially sued under the *Brown* ruling, the schools that have the highest Black-White segregation scores today are more often states in the North, such as Michigan, Illinois, New Jersey, and Ohio.[23]

The goal of the litigants in *Brown* was to integrate the public schools and end second-class citizenship. They considered racial integration necessary if African Americans and other minorities were to attain a quality education and achieve the most direct pathway to the American dream. *Brown* no doubt was an important milestone that heartened Blacks and other minorities in their hope that equal opportunity in America was a realizable goal. The decision's impact, however, focused as it was on the policy area of education, quite logically did not (or could not) address equality in other policy areas such as housing, employment, or voting rights. Thus some minority citizens still had to overcome substantial, additional legal barriers in the integration of higher education, recreational facilities, and public accommodations.[24]

Affirmative Action in the Schools

By the time John F. Kennedy became president in 1961, the Civil Rights Movement was gathering momentum. Through nonviolent demonstrations, bus boycotts, sit-ins, freedom rides, and voter registration drives, African Americans asserted their right to full citizenship. (See Chapter 7.) Congress was controlled by Southern, segregationist Democrats, which made the legislative route to policy change impassable. Consequently, Kennedy's response was to issue Executive Order 10925. It mandated "federally funded projects 'take affirmative action'

Figure 10.3   Exposure to White Students for the Typical Black Student in Public Schools

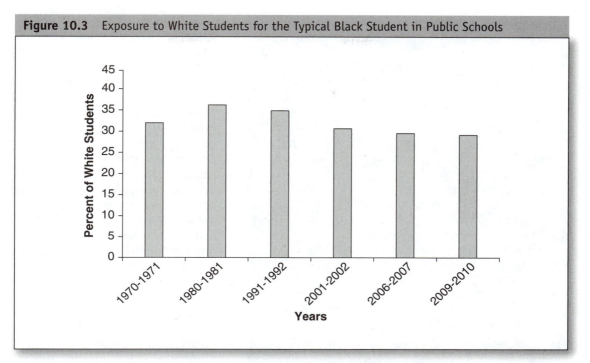

Source: Richard Rothstein, "For Public Schools, Segregation Then, Segregation Since: Education and the Unfinished March" (Washington, DC: Economic Policy Institute, 2013), 14.

to ensure that hiring and employment practices are free of racial bias." **Affirmative action** became a vast array of public and private policies and programs intended to remedy past racial and gender discrimination in employment and education through the hiring and admission of racially underrepresented groups.[25]

After Kennedy's death in 1963, President Lyndon B. Johnson implemented a sweeping domestic policy agenda. Johnson was persuaded that the *Brown* decision would not usher in the hoped-for equality without additional federal laws. His legislative agenda was motivated by a broad vision of a Great Society open to all of its citizens; thus he asked Congress to create various administrative units empowered to pursue equality goals, such as the Office of Economic Opportunity, Volunteers in Service to America (VISTA), and Head Start—a program to tackle early childhood educational disparities. In 1965 at Howard University, Johnson articulated his rationale for affirmative action: "You do not take a person who, for years, has been hobbled by chains and liberate him, bring him up to the starting line in a race and then say, 'You are free to compete with all the others,' and still justly believe that you have been completely fair."[26] Johnson directed the Office of Federal Contract Compliance and the Equal Opportunity Commission to require federal contractors and grantees to submit extensive plans stating their goals and timetables for recruiting and hiring more Black employees based on the present labor market. This was eventually extended to include Hispanics, Asian Americans, and Native Americans.[27]

Many Whites angrily resisted the Supreme Court–mandated change ending segregation in schools and staged antibusing protests in 1974–1975. Black students often faced the wrath of angry Whites as they were bused to newly integrated schools. To forestall or limit violence, it was not uncommon for buses of Black students to receive police escorts. While the hard barrier of segregation was dismantled in the schools, additional legal barriers remained to be surmounted.

Affirmative action soon had its opponents in the business sector, as well as in universities, where some believed that policies of preferential treatment of minorities constituted **reverse discrimination,** or a form of racial inequality that is unfair to Whites. Although this debate continues, such preferential treatment is not unique. Athletes and persons whose parents attended a university or college (known as legacies) are among those groups that also have been given special consideration in college admissions. Athletes are often admitted because they can help produce a winning team, and legacies are admitted to induce generous alumni giving. In both cases, the GPA and test scores for these groups might be lower than the cutoff for other applicants. In applying affirmative action policies, university admissions committees began to take into consideration factors in addition to grades, test scores, and letters of recommendation. Because diversity is a goal that may reinforce excellence—the greater the choices, the better the outcomes—factors such as an applicant's race, income level, and previous conditions of hardship were considered valid factors in granting admission, especially in state universities. This angered some White applicants who felt that they were denied a seat that was taken by a less qualified person of color.[28]

College Admissions Policies and Challenges to Affirmative Action

Prior to the 1960s, a handful of mostly Northern colleges and universities admitted small numbers of African Americans and other minorities with the expressed aim of fostering cultural diversity within their student bodies and giving minority students an equal opportunity for a quality education. The Oberlin College board of trustees in Oberlin, Ohio, for example, stated as far back as 1835 that "the education of people of color is a matter of great interest and should be encouraged and sustained in this institution."[29] But by 1965, still only a paltry 1 percent of students

enrolled in all law schools and 2 percent of students in medical schools were Black, not including
the enrollees of historically Black institutions such
as Howard University and Meharry Medical
College. Thus, with President Johnson's call to take
affirmative action, elite institutions such as
Harvard and Yale Universities, pressured in large

> Is there a basic clash between a col-
> lege encouraging academic excel-
> lence among its students and its
> attempting to racially and ethnically diversify
> its student body?

part by the civil rights debates of the 1960s and later by student protests, began to consciously
admit Black students in larger numbers. Throughout the 1960s and well into the 1980s, it was often
student protests on majority-White campuses that pressured college and university administrators
to consider how to racially and ethnically diversify their student enrollments. Ivy League institutions witnessed dramatic Black student enrollment increases in short periods of time—from 2.3
percent in 1967 to 6.3 percent in 1976. Other elite institutions witnessed increases of 1.7 percent
to 4.8 percent. And by 1975 the number of Black students in medical schools rose from 2 percent
to 6.3 percent, and the number of Black law students grew from 1 percent to almost 5 percent.[30]

The wider implementation of affirmative action policies in higher education became a contentious issue as battle lines were drawn between those who took a **race-neutral** position,
believing that race should have no consideration in admission decisions, versus those with a
race-conscious position, believing that race should be only one of many considerations.
Questions arose as to whether university admissions procedures were fair to all applicants, or
whether they were tilted toward less-qualified African Americans and Latinos. In 1978 Alan
Bakke, a White male who questioned race-conscious admissions policy, sued for admission to
the medical school of the University of California at Davis. The case, known as *Regents of the
University of California v. Bakke,* centered on the medical school's admission policy that took
race into consideration. Bakke was an unsuccessful applicant to the medical school in 1973 and
1974 because he did not meet the requisite cutoff score. In both years, however, applicants with
at least modestly lower scores than Bakke were admitted. He alleged that a special admissions
program excluded him on the basis of race. The University of California at Davis had opened a
medical school in 1968 with eighty-four of the seats to be filled through a regular admissions
program. The remaining sixteen positions were to be filled by a special admissions program for
applicants who were considered "economically and/or educationally disadvantaged," including
Blacks, Hispanics, Asians, or American Indians. Disadvantaged applicants who did not have a
2.5 grade-point average were reviewed by a special admissions committee. A number of Whites
who did not meet this minimum GPA applied for special admission, but none was admitted.

The U.S. Supreme Court could not reach a majority opinion in the *Bakke* case. Instead, the justices wrote six separate opinions. Justice Lewis Powell's opinion garnered the most support on the
Court, holding that "ethnic diversity . . . is only one element in a range of factors a university
properly may consider in attaining the goal of a heterogeneous student body." Furthermore, the
Court found that "the University of California admissions . . . program does not establish a quota
in the invidious sense of a ceiling on the number of minority applicants to be admitted. . . . Davis'
special admissions program cannot be said to violate the Constitution."[31] Three dissenting justices
found that the university's special admissions program violated Title VI of the Civil Rights Act of
1964, which prohibits discrimination in a program or activity receiving federal funding assistance,
and that Bakke had suffered discrimination due to his race. Although the justices were divided in
their opinions, the *Bakke* decision provided the legal doctrine for affirmative action in higher
education admissions. It established the principle that a **racial quota,** or an explicit effort to

reserve an admission slot based on race in order to guarantee the outcome of minorities being a specific percentage of an entering class, is not constitutional, but goals and timetables that consider race and ethnicity as one of many factors in admission are constitutional.

Two other sets of cases challenged affirmative action precedents and became part of a debate in the 1980s and 1990s when considering, in the words of President Bill Clinton, whether we should "mend it, not end it."[32] First, in the 1996 case of *Hopwood v. Texas,* four White Texas residents claimed that the University of Texas law school's affirmative action admissions program violated the Equal Protection Clause of the Fourteenth Amendment and Title VI of the Civil Rights Act. The U.S. Court of Appeals for the Fifth Circuit held that the law school could not use race as an admissions factor in order to have a diverse student body. This decision was the opposite of Justice Powell's Supreme Court opinion in *Bakke,* but the Court refused to hear the case, and the decision stood at the state level. This case occurred around the same time that the Proposition 209 ballot amendment was being debated in California, and it encouraged anti–affirmative action groups to extend their efforts to other states.[33]

Second, there were the 2003 cases of *Gratz v. Bollinger,* regarding undergraduate admissions, and *Grutter v. Bollinger,* concerning law school admissions—both in the state of Michigan. Twenty-five years after the *Bakke* decision, *Gratz* and *Grutter* questioned whether Justice Powell's opinion set a precedent that established diversity as a constitutional justification for race-conscious admissions. In *Gratz,* two White residents of Michigan were denied admission to the University of Michigan undergraduate College of Literature, Science, and the Arts. Jennifer Gratz and Patrick Hamacher filed a class-action suit, alleging a violation of their rights under the Fourteenth Amendment and the Civil Rights Act of 1964. The Court found the university's use of an explicit rating system that granted a number of points simply based on whether an applicant was a racial or ethnic minority to be unconstitutional.

In *Grutter v. Bollinger,* a white Michigan resident was rejected from the University of Michigan's law school. Barbara Grutter alleged that her application was rejected because the law school used race as a "predominant" factor, which gave applicants from certain minority groups "a significantly greater chance of admission than students with similar credentials from disfavored racial groups."[34] The law school asserted that it had a compelling interest in obtaining the educational benefits derived from a diverse student body. Justice Sandra Day O'Connor, the swing vote on a narrowly divided conservative-to-liberal Court, delivered the majority opinion:

> Public and private universities across the nation have modeled their own admissions program on Justice Powell's views on permissible race-conscious politics . . . . Our conclusion that the Law School has a compelling interest in a diverse student body is informed by our view that attaining a diverse student body is at the heart of the Law School's proper institutional mission. . . . We are satisfied that the law school's admissions program . . . does not operate as a quota. . . . The law school's race-conscious admissions program does not unduly harm nonminority applicants.[35]

These cases are significant because they reaffirmed Justice Powell's opinion in *Bakke.* Race can be considered in the admissions process in the interests of attaining a diverse student body. Such a procedure is constitutional because it is not a quota system; nor does it injure nonminority applicants. In June 2013, the Supreme Court in a 7–1 verdict decided to return a recent case in which a White student, Abigail Fisher, sued the University of Texas for its affirmative action policies, to lower courts for review. In effect, the Court placed questions about the continued constitutionality of affirmative action on hold. There will likely be further challenges.[36]

BOX 10.2 ROAD SIGN

The Education DREAM for Children of Unauthorized Immigrants

Dan-el Padilla Peralta is a young man of both Hispanic and Black ancestries whose parents are from the Caribbean island nation of the Dominican Republic. He had somewhat of an American rags-to-riches story because at one point his mother and family faced such great poverty that for a time they had to reside in a homeless shelter, but Padilla's brilliance won him a scholarship to study Latin and the classics at Princeton University. While a student there, he earned an impressive 3.9 grade-point average, among many other honors, and was named the salutatorian of his class. A Princeton faculty member once asserted that "he will be one of the best classicists to emerge in his generation."

After winning several other academic awards he was awarded a two-year scholarship to study abroad at Oxford University. But in 2006, U.S. Citizenship and Immigration Services threatened not to permit him to re-enter the United States and to deport him to the Dominican Republic because his mother's immigration visa had long since expired. Since Dan-el had lived in the United States since he was four years old, it had become home to him. It is talented young people that the Obama administration tried but failed to retain through the Development, Relief and Education for Alien Minors, or DREAM. Act.[37]

Addressing the Achievement Gap

Along with the failure of schools to fully integrate came a new revelation concerning educational achievement. Students within urban schools began to show consistently lower test scores, primarily for African American and

> Should the children of unauthorized immigrants be allowed to attend U.S. universities?

Latino students. With this test gap, often called the **achievement gap,** questions were raised about how to improve public education and bring all schools up to a minimum standard.[38] Educational policy, curriculum innovations, and targeted resources have begun to close the gaps or disparities between various racial and ethnic groups on standardized tests, as well as in overall scholastic performance. Between 1978 and 2008, African Americans and Latinos made the greatest progress in their basic proficiency of mathematics, though they still lagged behind Whites. While a much higher percentage of Whites had advanced proficiency in mathematics, no group experienced appreciable improvements when we note the differences between 1978 and 2008. This matters because a proficiency in math serves as a gateway to success in higher education, and often in high-paying careers.[39]

Table 10.1 displays group disparities via a fundamental indicator of whether a college-bound senior is likely to be admitted into one of America's high-quality, selective institutions—the Scholastic Aptitude Test (SAT). This table highlights an interesting feature about race and ethnicity as they operate today—not all racial and ethnic minorities are at absolute or decisive educational disadvantage in comparison to Whites, or not all minorities are at a disadvantage to the same degree. Some groups have made significant headway. Between 1990 and 2010, Asian/Pacific Islander students had the best combined reading and math scores, followed by Whites,

Table 10.1   SAT Combined Average Reading and Math Scores of College-Bound Seniors, by Race and Ethnicity, 1990–2010

Racial/Ethnic Group	Average Total Score	Average Math Score	Average Reading Score
Asian/Pacific Islander	1,078	573	506
White	1,059	532	527
All students	1,018	514	504
American Indian/Alaska Native	968	485	482
Other Hispanic	923	464	459
Mexican American	913	461	452
Puerto Rican	906	451	455
Black	858	426	432

Source: Statistics, National Center for Education. "Fast Facts: Sat Scores." Institute for Education Sciences, U.S. Department of Education, Table 141, http://nces.ed.gov/fastfacts/display.asp?id=171.

and then Americans Indians, Latinos, and Blacks. Those groups that experienced the greatest improvement in their combined scores were Asian/Pacific Islanders, American Indians/Alaskan Natives, and Whites. Blacks, Mexican Americans, and other Latinos experienced the smallest improvements. We will later summarize some of the reasons—the whys—for these outcomes.

As we've noted, ideology matters in the politics of educational policy. Racial conservatives such as political scientist Charles Murray and experimental psychologist Richard Herrnstein argue that there is a socioeconomic bell curve. Put simply, one's class background determines one's access or exposure to high-quality education, as well as social/family networks that promote intelligence. Because of a lack of exposure to such resources, certain minority groups and low-income persons are not as academically successful as are more affluent persons, who have become a so-called cognitive elite. Racial liberals such as evolutionary biologist Stephen Jay Gould and education scholar Joe Kincheloe strongly reject this view and argue that historical and structural inequalities provide certain groups with cumulative advantages and others with cumulative disadvantages that find their own way into academic outcomes.[40] The approach of this book agrees with the racial liberal perspective—where a group stands now depends on the road they traveled to get here.

Groups of policymakers, parents, teachers, and other concerned parties have made efforts to address these persistent achievement gaps. One major way the federal government has attempted to motivate school systems to bridge these gaps is through funding and performance mandates that require minimal educational standards, such as the **No Child Left Behind (NCLB) Act of 2001**. NCLB was proposed by the administration of President George W. Bush. The president used the phrase "the soft bigotry of low expectations" to directly articulate his administration's view that minority and low-income students were being greatly underserved by the then-present educational standards. [41] NCLB instituted accountability standards for schools by measuring adequate yearly progress for all students and subgroups of students defined by socioeconomic background, race/ethnicity, English language proficiency, and disability.

Diverse segments of the policy community originally considered NCLB to be a positive step in improving educational standards. In reality, it turned out to be quite flawed because of the wide range of public school quality levels across the states. Charter schools play into this range of quality. In a continuing effort to achieve quality public education, since the 1990s especially certain parts of the country have been swept by the school choice movement, where parents seek more educational options through voucher programs or charter schools. Technically, charter schools are part of the public school system, but they are free to innovate and operate outside of traditional bureaucratic requirements. Since there is no uniform definition of what constitutes a charter school, they differ in terms of accountability measures, teacher certification, and enrollment guidelines from state to state. At this point there is no consensus on whether charter schools provide a better education than do public schools, and the lack of uniform standards makes gauging their quality difficult to achieve. [42]

RACE, ETHNICITY, AND EDUCATION POLICY OUTCOMES

Up to this point, we have focused on the impetus for different policies, such as integration, affirmative action in school admission policies, and No Child Left Behind. We have examined the motivations behind these policies from various perspectives—racial conservative, racial liberal, race-neutral, and race-conscious. Understanding why and how certain policies are made provides important contexts for examining policy outcomes. Given that schools today continue to be largely segregated by race and that minority students often attend poor-quality, inner-city public schools, it would be easy to say that little has changed since the *Brown* ruling. It is true that substantial challenges remain if we are to provide equal opportunity to quality education for all, yet though the road has not been smooth, progress has been made.

Roughly fifty years after the initiation of affirmative action and job nondiscrimination statutes via the 1964 Civil Rights Act, racial minorities have made inroads with various occupations in the education field. As Figure 10.1 illustrates, overall, minorities are best represented among the ranks of preschool and kindergarten teachers, and they comprise a significant number of education administrators. This last fact, in particular, is an encouraging indicator because it means that minorities are attaining positions of power in the education field from which they can exert influence to better effect policy change. From these positions, they can also serve as role models to students. The foothold of each group in education occupations varies as a result of student demographic shifts, affirmative action recruitment, and native/immigrant status; career pathways have differently affected each group as well. [43]

Patterns of student enrollment are shifting. Between 1989 and 2009, more of the students enrolled in public schools from kindergarten to the twelfth grade have been Latino, Black, or of some other racial or ethnic identity. This both reflects that increasing birthrates among Latinos and other minorities are outpacing White families, and that in this post-*Brown* period, fewer White students are enrolling in public schools and instead opting to attend private schools or academies. The percentage that White students comprised of total public school enrollment dropped from 68 percent in 1989 to 55 percent in 2009. The Latino student share of the total enrollment, on the other hand, doubled from 11 percent in 1989 to 22 percent by 2009. But African American student enrollment in public schools has slightly declined, from 17 to 15 percent of the total.[44]

One of the most challenging problems facing minority students in public education is poverty. Nearly 50 percent of Black and Hispanic students attend public schools in neighborhoods with high poverty both at the elementary and secondary levels. To a lesser degree, this is also the case for Native American students, although it is much less so for Asian American students. Figure 10.4 breaks down the percent of students in high-poverty schools for the 2008–2009 school year. While Blacks and Hispanics make up nearly half of all students in high-poverty schools, White students are the least represented, at around 5 percent for elementary school and a mere 2 percent for secondary school. The implications of these data are numerous. Students attending high-poverty schools often receive a lower-quality education, and many may drop out of school entirely. This limits their opportunities for higher education, which in turn impacts their future earning potential. Looking even further into the future, the children of these students may also attend high-poverty schools, and the cycle repeats itself.[45]

Figure 10.4 Public School Students in High-Poverty Schools by Race and Ethnicity, 2008–2009

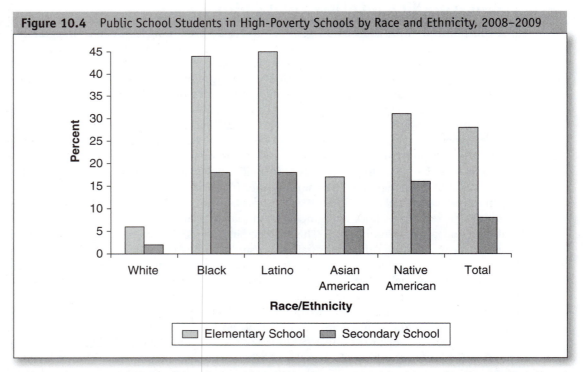

Source: Susan Aud et al., "The Condition of Education 2011" (Washington, DC: National Center for Education Statistics and American Institutes for Research, 2011), Figure 28.1.

High-poverty schools will continue to serve as a roadblock to equal education for minorities, though this is changing in certain places. KIPP's high school in Washington DC's lowest income neighborhood has 100 percent of students going to college. The level of education that minorities achieve has grown steadily since 1970, although it has grown more quickly for some than for others. Figures 10.5 and 10.6 report the advancement—and gaps—in educational attainment between 1970 and 2009. Figure 10.5 focuses on high school graduation rates, and we can see that the gap between Asian Americans, White Americans, and African Americans closed significantly. The figure also illustrates one of the important success stories of the post-*Brown* period, and that is that all three of these groups have virtually the same percentage of people age twenty-five and older who report graduating from high school (around 85 percent). The Latino graduation rate progress has also been significant but still lags far behind the other groups. This lag is partly explained by the diversity of the immigrant populations who comprise the Latino student population and lower levels of high school

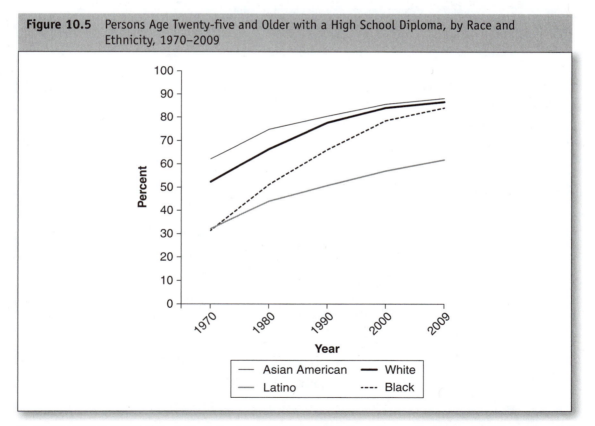

Figure 10.5   Persons Age Twenty-five and Older with a High School Diploma, by Race and Ethnicity, 1970–2009

Source: "The 2011 Statistical Abstract: The National Data Book." 2011. U.S. Census Bureau. Washington, DC: U.S. Department of Commerce, Table 225.

Note: Averages were substituted for missing data for Asian American educational attainment.

enrollment of newer immigrants. Examining the data with a wide lens, the most significant advances have been made by African Americans, who in 1970 had a high school graduation rate of just over 30 percent, and by 2009 saw 75 percent of students obtaining diplomas.

Our present economy increasingly demands a college degree for gainful employment, and Figure 10.6 indicates that while much progress has been made in high school education, wide disparities exist in the attainment of college degrees. Since 1970, each group has experienced a slow, fairly steady increase in the numbers who have attained college degrees, but we need to consider the wider context when we look at these data—where each group has ended up depends on where it began. Notice that in the early 1970s—shortly after the 1965 Immigration and Naturalization Act permitted in larger numbers of immigrants if they were well educated and had resources—roughly 20 percent of Asian Americans age twenty-five and older had college degrees; this is significantly more than any other group shown in that year. In the ensuing years, Asian Americans experienced a steep increase, more than doubling their percentage

Figure 10.6   Persons Age Twenty-five and Older with a College Degree by Race and Ethnicity, 1970–2009

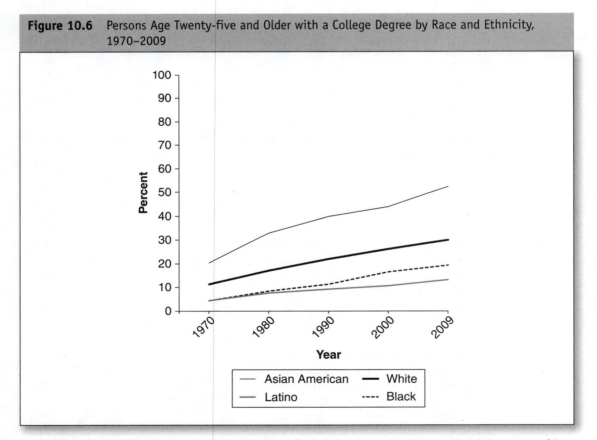

Source: "The 2011 Statistical Abstract: The National Data Book," U.S. Census Bureau (Washington, DC: U.S. Department of Commerce, 2011), Table 225.

Note: Averages were substituted for missing data for Asian American and Latino educational attainment.

of college graduates (from 20 percent to about 40 percent), when all other groups had a much slower increase. Thus the data in this figure partly undermine the model minority myth that argues that the cultural values and the work ethic of Asian Americans greatly determine their status—it is clear that public policy, especially an immigration policy that values those with skills and education, also matters, for it determines the baseline, or starting point, from which a group begins. While White college graduates are far behind their Asian American counterparts, their rates are still nearly twice that of Hispanics, and at least ten percentage points higher than that of Black college graduates. Race and ethnicity still matter, but in varying ways.

While significant inequalities remain when it comes to the attainment of college degrees, rates are increasing. If this trend continues in the long term, it should have a positive impact on minorities' earning potential as they obtain more-skilled jobs with higher incomes. This, in turn, may contribute to fewer minority students attending high-poverty schools as their parents move to more affluent neighborhoods. Consequently, schools may also become more integrated as class inequities are minimized. These examples illustrate how education equality can minimize or remove roadblocks and provide greater opportunities for minorities. But education is not yet equal, and it will remain a battleground policy area.

Under President Obama, an effort was made to increase the number of students who attend community colleges and to encourage college dropouts to finish their degrees, though it is too early to tell whether these efforts have paid off. At the high school level, the dropout rate in many urban areas is declining, but only a little more than half of Black males, or 52 percent, and of Latino males, or 58 percent, graduate after four years; this is compared to 78 percent of non-Hispanic White males. Young male dropouts often end up in the juvenile justice system, with nowhere to turn.[46] From juvenile justice, many go on as adults to serve time in prison, and there is a growing concern that the lack of educational opportunities for low-income persons, especially racial and ethnic minorities, too often leads to a "school-to-prison pipeline." When a quality education is not available, a minority of low-income citizens may feel compelled to resort to incomes from criminal activities to meet their vital needs, which in turn impacts rates of arrest and imprisonment. While public schools struggle to serve as an equalizing force for all Americans, criminal justice policy contains stark racial disparities that further alienate minorities from mainstream society and limit their opportunities for equality.[47]

 Can disadvantages like a poor education in elementary and secondary school be overcome with hard work?

THE CRIMINAL JUSTICE SYSTEM: BARRIERS AND ROADBLOCKS

The criminal justice system is a public policy domain that produces stark racial disparities between Blacks and Whites in the United States. But as this book points out, we cannot simply presume that Blacks and Hispanics constitute a similarly situated subordinate group, although Hispanics likewise confront inequalities as compared to non-Hispanic Whites. Race and legal studies scholar Michelle Alexander argues that the criminal justice system creates a second-class citizenship for Blacks (especially Black men) akin to the creation of a "New Jim Crow": "Once you're labeled a felon, the old forms of discrimination—employment discrimination, housing discrimination, denial of the right to vote, denial of education opportunity, denial of food stamps and other public benefits, and exclusion from jury service—are suddenly legal. As a criminal, you have scarcely more rights, and arguably less respect, than a black man living in Alabama at the height of Jim Crow. We have not ended racial caste in America; we have merely redesigned it."[48] In our examination of the outcomes of criminal justice policy, we will touch on core problems that prompt Alexander to her conclusions, and we will also consider how the increasing criminalization of immigration policy expands the color line of federal incarceration to include Latinos as an increasingly disadvantaged group.

When it comes to crime in the United States, there are often misconceptions about where minorities fall on the scale of law-abiding and law-breaking. For instance, one common misconception is that African Americans comprise a larger segment of drug users than Whites. Data reveal that Blacks are no more likely than their White counterparts to abuse illegal drugs. What accounts for these inaccurate impressions? Popular understanding of crime and criminals is in part affected by the racialization of minority populations—consciously or unconsciously. These same racialized views contribute to criminal justice policy and stark disparities in the arrest, sentencing, and treatment of minorities by law enforcement. It is these differences and the ripple effect from them—denial of the right to vote and of certain public benefits like food stamps, as well as employment and housing discrimination—that create a population of second-class citizens who do not have equal access to the rights and opportunities granted to all Americans.

The United States today might be termed a carceral, or prison, state. Prisons have literally become an industry (and in some instances they are for-profit industries), sponsored and maintained by state and federal governments. At the same time, there is little discussion in public policy circles about attacking the underlying poverty that may inspire crime—some of the very roadblocks to opportunity that this book has discussed. Sociologists Lawrence Bobo and Victor Thompson observe "a large-scale shift toward formal incarceration as our collective response to crime."[49]

As evidence of just how high the incarceration rate is, in 1980 just over 300,000 persons were in prison, but by 2010, the number reached over 1.5 million. That's a five-fold increase. As of 2010, more than 7 million persons—or, by comparison, nearly the entire population of the state of Virginia—were under the supervision of correctional systems. If we consider just the number of prison inmates who are males in comparison to the total U.S. male population, there has been an extremely dramatic rise in incarceration. In 1975 fewer than 300 males per every 100,000 were inmates; by 2007, about 1,000 males per every 100,000 were inmates. As one *New York Times* writer editorialized: "The 50 states last year [2007] spent $44 billion in tax dollars on corrections, up from nearly $11 billion in 1987. . . . Vermont, Connecticut, Delaware, Michigan, and Oregon devote as much money or more to corrections as they do to higher education."[50]

Not only does the United States imprison more people than it has in past decades, but on average U.S. courts assign longer and more punitive sentences, such as the death penalty, and are more willing to convict juveniles at a younger age. One key reason for mushrooming rates of incarceration is that the escalated criminalization of drugs in the 1980s greatly increased the numbers of persons arrested, convicted, and imprisoned on drug-related charges. This drug criminalization policy has much more heavily impacted minorities and especially African Americans than it has Whites, even though, as we noted, Blacks are no more likely than their White counterparts to illegally use drugs.[51]

The racial disparities in U.S. criminal justice policy are greatly influenced by, although not solely due to, the persistent racial inequalities of the South. For example, African Americans comprise exponentially higher national percentages of those on death row and of those executed in comparison to their percentage of the total U.S. population. The South often drives these disparities. Between 1977 and 2010, Blacks comprised 41 percent of all persons on death row and 34 percent of those executed. Of the 1,234 persons executed between 1977 and 2010, a whopping 82 percent were in the South—432 in Texas alone. In fact, during this period a large majority of the 432 Blacks who were executed and the 3,225 who were on death row were located in the South. African Americans in 2010 comprised 47 percent of all Southerners on death row and about 22 percent of those executed. But the South is not alone in these disproportionate numbers: in 2010 Blacks and Hispanics combined made up 60 percent of all of those on death row in the Northeast, at 135 out of 226 death row inmates. They were 36 percent of the 699 persons on death row in the state of California.[52] As the remainder of this chapter will show, it was Southern efforts to establish a new racial order that helped set us on the current path in criminal justice policy. This is especially true in the era during and shortly after the Civil Rights Movement.

New Jim Crow: Race, Criminal Justice, and the South

Race and legal studies scholar Michelle Alexander labeled current racial disparities in the criminal justice system "the New Jim Crow" because she saw strong evidence that our system has created a new, impoverished racial caste of minority inmates. The term **New Jim Crow** evokes the period after the Civil War and before the Civil Rights Movement during which racial separation was sanctioned by law and custom and often referred to as Jim Crow. As journalist Douglas A. Blackmon noted, the criminal justice system, shortly after the Civil War and Reconstruction periods, created a form of "slavery by another name" because of the arbitrary and harsh ways in which it meted out punishment that directly targeted African Americans.[53] (See Chapter 3.)

This new form of slavery, or New Jim Crow, can be seen in the Virginia Supreme Court case of *Ruffin v. Commonwealth* (1871). In this case, the line between slave and convict was negated when the court concluded of Amber Ruffin: "He has, as a consequence of his crime, not only forfeited his liberty, but all his personal rights except those which the law in its humanity accords to him. He is for the time being a slave of the State."[54] Convicts as slaves were a very important element of a larger system of political, social, and economic control in the early twentieth century, the purpose of which was to resubjugate African Americans as a racial caste—despite the passage of the Thirteenth (antislavery), Fourteenth (equal protection), and Fifteenth (voting rights) Amendments.[55]

In particular, the criminal justice system in the Southern states, where 75 percent of all African Americans resided by the 1900s, used the law to economically exploit thousands of African American laborers. They criminalized behaviors as innocent as "vagrancy" or loitering; swiftly and arbitrarily convicted alleged offenders and handed out extreme sentences; and generated needed tax revenue by selling or leasing convict labor to companies and corporations that demanded workers do backbreaking, dangerous jobs such as pick cotton, mine coal, cut timber, work in iron or steel foundries, and clear massive boulders for road construction in the industrializing New South. These prisoners were housed under inhumane and

ASSOCIATED PRESS

U.S. criminal justice policy sends a disproportionate number of African Americans to prison, and for longer terms than it does Whites. This and other inequalities in the criminal justice system have given rise to what some label the New Jim Crow, for a system that unfairly disadvantages minorities.

unsanitary conditions that led to mass outbreaks of disease. They were fed terrible food, punished by brutal methods, and at times literally worked to death because employers could always lease or buy another convict from the state. This was during the period of Jim Crow, when race was a decisive and nearly absolute barrier to African American equality. Also recall from earlier chapters that this same period in the late 1890s and early 1900s when Blacks were treated as second-class citizens and menial workers was also when Chinese laborers faced exploitation and exclusion, especially in the West and Northeast, and when Mexicans and Mexican Americans confronted continued denial of their civil liberties and land rights in the Southwest.[56]

It is from this foundation of early-twentieth-century racialization in U.S. criminal justice policy and practices that we arrive at modern policy and its outcomes. The "tough on crime" measures of the later twentieth century resulted in a marked increase in mass incarcerations, while racial profiling reveals the distinct disparity between how Whites and non-Whites are viewed—on the surface—by many in law enforcement and the judicial system. For example, being stopped by police officers often for little to no cause is a common occurrence for many African American men, and Blacks and Latinos are ever more likely to be convicted and sentenced to longer prison terms than are White defendants. These modern truths present decisive roadblocks for minorities on their roads to equal rights and opportunities.

Law and Order: The Racial Origins of Mass Incarceration

The period from World War II to the mid-1960s witnessed remarkable political reforms led by various minority groups—including African Americans, Native Americans, and Latinos—who led different civil rights movements. Using their access to the laws, institutions, and resources of the polity through means of court cases, mass protest, and voting for candidates who reflected their beliefs, among other actions, minority efforts slowly overturned explicit government-sanctioned racial discrimination and, in effect, led to the death of the old methods of maintaining the color line. Therefore, "those committed to racial hierarchy," states Michelle Alexander, "were forced to search for new means of achieving their goals according to the new rules of American democracy." This meant that with the old ways of minority oppression no longer available, new means were sought to perpetuate discrimination, including the use of race-neutral terms for policies with very specific racial outcomes, such as the war on drugs and other crime policies.

Urban riots in the late 1960s broke out across the nation in cities like Detroit; Rochester, New York; and Los Angeles. Often ignited by police brutality in Black and other minority communities and fueled by persistent inequalities, these riots destroyed city infrastructure and garnered much media attention. The costliest of these riots was in Detroit in 1967, with some $50 million in damages, forty-three people killed (thirty of them Black), over three hundred hurt, and nearly four thousand arrested. Televised images of angry Blacks were viewed in homes across the nation. As the nation's minorities struggled for equal civil rights, many in the majority society remained too frightened or intolerant to change, and the images from these riots fueled moral panics around crime and criminality. Calls for "law and order" quickly became the new mantra that racial conservatives used to oppose racial reforms.[57]

The most ardent segregationists argued that integration caused crime. Governor John Bell Williams of Mississippi stated that Black migration out of the South to various cities sparked "a wave of crime," and thus, "Segregation is the only answer as most Americans—not the politicians—have realized for hundreds of years."[58] While federal laws were changing to support integration in the wake of rulings like *Brown v. Board of Education* and to encourage greater equality among all citizens, criminal justice policy in many ways changed its language more than its content. Republican candidates for president, including Senator Barry Goldwater in 1964 and more notably Vice President Richard Nixon in 1968, argued that the country—due to turbulent protests for civil rights and women's rights, and against the Vietnam War, among other causes—must again become "a nation of laws." They and others justified "get tough on crime" public policies and aggressive actions by police agencies. Many persons responded positively to language like "get tough on crime," so even as minorities were most affected by these measures, the racial impact was less public because the policy, on its surface, was presented in race-neutral terms. Also during this time, the Federal Bureau of Investigation launched its now-infamous Counterintelligence Program (COINTELPRO) that spied on, interrogated, and disrupted a wide number of leaders and groups it feared were too militant and capable and/or willing to overthrow the U.S. government. These included Dr. Martin Luther King Jr., the Black Panther Party, and the American Indian Movement.[59]

It was in this context that Vice President Nixon and his campaign aides formulated the "Southern Strategy" in his 1968 run for the presidency. It was an effort by Republican leaders to counter the Democratic Party's emerging coalition of Blacks and other minority voters, labor union members, urban dwellers, and others by attracting disaffected White Southerners, suburbanites, and affluent and middle-class voters. John Ehrlichman, Nixon's legal counsel, once brashly characterized it as, "We'll go after the racists."[60] The strategy purposely sought to foster racial polarization in the votes cast for Democratic and Republican candidates, and over the course of the 1980s and into the 1990s it worked—Whites became more likely to support Republicans, and minority voters more likely to support Democrats. In fact, by the first decade of the twenty-first century, the Republican Party acknowledged that it needed to reach out more to minority voters if it was to maintain its relevance in a nation anticipated to become majority-minority by 2040.[61]

From its inception, the Southern Strategy used race-neutral code words like *crime* and *criminals* to attract voters; and, against the backdrop of debates about urban poverty and the deserving and undeserving poor in the mid-1960s and 1970s, Republican candidates attacked the liberal and Democratic agenda of civil rights and economic opportunity. When President Nixon rhetorically called for a war on drugs in 1971 or increased penalties and policing of drug crimes, already about 81 percent of Americans believed that "law and order [had] broken down in the country," and over 50 percent said that "Negroes who start riots" and "communists" were responsible.[62] In 1973 Nelson Rockefeller, the moderate Republican governor of New York, enacted what became known as the "Rockefeller drug laws," a series of laws that established New York as having among the toughest drug penalties in the nation, with a mandatory minimum sentence for drug possession. Massachusetts, Michigan, Florida, Pennsylvania, and Oregon subsequently passed similar laws. In 1986, a few years after President Ronald Reagan announced his antidrug policy, Congress passed the Anti–Drug Abuse Act, which required very long mandatory minimum sentences for first-time drug offences—five to ten years. Many states followed suit, and it was in the 1980s that we witnessed the exponential growth in the prison population previously discussed, along with the dramatic racial disparities the mandatory minimum policies created.

As part of the get tough on crime effort, policy toward drug offenses has resulted in **mass incarceration,** or the widespread imprisonment of various groups. As of 2010, over 50 percent of all federal inmates were imprisoned on drug-related charges and comprised about 20 percent of all persons in state prisons. Of the total number of persons in state prisons on drug-related sentences, about 45 percent were African American. As previously noted, African Americans are no more likely than Whites to use illegal drugs, yet they *are* more likely to be convicted than are White offenders—a fact that we'll explore in greater detail below. While policymakers believe that sending people to prison for illegal drug use or distribution at the street level is an effective deterrent, much of the empirical evidence tells us that, according to criminologist Michael Tonry, "sending people to prison makes them more likely to commit new crimes than if they were punished in some other way."[63] One simple fact with regard to illegal drugs is that the street-level price of cocaine, as one example, has decreased over many years. If interdiction, drug arrests, and convictions were making it more difficult to conduct business, then market logic dictates that the price should have increased. Advocates for treating illegal drugs as a public health issue or for some level of decriminalization continue to raise this point, to little avail.[64]

 Are race-neutral terms still used in criminal justice policy today? What are some examples?

Contemporary Racial Profiling and Policing

There have been extensive debates about the practice of the police and other law enforcement agencies using race and ethnicity as factors to determine if someone is likely to commit or already has committed a crime, a practice called **racial profiling.** Police officers are guided not only by their personal views and biases but also by those of the larger public. There is a large body of research that demonstrates that the public, and in particular White citizens, unconsciously believe African Americans and some Latinos, especially those with darker complexions, are more likely to commit crimes than those persons with lighter complexions. The Implicit Association Test (IAT) has found that individuals may unconsciously associate a number of negative characteristics with being Black, even if these individuals do not consciously express anti-Black prejudice. A person who holds unconscious, negative stereotypes about another racial or ethnic group has what is called **implicit bias.** This psychological feature of race and ethnicity matters when a police officer has to quickly decide to draw his or her weapon in self-defense, stop a motorist, arrest a suspect, and decide what charge is relevant—especially if she or he must enforce Arizona's or Alabama's immigration law authorizing the police to stop those they suspect are illegally in the country.

There is a long history of cases in which the police or ordinary citizens were suspected of using racial profiling to determine whether a minority suspect presented a threat to life or property. The 2012 shooting of a Black Florida teen, Trayvon Martin, by George Zimmerman, who is of mixed White and Hispanic heritage and was a neighborhood crime watch leader, is just one in a long line of cases. Police officers, along with prosecutors and judges, have become more sensitized to the influences that racial and ethnic stereotypes exert on their judgments. The infamous 1992 Rodney King verdict is partly responsible for this shift. King, an African American, was detected speeding in Los Angeles, and he feared that being pulled over would result in revocation of his probation. He led police on a high-speed chase before he was stopped, tasered, and beaten. Blacks believed King was, from the start, targeted by racial profiling, but in 1992 the jury in a majority White county acquitted the police officers. The Los Angeles African American community erupted in outrage and rioting that resulted in $1 billion in damages and the deaths of fifty-three people.

More than twenty years after the King verdict, law enforcement officials still have wide discretion in their conduct, and subsequent cases of arrest and violence toward suspects have raised accusations of racial profiling. Evidence from studies and incentives for police performance indicates that race and ethnicity still can matter in the practice of policing.[65] For example, in August of 2014, a routine police matter resulted in the death an unarmed 18-year old Black man, Michael Brown. He was shot and killed by a White police officer, Darren Wilson, in Ferguson, Missouri, after he supposedly stopped Brown for walking in the middle of the street. The lack of transparency by the police department and other investigators, combined with the aggressive, anti-riot tactics of the police, incensed many in the community and led to several nights of protest and unrest. A number of studies of the policing practices of highway patrol officers found that minorities are more frequently stopped by the police out of proportion to the actual likelihood that they have broken a traffic law or are probable crime suspects—sarcastically referred to as the problem of **driving while Black** or driving while brown. As mentioned earlier, this is when African American or Latino motorists are more readily stopped by police officers for minor or nonexistent infractions in comparison to Whites, who are not readily stopped. For example, a University of Toledo law professor found in 1999 that Illinois state patrol officers stopped African American and Hispanic motorists greatly out of disproportion to their likelihood of being involved in a drug crime. While Blacks on average were only 6.4 percent of the motorists in targeted drug neighborhoods, they were almost 24 percent of those stopped. While Hispanics on average were a mere 2.8 percent of the motorists in the same targeted neighborhoods, they were 21 percent of those stopped. The latter ratio is a whopping 1 to 10 disparity! Additional studies have also confirmed that minorities are no more likely to use illegal drugs than are their White counterparts.

In addition to these conscious or unconscious racial biases by law enforcement, there are many incentives, most especially public pressure, for police to demonstrate successful arrest rates in stemming crime by targeting certain neighborhoods and sections of a city or town. Minority and low-income communities are more likely to be targeted in drug busts because low-level distributors and users in these communities are more compelled to conduct business on the street or in so-called open air markets. These communities are also targeted because low-income users are more likely to use a drug like crack cocaine while middle-income users prefer powder cocaine. In turn, the latter group is more likely to obtain their drugs through very private exchanges and to use them in the privacy of their homes. Thus they are much less susceptible to police surveillance. Additionally, there is a clear political cost for the police to target a very affluent suburban community for a drug bust over a low-income neighborhood street. As we have shown, however, there is also a racial/ethnic impact to the decision making of where—and on whom—law enforcement focuses its attention.[66] This, in turn, affects incarceration rates.

> Have you been the victim of racial profiling? Have you ever found yourself profiling someone else? Under what circumstances?

Disparities in Arrest, Sentencing, and Imprisonment

As the second half of this chapter has described, the legal and law enforcement system's response to prospective or actual crime is racially biased. African Americans comprise roughly the equivalent percentage of monthly drug users as their percentage of the U.S. population—14.5 versus 11.9 percent. The anticrime institutions of the government, however, react to this minority community in a disproportionate way. As Figure 10.7 illustrates, Blacks are 33.9 percent of those arrested for drugs (more than twice the proportion of users). They are 46 percent of those convicted for drug use at the state level (more than three times the proportion of users). And they are 45.1 percent of those sentenced to state prisons on drug sentences (roughly three times the proportion of users).

Across other categories of crime, criminologist Michael Tonry refutes claims that African Americans are arrested and imprisoned at higher rates because they commit disproportionately more violent crime. Rather than increasing rates of African American criminality, the opposite is true. While violent crime for all groups—but especially Blacks—declined from the late 1980s into the early 2000s, rates of imprisonment for Blacks steadily increased. Additionally, as mentioned at the start of the criminal justice policy section, the further criminalization of illegal immigration is resulting in Hispanics representing higher and higher percentages of persons in federal prisons. In short, race and ethnicity remain consequential in the U.S. criminal justice system, while the actual behaviors of groups do not matter as much.[67]

Figure 10.7   Race, Criminal Justice, and the Drug War

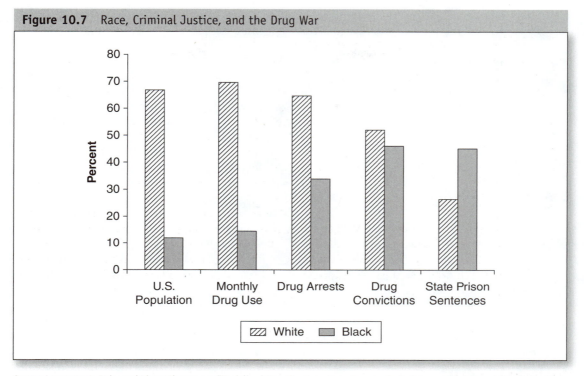

Source: Lawrence D. Bobo and Victor Thompson, "Racialized Mass Incarceration: Poverty, Prejudice, and Punishment," in *Doing Race: 21 Essays for the 21st Century,* ed. Hazel Rose Markus and Paula M. L. Moya (New York: W. W. Norton, 2010), 332.

In the end, public perceptions matter. As we referenced earlier, there is a growing body of research demonstrating that the public, and in particular White citizens, hold the view that persons who are browner in their skin complexions are more likely to commit crimes. A study by Jennifer Hochschild and Vesla Weaver (2007) finds that there is a "dark-skinned" discrimination, or **colorism,** that occurs: "Relative to their lighter-skinned contemporaries, dark-skinned blacks have lower levels of education, income, and job status." When this premise is extended to criminal justice, the authors find in a study of sixty-seven thousand Georgia convicts: "Controlling for type of offense, socioeconomic characteristics, demographic factors, light-skinned black defendants received sentences indistinguishable from those of whites. Medium- and dark-skinned black defendants received longer sentences."[68]

All of this is fascinating, but unfortunately is it not surprising in a society where skin color continues to matter.

Given that African Americans and Latinos confront disproportionately higher rates of arrest and incarceration, and typically get lengthier sentences as compared to non-Hispanic Whites, it is not difficult to understand how such barriers lead to these minority groups traveling quite uneven roads of public policy outcomes and opportunities. Let us consider the issue of felon disenfranchisement, or persons not being able to vote because they have served jail time, been

A youth holds a sign during a rally in New York City that was part of a national day of action in support of justice for Trayvon Martin, a teenager shot and killed by George Zimmerman, who was acquitted of all charges. The case raised an intense, nationwide debate about "stand your ground laws" passed in various states, and whether Martin was a victim of racial profiling.

arrested, or are on parole. In 2010 nearly six million Americans in the United States were disenfranchised, or not permitted to vote, due to arrests or previous convictions—this is a little less than 4 percent of the total number of persons who turned out to vote in 2008. As many as two million, or more than 60 percent, of these disenfranchised people were African Americans, and nationwide, one out of eight adult Black men (or about 13 percent) was ineligible to vote.

Why does this matter? During the state house and midterm congressional elections of 2010, the disenfranchisement of these Black voters likely made a key difference. Some of them were disenfranchised in states like Florida (23 percent), Virginia (20 percent), Tennessee (19 percent), and Alabama (15 percent), which had elected majorities of conservative representatives to state houses and the U.S. Congress. Black voters typically support moderate to liberal candidates in favor of increased government spending and expanded civil rights protections. The denial of the vote based upon arrests and convictions has real consequences on who makes the laws.[69]

RACE, ETHNICITY, AND CRIMINAL JUSTICE POLICY OUTCOMES

In our examination of U.S. criminal justice policy, we have focused on how it has been used to continue discriminatory practices against minorities, including the use of race-neutral language to mask overt discriminatory intent, and how the South instituted a New Jim Crow that allowed convicted Blacks to be worked as slaves. We have also examined the growing modern disparities in incarceration and sentencing across minority groups and how they came about, including racial profiling. From this context, we turn to criminal justice policy outcomes, which represent an institutionally supported barrier to group and individual progress.

Figure 10.8 starkly represents the very wide disparity of incarceration rates across race and ethnicity. While rates of imprisonment disproportionately affect racial and ethnic minorities, they most clearly affect Black males. It is striking how many more Black males are in federal,

Figure 10.8   Black, White, and Hispanic Male Inmates in Federal, State, or Local Prisons per 100,000 U.S. Residents

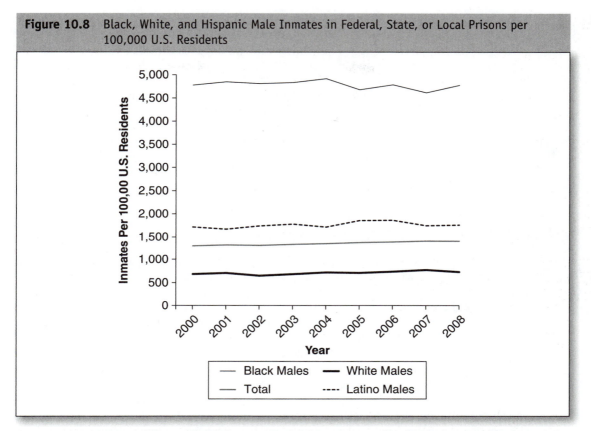

Source: Heather C. West and William J. Sabol, "Prison Inmates at Midyear 2008—Statistical Tables," Bureau of Justice Statistics, Table 18, p. 18, http://www.bjs.gov/content/pub/pdf/pim08st.pdf.

Note: Total includes American Indians, Alaskan Natives, Asian Americans, Native Hawaiians, other Pacific Islanders, and persons identifying as two or more races.

state, or local prisons than any other race or ethnicity, and particularly out of the total number of inmates per 100,000 residents. Hispanic males constitute a second group of disparities above the total, and White males fall significantly below. It is no wonder that civil rights advocates have begun to argue that such gaping inequalities are, in their view, becoming the civil rights issue of the twenty-first century.[70]

While the racial and ethnic disparities in sentencing are significant, they are not the end of the story. Criminal justice policy does disproportionately affect minority populations—especially African Americans and, increasingly, Latinos—and it has long-term impacts that affect these individuals long after they are released from prison. Earlier in this chapter we discussed the problem of "collateral consequences," or all of the adverse outcomes that stem from being arrested. Sociologist Darren Wheelock listed a number of restrictions some states and local governments have placed upon persons convicted of felonies even if they committed nonviolent crimes, and even after these persons have served their sentences: disenfranchisement (or loss of voting rights); exclusion from juries; ineligibility in running for office; restrictions of various benefits, including public assistance, public housing, and military service benefits; denial of employment in government and the right to gain various licenses (e.g., barber license or beautician license); loss of custody of a child; and, if an immigrant, deportation. Furthermore, various employers may simply refuse to hire anyone with a criminal background. The denial of rights based on previous arrest or conviction is so severe in a few cases that by one view it might constitute these persons experiencing a "civil death," in which they have little to nearly no citizenship rights and/or equal opportunities.[71]

 How, if at all, do the social consequences of incarceration compound racial and ethnic inequalities?

CONCLUSION: PUBLIC POLICY DESTINATIONS

As we've maintained throughout this book, where one starts on the road to equality and opportunity affects where one ends up. When it comes to education and criminal justice policies, minority populations begin with an oftentimes distinct disadvantage. Those for whom strong color lines exist, as is the case with Blacks and Latinos and imprisonment rates, face far more decisive barriers than those for whom the color lines are blurry, as is the case with non-Hispanics and high school graduation rates or Asian American college degree attainment. An individual or group facing a strong color line is likely to experience more roadblocks and disadvantages.

As areas of public policy, education and criminal justice are very important to consider when understanding when, why, and how race matters to a group enjoying full citizenship and equal opportunities. These policies have mattered most during those periods in contemporary U.S. politics and in those political contexts when there have been intense disagreements about how to strike a balance between ensuring a racial or ethnic group is given an equal opportunity to succeed versus the need to ensure that all are treated equally before the law. For example, affirmative action became such a hotly contested policy in the 1990s and early 2000s at prestigious public universities like the University of Michigan precisely because in this period, well after the Civil Rights Movement, this institution was compelled by student movements and their allies to use such policies to recruit and matriculate larger numbers of minority students—whereas critics saw this as a form of reverse discrimination against Whites.[72] Education and criminal justice policy have mattered in explaining a racial/ethnic group's well-being to the degree that there have been strong debates about the whys or the rationales, however erroneous or not, for believing a group is or is not unfairly affected by a policy. For example, whether a person believes New York City police officers unfairly used racial profiling or they aggressively reduced drug crime and gun violence when they widely 'stopped and frisked' pedestrians in minority neighborhoods depends upon a person's beliefs or reasoning about what is a racially fair or evenhanded way to guarantee the public safety of minority and all other neighborhoods.[73]

Education and criminal justice policy have mattered in understanding how policy affects a racial/ethnic group's well-being as we understand the outcomes of specific processes, groups, and actors. For example, it is important to understand how residential segregation or the racial segregation of certain neighborhoods remains several decades after *Brown v. Board of Education* and provides for segregated public schools. Government, as an institution, cannot require White families to remain within racially/ethnically diverse school districts.[74] Blacks and other racial/ethnic minorities are no less likely to use illegal drugs than their White counterparts. But policing policies that target perceived high-crime communities (more often minority), differences in the availability of legal counsel, and juries' misperceptions that minority defendants are more likely to be guilty than White defendants, are how criminal justice processes and institutions produce uneven outcomes for minority groups.[75]

Ultimately, education and criminal justice policies are just two of many examples of how public policy can produce racial and ethnic differences in a group's barriers or gateways to citizenship rights and equal opportunities. Education can provide opportunities, just like policies that foster homeownership or employment. Criminal justice can provide barriers, just like policies that adversely affect one's lifespan. In the end, the degree to which a group will or will not be adversely racialized—the degree to which the outcomes of policies are racially decisive or inconsequential to the group's well-being—depends upon the equitable provision of education and the color-blind administration of justice.

DISCUSSION QUESTIONS

1. With educational and criminal justice policy, can you identify the conservative and liberal perspectives with regard to race? What is your evaluation of the effectiveness of these policies? What are these perspectives on other types of policies?

2. In what ways are the legacies of racial/ethnic segregation still evident in the public education system, even all of these decades after the *Brown v. Board of Education* decision?

3. What are the main factors contributing to the persistence of educational quality and achievement gaps between minorities and Whites? What policies may best diminish these gaps?

4. Are the policies that result in the mass incarceration of minorities today purposefully unfair/unjust, or is that an unintended consequence? What changes should be made to criminal justice policy to ensure equal treatment under the law?

5. Do the collective consequences of U.S. criminal justice policy create insurmountable disadvantages for minorities? Explain your answer.

KEY TERMS

achievement gap (p. 309)

affirmative action (p. 305)

Brown v. Board of Education of Topeka (1954–1955) (p. 302)

color-blind society (p. 297)

de facto racial discrimination (p. 296)

de jure racial discrimination (p. 296)

driving while Black
(p. 321)
implicit bias (p. 321)
mass incarceration
(p. 320)
New Jim Crow (p. 317)

No Child Left Behind Act
of 2001 (p. 310)
public policy (p. 295)
race-conscious (p. 307)
race-neutral (p. 307)
racial conservative (p. 296)

racial liberal (p. 296)
racial profiling (p. 320)
racial quota (p. 307)
reverse discrimination (p. 306)
White flight (p. 304)

11 Immigration Policy: The Road to Settlement and Citizenship

Give me your tired, your poor,

Your huddled masses yearning to breathe free,

The wretched refuse of your teeming shore.

Send these, the homeless, tempest-tost to me,

I lift my lamp beside the golden door!

Emma Lazarus, "The New Colossus"[1]

Many presidents throughout U.S. history have identified one of the country's central organizing myths and ongoing realities: the understanding of the United States as a nation of immigrants. In 1783 President George Washington said, "The bosom of America is open to receive not only the Opulent and respected Stranger, but also the oppressed and persecuted of all Nations and Religions; whom we shall welcome to a participation of all our rights and privileges, if by decency and propriety they appear to merit the enjoyment."[2] More than two hundred years later, President Barack Obama in 2010 invoked that same imagery of a welcoming nation when he said:

> I believe we can appeal not to people's fears but to their hopes, to their highest ideals, because that's who we are as Americans. It's been inscribed on our nation's seal since we declared our independence. "E pluribus unum."

Box 11.1 Chapter Objectives

- Identify the three different types of immigrants.
- Describe early immigration policies and how restrictions grew out of domestic and international pressures.
- Explain how the Immigration and Nationality Act Amendments of 1965 provided the foundation for contemporary U.S. immigration law.
- Describe incorporation policies at the national, state, and societal levels.
- Distinguish between the varying perspectives in the contemporary debate over comprehensive immigration reform.

329

ASSOCIATED PRESS

Many immigrants in the United States settle into the country and seek citizenship. Those seeking formal membership in U.S. society must naturalize as U.S. citizens. This process requires an exam before a U.S. official, payment of a fee, and a background check. After completion of this process, naturalizing citizens take an oath of allegiance to the United States at a public ceremony.

Out of many, one. That is what has drawn the persecuted and impoverished to our shores. That's what led the innovators and risk-takers from around the world to take a chance here in the land of opportunity.[3]

Yet Obama also acknowledged: "Each new wave of immigrants has generated fear and resentments towards newcomers, particularly in times of economic upheaval. . . . So the politics of who is and who is not allowed to enter this country, and on what terms, has always been contentious."[4]

Both Washington and Obama recognize the tension inherent in building a nation through large numbers of immigrants from throughout the world. Washington speaks of the need to welcome new immigrants, but cautions that they must "appear to merit the enjoyment" of the rights and privileges of being an American. President Obama, with the benefit of historical hindsight—and in an effort to build support for legislation intended to significantly reform the structure of U.S. immigration policy—acknowledged that the long-term reverence for immigrants has been balanced by contentious relations between native-stock populations and newcomers and ongoing efforts to restrict immigration.

These debates continue today. In this chapter, we trace the development of U.S. immigration and immigrant incorporation policies to better understand the debates that the nation and Congress are engaged in as they build new foundations for U.S. immigration law (the "how" question of this chapter); we look also at the role that racial attitudes and perceptions of racial difference between native-stock populations and immigrants played in the making of immigration policy (which partially answers the "why" question in immigration policy). In recent sessions, Congress has unsuccessfully debated bills for widespread reform of U.S. immigration law. These comprehensive reform debates resulted from broad dissatisfaction in the American public and among employers about the operation of current U.S. immigration law. The current law, passed in 1965, emerged from the reformist spirit of the Civil Rights era that we have argued establishes the foundation for today's U.S. minority politics. The nation is too divided to enact a similar reform in the current era.

Immigration is an issue of continuing importance to the nation. Its status has waxed and waned, depending on domestic and international events. For instance, immigration—and race/ethnicity—tends to matter more during times of economic hardship and war than in times of peaceful prosperity. These periods of *when* immigration and race matter in the United States have historically been tied to *why* it matters—often in response to concerns among native U.S. citizens that immigrants are taking needed jobs or represent a security threat. *How* immigration and race matter is played out in shifting policies, which this chapter examines in depth. As we explore when, why, and how immigration and race matter when it comes to U.S. immigration and immigrant integration policies, we will also come to understand the ways in which U.S. laws, institutions, and resources have been used both to establish discriminatory policies and procedures and to create more equal opportunity.

IMMIGRANT STATUS AND NUMBERS

Relative to most other countries, the United States admits more immigrants and has done so through most of its history, but not all immigrants have the same status. Immigrant status may vary from legal permanent residents, guest workers, and unauthorized immigrants. (See Figure 11.1 for an overview of immigration.) More than one million people who enter the United States each year are designated as **legal permanent residents.** Immigrants to permanent residence enter the United States with "green cards" that permit work in the United States and access to many of the rights enjoyed by the U.S.-born. After no more than five years, these immigrants to permanent residence can naturalize as U.S. citizens.

The United States also admits large numbers of **guest workers,** business people, and other temporary visitors; these are effectively immigrants who have the right to stay in the United States only until the end of their contract or visa period. For these guests, there is no road to becoming part of the United States unless they can establish the eligibility to immigrate as permanent residents. In 2012 guest workers numbered approximately 2.8 million people.

Other temporary visitors numbered 47.7 million: approximately 42 million people entered the United States as temporary visitors for pleasure, and 5.7 million entered as temporary visitors for business.[5]

Finally, the United States is home to a large number of immigrants who do not possess valid visas to be in the United States. These **unauthorized immigrants**—who are estimated to have numbered 11.7 million in 2012—include migrants who crossed the border without authorization and others who entered on a short-term visa and did not leave the United States prior to the expiration of that visa.[6] Unauthorized immigrants are often referred to derogatorily as illegal immigrants. These immigrants, many of whom have resided in the United States for years, are seeking to find a road that will lead to membership in the U.S. polity.

Immigration is contentious in today's society, and has been at several points in U.S. history. Between 2000 and 2009, more than ten million immigrants entered the United States. With this influx, native-stock populations fear the competition for jobs and resources from

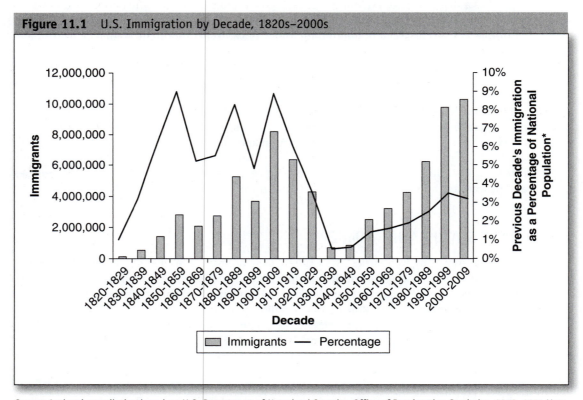

Figure 11.1 U.S. Immigration by Decade, 1820s–2000s

Source: Authors' compilation based on U.S. Department of Homeland Security, Office of Immigration Statistics. 2012. 2011 Yearbook of Immigration Statistics. Washington, DC: U.S. Department of Homeland Security. Available at http://www.dhs.gov/sites/default/files/publications/immigration-statistics/yearbook/2011/ois_yb_2011.pdf.

* Percentage of national population from the start of the next decade.

these immigrants. Many also fear that immigrants—who are often racially/ethnically distinct from the majority of the native-stock population—will bring major cultural change to the United States. These racial, ethnic, and cultural differences often lead to the assertion that immigrants are insufficiently committed to American values.[7] In the current debate, unauthorized migrants are a particular concern for native-stock populations and for policymakers. Their willingness to violate U.S. law to enter or to stay in the country and, often, to work in the United States (also in violation of law) adds to the suspicions held by native-stock populations of immigrants more generally.

 Is the U.S. system of classifying immigrants too simple? Should there be other categories?

These fears, particularly of unauthorized immigrants—who in 2012 were estimated at 11.7 million—are often countered in legislative debates by business leaders and others in U.S. society who benefit from immigrant labor, as well as by ethnic leaders and communities who seek to ensure that their co-ethnics have rights to immigrate comparable to those who arrived earlier in U.S. history. Additionally, some descendants of immigrants from earlier eras also argue on behalf of continuing immigration. These ongoing tensions of support for immigration and concerns about its effects on U.S. society were highlighted by both Presidents Washington and Obama, illustrating that for a nation founded by immigrants, immigration has always been highly debated by policymakers and the populace as a whole.

IMMIGRATION POLICIES BEFORE 1965

In the late eighteenth and nineteenth centuries, there were few limits on immigration and relatively minimal standards for White immigrant men to naturalize as U.S. citizens. By the early 1900s, the nation had moved to a significantly more restrictive set of policies on who could immigrate to the United States and modestly increased standards for naturalizing as a U.S. citizen.[8] (This is discussed in greater depth later in the chapter.) Of equal importance, as the United States expanded its regulation of who could immigrate, it established an international bureaucracy for enforcement.[9] Over the past two decades in particular, the United States has added considerably to the enforcement of its land borders, particularly the border with Mexico, including the construction of seven hundred miles of wall along the southern border. At this writing, the United States is in a period of particular growth in technologies of immigration enforcement, both on the borders and in the interior of the country.

As the regulation of immigration has changed over the nation's history, so too did its composition. Prior to 1965, the overwhelming majority of immigrants to the United States came from Europe. Only in the years just before 1965 did migrants from Latin America and Asia begin to arrive in large numbers. Here, we will explore the foundations of U.S. immigration policies and identify growing restrictions as a result of domestic and international pressures.

The Open Foundations of U.S. Immigration Policies, 1780s–1860s

At the time of the nation's founding, leaders did not believe that immigration could be regulated. Anyone who was able to get to U.S. shores was thought to be eligible to stay in the country.

Copyright Piotr Redlinski/Corbis/APImages

In response to national concerns about unauthorized migration, the United States in 2007–2008 built a wall along approximately 700 miles of the 1,900-mile U.S.-Mexico border.

Naturalization, on the other hand, could be regulated. **Naturalization** is the process by which an immigrant becomes a legal U.S. citizen. The desire to populate the country mandated that citizenship be relatively easily achieved, at least for those immigrants with characteristics desired by the new country. Thus, among the few powers expressly delegated to the new national government in the Constitution was the power to "establish a uniform rule of naturalization" (Article I, Section 8). Using this power, Congress enacted the first naturalization law in 1790, which provided that White men could naturalize after two years of residence (extended to five years in 1795) as long as they were of "good moral character" (which has been interpreted differently over time) and were willing to swear their loyalty to the United States. Race, then, was an absolute barrier to non-White immigrants seeking naturalization.

Women could not naturalize on their own until the 1920s; a woman's citizenship status followed that of her husband, or her father if she was unmarried, so nineteenth-century immigrant women became U.S. citizens when their husbands or fathers did.[10] If a nineteenth-century woman who was a citizen married a noncitizen, her citizenship was revoked. This policy remained in place until 1922 for U.S. citizen women marrying a foreign national from a country eligible to naturalize. U.S.-born women most often lost their citizenship under this law by marrying an immigrant from Asia. Only in 1931 did U.S. citizen women not lose their citizenship if they married a national of a country ineligible to naturalize.

As the number of immigrants grew in the 1800s and the relations between native-stock and immigrant populations became more contentious, the nation's philosophy about whether it could regulate immigration changed. With the exception of the prohibition on the migration of immigrants destined for slavery (all of whom were African) after 1808, these initial efforts at regulation were very tentative. In 1819 Congress required that ship captains provide a list of immigrant passengers upon arrival in a U.S. port. For this reason, we begin to have data on how many people immigrated in 1821; before that, no official records existed.

It was not until 1862 that Congress barred certain newcomers—labor migrants from China—and then only because Congress believed that it could regulate ships sailing under the authority (the "flag") of the United States. After 1862, Chinese labor migrants could only come to the United States if they traveled on ships sailing under the flag of another nation's government. This legislation's goal was to slow Chinese migration, but Congress did not believe that it had the authority to prohibit it outright. The ships of other nations were more than willing to bring these migrants to the United States, and the number of Chinese migrants increased from 35,933 in the 1850s, to 54,028 in the 1860s, and 133,139 in the 1870s.[11]

Increasing Restrictions and Prohibitions, 1870s–1964

As the nation urbanized and industrialized after the Civil War (1861–1865), its governing philosophy toward immigration regulation shifted. Between 1875 and 1921, Congress enacted steadily more restrictive legislation on who could migrate, and it established an administrative bureaucracy to enforce this legislation.[12] This period saw the prohibition of all labor migrants from China through the 1882 Chinese Exclusion Act; the expansion of these prohibitions to all Chinese immigrants and to all Asian migrants regardless of class between 1892 and 1917 in what was called the Barred Zone (see Chapter 5); and the steady expansion of classes of immigrants ineligible for migration based on health, beliefs, memberships, and literacy.[13] What began as a racial barrier to naturalization became a near-absolute racial barrier to immigration for people born in Asia.

In the 1920s, Congress passed the most restrictive immigration legislation in the nation's history, the **national origin quotas.** This legislation severely restricted the total number of migrants to the United States and sought to freeze the nation's ethnic composition at what it was in 1890. The law achieved this by allocating the number of visas to 1 percent of the people from that country counted in the 1890 census. This meant that there were few visas available to migrants from countries who began migrating in large numbers after 1890—largely Southern and Eastern Europeans. (See Chapter 6.) As these were the more recent immigrants at the time the national origin quota legislation passed, there was more demand to immigrate from these countries. Racial exclusion thus expanded from Asians to include Southern and Eastern Europeans as well.

A bureaucracy to enforce these rules was slower to develop. By 1921, immigrants entering the country through a seaport (not overland) needed a visa issued by a U.S. consulate abroad. A **visa** is written evidence that the immigrant has been authorized to immigrate; today, the visa often appears as a stamp in a passport. The first tentative efforts to regulate who could cross U.S. land borders also appeared in this period. While the 1920s ended with very restrictive legislation, it is important to note that even as native-stock attitudes toward immigrants soured, immigrants themselves and their children were able to slow restrictionist efforts.[14] Supporters of

 How does the changing shape of U.S. immigration and naturalization laws up to 1965 illustrate shifting perceptions of race?

immigration (including both business interests that wanted to maintain the flow of cheap labor and immigrant/ethnic communities that wanted to ensure relatives and co-ethnics could continue to migrate) used the legislative process to slow restrictions on immigration.

The effort to limit migration from Southern and Eastern Europe, however, did not slow the demand for immigrant labor. The national origin quota laws exempted migrants from the Western Hemisphere from their restrictions (those from the Western Hemisphere were subject to other requirements of immigration law, such as literacy in their native language, after 1917). The consequence of this decision was to speed up migration from Mexico and the Caribbean, which had previously made up a small share of U.S. migration. (See Table 11.1.) These new labor migrants continued to increase in number over the remainder of the twentieth century and into the twenty-first century.

The national origin quota laws remained in effect from 1921 until 1965, but the demands of the growing U.S. economy after World War II sealed their demise. At the beginning of the war, the United States removed the prohibitions on Asian migration. The fact that several of the countries in the Barred Zone were allies in the war necessitated a rethinking about

Table 11.1 Four Largest Immigrant Nationalities by Decade, 1900s–2000s

Decade/Country	Number of Immigrants	% of Decade's Immigration	Decade/Country	Number of Immigrants	% of Decade's Immigration
1900s	**8,202,388**		**1960s**	**3,213,749**	
Austria-Hungary	2,001,376	24.4	Mexico	441,824	13.7
Italy	1,930,475	23.5	Canada and Newfoundland	433,128	13.5
Russia	1,501,301	18.3	United Kingdom	220,213	6.9
United Kingdom	469,518	5.7	Germany	209,616	6.5
1910s	**6,347,380**		**1970s**	**4,248,203**	
Italy	1,229,916	19.4	Mexico	621,218	14.6
Austria-Hungary	1,164,727	18.3	Philippines	337,726	7.9
Russia	1,106,998	17.4	Cuba	256,497	6
Canada and Newfoundland	708,715	11.2	Korea	241,192	5.7
1920s	**4,295,510**		**1980s**	**6,244,379**	
Canada and Newfoundland	949,286	22.1	Mexico	1,009,586	16.2
Italy	528,133	12.3	Philippines	502,056	8
Mexico	498,945	11.6	Korea	322,708	5.2
Germany	386,634	9	India	231,649	3.7

Decade/Country	Number of Immigrants	% of Decade's Immigration	Decade/Country	Number of Immigrants	% of Decade's Immigration
1930s	**699,375**		**1990s**	**9,775,398**	
Canada and Newfoundland	162,703	23.3	Mexico	2,757,418	28.2
Germany	119,107	17	Philippines	534,338	5.5
Italy	85,053	12.2	China	458,952	4.7
United Kingdom	61,813	8.8	Russia	433,427	4.4
1940s	**856,608**		**2000s**	**10,299,430**	
Canada and Newfoundland	160,911	18.8	Mexico	1,704,166	16.5
United Kingdom	131,794	15.4	China	649,294	6.3
Germany	119,506	14	India	590,464	5.7
Mexico	56,158	6.6	Philippines	545,463	5.3
1950s	**2,499,268**				
Germany	576,905	23.1			
Canada and Newfoundland	353,169	14.1			
Mexico	273,847	11			
United Kingdom	195,709	7.8			

Source: U.S. Department of Homeland Security, *2009 Yearbook of Immigration Statistics* (Washington, DC: Office of Immigration Statistics, 2010), http://www.dhs.gov/xlibrary/assets/statistics/yearbook/2009/ois_yb_2009.pdf, Tables 1 and 2.

Notes: Prior to 1919, the Russia category included immigrants from parts of today's Poland.

Recipients of legalization under the Immigration Reform and Control Act of 1986 appear as legal immigrants in the year in which they obtained legal permanent resident status. For most Immigration Reform and Control Act recipients, this occurred between 1989 and 1993.

China includes Hong Kong beginning in 1990.

national policies (if not the bias in the general public that inspired them). The national origin quota legislation, however, ensured that few potential Asian migrants would get visas. Also, during World War II, the United States and Mexico entered into a bilateral agreement to provide seasonal agricultural labor to the U.S. farmers and agricultural processors, called the ***Bracero* program**. This program far outlived the war. The *Bracero* program was arguably one of the foundations of large-scale unauthorized migration from Mexico in the final third of the twentieth century, in that it encouraged Mexican migrants to come to the United States for work. Although the program was discontinued in 1964, U.S. companies continued to seek cheap labor, and Mexican workers were willing to continue supplying it, even if doing so meant that both the companies and the workers violated U.S. law. The fact that the United States had to establish the *Bracero* program demonstrates the failure of immigration levels under the national origin quota system to meet the nation's growing labor needs.[15]

THE 1965 IMMIGRATION AND NATIONALITY AMENDMENTS

By 1965, the nation had outgrown the **nativism**—policies and social practices that limit the rights and social standing of newcomers in society based on the assumption that the newcomers are less worthy and less likely to adopt the values and practices of the established groups in society—that guided the enactment of the national origin quotas.[16] That alone might not have led to their replacement, yet as the *Bracero* program demonstrated, the economy dictated a change. After minimal debate, Congress established the foundation for today's immigration system. Although they are not often compared, the inclusive goals of the 1965 immigration legislation reflected some of the reformist impulses that shaped the Voting Rights Act of 1965 and the Civil Rights Act of 1964; in each case, the legislation sought to use the power of the federal government to enforce equal protection of the laws. (See Chapter 7.) This legislation diminished the importance of nationality—and consequently race—in determining who could and could not migrate to the United States.

The **Immigration and Nationality Act Amendments of 1965** established the foundation for today's immigration law. It recognized three paths to eligibility for immigration to permanent residence: close family in the United States, job skills or professional training needed in the U.S. economy or by specific U.S. employers, or being a **refugee** who cannot safely return to one's country of citizenship. The 1965 act also sought to reduce the national origin bias and to eliminate the national origin quotas that privileged migrants from Northwestern Europe in U.S. immigration law. It established annual limits of 20,000 migrants from any country, but exempted from these limits immediate relatives of U.S. citizens and, in some cases, permanent residents. The law established no limit on overall migration to the United States. At the time the bill passed, approximately 300,000 immigrants arrived annually in the United States as permanent residents; by the early twenty-first century, this number had grown to approximately one million annually. In the 1960s, approximately 65 percent of immigrant visas were based on family connections. This share has declined somewhat in the intervening years, though family-based visas continue to make up the majority of those issued.

Although it does not say so explicitly, the 1965 immigration act also created a large pool of people globally who would never be able to migrate to the United States: those without close relatives, job skills, or a recognized refugee status. It also tells some potential immigrants that although they will someday be eligible to migrate, they will have to wait many years to be awarded a visa (such as adult children of U.S. citizens and siblings of U.S. citizens, who have a very low priority under the 1965 law to immigrate and are subject to numerical limits on the numbers who can migrate from each country). For those who will never have eligibility to migrate, or for family members of U.S. citizens or permanent residents who will have to wait many years, there is an incentive to migrate anyway, as an unauthorized immigrant. At the time the 1965 act was passed, enforcement along the border was minimal and largely nonexistent in the nation's interior, laying the foundation for subsequent immigration controversies that would come to have an explicitly nativist and racial/ethnic dimension.

The Controversy of Unauthorized Migration Post-1965

In the years since the passage of the 1965 act, debates over immigration have primarily focused on unauthorized migration and the lengths to which the country should go to enforce immigration laws. Most recently, debates have also included questions over the numbers of legal immigrants who should be admitted annually and the skills they should have; the degree of access that immigrants to permanent residence should have to social welfare programs; and the standards for deportation of legal immigrants prior to naturalization. In the period since the passage of the 1965 immigration act, the overwhelming majority of immigrants are Latino and Asian American, so anti-immigrant rhetoric often introduces race into the immigration debate to tap native-stock fears of immigrant cultural difference (and immigrant potential to adopt American values) as a tool to motivate restrictionist policies. In this pattern, the contemporary era shares similarities with the period prior to the passage of the national origin quota laws.

Since 1965, Congress has sought to reduce the incentives to unauthorized migration in several ways. In 1986, as part of the **Immigration Reform and Control Act (IRCA),** Congress mandated that employers verify the work eligibility of all new employees within the first three days of employment and created legal penalties ("employer sanctions") for employers who knowingly hired unauthorized workers. It is for this reason that all new employees complete an I-9 form and present identification, including state-issued photo identification, to their employer. Ultimately, the easy availability of fraudulent identity documents undermined the effectiveness of this legislation.

In the early 1990s, Congress and the executive branch began to considerably expand enforcement efforts to control unauthorized immigration, initially along U.S. borders and, more recently, in the interior of the country, focusing particularly on work sites. These efforts, which began in 1993, have spurred a rapid growth in the size, training, and compensation of the border patrol, the construction of a seven-hundred-mile fence along part of the U.S. border with Mexico, and the use of advanced technologies (such as motion and heat detectors in the ground and aerial drones) to create a "virtual fence" along other parts of the border. The United States is also developing a database of employment records so as to target workplace raids; to deport unauthorized workers; and to

 Should the United States have erected a fence along its border with Mexico?

fine and, in some cases, imprison employers who knowingly hire unauthorized workers. The number of deportations has also steadily increased. During the first four years of the Obama presidency, the Department of Homeland Security deported an average of 400,000 foreign nationals annually, an increase of at least 10 percent over the previous record-high levels of the George W. Bush administration.[17]

Despite the dramatic increase in staffing, technology, and deportations over the past seventeen years, it is not possible to assess their effectiveness. Until the 2008 economic downturn, the number of unauthorized immigrants in the United States grew each year by as many as five hundred thousand. With the 2008 recession, unauthorized migration declined, but has slowly begun to rise again with the partial recovery of the U.S. economy. The post-2008 decline could represent evidence of success of the new enforcement regime or could instead reflect slowed new migration and some return migration (people returning to their home countries) in the face of economic difficulties in the United States. Better evidence of success of the vast expansion of border and interior enforcement policies will be available when the U.S. economy more fully recovers.

The Controversy of Immigration Levels Post-1965

Unauthorized migration has not been the only point of controversy in the 1965 act. Policymakers and the citizenry have been concerned by the overall levels of legal immigration, by the perception that legal immigrants are not contributing economically, by fears that legal immigrants are too hard to deport, and by the sense that some countries are largely excluded from contemporary migration because they have few recent migrants in the United States to seek family reunification visas. Congress has reformed aspects of the 1965 law to address all of these concerns, except for the issue of the overall number of legal immigrants; but the structure established in 1965 remains the law of the land.

In 1996 Congress eliminated the eligibility of some permanent residents for needs-based social welfare programs, such as food stamps and Medicaid, while allowing states to provide this access if they so choose. In this same period, Congress also sought to address concerns about the economic contributions of legal immigrants by increasing the income requirements for permanent residents and their sponsors. The sponsor is the U.S. citizen, permanent resident, or company that petitions for the immigrant visa. In the 1990s and after September 11, 2001, Congress also made it easier to deport nonnaturalized permanent residents and added to the crimes that resulted in deportation. The new crimes that made an immigrant subject to deportation included gang involvement and some misdemeanors. These policy changes reflect the ongoing concern that immigrants are less likely than their immigrant predecessors to become equal contributors to American society. There is often little social science–based evidence to support these concerns. Instead, the fear of difference—often racial/ethnic difference—is at the root of such insecurities.

After 9/11, Congress added to the background checks conducted prior to immigration and sped deportation for legal immigrants with suspected ties to terrorist organizations. In 1990, it also expanded the pool of immigrants eligible for legal immigration by creating a "diversity visa" lottery, to which potential immigrants from countries that have not been sending large numbers to the United States could apply. In 2012, 14.8 million people worldwide entered the lottery for the fifty-five thousand visas available annually through this program.[18] These new "diversity immigrants" expanded opportunities for Africans to migrate to the United States, but they also created opportunities for European migrants, who had not arrived in large numbers since the 1920s. Interestingly, here, Congress expanded the racial diversity of immigrants to the United States. Prior to the establishment of the diversity visa program, few potential

African migrants met the eligibility standards for immigration to the United States (having a close family member in the United States or having a needed job skill). As a result, most African nations had not sent many immigrants to the United States. In the years since its enactment, many more migrants from Africa have immigrated and create eligibility for their immediate family members to apply for permanent resident visas.

Recent changes in immigration law have not included an overall limit on annual levels of legal immigration. In 1990, at the same time it created the diversity visa lottery, Congress debated whether to pass an annual cap on legal immigration, but it rejected the proposal. Immigration caps have also appeared in some of the comprehensive immigration reform legislation (discussed later in the chapter). These proposals failed as a result of Congress's inability to craft an immigration compromise. When Congress does pass comprehensive immigration reform, it is likely that this range of immigration-related issues will supplement legislative efforts to control unauthorized migration as part of a new national immigration law that will replace the 1965 immigration and nationality law in whole or in large part.

U.S. IMMIGRANT INCORPORATION POLICIES

Despite the fact that throughout its history the United States has been "a nation of immigrants," there are relatively few formal policies to ensure that immigrants and their children make the transition from immigrant to equal citizen. These **incorporation policies** are considerably less debated than immigration policies. Also unlike immigration, naturalization is less measured. Until 1907, there was no centralized record of who naturalized as a U.S. citizen and no count of total number of immigrants who naturalized. Between 1907 and 2010, more than twenty-four million immigrants became new U.S. citizens. (See Figure 11.2.)

While immigration regulation has changed considerably over the past 225 years, U.S. rules for naturalization—the core of its incorporation policies—were established early in its history. Among the first acts of Congress was the passage of a naturalization law that set a pattern for those that would follow: a minimal residency requirement for those immigrants desired by the nation. In the case of the 1790 legislation, the residency requirement was set at two years, and naturalization was only available to White men. The period of residence was extended to five years in 1795, and this has remained largely unchanged since. Several new standards were added in 1795, such as "good moral character" and attachment to the principles of the U.S. Constitution. Although these standards have since been supplemented, the basic structure remains. In the early twentieth century, Congress required that naturalizing citizens demonstrate the ability to speak, read, and write English, and at midcentury, it required that naturalizing immigrants demonstrate a basic knowledge of U.S. history and civics. By midcentury, race was removed as a bar to naturalization.

Unlike in many other countries, the formal process of immigrant incorporation in the United States—naturalization—is only a concern for immigrants. The Fourteenth Amendment to the Constitution, drafted in large part to provide U.S. citizenship for former slaves, also provided for **birthright citizenship,** or the grant of U.S. citizenship to all persons born in the United States. At the time of its ratification, this provision was largely noncontroversial and reflected prevailing practice in the nation. In the years since immigrant

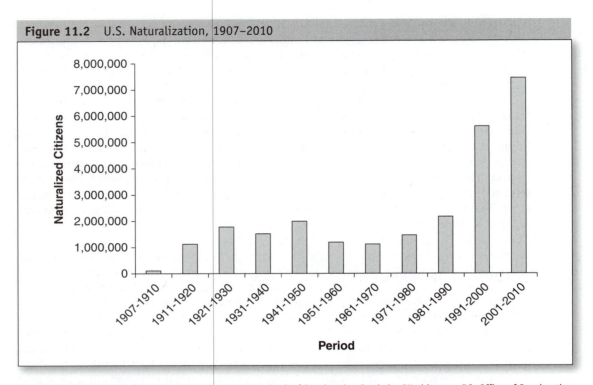

Figure 11.2   U.S. Naturalization, 1907–2010

Source: U.S. Department of Homeland Security, *2009 Yearbook of Immigration Statistics* (Washington, DC: Office of Immigration Statistics, 2010), http://www.dhs.gov/xlibrary/assets/statistics/yearbook/2009/ois_yb_2009.pdf, Table 20.

Notes: The U.S. government did not collect naturalization data before 1907. There are no comprehensive data on the number of naturalizing citizens between 1787 and 1906. Records for individuals who naturalized prior to 1907 are sometimes available from the states and cities where they naturalized.

regulation began and some newcomers arrived as unauthorized migrants, however, it has become more controversial, particularly for the U.S.-born children of unauthorized immigrants.[19] Whether intentional or not, birthright citizenship has sped the incorporation of immigrants' children and grandchildren in the United States and removed race as a barrier to citizenship for people born in the United States. While they have undoubtedly faced cultural and economic barriers to incorporation relative to the native stock, the children and grandchildren of immigrants—regardless of the immigration status of the immigrant ancestor—have not had to contest their right to participate in governance based on the status of the immigrant ancestor.

State and Societal Incorporation Policies

Immigrant incorporation, arguably, should be thought of more expansively than simply as a set of rules to allow for the legal transition from immigrant to citizen. Yet the United States has not established a formal incorporation system at the federal level, and instead has largely left it to the states and the society at large to handle. States have traditionally provided the most important resource to ensure that immigrants and their children make the transition to becoming Americans: public education. In fact, public primary education—the roots of today's public K–12 education—emerged in the 1820s and 1830s in part as a strategy to ensure that the children of immigrants were socialized into American values and civics. States have continued to absorb this responsibility for immigrant incorporation in the years since, and—as they frequently tell the federal government—the cost as well.

States also bear the primary responsibility for much of the incorporation that adult immigrants seek in the United States, including adult English language and civics classes, job retraining, and establishing licensing standards for different professions. While the federal government offers partial reimbursements to states for providing these services—particularly to refugees, for whom the federal government has traditionally taken a greater responsibility—the states largely determine what services are provided and which immigrants are eligible. Beginning in 1996, the federal government changed national social welfare policies and removed the requirement that legal permanent residents be eligible for needs-based social welfare programs, such as Medicaid, Temporary Aid to Needy Families, or Supplemental Security Income for the elderly poor, during their first five years of residence. States, however, had the authority to include recent immigrants as long as they would assume some of the costs.[20]

The private and philanthropic sectors, community-based organizations, and trade unions have also assumed responsibilities for ensuring the incorporation of immigrants. These efforts have historically included job training and retraining, capacity-building, social service provision, and leadership training.[21] Such efforts have ebbed and flowed over time, but they have become an increasing focus of philanthropy in recent years, as the number of immigrants in the United States has grown. The philanthropic sector also responds in periods when immigrants organize to make demands on the society. In periods of high demand for naturalization, for example, community-based organizations are on the front lines providing classes, form assistance, legal representation, and sometimes even loans to help immigrants prepare for naturalization and to pay the application fees. A few cities, such as New York, provide some naturalization assistance, but the vast majority are delivered by community organizations relying on philanthropic support.

The Incorporation of Unauthorized Immigrants

A final component of immigrant incorporation is traditionally discussed more as immigration policy than in terms of immigrant incorporation policy, but we see it more as the latter. When the nation began to recognize some potential immigrants as eligible to immigrate and others not, it created a new category of immigrant: the "unauthorized" immigrant. Over time, Congress has created the opportunity for some unauthorized immigrants to become legal permanent residents (and eventually, through a separate application, to become U.S. citizens). Congress has extended this opportunity to legalize one's immigration status to long-term unauthorized residents of the United States—arguably immigrants who have begun to make the connections to the United States that the nation expects of its newest members. For this reason, we see legalization programs as part of the nation's immigrant incorporation policies.

TIME TO GET SERIOUS ON THE IMMIGRATION ISSUE !!

DAVE GRANLUND © www.davegranlund.com

Courtesy of Cagle Cartoons

The number of unauthorized immigrants began to grow dramatically in the 1920s, with the passage of the national origin quota laws. Interestingly, soon after the number of unauthorized immigrants grew, Congress passed legislation to regularize the status of this population (to "legalize" them, in the contemporary usage). The first large-scale legalization plan was enacted in 1929 and provided the opportunity to move into permanent resident status for immigrants who could prove that they had been resident without legal status in the United States since 1921. The year of migration for long-term unauthorized immigrants has been updated several times. Under current law, unauthorized immigrants who have been resident in the United States since 1972 can become legal permanent residents. The year of eligibility was last updated in 1986.

As part of the 1986 Immigration Reform and Control Act, Congress created a less direct path to legal status for immigrants who had shorter periods of unauthorized residence. Unauthorized immigrants who had been resident in the United States since 1981 could apply for a temporary legal status that could be made permanent after an additional eighteen months and after the formerly unauthorized immigrants demonstrated knowledge of U.S. history, civics, and English. Alternatively, they could also meet the last requirement if they could prove that they were taking classes to develop this knowledge. IRCA also established a legalization program for agricultural workers with shorter periods of unauthorized residence.

Approximately two million long-term unauthorized immigrants legalized under the provisions of IRCA. An additional one million agricultural workers legalized under the program that required shorter periods of unauthorized residence. While many have criticized the employer sanctions provisions of IRCA, the legalization programs were implemented very successfully. The number of applicants was larger than expected, and the immigration bureaucracy was able to respond successfully to this demand. Most immigrants who legalized under IRCA had achieved permanent status by 1992. A study conducted in 2009 found that 53 percent of those had naturalized as U.S. citizens by 2009. The share who had naturalized was somewhat lower—34 percent—for unauthorized immigrants who had legalized after shorter periods of residence based on their labor in agriculture or agricultural processing.[22] Arguably, these programs were very successful, as they allowed immigrants to incorporate more fully into U.S. society and allowed greater protections for their U.S. citizen and permanent resident family members.

Naturalization Policy and Outcomes in the Contemporary Era

Considering the major debates surrounding immigration policy in the United States, naturalization is largely taken for granted by policymakers. Many assume, incorrectly, that all immigrants naturalize soon after they become eligible. On the contrary, a large share of eligible immigrants never naturalize. What perhaps should be understood by policymakers is that many eligible immigrants seek naturalization in some tangible way, but are unable to complete its bureaucratic requirements.

The absolute number of citizenship-eligible, nonnaturalized immigrants is not known. The best estimates are that 7.9 million citizenship-eligible permanent residents resided in the United States in 2009.[23] Although the exact numbers change each year, approximately 740,000 immigrants naturalized each year in the first decade of the twenty-first century. The citizenship-eligible population, however, increases by as many as 1 million each year as permanent residents achieve the statutory minimum residence for naturalization, so the number of citizenship-eligible immigrants will increase over time.

Why do some immigrants naturalize and others do not? The most obvious explanation is probably the least likely one. Many assume that immigrants do not naturalize simply because they don't want to be U.S. citizens. Survey evidence suggests that this is not the case. Most permanent residents and, of particular importance, most permanent residents with five years of residence in the United States indicate that they desire U.S. citizenship, and a large share have made concrete steps to naturalize.[24] Surveys of Latinos show that significant majorities of citizenship-eligible immigrants intend someday to naturalize. Many who have not completed the naturalization application process are either in the process of formally applying for U.S. citizenship or have done something concrete to naturalize, such as taking classes to prepare for the civics, history, or English exams, or obtaining the naturalization application form.[25] The United States does not promote naturalization among citizenship-eligible immigrants. (See Box 11.2.)

The potential applicants who succeed in their pursuit of citizenship generally have higher income levels and higher levels of education. Income and education provide immigrants with the resources to naturalize (the application costs $595 and applicants are required to pay an additional $85 for biometrics [fingerprints]), as well as increasing the odds that applicants will have the coping skills necessary to negotiate the lengthy application bureaucracy. Immigrants seeking citizenship are also advantaged if they have longer periods of residence in the United States and are older. These applicants are exempt from the English reading, speaking, and writing requirement, and they can take the civics and history exam in their native language. Eligible immigrants are more likely to naturalize if they migrated from an English-speaking country or were exposed to English-language media before they migrated. Those from Asia generally naturalize more rapidly than immigrants from the Americas and the Caribbean. Finally, one factor seems to consistently disadvantage eligible immigrants from moving toward U.S. citizenship—proximity to the United States. Controlling for other factors, immigrants from Mexico and Canada are less likely than immigrants from other countries to naturalize as U.S. citizens.[28]

> Should naturalization be reformed to ensure more equitable outcomes among immigrants eligible for and interested in becoming U.S. citizens? How?

BOX 11.2 ROAD SIGN

U.S. Promotion of Naturalization

The barriers to naturalization for immigrants to the United States have traditionally been lower than for other advanced democracies. While the United States has historically barred some immigrants from naturalizing, for those who are eligible, naturalization is popularly understood to occur soon after immigration. Today, immigrants to permanent residence can naturalize after five years of U.S. residence. They must complete a lengthy application form; pass a background check; pay a fee of $680 ($595 as an application fee and $85 for "biometrics" used in the background check of all applicants); and demonstrate knowledge in two areas: U.S. history/civics and the ability to read, write, and speak English. The language requirements are waived for older applicants who have resided in the United States for more than fifteen years.

Not all eligible immigrants naturalize. As this chapter discusses, the available evidence suggests that most naturalization-eligible immigrants who have not naturalized see their futures in the United States and want to naturalize eventually. Some are confused as to how to proceed, or how to prepare for naturalization. Should the United States do more to encourage naturalization among the eligible?

Through most of its history, the United States has seen naturalization as an individual decision. It provides some support for the production of citizenship texts and for localities to offer adult education classes to prepare immigrants for the citizenship exam. In recent years, it has also made small grants to immigrant-serving, community-based organizations to allow them to offer direct citizenship training and assistance. With very narrow exceptions, particularly among active-duty military and during a short window in the 1990s, it has not promoted naturalization directly among eligible immigrants.

Canada offers an alternative model.[26] Like the United States, Canada receives a large number of immigrants annually relative to its population and has relatively low barriers to naturalization. Yet, overall, it has higher rates of naturalization among its immigrants. Among the possible explanations for this difference in outcomes is that Canada informs immigrants when they become eligible to naturalize and provides training for the exam directly to immigrants; also, it allows Canadian-born citizens to go through the naturalization process with immigrants to create a shared experience of being Canadian.

Should the United States follow the Canadian model and more actively promote naturalization? History offers a lesson as to why the United States is less encouraging. In the mid-1990s, the Clinton administration moved to change the long-standing policy and more actively promote naturalization. Congressional Republicans (President Bill Clinton was a Democrat) immediately challenged these efforts and asserted that the president was using government resources to build the pool of future Democrats. After much investigation, there was no evidence found to support these allegations; in fact, evidence showed that naturalization promotion reached out to immigrants just as likely to become Republicans as Democrats.[27] The charges and investigations, however, had the desired effect. The Clinton administration backed away from active naturalization promotion, and no subsequent president has sought to change this policy. Arguably, the United States pays a price for inaction; many immigrants eligible for U.S. citizenship fail to apply due to lack of knowledge about how to proceed or inaccurate understanding of the potential consequences of applying and not receiving U.S. citizenship. The pool of naturalization-eligible immigrants has steadily grown since the mid-1990s and will continue to for the foreseeable future.

IMMIGRATION REFORM IN THE UNITED STATES TODAY

As we indicated at the beginning of this chapter, as important as immigration is to the ongoing development of the United States, it is a highly contentious policy. The United States is again at a point in its national development where many in the country are profoundly dissatisfied with immigration policies and, to a much lesser degree, with immigrant incorporation policies. Race and the perception of large-scale cultural change driven by immigration at current levels is one factor, but certainly not the only factor, that drives this mass (and elite) dissatisfaction. Evidence of this dissatisfaction can be seen in the fact that some have joined informal militias to defend the border—such as members of the Minuteman Civil Defense Corps who "defended" the U.S.-Mexican border in areas where the U.S. Border Patrol was not present—and others have joined mass protests over specific policies—such as the approximately five million immigrant rights marchers who protested in 2006 in cities across the country. Immigration has shaped national and local elections as recently as 2012 and will likely do so again in 2016. States such as Arizona have passed laws that arguably usurp federal prerogatives to make and enforce immigration law. Arizona SB 1070 made it a state crime for immigrants to be in the United States without evidence that they were in the nation legally, and it gave state police the authority to enforce this law. Opponents countered that immigration law is a federal, not state, responsibility, and that such a law would encourage racial profiling (the disproportionate identification of some racial groups—Latinos in this case) for enforcement, whether they were unauthorized immigrants or not. The Supreme Court held much of the law to be unconstitutional, but this heightened level of national concern reflected in SB 1070 and the other manifestations of mass interest in immigration policy demonstrate a widespread demand for change, but not necessarily an agreement on what must be done.

Public opinion is mixed on immigration reform. The loudest popular voices on immigration generally support restrictions and added enforcement to control unauthorized migration. Most people in the United States do not rank immigration among the most important issues that the nation faces, and employers are increasingly vocal in their complaints that they cannot find sufficient workers in the domestic labor force. In Latino and, to a lesser degree, Asian American communities, demands for immigration reform—including a path to legalization for many of the nearly twelve million unauthorized immigrants in the United States—have been central to community politics since 2006. In that year, immigrant rights protests included as many as five million people, who marched in more than 150 cities.[29]

Congress has engaged in an extended debate on immigration policies several times since 2005, but it has failed to pass a **comprehensive immigration reform** bill.[30] (See Box 11.3.) In the discussion that follows, we highlight the likely components of such a bill—a reform that will serve as the foundation for the next generation of immigration and immigrant incorporation policies in the United States. As will be evident, this reform will require compromises that will be uncomfortable for many in U.S. society and Congress, for reasons detailed below. Only with compromises such as these, however, will the nation be able to craft a new set of policies that will build on or replace the framework established in 1965.

Any new immigration legislation will have to serve the needs of the labor market. Arguably, this has been the primary purpose of U.S. immigration policy since the nation's first days. In comparison to other countries, the United States has a low number of people relative to its large land mass, so it has always been population-short and has attempted to overcome this deficit by selectively encouraging immigration.[31] Employers will seek to ensure that they have access not just to skilled workers, but also to low-skilled workers who work in jobs that native-stock workers are less likely to accept, such as service-sector jobs or work in agriculture and light industry. Employers and their congressional advocates will seek to ensure that more immigrants can migrate and that these opportunities extend to low-skilled as well as skilled workers. This perceived need for labor—both skilled and unskilled—is not necessarily shared by many workers in society. Immigrant workers can, but do not always, compete with native-stock workers, and they have the potential to lower wage rates in sectors of the economy where immigrant and native-stock workers compete. Much of contemporary low-skilled immigrant labor, however, does not directly compete with the labor of native-stock workers.

Many perceive that the 1965 act does not provide enough visas to skilled workers, and that Congress will be pressured to expand the number of immigration visas available to skilled workers and their families. These new immigration opportunities could be provided over and above the number of visas currently being offered, meaning an overall increase in immigration could come at the expense of family-preference immigration opportunities. At the same time, it might be easy to suggest that the nation should prefer skilled workers over family members of U.S. citizens and permanent residents, who tend to be less skilled, but employers argue that immigration law must account for their needs for low-skilled workers. Opposition to immigration eligibility based on family connections has a racial dimension in contemporary U.S. society; approximately 80 percent of contemporary immigrants are Latino or Asian American. It is these recent immigrants who would most likely have immediate family members abroad and be able to petition for their immigration to permanent residence.

To meet employer needs for these workers, employers will advocate for additional guest worker programs in any comprehensive reform of immigration. The nation already has many guest workers (as many as 2.8 million annually), but these are all limited to specific industries—agriculture/agricultural processing, high technology, seasonal entertainment/recreation, and child care. As part of a comprehensive reform, employers will seek a labor market–wide guest worker program that would allow guest workers to move from job to job throughout the economy for a set period of time (often three years, renewable once) before having to return to their country of origin. This would reduce the overall costs of employing these types of workers; guest workers would likely work for lower wages than native-stock workers, and would be more dependent on making the employer happy in order to maintain their job and their ability to work in the United States legally.

Public Concerns with Immigration Reform

The need for labor, however, is not the aspect of the 1965 immigration bill that most angers the general public. Nor, at least at present, is the overall level of immigration to the United States. Instead, unauthorized immigration shapes popular perceptions of the perceived failure of U.S. immigration policy. The border militias are just one manifestation of popular anger over unauthorized migration. Any immigration reform, particularly any reform that

BOX 11.3 ROAD SIGN

Comprehensive Immigration Reform in Congress and the Growth of the National Democratic Majority

The results of the 2012 election were a wakeup call for many Republican leaders. Many—including their presidential candidate, Governor Mitt Romney of Massachusetts—expected a close election and, perhaps, a Republican presidential victory. Instead, President Obama won a solid victory in the popular vote and state-level victories in all but one of the competitive "battleground" states, leading to a sizeable majority in the Electoral College. The magnitude of this Democratic victory (as well as the party's ability to hold onto a majority in the U.S. Senate) was attributed by many to a growth in the number of minority voters and the increasing share of their votes for the Democrats. One of the key issues that drove minority—particularly Latino and Asian American—voters to the Democrats was the perception that Democrats took positions on immigration policy closer to those of minority communities.

After the election, the Speaker of the House, Republican John Boehner, seemed to acknowledge this reality and the desire of establishment Republicans to reverse the trend. Two days after the election, he told the national media: "This issue [immigration reform] has been around far too long. A comprehensive approach is long overdue, and I'm confident that the president, myself, and others can find the common ground to take care of this issue once and for all." Many saw this as the beginning of the end of the debate over comprehensive immigration reform, with the likelihood of a quick compromise being reached that would include a path to legalization for many of the nation's unauthorized immigrants.

In times of more normal politics, this would have been a safe prediction. The nation's leading Democrat (the president) and leading Republican (the Speaker) seemed to be on a similar page and each for his own reasons was willing to compromise. To some degree, expectations for a compromise were realized in the summer of 2013, when the Senate passed a comprehensive immigration reform bill with the votes of fourteen Republicans. Expectations for a congressional compromise, however, didn't account for the weak level of control the Speaker had over his caucus (the Republicans in the House of Representatives) and the absolute opposition of Tea Party Republicans to any reform that included a path to legalization for unauthorized immigrants. The intransigence of between sixty and one hundred Republican members of the House has prevented consideration of this Senate bill or of a House-drafted comprehensive bill that might more closely reflect the positions of House members interested is passing immigration legislation. Speaker Boehner has several times sought to move forward on immigration reform, only to reverse himself when he saw the depth of opposition in his caucus.

Speaker Boehner does have another option. He could bring a bill to the floor—perhaps the bill passed by the U.S. Senate—and let it pass primarily with Democratic votes. He has done this several times in his Speakership, including with important legislation such as the bill to allow an increase in the federal government's debt limit. Were Boehner to follow this path on immigration, he would enrage his caucus and, perhaps, end his Speakership. He would quite likely also do his party a great favor. By diminishing the importance of immigration as a policy issue in the 2016 election, he would increase the Republicans' odds of winning the presidency and, perhaps, taking majority control of the U.S. Senate. As long as immigration reform remains unresolved, minority voters will become more Democratic and will be more highly motivated to turn out and vote.

includes new routes to legal immigration, will need to convince the public that the United States has designed a system to prevent or drastically reduce future unauthorized migration. As we have discussed, the nation has invested a great deal over the past twenty years to increase border enforcement, to increase staff of Immigration and Customs Enforcement, and to routinize interior enforcement. To date, these new investments have not proven that they successfully deter new unauthorized immigration, particularly when the U.S. economy is strong and U.S. employers are seeking new workers. New technologies are probably available to reduce the likelihood of new unauthorized migration, but these might limit the freedoms of U.S. citizens and hence would be highly controversial. Most obvious of these would be a counterfeit-proof national identification card that citizens and immigrants with legal status would need to provide to government authorities and, potentially, to employers and health care providers. Whether this is the appropriate solution or not, it seems unlikely that comprehensive immigration reform will be possible without added guarantees that new unauthorized migration will slow considerably or stop entirely.

The general public is also suspicious of guest worker programs. Some express concern that guest workers will compete with native-stock workers for jobs. Others fear that guest workers will be exploited and will lower the standard of treatment of workers generally or weaken the ability of trade unions to organize. Finally, many worry that guest workers will not willingly leave the country at the end of their contracts and will become the next generation of unauthorized immigrants. Based on the experiences of previous guest worker programs in the United States and Europe, these assessments are well grounded. Guest workers will also likely be racially distinct from the native population, adding to the perception that immigration is leading to massive cultural and racial change.

Immigrant and ethnic interests will also need to be addressed as part of comprehensive immigration reform. Immigrant communities and their U.S.-born co-ethnics are closest to the immigration experience. Hence, immigration and immigrant incorporation are more salient for Latinos and Asian Americans than they are for many others in U.S. society. That alone does not give them a voice were the rest of the country to be allied against their interests (which we do not believe is the case). As a practical matter, the votes of Latinos, Asian Americans, and African Americans will be crucial to the success or failure of comprehensive immigration reform in Congress. Later in the chapter, we will return to the question of how unified these communities' interests are on immigration.[32]

For immigrant and ethnic communities, fair treatment of immigrants is the central issue. A plan for legalization of unauthorized immigrants already resident in the United States tops their goals for immigration reform. Immigrant and ethnic communities express concern about how guest workers will be treated and question the fairness of a system that uses people's labors, but doesn't offer them the rights or citizenship or many protections in labor law. They will likely be even more opposed than the population as a whole to any national guest worker program that does not allow for a transition to permanent resident status at the end of the guest worker period. Finally, and contrary to the assertions often made by opponents of immigration at current levels, immigrant ethnic communities do *not* advocate for an expansion of overall immigration. Many, however, do seek to be able to allow their relatives to immigrate. Consequently, they will be cautious about any significant change to the current balance in the immigration system between skilled migrants and family-preference migrants.

Like other areas of policy in the United States, some actors have louder voices in immigration reform debates than others. The agriculture and agricultural processing sectors, for example, often ensure that their needs are met before those of other employers. Comprehensive immigration reform will probably include some special benefits for agricultural employers—such as additional targeted guest worker programs and reduced enforcement—more than those for employers in general. Cuban Americans have tended to be treated more generously by immigration laws and policies since the early 1960s than have other groups (see Chapter 4), and this too would likely continue under a new immigration structure. Refugee policy, which has largely been left to the U.S. State Department as a tool of foreign policy, might become more regulated (limited and managed by Congress rather than the State Department) as part of a new reform.

Although the exact contours of a new or significantly revised U.S. immigration policy cannot be predicted, it is safe to say that all interests will have to make significant compromises for reform to occur. Until then, the current structure and the large numbers of unauthorized immigrants that it encourages will be a part of the nation's fabric. Despite the high levels of public anger spurred by the current system, it is important to note that the status quo serves many, particularly employers in certain sectors who need a steady supply of low-skilled/low-wage workers who do not require extensive training, and immigrant families seeking to live with family members who cannot migrate legally. Having so many people outside of the protections of the U.S. government, however, raises long-term concerns about how well they and their children can be integrated into the American mainstream.[33]

Reform Efforts and Immigrant Incorporation

In congressional debates over comprehensive immigration reform from 2007 to 2014, immigrant incorporation policies have rarely been discussed. One proposal would have reduced the waiting period for naturalization to four years for immigrants with college educations. Implicit in the debates, however, was what could potentially have been a major incentive for large-scale immigrant incorporation. Any legalization proposal would have required that legalizing immigrants demonstrate both English language skills and knowledge of U.S. history and civics. The debates never reached the stage where the specific expectations were set—for example, whether taking classes to learn English, history, and civics would be sufficient, or whether legalizing immigrants would have to pass a test on these subjects. Should comprehensive immigration reform pass Congress and some of today's 11.7 million unauthorized immigrants become eligible for legalization, the legislation would spur unprecedented demand for states and localities to increase the classes that they offer and would encourage community-based organizations to increase their resources to help immigrants prepare for government forms and tests. (See Box 11.4 for student efforts in support of immigration reform.)

Despite the very contentious debates over immigration policy, immigrant settlement policy is largely not debated at the national level (nor, for the most part, in the states). Some polemicists assert that immigrants are not incorporating or that they are seeking to change the political or cultural makeup of the nation,[34] but their evidence often doesn't stand up to scholarly tests.[35] More important, while the native stock may express some concerns about the effects of immigration generally on the United States, the majority indicate that they believe that immigrants contribute to U.S. society and are joining the cultural and political mainstream. (See Table 11.2.) Thus their concerns about migration do not extend to legal immigrants. Although the numbers vary somewhat based on the polling source, the majority of Americans generally favor providing legalization to unauthorized immigrants as part of a comprehensive immigration reform.[36]

Americans are somewhat more divided on an increasingly debated aspect of immigrant incorporation. Concerns about unauthorized migration have spurred many to seek a change in the birthright citizenship provisions of the Fourteenth Amendment. Changing

Table 11.2   U.S. Attitudes toward Immigration and Immigrants

"In your view, should immigration be kept at its present level, increased, or decreased?" [2000, 2005, and 2010]

	2000	2005	2010
Increased	13%	16%	17%
Maintained at present levels	41%	34%	34%
Decreased	38%	46%	45%

"Do you think that the number of LEGAL immigrants from foreign countries who are permitted to come to the United States to live should be increased, decreased, or left the same as it is now?" [2010]

	Increased	Decreased	Left the Same
All	17%	35%	47%
Hispanics	25%	16%	57%

"On the whole, do you think immigration is a good thing or a bad thing for this country today?" [2003, 2006, 2008, and 2010]

	2003	2006	2008	2010
Good thing	58%	67%	64%	57%
Bad thing	36%	28%	30%	36%

"Which of these statements comes closer to you own views—even if neither is exactly right? Immigrants today strengthen our country because of their hard work and talents, or immigrants today are a burden on our country because they take jobs, housing, and health care?" [2010, General Population and Latinos]

	2010 General population	2010 Latinos
Strengthen country	44%	78%
Burden on country	42%	13%

Sources: Lymari Morales, "Amid Immigration Debate, Americans' Views Ease Slightly," Washington, DC: Gallup Poll, AP-GfK Poll. 2010. AP-GfK Roper Public Affairs and Media Poll May 7–11, 2010; AP-Univision Poll. 2010. AP-GfK Roper Public Affairs and Media Poll May 7–11. Mark Hugo Lopez, Rich Morin, and Paul Taylor, *Illegal Immigration Backlash Worries, Divides Latinos* (Washington, DC: Pew Hispanic Center, 2010).

this provision would likely require a constitutional amendment, though some argue that it can be done through legislation. Constitutional amendments are rare in the United States because they require support from two-thirds of the members of both houses of Congress and ratification by three-quarters of the states (or through a constitutional convention). Americans are nearly equally divided on whether the Constitution should be amended to eliminate birthright citizenship.[37]

One aspect of immigrant behaviors that has changed in recent years concerns some critics, but may ultimately speed the process of incorporation. Today's immigrants are able to engage with the lives of their family members abroad, the civic life of their home communities, and in some cases the politics of their home countries in a way that few immigrants could in the past. This transnational engagement is not fundamentally new. Immigrants have always wanted to maintain these ties, but until relatively recently, few have been able to do so. What is new is the share of immigrants who are able to take part in such activities. We discuss this phenomenon more thoroughly in Chapter 12, but here we want to indicate that the available evidence indicates that the transnationally engaged are no less likely to become civically and politically incorporated and may, in fact, be sped in this process by their transnational engagement.[38]

BOX 11.4 COALITIONS IN ACTION

Strange Bedfellows for Comprehensive Immigration Reform

Comprehensive immigration reform has spurred previously unseen coalitions in American politics. Perhaps most notably, organized labor has worked with the Chamber of Commerce (which represents employers) to craft a compromise that both can accept on the expansion of the number of guest workers in the U.S. economy. Recognizing the changing composition of the American workforce, particularly in the service and light industrial sectors of the economy that have relatively high levels of unionization, organized labor has also become a strong advocate of legislation for unauthorized immigrants in U.S. society. In the past, organized labor feared the labor competition that would come from newly legalized workers.

Ultimately, though, the success and inclusiveness of comprehensive immigration reform will result from the demands of immigrant-ethnic communities, particularly Latinos and Asian Americans, for policies that are fair to all in U.S. society. Republicans and Democrats could have easily settled their differences over most aspects of immigration policy and passed new legislation that would have built on and partially replaced the 1965 immigration law. So far, one element of comprehensive immigration reform has prevented compromise—a path to legal status for many of the 11.7 million unauthorized immigrants in the United States. Here, minority leaders and minority voters spoke with near-unanimity and ensured that Democrats would not compromise. Nor, for that matter, have Tea Party Republicans, leading to the current immigration stalemate. When viewed from the perspective of previous immigration debates, this outcome—though not in the nation's long-term interests—suggests a new and important role for Latino, Asian American, and African American communities on issues of central importance to them.

Among the most vocal advocates of comprehensive immigration reform are young adult unauthorized immigrants who came to the United States as children. Early versions of immigration reform legislation created a special legalization path for these immigrants, the so-called DREAMers.

ASSOCIATED PRESS

Minority Communities and Minority Coalitions in the Immigration Reform Debate

The debates over reforming immigration policy are of greater importance in Latino and Asian American communities than for African Americans or Native Americans. It is perhaps a truism in American politics that Native Americans have been most disadvantaged by migration to the United States. In the current era, Native American leaders do not engage in debates over U.S. immigration policy except to the degree that it directly affects tribal lands, such as reservations that cross the U.S.-Mexico or U.S.-Canada borders.

The African American community, though grounded in migration, has also paid a price for the long-term policy to encourage migration. To explain these costs, it is necessary to briefly discuss the economic effects of migration on the United States. Although there are extensive debates about the short-term economic costs of migration, economists largely agree that in the long term, migration has been a considerable economic benefit to the country. Migrants have traditionally offered the people, the labor, the ingenuity, and the creativity that have allowed the United States to grow into the North American continent and to tap its resources to become a world power. In the short term, however, immigrants offer competition for domestic workers to the degree that they work in the same sectors of the economy. The presence of large numbers of low-skilled immigrants who are frequently willing to work for lower wages, who expect less of their employers, and who seek fewer services from and make lesser demands on government reduce the pressures on society to improve conditions for the least advantaged of the native-stock populations. African Americans have often been the group in U.S. society that would be most advantaged by lower levels of immigration (in the twentieth century, they were joined by Puerto Ricans and Mexican Americans). Without a large pool of immigrants, employers would have greater incentives to train and reward domestic workers, as well as to invest in new labor-saving technologies that would reduce demands for labor.

What principles should guide Congress in its efforts at comprehensive immigration reform? What compromises need to be made in order to implement these principles?

Despite the relatively higher costs paid by African American communities and others to support national policies that encourage large-scale migration, it is important to note that U.S. residents, including African Americans, see immigrants as an asset to U.S. society. (See Table 11.2.) African American leaders and organizations such as the National Association for the Advancement of Colored People (NAACP) have also seen immigrants and immigration more broadly through a separate lens—that of civil rights. The premise of the Civil Rights Movement—that government has a fundamental responsibility to ensure equal protections of the law—is understood by many in the African American community to extend to immigrants as well as to native-stock citizens. Equally important, African American civil rights leaders and organizations have generally understood immigration policies and the rights of immigrants as civil rights and, hence, as broadly a part of the agenda of the African American community. This understanding is undoubtedly enhanced by the fact that African and Afro-Caribbean immigrants are steadily making up a larger share of the immigrant population (making up approximately 13.1 percent of immigrants between 2000 and 2009),[39] but it also reflects a broader recognition by African Americans of the need to protect the rights of the disadvantaged in U.S. society.

Latinos and Asian Americans are also more likely than nonminority U.S. populations to recognize the contributions of immigrants to U.S. society and to support policies that ensure the incorporation of immigrants. It is important to note, however, that their greater support for immigrant rights and immigrant incorporation does not mean that minority communities advocate an expansion in immigration. Like most Americans, Blacks, Latinos, and Asian Americans advocate either maintaining immigration at current levels or reducing overall immigration; less than 20 percent advocate an increase in immigration.

Where minority communities differ from Whites, and where they see the foundation for cross-group alliance, is in policies that ensure that immigrants are able to incorporate into U.S. society. These include policies that allow for education, including adult education, to be available to immigrants; for professional licenses earned abroad to be recognized in the United States; for immigrants (particularly immigrants to permanent residence) to be eligible for participation in U.S. social welfare benefit programs; and for long-term unauthorized residents to be able to earn legal status. Although support for these immigrant incorporation policies is not universal in minority communities, it is more likely to come from Latinos, Asian Americans, and African Americans than from non-Hispanic Whites. As such, these minority communities offer one pillar for minority politics in the United States.

CONCLUSION: A TURNING POINT FOR U.S. IMMIGRATION POLICY

President Obama observed that the United States is "a place of refuge and freedom for, in Thomas Jefferson's words, 'oppressed humanity,'" but that it has often not lived up to these goals. This failure to ensure the incorporation of immigrants has spawned several of the uneven roads that are the focus of this book. We are at another of these turning points in American politics today. If we fail to ensure that today's immigrants—legal and unauthorized, and, more important, their children—incorporate into the polity and into the society, the nation will face generations of steadily more diverging roads and, ultimately, a dual society in which the roads never cross. If, on the other hand, the United States continues as it has with many immigrants—particularly White immigrants—in the past and creates incentives to ensure that immigrants are able to become part of the nation's civic life and economic vitality, immigrant status will simply be the local lane that will eventually merge with the main highway.

As Congress debates changes to immigration policy, it will set the foundation for the nation's ethnic composition for the rest of the twenty-first century. Changes currently being debated in Congress could ultimately reduce migration from some countries that sent large numbers of immigrants in the twentieth century (Mexico, in particular), but extend new opportunities for Latin American, Asian, and African migration that will add to the nation's racial and ethnic diversity.

Increasingly, then, immigration and immigrant incorporation will be issues of shared interest in Asian American, Latino, and African American communities, and of greater interest in these communities than in the non-Hispanic White community (where, it should be noted, there will also be new immigrants). Clearly, race is playing a different role in the current wave of immigration reform than it has in the past. The fear of immigrant-driven cultural change is certainly part of the debate, as it has been in the past, and a central aspect of the opposition to legalization of unauthorized immigrants as part of comprehensive immigration reform legislation. Unlike previous eras when Congress debated major changes to immigration policy, however, racial and ethnic minorities have a legislative voice and vote in large numbers. Their presence in Congress and in the electorate ensures that their interests must be a part of whatever compromise is ultimately reached.

As Congress undertakes this process of reform, however, it should be attentive to the concerns about immigrant incorporation raised by President Obama and assumed by President Washington. Through much of the nation's history, incorporation could safely be predicted as the likely outcome for most, and the costs to the country of those who were denied incorporation—who were put on the path of uneven roads—were not of concern to policymakers or to voters. In today's more diverse United States, immigration that leads to multigenerational uneven roads comes at far too high a risk, and one that will be disproportionately felt in minority communities.

DISCUSSION QUESTIONS

1. How do the three categories of immigrants—legal permanent residents, guest workers, and unauthorized immigrants—contribute to the shaping of support and opposition to U.S. immigration policy?

2. Consider the increasing restrictions and prohibitions on immigration in the late 1880s to 1965, and the data displayed in Table 11.1 on the largest immigrant nationalities by decade. How effectively did the restrictions enacted in this period contribute to the maintenance of a White-dominant society up to the 1960s? In what ways might these restrictions have encouraged the creation of a unified White identity versus various White ethnic identities?

3. What are the most notable similarities and differences between pre- and post-1965 immigration concerns? What distinctions can be made in comparing the motivations for these concerns?

4. Lacking a formal federal incorporation system, most of the responsibility for immigrant incorporation falls to the state and society. Should there be a formal federal system? If so, what should it address, and how should it steer state policies to encourage immigrant incorporation?

5. Today there exists a divergence between economic and mass interests on immigration policy. Does the racial and ethnic diversification of the electorate change this equation? If so, how? Will this be a permanent change?

KEY TERMS

birthright citizenship (p. 341)

Bracero program (p. 337)

comprehensive immigration reform (p. 347)

guest workers (p. 331)

Immigration and Nationality Act Amendments of 1965 (p. 338)

Immigration Reform and Control Act (ICRA) (p. 339)

incorporation policies (p. 341)

legal permanent residents (p. 331)

national origin quotas (p. 335)

nativism (p. 338)

naturalization (p. 334)

refugee (p. 338)

unauthorized immigrants (p. 332)

visa (p. 335)

12 Diasporic Politics and Foreign Affairs

We also value the contribution you [Indian Americans in the United States] have been making to India's progress and modernization. . . . Let me take this opportunity to extend an invitation to all Indian Americans and non-resident Indians who wish to return home to India in one capacity or another. You no longer have to make a choice between here and there. Modern technology and our flexible policies have opened possibilities of working in both places. . . . I hope you will be the bridge that will continue to connect our two nations and societies.

—Manmohan Singh (Prime Minister of India, 2004–2014)[1]

In our discussion so far, we have consciously conflated **immigrant** and ethnic communities with the term **immigrant-ethnic** to reflect our assessment that immigrants from a country or region and their U.S.-born co-ethnics often share many experiences in U.S. politics. We also discussed in Chapter 9 how these two populations are more similar to each other in terms of their political attitudes and behaviors than they are to the non-Hispanic White population. Here, however, we delve more deeply into what distinguishes immigrants from their U.S.-born co-ethnics as we explore immigrants' ties to their countries of origin (**diasporic politics**) and how these ties have the power to influence politics on both their native and adopted soils.

Immigrants have much stronger ties to their countries of origin and are more likely to act on those ties than are their U.S.-born descendants, the second and beyond generations (the population that we call "ethnic"). In this case, race and ethnicity matter less than the length of time individuals or their families have been in the United States. As a result, our discussion of diasporic politics—the politics of migrant populations relative to their country of origin, toward their country of destination, and toward ethnic/national conflicts in which their country of origin is involved—and foreign affairs within U.S. minority politics will primarily analyze efforts by immigrants to establish and maintain civic and political ties to their countries of origin. We will show that in rarer circumstances, immigrants seek to influence U.S. relations with their countries of origin or to shape the domestic politics of those countries. In contrast, and

> ## Box 12.1 Chapter Objectives
>
> - Describe different forms of transnationalism and why immigrants engage in these activities.
> - Identify transnational activities and émigré and sending-country motives for engaging in transnationalism.
> - Explain the motivations for immigrant-sending countries to engage their expatriates.
> - Discuss the extent to which foreign policy issues are the focus of minority organizations within the United States.

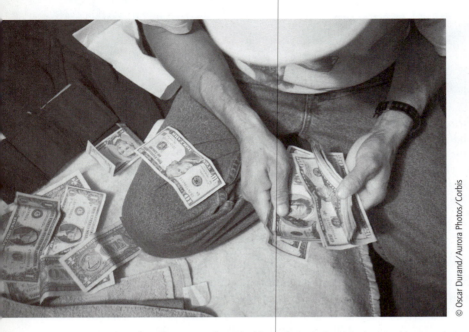

A migrant worker who comes to the United States for agricultural work counts his money from his room in upstate New York. Diasporic politics revolves in part around the money, or remittances, that migrants send back home to their families and communities.

© Oscar Durand / Aurora Photos / Corbis

with few exceptions, ethnic populations focus more on domestic U.S. political issues—where race and ethnicity may matter more—and rarely organize to ensure that their country of ancestry receives special treatment from the United States.

To build our understanding of diasporic politics, we will first briefly analyze efforts by immigrant and ethnic populations prior to the current era to maintain civic or political connections to their countries of origin or ancestry. With this context, we then explore more deeply efforts by contemporary minority populations to establish and maintain transnational connections, particularly transnational civic and political connections, with family members, communities of origin/ancestry, and countries of migration. We will also assess efforts by these countries to shape the depth and influence of émigré relations with domestic politics. Finally, we look at the positions of minority communities more generally on issues in U.S. foreign policy. Here, we will show that foreign policy issues, aside from transnational engagement primarily among immigrants, do not dominate the agendas of U.S. minority communities.

We should note at the outset that many of the examples we provide emerge from the experiences and behaviors of immigrants from the Americas and, particularly, Mexico. This reflects the fact that immigration from the Americas has made up the largest share of U.S. immigration in the modern era (since the immigration law was last subject to a comprehensive change in 1965 [see Chapter 11]). There is also generally more scholarship on the Latino immigrant experience than of migrants from other parts of the world in the contemporary era. We certainly look broadly at the diasporic experiences of all immigrants but will provide more evidence from the Latino experience. Where we don't have evidence from the experiences of other non-Latino contemporary immigrant communities, our reading is that the Latino exercise of diasporic politics and in terms of foreign affairs is not significantly different from the experiences of other contemporary immigrant groups.

As we have suggested, race/ethnicity is not the driving force that explains U.S. immigrant diasporic behaviors and attitudes. Instead, it is the desire that today's immigrants share with previous generations of immigrants to maintain ties to family members abroad and communities of origin abroad. As we will suggest, race and ethnicity could come to play more of a role in diasporic engagement and immigrant attitudes toward foreign policy if the United States seeks to exclude some immigrants from opportunities to incorporate in U.S. society based on race, ethnicity, or perceived ability to acculturate to the United States. In other words, if the road to joining the United States is slowed (see Chapter 11), the expanded opportunities to maintain ties to the country of origin will not be the supplement that we find they are now but instead an alternative. We discuss the largely inconsequential nature of race/ethnicity to immigrant diasporic engagement in contemporary U.S. society in the chapter that follows.

Throughout this chapter, the terms **immigrant, emigrant, migrant, and émigré are used**. Broadly, these terms all refer to *migrants,* people who have moved from one place to another—the broadest of the terms. Technically, we mean international migrants—in other words, people who reside in a country other than their country of birth. When referred to as *immigrants,* we are focusing on their status in the receiving society; *emigrant* and *émigré* focus on their departure from and possibly continuing ties to the country of origin.

THE GROWING EASE OF TRANSNATIONAL ACTIVITY

It has become much easier in recent years for immigrants to maintain connections to their family members abroad and with their communities and countries of origin or ancestry—in other words, to be **transnational**. The Internet and continually declining prices for voice communication make daily engagement possible, and transportation between the United States and immigrant-sending countries is much less expensive and less time consuming today than it was before the commercialization and deregulation of international air travel in the 1980s. Thus the "how" of diasporic connections is easier and cheaper than it has ever been in the past. As a result, immigrants are able to maintain their connections to their countries of origin to a greater degree today than in the past. Yet the greater frequency of transnational engagements today should not obscure the fact that immigrants have long wanted to maintain connections to their countries of origin, and did so.

Even when international transportation required travel by sailing ships and many weeks of travel to cross the Atlantic or the Pacific prior to the mid-nineteenth century, there is ample evidence of immigrants returning to their countries of origin for visits. And for the literate, letters allowed émigrés to keep up with their families and their sending communities. The degree to which migrants availed themselves of these opportunities to maintain ties with their families and communities undoubtedly varied and responded to the difficulty of travel, the opportunities perceived in the receiving society, and the political environment of the **sending country** (the country from which the immigrant emigrated). A study of European migrants to the United States between 1908 and 1923, for example, found that just 5 percent of Jewish (mostly Eastern European) migrants returned to their countries of origin.[2] The rates of return for Bulgarian, Serbian, and Montenegrin migrants, on the other hand, were as high as 89 percent. Jewish migrants in this era had little to return to, and in many cases, feared for their safety if they did. For the Bulgarians, Serbians, and Montenegrins, on the other hand, short-term migration was the norm, and many would migrate and return many times during their working years.

This geographic fluidity in immigrants' lives also offered the foundation for political organizing. Émigrés could use the United States' relative political freedom to organize

Why do migrants engage in transnationalism? When are these activities political?

around issues of importance in their country of origin. Such political organizing has probably appeared in all immigrant populations that achieved even modest levels of concentration in the United States. In many cases, the organizing focused on support for the politics or policies of the sending country or of major political movements in those countries. In

some cases, the organizing served as a foundation for challenging the political institutions of the sending country's government. Nineteenth-century Irish immigrants in the United States, for example, organized in support of Irish nationalism and challenged British control of Ireland. Many Latin American revolutions in the nineteenth and twentieth centuries were organized by émigrés in the United States and at least partially funded by émigrés abroad. Leaders of twentieth century Asian revolutions often had periods of forced exile abroad. For example, Ho Chi Minh, leader of the Vietnamese Communist Party, spent much of the period between 1912 and 1923 in the United States and Europe, during which his political philosophy crystallized. In the United States, his influences included Marcus Garvey, an advocate of Black nationalism, pan-African movements, and Back-to-Africa movements in U.S. African American communities; he also was inspired by Korean nationalists organizing in the United States to secure Korean independence from Japan.[3]

These historical forms of transnational organizing included many efforts by émigrés to support their countries of origin (or ancestry), not just to destabilize them. In the period before World War II, some in the American Jewish community strongly advocated for Zionist movements to create the state of Israel, and since Israel's founding, many American Jews have been advocates of U.S. policies to support it and have used U.S. Jewish philanthropy to finance Israeli causes. A traditional part of American ethnic politics has been presidential (and sometimes candidate) visits to the countries that have sent immigrants to the United States. In 2011, for example, President Barack Obama's trip to Ireland included a visit to Moneygall, the town from which his great-great-great-grandfather migrated. President Obama both conducted U.S. diplomacy (speaking with government leaders and the Irish people about shared binational concerns) and U.S. ethnic politics (visiting Moneygall, having a Guinness at the local pub, and identifying as one of the "Moneygall Obamas" in search of the lost apostrophe [O'Bama would make the Kenyan ancestry name more phonetically Irish]).

Our goal here is not to discuss the many historical incidences of political transnationalism. Instead, it is to suggest that many immigrants have sought the opportunity to maintain connections with the people and places they have left behind. Without question, it is easier to do this in today's globalized world, but the relative difficulty and expense in the past should not be interpreted to mean that transnationalism is new. What is new is the ease with which immigrants can maintain home-country ties and the emerging efforts by many immigrant-sending countries to organize the transnational energies of emigrants in support of the sending country's political goals.

THE ROOTS OF CONTEMPORARY TRANSNATIONAL ENGAGEMENT: FAMILY AND COMMUNITY TIES

Few migrants set out to be politically engaged in their country of origin from abroad. Instead, their initial need to adapt to their new society and to ensure that they are able to support themselves and their families guides their energies and focus. Regardless of whether émigrés seek a long-term home in the country of migration or plan eventually to return to their country of origin, most, if not all, seek to maintain ties with their families and the communities they left behind. This, we argue, is the root of many transnational civic and political activities. The desire for ongoing connections with family members abroad can remain for many years after migration; it does, however, decline with time, particularly if immediate family members subsequently migrate.

ASSOCIATED PRESS

President Barack Obama and First Lady Michelle Obama greet well-wishers in the president's ancestral home of Moneygall, Ireland, in 2013. The trip gave Obama a chance to highlight his immigrant-ethnic roots.

One particular form of these connections between migrants and their families has considerable civic and political implications—**remittances,** or the sending of money from émigrés to family members in the country of origin. Remittances are a very common form of transnational engagement, and one of the few in which the second generation (the children of immigrants born in the United States) continues to engage at a notable rate. The sheer volume of these money transfers—estimated to be as much as $414 billion globally in 2013, of which $51 billion is sent from the United States[4]—makes the sending of remittances highly political. These funds are often used for the subsistence needs of family members, and by sending them, migrants reduce the demand on immigrant-sending countries to provide basic social services. They also add to the pool of foreign exchange (monies from the developed nations) available in the developing world. This foreign exchange allows immigrant-sending countries to buy more goods and services from other countries and to reduce their international borrowing. Immigrant-sending countries see these resources as one of the advantages of high emigration rates.[5] Figure 12.1, using a slightly more expansive definition of remittances than the one provided here, lists the ten countries with the highest numbers of immigrants resident in the United States in 2010, and the World Bank's estimates for remittances from these migrants to each of these countries.

The propensity to remit varies by immigrant population and the relationship between the United States and the country of origin, so it is not possible to tell a single story about the likelihood of immigrants remitting. A recent survey of Latino migrants, however, offers some important insights. Although these exact rates of remittance may not reappear among migrants from other parts, the broader pattern is likely common across groups. More than two-thirds of Latino immigrants who migrated as adults remit on occasion. Almost half of these immigrants who do remit do so at least once a month. Latino immigrants who migrated as children are somewhat less likely to remit and, among those who do, send money less frequently than Latino immigrants who migrated as adults. The average remittance varies, based on whether immigrants are regular remitters. Among respondents who reported that they did send money to family members abroad, the annual total of these remittances averaged approximately $2,500 in 2006.[7]

Figure 12.1 Top Ten Immigrant Populations and Remittances to Each Country, 2010

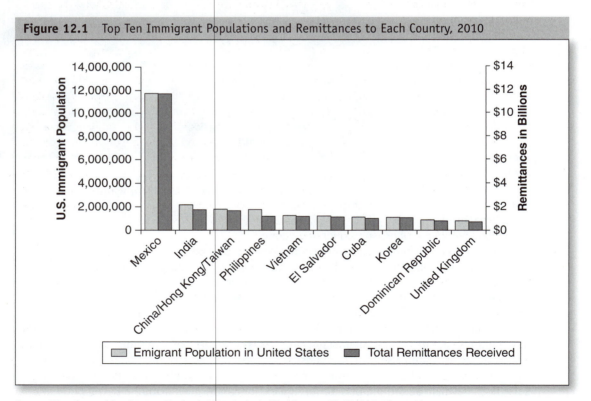

Source: Migration and Remittances Factbook 2011, 2nd ed. (Washington, DC: World Bank, 2011).

Note: The World Bank uses a somewhat narrower definition of remittances than other sources. It does, however, allow for global comparisons.[6]

We would anticipate that the likelihood of remitting varies considerably; migrants from more developed countries and migrants who migrate with their immediate family members are less likely to remit than are many Latino migrants, who are more likely to migrate without their immediate family members. That said, remittances are very much a part of the immigrant experience, and are a resource to maintain connections with family and community in all immigrant populations.

Most remittances are sent to family members and are largely used to meet short-term needs rather than as savings or investments. Some remittances, however, are directed to collective needs for the communities of origin of immigrants. These **collective remittances** are often the product of community-wide efforts among émigrés from a village or town who are living in the same place of destination. For example, members of a U.S.-based hometown association of people from a specific town in the Mexican state of Oaxaca will raise monies to build a road to that town or to repair the town's church or town hall.[8] Another form of collective remittance is relief in response to natural disasters such as typhoons in Asia or earthquakes in Haiti. This form of collective remittance often includes funds from emigrants, ethnics who trace their ancestries to the location of the natural disaster, and others with no direct ties who are motivated by humanitarian concerns.

Some immigrant-sending countries seek to encourage these collective remittance efforts and channel them by offering to use federal and state-level funds to match those sent by émigrés (or, in some cases, to more than match) to specific communities. Mexico has been the most aggressive in promoting such a program. These collective remittance efforts make up a small share of the total flow of remittance funds worldwide—or, more specifically, from the United States. In 2004 approximately $17 billion was remitted from the United States to Mexico. Of this, just $14.2 million (less than one-tenth of 1 percent) were collective remittances funneled into the program that matched émigré contributions with a three-for-one match from Mexico and Mexican state governments.[9] Collective remittances are nevertheless important because they show how remittance sending can become very political, both in the country of destination and in the country of origin. It takes **collective action**—cooperative action to achieve a collective goal—in the migrants' country of destination to raise these funds. The fund-raising often takes the form of social activities such as fairs and cultural events focused on the culture of the sending community. Once the funds are raised, the émigrés need to establish a procedure to decide how they should be used and to oversee that the funds are used well. This sometimes involves negotiation with state or national governments in the sending countries.

> Should immigrant-receiving countries be concerned about the volume of the remittances sent from them?

Remitting on a routine basis is more common for immigrants more recently arrived, for those with immediate family members in the country of origin, and for those who do not have legal status in the United States. Although there are no comprehensive studies of immigrants to the United States from throughout the world, there do appear to be some national origin differences in the likelihood of sending remittances. In several studies of migrants from Latin America, migrants from Central American countries appear to be somewhat more likely to send remittances than are those from elsewhere in the Americas.[10] In addition to routine remittances, those sent in times of crisis, such as after environmental disasters, are less predictable but seem to be more common among longer-term immigrants who do not remit as regularly and those without immediate family ties to the country of origin. A natural disaster such as an earthquake or a devastating hurricane reminds migrants and their children of sometimes lost ties to ancestral homelands.

Second and later generation migrants also remit, though in relatively small numbers. In the survey of Latinos discussed previously, 64 percent of second generation Latinos and 82 percent of third and beyond generation Latinos never remit. In this case, race or ethnicity seems relatively inconsequential in the decision to remit; instead, the driving force is close ties to family members and communities abroad. (See Figure 12.2 for an overview of transnational activities.)

Figure 12.2   Immigrants' Transnational Engagement

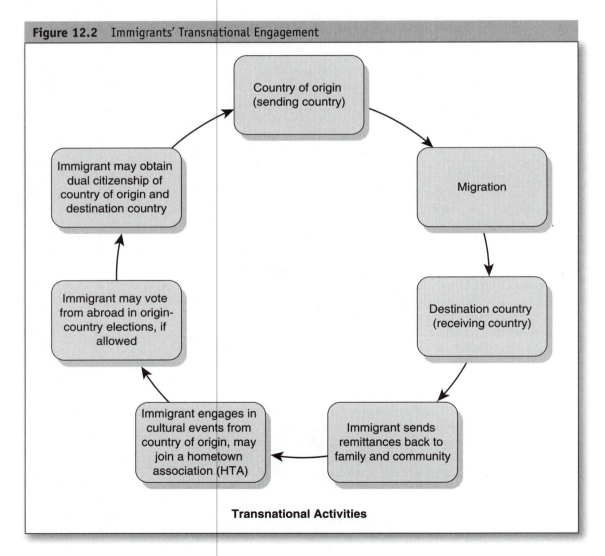

Transnational Activities

Emigrants and Country of Origin–Focused Civic Life

While remitting to maintain personal and civic connections with their countries of origin comprise the bulk of monies sent home by migrants, remittances are used in other ways as well. These can be divided into activities that focus on serving the country of origin and activities that focus primarily on co-nationals in the United States—in other words, as a form of U.S. civic activity among immigrants. For immigrants who do participate in transnational activities, these civic and political outlets potentially have two important political consequences that shape the politics of both the United States and the immigrants' countries of origin. First, they offer a new collective voice that can influence the politics of the countries of origin, particularly in countries like Mexico and India that facilitate transnational connections with their émigrés. In many cases, one of the factors that spurred migration in the first place was the migrants' perception that they would not have an influence in the national politics of the sending country, so this opportunity to influence home-country politics can be particularly welcome.[11] Second, transnational civic and political activities offer a training ground for immigrants that can easily be refocused to their needs in the United States. As we have shown in Chapters 7 and 11, immigrants participate in U.S. politics at lower rates than the U.S.-born. Immigrants who are involved in transnational civic and political behaviors will likely become more quickly engaged in U.S. civic and political activities.[12] Thus the training ground of transnationalism can overcome some of the costs of race/ethnicity on U.S. political participation.

The immigrant desire to help family members and communities increasingly takes another form of assistance, that of membership in **hometown associations (HTAs)**—organizations of immigrants from the same city or region of origin who reside in the same part of the country of destination who band together to provide material support to the place of origin (while also building community in the destination country). Migrants from a specific town often come to the same place in the country of destination, so these associations reflect unique bilateral connections between sending and receiving societies.

HTAs are not unique to migrants in the United States. They have emerged in many émigré populations. Estimates suggest that there are as many as three thousand Mexican HTAs, one thousand Filipino HTAs, and five hundred Ghanaian HTAs in the United States. Hometown associations have also formed in Europe and Asia.[13] Their core mission is to create community. The main resource to do so is the shared tie to the place or region of origin and the desire to maintain shared cultural connections and to help people in that place of origin. HTAs promote the culture of the country of origin, create social networks, raise money to send as collective remittances for community development, and nurture the shared memories of the members. Fund-raising takes a variety of forms, including cultural fairs, beauty contests, sports leagues, and business sponsorships.

Although these networks form because of the shared ties to a community or region abroad and the desire to assist the place of origin, their organizational focus can shift to the United States when their members are facing a shared challenge.[14] For example, when the U.S. House of Representatives passed legislation in 2005 to make unauthorized presence in the United States a criminal offense (H.R. 4437), HTAs became a prime recruitment resource to turn out people to protest this legislation. Over several months, more than five million people joined these protests in more than 125 cities nationwide. Congress quickly dropped this proposal.[15]

HTAs have long existed in some form, but their numbers have exploded in recent years. In part, this rapid growth is a result of growing migration and increased immigrant abilities to maintain frequent contact with the friends and family in their community of origin. It also results, in part, from efforts by some immigrant-sending countries to encourage the establishment of HTAs and to connect HTAs from the same states of origin. Mexico has been particularly active in these efforts and has created a governing body for Mexican HTAs that advises the Mexican foreign affairs ministry (discussed later). Despite this growth, the share of immigrants who participate in HTA activities is small. Among Latino immigrants surveyed in 2007, just 5 percent reported HTA membership.[16]

Transnational civic activities can also focus primarily on migrants in the United States. Embassies and consulates, for example, offer cultural and educational events focused on the country of origin, often attended by migrants. U.S.-based organizations of émigrés from a country or a region (such as the Federación de Clubes Zacatecanos del Sur de California [the federation of hometown associations from the Mexican state of Zacatecas]) exist to promote cultural and political ties with these countries, whose political issues can be the focus of U.S. political organizing. Surveys of immigrants suggest that with one exception, these sorts of activities see participation from some immigrants, but the share is relatively small compared to the share that participates in HTAs.[17] An exception to the pattern of low rates of immigrant engagement is attending a cultural or educational event related to the home country within the last year.

Emigrants and Country of Origin Electoral Politics

The opportunity to participate in home-country electoral politics varies dramatically for contemporary U.S. immigrants. Most immigrant-sending countries either bar voting from abroad or make it very difficult. A few encourage it and structure the opportunity to vote either by mail or at embassies and consulates, and/or provide representation for nationals residing abroad in the national parliament.

Mexico, the largest source of immigrants to the United States, has traditionally been an example of the former model, so few Mexicans resident in the United States have voted from abroad. In the 1990s and early 2000s, Mexican émigrés pressured Mexico to ease its regulations on voting from abroad. In response, Mexico liberalized its policies and allowed a mail vote from abroad in the 2006 election. Mexico did, however, find ongoing strategies to limit the voice of the Mexican diaspora in its elections, specifically by creating a very high barrier to voter registration.[18] In the 2012 presidential election, the second Mexican presidential election with voting from abroad, just 41,000 of the approximately twelve million Mexican subjects in the United States voted. This very low turnout is all the more remarkable considering the high levels of Mexico-focused HTAs discussed earlier in this chapter.

Although less common among countries sending immigrants to the United States, some do encourage voting from abroad. Italy, the Dominican Republic, and Colombia are representatives of this latter model. Each allows registered voters from abroad to vote by mail in national elections for president or the national parliament. Each also created parliamentary representatives for nationals living abroad who are elected by voters living outside of the country—what Italy calls the **overseas constituency**.[19] Some countries allow voting from abroad but require that it take

ASSOCIATED PRESS

Immigrants and activists carry flags through downtown Chicago during an immigration reform rally. The march was part of a nationwide effort to demand comprehensive immigration reform. The collective action of immigrants within the receiving country can influence domestic policies and at times even affect foreign affairs to some degree.

place at the consulate or other designated locations, which limits participation. Iraq's first election after Saddam Hussein was deposed followed this model. Although turnout among the expatriate populations of these countries that encourage overseas voting is higher than it is for expatriate Mexicans, electoral turnout overall remains low as a percentage of all nationals of those countries living abroad.

It should come as little surprise, then, that relatively few immigrants in the United States have voted in the elections of their countries of origin since migration. A national survey of Latinos found that approximately 4 percent report having voted since migration. Of these, 44 percent had voted in the United States and 56 percent by returning to the country of origin.[20] There are no comparable data for immigrants from other regions of the world.

Voting is just one form of electoral engagement. The national politics of some of the countries with large émigré populations in the United States now routinely include campaign events in the United States. It is not clear if the goal of these efforts is votes, fund-raising, or simply word of mouth to co-nationals in the country of origin, but these events do bring the candidates and issues of the home country directly to the United States. Arguably, they should increase electoral turnout among émigrés, but there is no research on this question. Some countries, perhaps fearing the effects of émigrés and their issues on home-country politics, prohibit campaigning abroad. Mexico is one of these countries, though some fund-raising does take place in the United States. It is likely that visits to the United States by candidates in immigrant-sending country elections will increase in the future as the numbers of migrants and transnational connections increase.

Over time, home-country electoral participation by immigrants in the United States is also likely to increase. Immigrants increasingly see voting as part of the package of opportunities for transnational engagement. Among Latinos, approximately 58 percent of immigrants believe that it is appropriate for émigrés to vote in their national elections. Interestingly, the majority of second and beyond generation immigrants are also more likely to agree with this position than to oppose it.[21] As immigrant-sending nations seek to solidify their connections with their long-term émigré populations, they will likely provide for increased opportunities to vote from abroad and, potentially, establish specific legislative seats designated for people living outside of the country. Evidence from the countries that do allow international voting shows that the turnout will likely be low, adding to the incentives to offer a limited form of international voting.

Dual Citizenship: Sustaining Connections

Dual citizenship—the establishment and maintenance of political membership in two countries—is the most formal and, arguably, the most politically consequential form of trans-national engagement. Citizenship establishes a formal set of privileges and responsibilities for the subject and the state. Dual citizenship requires the subject to provide his or her fealty to two countries, potentially to pay taxes and provide military service to both, and for both countries to protect the citizen under international law.

Many immigrants see dual citizenship as their only logical path—though, as we will suggest, many probably do not meet all of the requirements by both the sending country and the **receiving country,** or destination country, to be dual citizens. They have little desire to renounce their political connection to their country of origin but want to demonstrate their connections and loyalty to their country of residence.

Both immigrant-receiving and immigrant-sending countries have traditionally resisted immigrant desires for dual citizenship, though this resistance is declining. Traditionally, immigrant-sending countries did not like to admit that they were losing their connections to their émigrés, and they resisted allowing them to maintain the sending-country citizenship after the emigrant naturalized in another country. Immigrant-receiving countries want to be assured that they will have the full political loyalty of their new, voluntary citizens. The resistance of immigrant-sending countries has been diminishing, as they have come to see the advantages in having émigrés with ongoing connections to the sending country *and* to the often more developed countries to which they migrate. Immigrant-receiving countries seek to ensure that the loyalty of the newly naturalizing citizen is absolute, so they have sought, at least rhetorically, to prevent dual citizenship. The U.S. naturalization oath, for example, requires that all naturalizing U.S. citizens take an oath that they "absolutely and entirely renounce and abjure all allegiance and fidelity to any foreign prince, potentate, state, or sovereignty, of whom or which I have heretofore been a subject or citizen." (See Box 12.2 for the full naturalization oath.)

BOX 12.2

U.S. Naturalization Oath

I hereby declare, on oath, that I absolutely and entirely renounce and abjure all allegiance and fidelity to any foreign prince, potentate, state, or sovereignty, of whom or which I have heretofore been a subject or citizen;

that I will support and defend the Constitution and laws of the United States of America against all enemies, foreign and domestic;

that I will bear true faith and allegiance to the same;

that I will bear arms on behalf of the United States when required by the law;

that I will perform noncombatant service in the Armed Forces of the United States when required by the law;

that I will perform work of national importance under civilian direction when required by the law; and

that I take this obligation freely without any mental reservation or purpose of evasion; so help me God.

In some cases, the U.S. Department of Citizenship and Immigration Services allows the oath to be taken without the following clauses:

. . . that I will bear arms on behalf of the United States when required by law;

that I will perform noncombatant service in the Armed Forces of the United States when required by law. . . .

Despite the hesitancy of some immigrant-sending and immigrant-receiving countries to recognize dual citizenship, immigrants have increasingly pursued this status, and it has become more common. In the case of the United States, naturalizing citizens formally renounce their former citizenship as part of the naturalization ceremony. As U.S. citizens, however, they can reestablish their former citizenship if their country of origin is willing to extend the privilege to them as "former" nationals (the sending country does not have to recognize the renunciation of citizenship). Increasingly, immigrant-sending countries see an advantage to having their former nationals also holding U.S. citizenship as a means to maintain political and cultural connections to émigrés for longer and to ensure that the émigrés are able to exercise more rights and privileges in their country of destination than would immigrants who have not naturalized. As a result, some countries have modified their policies to make the reestablishment of citizenship easier.[22] Canada, for example, explicitly tells its subjects thinking of naturalizing as U.S. citizens that the only way that they can renounce their Canadian citizenship is before an official of the Canadian government. The promise to "renounce and abjure" the "allegiance and fidelity" to Canada in the U.S. naturalization oath is only meaningful when it takes place before a Canadian official.

This ability of U.S. citizens to establish a second citizenship has long been a part of U.S. law and is exercised by native-born U.S. citizens who migrate to and become citizens of other countries. Like Canada, the United States requires that its citizens seeking to terminate their U.S. citizenship formally renounce the citizenship before a U.S. government employee (usually a consular official in a U.S. embassy or consulate). From the perspective of the United States, naturalizing as a foreign subject does not affect a person's U.S. citizenship.

Mexico, as the largest source of immigrants to the United States, somewhat complicates the story of increasing levels of perceived and actual dual citizenship. Mexico follows a more traditional pattern toward its émigrés and has long resisted dual citizenship for its nationals who naturalize in another country. As part of a broader effort to reach out to its émigrés (discussed in more detail below), the Mexican constitution was amended in 1998 to allow for dual nationality, in which the "national" can exercise rights granted by Mexican law but is not a citizen.[23] While this term might seem like a semantic difference, it in fact suggests more. By creating this new category of membership short of citizenship, Mexico retains the ability in the future to eliminate the status or to limit the rights of "nationals." At the time the status was established, Mexico limited the rights of nationals relative to citizens. Nationals, for example, could only vote in Mexican elections if they were resident in Mexico in the 1990s and had a valid Mexican voter identification from that period. As we have noted earlier in the chapter, it is difficult for Mexican citizens to vote from abroad, and few do.

> Do the efforts of U.S. immigrants to become dual citizens potentially add to the political distinctiveness or racialization of immigrants from the Americas, Asia, and Africa?

Many countries extend the privilege of citizenship to the children of their nationals born abroad, although each has its own requirements. Frequently these requirements include some period of residence in the country of ancestry prior to adulthood, though some countries, like the United States, do not have such a requirement. Children of U.S. citizens are themselves U.S. citizens regardless of where they are born, as long as at least one of their parents has resided in the United States or its outlying territories for the amount of time required in U.S. law.[24]

As important as dual citizenship (or dual nationality) could *potentially* be to the United States—because the dual citizens/dual nationals might have a different understanding of the rights and responsibilities of their U.S. citizenship—it is not possible to provide a count of dual citizens in the country. Many immigrants who have naturalized as U.S. citizens may think of themselves as dual citizens, but in many cases they haven't done what they need to do for their country of former citizenship to again recognize them as citizens (such as reapplying for that country's passport). They can do this at any point in the future, however, making them potential rather than actual dual citizens. The United States does not keep records of how many of its citizens by birth naturalize in another country, so this population cannot be counted, either. Finally, as noted, some countries including the United States extend citizenship to the children of their citizens who are born abroad. It is not possible to know what share of these potential dual citizens will exercise that citizenship when they reach adulthood.

With the rapidly increasing number of global migrants and the steadily decreasing national barriers to dual citizenship, the rights of dual citizens and the responsibilities of countries of citizenship in which they do not regularly reside will likely be an increasingly contentious political issue in the future, one that might lead to renewed national efforts to limit dual citizenship.[25] Although the United States does not today regulate dual citizens differently, it could in the future. Were such policies to be developed, they would likely focus on the racial/ethnic characteristics of the majority of dual citizens, particularly dual citizens who had naturalized as U.S. citizens. While race and ethnicity are inconsequential for the exercise of transnationalism and dual citizenship today, the steadily increasing numbers of immigrants and, by extension, transnationally engaged immigrants, ensure that race/ethnicity could come to be more important in this dimension of politics in the future.

BOX 12.3 ROAD SIGN

Boston Marathon Bomber Not Tried as an Enemy Combatant

Brothers Tamerlan and Dzhokhar Tsarnaev lived in several different republics of the former Soviet Union before immigrating to the United States. College student Dzhokhar became a naturalized citizen, while his older brother's application for naturalization was denied because of a criminal conviction. On April 15, 2013, the brothers allegedly carried out an attack on the Boston Marathon, killing five and injuring more than two hundred. In the aftermath of the attack, many called for Dzhokhar Tsarnaev, the surviving attacker, to be tried as an unlawful enemy combatant, in part based on his being a naturalized, rather than natural-born, U.S. citizen. The Obama administration rejected the call and tried Tsarnaev in federal court. Had the Obama administration heeded these calls, the rights of all U.S. citizens would have been diminished.

While Tamerlan Tsarnaev was shot and killed by police, evading capture, Dzhokhar was captured, hospitalized, and questioned. Fearing that the Boston Marathon bombings were part of a larger conspiracy, police did not initially provide a Miranda warning, which notifies suspects that anything they say could be used against them in court and that they have the right to have an attorney present. Courts have allowed a temporary public safety exception to the Miranda warning, and the investigators in this case extended the notion of "temporary" to sixteen hours. Once Tsarnaev received his Miranda warning, he stopped speaking with investigators without an attorney present. As an enemy combatant, Tsarnaev would have no Miranda warning and would have been subjected to more rigorous questioning without an attorney present.

Historically, the concept of enemy combatants referred to members of the armed forces of a state with which one was at war. These combatants were entitled to protections under international treaties such as the Geneva Conventions. The concept became muddied in the modern era, however, when many combatants, such as members of al-Qaeda, were not affiliated with a state. It is this group that some refer to as "unlawful" enemy combatants. After the September 11, 2001, attacks, the Bush administration issued a Presidential Military Order stating that enemy combatants could be held in

(Continued)

(Continued)

military prisons and tried in military courts absent protections of the U.S. Constitution.[26] These assertions of presidential power were limited by the federal courts,[27] but the premise that the president has the authority to determine who is an enemy combatant and that enemy combatants could face more rigorous forms of interrogation remains, and is at the core of demands that Dzhokhar Tsarnaev be recognized as one.

On their face, there are few merits to this demand. Tamerlan Tsarnaev may have developed some contacts with Chechen separatists during an extended visit to Chechnya in the year prior to the attack, but there is no evidence that either brother had ties to al-Qaeda, the Taliban, or related forces—the targets of the post-9/11 legislation on which the Bush administration based policies toward enemy combatants. When he was arrested, Dzhokhar Tsarnaev was not just a U.S. citizen, he

was also on U.S. soil. He could thus be tried in U.S. courts. He was charged with using weapons of mass destruction, a federal charge that could result in the death penalty, as well as state charges including murder. In the years since 9/11, federal law enforcement has successfully prosecuted nearly five hundred terrorism-related cases.[28] There is no reason to assume that they would not be able to prosecute this one as well.

The Obama administration's decision to forgo the path of treating Dzhokhar Tsarnaev as an enemy combatant offers protections not just for Tsarnaev. If his status as a naturalized citizen were to be used to reduce his constitutional protections (and were that diminished status to be upheld by the federal courts), immigrants would remain in a permanent second-class status. Ultimately, this would reduce the substantial meaning of U.S. citizenship for all U.S. citizens.

TRANSNATIONAL ACTIVITY: BEYOND THE IMMIGRANT GENERATION

Transnational political and civic activity is less often seen among their U.S.-born children. These children frequently have considerable cultural interest in their parents' country of origin and maintain symbolic ties, but are less likely to send money, organize civically or politically, or seek citizenship in that country. As well, language is often a barrier for the U.S.-born children of immigrants, particularly by the time they reach adulthood. There certainly are exceptions to these generalizations, but they are few in the contemporary United States.

This pattern of low levels of transnational engagement in the second generation could certainly change. As we have suggested, however, change would probably require a more sustained connection between immigrant families (including their U.S.-born children) and the community of origin. We understand transnational activity to emerge from personal ties to both family and community in immigrant-sending countries rather than from an instrumental effort by migrants to become civically engaged or political. If this understanding is correct, and should immigration slow in the future, it is likely that the levels of new transnational engagement will also diminish. Somewhat counterintuitively, however, a decline in immigration rates would also increase the number of family members who remain abroad, which might create an incentive for more sustained, multigenerational transnational connections.

Transnationalism from Above: Sending-Country Efforts to Shape Engagement

Just as immigrants' interest in maintaining civic and political ties to their countries of origin have grown in recent years, immigrant-sending countries have increasingly also sought to structure the opportunities for their émigrés to involve themselves in the politics of the home country. These efforts can be passive, such as allowing émigrés who naturalize as citizens of another country to maintain both citizenships or by providing representation for nationals abroad in the national legislature. The efforts can also be more active by creating civic structures in the country of migration through which émigrés can directly influence governance in the home country, such as creating a body to represent émigrés abroad in some aspect of governance or allowing voting from abroad.

Contemporary efforts by immigrant-sending countries to shape their émigrés' relationship with them are not new. In the 1920s and early 1930s, for example, Mexico reached out to its émigrés and sought to serve as their representative before U.S. and state governments. These efforts, however, came to be seen as manipulative by Mexican American communities, who feared that Mexico was seeking to profit from their labor in the United States by undercutting efforts to build independent, U.S.-based unions.[29] The Mexican government's efforts soon collapsed as Mexico began to focus on other issues and again began to neglect its émigrés in the United States.

Immigrant-ethnic populations also potentially pay a price for perceived connections between the sending country and its émigrés. The justification for the internment of Japanese Americans during World War II was an example of faulty logic that they would conspire with Japan to undermine the U.S. war effort.[30] Some Italian Americans and German Americans also faced internment during World Wars I and II, though their numbers were small compared to the Japanese Americans interned during World War II, for whom it was a near-universal experience.[31] It should be noted that these connections were, in almost all cases, not demonstrated. Although the Japanese, German, and Italian governments did establish spy networks in the United States (as did the Soviet Union and China), the agents were not, for the most part, immigrants or their U.S.-resident children. In contemporary U.S. society, Muslim immigrants also face heightened scrutiny about their loyalty to the United States and are more often subject to detention than are other immigrants. (See Road Sign, "Boston Marathon Bomber Not Tried as an Enemy Combatant.")[32]

 To what extent are Muslim immigrants racialized in contemporary U.S. society?

In the contemporary era, immigrant-sending countries' efforts to shape the transnational experiences of their émigrés have been more benign and more overt than the Mexican effort to structure the relationship between Mexican labor and U.S. employers in the 1920s. At a minimum, most countries with large numbers of émigrés in the United States monitor those emigrants' HTAs and other transnational organizing activities. This responsibility is housed in the embassy and consulates; the quality of the record keeping can be seen as an indicator of the sending country's level of interest in émigrés. For countries that are interested in establishing formal connections to émigré organizations, the next step is frequently financial resources for network building. This funding can be used to facilitate meetings of HTA leaders at the city or national level, or in some cases for travel for some leaders to the country of origin.

With the steady increase in migration, some immigrant-sending countries have sought not just to monitor HTAs and facilitate networking among their leaders but also to coordinate their efforts. In terms of migrant populations in the United States, Mexico offers a prime example of this new model of transnationalism from above and its evolution. In the early 1990s, in an effort to coordinate Mexican efforts to reach out to the expatriate community, Mexico established the Program for Mexican Communities Living Abroad. The establishment of this program within the Mexican foreign ministry was an important first step in developing a coordinated relationship between Mexico and its émigrés. It created a structure within which consulates could interact with and support transnational organizing abroad.[33] It was this network that coordinated demands for voting from abroad, among other issues. Mexican immigrants, or at least those active in the organization, created networks that they would not have otherwise developed, and the Mexican government learned that Mexican émigré interests were not necessarily aligned with those of Mexico.

When he was elected in 2000, Mexican president Vicente Fox reached out to the émigré community and established an administrative foundation for Mexico to be better able to communicate with the leaders of its diaspora. Initially, he achieved this aim by establishing a presidential-level Office of Mexicans Abroad. The office was directed by a Mexican immigrant residing in Texas and appointed by Fox to this cabinet-level position. The Office of Mexicans Abroad offered President Fox a direct communications channel to Mexican emigrants, bypassing the Mexican foreign ministry. After two years, the office was replaced by one that returned to the control of the foreign ministry (the Institute of Mexicans Abroad, or IME, based on its name in Spanish). In something of an innovation, the IME established an advisory council made up of one hundred representatives from Mexican communities abroad who had at least nominal control of setting the priorities of the office and ensuring that it would not be swallowed by the foreign ministry.[34] Most of the representatives on this council are HTA leaders, though the council includes some scholars and religious leaders. Most are elected by the leaders of HTAs recognized by the Mexican government. The council meets annually and has set four priorities for the office—collecting data on Mexicans abroad, promoting the vote from abroad, communicating issues of importance to the diaspora through regular e-mails and web communication, and conducting scholarly studies of the Mexican émigré experience.

Mexico's efforts are relatively recent, so it is not possible to assess whether they will succeed in the long term. What is evident is that the commitment of Mexico's presidents will likely vary from administration to administration. Mexico's efforts, however, establish an important model for countries seeking to build trust and develop an ongoing relationship with their émigrés—or, at least, émigré leaders—abroad. That said, we certainly do not expect all countries—or many, for that matter—to follow the Mexican model. The proximity of Mexico to the United States ensures that Mexico has easier access to its émigrés and that its émigrés have easier access to their families in Mexico than do most others. The Mexican diaspora is also larger than that of most émigré populations. Approximately 15 percent of people born in Mexico now reside in the United States. Finally, Mexican migration to the United States has a longer history than most others, with large numbers of Mexicans beginning to migrate to the United States in the early twentieth century.

Embassies and consulates often also provide another form of transnationalism that is directed at individuals rather than organizations. These focus on cultural and civic outreach to émigrés and their children through such programs as language classes for the children of immigrants, cultural performances, presentations by national leaders, and cultural celebrations. Some also offer legal assistance, loan programs for migrants in distress, and repatriation for those who die abroad and whose families cannot afford the costs of a funeral and transportation of the remains. Nations with many emigrants have a rich consular structure. Canada, for example, has seventeen throughout the United States (supplemented by thirteen honorary consuls who, for the most part, do not have resources to reach out to émigré populations, but who serve as official representatives of Canada in different cities);[35] Korea has twelve consulates and fourteen honorary counsels. In these cases, the more individually focused forms of transnational outreach can reach many or most émigrés. Countries with fewer émigrés may only have a presence in Washington DC, so the outreach doesn't reach as high a share of immigrants. (See Figure 12.3 for a summary of sending-country efforts to influence engagement.)

Figure 12.3   Sending-Country Efforts to Influence Émigré Engagement

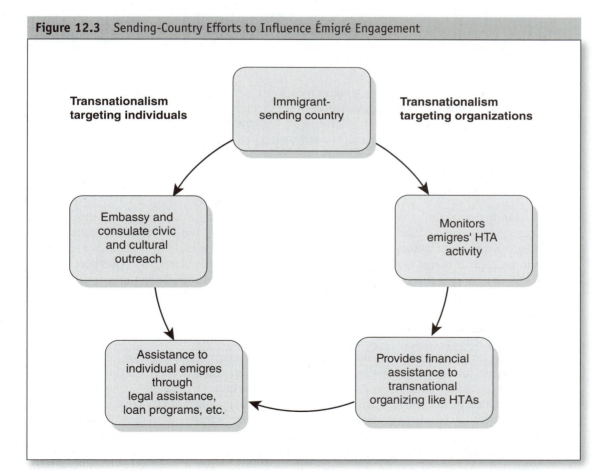

Receiving-Country Concerns about Transnationalism

The dramatic increase in opportunities for immigrant transnational engagement has led to concerns by some in the United States that if immigrants are more engaged in the civic and political life of their home countries, they will be slower to make connections to U.S. political institutions and to formalize their political loyalty to the United States through naturalization. Political theorist Stanley Renshon, for example, characterizes the transnationally active as "50% Americans" who are failing to make the transition to full participation in U.S. civic life and politics.[36] According to Renshon, this immigrant failure to accept American political identity has costs both for immigrants and for the United States. For the immigrants, the 50 percent American status will slow their economic, social, and cultural adaptation as well, so that transnational immigrants will remain marginal in U.S. society. For the nation, the risks are perhaps greater. These marginalized residents will provide a point of access to the United States for nations and movements antithetical to the interest of the nation.

Renshon's concerns are echoed by political theorist Samuel Huntington, who characterizes many immigrants—particularly immigrants from the Western hemisphere—as "ampersands," people who have "two countries, two homes."[37] Huntington is particularly concerned about Mexican immigration because of its overall volume and the long period of high migration from Mexico. He characterizes this as the following:

[The] reconquista of areas Americans took from Mexico by force in the 1830s and 1840s. . . . It is also blurring the border between Mexico and America, introducing a very different culture, while also promoting the emergence, in some areas, of a blended society and culture, half-American and half-Mexican. Along with immigration from other Latin American countries, it is advancing Hispanization throughout America and social, linguistic, and economic practices appropriate for an Anglo-Hispanic society.[38]

Huntington's concerns extend beyond the effects of Mexican/Latino immigration on U.S. society. He believes that the "blurring of the border" and the "ampersand" culture slow Mexican and other Latino adaptation to U.S. society both in formal forms of political connectedness, such as naturalization, and in terms of economic and cultural incorporation.

These concerns about **immigrant adaptation,** or specifically Mexican immigrant adaptation to U.S. society, are not new and undoubtedly have an underlying racial dimension for many who are suspicious of whether people who are racially different from the majority can be equals in U.S. society. As we discussed in Chapters 6 and 11, large and culturally distinct immigrant populations have long been blamed for failing to incorporate into U.S. society, only to become part of the national mainstream within a couple of generations. For example, early in the nation's history Benjamin Franklin feared Pennsylvania was becoming a German colony in which "the Dutch under-live, and are thereby enabled to under-work and under-sell the English; who are thereby extremely incommoded, and consequently disgusted, so that there can be no cordial affection or unity between the two nations."[39] Similarly, Madison Grant feared an influx of the "increasing number of the weak, the broken and the mentally crippled of all races drawn from the lowest stratum of the Mediterranean basin and the Balkans, together with the wretched, submerged populations of the Polish Ghettos."[40] While time has proven these fears to be unfounded for previous waves of immigrants, similar concerns continue to arise regarding today's immigrants, suggesting that the racialization of immigrants continues in contemporary society. What is different about the current era, however, is that concerns about the adaptability of many immigrants to U.S. society focus on their transnational engagement, both in terms of where their political loyalties lie and the negative consequences of cultural or political connections to the home country on U.S. incorporation.

> What sensitivities should transnationally engaged immigrants and immigrant-sending countries have about U.S. public opinion? Should they have any at all?

Study of contemporary immigrant populations, however, suggests that these concerns, particularly in terms of immigrant political identifications and loyalties, are not substantiated by immigrants' attitudes and behaviors. Immigrants themselves don't see a contradiction between feeling connected to the country of origin and identifying as American. Analysis of the largest national study of Latino immigrants, conducted by Luis Fraga and colleagues in 2006, finds that immigrants do not choose one identity at the expense of another, "but rather that immigrants hold these identities simultaneously—becoming more 'American' even as they keep strong attachments to both their country of origin and a large sense of being Latino or Hispanic."[41] Although less a focus of concern among scholars fearful of the domestic costs of immigrant transnational engagement, immigrants from Asia show a similar pattern.[42] Asian immigrants who maintain political ties to their countries of origin show comparable levels of attachment to U.S. values and interest in pursuing U.S. citizenship as Asian immigrants with no transnational engagement.

Contrary to the expectations of scholars who anticipate a negative effect on U.S. political engagement from transnational participation, evidence indicates that immigrants who are transnationally engaged are more likely to be involved in civic organizations in the United States, more likely to report an intention to make the United States a permanent home, and more likely to have naturalized as a U.S. citizen. The positive effects of transnational engagement are stronger for the first two of these measures than for naturalization.[43] Thus the evidence demonstrates that transnational engagement serves as a training ground for U.S. civic and political engagement, rather than a barrier, and can serve to overcome racial/ethnic barriers to civic and electoral participation in U.S. society. Thus the scholarly evidence suggests that concerns about transnationally engaged immigrants being somehow less than fully American are unsubstantiated.

U.S. FOREIGN POLICY AND MINORITY COMMUNITIES

Public opinion surveys of African Americans, Latinos, and Asian Americans tell a consistent story—U.S. minority communities do not place foreign policy issues at the top of their issue agenda except during periods when the United States is in the early phases of war abroad. In this pattern of low interest in foreign policy, minority communities follow a pattern very similar to non-Hispanic Whites. During times of war, Americans pay more attention and express more concern about international issues. Similarly, after natural disasters, Americans' attention turns to the victims. This phenomenon is stronger among émigrés from the place of the disaster and ethnics who trace their ancestry to that country or region. These exceptions pass quickly, however, and the policy focus of minority communities returns to a more domestically focused agenda.

The Hindu community in New York City participates in a parade celebrating Lord Krishna's birthday. U.S. immigrant/ethnic communities may retain some interest and involvement in their country of origin, but this tends to be narrow in focus; they are much more concerned with U.S. domestic issues. Here, New York City mayoral candidate John Liu joins in the celebration as he reaches out to potential voters in 2013.

Minority organizations, however, seek to ensure that there are minority voices in U.S. foreign policy debates. The focus of these organizational efforts is most often on the countries or regions to which each racial/ethnic group traces its ancestry—for example, Latin America for Latinos or Africa for African Americans. The interests of national origin–focused organizations are frequently more narrowly focused, such as the Dominican Republic among Dominican immigrant or Dominican American organizations, and consequently include some foreign policy issues on their agendas. This is particularly evident among national origin–focused organizations in immigrant/ethnic communities with large shares of political refugees, such as Cuban, Vietnamese, or Nicaraguan communities.

African Americans have had more of an influence on U.S. foreign policy than other racial and ethnic populations and, because of the history of African migration, this organizing has focused on the continent of Africa. Perhaps the most notable success was the ongoing challenge to South African apartheid.[44] African American organizations, often in alliance with college students of all races, organized to ensure that public institutions, such as colleges and philanthropies, did not own stock in companies that did business with the White-ruled government of South Africa. This demand for "divestment" added pressure to publicly held companies not to do business with South Africa. This economic pressure added to the political pressure on the White rulers of South Africa that spurred the release of Nelson Mandela from prison and, ultimately, the democratization of South Africa.

What contemporary foreign policy issues are supported by a U.S. minority community? Why are these issues important to its members?

The national civil rights organizations do not invest heavily in foreign policy advocacy issues, except in moments of international crisis. The National Association for the Advancement of Colored People, for example, identifies nine issue areas and two sets of issue-focused activities as central to its advocacy and issues agenda.[45] All of these focus on domestic issues. The National Council of La Raza identifies eight issue areas and one strategy as part of its issues and programs. One of these—immigration—potentially has implications for U.S. foreign policy and international relations, but each of the sub-issues identified are more domestically focused, such as immigration reform, state and local initiatives, and naturalization through the DREAM Act.[46] The Asian American Legal Defense and Education Fund does include one internationally focused issue among its nine-policy issue foci—antitrafficking of low-wage and sex workers.[47] Not surprisingly, immigration also appears on its list of issues, but the focus is almost exclusively on the United States, centered on immigrant rights and post-9/11 civil liberties.

These organizations do not represent all racial and ethnic minority organizations, by any means, but their low level of interest in international issues or U.S. foreign policy should suggest that the organizational leadership of U.S. minority communities, like U.S. racial and ethnic populations, is primarily focused on a domestic policy agenda. In the future, it is likely that more specialized organizations with a focus specifically on foreign policy issues at a regional (or pan-ethnic) level will appear in U.S. racial and ethnic communities. At present, this sort of specialized, foreign policy–focused organizing appears only in the African American community among the United States' racial and ethnic populations.[48]

CONCLUSION: THE POLITICAL VALUE OF TRANSNATIONAL POLITICS

With immigrants and their children making up a large and growing share of the U.S. minority population, transnational politics is critical to understanding the future of U.S. minority politics. The range of transnational civic and political venues is increasing, and immigrant-sending countries are more often facilitating émigré participation than they have in the past. As a result, the relatively low share of immigrants who are participating in these activities today should not be read as a prediction that a low share will always participate. Instead, immigrant frustrations with their opportunities to adapt to U.S. society and to shape U.S. political outcomes could drive immigrants to use transnational politics as a tool to achieve political efficacy, if they come to perceive that the immigrant-sending country will be more responsive to their organization and demands than is the United States. If this should happen, and we think it unlikely, it would be a considerable supplement to the roots of much of today's transnational engagement—those roots being the desire that has always existed among immigrants to maintain connections with their families and communities in the country of origin.

Should the United States fear transnational engagement among its immigrants? The evidence from today's migrants says no. On the contrary, the transnationally engaged are also more engaged in U.S. civic life and are more likely to naturalize as U.S. citizens. We suspect this reflects the fact that some people are simply more political than others, and that those who are find opportunities to act collectively. Immigrants who fit this profile don't necessarily make a distinction between community and civic efforts focused on the country of origin or focused on co-nationals in the United States (just as they don't see a contradiction between being American and being attached politically to the country of origin). The skills they learn in one venue can easily translate to the other. Ultimately, this serves as a resource for the United States. Americans today generally are less civically and politically involved than they have been in the past, so resources to encourage involvement and train people to participate are an important asset. Transnationalism should be embraced as a tool for immigrant incorporation and not feared as a barrier.

A second question that emerges from immigrant transnational engagement is whether increased engagement will add foreign policy issues to the agendas of U.S.-born co-ethnics or to the agendas of the national U.S. racial and ethnic civil rights organizations. For example, will increasing numbers of immigrants from China increase the need for Asian American organizations to develop a policy agenda on U.S. economic or political relations with China? There is less evidence to answer this question. Despite the growth of transnational organizing over the last two decades, the agendas of national organizations have not become more internationally focused. In this, they reflect a long-standing characteristic of Americans of all races and ethnicities to focus on domestic concerns more than international ones. Thus, in terms of relative interest in foreign policy, race/ethnicity proves largely inconsequential.

Immigrants and their children may be able to make the United States somewhat more international in terms of language and cultural practices, but their effect will ultimately be muted by the fact that the political interests of émigrés and their children will likely focus on their country of origin or ancestry rather than adopt a regional or international focus more generally. The second generation's interests will likely be more on their ancestral culture rather than questions of politics. Over time, then, it is more likely that the descendants of today's immigrants will follow the pattern of those of previous generations and focus their political energies increasingly on domestic concerns—except in times of crisis, when ancestry overlaps with humanitarian impulses.

DISCUSSION QUESTIONS

1. What are the implications of the growing ease of transnational engagement?

2. In what ways does the desire among emigrants to maintain cultural, social, civic, and political ties to their communities of origin contribute to the establishment of civic life in the receiving country?

3. Compare the motivations and benefits of transnational activity for the sending and receiving countries. Which receives the greater advantage, and how so?

4. Race and ethnicity do not drive the likelihood of immigrant transnational engagement in today's society. If policies were to change and immigrant transnational engagement were to be discouraged by the U.S. government or the states, would race/ethnicity become more or less important as a predictor of various forms of immigrant transnationalism? Explain your answer.

KEY TERMS

collective action (p. 365)
collective remittances (p. 365)
diasporic politics (p. 359)
dual citizenship (p. 370)
emigrant (p. 361)
émigré (p. 361)
hometown associations
  (HTAs) (p. 367)

immigrant (p. 359)
immigrant adaptation (p. 378)
immigrant-ethnic (p. 359)
migrant (p. 361)
overseas constituency (p. 368)
receiving country
  (or destination country) (p. 370)

remittances (p. 363)
sending country (or country
  of origin) (p. 361)
transnational (p. 361)

13 Beyond Race: Intersections of Race, Gender, Class, and Sexual Orientation

As opposed to examining gender, race, class, and nation as separate systems of oppression, intersectionality explores how these systems mutually construct one another . . . across multiple systems of oppression and serve as focal points or privileged social locations for these intersecting systems.

—Patricia Hill Collins[1]

In *Uneven Roads* we have examined the journeys of Whites, Blacks, Latinos, Asian Americans, and Native Americans as they sought inclusion in the U.S. political system and society. Beginning in the colonial times of the late 1700s when the American Republic was first founded up to today, those persons considered White have remained the dominant group to lead the polity and shape the society.[2] But that is only part of this broader story. We have presented an *Uneven Roads* racialization framework to explain why race, racism, and ethnicity are not the same today as they were 50 years ago, let alone 250 years ago. They are more complex processes in the early twenty-first century and are, in many cases, literally not as black and white as long ago, though they have never been simple. We have had you think about *when* (the periods in time and the contexts), *why* (the rationales), and *how* (the processes and institutions) race

> ## Box 13.1 Chapter Objectives
>
> - Contrast the racial status of various racial and ethnic groups.
> - Discuss identity politics and how it led to mass movements that matter today.
> - Describe "intersectionality" and its role in politics today.
> - Explain the role of illuminated individualism in countering implicit bias.

Some inequality concerns are not a matter of race or ethnicity but of class, gender, or sexual orientation. The Occupy Movement began in 2011 in response to economic inequality, with people of all backgrounds joining the protest. Issues such as these affect people of all races and ethnicities and bring them together in a common cause.

has ranged from being an absolute to an inconsequential barrier to a group's well-being. From controversies surrounding the enforcement of voting rights to the usefulness of affirmative action, there remains a large debate in American society about whether race, racism, and ethnicity present consequential barriers or roadblocks for racial and ethnic minorities.

In fact, we began this text by remarking that when Barack Obama won both the 2008 and 2012 presidential elections some pundits concluded that we now live in a "postracial America." They saw race as becoming an inconsequential factor in American politics because, for the first time in U.S. history, an African American had won two presidential elections with levels of support from White voters comparable to those of other Democratic candidates, all of whom had been White. In April 2014 Donald Sterling, the owner of the professional basketball team the Los Angeles Clippers and who is White, was caught remarking to his girlfriend that he did not want her associating with Black people, even though they comprise 76 percent of the National Basketball Association's (NBA's) players. That these remarks were unanimously condemned by public figures on the political left, including President Barack Obama and U.S. House of Representatives minority leader Nancy Pelosi, and the right, such as U.S. House of Representatives Speaker John Boehner and Senate minority leader Mitchell McConnell, was taken as evidence by conservative commentator Rush Limbaugh that there is no more racism in the contemporary United States.[3] We hope we have convinced you otherwise, even while we can certainly disagree about the extent of the problem. Despite enormous racial progress in the United States in the last fifty years, we contend that race and racism still matter in American society and politics. For most racial and ethnic minorities, various barriers have not disappeared as they have pursued full citizenship rights, fought for economic and educational opportunities, and run for political office. For White Americans of various European ethnic ancestries, race or ethnicity are currently not barriers as they pursue their citizenship rights and economic opportunities, and in fact are most often an advantage, according to scholars of White privilege.[4]

This final chapter has two main purposes. First, we will explain the book's main conclusion that race and ethnicity still matter. We will focus on issues beyond race and discuss how race is interrelated to or intersected by other forms of identity and discrimination, including sexism, classism, and homophobia or heterosexism. Second, we will discuss the formation of successful political coalitions that have confronted the barriers and divides of race and ethnicity, among other things, and also give you food for thought as to what you can do as an individual and with groups to confront these barriers and divides.

THE STILL UNEVEN ROADS OF RACE, RACISM, AND ETHNICITY

Even with the passage of the 1965 Immigration and Nationality Act and the civil rights reforms of the 1964 Civil Rights Act, the 1965 Voting Rights Act, and the 1968 Fair Housing Act, racial and ethnic minorities are still pushing for inclusion in the polity—that is the broad governing framework within which political and economic interaction occurs. For example, Blacks and Latinos seek unfettered access to voting without the restrictions of the voter identification laws that they feel could subtly discriminate against them, and Native Americans continue to push for greater enforcement of long-standing treaty commitments.[5] True to the main theme of this book, racial and ethnic groups in the United States have traveled along uneven roads toward full citizenship and equal opportunities. These roads began in widely varying places and, given the contours of each, have ended at different destinations. As the previous chapters have noted, these roads are quite different in terms of whether they are curved, smooth, bumpy, hilly, or filled with potholes. Whites have been citizens from the founding of the Republic, but various groups have experienced different qualities of citizenship, depending on whether they were in the most desired category of Northern European and/or Protestant (such as English and German), or instead were Southern European and/or Catholic (such as Irish and Italian). Not until the mid–twentieth century did the idea of one White racial identity comprised of all who were of European ancestry arise.[6] (See Chapter 6.) Initially, there were no roads for African Americans, Chinese (later all Asians), and Native Americans to become U.S. citizens. Court cases and the *Congressional Record* indicate that the U.S. government believed that Blacks, Asians, and Native Americans did not fit the image of U.S. citizens and would never assimilate into American culture. In the case of Native Americans, obtaining U.S. citizenship was not their goal; instead, they sought—and seek—sovereignty rights for their lands. (See Chapter 2.) Latinos were very unevenly incorporated into American citizenship through very different processes, depending on the nature of the relationship the United States established with the nation from which they emigrated.[7] (See Chapter 4.)

To return to our racialization framework, each group has traveled along a progression and is now experiencing different qualities of citizenship and opportunities. Figure 13.1 illustrates that from a key point in a group's history until today, it has had to progress through the factors of racialization that have resulted in race and ethnicity mattering in very different ways. Table 1.3 in Chapter 1 is an important reference point in helping you to understand Figure 13.1, which applies that table to all of the groups. The arrows in Figure 13.1 are not meant to indicate that each group has experienced a straight path of progression. Rather, they indicate the range and strength of barriers each group has confronted that would lead to race being an absolute, decisive, insufficient, or inconsequential factor. At the end of each arrow is a bracket that indicates the current range in which a majority of persons in that group falls. If you review the economic and educational well-being of each group as discussed in Chapter 1 (coupled with an understanding of the group's political history, considered in Chapters 2 through 6, and current issues of concern, described in Chapters 7 through 12), you will see how we have reached our conclusions.

Our three broad conclusions are somewhat influenced by sociologist Eduardo Bonilla-Silva's theory of America's evolving tri-racial system, whereby racism is based not just on race but also on other indicators of social status, including class or economic standing.[8] First, as Figure 13.1 shows, the ranges of racial and ethnic barriers that many Native Americans, Blacks, and Latinos confront have led to racism being everything from a decisive, to insufficient, barrier to their present well-being. These groups most often occupy a **subordinate racial position** in the U.S. polity and society relative to Whites, meaning they are the most politically and economically disadvantaged. As indicated by the brackets, however, there is a very wide range of possibilities with regard to race decisively mattering or not mattering enough to produce an adverse outcome for members of these groups. Second, the ranges of racial and ethnic barriers Asian Americans confront have led to racism being everything from a decisive, to a nearly inconsequential, barrier to their present well-being. These groups at times occupy an **intermediary racial position** in the polity and society. They neither have all of the advantages of the dominant group (Whites) nor all of the disadvantages of subordinate groups (Native Americans, Blacks, and Latinos). Despite the moderate to great economic or educational success of Asian Americans, the model minority stereotype referenced in Chapter 5 is still active. As evident from post-9/11 racial/ethnic profiling, Whites sometimes racialize Asian Americans as foreigners or alien others and perceive them as racial threats worthy of surveillance, containment, or violence.[9] Last, the ranges of racial and ethnic barriers that Whites confront in the current era have led to racism being an insufficient to inconsequential factor to the group's well-being. Thus Whites occupy a **superordinate racial position,** the most advantaged or the most powerful position in the U.S. polity and society relative to all other racial and ethnic groups.[10]

How well does the theory of a tri-racial system apply to the United States?

Having reached these three conclusions, we want you to note that for none of the groups discussed do we believe that race is an absolute barrier as it might have been in the past. There is a difference between the seventeenth-century enslavement of Africans or the nineteenth-century military annihilation of Native Americans versus the issues of the present-day mass incarceration of African Americans and the poverty of Native Americans.[11] We also remind you that the brackets in Figure 13.1 indicate a range of possibilities concerning how race matters today—from decisive to inconsequential. Because there is such a broad range of contemporary possibilities, we explain some of the other factors that intersect with or mediate race, including gender, class, and sexual orientation.

To mediate race means that individuals and groups within racial and ethnic groups experience racism and racial discrimination in very different ways as a result of factors other than race. For example, there is a difference between Donald Sterling—the wealthy (now former) owner of the Los Angeles Clippers basketball team, who is White—making private, anti-Black comments about legendary former basketball player Magic Johnson, who is also wealthy, versus Sterling as an owner of apartment buildings publicly discriminating against working-class and low-income Blacks and Hispanics by refusing to rent them units. In this specific case, it is at least true that class or socioeconomic status is mediating race, so that a wealthy African American man or woman (for instance, media mogul Oprah Winfrey) may understandably experience psychological pain from being victimized by racial prejudice or bigotry. But they do not experience the same economic hardships as working-class Blacks or Latinos because such wealthy people can effectively resist or fight Sterling's racism (or that of other Whites) in ways that are not true for low-income African Americans and Latinos who seek to be Sterling's tenants.[12] Another way to think of this is that poor women or LGBT persons experience a greater sense of **marginalization,** whereby a dominant group—for instance, men, rich corporations, or heterosexuals—discriminate against them and relegate them to the less visible and powerful sectors of society and the polity.[13]

THE UNEVEN ROADS OF IDENTITY POLITICS

Before we discuss how race is often mediated by other factors, let us briefly consider the background of the other marginalization factors of gender, class, and sexual orientation in the United States. **Identity politics** stems from the liberal social movements of the 1960s and 1970s and refers to the new political consciousness various groups developed as they became more aware of the institutional inequalities or structural discrimination they faced in relation to more powerful groups and institutions.[14] Between 1950 and 2000 the fight for equal rights took place in various arenas and through mass movements as Blacks and other racial minorities, workers, women, lesbians and gays, as well as others asserted their grievances about their lack of equal opportunity. These movements raised questions about group identity as individuals within larger groups felt oppressed and exploited.[15]

There are several examples of the new identities that emerged in the 1960s and 1970s in which groups rejected old group labels and assumed what they saw as more positive names. Civil Rights and later Black Power Movement activists began to reject the term *Negro* in favor of *Black, Afro-American*, and in some cases *African;* they saw the latter terms as less racially demeaning (some racists would pronounce Negro *Niggra*) and as consistent with a proud

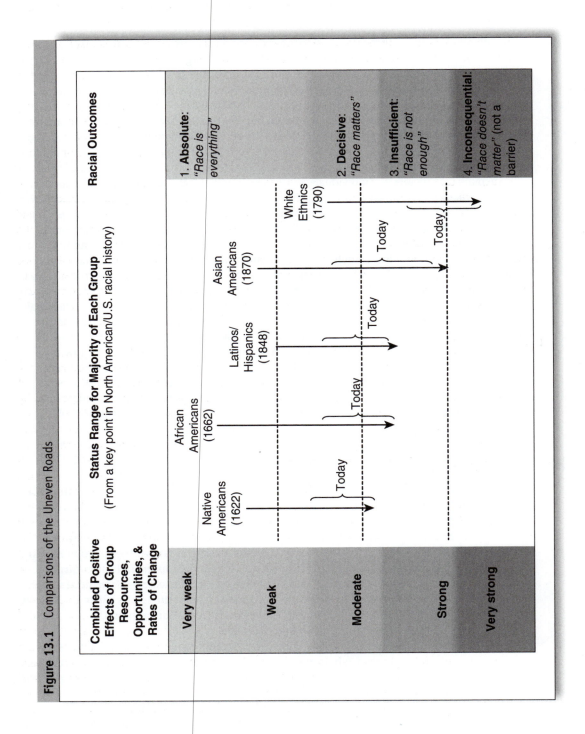

Figure 13.1 Comparisons of the Uneven Roads

Combined Positive Effects of Group Resources, Opportunities, & Rates of Change

- Very weak
- Weak
- Moderate
- Strong
- Very strong

Status Range for Majority of Each Group
(From a key point in North American/U.S. racial history)

- Native Americans (1622)
- African Americans (1662)
- Latinos/Hispanics (1848)
- Asian Americans (1870)
- White Ethnics (1790)

Today

Racial Outcomes

1. **Absolute:** *"Race is everything"*
2. **Decisive:** *"Race matters"*
3. **Insufficient:** *"Race is not enough"*
4. **Inconsequential:** *"Race doesn't matter"* (not a barrier)

African past. Women's liberation movement activists rejected the belittling sexism of grown women being referred to as *girls* and insisted on being called *women* and addressed by the professional honorific of *Ms.* versus *Miss* and *Mrs,* which introduced women according to marital status.

There are other examples in which groups in the 1960s and 1970s inverted the previously negative connotations or meanings of group labels and rebranded them as positive. Brown Power Movement activists began to reject the terms *Mexican* or *Spanish-speaking* for *Chicano,* a word that previously had a negative connotation, for they now saw the latter as more culturally in sync with their language and heritage. Gay Rights Movement activists took the antigay slur of *queer* and in some cases rebranded it to all persons who do not fit into mainstream ideas of sexuality and gender expression, including lesbian women or gay men, bisexual persons, and transgender persons (who feel there is some disjuncture between their biological sex and their true gendered sense of self).[16] Today, these communities are included under the acronym of LGBT.[17] The 1950s–1960s Civil Rights Movement among African Americans and their allies marked the beginning of an entrenched fight for the rights of all Americans. (See Chapter 7.) Every group that followed the Black push for equality built on the techniques of the Civil Rights Movement to make the public aware of the discrimination they had experienced and the need for government enforcement of their rights.

Gender and the Women's Movement

Discrimination or marginalization based on one's being a woman is referred to as **sexism**—or, in its most violent forms, as misogyny. The spark that ignited the Women's Movement of the mid–twentieth century in the U.S. was the 1963 publication of *The Feminine Mystique* by Betty Friedan. This period has been called "second-wave feminism" because it followed the eighteenth- and early nineteenth-century women's suffrage and early women's rights movements that first challenged society's traditional ideas about women and **gender** (the presumptions, roles, and practices a society assigns to the biological sexes of male and female). In Friedan's describing "the problem that had no name," or society ignoring how it confined women to play very limited roles—mother, housewife—she focused on the frustration of one segment of the female population—suburban, college-educated, middle-class White women who felt that they were unfulfilled because they had no identity other than as housewives.[18] In moving from author to organizer, Friedan helped to found the **National Organization for Women (NOW)** in 1966, with the goal of bringing women into the American mainstream and challenging gender inequalities.[19] Inspired by the Civil Rights Movement—and Simone de Beauvoir's The Second Sex—Friedan and the founders of NOW questioned the limited rights of women in American society. Women benefited from the legislative gains of the Civil Rights Movement by noting that the 1964 Civil Rights Act prohibited discrimination on the basis of sex as well as race, color, religion, or national origin. U.S. Representative Howard Smith of Virginia had the word *sex* included in the bill as a joke because he assumed that requiring gender equality would make it impossible to pass. Through the efforts of U.S. Representative Martha Griffiths of Michigan, however, the bill passed when Congressman Smith was absent.[20]

Up until the early twentieth century, women were constrained by the common law doctrine of coverture, which considered the husband and wife as one entity. In many states married women could not own property in their own name, file lawsuits, be sued separately, or execute

Gender inequalities brought women together in coalitions to press for greater rights, including the right to own property in their own name and to be free from discrimination based on marital status. The proposed Equal Rights Amendment aimed to ensure that women were guaranteed the same rights as men in U.S. society, but in 1982 it failed to obtain ratification.

contracts.[21] By the 1960s and 1970s, NOW broadcast its message widely through various efforts: organizing a march down New York's Fifth Avenue; promoting books such as *Our Bodies, Ourselves;* leading consciousness-raising sessions where people gathered and read and discussed materials that focused on sexism and gender inequality; as well as supporting publications such as *Ms.* magazine, and edited by Gloria Steinem and Letty Cottin Pogrebin. NOW focused on discrimination in the workplace, where women were usually relegated to (then especially) low-paying jobs such as teachers, nurses, or secretaries, with little room for advancement. Women also faced considerable barriers in entering professional schools such as medicine or law. All the professional managerial positions had previously been designated for males.[22]

One major problem for solidarity among women was that the public face of the Women's Movement was middle-class and upper-class White women, even though Black women and later Latinas were also vital leaders. The feminist activism of African American lawyers Pauli (Anna Pauline) Murray and Flo (Florynce) Kennedy overlapped with their Civil Rights Movement activism. Murray was a founding member of the Congress of Racial Equality (CORE) in 1942, and subsequently a founding member of NOW. She is credited with having persuaded Betty Friedan that "the country needed an NAACP for women." The outspoken activist Flo Kennedy was also a founder of NOW as a well as publicly self-identified or "out" lesbian and contributor to the Gay Rights Movement. Kennedy was known for her wit and joined Gloria Steinem on a lecture tour in the 1970s. Her philosophy on how to secure women's rights was, "When you want to get to the suites, start in the streets." She was a founder of the Women's Political Caucus and the Media Workshop to combat racism in journalism. Just as the media presented an inaccurate image of the African American Civil Rights Movement when it highlighted the leadership of Black men, all the leaders of the Women's Movement certainly were not White women. Eventually, Black feminists formed two new organizations: the National Black Feminist organization (NBFO) and Black Women Organized for Action (BWAO).[23]

Although there were racial differences among feminists, obtaining economic rights and opportunities were major battles for the entire movement. Through their protest efforts, women had their rights affirmed in the Equal Pay Act of 1963, which eliminated wage differentials based on sex to ensure that women would get equal pay for equal work. Obtaining credit in their own name had been a huge obstacle for women, especially divorced women. Finally, in 1974 the Equal Credit Opportunity Act prohibited discrimination on the basis of marital status, age, race, religion, gender, or ethnic background. [24] Both of these acts benefitted all women. A proposed **Equal Rights Amendment (ERA)** stated, "Equality of rights under the law shall not be denied or abridged by the United States or by any State on account of sex." Passage of the ERA was considered key to ensuring that women had all the rights of men in American society. When the amendment was sent to the states, only thirty-five states out of the needed thirty-eight ratified it before the 1982 deadline. This was a major blow to NOW and the over two hundred organizations that had supported passage of the amendment. [25]

The 2009 Lilly Ledbetter Fair Pay Act, an amendment to the 1964 Civil Rights Act that extended the time a plaintiff may file a suit of gender wage discrimination, continues the fight to close pay disparities. Despite this legislation, today there remains a significant disparity in the ratio of women's earnings to those of men. In 2013 women only took home a median of about 82 percent of the weekly earnings of men, even when they had the same occupation. This 82 percent is a significant improvement, when in the mid-1970s women only earned a little more than 60 percent of the weekly earnings of men. In some cases, the gap is even larger when we take race and ethnicity into account. In 2013 White women earned 80.1 percent of the earnings of White men, but the figures were 68.1 percent for Black women, 59.3 percent for Latinas, and 87.6 percent for Asian American women. [26]

Class and Economic Justice Movements

Another component of an individual's identity and a determinant of equal opportunity is class. Class or **socioeconomic status** is comprised of the combination of an individual's education, income, and occupation. Discrimination or marginalization based on one's having a lower income or being poor is referred to as **classism.** The American labor movement has been an advocate for the rights of workers. Its history stems back to the mid–eighteenth century and witnessed significant breakthroughs in the 1930s with the passage of the National Labor Relations Act, which established the right of workers to organize unions and to collectively negotiate with their managers. But the movement has witnessed a significant decline in membership over the past several decades. In 2013 only 11.3 percent (14.5 million) wage and salary workers in the United States belonged to unions, as compared to 20.1 percent (17.7 million) in 1983. Part of these declines in membership are due to federal and state court and legislative actions that either have weakened the right of workers to organize unions or to collectively bargain for wage increases, especially in the South. [27]

Despite declines in labor movement membership, there has been extensive public discussion about the rising levels of **income inequality** in the United States, or the problem that the very rich own an increasing share of the income and wealth of the nation and average wages and income are not increasing, even as the productivity of American workers is increasing. In the United States there are wide disparities in income and class standing, even though most people identify as middle class. Economists Estelle Sommeiller and Mark Price of the Economic Analysis and Research Network stated in a 2014 report: "Between 1979 and 2007, the top 1 percent took home well over half (53.9 percent) of the total increase in U.S. income. Over this period, the average income of the bottom 99 percent of U.S. taxpayers grew by 18.9 percent. Simultaneously, the average income of the top 1 percent grew over 10 times as much—by 200.5 percent."[28] The income inequality witnessed under the Great Recession of 2008–2009 was the highest on record since the 1920s and the Great Depression of the 1930s. As noted previously, when we factor in race, such gaps are also quite large. Between 1984 and 2009, for example, the Black-White family wealth gap increased from $85,000 to a nearly triple figure of $236,500.

Although the labor movement remains an important factor in challenging today's issues of economic inequality or unfairness, there are a number of other movements that have emerged to lead this challenge. Immigrants to the United States are captivated by the idea of the American Dream, a national belief that the United States is a land of enormous opportunity where nearly everyone can succeed if they simply work hard. The previous data we discussed significantly qualify this belief.

On September 17, 2011, a group of people who were disgusted with how little the government was doing to level rising income and wealth inequality as well as to stop the greed and corruption of Wall Street and large corporations decided to begin a sit-in protest in New York City's Zuccotti Park. Labeling themselves the 99 Percent Movement (or the 99 percent of all persons who do not own a majority of the nation's income) or Occupy Movement, they protested against the 1 percent (or the most wealthy families and individuals in the United States), as symbolized by Wall Street. The financial sector was blamed for greed, the widening income gap between the 1 percent and the other 99 percent, and influencing the federal government to enforce the weak regulations of the financial industry. The protesters were a relative cross-section of the population, with surveys showing a mean age of thirty-three and a breakdown of 68 percent White, 10 percent Hispanic, 10 percent Black, 7 percent Asian American, and 5 percent claiming the ethnic identity of "other." Economically, about half were employed, and most considered themselves political independents.[29] This is just one of many other economic justice movements that have emerged in the United States since the 1960s. Others include the Welfare Rights Movement led by Johnnie Tillmon, Beulah Sanders, and Annie Smart of the National Welfare Rights Organization as well as the living wage movement.[30]

Sexual Orientation and the LGBT Movement

A third form of identity politics is rooted in **sexual orientation,** or the sexual-attraction identity individuals privately and/or publicly embrace in affirming they are a lesbian woman, a gay man, a bisexual person, or a transgender person. Like the Women's Movement and economic justice movement, the LGBT movement has a history rooted in discriminated individuals developing new forms of self-awareness and consciousness, uniting together, and challenging their marginalization. Discrimination or marginalization based on one's being LGBT is referred to as **homophobia,** or heterosexism. The concept of one's being "homosexual" is a fairly recent one (late nineteenth into the twentieth century), although persons having sex with others of their own sex is an ancient practice. Given contemporary religious and cultural beliefs and norms that frequently considered homosexuality abhorrent or alien,

LGBT persons have been greatly marginalized in American society until most recently. In fact, not until 1973 did the American Psychiatric Association stop classifying homosexuality as a mental disorder.

There were various waves of overt and underground activism between the 1940s and the 1960s.[31] The 1969 Stonewall Uprising is the event that the modern LGBT movement sees as its most prominent point of origin. This series of riots sprung from a June 28, 1969, police raid on a gay club in Greenwich Village, New York City, the Stonewall Inn. It was a common practice of police in New York and many other cities to aggressively enforce state and local ordinances outlawing homosexuality and thus gay clubs. Angered by yet another instance of harassment and marginalization, those at the club, some of whom were Black and Latino, retaliated against the police and rioted for several days, and in turn sparked what came to be known as the Gay Liberation Movement, or what we refer to as the Gay Rights Movement.[32]

By the 1970s, the first Gay Pride parades took place in New York as well as Los Angeles and Chicago, and a multitude of grassroots and national gay rights organizations and institutions formed, including the Lambda Legal Defense and Education Fund, the Gay Rights Alliance of New York City, the National Gay Task Force, and eventually the Human Rights Campaign. There had long been a struggle within the movement about its strategy. Should it be one of overt public activism and lawsuits that challenged norms and laws that marginalized LGBT persons—such as antisodomy laws that made homosexual sex and, more broadly, "homosexual conduct" a crime, and the hiring of openly gay teachers illegal? Should the movement take a more moderate, conservative approach of quietly changing public attitudes about LGBT persons—demonstrating they were just like everyone else—in the hope of eventually changing the laws? [33]

Actions and court cases such as *Doe v. Commonwealth's Attorney for the City of Richmond* dealt the activist strategy and the whole movement significant setbacks. In this 1975 case a federal district court and the U.S. Supreme Court affirmed that Virginia's sodomy laws were constitutional. During this period, entertainer and religious conservative Anita Bryant successfully campaigned in the state of Florida to repeal local gay rights ordinances in the Sunshine State. Despite these setbacks, the movement continued forward in many respects, including the election of openly gay public officials, such as the 1977 seating of the legendary San Francisco Board of Supervisors member Harvey Milk (who was later murdered in his office); the 1979 National March on Washington for lesbian and Gay Rights, which gathered a record 75,000 demonstrators; and the 1980 National Democratic Convention, which included gay rights as a civil rights issue in its platform—the first time a major political party had taken such an action. It was the early to mid-1980s discovery of HIV/AIDS—an epidemic that ravaged the LGBT community, with record numbers of gay men dying from this disease transmitted through blood and bodily fluids—that in 1987 prompted a new urgency and sparked the creation of extremely activist groups such the AIDS Coalition to Unleash Power (ACT UP). This group advocated for the eventual passage of the 1990 Ryan White Care Act, which provided federal funding to support victims of HIV/AIDS.[34]

In the 1990s and 2000s, there had been a transformation in the public attitudes and some of the laws that have marginalized LGBT

Does today's discrimination based on gender, class, or sexual orientation create greater barriers to full citizenship and equal opportunity than discrimination based on race?

communities. The period effectively began when Democratic president Bill Clinton reluctantly implemented the 1993 **Don't Ask, Don't Tell** policy, which affirmed the ban of openly gay and lesbian persons from the U.S. military but also in theory prohibited people from being asked their sexual orientation (it did not work, because gays and lesbians were instead targeted). It continued in 1996, when Clinton signed the **Defense of Marriage Act (DOMA).** The latter gave a federal definition of marriage as a legal union between one woman and one man; it also allowed states not to have to observe same-sex marriages performed in other states.

The current period has witnessed great progress. The U.S. Supreme Court declared elements of DOMA unconstitutional and affirmed a lower court overturning a California ban on same-sex marriage. The Obama administration successfully encouraged the U.S. Senate to repeal Don't Ask, Don't Tell, and among its other pro–LGBT rights pronouncements said it will permit legally married same-sex couples to jointly file federal taxes and to share in federal employee benefits like health care.[35] Led in part by the group Freedom to Marry, the Marriage Equality Movement has made great strides in the last decade. As of mid-2014, nearly twenty states have passed laws that permit same-sex marriage, including the mid-Atlantic state of Maryland. In a little more than a decade, there has been a major cultural shift in American public opinion toward LGBT persons and same-sex marriage. Whereas in 2001, a solid majority or 57 percent of Americans opposed and 35 percent favored same-sex marriage, in 2014 a solid majority of 54 percent approved and 39 percent opposed it, with a whopping 69 percent of the younger generation approving.

With all of this progress, a number of states continue to permit (and in some cases encourage) job and housing discrimination against LGBT persons as well as outright bans against same-sex marriage. Researcher Randy Albelda and her coauthors on a Williams Institute report found that as many as 25 percent of lesbian households live below the poverty line, as compared to 19 percent of their heterosexual counterparts; and children in gay and lesbian–couple families are twice as likely to live in poverty as children in heterosexual households. Racial discrimination compounds this economic discrimination against LGBT persons, with 14.4 percent of Black gay male households and 21.1 percent of Black

AFP/Getty Images

On June 26, 2013, gay rights activists outside the U.S. Supreme Court celebrate the ruling that struck down the Defense of Marriage Act, which defined marriage as a legal union between one woman and one man. As public opinion changes, several states have passed laws such as those allowing same-sex marriage, but discrimination against LGBT persons continues to present roadblocks to their equal treatment.

lesbian households living in poverty, compared to only 9.3 percent of Black heterosexual households. It is important to note that LGBT persons of color, such as the poet and civil rights leader Audre Lorde, and the civil rights leader and organizer of the 1963 March on Washington, Bayard Rustin, have made fundamental contributions to the strides made by the LGBT movement.[36]

INTERSECTING ROADS: RACE, GENDER, CLASS, AND SEXUAL ORIENTATION

We now turn to our previous discussion of understanding how gender, class, and sexual orientation mediate race through a process of **intersectionality**. We use the term *intersectionality* as a framework or scholarly lens through which to examine how various factors have interacted with race to determine the political experience or status of all groups, but especially subordinate and intermediary racial groups. This approach assumes that there are many or multiple barriers and opportunities an individual or group can face that explain their status in a polity or society. Individuals in turn have many or multiple group identities, even when one identity appears to be dominant—for instance, a Latino person may in fact be a "Latina" or a "woman" who also is "middle class"; a man may also be "gay" and "working class" and "Filipino."

Intersectionality is a framework first devised by scholars of feminist studies, racial and ethnic studies, and legal studies. Kimberle Crenshaw, a law professor and a scholar of feminist and racial/ethnic studies, explains, for example, how best to analyze the circumstances of Black women: "Because the intersectional experience is greater than the sum of racism and sexism, any analysis that does not take intersectionality into account cannot sufficiently address the particular manner in which Black women are subordinated."[37] This approach is more complex than simply saying Black women are subordinated due to racism and sexism. Later in this chapter we will present the concept of illuminated individualism by political essayist Tim Wise. It borrows from the intersectionality framework and provides a way for us to get beyond race, and possibly racism, by "respect[ing] the uniqueness of all persons and communities."[38]

Intersectionality: Barriers and Bridges to Opportunity

Intersectionality is very helpful in two regards. First, it can help us understand just how difficult it is to overcome present-day racism or racial inequality because it is combined with other factors that greatly disadvantage individuals and groups. These factors may also be what are driving apparent racial disparities. For instance, past housing loan discrimination against African American families means they have less equity (accumulated value in their homes) and thus less wealth to pass on to future generations for college educations or home purchases. Likewise, racial disparities may be hiding behind these other factors. For example, the average gap in comparable pay between men and women is many times larger between White men and Latina women.[39]

Second, intersectionality can also help us understand how various group differences can build bridges of commonality between groups that may, in turn, create coalitions. At the end of this chapter, we will discuss how racial and ethnic groups can build multi-identity coalitions in politics. We want you to understand how you can conduct an intersectional analysis both of the larger polity and society as well as the immediate world around you, to move our discussion a little further beyond race and ethnicity.

Intersecting Barriers. With regard to present-day barriers, race and ethnicity remain dominant factors in determining one's place in the United States, but they in turn directly affect one's class standing. While one widely held American belief has been life, liberty, and the pursuit of happiness, the road to social mobility, or opportunities for educational and social advancement and for making a higher income, is uneven. Some of the factors that create potholes along this road include continued racial stereotypes about Black employees, gender disparities in pay, barriers against unionization and fairer wages, as well as job discrimination because one is openly lesbian, gay, or transgender. One Texas Supreme Court case further illustrates how difficult it is to achieve equality when race and class intersect. The basis for the case was income disparities, but these income disparities had and still have racial impacts. The 1973 case of *San Antonio School District v. Rodriquez* [40] questioned the issue of whether the financing of public schools based on county property taxes violated the Equal Protection Clause of the Fourteenth Amendment. Education is a local matter that is not mentioned in the U.S. Constitution, and states greatly differ as to how they fund their public schools. The *San Antonio School District* case considered inequality that resulted from meager financial resources obtained through local property taxes. Because income and wealth are not evenly distributed, some communities are able to spend more on education, and this of course provides greater resources to pupils.

The basis for the San Antonio case is that "children in less affluent communities necessarily received an inferior education because those communities had fewer resources. . . . The contention was that the Texas system's reliance on local property taxes favored the more affluent and violated equal protection requirements because of disparities between districts in per-pupil expenditures." [41] The U.S. Supreme Court held that education was not implicitly protected by the Constitution. It further stated that the Texas system of financing schools resulted in unequal expenditures between children who happened to reside in different districts, but that "such disparities are the product of a system that is so irrational as to be invidiously discriminatory." [42] The majority found that even though there were differences between school districts, it did not constitute direct discrimination. Four out of the nine justices dissented because they saw the poor as being subject to discrimination since there was no constitutional protection. [43] In this case low-income Latinos were denied equality when the Supreme Court found that the Equal Protection Clause did not cover education. This relegated Latinos to inferior schools because property taxes were insufficient to improve the quality of the schools. Despite today's emphasis on achieving diversity, inclusion or equality is not often achieved because laws are not always strictly enforced.

Intersecting Bridges. For all that barriers continue to exist and disadvantage minorities, bridges are also providing avenues to potentially overcome them. A recent mayoral election in New York provides an opportunity to understand how intersectionality builds bridges. New York City is the quintessential American city that reflects all of the diversities we have discussed—racial, ethnic, cultural, class, and sexual orientation. Since the early nineteenth century, New York political parties have selected candidates with a goal of balancing ethnic, racial, and geographical considerations on a ticket. A balanced mayoral ticket would often include a Jew, an Italian, and an Irishman to appeal to voters across ethnic communities. In the twentieth century this widened to include Blacks and Puerto Ricans, as well as women and LGBT candidates. In the 2013 mayoral election, Bill de Blasio was the Democratic candidate for mayor after beating a Black candidate and White lesbian in the primary election. Chinese Americans were represented by John C. Liu, who received most of the Asian community's support. As *New York Times* reporter Sam Roberts noted, de Blasio received 42 percent of the Black vote, 36 percent of the women's vote, and 47 percent of the gay vote. Roberts called this "identity politics in a brand-new form."[44] The assump-

AFP/Getty Images

Bill de Blasio, right, is sworn in as mayor of New York City by former president Bill Clinton in 2014 as his family looks on. De Blasio received a substantial portion of his votes from African Americans, women, and gays, who found in him an intersection of their interests.

tion that voters would vote strictly based on identity politics did not hold true; de Blasio was so popular that he pulled votes from across New York's diverse communities.

De Blasio's candidacy moved from just balancing racial and ethnic identities among candidates to the more complex intersection of identity characteristics represented in his own family. As a White male, de Blasio had Italian heritage on his mother's side and German heritage on his father's. He decided to identify with his Italian relatives, who had reared him, by changing his name from Warren Wilhelm to Bill de Blasio. His 1994 marriage to Chirlane McCray, a Black woman of Barbadian descent, produced biracial children. Their son, Dante, who wears a large Afro, has been called "his father's 'most interesting surrogate.'"[45] His wife, Chirlane, a writer and poet, is known for her 1979 article in *Essence* magazine entitled "I Am a lesbian." When questioned about her sexual orientation, McCray explained that in the 1970s she wrote about her identification as a lesbian, but after meeting de Blasio in 1991 she put aside her assumptions about the form and package her love would assume.[46] The racial diversity within de Blasio's family did not hinder his general election; he won with 73 percent of the vote. In New York City it appears that no one is questioning how many votes were cast because of race, or sexual orientation. This election is just one example of how more complex politics and the road to equality have become.[47]

 Is New York City's 2013 mayoral election the sign of greater social acceptance or an exception to the norm?

ILLUMINATED INDIVIDUALISM AS A RESPONSE TO UNEVEN ROADS

As indicated earlier, political commentator Tim Wise believes that we cannot solve racial inequality and other forms of inequality in the American polity and society by acting in a color-blind fashion that pretends these inequalities do not exist and/or do not matter. He feels we must instead be directly aware of the implicit biases—any ingrained stereotype and/or negative reactions to differences in others—whether they are within ourselves and/or the larger society. He advises us to practice what he calls **illuminated individualism,** whereby we do not assume that any characteristic "automatically tells us what we need to know about a person or their background—while yet acknowledging the general truth that to be white, a person of color, indigenous, or an immigrant continues to have meaning in the United States." He goes on to state that "only by illuminating our own individual and community uniqueness—including our own individual and community uniqueness—including our personal biases—can we hope to check the tendency to disadvantage and exclude."[48] Below are some of the many recommendations Wise makes to practice illuminated individualism:

1. More parents must talk to their children about the issues and problems of race and other inequalities so that young people develop an awareness of these issues and problems.

2. Teachers (from kindergarten to college) must be aware of their implicit biases and those of the society and encourage students who are from minority or nondominant groups to excel by combining "constructive criticism" with a "consistent belief . . . in their potential."

3. Government must require "racial impact statements" for all proposed legislation or policies, in which it analyzes what will be the direct or indirect consequences of this legislation or policy on minority or nondominant communities.

4. Prohibit companies that are guilty of "intentional racial discrimination from receiving government contracts, tax breaks or direct subsidies for a period of at least ten years" and apply a less punitive, "two-strike" policy for companies that have unintentionally discriminated.

5. Target "stimulus and investment in communities where the residents are at least 50 percent persons of color, and all communities with poverty rates that are 150 percent of the national average."[49]

What are some implicit biases evident in today's social and political concerns? How do these biases present roadblocks?

Multi-Identity Coalition-Building

Much of the focus of this book has been on the political and economic dynamics between Whites and racial and ethnic minorities. It is important to recognize, however, that it is quite common for there not only to be practices of discrimination between racial and ethnic groups—such as conflicts between African American customers and Korean American grocers—but also within a racial or ethnic group that marginalizes other group members based on an identity characteristic that is not shared—for instance, heterosexual Irish Americans objecting to LGBT Irish communities marching in a St. Patrick's Day Parade.[50] If we are able to follow Tim Wise's advice and overcome elements of both forms of bias and exclusion, then it may be possible to build multi-identity bridges that may not eliminate racial and other differences, per se, but also are not completely prevented by them.

Political scientists Shaun Bowler and Gary Segura, among other scholars of racial and ethnic politics, have concluded that multiracial coalitions are possible under certain circumstances. We adapt these conclusions and consider how they might apply across various factors of difference. They include the following: (1) political leaders and elites must be able and willing to see or seek an understanding of common interests between communities and use this understanding to mobilize support or agreement within their communities; (2) common economic concerns are often a good basis for coalition-building in situations that are noncompetitive, such as the creation of policy versus direct competition for jobs; (3) political contexts greatly vary and thus leaders and communities must build coalitions according to their our own circumstances; and (4) it is all right for alliances or coalitions to be "quite fragile" so that leaders and communities remain vigilant and responsive to maintaining them and not take their allies for granted.[51]

CONCLUSION: PROSPECTS FOR THE FUTURE

Experts predict that by the year 2050 there will be no racial or ethnic majority in the United States; Whites will comprise 49 percent or less of the total population, and thus it may no longer make sense to use the term *minority*.[52] Simply because a few decades from now the United States will be a very multiracial polity and society in its demographic composition does not necessarily mean that the roads to full citizenship and equal opportunity will be completely even for all. Think about what we all will have to do now in order to overcome the remaining barriers on various uneven roads, but especially on the roads of racial and ethnic politics. How will issues like affirmative action, continued economic disparities, racial profiling, educational achievement gaps, and access to the right to vote further complicate our overcoming these barriers?

Among other states, California, Texas, Florida, and Michigan have decided that affirmative action should be abolished in university admissions, and it is being further challenged in the courts. Will affirmative action have to be tailored to better serve the interests of intermediary communities like Asian Americans, who in some respects are well represented in college and university admissions?[53] While Blacks and Latinos have benefitted from affirmative action, it appears that Asian Americans have benefitted in states that abolished it. In California, Asian Americans' college enrollments increased from 37.3 percent in 1995 to 43.6 percent in 2000. While Latinos make up a larger percentage of the population in California, Texas, and Florida than do Blacks, their enrollment peaked at 16.1 percent in 1995, with a low of 12.5 percent in 2000.[54] Another irony is that the gender equity provisions of affirmative action mean that this policy benefits Whites—particularly White females—to a greater extent than it does racial and ethnic minorities. A 1995 study (the most recent available) of six million women found that White women gained more jobs than did minorities in both the public and private sector because of affirmative action requirements.[55]

Will racial profiling continue to erode constitutional principles because it unfairly targets people of color? Once considered a problem primarily for Black males who were stopped while driving, the scope of the problem has widened. Some considered "driving while Black" to be a joke until these police tactics were used against the Muslim, Arab, and South Asian communities. The Latino community did not escape scrutiny either, because in southwestern states the search for undocumented immigrants is constant.[56] In all of these cases the premise is based on stereotypical images of who is a criminal, a terrorist, or an unauthorized immigrant.

Will the ongoing transformation of the U.S. economy produce continued hardships for and competition between Americans of various racial and ethnic backgrounds seeking to get into the middle class? As we have noted, since the 2008–2009 recession, the gap between the rich and poor has further widened. Reporter Nelson Schwartz of the *New York Times* notes, "The post-recession reality is that the customer base for businesses that appeal to the middle class is shrinking as the top tier pulls even further away."[57] Retailers to the middle class, Sears and J. C. Penney, "have fallen more than 50 percent since the end of 2009," while upscale stores such Nordstrom and bargain stores such as Dollar Tree "have more than doubled in value over the same period."[58]

Will the educational achievement gap between Blacks and Whites, which has been measured frequently since the 1954 decision in *Brown v. Board of Education,* widen in ways that reflect class inequalities as much as racial inequalities? In 2012 this gap narrowed for Blacks and Whites, while the rich–poor gap had increased to 40 percent. Consequently, in poorer school districts class differences will affect the quality of schools, thwarting the aspirations of children who seek to enter the middle class.[59]

Will the basic American right of access to the ballot box prove to be a barrier for the growing Latino electorate? This was a right that was long denied to southern Blacks, but recently it has become more of an issue for new American citizens who speak English as a second language, and for all groups who have less access to government-issued identification such as driver's licenses. Will this continue to be a concern also due to a requirement that the Voting Rights Act be reauthorized every few years, and to the U.S. Supreme Court striking down key VRA provisions when Congress and the president are too divided to update them?[60]

In conclusion, we know we have asked more questions than we have answered. But we want you—the student, the young person who will live your life and may raise a family in the America of 2050 and beyond—to think about what paths we should take if that future is to be politically and economically inclusive of and provide greater opportunities to all who live in this nation. We hope that by thoroughly examining the roads we have taken to be where we are now, we have helped you to chart a better, more informed course to that future America.

DISCUSSION QUESTIONS

1. What conclusions do the authors of this text reach in comparing the racial positions of Native Americans, Blacks, Hispanics, Asian Americans, and Whites? What explains the range of positions occupied within a group (the end of the arrows), as illustrated by Figure 13.1?

2. How do gender, class, and sexual orientation contribute to a different if often related identity politics? How would you describe the different, uneven roads women, the poor and working class, and LGBT persons have had to travel since the 1960s?

3. How does intersectionality provide barriers as well as bridges regarding opportunities? How can race and racism be part of a broader discrimination experienced by groups also facing sexism, classism, and/or homophobia/heterosexism?

4. Describe the concept of illuminated individualism and the types of measures it recommends we take in order to bridge various divides and inequalities, including those created by race and racism.

5. Describe the challenges and opportunities that may exist in the year 2050 in terms of overcoming the uneven roads of race in the United States as well as other forms of discrimination.

KEY TERMS

classism (p. 391)

Defense of Marriage Act (DOMA) (p. 394)

Don't Ask, Don't Tell (p. 393)

Equal Rights Amendment (ERA) (p. 391)

gender (p. 398)

homophobia (p. 392)

identity politics (p. 387)

illuminated individualism (p. 398)

income inequality (p. 391)

intermediary racial position (p. 386)

intersectionality (p. 395)

marginalization (p. 387)

National Organization for Women (NOW) (p. 389)

sexism (p. 389)

sexual orientation (p. 392)

socioeconomic status (p. 391)

subordinate racial position (p. 386)

superordinate racial position (p. 386)

tri-racial system (p. 386)

References

A Tale of Two Schools: Race and Education on Long Island. Documentary. 2012. Available at http://eraseracismny.org/our-work/education/a-tale-of-two-schools-race-and-education-on-long-island.

Adelman, Larry, director. 2003. *Race: The Power of an Illusion.* California Newsreel, episodes 1–3.

Aguilar-San Juan, Karin. 1994. *The State of Asian America: Activism and Resistance in the 1990s.* Cambridge, MA: South End Press.

Alba, Richard. 2009. *Blurring the Color Line: The New Chance for a More Integrated America.* Cambridge, MA: Harvard University Press.

Alexander, Michelle. 2010. *The New Jim Crow: Mass Incarceration in the Age of Colorblindness.* New York and London: The New Press.

Barreto, Matt. 2010. *Ethnic Cues: The Role of Shared Ethnicity in Latino Political Participation.* Ann Arbor: University of Michigan Press.

Baxandall, Rosalyn, and Linda Gordon. 2002. "Second Wave Feminism." *A Companion to American Women's History.* New York: John Wiley and Sons, 414–432.

Black, Latino and Asian Caucus of the New York City Council. Available at http://council.nyc.gov/html/about/bla.shtml.

Bobo, Lawrence, and Vincent L. Hutchings. 1996. "Perceptions of Racial Group Competition: Extending Blumer's Theory of Group Position to a Multiracial Social Context." *American Sociological Review* 61, no. 6 (96/12): 951–972.

Bonilla-Silva, Eduardo, Amanda Lewis, and David G. Embrick. 2004. "I Did Not Get That Job Because of a Black Man . . .": The Story Lines and Testimonies of Color-Blind Racism." *Sociological Forum* 19, no. 4 (December): 555–581.

Bowler, S., and G. Segura. 2012. *The Future Is Ours: Minority Politics, Political Behavior, and the Multiracial Era of American Politics.* Washington, DC: CQ Press.

Bowler, Shaun, and Gary M. Segura. 2012. *The Future Is Ours: Minority Politics, Political Behaviors and the Multicultural Era of American Politics.* Washington, DC: CQ Press.

Broken on All Sides: Race, Mass Incarceration, and New Visions of Criminal Justice in the U.S. Documentary. 2012. Available at http://brokenonallsides.com.

Burke, Joseph C. 1969. "The Cherokee Cases: A Study in Law, Policies, and Morality." *Stanford Law Review* 21 (February): 500–531.

Cherokee Nation v. Georgia, 300 U.S.1 (1831).

"The Chapters of Freedom" National Archives. Available at http://www/archives.gov/exhibits/chapters.

Choy, Christine. 1988. *Who Killed Vincent Chin?* 82 min. Detroit, MI: Film News Now Foundation, WTVS/Detroit.

Crawford, Vicki, Jacqueline Anne Rouse, and Barbara Woods. 1993. *Women in the Civil Rights Movement.* Bloomington: Indiana University Press.

Dawson, Michael C. 1994. *Behind the Mule: Race and Class in African American Politics.* Princeton, NJ: Princeton University Press.

Dawson, Michael. 2001. *Black Visions: The Roots of Contemporary African-American Political Ideologies.* Chicago: University of Chicago Press.

de la Garza, Rodolfo O., and Briant Lindsay Lowell, eds. 2002. *Sending Money Home: Hispanic Remittances and Community Development.* Lanham, MD: Rowman and Littlefield.

Deloria, Vine, Jr. 1970. *Custer Died for Your Sins: An Indian Manifesto.* New York: Avon Books.

Deloria, Vine, Jr. 1974. *Behind the Trail of Broken Treaties.* New York: Delacorte Press.

Deloria, Vine, Jr., and Clifford M. Lytle. 1984. *The Nations Within: The Past and the Future of American Indian Sovereignty.* New York: Pantheon Books.

Deloria, Vine, Jr., and David Wilkins. 1999. *Tribes, Treaties, and Constitutional Tribulations.* Austin: University of Texas Press.

Ducat, Vivian. 1999. "Hawaii's Last Queen." In *The American Experience*, 56 min. Boston, MA: A Ducat Segal Productions, Inc. Film; Public Broadcasting System.

Eckstein, Susan Eva. 2009. *The Immigrant Divide: How Cuban Americans Changed the U.S. and Their Homeland.* New York: Routledge.

Encyclopedia of United States Indian Policy and Law. 2009. Edited by Paul Finkelman and Tim Alan Garrison. 2 vols. Washington, DC: CQ Press. Available at http://library.cqpress.com/ipl.

Evers, Myrlie. 1996. *For Us, the Living.* Jackson: Banner Books/University Press of Mississippi.

Eyes on the Prize: America's Civil Rights Movement 1954–1985. Public Broadcasting Service. Available at http://www.pbs.org/wgbh/amex/eyesontheprize.

Fitzgerald, David. 2009. *A Nation of Emigrants: How Mexico Manages Its Migration.* Berkeley: University of California Press.

Fletcher v. Peck, 10 U.S. 87 (1810).

Fournier, Eric P. 2006. *Of Civil Wrong and Rights: The Fred Korematsu Story.* 70 min. New York: Fred Korematsu Film Project.

Fraga, Luis R., John A. Garcia, Rodney E. Hero, Michael Jones-Correa, Valerie Martinez-Ebers, and Gary M. Segura. 2011. *Latinos in the New Millennium: An Almanac of Opinion, Behavior, and Policy Preferences.* New York: Cambridge University Press.

Fraga, Luis R., John A. Garcia, Rodney E. Hero, Valerie Martinez-Ebers, and Gary M. Segura. 2012. *Latinos in the New Millennium: An Almanac of Opinion, Behavior, and Policy Preferences.* New York: Cambridge University Press.

Franklin, John Hope, and Evelyn Higginbotham. 2010. *From Slavery to Freedom.* New York: McGraw-Hill Humanities/Social Sciences.

García Bedolla, Lisa, and Melissa R. Michelson. 2012. *Mobilizing Inclusion: Transforming the Electorate through Get-Out-the-Vote Campaigns.* New Haven: Yale University Press.

Geron, Kim, Enrique de la Cruz, Leland T. Saito, and Jaideep Singh. 2001. "Asian Pacific Americans' Social Movements and Interest Groups." *PS: Political Science and Politics* 34, no. 3, 618–624.

Gilliam, Franklin, Jr. 2001. *Farther to Go: Readings and Cases in African American Politics.* New York: Harcourt Brace.

Gonzalez, Juan. 2010. *Harvest of Empire: A History of Latinos in America.* New York: Viking.

Grant, Madison. 1918. *The Passing of the Great Race; or, The Racial Basis of European History.* New York: Charles Scribner's and Sons.

Gutiérrez, David G. 1995. *Walls and Mirrors: Mexican Americans, Mexican Immigrants, and the Politics of Ethnicity.* Berkeley: University of California Press.

Haggis, Paul, director. 2004. *Crash.*

Haney-Lopez, Ian. 1996. *White by Law: The Legal Construction of Race.* New York: New York University Press.

Harris, Frederick C. 2012. *The Price of the Ticket: Barack Obama and the Rise and Decline of Black Politics.* New York: Oxford University Press.

Horseman, Reginald. 1971. *Race and Manifest Destiny: The Origins of American Racial Anglo-Saxonism.* Cambridge, MA: Harvard University Press.

Inequality for All. 2013. Documentary.

Johnson v. M'Intosh, 21 U.S. 543 (1823).

Keyssar, Alexander. 2000. *The Right to Vote: The Contested History of Democracy in the United States.* New York: Basic Books.

Kim, Claire Jean. 2000. *Bitter Fruit: The Politics of Black-Korean Conflict in New York City.* New Haven: Yale University Press.

Laguerre, Michel S. 2013. *Parliament and Diaspora in Europe.* New York: Palgrave Macmillan.

Latino Civil Rights Timeline. Available at www.tolerance.org/latino-civil-rights-timeline.

Leadership Conference on Civil Rights—Members. Available at http://www.civilrights.org/about/the-leadership-conference/coalition_members.

Lee, Mun Wah, director. 2008. *The Color of Fear.*

Legislator's Guide to North Carolina Legislative and Congressional Redistricting, 2011 General Assembly. 2011 Regular Session 2011 (March 2011). Research Division, N.C. General Assembly. Available at http://www.ncleg.net/GIS/Download/Maps_Reports/2011Redistricting Guide.pdf.

LeMay, Michael, and Elliott Robert Barkan. 1999. *U.S. Immigration and Naturalization Laws and Issues: A Documentary History.* Westport, CT: Greenwood Press.

Levitt, Peggy. 2001. *The Transnational Villagers.* Berkeley: University of California Press.

Madrid, E. Michael. 2008. "The Unheralded History of the Lemon Grove Desegregation Case." *Multicultural Education* (Spring): 15–19.

Marcus, Hazel Rose, and Paula M. L. Moya, eds. 2010. *Doing Race: 21 Essays for the 21st Century.* New York: W. W. Norton.

Masuoka, Natalie, and Jane Junn. 2013. *The Politics of Belonging: Race, Public Opinion, and Immigration.* Chicago, IL: University of Chicago Press.

McClain, Paula D., and Joseph Stewart Jr. *"Can We All Get Along?" Racial and Ethnic Minorities in American Politics.* 5th ed. Boulder, CO: Westview Press.

McLaughlin, Elliot. 2014. "What we know about Michael Brown's shooting." 15 August. CNN on-line. http://www.cnn.com/2014/08/11/us/missouri-ferguson-michael-brown-what-we-know/

Morris, Aldon. 1986. *The Origins of the Civil Rights Movement: Black Communities Organizing for Change.* New York: The Free Press.

Ogletree, Charles J., Jr. 2004. *All Deliberate Speed: Reflections of the First Half Century of* Brown v. Board of Education. New York and London: W. W. Norton.

Oliver, J. Eric, and Janelle Wong. 2003. "Intergroup Prejudice in Multiethnic Settings." *American Journal of Political Science* 47, no. 4, 567–582.

Oliver, M. L., and T. M. Shapiro. 2006. *Black Wealth, White Wealth: A New Perspective on Racial Inequality.* New York: Routledge.

Ong, Aihwa. 1999. *Flexible Citizenship: The Cultural Logics of Transnationality*. Durham, NC: Duke University Press.

Padilla, Felix. 1985. *Latino Ethnic Consciousness: The Case of Mexican Americans and Puerto Ricans in Chicago*. Notre Dame, IN: University of Notre Dame Press.

Parker, Frank R. 1990. *Black Votes Count: Political Empowerment in Mississippi after 1965*. Chapel Hill: University of North Carolina Press.

Payne, Charles. 1995. *I've Got the Light of Freedom*. Oakland: University of California Press.

Perdue, Theda, and Michael Green. 2007. *The Cherokee Nation and the Trail of Tears*. New York: Penguin Books.

Porter, Kenneth Wiggins. 1996. *The Black Seminoles: History of a Freedom-Seeking People*. Edited by Thomas Senter and Alcione Amos. Gainesville: University of Florida Press.

Provine, Marie Doris, and Roxanne Lynn Doty. 2011. "The Criminalization of Immigrants as a Racial Project." *Journal of Contemporary Criminal Justice* 27, no. 3: 261–277.

Prucha, Francis Paul. 1984. *The Great Father: The United States Government and the American Indians*. Lincoln: University of Nebraska Press.

Ramírez, Ricardo. 2013. *Mobilizing Opportunities: The Evolving Latino Electorate and the Future of American Politics*. Charlottesville: University of Virginia Press.

Riggs, Marlon T., Nicole Atkinson, and Christiane Badgley, directors. 1995. "Black Is . . . Black Ain't." California Newsreel, San Francisco, CA.

Rivers, Christina. 2014. *The Congressional Black Caucus, Minority Voting Rights, and the U.S. Supreme Court*. Ann Arbor: University of Michigan Press.

Roediger, David R. 2005. *Working toward Whiteness: How America's Immigrants Became White*. New York: Basic Books.

Rothstein, Richard. "For Public Schools, Segregation Then, Segregation Since: Education and the Unfinished March." 2013. Washington, DC: Economic Policy Institute.

Schrag, Peter. 2010. Not *Fit for Our Society: Immigration and Nativism in America*. Berkeley: University of California Press.

Schuman, Howard. 1997. *Racial Attitudes in America: Trends and Interpretations*. Cambridge, MA: Harvard University Press.

Sears, David O., Jim Sidanius, and Lawrence Bobo. 2000. *Racialized Politics: The Debate about Racism in America*. Chicago, IL: University of Chicago Press.

Segura, Gary, and Shaun Bowler. 2012. *The Future Is Ours: Minority Politics, Political Behavior, and the Multiracial Era of American Politics*. Washington, DC: CQ Press.

Smedley, Audrey. 1993. *Race in North America: Original and Evolution of a Worldview*. Boulder, CO: Westview Press.

Smith, Michael Peter, and Matt Bakker. 2008. *Citizenship across Borders: The Political Transnationalism of El Migrante*. Ithaca, NY: Cornell University Press.

Smithsonian Institution. "National Museum of the American Indian." Available at http://nmai.si.edu/home.

Stein, Marc. 2012. *Rethinking the Gay and Lesbian Movement*. New York: Routledge.

Stonewall Uprising. 2010. Documentary.

Sucheng Chan. 1991. *Asian Americans: An Interpretive History*. Detroit: Twayne Publishers.

Takaki, Ronald. 1998. *Strangers from a Different Shore: A History of Asian Americans*. New York: Back Bay Books.

The Center for the Study of Race and Equity in Education. Available at http://www.gse.upenn.edu/equity.

The Sentencing Project. Available at http://www.sentencingproject.org/template/index.cfm.

Thorton, Russell. 1987. *American Indian Holocaust and Survival: A Population History since 1492*. Norman: University of Oklahoma Press.

Tichenor, Daniel J. 2002. *Dividing Lines: The Politics of Immigration Control in the United States*. Princeton, NJ: Princeton University Press.

Tonry, Michael. 2011. *Punishing Race: A Continuing American Dilemma*. New York: Oxford University Press.

Trans-Atlantic Slave Trade Database—Voyages. Available at http://slavevoyages.org/tast/index.faces.

Trías Monge, José. 1997. *Puerto Rico: The Trials of the Oldest Colony in the World*. New Haven: Yale University Press.

U.S. Census Bureau. 2010 Census Briefs. Available at http://www.census.gov/2010censusdata/2010-census-briefs.php.

U.S. Census. 2010. Interactive Population Map. Available at http://www.census.gov/2010census/popmap.

U.S. Department of Homeland Security, Office of Immigration Statistics. 2012. *2011 Yearbook of Immigration Statistics*. Washington, DC: U.S. Department of Homeland Security. Available at http://www.dhs.gov/sites/default/files/publications/immigration-statistics/yearbook/2011/ois_yb_2011.pdf.

U.S. Senate. Ethnic Diversity in the Senate. Available at http://www.senate.gov/artandhistory/history/common/briefing/minority_senators.htm.

Verba, Sidney, Kay Lehman Schlozman, and Henry E. Brady. 1995. *Voice and Equality: Civic Voluntarism in American Politics*. Cambridge, MA: Harvard University Press.

"We Shall Remain." *American Experience*. Public Broadcasting Service. Available at http://www.pbs.org/wgbh/amex/weshallremain.

Wilkins, David. 2002. *American Indian Politics and the American Political System*. Lanham, MD: Rowman and Littlefield.

Wise, T. 2013. *Colorblind: The Rise of Post-Racial Politics and the Retreat from Racial Equity*. San Francisco: City Lights Books.

Wong, Janelle, S. Karthick Ramakrishman, Taeku Lee, and Jane Junn. 2011. *Asian American Political Participation*. New York: Russell Sage Foundation.

Wong, Janelle, S. Karthick Ramakrishnan, Taeku Lee, and Jane Junn. 2011. *Asian American Political Participation: Emerging Constituents and Their Political Identities*. New York: Russell Sage Foundation.

Wong, Janelle, S., Karthick Ramakrishnan, Taeku Lee, and Jane Junn. 2011. *Asian American Political Participation: Emerging Constituents and Their Political Identities*. New York: Russell Sage Foundation.

Worcester v. Georgia, 31 U.S. 515 (1832).

Wu, Ellen D. 2013. *The Color of Success: Asian Americans and the Origins of the Model Minority*. Princeton, NJ: Princeton University Press.

Zolberg, Aristide R. 2006. *A Nation by Design: Immigration Policy in the Fashioning of America*. Cambridge, MA, and New York: Harvard University Press and Russell Sage Foundation Press.

Glossary

1808 Prohibition. Clause in Article I of the U.S. Constitution that prohibited Congress from passing any law that ended the importation of slaves from Africa into the United States until twenty years after the Constitution was ratified.

achievement gap. The difference in school performance between White students and African American and Latino students.

affirmative action. Programs designed to ensure that African Americans and other racial/ethnic minorities gain greater access to societal resources, particularly higher education, government jobs, and government contracts.

anti-Asian Movement. Increased White resentment of the Chinese and eventual anti-Chinese violence in California and elsewhere in the 1870s, spurred by economic and racial tensions.

Asian American ethnic associations: Refers to a range of early Asian American organizations in the late 19th century and early 20th century, especially among Chinese, Japanese, and Filipino communities, that promoted the perceived cultural, civic, and in some cases political interests of these communities.

at-large election. An election conducted on a city- or county-wide basis instead of on a system of smaller districts.

Barred Zone. Swath of countries barring the immigration of Asian Indians as part of the 1917 Immigration Act. Included most of the Middle East, Central Asia, South Asia, and Southeast Asia.

birthright citizenship. The grant of U.S. citizenship to persons born in the United States.

Black Power. Movement that challenged racial integration as the primary means to achieve African American empowerment and was inspired by Black Nationalism and the example of Malcolm X as it was initially led by Stokely Carmicheal.

Bracero **program.** A bilateral agreement between the United States and Mexico during World War II to provide seasonal agricultural labor to the U.S. farmers and agricultural processors.

Bradley effect. Occurs when a Black and White candidate compete and a sizeable proportion of Whites assert in polls that they are undecided (social desirability), when ultimately they vote for the White candidate.

Brown v. Board of Education of Topeka, Kansas **(1954).** Landmark Supreme Court decision that declared that "separate but equal" accommodations in public schools were unconstitutional.

Bureau of Indian Affairs (BIA). The office of the federal government responsible for managing Indian relations; established in the early nineteenth century, the BIA oversaw the execution of policies such as assimilation and termination.

Burlingame-Seward Treaty (1868). U.S.-China agreement that prohibited Chinese from naturalizing as U.S. citizens but established the right of citizens to mutually emigrate between both nations to fulfill the increasing labor demands of the United States.

Cable Act. Legislation mandating that any White female citizen who married a noncitizen who was ineligible to naturalize would be stripped of her citizenship.

Carlisle Indian School. Boarding school run by Whites to assimilate Indian children into White culture, often involuntarily.

Chinatown. Predominantly Chinese community within a city. Initially formed as the Chinese adapted to the increasing racial strictures placed upon their businesses and often their residential communities, as Whites viewed them as alien and threatening.

Chinese Exclusion Act (CEA) (1882). Congressional act that prohibited the reentry of Chinese laborers for ten years after they departed the United States, exempting students, diplomats, merchants, and teachers.

classism. Discrimination or marginalization based on one having a lower income or being poor.

civic voluntarism. Activity that has the intent or effect of influencing government action—either directly by affecting the making or implementation of public policy or indirectly by influencing the selection of people who make those policies.

civilization program. The policy adopted under President Thomas Jefferson that aimed to "civilize" Native Americans to the ways of Whites, thus incorporating them into the growing majority culture.

civil right. The enforceable rights or privileges of citizens to political and social freedoms, such as free speech, assembly, and free press.

Civil Rights Act (1866). Federal legislation that stated all persons born in the United States were citizens of their state and of the nation. Outlawed the Black Codes, which many southern governments enacted to try to control freed African Americans by curtailing their economic and political rights.

Civil Rights Act (1957). Federal legislation that created basic civil rights administrative infrastructure in the federal government, including a bipartisan Commission on Civil Rights and a Civil Rights Division within the Department of Justice.

Civil Rights Act (1964). Federal legislation that addressed a variety of areas, including voting rights, relief against discrimination in places of public accommodation, desegregation of public facilities and public education, equal employment opportunity, and registration and voting statistics, among others.

Civil Rights Movement. Actions by Blacks that opened the franchise and electoral participation for Blacks and other minority groups.

Classical Prejudice Model. Theory that asserts interracial hostility depends on individual psychological dispositions rather than objective reality.

collective action. Cooperative efforts to achieve a collective goal.

collective memory. Process whereby historical events not only shape the political views of an immediate generation but prompt the political interpretations of succeeding generations guided by these events.

collective remittance. Money pooled by a group of immigrants and sent to their common community of origin.

color-blind society. An ideological debate as to whether—across a host of public policy arenas such as voting and election laws, education, criminal justice, housing and mortgage lending, job hiring, and college admissions—we should not pay attention to—or be *blind* to—the racial and ethnic background of individuals.

color line. An absolute political boundary in which those considered to be not White were barred from inclusion.

Declaration of Indian Purpose. Document drafted by collectively organized Native Americans in 1961 and presented to President John F. Kennedy, calling for educational reforms, tribal control of resources and social services, and an end to the termination policy.

de facto racial discrimination. Legally permissible inequality that persists without explicit references to race and ethnicity.

Defense of Marriage Act (DOMA). 1996 act that provided a federal definition of marriage as between one woman and one man and allowed states to not have to observe same-sex marriages performed in other states; later overturned by the U.S. Supreme Court.

de jure racial discrimination. Discrimination sanctioned by law.

descriptive representation. Representation by a person of the same racial or ethnic group as the majority of voters in the district.

diasporic politics. Immigrant ties to their countries of origin and how these ties have the power to influence politics on both their native and adopted soils.

discriminatory intent. The intent to disadvantage Blacks or another minority population through a policy or practice.

discriminatory results standard. Part of the 1982 extension of the Voting Rights Act designed to make it possible to prove discrimination in the use of at-large electoral systems, and allow for a remedy in the creation of a number of legislative districts for city councils and/or state legislatures.

disenfranchisement. The act of denying voting access to a certain group.

Don't Ask, Don't Tell. Policy that affirmed the ban of openly gay and lesbian persons from the U.S. military but also in theory prohibited persons from being asked their sexual orientation.

***Dred Scott v. Sandford* (1857).** Supreme Court case in which enslaved Dred Scott sued for his freedom after he moved from a slave state (Missouri) to the Wisconsin Territory (a free jurisdiction). The Court decided that the U.S. Constitution did not apply to Black people, because they "had no rights which the white man was bound to respect."

driving while Black. The policing practices of highway patrol officers whereby minorities, especially African

Americans, are more frequently stopped out of proportion to the actual likelihood that they have broken a traffic law or are probable crime suspects.

dual citizenship. The establishment and maintenance of political membership in two countries.

dual nationality. Status in which an immigrant, called a "national," can exercise rights granted by the law of the country he or she emigrated to, but is not considered a citizen.

El Congreso de Pueblos que Hablan Español (the **Congress of Spanish Speaking Peoples**). Group formed in 1939 to organize the "Spanish speaking" regardless of nativity and call for an end to discrimination against the foreign-born and an end to large-scale deportations.

Election-Day registration. A system that allows for voter registration up to and on Election Day.

Electoral College. Indirect mechanism by which the president is formally elected, made up of delegates from each state.

emigrant. A person who leaves his or her native country for another.

émigré. A person who leaves his or her native country for another country; a person who emigrates.

enfranchisement. The act of opening up access to voting to a certain group.

Enumeration Clause. See Three-Fifths Clause.

Equal Rights Amendment (ERA). Proposed amendment to the U.S. Constitution that sought to ensure equality of rights for all sexes, it failed to achieve the required number of votes in ratification in 1982.

ethnicity. The label used to organize and distinguish peoples based primarily on their cultural practices or national or regional ancestries.

Executive Order 8802. Passed by Roosevelt in July 1941; established broad anti-discrimination guidelines as well as a Fair Employment Practices Committee (FEPC) that had limited powers to monitor hiring practices in war industries.

Executive Order 9066. Along with Public Law 503, presidential order that prohibited all persons of Japanese ancestry from living in areas and regions designated as vital to national security and authorized the Army and other agencies (especially the War Relocation Authority) to provide for the evacuation of such persons to in-land concentration camps.

explicit racial attitude. Overt racially prejudicial or racist views held by groups against other groups or individuals.

federalism. A system of government in which both the national government and sub-national governments—the states in the case of the United States—have independent powers and responsibilities to their citizens.

Fifteenth Amendment (1870). Amendment to the U.S. Constitution that prohibited state governments from denying a citizen the right to vote based on race or former enslavement.

filibuster. The procedural rule in the United States Senate that ending debate requires the votes of 60 of the 100 Senators.

Five Civilized Tribes. Term used by Whites to describe the Choctaw, Creek, Chickasaw, Seminole, and Cherokee, who adapted to White culture and effectively operated along democratic principles and had efficient economies.

Fourteenth Amendment (1868). Amendment to the U.S. Constitution that enshrined the tenet of the Civil Rights Act of 1866, holding that persons born in the United States were automatically granted citizenship. Also extended equal protection of the laws to all, and provided sanctions against state governments that did not comply with new civil rights standards in their constitutions and laws.

Freedmen's Bureau. Temporary agency established under the War Department charged with helping newly emancipated African Americans in their transition to freedom. Also provided aid to White Southerners affected by the devastation of the Civil War.

Fugitive Slave Act. Part of the 1850 Compromise, it authorized and monetarily compensated federal marshals and bounty hunters to forcibly return escaped slaves to their masters, holding not only state and local governments but individual civilians liable if they did not comply with the law; also referred to as the Fugitive Slave Clause.

gender. The presumptions, roles, and practices a society assigns to the biological sexes of male and female.

Gentlemen's Agreement (1907). Pact between the United States and Japan whereby Japan imposed restraints on the numbers of Japanese who could apply for emigration to the United States.

G.I. Bill of Rights. Legislation passed near the end of World War II that sought to assist veterans in adapting to civilian life through low-cost mortgages, low-interest loans to start a business, and cash payments of tuition and living expenses to attend college or vocational schools.

grassroots activism. A form of political action that assumes ordinary citizens can confront maldistributions of power by organizing as communities of geographic or ascriptive identity (race, class, and gender) and use their indigenous creativity, leadership, and resources.

Great Migration. Period between 1910 and 1930 when nearly two million African Americans migrated from the rural South to urban areas throughout the country.

group interests. The individual's belief that a group with which he or she closely identifies has common public policy needs and preferences—for instance, health care, affordable housing, nondiscrimination with jobs—and that those interests should be advocated in the public arena.

Group Position/Group Threat Theory. Historically and collectively developed judgments about the positions in the social order that in-group members should rightfully occupy relative to members of an out-group.

guest worker. Immigrant who comes to the United States to work and who has the right to stay in the United States only until the end of his or her contract or visa period.

Homestead Act (1862). Law that allowed for the transfer of 285 million acres—nearly 10 percent of the land mass of the United States—to individual landholders who were able to purchase 160 acres of public land for modest sums after occupying the land for five years. Designed to encourage Westward expansion.

hometown associations (HTAs). Organizations of immigrants from the same city or region of origin who reside in the same part of the country of destination and band together to provide material support to the place of origin.

homophobia. Discrimination or marginalization based on one being Lesbian, gay, bisexual, or transgender. Sometimes used interchangeably with the term heterosexism.

hypodescent. Process by which the legal status of a child of an enslaved mother is assigned the mother's social status, regardless of the social status of the father.

identity politics. Political consciousness various groups developed as they became more aware of the institutional inequalities or structural discrimination they faced in relation to more powerful groups and institutions.

ideology. The groups of fundamental beliefs and ideas that shape an individual's understanding of the political system.

iluminated individualism. Practice by which one does not assume that any characteristic reveals complete information about a person or his or her background, but also acknowledges that those characteristics, such as race or ethnicity, have meaning.

immigrant. Person who moves from one country to another in anticipation of a much longer--if not permanent—residence in the destination country, often for familial, economic, and political reasons.

immigrant-ethnic. Assessment that immigrants from a country or region and their U.S.-born co-ethnics often share many experiences in U.S. politics.

Immigration and Nationality Act (1924). Law halting the immigration of Chinese, Japanese, Koreans, and Asian Indians to the United States.

Immigration and Nationality Amendments (1965). Legislation that established three paths to eligibility for immigration to permanent residence. close family in the United States, job skills or professional training needed in the U.S. economy or by specific U.S. employers, or being a refugee who cannot safely return to one's country of citizenship.

Immigration Reform and Control Act (IRCA) (1986). Legislation in which Congress mandated that employers verify the work eligibility of all new employees within the first three days of employment and created legal penalties ("employer sanctions") for employers who knowingly hired unauthorized workers.

Implicit Association Test. Assessment measuring a subject's reactions to covert, subtle cues—matching-words, facial features, skin color—to understand if he or she has an automatic positive or negative bias.

implicit bias. Unconscious, negative stereotypes about another racial or ethnic group.

implicit racial attitudes. Subconsciously held negative biases or prejudicial feelings against other groups.

income inequality. Disparity in the distribution of wealth, in which the very rich own an increasing share of the income and wealth, while average wages and income are not increasing.

incorporation policy. Formal policy to ensure that immigrants and their children make the transition from immigrant to equal citizen.

indentured servant. Individual bound to a time-limited period of service during Colonial times; different from a permanent slave.

Indian Civil Rights Act. Measure passed by Congress in 1968 that extended Bill of Rights protections to Native

Americans and encouraged the development of tribal courts and tribal law.

intermediary racial position. Group or individual who has neither all of the advantages of the dominant group nor all of the disadvantages of subordinate groups.

intersectionality. Various ways in which other factors interact with race to determine the political experience or status of all groups, but especially subordinate and intermediary racial groups.

Jim Crow politics. Customary and official government sanction of anti-Black racial discrimination, racial separation, and violence following the Civil War and into the twentieth century.

Jones Act. Legislation that granted U.S. citizenship to Puerto Ricans and established Puerto Rico as a self-governing, unincorporated territory of the United States.

League of United Latin American Citizens (LULAC). The first local civic organization for Mexican Americans, formed in the Southwest in 1929, whose early members reflected a small, newly emerging middle class.

legal permanent resident. An immigrant who enters the United States with a "green card" that permits work in the United States and access to many of the rights enjoyed by the U.S.-born.

Linked or common fate. Process where the individual through a number of factors (ethnic and cultural ties, the group's treatment, and political circumstances) perceives that his or her well-being is, generally speaking, associated with an assessment of the group's well-being.

lynching. The extralegal use of torture and murder, including hanging, burning, castration, and dismemberment of victims, most often Black, who were accused of alleged and most often false crimes.

majority-minority district. A congressional district drawn so that it has a majority made up of minority voters.

marginalization. Process by which a dominant group discriminates against a minority and relegates them to the less visible and powerful sectors of society and the polity.

Mariel boatlift. Event in which the Castro regime in Cuba opened the port of Mariel to those seeking to flee the country after a long period in which emigration was barred; many refugees were later found to be criminals released from prison and forced to leave.

Marshall Doctrine. The collective term for three key court cases, *Johnson v. M'Intosh* (1823), *Cherokee Nation v.*

Georgia (1831), and *Worcester v. Georgia* (1832), that determined the limits of Indian sovereignty.

mass incarceration. The widespread imprisonment of various groups.

migrant. A person who leaves his or her native country for another.

minority vote dilution. Condition when the votes of a minority population are unlikely to result in the election of an official representing the interests of that minority.

miscegenation. Racial mixing; an activity discouraged by polygenists and others who felt that it would result in another, weaker race.

model minority. Societal distinction granted to certain racial and ethnic minorities (such as Asian Americans) that are considered highly intelligent, industrious, and politically passive or apolitical, and thus by implication ideal workers in comparison to other minorities.

Morrill Land-Grant College Act of 1862. Act by which the federal government made large tracts of public lands available to each state in exchange for the establishment of state colleges devoted to the "agricultural and mechanical arts."

mutualist organization. Mass organization designed to meet specific collective needs of a racial or ethnic group, such as Mexican Americans, that could not or would not be met by Anglo organizations.

National Association for the Advancement of Colored (NAACP). Organization created in 1909 to ensure the political, educational, social, and economic equality of rights of Blacks and all persons, and to eliminate race-based discrimination.

National Organization for Women (NOW). Organization founded in 1966 with the goal of bringing women into the American mainstream and challenging gender inequalities.

national origin quotas. Restrictions on immigration passed in the 1920s; designed to freeze the ethnic composition of the United States by allocating visas based on the percentage of a nation's émigrés resident in the United States at the time of the 1890 census.

native stock. U.S.-born adults of U.S.-born parents.

nativism. Policies and social practices that limit the rights and social standing of newcomers in society based on the assumption that the newcomers are less worthy and less likely to adopt the values and practices of the established groups in the society.

naturalization. Process by which an immigrant becomes a legal U.S. citizen.

Naturalization Act (1790). Legislation that limited immigrants' ability to naturalize (to become voluntary U.S. citizens) to "free white persons" who had lived in the United States for two years.

New Deal. The collection of federal programs implemented by Franklin Roosevelt in the 1930s to assist the citizenry and move the nation out of the Great Depression.

New Deal (Democratic) Coalition. A more liberal, national coalition of the Democratic Party formed in response to the Roosevelt economic reform agenda. Comprised of labor and the White working class, Catholics and Jews (or some White immigrants), the elderly, women, and minority voters, including African Americans.

New Jim Crow. Term for contemporary racial disparities in the criminal justice system that many allege unfairly target African Americans and other racial and ethnic minorities, putting them at a significant disadvantage.

No Child Left Behind (NCLB) Act (2001). National legislation that instituted accountability standards for schools by measuring adequate yearly progress for all students and subgroups of students defined by socioeconomic background, race/ethnicity, English language proficiency, and disability.

one-drop rule. Assertion that emerged during the era of Jim Crow that anyone with even the smallest traces of African ancestry or "Black blood" clearly fell on the Black side of a color line separating Whites and Blacks.

overseas constituency. Parliamentary representatives for nationals living abroad who are elected by voters living outside of the country.

Page Act. Federal act of 1875 that closed the immigration doors to a variety people Congress presumed "undesirable," including Chinese women they feared would enter prostitution.

pan-ethnic identity. When the ancestral connection is to a region, rather than to a specific nation.

pan-ethnic group. Comprised of many ethnic-national communities.

partisanship. Preference for one political party over another.

plenary. Full and absolute power over the governance and jurisdiction of Indians.

***Plessy v. Ferguson* (1896).** Supreme Court decision that declared the practice of "separate but equal," or the segregation of public facilities, constitutional.

political culture. The attitudes or values, norms, and forms of social and artistic expression that define group membership and group interests relevant to political empowerment and the political system.

political efficacy. The degree to which a particular community can affect political outcomes.

political ideology. The arrangement of political attitudes into specific or systematic schemes that justify specific interpretations of what is in a community's best interests.

political opportunity. Those methods, periods, and contexts that can take advantage of a power structure's political vulnerabilities or weaknesses and make it attentive to the concerns of activists.

political refugee. A person who leaves his or her native country for political reasons, such as government oppression.

political socialization. The ways in which the historical and contemporary experience of a racial or ethnic group teach individuals about the group's political values, beliefs, and norms.

Principled Objection Model. Theory that asserts interracial hostility is due to a clash with the dominant American belief in individual opportunity.

Prohibition. The nationwide ban on the sale, production, importation, and transportation of alcoholic beverages that was enacted in the United States from 1920 to 1933.

Public Law 503. Legislation that, along with Executive Order 9066, prohibited all persons of Japanese ancestry from living in areas and regions designated as vital to national security and authorized the U.S. Army and other agencies (especially the War Relocation Authority) to provide for the evacuation of such persons to in-land internment camps.

public opinion. The various attitudes or views large communities of people hold about politics and the actions of government.

public policy. The formal outcome of governmental actions, such as regulations, laws, and court orders; also the political processes through which these outcomes are shaped, such as citizen and lobbyist interactions with bureaucracies, legislative processes, and judicial proceedings.

race. The macro-categories society assigns and the significance it attaches to perceived groupings of human physical distinction, including skin color, hair color and texture, lips, nose, eyes, body shapes, and sometimes cultural differences.

race conscious. Belief that race should be one of many factors considered in college admissions decisions.

race neutral. Belief that race should have no consideration in college admissions decisions.

racial assimilation. The practice of often intermarrying with "inferior races" but also demanding that they abandon their religions and cultures and assume those of the dominant group.

racial conservative. A person who does not believe that race, ethnicity, and racism have a significant impact on the current outcomes of public policy.

racial essentialism. Belief that one's racial essence is obvious from one's outer appearance.

racialization. Process whereby American society and individuals use macro-categorizations of race (White, Black, American Indian and Alaska Native, Asian American, etc.) to make assumptions about a person, group, or condition.

racial liberal. A person who believes that race, ethnicity, and racism have a significant impact on current public policy outcomes and that these factors are decisive, if not absolute, explanations for key political or economic differences between racial and ethnic groups.

racial profiling. The practice of the police and other law enforcement agencies of using race and ethnicity as factors to determine if someone is likely to commit or already has committed a crime.

racially polarized. The process of being markedly divided by race; in elections, when Whites vote for Whites and Blacks for Blacks.

racial quota. An explicit effort to reserve a college admission slot based on race in order to guarantee the outcome of minorities being a specific percentage of an entering class.

racial separation. Very strict lines of division between the dominant and subordinate races, including the forbidding of intermarriage and various kinds of contact; also called racial separatism.

racial superiority. The belief and practice that one's race (however defined) is morally, culturally, and intellectually more advanced than other races.

racial triangle. Process whereby Whites view Asian Americans as not fully equal to Whites (because they are foreign) but also as racially and ethnically superior to other minority groups.

racism. The use of perceived racial differences to rank and order which group(s) enjoy full citizenship rights and opportunities according to where they fall within a system of racial classification.

redlining. Policies of residential discrimination designed to limit the opportunities of non-White veterans to move outside U.S. cities (particularly to the newly emerging suburbs).

Red Power movement. Militant Indian rights movement active during the late 1960s and 1970s that focused on holding the federal government accountable for its broken treaties and failed policies.

refugee. Someone who has left his or her native country and cannot safely return to it.

remittance. Money sent from émigrés to family members in their country of origin.

restrictive covenant. Enabled property owners to prohibit the sale of property based on race or ethnicity. Struck down in the 1947 decision *Sweatt v. Painter.*

reverse discrimination. A form of racial inequality that is unfair to Whites.

scientific racism. The fallacious use of empirical methods to justify assumptions of racial superiority and inferiority.

Section 203. Part of the 1975 extension of the Voting Rights Act that protects speakers of Spanish, Asian, and Native American languages by providing ballots and other forms in other languages.

self-determination. Policy of respect and support of Indian tribal sovereignty, especially regarding a tribe's authority to decide on actions to support its people and the right to control how those needs are met.

sending country. The country from which an immigrant emigrated.

"separate but equal" doctrine. Policy arising out of the 1896 case of *Plessy v. Ferguson,* in which the Supreme Court ruled that the Fourteenth Amendment's guarantee of equal protection under the law permitted states and businesses to segregate all facilities and communities by race.

settlement policy. Policies designed to assist in the incorporation of immigrants.

sexism. Discrimination or marginalization based on one's being a woman.

sexual orientation. The sexual-attraction identity individuals privately and/or publicly embrace in affirming they are a Lesbian woman, a gay man, a bisexual person, or a transgender person.

Shelby County, Alabama v. Holder (2013). Supreme Court ruling that the criteria for added federal monitoring of registration procedures and voting practices found in the Voting Rights Act were unconstitutional because they had been established in the 1960s and 1970s and not updated.

Simple Self-Interest Model. Theory that holds that hostility between members of two racial groups reflects an underlying clash of economic and political interests.

sit-in. A type of labor strike to protest discriminatory employment practices and laws condoned by White-controlled Southern governments and White-owned businesses; protesters would sit in a diner or other locale in silent, peaceful protest.

social capital. Strong relationships of trust and reciprocity that provide opportunities for participation with few costs.

social desirability effect. The assumption that survey respondents (especially Whites) are so concerned about revealing their racial biases that they sometimes will mask them in the answers they provide to pollsters.

socioeconomic status. A status composed of the combination of an individual's education, income, and occupation.

South Carolina v. Katzenbach (1966). Supreme Court decision that held the Fifteenth Amendment gave authority to the federal government to intervene in what had traditionally been the states' responsibility to manage elections.

subordinate racial position. The most politically and economically disadvantaged in a society.

substantive representation. An elected official that represents the particular interests of a minority group.

superordinate racial position. The most advantaged or the most powerful position in the U.S. polity and society relative to all other racial and ethnic groups.

Takao Ozawa v. United States. The 1922 Supreme Court case that decided a Japanese man who wanted to be a naturalized citizen was "yellow," and thus neither Caucasian nor White, according to the 1790 legal requirements.

Thirteenth Amendment. Amendment to the U.S. Constitution passed in 1865 that officially outlawed slavery everywhere in the United States.

Three-Fifths Clause. Clause from Article I of the U.S. Constitution that stipulated that each enslaved person would count as three-fifths of a free (White) person for the purposes of determining how many seats each state would be apportioned in the U.S. House of Representatives; also called the Enumeration Clause.

Transcontinental railroad. Railroad built primarily by Chinese laborers that ran the width of the continental United States. Considered one of the nineteenth century's technological marvels.

transnational. Describing an immigrant who maintains connections to his or her family members abroad and with his or her communities and countries of origin or ancestry.

Treaty of Fort Laramie (1868). Treaty in which the U.S. government agreed to relinquish its forts along the Bozeman Train and guarantee the Lakota possession of the half of South Dakota that includes the Black Hills, as well as parts of Montana and Wyoming.

Treaty of Guadalupe Hidalgo (1848). Agreement that ended the U.S.-Mexican War and transferred to the United States approximately half of what had been the prewar territory of Mexico; it also guaranteed citizenship to former Mexican subjects in the acquired territory.

Treaty of Paris (1898). Peace agreement that ended the Spanish-American War, under which the United States received the territories of Puerto Rico, Cuba, and the Philippines as colonies but did not guarantee the residents U.S. citizenship.

tri-racial system. System in which racism is based not just on race but also on other indicators of social status, including class or economic standing.

unauthorized immigrant. An immigrant who does not possess a valid visa to be in the United States.

Underground Railroad. The extensive formal and informal network of agents and allies who led and assisted enslaved Blacks in their flight to Northern states, and especially to the free nation of Canada.

United States v. Bhagat Singh Thind (1923). Supreme Court case that decided that Bhagat Singh Thind, according to science, was in fact Caucasian because he was Aryan (i.e., Indian) but clearly not White as commonly understood.

visa. Written evidence that the immigrant has been authorized to immigrate; today, it often appears as a stamp in a passport.

voter mobilization. Incentives and encouragement to get people to vote in elections.

voter registration requirement. A rule requiring potential voters to certify their eligibility to vote with the state in the weeks or months before the election.

Voting Rights Act (1965). Legislation designed to protect voting discrimination and voting rights in a more strategic and more administrative fashion, rather than handling each violation as an individual court case.

Voting Rights Act (1965), Section 4. Identified tests or devices by which states or subdivisions in any federal, state, or local election discouraged electoral participation, and specified that citizens could not be denied the right to vote.

Voting Rights Act (1965), Section 5. Required that any state or political jurisdiction that met the tests of Section 4 (a) had to seek agreement from the U.S. District Court for the District of Columbia (and later the Civil Rights Division of the Department of Justice) when it tried to administer new voting laws different from those in effect in November 1964.

white advantage. The concept of a person being more likely to automatically have or inherit greater opportunities and more advantages than those afforded to racial and ethnic minorities if society perceives/classifies that person as White; also called white privilege.

white flight. Mass movement of Whites away from city centers and into new suburban areas beginning in the 1950s.

White Man's Burden. Worldview popular in the late 1800s that White America and Europe should "civilize" less developed nations and their peoples while extracting their mineral resources and agricultural products.

Yellow Peril. Term based on a racist depiction from the late nineteenth and early twentieth centuries that portrayed Asian Americans as contaminating America with their foreign influences. Also described as the Oriental Problem.

***Yo Wick v. Hopkins* (1886).** Supreme Court decision finding local ordinances that racially discriminate against persons, whether aimed at citizens or noncitizens, violate the Fourteenth Amendment's Equal Protection Clause.

Notes

CHAPTER 1

1. Ronald Takaki, *A History of Asian Americans: Strangers from a Different Shore* (New York: Back Bay Books: Little, Brown and Company, 1998), 99–112, 485–486; Louis DeSipio and Rodolfo O. de la Garza, *Making Americans, Remaking America: Immigration and Immigrant Policy* (New York: Westview Press, 1998), 65–70; Linda Greenhouse, *Becoming Justice Blackmun: Harry Blackmun's Supreme Court Journey* (New York: Times Books, H. Holt and Co., 2005), 133.

2. CNN, "Election Center 2008," http://www.cnn.com/ELECTION/2008; Tucker Carlson and Ana Marie Cox, "Abortion, Affirmative Action, More," *Washington Post,* June 1, 2009. For a discussion of 2012 results, see "President Exit Polls," http://elections.nytimes.com/2012/results/president/exit-polls.

3. Andrew Grant-Thomas, "Does Barack Obama's Victory Herald a Post-Racial America?," RaceWire: The Colorlines Blog, http://www.racewire.org/archives/2008/12/does_barack_obamas_victory_her_1.html; Shelby Steele, "Obama's Post-Racial Promise: Barack Obama Seduced Whites with a Vision of Their Racial Innocence Precisely to Coerce Them into Acting out of a Racial Motivation," *Los Angeles Times,* http://www.latimes.com/news/opinion/commentary/la-oe-steele5–2008nov05,0,6553798.story; Tom Scocca, "Eighty-Eight Percent of Romney Voters Were White," *Slate,* http://www.slate.com/articles/news_and_politics/scocca/2012/11/mitt_romney_white_voters_the_gop_candidate_s_race_based_monochromatic_campaign.html.

4. Barack Obama, "Transcript: Barack Obama's Speech on Race" (2008), http://www.npr.org/templates/story/story.php?storyId=88478467; National Constitutional Center, "A More Perfect Union: A Virtual Exhibit of Barack Obama's Race Speech at the Constitution Center on March 18, 2008," National Constitutional Center, http://www.constitutioncenter.org/obamaracespeech.

5. Lynn Sweet, "Obama's N.A.A.C.P Speech, New York, July 16, 2009. Transcript," in *Lynn Sweet: The Scoop from Washington* (Chicago, IL: *Chicago Sun-Times,* 2009).

6. Amy Davidson, "Obama: Trayvon Martin Could Have Been Me," *New Yorker,* July 19, 2013. For a discussion of Obama's second inaugural address, see "President Obama's Second Inagural Address (transcript)," *Washington Post,* January 21, 2013.

7. James Bell, "Correcting the System of Unequal Justice," in *The Covenant with Black America,* ed. Tavis Smiley (Chicago, IL: Third World Press, 2006), 53.

8. Dalton Conley, *Being Black, Living in the Red: Race, Wealth, and Social Policy in America* (Berkeley: University of California Press, 1999), 32–42; Michael Powell and Janet Roberts, "Minorities Affected Most as New York Foreclosures Rise," *New York Times,* May 15, 2009; Debbie Gruenstein Bocian, Wei Li, and Keith S. Ernst, "Foreclosures by Race and Ethnicity: The Demographics of a Crisis, CRL Research Report" (Washington, DC: Center for Responsible Lending, 2010), 2; Bureau of Labor Statistics, "News: The Employment Situation, June 2009" (Washington, DC: United States Department of Labor, 2009), 1. For the Obama quotation, see Sweet, "Obama's N.A.A.C.P Speech."

9. Sonia Sotomayor, "Lecture: 'A Latina Judge's Voice,'" *New York Times,* May 14, 2009, http://www.nytimes.com/2009/05/15/us/politics/15judge.text.html.

10. Janet Hook, "Some Republicans Rebuke Limbaugh, Gingrich on Sotomayor Criticism," *Los Angeles Times,* May 30, 2009, http://articles.latimes.com/2009/may/30/nation/na-sotomayor30.

11. Sotomayor, "Lecture: 'A Latina Judge's Voice.'"

12. Melissa Nobles, *Shades of Citizenship: Race and the Census in Modern Politics* (Stanford, CA: Stanford University Press, 2000), 36.

13. Paula M. Moya and Hazel Rose Markus, "Doing Race: An Introduction," in *Doing Race: 21 Essays for the 21st Century,* ed. Hazel Rose Markus and Paula M. Moya (New York and London: W. W. Norton, 2010), 20–21; Audrey Smedley, *Race in North America: Origin and Evolution of a Worldview,* 3rd ed. (Boulder, CO: Westview Press, 2007), 13–17; Melissa Nobles, *Shades of Citizenship: Race and the Census in Modern Politics* (Stanford, CA: Stanford University Press, 2000), 6–8; Nancy Foner and George M. Frederickson,

eds., *Not Just Black and White: Historical and Contemporary Perspectives on Immigration, Race, and Ethnicity* (New York: Russell Sage Foundation, 2005), 23; Smedley, *Race in North America,* 14–15, 18–19.

14.   Karim Murji and John Solomos, *Racialization: Studies in Theory and Practice* (Oxford: Oxford University Press, 2005).

15.   Audrey Smedley, *Race in North America: Origin and Evolution of a Worldview,* 3rd ed. (Boulder, CO: Westview Press, 2007), 14–15, 18–19.

16.   Ronald Takaki. *Strangers from a Different Shore: A History of Asian Americans* (updated and revised), eBookIt.com, 2012, 110–111, 484–486.

17.   Ali Mazrui and Michael Tidy, *Nationalism and New States in Africa: From 1935 to the Present* (Nairobi and London: Heineman, 1984), 381–384; Smedley, *Race in North America,* 43–72.

18.   Smedley, *Race in North America,* 123–60; George M. Fredrickson, *White Supremacy: A Comparative Study in American and South African History* (New York: Oxford University Press, 1981).

19.   Nobles, *Shades of Citizenship: Race and the Census in Modern Politics.*

20.   Marcus W. Feldman, "The Biology of Ancestry: DNA, Genomic Variation, and Race," in *Doing Race: 21 Essays for the 21st Century,* ed. Markus and Moya; Paula Rothenberg, "The Social Construction of Difference: Race, Class, Gender, and Sexuality," in *Race, Class, and Gender in the United States: An Integrated Study,* ed. Paula Rothenberg (New York: St. Martin's Press, 2001), 8–10; Smedley, *Race in North America,* 1–7, 23–26, 30–35.

21.   Scott L. Malcomson, *One Drop of Blood: The American Misadventure of Race* (New York: Farrar, Straus and Giroux, 2000).

22.   Mark S. Weiner, "Black Trials: Citizenship from the Beginnings of Slavery to the End of Caste" (New York: Albert Knopf, 2004), 214–239; Michael Omi and Howard Winant, *Racial Formation in the United States: From the 1960s to the 1990s,* 2nd ed. (New York: Routledge, 1994), 53–54, 71–72.

23.   Sonya Tafoya, "Shades of Belonging," in *A Pew Center Project Report* (Washington, DC: Pew Hispanic Center, 2004); Linda Martin Alcoff, "Latinos/as, Asian Americans, and the Black-White Binary," *Journal of Ethics* 7 (2003); Gary M. Segura and Helena Alves Rodrigues, "Comparative Ethnic Politics in the United States: Beyond Black and White," *Annual Review of Political Science* 9 (2006); Pawan H. Dhingra, "Being American between Black and White: Second-Generation Asian American Professionals' Racial Identities," *Journal of Asian American Studies* (2003); Nancy S. Landale and R. S. Oropesa, "White,

Black, or Puerto Rican? Racial Self-Identification among Mainland and Island Puerto Ricans," *Social Forces* 81, no. 1 (2002); Eduardo Bonilla-Silva, "From Bi-Racial to Tri-Racial: Towards a New System of Racial Stratification in the USA," *Ethnic and Racial Studies* 27, no. 6 (2007).

24.   Stephen Cornell and Douglas Hartmann, *Ethnicity and Race: Making Identities in a Changing World* (Thousand Oaks, CA: Pine Forge Press, 1998), 15–16. For a discussion of pan-ethnicity, see Yen Le Espiritu, *Asian American Panethnicity: Bridging Institutions and Identities,* Asian American History and Culture Series (Philadelphia: Temple University Press, 1992). For a discussion of "Latino" as a new category with the census, see Clara E. Rodriguez, *Changing Race: Latinos, the Census, and the History of Ethnicity in the United States* (New York: New York University Press, 2000).

25.   Cornell and Hartmann, *Ethnicity and Race: Making Identities in a Changing World,* 15–16.

26.   Max Weber, "The Origins of Ethnic Groups," in *Ethnicity,* ed. John Hutchinson and Anthony D. Smith (Oxford; New York: Oxford University Press, 1996), 35; John Hutchinson and Anthony D. Smith, *Ethnicity,* Oxford Readers (Oxford; New York: Oxford University Press, 1996), 6–7.

27.   Cornell and Hartmann, *Ethnicity and Race: Making Identities in a Changing World,* 35; Dianne Pinderhughes, *Race and Ethnicity in Chicago Politics: A Reexamination of Pluralist Theory* (Urbana: University of Illinois Press, 1987), 109–140.

28.   Beverly Daniel Tatum, *"Why Are All the Black Kids Sitting Together in the Cafeteria?": And Other Conversations about Race* (New York: Basic Books, 2003), 7–13; Stokely Carmichael and Charles V. Hamilton, *Black Power: The Politics of Liberation in America* (New York: Vintage Books, 1967), 3–4.

29.   Linda F. Williams, *The Constraints of Race: Legacies of White Skin Privilege in America* (University Park: Pennsylvania State University Press, 2003); Joe R. Feagin, *Racist America: Roots, Current Realities, and Future Reparations* (New York: Routledge, 2000), 175–202.

30.   Robert Barnes, "Justice Rule for White Firemen in Bias Lawsuit," *Washington Post,* 2009.

31.   Clarence Thomas, "Victims and Heroes in the Benevolent State," in *Color, Class, Identity: The New Politics of Race,* ed. John Arthur and Amy Shapiro (Boulder, CO: Westview Press, 1996), 85.

32.   Omi and Winant, *Racial Formation in the United States,* 71, 72, 73; emphasis in original.

33.   The Atlanta-based Southern Poverty Law Center (SPLC) compiles data and creates a "hate map" based on its "hate watch" project of the United States. It

includes groups it believes preach racial separatism and/or racial superiority. The criteria the SPLC uses to compile these data are controversial to some, for the center counts *all* groups it believes preach racial separatism—whether they are Black Nationalist groups (for instance, the Nation of Islam and the New Black Panther Party), White Nationalist groups (like the Ku Klux Klan and the Neo-Confederate League), or other groups (like the Jewish Defense League). While the SPLC strongly believes the preaching of racial separatism by anyone is equally indefensible, and that "racism should be exposed in all of its forms," it also says it recognizes that "much black racism in America is, at least in part, a response to centuries of white racism." Mary R. Jackman and Marie Crane, "'Some of My Best Friends Are Black . . .': Interracial Friendship and Whites' Racial Attitudes," *Public Opinion Quarterly* 50, no. 4 (Winter 1986).

34. Eduardo Bonilla-Silva, "The New Racism: Racial Structure in the United States, 1960s–1990s," in *Race, Ethnicity, and Nationality in the United States: Toward the Twenty-First Century,* ed. Paul Wong (Boulder, CO: Westview Press, 1999); Eduardo Bonilla-Silva, *Racism without Racists: Color-Blind Racism and the Persistence of Racial Inequality in the United States,* 2nd ed. (Lanham, MD: Rowman and Littlefield, 2006).

35. See A. O. Scott, "A Harsh Hello for Visitors from Space," film review, *District 9, New York Times,* August 13, 2009; and Lorenzo Veracini, "*District 9 and Avatar:* Science Fiction and Settler Colonialism," *Journal of Intercultural Studies* 32, no. 4 (2011): 355–367.

36. Smedley, *Race in North America,* 169–170. One of the most influential books on the concept of "scientific racism" and especially "biological determinism" is Stephen Jay Gould, *The Mismeasure of Man,* rev. and expanded ed. (New York: Norton, 1996).

37. Moya and Markus, "Doing Race: An Introduction," 34–36.

38. Thomas Jefferson, Adrienne Koch, and William Harwood Peden, *The Life and Selected Writings of Thomas Jefferson,* 1st trade paperback ed. (New York: Random House, 1993), 238. For a detailed discussion of the relationship between Sally Hemings and her family and Thomas Jefferson and his family, see Smedley, *Race in North America,* chaps. 10, 11, and 12.

39. For a definition of "racist" racial project, see Omi and Winant, *Racial Formation in the United States,* 71; Nobles, *Shades of Citizenship: Race and the Census in Modern Politics,* 25.

40. Nobles, *Shades of Citizenship: Race and the Census in Modern Politics,* 27–62. Detailed accounts of this nineteenth-century racial and colonial history are found in the works of Ronald Takaki, *A Different Mirror: A History of Multicultural America* (Boston: Little, Brown and Company, 1993), and Howard Zinn, *A People's History of the United States* (New York: Harper and Row, 1980), chap. 12.

41. Nobles, *Shades of Citizenship: Race and the Census in Modern Politics,* 63–75.

42. Ibid., 75–84.

43. Rodriguez, *Changing Race: Latinos, the Census, and the History of Ethnicity in the United States.*

44. Kim M. Williams, *Mark One or More: Civil Rights in Multiracial America (The Politics of Race and Ethnicity)* (Ann Arbor: University of Michigan Press, 2006).

45. William N. Evans and Julie H. Topoleski, "The Social and Economic Impact of Native American Casinos" (Cambridge, MA: National Bureau of Economic Research, September 2002).

46. Bonilla-Silva, "From Bi-Racial to Tri-Racial: Towards a New System of Racial Stratification in the USA"; Ani Turner, "The Business Case for Racial Equity" (Altarium Institute, October 2013).

47. Takaki, *A Different Mirror: A History of Multicultural America.* Two very good examples of racial/ethnic revisions of pluralist theory include Pinderhughes, *Race and Ethnicity in Chicago Politics;* and Rodney E. Hero, *Latinos and the U.S. Political System: Two-Tiered Pluralism* (Philadelphia: Temple University Press, 1992).

48. Arthur M. Schlesinger, *The Disuniting of America: Reflections on a Multicultural Society,* rev. and enlarged ed. (New York: W. W. Norton, 1998), 20–22.

49. For a discussion of these American Indian, Black, and Italian examples, see Devon Mihesuah, *American Indians: Stereotypes and Realities* (Atlanta, GA: Clarity Press, 2004); John M. Goering, *Fragile Rights within Cities: Government, Housing, and Fairness* (Lanham, MD: Rowman and Littlefield, 2007); Jennifer Guglielmo and Salvatore Salerno, eds., *Are Italians White? How Race Is Made in America* (New York: Routledge Press, 2003).

50. Alan Kennedy-Shaffer, *The Obama Revolution* (Beverly Hills, CA: Phoenix Books, 2009).

51. Steven P. Erie, *Rainbow's End: Irish-Americans and the Dilemmas of Urban Machine Politics, 1840–1985,* California Series on Social Choice and Political Economy 15 (Berkeley: University of California Press, 1988); Karen Brodkin, *How Jews Became White Folks and What That Says About Race in America* (New Brunswick, NJ: Rutgers University Press, 1998).

CHAPTER 2

1. Vine Deloria Jr., *God Is Red: A Native View of Religion* (Golden, CO: Fulcrum Publishing, 2003), 115.
2. "Iroquois Influences on the U.S. Constitution," in *Encyclopedia of United States Indian Policy and Law,* ed. P. Finkelman and T. Garrison (Washington, DC: CQ Press, 2009), http://library.cqpress.com/ipl/eusipl_219.
3. Ibid.
4. Theda Perdue, interviewed by California Newsreel, 2003, edited interview transcript, *RACE—The Power of an Illusion,* Public Broadcasting Service, http://www.pbs.org/race/000_About/002_04-background-02-07.htm.
5. Karen Ordahl Kupperman, interviewed by California Newsreel, 2003, edited interview transcript, *RACE—The Power of an Illusion,* Public Broadcasting Service, http://www.pbs.org/race/000_About/002_04-background-02-10.htm.
6. Mason Wade, "French-Indian Policies in History of Indian-White Relations," in *Handbook of North American Indians,* ed. Wilcomb E. Washburn (Washington, DC: Smithsonian Institution), 20–28. Quoted in David E. Wilkins and K. Tsianina Lomawaima, *Uneven Ground: American Indian Sovereignty and Federal Law* (Norman, OK: University of Oklahoma Press, 2001), 30.
7. Ibid., 27.
8. Ibid., 31.
9. Wilkins and Lomawaima, *Uneven Ground,* 19–20.
10. Duane Champagne, *Social Change and Cultural Continuity among Native Nations* (Lanham, MD: AltaMira Press, 2007), 108, 110.
11. Ibid.
12. Robert J. Miller, "Louisiana Purchase," in *Encyclopedia of United States Indian Policy and Law,* ed. Finkelman and Garrison.
13. Albert Ellery Bergh, ed., *The Writings of Thomas Jefferson,* XI (Washington, DC: Thomas Jefferson Memorial Association, 1907), 102–103. Quoted in Frederick M. Binder, *The Color Problem in Early National America as Viewed by John Adams, Jefferson, and Jackson* (The Hague: Mouton and Co., 1968), 84.
14. Binder, *The Color Problem in Early National America as Viewed by John Adams, Jefferson, and Jackson,* 87.
15. Ibid., 88.
16. Ibid., 91.
17. Miller, "Louisiana Purchase."
18. Binder, *The Color Problem in Early National America as Viewed by John Adams, Jefferson, and Jackson,* 99.
19. Ibid., 100.
20. Miller, "Louisiana Purchase."
21. Bernard W. Sheehan, *Seeds of Extinction: Jeffersonian Philanthropy and the American Indian* (Kingsport, NC: University of North Carolina Press, 1973), 167.
22. David E. Wilkins. *American Indian Politics and the American Political System,* 2nd ed. (Lanham, MD: Rowman and Littlefield, 2007), 136.
23. *Fletcher v. Peck,* 10 U.S. 87 (1810); *Johnson v. M'Intosh,* 21 U.S. 543 (1823); *Cherokee Nation v. Georgia,* 300 U.S. 1 (1831); and *Worcester v. Georgia,* 31 U.S. 515 (1832).
24. Steven B. Jacobson, "*Johnson v. M'Intosh* (1823)," in *Encyclopedia of United States Indian Policy and Law,* ed. Finkelman and Garrison.
25. Ibid.
26. Lenore H. Stiffarm and Phil Lane Jr., "The Demography of Native North America," in *The State of Native America,* ed. M. Annette Jaimes (Boston: South End Press. 1992), 42; and Wilkins, *American Indian Politics and the American Political System,* 113.
27. Jacobson, "*Johnson v. M'Intosh* (1823)."
28. Robert J. Miller, "*Cherokee Nation v. Georgia* (1831)," in *Encyclopedia of United States Indian Policy and Law,* ed. Finkelman and Garrison.
29. Leonard J. Sadosky, "Compact of 1802," in *Encyclopedia of United States Indian Policy and Law,* ed. Finkelman and Garrison.
30. Miller, "*Cherokee Nation v. Georgia* (1831)."
31. Ibid.
32. Bruce Duthu, *American Indians and the Law* (New York: Penguin Books, 2008), 8; emphasis in original.
33. Ibid., 9.
34. Wilkins, *American Indian Politics and the American Political System,* 49.
35. Duthu, *American Indians and the Law,* 75.
36. Wilkins, *American Indian Politics and the American Political System,* 59.
37. Perdue, interview.
38. Ibid.
39. "Red Cloud," in *New Perspectives on the West,* Public Broadcasting Service, http://www.pbs.org/weta/thewest/people/i_r/redcloud.htm.
40. "Sitting Bull," in *New Perspectives on the West,* Public Broadcasting Service, http://www.pbs.org/weta/thewest/people/s_z/sittingbull.htm.
41. Ibid.
42. Mikaëla M. Adams, "Slavery: Enslavement of Indians," in *Encyclopedia of United States Indian Policy and Law,* ed. Finkelman and Garrison.
43. Nancy Matuszak, "Slavery Indian Holding," in *Encyclopedia of United States Indian Policy and Law,* ed. Finkelman and Garrison.
44. Brendan I. Koerner, "Blood Feud," *Wired* 13, no. 9 (September 2005), http://www.wired.com/wired/archive/13.09/seminoles.html.

45. The Africana Heritage Project, "Black Seminoles, Maroons, and Freedom Seekers in Florida, Part 1: Early Freedom Seekers in Florida," University of South Florida, http://www.africanaheritage.com/black_seminoles_1.asp.

46. Vine Deloria Jr. and David E. Wilkens, *Tribes, Treaties, and Constitutional Tribulations* (Austin: University of Texas Press, 1999), 142–143.

47. Senate Committee on the Judiciary, "The Effect of the Fourteenth Amendment on Indian Tribes," 41st Cong., 3rd sess., 1871, S. Rep. 268. Quoted in Deloria and Wilkens, *Tribes, Treaties, and Constitutional Tribulations,* 143.

48. Rebecca L. Robbins, "Self-Determination and Subordination: The Past, Present, and Future of American Indian Governance," in *The State of Native America,* ed. M. Annette Jaimes (Boston: South End Press. 1992), 92.

49. 25 U.S. Code Section 71.

50. Robbins, "Self-Determination and Subordination," 93.

51. *United States v. Kagama,* 118 U.S. 375 (1886).

52. Ibid.

53. Franke Wilmer, *The Indigenous Voice in World Politics* (Newbury Park, CA: Sage, 1993).

54. Robbins, "Self-Determination and Subordination," 93.

55. Wilkins, *American Indian Politics and the American Political System,* 116.

56. Champagne, *Social Change and Cultural Continuity among Native Nations,* 108.

57. Wilkins, *American Indian Politics and the American Political System,* 117.

58. Annette M. Jaimes, "Federal Indian Identification Policy: A Usurpation of Indigenous Sovereignty in North America," in *The State of Native America,* ed. M. Annette Jaimes (Boston: South End Press, 1992), 126.

59. Wilkins, *American Indian Politics and the American Political System,* 117.

60. Duthu, *American Indians and the Law,* 75.

61. Deloria, *Behind the Trail of Broken Treaties,* 135.

62. Francis E. Leupp, *The Indian and His Problem* (New York: Charles Scribner's Sons, 1910). Reprint (New York: Arno Press, 1971), 93. Quoted from Robbins, "Self-Determination and Subordination," 93.

63. Ibid.

64. Wilkins, *American Indian Politics and the American Political System,* 28.

65. Felix S. Cohen, *Handbook of Federal Indian Law,* reprint (Albuquerque: University of New Mexico Press, 1972), 2. Quoted in David E. Wilkins, *American Indian Politics and the American Political System,* 2nd ed. (Lanham, MD: Rowman and Littlefield, 2007), 30.

66. Jaimes, "Federal Indian Identification Policy: A Usurpation of Indigenous Sovereignty in North America," 126.

67. Merrill E. Gates, "Addresses at the Lake Mohonk Conferences," in *Americanizing the American Indians: Writings by the "Friends of the Indian," 1880–1900,* ed. Frances Paul Prucha (Cambridge, MA: Harvard University Press, 1973), 340. Quoted in Kevin Bruyneel, "Challenging American Boundaries: Indigenous People and the 'Gift' of U.S. Citizenship,'" *Studies in American Political Development* 18 (Spring 2004): 30–43, 32.

68. Bruyneel, "Challenging American Boundaries," 30–43, 34.

69. Deloria, *Behind the Trail of Broken Treaties,* 18.

70. Ibid.

71. Wilkins, *American Indian Politics and the American Political System,* 59.

72. Brian W. Dippie, *The Vanishing American* (Middletown, CT: Wesleyan University Press, 1982), 299.

73. Robbins, "Self-Determination and Subordination," 96.

74. Ibid., 93.

75. *Morton v. Mancari,* 417 U.S. 535 (1974).

76. Robbins, "Self-Determination and Subordination," 97.

77. Ibid.

78. Donald L. Fixico, *Termination and Relocation: Federal Indian Policy, 1945–1960* (Albuquerque: University of New Mexico Press, 1986), 81.

79. Robbins, "Self-Determination and Subordination," 99.

80. Wilkins, *American Indian Politics and the American Political System,* 121.

81. Robbins, "Self-Determination and Subordination," 100.

82. Ibid.

83. Vine Deloria Jr., *Custer Died for Your Sins: An Indian Manifesto* (1968; reprint, Norman: University of Oklahoma Press, 1988); and *We Talk, You Listen: New Tribes, New Turf* (New York: Macmillan Publishers, 1970).

84. Dennis Banks, "Forward," in *Native America: Portrait of the Peoples,* by Duane Champagne (Detroit: Visible Ink, 1994), xii.

85. George Horse Capture, Duane Champagne, and Chandler C. Jackson, eds., *American Indian Nations: Yesterday, Today, and Tomorrow* (Lanham, MD: AltaMira Press, 2007), 133.

86. Ibid., 194.

87. Vine Deloria Jr., "American Indians," in *Multiculturalism in the United States: A Comparative Guide to Acculturation and Ethnicity* (New York: Greenwood, 1992), 45. Quoted in David E. Wilkins, *American Indian Politics and the American Political System,* 2nd ed. (Lanham, MD: Rowman and Littlefield, 2007), 30.

88. Emily Langer, "Native American Activist Worked to Avenge Injustices," *Washington Post,* October 23, 2012.

89. Jennifer A. Terry, "Occupation of Wounded Knee (1973)," in *Encyclopedia of United States Indian Policy and Law*, ed. Finkelman and Garrison.

90. Mark Fogarty, "Inouye Set to Wire Indian Country," *Indian Country Today*, March 8, 2004, http://indiancountrytodaymedianetwork.com/2004/03/08/inouye-set-wire-indian-country-90058.

91. Department of Health and Human Services, Indian Health Service, *Facts on Indian Health Disparities* (January 2006), http://aiac.alabama.gov/DisparitiesFacts-Jan2006.pdf.

92. Palash Ghosh, "Native Americans: The Tragedy of Alcoholism," *International Business Times*, February 11, 2012, http://www.ibtimes.com/native-americans-tragedy-alcoholism-214046.

93. Wilkins, *American Indian Politics and the American Political System*, 261.

94. Associated Press, "As Casinos Struggle, Indian Tribes Seek More Federal Aid," *Syracuse: The Post Standard*, March 23, 2013, http://www.syracuse.com/news/index.ssf/2013/03/as_casinos_struggle_indian_tri.html.

CHAPTER 3

1. For an overview of the racial conditions confronting African Americans, see Christopher Foreman, ed., *The African-American Predicament* (Washington, DC: Brookings, 1999). Discussions of the status of Black Americans relative to other groups are found in the works of Eduardo Bonilla-Silva, "From Bi-Racial to Tri-Racial: Towards a New System of Stratification in the United States," *Ethnic and Racial Studies* 27, no. 6 (2004), and Cedric Herring, "Bleaching out the Color Line? The Skin Color Continuum and the Tripartite Model of Race," *Race and Society* 5 (2002).

2. Hanes Walton Jr. and Robert C. Smith, *American Politics and the African American Quest for Universal Freedom* (New York: Longman, 2012); Mary Frances Berry and John W. Blassingame, *Long Memory: The Black Experience in America* (New York and Oxford: Oxford University Press, 1982).

3. Joseph Holloway, ed., *Africanisms in American Culture*, 2nd ed. (Bloomington: Indiana University Press, 2005); Sterling Stuckey, *Slave Culture: Nationalist Theory and the Foundations of Black America* (New York and Oxford: Oxford University Press, 1987).

4. Herbert S. Klein, *The Atlantic Slave Trade: New Approaches to the Americas* (New York: Cambridge University Press, 2010); Phillip Curtin, *The Atlantic Slave Trade: A Census* (Madison: University of Wisconsin Press, 1969).

5. "The Charters of Freedom," National Archives, http://www.archives.gov/exhibits/charters/declaration_transcript.html.

6. Jan Lewis and Peter S. Onuf, *Sally Hemings and Thomas Jefferson: History, Memory, and Civic Culture* (Charlottesville: University of Virginia Press, 1999), Appendix C: Thomas Jefferson to Francis Gray, 4 March 1815, 262–263; Thomas Jefferson, *Notes on the State of Virginia*, ed. William Peden (Chapel Hill: University of North Carolina Press, 1955), quotation on p. 138.

7. "People and Events: Bacon's Rebellion, 1675–1676," *Africans in America*, Public Broadcasting Service, http://www.pbs.org/wgbh/aia/part1/1p274.html; Darlene Clark Hine, William C. Hine, and Stanley Harrold, *The African-American Odyssey*, 4th ed. (Upper Saddle River, NJ: Pearson Prentice Hall, 2010), 61.

8. Audrey Smedley, *Race in North America: Origin and Evolution of a Worldview*, 3rd ed. (Boulder, CO: Westview Press, 2007), 117–118.

9. John Hope Franklin and Evelyn Higginbotham, *From Slavery to Freedom: A History of African Americans* (New York: McGraw-Hill, 2010), 54–59. For a discussion of Bacon's Rebellion and the rationale for racializing slavery, see Audrey Smedley, *Race in North America: Origins and Evolution of a Worldview* (Boulder, CO: Westview Press, 2007), 99–118.

10. Darlene Clark Hine, William C. Hine, and Stanley Harrold, *African Americans: A Concise History*, 4th ed. (New York: Pearson, 2012), 56–59.

11. Philip A. Klinkner and Rogers M. Smith, *The Unsteady March: The Rise and Decline of Racial Equality in America* (Chicago, IL: University of Chicago Press, 2002), quoted on p. 14.

12. Hine, Hine, and Harrold, *African Americans: A Concise History*, 78–90. Quotation is from Berry and Blassingame, *Long Memory: The Black Experience in America*, 55.

13. Edward F. Larson and Michael P. Winship, eds., *The Constitutional Convention: A Narrative History from the Notes of James Madison* (New York: Modern Library, 2005).

14. David Waldstreitcher, *Slavery's Constitution: From Revolution to Ratification* (New York: Hill and Wang, 2009). For an excellent discussion of the slave interests of the American founders, see Paul Finkelman, *Slavery and the Founders: Race and Liberty in the Age of Jefferson*, 2nd ed. (New York: M. E. Sharpe, 2001).

15. The Mason-Dixon was associated with a line laid in the 1760s to settle a boundary dispute by an English surveyor, Jeremiah Dixon, and an English astronomer, Charles Mason. It was later used to demarcate the boundary between slave and free regions in the

United States during the political debate over the Missouri Compromise in 1820. Bijal P. Trivedi, "Saving the Mason-Dixon Line," National Geographic News, April 10, 2002, http://news.nationalgeographic .com/news/pf/62376481.html.

16. Brown was a deeply committed abolitionist and supporter of many activities of free Blacks including Frederick Douglass. See, for example, "John Brown's Harpers Ferry Raid," Civil War Trust, http://www .civilwar.org/150th-anniversary/john-browns-harpers -ferry.html.

17. "The Fugitive Slave Law," speech to the National Free Soil Convention in Pittsburgh, August 11, 1852; Frederick Douglass paper, August 1852, University of Rochester Frederick Douglass Project, http://www .lib.rochester.edu/index.cfm?PAGE = 4385.

18. Steven Hahn, *A Nation under Our Feet: Black Political Struggles in the Rural South from Slavery to the Great Migration* (Cambridge, MA, and London, England: Belknap Press of Harvard University Press, 2003), 6.

19. The experiences of Solomon Northup were recently revisited in the film *12 Years a Slave,* released in 2013; this was originally published by Northup in 1853 as *Twelve Years a Slave: Narrative of Solomon Northup, a Citizen of New-York, Kidnapped in Washington City in 1841, and Rescued in 1853* (Auburn, NY: Derby and Miller, 1853).

20. Berry and Blassingame, *Long Memory: The Black Experience in America*, 33–59; Hine, Hine, and Harrold, *African Americans: A Concise History*, 148–166; Kathleen Sullivan, "Charleston, the Vesey Conspiracy, and the Development of the Police Power," in *Race and American Political Development*, ed. Joseph Lowndes, Julie Novkov, and Dorian T. Warren (New York: Routledge, 2008), 59–70, quotation on pp. 63–68.

21. For an excellent discussion of the religion of enslaved African Americans, see Albert Raboteau, *Slave Religion: The Invisible Institution in the Antebellum South*, updated ed. (New York: Oxford University Press, 2004).

22. Hahn, *A Nation under Our Feet,* 16, 34–51; Sylvia Frey, *Water from the Rock: Black Resistance in a Revolutionary Age* (Princeton, NJ: Princeton University Press, 1991), 5–44. For a discussion of the dynamics of slave communities, see the classic work by John W. Blassingame, *The Slave Community: Plantation Life in the Antebellum South* (Oxford: Oxford University Press, 1979).

23. Franklin and Higginbotham, *From Slavery to Freedom: A History of African Americans*, 108–112.

24. Ibid., 186–93, 99–203, with quotation on p. 193.

25. Michael Dawson, *Black Visions: The Roots of Contemporary African-American Political Ideologies* (Chicago and London: University of Chicago Press, 2001); Paula Giddings, *When and Where I Enter: The Impact of Black Women on Race and Sex in America* (New York: Pereninal, 2001); Stuckey, *Slave Culture: Nationalist Theory and the Foundations of Black America.*

26. Hine, Hine, and Harrold, *African Americans: A Concise History*, 203–206; Franklin and Higginbotham, *From Slavery to Freedom: A History of African Americans*, 151–158. For a good discussion of the concept of infrapolitics as a part of the politics of ordinary Black people, see Robin Kelley, "The Black Poor and the Politics of Opposition in a New South City, 1929–1970," in *The Under Class: Views from History*, ed. Michael Katz (Princeton, NJ: Princeton University Press, 1993).

27. Darlene Clark Hine, William Hine, and Stanley Harrold, *The African-American Odyssey, Combined Volume, Special Edition* (Upper Saddle River, NJ: 2010), 268.

28. The quotations are from Hine, Hine, and Harrold, *African Americans: A Concise History*, 234. For a comprehensive summary of the history of the period, see Eric Foner, *Reconstruction: America's Unfinished Revolution, 1863–1877* (New York: Harper and Row, 1988), 1–34.

29. W.E.B. DuBois, *Black Reconstruction in America, 1860–1880* (New York: Atheneum, 1935), with quotation on p. 715.

30. Manning Marable, *Race, Reform, and Rebellion: The Second Reconstruction and Beyond in Black America, 1945–2006*, 3rd ed. (Oxford, MS: University Press of Misssissippi, 2007), 3–5.

31. Ibid.

32. Foner, *Reconstruction: America's Unfinished Revolution, 1863–1877*, 60–76, 124–170; Linda Faye Williams, *The Constraint of Race: Legacies of White Skin Privilege in America* (State College, PA: Pennsylvania State University Press, 2004).

33. Williams, *The Constraint of Race: Legacies of White Skin Privilege in America*, 25-68; Foner, *Reconstruction: America's Unfinished Revolution, 1863–1877*, 56–57, 153–169, 243–247, 446–449, 553–556.

34. Foner, *Reconstruction: America's Unfinished Revolution, 1863–1877*, 281–291.

35. Rayford Logan, *The Betrayal of the Negro: From Rutherford B. Hayes to Woodrow Wilson* (New York: De Capo Press, 1997 [1965]); Foner, *Reconstruction: America's Unfinished Revolution, 1863–1877*, 564–601; Franklin and Higginbotham, *From Slavery to Freedom: A History of African Americans*, 256–268, with Till quotation on p. 267.

36. For a discussion of lynching and the activism of Wells, refer to Giddings, *When and Where I Enter,* 26–30; Hine, Hine, and Harrold, *African Americans: A Concise History,* 320–322; and Phillip Dray, *At the Hand of Persons Unknown: The Lynching of Black America* (New York: Random House, 2003). A chilling but brilliant book that portrays grisly glimpses of this method is by James Allen, *Without Sanctuary: Lynching Photography in America* (New York: Twin Palms Press, 2010).

37. David Pilgrim, "Who Was Jim Crow?," Jim Crow Museum of Racist Memorabilia, http://www.ferris.edu/htmls/news/jimcrow/who.htm; Pilgrim, "What Was Jim Crow?," Jim Crow Museum of Racist Memorabilia, http://www.ferris.edu/htmls/news/jimcrow/what.htm.

38. Douglas A. Blackmon, *Slavery by Another Name: The Re-Enslavement of Black America from the Civil War to World War II* (New York: Random House, 2009); Franklin Gilliam Jr., *Farther to Go: Readings and Cases in African American Politics* (New York: Harcourt Brace, 2001), 36.

39. For a discussion of the entire issue of Black education in the post-Reconstruction South, refer to James Anderson, *The Education of Blacks in the South, 1860–1935* (Chapel Hill and London: University of North Carolina Press, 1988). For a discussion of the politics of Washington's approach, see Hine, Hine, and Harrold, *African Americans: A Concise History,* 267–269, 336–343, as a summary; and the following outstanding biographies for greater detail: Louis R. Harlan, *Booker T. Washington: The Wizard of Tuskegee, 1901–1915* (New York and Oxford: Oxford University Press, 1983), and David Levering Lewis, *W .E. B. Du Bois: Biography of Race* (New York: Henry Holt and Company, 1993).

40. C. Eric Lincoln and Lawrence H. Mamiya, *The Black Church in the African American Experience* (Durham: University of North Carolina Press, 1990); Hine, Hine, and Harrold, *African Americans: A Concise History,* 342–345, 53–57, 410–412.

41. W. E. B. Du Bois, *The Souls of Black Folk: A Norton Critical Edition,* ed. Henry Louis Gates Jr. and Terri Hume Oliver (New York: W. W. Norton, 1999), 17.

42. Hine, Hine, and Harrold, *African Americans: A Concise History,* 368–378, 83–90. For a very good history of the NAACP, refer to Patricia Sullivan, *Lift Every Voice: The NAACP and the Making of the Civil Rights Movement* (New York: The New Press, 2009).

43. For an excellent discussion of the Black Women's Club Movement, refer to Giddings, *When and Where I Enter: The Impact of Black Women on Race and Sex in America,* 95–117. Historian Kevin Gaines argues that there was a shared, elitist "uplift" philosophy that many Black leaders embraced at the turn of the century, including Du Bois, as influenced by American thinking about the Protestant work ethic, intelligence, and culture. It is also true that despite these ideals, the various Black leaders and White allies who established the movement, even in their moderate views, were fundamentally challenging prevailing ideas about race and the racialization of African Americans as second-class citizens. Refer to Kevin Kelly Gaines, *Uplfiting the Race: Black Leadership, Politics, and Culture in the Twentieth Century* (Chapel Hill and London: University of North Carolina Press, 1996).

44. Nancy Weiss, *Farewell to the Party of Lincoln: Black Politics in the Age of FDR* (Princeton, NJ: Princeton University Press, 1983).

45. Dona Cooper Hamilton and Charles V. Hamilton, *Dual Agenda: The African-American Struggle for Civil and Economic Equaliy* (New York: Columbia University Press, 1997); Franklin and Higginbotham, *From Slavery to Freedom: A History of African Americans,* 433–440; Marable, *Race, Reform, and Rebellion: The Second Reconstruction and Beyond in Black America, 1945–2006,* 13–39; Lawrence S. Wittner, "The National Negro Congress: A Reassessment," *American Quarterly* 22, no. 4 (Winter, 1970): 883–901.

46. "Facts about the 442nd: What Was the 442nd Regimental Combat Team?" *442nd Regimental Combat Team,* http://www.the442.org/442ndfacts.html; Robert D. McFadden, "Daniel Inouye, Hawaii's Quiet Voice of Conscience in Senate, Dies at 88," *New York Times,* December 17, 2012, http://www.nytimes.com/2012/12/18/us/daniel-inouye-hawaiis-quiet-voice-of-conscience-in-senate-dies-at-88.html?pagewanted = 1&ref = danielkinouye.

47. Weiss, *Farewell to the Party of Lincoln: Black Politics in the Age of FDR;* Steven F. Lawson, *Running for Freedom: Civil Rights and Black Politics in America since 1941,* 2nd ed. (New York: McGraw-Hill, 1997), 1–37, 40–43.

48. Charles Payne, *I've Got the Light of Freedom: The Organizing Tradition and the Mississippi Freedom Struggle* (Berkeley and Los Angeles: Unversity of California Press, 1995); Hine, Hine, and Harrold, *African Americans: A Concise History,* 504–509; Williams, *The Constraint of Race: Legacies of White Skin Privilege in America;* Ira Katznelson, *When Affirmative Action Was White: An Untold History of Racial Inequality in Twentieth-Century America* (New York and London: W. W. Norton and Company,

2005); Melvin Oliver and Thomas Shapiro, *Black Wealth, White Wealth: A New Perspective* (New York: Routledge, 2006); Christopher Parker, *Fighting for Democracy: Black Veterans and the Struggle against White Supremacy in the Postwar South* (Princeton, NJ: Princeton University Press, 2009).

49. Marable, *Race, Reform, and Rebellion: The Second Reconstruction and Beyond in Black America, 1945–2006*, 13–39.

50. Doug McAdam, *Political Process and the Development of Black Insurgency, 1930–1970* (Chicago: University of Chicago Press, 1982); David Meyer and Debra Minkoff, "Conceptualizing Political Opportunity," *Social Forces* 82, no. 4 (2004); William Gamson, *The Strategy of Social Protest*, 2nd ed. (Bellmont, CA: Wadsworth, 1990).

51. William Bradford Huie, "What's Happened to the Emmett Till Killers?" *Look* 22 (January 1957): 63–66, 68, http://www.emmetttillmurder.com/Look%201957.htm.

52. Franklin and Higginbotham, *From Slavery to Freedom: A History of African Americans*, 507–517; Hine, Hine, and Harrold, *African Americans: A Concise History*, 504–516. To understand the implications of the *Brown* decision and the Civil Rights Movement, refer to Peter F. Lau, ed., *From the Grassroots to the Supreme Court:* Brown v. Board of Education *and American Democracy* (Durham and London: Duke University Press, 2004).

53. Marable, *Race, Reform, and Rebellion: The Second Reconstruction and Beyond in Black America, 1945–2006*, 61–85.

CHAPTER 4

1. Quote taken from United Farm Workers, History, http://www.ufw.org/_page.php?menu = research&inc = history/09.html.

2. Juan Gonzalez, *Harvest of Empire: A History of Latinos in America* (New York: Viking, 2010).

3. Richard Griswold del Castillo, *The Treaty of Guadalupe Hidalgo: A Legacy of Conflict* (Norman: University of Oklahoma Press, 1990).

4. Martha Menchaca, "Chicano Indianism: A Historical Account of Racial Repression in the United States," *American Ethnologist* 20, no. 3 (August 1993): 583–603.

5. *In re Ricardo Rodríguez* 81 F. 337 (1897).

6. Arnoldo De León, *In re Ricardo Rodríguez: An Attempt at Chicano Disenfranchisement in San Antonio, 1896–1897* (San Antonio: Caravel Press, 1979).

7. Rodolfo O. de la Garza and Louis DeSipio, "Save the Baby, Change the Bathwater, and Scrub the Tub: Latino Electoral Participation after Seventeen Years of Voting Rights Act Coverage," *Texas Law Review* 71, no. 7 (June 1993): 1479–1539.

8. Alexander Keyssar, *The Right to Vote: The Contested History of Democracy in the United States* (New York: Basic Books, 2000).

9. Linda Gordon, *The Great Arizona Orphan Abduction* (Cambridge, MA: Harvard University Press, 1999).

10. Alan Knight, *The Mexican Revolution,* 2 vols. (New York: Cambridge University Press, 1986).

11. Gilbert González, *Mexican Consuls and Labor Organizing: Imperial Politics in the Southwest* (Austin: University of Texas Press, 1999).

12. Benjamin Márquez, *LULAC: The Evolution of a Mexican American Political Organization* (Austin: University of Texas Press, 1993).

13. George J. Sánchez, *Becoming Mexican American: Ethnicity, Culture, and Identity in Chicano Los Angeles, 1900–1945* (New York: Oxford University Press, 1993); Mario T. García, *Memories of Chicano History: The Life and Narrative of Bert Corona* (Berkeley: University of California Press, 1994).

14. Julie Leininger Pycior, *LBJ and Mexican Americans: The Paradox of Power* (Austin: University of Texas Press, 1997).

15. Kenneth C. Burt, *The Search for a Civic Voice: California Latino Politics* (Claremont, CA: Regina Books, 2007).

16. Robert Caro, *Means of Ascent: The Years of Lyndon Johnson* (New York: Knopf, 1990); Ignacio M. García, *Viva Kennedy: Mexican Americans in Search of Camelot* (College Station, TX: Texas A&M University Press, 2000).

17. Louis DeSipio, "The Pressures of Perpetual Promise: Latinos and Politics, 1960–2003," in David Gutiérrez, ed., *The Columbia History of Latinos in the United States since 1960* (New York: Columbia University Press, 2004), 421–465.

18. F. Chris García and Rodolfo O. de la Garza, *The Chicano Political Experience: Three Perspectives* (North Scituate, MA: Duxbury Press, 1977); Louis DeSipio, "The Pressures of Perpetual Promise: Latinos and Politics, 1960–2003," in Gutiérrez, ed., *Columbia History of Latinos in the United States since 1960,* 421–465.

19. Jorge Duany, *The Puerto Rican Nation on the Move: Identities on the Island and in the United States* (Chapel Hill: University of North Carolina Press, 2002); Louis A. Pérez Jr., *The War of 1898: The United States and Cuba in History and Historiography* (Chapel Hill: University of North Carolina Press, 1998).

20. The United States granted the Philippines commonwealth status in 1935. After a period of Japanese

occupation during World War II, the Philippines became independent in 1946.

21. José Trías Monge, *Puerto Rico: The Trials of the Oldest Colony in the World* (New Haven: Yale University Press, 1997).

22. Virginia E. Sánchez Korrol, *From Colonia to Community: The History of Puerto Ricans in New York City* (Berkeley: University of California Press, 1994 [1983]).

23. James Jennings and Monte Rivera, eds., *Puerto Rican Politics in Urban America* (Westport, CT: Greenwood Press, 1984).

24. Felix Padilla, *Latino Ethnic Consciousness: The Case of Mexican Americans and Puerto Ricans in Chicago* (Notre Dame, IN: University of Notre Dame Press, 1985).

25. Maria de los Angeles Torres, *In the Land of Mirrors: Cuban Exile Politics in the United States* (Ann Arbor: University of Michigan Press, 1999).

26. Susan Eva Eckstein, *The Immigrant Divide: How Cuban Americans Changed the U.S. and Their Homeland* (New York: Routledge, 2009).

27. Alejandro Portes and Alex Stepik, *City on the Edge: The Transformation of Miami* (Berkeley: University of California Press, 1993).

28. Ira Katznelson, *When Affirmative Action Was White: An Untold History of Racial Inequality in Twentieth Century America* (New York: W. W. Norton, 2005).

29. Padilla, *Latino Ethnic Consciousness*.

30. Miguel Melendez, *We Took the Streets: Fighting for Latino Rights with the Young Lords* (New York: St. Martin's Press, 2003).

31. Armando Navarro, *Mexican American Youth Organization: Avant-Garde of the Chicano Movement in Texas* (Austin: University of Texas Press, 1995); Armando Navarro, *The Cristal Experiment: A Chicano Struggle for Community Control* (Madison: University of Wisconsin Press, 1998); Melendez, *We Took the Streets*.

32. De la Garza and DeSipio, "Save the Baby, Change the Bathwater, and Scrub the Tub."

CHAPTER 5

1. Carlos Bulosan, *America Is in the Heart: A Personal History* (Seattle: University of Washington Press, 2014 [1946]).

2. Philip S. Foner and Daniel Rosenberg, eds., *Racism, Dissent, and Asian Americans from 1850 to the Present: A Documentary History* (Westport, CT: Greenwood Press, 1993), 18.

3. *United States v. Bhagat Singh Thind*, 261 U.S. 204 (1923).

4. Claire Jean Kim, "The Racial Triangulation of Asian Americans," *Politics and Society* 27, no. 1 (1999): 113–114; Frank D. Gilliam Jr., *Farther to Go: Readings and Cases in African-American Politics* (Los Angeles: University of California Press, 2002), 11. In fact, John Marshall Harlan, a U.S. Supreme Court associate justice, agreed that this color line at the end of the nineteenth century was very arbitrary and implied that it presented Asian Americans with a mixture of absolute and decisive barriers. He was the lone dissenting vote in *Plessy v. Ferguson* (1896). The Court upheld as constitutional the Southern states' "Jim Crow" laws that required racially segregated public facilities, and Harlan stated, "There is a race so different from our own [Whites] that we do not permit those belonging to it to become citizens of the United States. Persons belonging to it are, with few exceptions, absolutely excluded from our country. I allude to the Chinese race." But he argued that Chinese who had no citizenship rights often could use the same public accommodations as Whites, whereas Blacks who were citizens could not. See United States Supreme Court, *Plessy v. Ferguson*, 163 U.S. 537 (1896).

5. Neil T. Gotanda, "Citizenship Nullification: The Impossibility of Asian American Poltiics," in *Asian Americans and Politics: Perspectives, Experiences, Prospects*, ed. Gordon H. Chang (Washington DC and Stanford, CA: Woodrow Wilson Center Press and Stanford University Press, 1999), 81–83.

6. Gordon H. Chang, *Asian American Politics: Some Perspectives from History*, ed. Gordon H. Chang, Asian American Politics: Perspectives, Experiences, Prospectives (Washington DC and Stanford, CA: Woodrow Wilson Center and Stanford University Press, 2001), 17, 21–22; "Eternally Foreign: Asian Americans, History, and Race," in *Doing Race: 21 Essays for the 21st Century*, ed. Hazel Rose Markus and Paula M. Moya (New York and London: W. W. Norton & Company, 2010), 218–219.

7. U.S. Census Bureau, "The Asian Population: 2000 Census 2000 Brief" (U.S. Department of Commerce, Economics and Statistics Administration, U.S. Census Bureau, 2002), 1.

8. Ibid.; Pei-te Lien, Magaret Conway, and Janelle Wong, *The Politics of Asian Americans: Diversity and Community* (New York and London: Routledge, 2004), 2.

9. Pei-te Lien, Margaret Conway, and Janelle Wong, *The Politics of Asian Americans: Diversity and Community* (New York: Routledge, 2004); Sucheng Chan, *Asian Americans: An Interpretive History* (New York: Twayne Publishers, 1991), 20.

10. Paul Wong et al., "Asian Americans as a Model Minority: Self-Perceptions and Perceptions by Other

Racial Groups," *Sociological Perspectives* 41, no. 1 (1998): 95–96.

11. Ibid; U.S. Census Bureau. "The Asian Population: 2010," in 2010 Census Briefs, 1-23 (Washington, DC: U.S. Department of Commerce, Economics and Statistics Administration, 2012); Lien, Conway, and Wong, *The Politics of Asian Americans: Diversity and Community*, 7–8.

12. Ronald Takaki, *A Different Mirror: A History of Multicultural America* (Boston: Little, Brown and Company, 1993), 101.

13. Chang, "Eternally Foreign: Asian Americans, History, and Race"; Ronald Takaki, *A History of Asian Americans: Strangers from a Different Shore* (New York: Back Bay Books: Little, Brown and Company, 1998), 101.

14. Kim, "The Racial Triangulation of Asian Americans," 10–13, 105–108.

15. Gary Y. Okihiro, *The Columbia Guide to Asian American History* (New York: Columbia University Press, 2001), 1–6; quotation on p. 6; Immanuel Wallerstein, *The Modern World-System III: The Second Era of Great Expansion of the Capitalist World-Economy, 1730–1840s* (San Diego, CA: Academic Press, Inc., 1989).

16. Audrey Smedley, *Race in North America: Origin and Evolution of a Worldview*, 3rd ed. (Boulder, CO: Westview Press, 2007), 219.

17. Takaki, *A History of Asian Americans: Strangers from a Different Shore*, 132–175; Gary Okihiro, *The Columbia Guide to Asian American History*, 17, 178–181.

18. Chan, *Asian Americans: An Interpretive History*, 3–4. The quotation is found on p. 7.

19. Ibid., 7–9.

20. Okihiro, *The Columbia Guide to Asian American History*, 12–13; Chan, *Asian Americans: An Interpretive History*, 5–12.

21. *Asian Americans: An Interpretive History*, 12–16.

22. Ibid., 16–17. The quotation is from E. San Juan Jr., "The Predicament of Filipinos in the United States: 'Where Are You From? When Are You Going Back?'," in *The State of Asian American: Activism and Resistance in the 1990s*, ed. Karin Aguilar-San Juan (Boston, MA: South End Press, 1994), 206.

23. Suman Kakar, "Asian Indian Families," in *Minority Families in the United States: A Multicultural Perspective*, ed. Ronald Taylor (Upper Saddle River, NJ: Prentice Hall, 1998), 209–11; Chan, *Asian Americans: An Interpretive History*, 20–23.

24. Jan Lin, "Chinese Americans: From Exclusion to Prosperity," in *The Minority Report: An Introduction to Raical, Ethnic, and Gender Relations*, ed. Anthony Gary Dworkin and Rosalind J. Dworkin (New York:

Harcourt Brace College Publishers, 1999), 323–323; Takaki, *A History of Asian Americans: Strangers from a Different Shore*, 179.

25. Takaki, *A History of Asian Americans: Strangers from a Different Shore*, 80.

26. Ibid., 80–82.

27. Shehong Chen, "Chinese American Experiences in a New England Mill City: Lowell Massachusetts, 1876–1967," in *Remapping Asian American History*, ed. Sucheng Chan (Walnut Creek and Lanham: Altamira Press, 2003); Xiaolan Bao, "Revisiting New York's Chinatown, 1900–1930," ibid.; Chan, *Asian Americans: An Interpretive History*, 30–32.

28. *Asian Americans: An Interpretive History*, 27, 35; Takaki, *A History of Asian Americans: Strangers from a Different Shore*, 132–152.

29. Paula D McClain and Joseph Stewart Jr., *'Can We All Get Along?' Racial and Ethnic Minorities in American Politics*, 5th ed. (Boulder, CO: Westview Press, 2010), 246; E. Michael Madrid, "The Unheralded History of the Lemon Grove Desegregation Case," *Multicultural Education* (Spring 2008).

30. Chan, *Asian Americans: An Interpretive History*, 78.

31. Ibid.; Takaki, *A History of Asian Americans: Strangers from a Different Shore*, 179–197, 239–257.

32. Chan, *Asian Americans: An Interpretive History*, 104.

33. Ibid., 103–112.

34. Foner and Rosenberg, *Racism, Dissent, and Asian Americans from 1850 to the Present: A Documentary History*, 181.

35. Chan, *Asian Americans: An Interpretive History*, 48–50; Foner and Rosenberg, *Racism, Dissent, and Asian Americans from 1850 to the Present: A Documentary History*, 180–182.

36. Okihiro, *The Columbia Guide to Asian American History*, 14–15; Foner and Rosenberg, *Racism, Dissent, and Asian Americans from 1850 to the Present: A Documentary History*, 24; Chan, *Asian Americans: An Interpretive History*, 54–56.

37. Paula D. McClain and Joseph Stewart Jr., *"Can We All Get Along?": Racial and Ethnic Minorities in American Politics* (New York: Westview Press, 2010), 269, 270.

38. Claire Kim, "The Racial Triangulation of Asian Americans," 114.

39. Ibid.; Chan, *Asian Americans: An Interpretive History*, 94, 95, 116; Takaki, *A Different Mirror: A History of Multicultural America*.

40. Chan, *Asian Americans: An Interpretive History*, 83–89.

41. Manning Marable, *Race, Reform, and Rebellion: The Second Reconstruction and Beyond in Black America, 1945–2006*, 3rd ed. (Oxford, MS: University Press of Misssissippi, 2007).

42. Chang, "Eternally Foreign: Asian Americans, History, and Race," 223.

43. Kerrily J. Kitano and Harry H. Kitano, "The Japanese-American Family," in *Ethnic Families in America: Patterns and Variables*, ed. Charles H. Mindel, Robert H. Habenstein, and Roosevelt Wright Jr. (Upper Saddle River, NJ: Prenctice Hall, 1998), 316–317; Chang, "Eternally Foreign: Asian Americans, History, and Race," 222–226; quotation taken from Takaki, *A Different Mirror: A History of Multicultural America*, 378.

44. Chan, *Asian Americans: An Interpretive History*, 121–134.

45. Ibid., 135–139.

46. Frank Wu, "Profiling in the Wake of September 11: The Precedent of the Japanese American Internment," *Criminal Justice* (2002); Edmund Fong, "Beyond the Racial Exceptionalism of Japanese Internment," *Politics, Groups, and Identities* 1, no. 2 (2013).

47. Post-9/11 Civil Rights Summit, "Confronting Discrimination in the Post-9/11 Era: Challenges and Opportunities Ten Years Later" (Washington, DC: Civil Rights Division, U.S. Department of Justice, 2011).

48. Chan, *Asian Americans: An Interpretive History*, 121–122.

49. Sanjeev Khagram, Manish Desai, and Jason Varughese, "Seen, Rich, but Unheard? The Politics of Asian Indians in the United States," in *Asian American Politics: Perspectives, Experiences, Prospects*, ed. Gordon H. Chang (Washington DC and Stanford, CA: Woodrow Wilson Center Press and Stanford University Press, 2001), 266.

50. Yasmine Hafiz, "Amy Chua in 'The Triple Package' Claims Jews and Mormons Produce More Successful People," in *Huffington Post,* 2014; Rosalind S. Chou and Joe R. Feagin, *The Myth of the Model Minority: Asian Americans Facing Racism* (Boulder and London: Paradigm Publishers, 2008), 28; Steven Yaccino, Michael Schwirtz, and Marc Santora, "Gunmen Kills 6 at a Sikh Temple near Milwaukee," *New York Times,* 2012; Nick Carbone, "Timeline: A History of Violence against Sikhs in the Wake of 9/11," in *Time,* 2012.

51. Chou and Feagin, *The Myth of the Model Minority: Asian Americans Facing Racism*, 28; Brian Montopoli, "SC Lawmaker Refers to Obama and Nikki Haley as 'Raghead'," in *CBS News,* 2010.

52. Gail M. Nomura, "Significant Lives: Asia and Asian Americans in the History of the U.S. West," *Western Historical Quarterly* 25, no. 1 (1994).

CHAPTER 6

1. Quoted in Edward S. Morgan, *Not Your Usual Founding Father: Selected Readings from Benjamin Franklin* (New Haven: Yale University Press, 2006), 149–150.

2. Madison Grant, *The Passing of the Great Race; or, The Racial Basis of European History* (New York: Charles Scribner's and Sons, 1918), 89–90.

3. Ian Haney-Lopez, *White by Law: The Legal Construction of Race* (New York: New York University Press).

4. See, for example, *Dred Scott v. Sandford,* 60 U.S. (19 How.) 393 (1857), which held that people of African descent and held as slaves as well as their descendants could never be citizens of the United States; *In re Ah Yup,* 1 Fed.Cas. 223 (D.Cal.Cir.Ct. 1878), which held that a Chinese immigrant who was of the "Mongolian race" was not White and not eligible for naturalization; or *In re Ahmed Hassan,* 48 F. Supp. 843 (E.D. Michigan 1942), which held that Arabs were not White and not eligible for naturalization.

5. Vine Deloria Jr. and Clifford M. Lytle, *The Nations Within: The Past and Future of American Indian Sovereignty* (Austin: University of Texas Press, 1984).

6. Aristide R. Zolberg, *A Nation by Design: Immigration Policy in the Fashioning of America* (Cambridge, MA, and New York: Harvard University Press and Russell Sage Foundation Press, 2006).

7. Thomas J. Carty, *A Catholic in the White House? Religion, Politics, and John F. Kennedy's Presidential Campaign* (New York: Palgrave Macmillan, 2004).

8. David R. Roediger, *Working toward Whiteness: How America's Immigrants Became White* (New York: Basic Books, 2005).

9. Thomas A. Gugliemo, *White on Arrival: Italians, Race, Color, and Power in Chicago 1890–1945* (New York: Oxford University Press, 2003); Robert Dahl, *Who Governs? Democracy and Power in an American City* (New Haven: Yale University Press, 1961); Steve Garner, *Whiteness: An Introduction* (New York: Routledge, 2007).

10. Noel Ignatiev, *How the Irish Became White* (New York: Routledge, 1995).

11. David R. Roediger, *The Wages of Whiteness: Race and the Making of the American Working Class* (New York: Verso, 1991); Roediger, *Working toward Whiteness: How America's Immigrants Became White.*

12. Jonathan D. Sarna, *When General Grant Expelled the Jews* (New York: Schocken Books, 2012).

13. Ibid.

14. Naomi W. Cohen, "Anti-Semitism in the Gilded Age: A Jewish View," *Jewish Social Studies* 41, nos.3/4 (Autumn 1979): 187–210.

15. Ivan Hannaford, *Race: The History of an Idea in the West* (Washington, DC, and Baltimore, MD: Woodrow Wilson Center Press and Johns Hopkins University Press, 1996).

16. Marguerite Ross Barnett, "A Theoretical Perspective on American Racial Public Policy," in Marguerite Ross Barnett and James A. Hefner, eds., *Public Policy for the Black Community: Strategies and Perspectives* (Port Washington, NY: Alfred Publishing Company, 1976),1–53.

17. Gerald H. Gamm, *The Making of New Deal Democrats: Voting Behavior and Realignment in Boston, 1920–1940* (Chicago, IL: University of Chicago Press, 1986); Lizabeth Cohen, *Making a New Deal: Industrial Workers in Chicago, 1919–1939* (New York: Cambridge University Press, 1990); Kristi Andersen, *The Creation of a Democratic Majority, 1928–1936* (Chicago, IL: University of Chicago Press, 1979).

18. Daniel Okrent, *Last Call: The Rise and Fall of Prohibition* (New York: Scribner, 2011).

19. Robert A. Slayton, *Empire Statesman: The Rise and Redemption of Al Smith* (New York: Free Press, 2001).

20. See, for example, Norman Mailer, *The Naked and the Dead* (New York: Rinehart and Company, 1948).

21. Mary E. Waters, *Ethnic Options: Choosing Identities in America* (Berkeley: University of California Press, 1990).

22. Richard Alba, *Blurring the Color Line: The New Chance for a More Integrated America* (Cambridge, MA: Harvard University Press, 2009).

23. Matthew Frye Jacobson, *Roots Too: White Ethnic Revival in Post–Civil Rights America* (Cambridge, MA: Harvard University Press, 2006).

24. Linda Faye Williams, *Legacies of White Skin Privilege in America* (University Park: Pennsylvania State University Press, 2003); Dona C. Hamilton and Charles V. Hamilton, *The Dual Agenda: Race and Social Welfare Policies of Civil Rights Organizations* (New York: Columbia University Press, 1997).

25. Alexander Keyssar, *The Right to Vote: The Contested History of Democracy in the United States* (New York: Basic Books, 2000).

26. Tyler Anbinder, *Five Points: The 19th-Century New York City Neighborhood That Invented Tap Dance, Stole Elections, and Became the World's Most Notorious Slum* (New York: The Free Press, 2001); Steven P. Erie, *Rainbow's End: Irish-Americans and the Dilemmas of Urban Machine Politics, 1840–1985* (Berkeley: University of California Press, 1988).

27. Dennis W. Johnson, *The Laws That Shaped America: Fifteen Acts of Congress and Their Lasting Impact* (New York: Routledge, 2009), chap. 3.

28. Trina R. Williams, "Asset-Building Policy as a Response to Wealth Inequality: Drawing Implications from the Homestead Act of 1862," *Social Development Issues* 24, nos. 1/2 (Spring/Fall 2003): 47–58.

29. Johnson, *The Laws That Shaped America,* chap. 3.

30. Jean Preer, "'Just and Equitable Division': Jim Crow and the 1890 Land-Grant College Act," in Donald G. Nieman, ed., *African Americans and the Emergence of Segregation 1865–1900* (New York: Garland Publishers, 1994), 299–311.

31. Thomas M. Shapiro, *The Hidden Cost of Being African American: How Wealth Perpetuates Inequality* (New York: Oxford University Press, 2004).

32. Williams, *The Constraint of Race,* 73.

33. Ira Katznelson, *When Affirmative Action Was White: An Untold History of Racial Inequality in Twentieth Century America* (New York: W. W. Norton, 2005).

34. Williams, *The Constraint of Race,* 79.

35. Marguerite Ross Barnett, "A Theoretical Perspective on American Racial Public Policy."

36. Nick Kotz, *Judgment Days: Lyndon Baines Johnson, Martin Luther King, Jr., and the Laws That Changed America* (New York: Houghton Mifflin, 2005), chap. 12.

CHAPTER 7

1. Lyndon B. Johnson's commencement address at Howard University, "To Fulfill These Rights," June 4, 1965. Lyndon Baines Johnson Presidential Library, University of Texas at Austin, http://www.lbjlib.utexas.edu/johnson/archives.hom/speeches.hom/650604.asp.

2. For examples, see Chapter 9's Road Sign for a discussion of the creation and implementation of voter ID requirements by over thirty states by 2011, as well as reduced early voting hours.

3. Frank Parker, *Black Votes Count: Political Empowerment in Mississippi after 1965* (Chapel Hill: University of North Carolina Press,1990), offers comments on the 1965 VRA; voter identification, felon disenfranchisement, and efforts to limit early voting are examples of efforts at disenfranchisement.

4. Daniel McCool, Susan M. Olson, and Jennifer L. Robinson, *Native Vote: American Indians, the Voting Rights Act, and the Right to Vote* (New York: Cambridge University Press, 2007), 9. Original quotation by Helen L. Peterson, "American Indians and

American Life," *Annals of the American Academy of Political and Social Science* 311 (May 1957): 116–126; quotation on p. 121. Number of Native Americans in World War II based on ibid., 123. Correspondence on Choctaws' responsibility for responding to the draft based on Alison Bernstein, *American Indians and World War II: Toward a New Era in Indian Affairs* (Norman: University of Oklahoma Press, 1991), 24.

5. McCool, Olson, and Robinson, *Native Vote,* 9; David Wilkins, *American Indian Politics and the American Political System,* 3rd ed. (Lanham, MD: Rowman and Littlefield, 2011); ACLU Voting Rights Project, "Voting Rights in Indian Country: A Special Report of the Voting Rights Project of the American Civil Liberties Union" (Atlanta, GA: September 2009), 15–16.

6. "1970s: The Early Years," LatinoJustice, https://latinojustice.org/about/history_1970s.

7. Pei-te Lien, Dianne M. Pinderhughes, Carol Hardy-Fanta, and Christine M. Sierra, "The Voting Rights Act and the Election of Nonwhite Officials," *PS* (July 2007): 489–494.

8. Jeffrey S. Passel and D'Vera Cohn, "U.S. Population Projections: 2005–2050," Pew Research Hispanic Trends Project, February 11, 2008, http://www.pewhispanic.org/2008/02/11/us-population-projections-2005-2050.

9. "Biography of Patsy Takemoto Mink, 1927–2002," U.S. House of Representatives, http://history.house.gov/People/detail/18329.

10. See, for example, the Blackside Inc. PBS series *Eyes on the Prize: America's Civil Rights Movement, 1955–1985.* See especially "Ain't Scared of Your Jails," http://www.pbs.org/wgbh/amex/eyesontheprize/about/fd.html; David Garrow, *Protest at Selma: Martin Luther King, Jr., and the Voting Rights Act of 1965* (New Haven: Yale University Press, 1980); Charles Payne, *I've Got the Light of Freedom* (Oakland: University of California Press, 1995); Barbara Ransby, *Ella Baker and the Black Freedom Movement: A Radical Democratic Vision* (Durham: University of North Carolina Press, 2005).

11. Voter Education Project, "Martin Luther King, Jr. and the Global Freedom Struggle," Stanford University, http://mlk-kpp01.stanford.edu/index.

12. "Freedom Summer (1964)," Encyclopedia, Martin Luther King, Jr., and the Global Freedom Struggle, http://mlk-kpp01.stanford.edu/index.php/encyclopedia/encyclopedia/enc_freedom_summer_1964.

13. Transcript of Civil Rights Act (1964), Our Documents Website: 100 Milestone Documents, http://www.our-documents.gov/doc.php?flash = true&doc = 97&page = transcript.

14. Frederick M. Wirt, *The Politics of Southern Equality: Law and Social Change in a Mississippi County* (Rutgers, NJ: Aldine Transaction, 2008), offers a detailed analysis of the challenges the Department of Justice faced in developing the evidence of discrimination, and in prosecuting cases.

15. Transcript of Voting Rights Act (1965), Our Documents Website: 100 Milestone Documents, http://www.ourdocuments.gov/doc.php?doc = 100&page = trans.

16. Ibid.

17. Nathaniel Persily, "The Promise and Pitfalls of the New Voting Rights," *Yale Law Journal* 117, no. 2 (November 2007): 174–254, http://www.jstor.org/stable/20455790; quotation on p. 177, emphasis added.

18. Janelle Wong, *Democracy's Promise: Immigrants and American Civic Institutions* (Ann Arbor: University of Michigan Press, 2006). Language issues remain current; for example, recent surveys of Asian Americans were conducted in seven Asian languages. Janelle Wong, S. Karthick Ramakrishnan, Taeku Lee, and Jane Junn, *Asian American Political Participation: Emerging Constituents and Their Political Identities* (New York: Russell Sage Foundation, 2011).

19. Ronald Schmidt Sr., Yvette Alex-Assensoh, Andrew Aoki, and Rodney Hero, *Newcomers, Outsiders, and Insiders: Immigrants and American Racial Politics in the Early Twenty-first Century* (Ann Arbor: University of Michigan Press, 2009).

20. Abigail Thernstrom, *Voting Rights—and Wrongs: The Elusive Quest for Racially Fair Elections* (Washington, DC: American Enterprise Institute Press, 2009).

21. *South Carolina v. Katzenbach,* 383 U.S. 301 (1966).

22. David Bositis, *Black Elected Officials: A Statistical Summary, 2001* (Washington, DC: Joint Center for Political and Economic Studies, 2003), Table 1, p. 13.

23. "Voting Rights, 1970 Legislative Chronology," in *Congress and the Nation, 1969–1972,* Vol. 3 (Washington, DC: CQ Press, 1973), 498, http://library.cqpress.com.proxy.library.nd.edu/catn/document.php?id = catn69-0008168863&type = toc&num = 28. After disagreement on this, the Twenty-Sixth Amendment to the Constitution was passed, reaffirming the vote for eighteen-year-olds.

24. The Voting Rights Act Summary and Text, United States Commission on Civil Rights, Clearinghouse Publication, No. 32, September 1971, 6–8, http://www.law.umaryland.edu/marshall/usccr/documents/cr11032.pdf.

25. Biographies and autobiographies of the men include Jack Santino, *Miles of Smiles, Years of Struggle: Stories of Black Pullman Porters* (Urbana:

University of Illinois Press, 1991); Andrew E. Kersten, *A. Philip Randolph: A Life in the Vanguard* (Lanham, MD: Rowman and Littlefield, 2006); Cornelius L. Bynum, *A. Philip Randolph and the Struggle for Civil Rights* (Urbana: University of Illinois Press, 2010); Roy Wilkins and Tom Mathews, *Standing Fast: The Autobiography of Roy Wilkins* (Cambridge, MA: Da Capo Press, 1994); Yvonne Ryan, *Roy Wilkins: The Quiet Revolutionary and the NAACP* (Lexington: University Press of Kentucky, 2013).

26. Dianne M. Pinderhughes, "Black Interest Groups and the 1982 Extension of the Voting Rights Act," in *Blacks and the American Political System,* ed. Huey L. Perry and Wayne Parent (Gainesville: University Press of Florida, 1995), 203–224; quotation on p. 211. Policy decisions in the Leadership Conference were made by an executive committee of about twenty members, by unanimous vote. The NAACP as a founding member is regularly a member of this group. See footnote 24, p. 223.

27. Quotation from "Minority Language Citizens: Section 203 of the Voting Rights Act," Civil Rights Division, United States Department of Justice, http://www.justice.gov/crt/about/vot/sec_203/203_brochure.php. Emphasis added.

28. A Voice: African American Voices in Congress website, "Voting Rights Act," http://www.avoiceonline.org/voting/legislation.html; and "Voting Rights Act Amendments of 2006," Determinations Under Section 203, Department of Commerce, Bureau of the Census, *Federal Register* 76, no. 198 (October 13, 2011): 1.

29. Pinderhughes, "Black Interest Groups and the 1982 Extension of the Voting Rights Act."

30. The attorneys were also prolific writers, later documenting their experiences in an array of biographical, policy, and philosophically based volumes on their work. Frank R. Parker, *Black Votes Count: Political Empowerment in Mississippi after 1965* (Chapel Hill: University of North Carolina Press, 1990); Laughlin McDonald, *A Voting Rights Odyssey: Black Enfranchisement in Georgia* (New York: Cambridge University Press, 2003); Lani Guinier, *The Tyranny of the Majority: Fundamental Fairness in Representative Democracy* (New York: The Free Press, 1994). By early 2011, Mississippi's Chief of the Highway Patrol was an African American, Colonel Donnell Berry. See the website for the State of Mississippi's Department of Public Safety: http://www.dps.state.ms.us/department-of-public-safety-leadership. "A Guide to the Frank R. Parker Papers, 1963–1997" (Lexington, VA: Washington and Lee

University), http://ead.lib.virginia.edu/vivaxtf/view?docId = wl-law/vilxwl00006.xml;query = .

31. 1980 census data: "Table 1, Alabama—Race and Hispanic Origin for Selected Large Cities and Other Places: Earliest Census to 1990, http://www.census.gov/population/www/documentation/twps0076/ALtab.pdf; City of Mobile website, http://www.cityofmobile.org/departments_full.php?view = 6. By 2010 Mobile's population was 195,111, when it reached 50.6 percent Black. "Mobile, Alabama Race and Hispanic or Latino Origin, 2010," http://factfinder2.census.gov/faces/tableservices/jsf/pages/productview.xhtml?pid = DEC_10_SF.

32. Peyton McCrary, Jerome Gray, Edward Still, and Huey L. Perry, "Alabama," in *Quiet Revolution in the South: The Impact of the Voting Rights Act, 1965–1990,* ed. Chandler Davidson and Bernard Grofman (Princeton, NJ: Princeton University Press, 1994), 38–66.

33. Chandler Davidson, "The Recent Evolution of Voting Rights Law Affecting Racial and Language Minorities," in *Quiet Revolution in the South,* ed. Davidson and Grofman, 21–37.

34. Pinderhughes, "Black Interest Groups and the 1982 Extension of the Voting Rights Act," 216.

35. Ibid.

36. See Chapter 4, Table 4.2, for the Latino population by decade. For Spanish-speaking percentages for 2000, see table, "America Speaks: A Demographic Profile of Foreign-Language Speakers for the United States: 2000," http://www.census.gov/hhes/socdemo/language/data/census/amspeaks/index.html.

37. For the Asian population, see "We the Americans: Asians." Bureau of the Census, 1993, p. 1; language data and quotation on p. 5. The definition of *linguistic isolation* "refers to persons in households in which no one 14 years old or over speaks only English and no one who speaks a language other than English speaks English 'very well.'" Quotation is a note from Table 2, p. 5.

38. Pei-te Lien, *The Making of Asian America through Political Participation* (Philadelphia: Temple University Press, 2001), 110.

39. Ibid.; also see footnote 18.

40. Ibid.

41. "Everything You Always Wanted to Know About Redistricting but Were Afraid to Ask," American Civil Liberties Union Foundation, Voting Rights Project, 2010, http://www.aclu.org/files/assets/2010_REDISTRICTING_GUIDE_web_0.pdf.

42. Ibid.

43. See Laughlin McDonald, *A Voting Rights Odyssey: Black Enfranchisement in Georgia* (New York:

Cambridge University Press, 2003), for his discussion of redistricting in the 1980s and 1990s.

44. Quotation from Justice Stephen Breyer, writing for the majority in *Hunt v. Cromartie* (2001) decision. Research Division, N.C. General Assembly. *Legislator's Guide to North Carolina Legislative and Congressional Redistricting, 2011,* General Assembly 2011 Regular Session 2011, March 2011, http://www.ncleg.net/GIS/Download/Maps_Reports/2011RedistrictingGuide.pdf, p. 32.

45. Daniel P. Tokaji, "The Story of *Shaw v. Reno*: Representation and Raceblindness," Ohio State Public Law Working Paper No. 53, Race Law Stories, 2007, http://ssrn.com/abstract = 896560; Ed O'Keefe and Paul Kane, "Senate Confirms Patricia Millett, Mel Watt Using New Majority Rules," *Washington Post,* December 10, 2013, http://www.washingtonpost.com/blogs/post-politics/wp/2013/12/10/senate-proceeding-as-scheduled-tuesday.

46. Tal Kopan, "NAACP, Democrats Fume at Open North Carolina Seat," *Politico,* January 14, 2014, http://www.politico.com/story/2014/01/naacp-democrats-north-carolina-seat-102156.html.

47. *1992 Census of Governments.* Vol. 1, Government Organization, No. 2, Popularly Elected Officials. Table 1, Elected Officials of State and Local Governments by Region and Type of Government: 1992, Table 1, p. 1.

48. Katherine Tate, "Black Politics, the GOP Southern Strategy, and the Reauthorization of the Voting Rights Act," *The Forum* 4, no. 2 (2006): 1. The Republican chair of the House Judiciary Committee wanted the reauthorization during his term, and because that term was due to expire in 2006, the legislative process was moved up one year. See Persily, "The Promise and Pitfalls of the New Voting Rights Act," 181. This article offers a more complicated picture and shows that President George W. Bush helped move the legislation toward a final resolution, despite opposition from Republicans in the House and Senate.

49. Quotation from Seth Stern, "Voting Rights Extension's Four Rejected Amendments," *CQ Weekly* (July 17, 2006): 1965, http://library.cqpress.com/cqweekly/weeklyreport109-000002334197.

50. Ibid.; Seth Stern, "House Vote 372: Voting Rights Reauthorization," *CQ Weekly* (January 1, 2007): 64, http://library.cqpress.com/cqweekly/document.php?id = weeklyreport109-000002422010&type = hitlist&num = 53&PHPSESSID = 83kp5ps0611c3bbsos5i502e16.

51. Stern, "House Vote 372."

52. David J. Becker, "Saving Section 5: Reflections on *Georgia v. Ashcroft,* and Its Impact on the Reauthorization of the Voting Rights Act," in *VRA: Voting Rights Act: Reauthorization of 2006: Perspectives on Democracy, Participation and Power,* ed. Ana Henderson (Berkeley: University of California, Berkeley Public Policy Press, 2007). Quotation on p. 223.

53. Ibid., 235.

54. Ibid., 240. Memorandum of Law in Opposition to Plaintiff's Motion for Summary Judgment and in Support of Defendants' Motion for Summary Judgment," *State of Florida v. Holder,* quotations on p. 6, http://www.justice.gov/crt/about/app/briefs/floridabrief.pdf.

55. Persily, "The Promise and Pitfalls of the New Voting Rights," 207.

56. Ibid., 217; "Party Divisions of the House of Representatives, 1789–Present," U.S. House of Representatives, http://history.house.gov/Institution/Party-Divisions/Party-Divisions.

57. Adam Liptak. "Voting Rights Law Draws Skepticism from Justices," *New York Times,* February 27, 2013, http://www.nytimes.com/2013/02/28/us/politics/conservative-justices-voice-skepticism-on-voting-law.html. For a discussion of the Tea Party, see Theda Skocpol and Vanessa Williamson, *The Tea Party and The Remaking of Republican Conservatism* (New York: Oxford University Press, 2012).

58. "Voting Rights Act: H.R. 3899: The Voting Rights Amendment Act of 2014." Website for Congressman Jim Sensenbrenner, http://sensenbrenner.house.gov/legislation/voting-rights-act.html.

59. Persily, "The Promise and Pitfalls of the New Voting Rights," 252.

60. Liptak, "Voting Rights Law Draws Skepticism from Justices."

CHAPTER 8

1. Hanes Walton Jr., *Invisible Politics: Black Political Behavior* (Albany: State University of New York Press, 1985), 7–19. For different discussions of political attitudes and ideology, see John Zaller, *The Nature and Origins of Mass Opinion* (Cambridge: Cambridge University Press, 1992), as well as Michael Dawson, *Black Visions: The Roots of Contemporary African-American Political Ideologies* (Chicago and London: University of Chicago Press, 2001), 4–5, 47–66.

2. Marion Orr, *Black Social Capital: The Politics of School Reform in Baltimore* (Lawrence: University Press of Kansas, 1999); Edward G. Goetz, "The Community-Based Housing Movement and Progressive Local Politics," in *Revitalizing Urban Neighborhoods*, ed. W. Dennis Keating, Norman Krumholz, and Philip Star (Lawrence: University Press of Kansas, 1996); Melissa Checker, *Polluted Promises: Environmental Racism and the Search for Justice in a Southern Town* (New York and London: New York University Press, 2005); Eric D. Knowles, Brian S. Lowery, and Rebecca L. Schaumberg, "Racial Prejudice Predicts Opposition to Obama and His Health Care Reform Plan," *Journal of Experimental Social Psychology* 46, no. 2 (2010).

3. Henri Tajfel et al., "Social Categorization and Inter-Group Behavior," *European Journal of Social Psychology* 1, no. 2 (1971); John Turner et al., "Self and Collective: Cognition and Social Context," *Personality and Social Pyschology Bulletin* 20, no. 5 (1994); Michael A. Hogg, "Social Categorization, Depersonalization and Group Behavior," in *Blackwell Handbook of Social Psychology: Group Processes*, ed. Michael A. Hogg and Scott Tindale (Malden, MA: Blackwell Publishing Ltd, 2002).

4. Herbert Gans, "Symbolic Ethnicity and Symbolic Religiosity: Towards a Comparion of Ethnic and Religoius Acculturation," *Ethnic and Racial Studies* 17, no. 4 (1994); Allen Fredrickson, "Gunman Kills 6 at a Sikh Temple near Milwaukee," *New York Times,* August 5, 2012.

5. Lawrence Bobo and James R. Kluegel, "Opposition to Race-Targeting: Self-Interest, Stratification Ideology, or Racial Attitudes?," *American Sociological Review* 58, no. 4 (1993); Lawrence Bobo and Vincent L. Hutchings, "Perceptions of Racial Group Competition: Extending Blumer's Theory of Group Position to a Multiracial Social Context," *American Sociological Review* 61, no. 6 (1996); Claire Jean Kim, *Bitter Fruit: The Politics of Black-Korean Conflict in New York City* (New Haven: Yale University Press, 2000); Paula McClain and Albert Karnig, "Black and Hispanic Socioeconomic and Political Competition," *American Politiacl Science Review* 84, no. 2 (1990).

6. Shaun Bowler and Gary M. Segura, *The Future Is Ours: Minority Politics, Political Behavior, and the Multiracial Era of American Politics* (Washington, DC: CQ Press, 2011).

7. Ronald Walters, *White Nationalism, Black Interests: Conservative Public Policy and the Black Community* (Detroit, MI: Wayne State University Press, 2003); Laura Pulido, *Black, Brown, Yellow and Left: Radical Activism in Los Angeles* (Los Angeles: University of California Press, 2005).

8. Mark Potok, "The Year in Hate and Extremism," Southern Poverty Law Center, 2013; Jennifer Agiesta and Sonya Ross, "Poll Finds Majority in U.S. Hold Racist Views: Prejudice Has Risen Since 2008 Obama Victory," Associated Press, October 28, 2012.

9. Tatishe M. Nteta and Jill S. Greenlee, "A Change Is Gonna Come: Generational Membership and White Racial Attitudes in the 21st Century," *Political Psychology* 34, no. 6 (2013): 889–890.

10. Mary J. Fischer, "Interracial Contact and Changes in the Racial Attitudes of White College Students," *Social Psychology of Education* 14, no. 4 (2011): 569.

11. Susan Herbst, "The History of Public Opinion," in *New Directions in Public Opinion*, ed. Adam J. Berinksy (New York: Taylor and Francis, 2012); Dawson, *Black Visions: The Roots of Contemporary African-American Political Ideologies;* Katherine Tate, *What's Going On? Political Incorporation and the Transformation of Black Public Opinion* (Washington, DC: Georgetown University Press, 2010).

12. J. Eric Oliver and Tali Mendelberg, "Reconsidering the Environmental Determinants of White Racial Attitudes," *American Journal of Political Science* 44, no. 3 (2000); Tali Mendelberg, *The Race Card: Campaign Strategy, Implicit Messages, and the Norm of Equality* (Princeton, NJ: Princeton University Press, 2001); Bobo and Hutchings, "Perceptions of Racial Group Competition: Extending Blumer's Theory of Group Position to a Multiracial Social Context"; Paul M. Sniderman et al., "The New Racism," *American Journal of Political Science* 35, no. 2 (1991); Taeku Lee, *Mobilizing Public Opinion: Black Insurgency and Racial Attitudes in the Civil Rights Era* (Chicago, IL: University of Chicago Press, 2002); Donald Kinder and Lynn Sanders, *Divided by Color: Racial Politics and Democratic Ideals* (Chicago and London: University of Chicago Press, 1996).

13. Hanes Walton Jr. and Robert C. Smith, *American Politics and the African American Quest for Universal Freedom* (New York: Longman, 2012), 51–60; Daniel J. Elazar, *The American Mosaic: The Impact of Space, Time, and Culture on American Politics* (Boulder and San Francisco: Westview Press, 1994); Richard Iton, *Solidarity Blues: Race, Culture, and the American Left* (Chapel Hill and London: University of North Carolina Press, 2000); Lester K. Spence, *Stare in the Darkness: The Limits of Hip-Hop and Black Politics* (Minneapolis and London: University of Minnesota Press, 2011).

14. Walton and Smith, *American Politics and the African American Quest for Universal Freedom*, 62–70;

Frederick C. Harris, "It Takes a Tragedy to Arouse Them: Collective Memory and Collective Action during the Civil Rights Movement," *Journal of Social, Cultural, and Political Protest* 5, no. 1 (2007); Benjamin G. Bishin and Casey A. Klofstad, "The Political Incorporation of Cuban Americans: Why Won't Little Havana Turn Blue?," *Political Research Quarterly* 65, no. 3 (2012).

15. For two articles that discuss how political scientists and other social scientists can use such racial tragedies to argue for changes in racial attitudes and larger public policies, see Michael C. Dawson, "Racial Tragedies, Political Hope, and the Tasks of American Political Science," *Perspectives on Politics* 10, no. 3 (2012): 669–673; and Vickie M. Mays, Denise Johnson, Courtney N. Coles, Denise Gellene, and Susan D. Cochran, "Using the Science of Psychology to Target Perpetrators of Racism and Race-Based Discrimination for Intervention Efforts: Preventing Another Trayvon Martin Tragedy," *Journal for Social Action in Counseling and Psychology* 5, no. 1 (2013): 11.

16. Howard Schuman, *Racial Attitudes in America: Trends and Interpretations* (Cambridge, MA: Harvard University Press, 1997); Jennifer Agiesta and Sonya Ross, "Poll Finds Majority in U.S. Hold Racist Views: Prejudice Has Risen since 2008 Obama Victory," Associated press, October 28, 2012.

17. Thomas Craemer, "Nonconscious Feelings of Closeness toward African Americans and Support for Pro-Black Policies," *Political Psychology* 29, no. 3 (2008); Thomas Craemer et al., "'Race Still Matters, However . . . ': Implicit Identification with Blacks, Pro-Black Policy Support and the Obama Candidacy," *Ethnic and Racial Studies* (2011); Jeffrey S. Nevid and Nate McClleland, "Measure of Implicit and Explicit Attitudes toward Barack Obama," *Psychology & Marketing* 27, no. 10 (2010).

18. Daniel Hopkins, "No More Wilder Effect, Never a Whitman Effect: When and Why Polls Misled about Black and Female Candidates," *Journal of Politics* 71, no. 3 (2009).

19. Michael Dawson, *Behind the Mule: Race and Class in African American Politics* (Princeton, NJ: Princeton University Press, 1994); Bobo and Hutchings, "Perceptions of Racial Group Competition: Extending Blumer's Theory of Group Position to a Multiracial Social Context," 955.

20. James S. Jackson, Vincent L. Hutchings, Ronald E. Brown, and Cara Wong, "National Politics Study" (Ann Arbor: Program for Research on Black Americans, Center for Political Studies; University of Michigan's Institute for Social Research, 2004).

21. David R. Roediger, *Working toward Whiteness: How America's Immigrants Became White: The Strange Journey from Ellis Island to the Suburbs* (New York: Basic Books, 2005). See also Nell Irvin Painter, *The History of White People* (2010). The term *double consciousness* can be found in the classic work by W. E. B. DuBois, *The Souls of Black Folk,* ed. David Blight and Robert Gooding-Williams (Boston and New York: Bedford Books, 1997).

22. Frederick C. Harris, "Survey on Race, Politics and Society" (New York: ABC News, *USA Today,* and the Center on African American Politics and Society, 2008), 6.

23. Bobo and Hutchings, "Perceptions of Racial Group Competition: Extending Blumer's Theory of Group Position to a Multiracial Social Context," 54–55, 953.

24. To see the recent "hate map" of the Southern Poverty Law Center that tracks a number of groups it labels "hate groups" (though some of these groups are led by racial/ethnic minorities), follow this link: http://www.splcenter.org/get-informed/hate-map.

25. Tate, *What's Going On? Political Incorporation and the Transformation of Black Public Opinion*; Linda Lopez and Adrian D. Pantoja, "Beyond Black and White: General Support for Race-Conscious Policies among African Americans, Latinos, Asian Americans, and Whites," *Political Research Quarterly* 57, no. 4 (2004).

26. Tate, *What's Going On? Political Incorporation and the Transformation of Black Public Opinion.*

27. For a discussion of this disjuncture among African Americans, see Robert Charles Smith and Richard Seltzer, *Race, Class, and Culture: A Study in Afro-American Mass Opinion* (New York: State University of New York Press, 1992).

28. Walton and Smith, *American Politics and the African American Quest for Universal Freedom,* 69.

29. For a review of the complexities of the immigration issue, see Kenneth Jost, "Immigration Conflict," in *Issues in Race and Ethnicity: Selections from the CQ Researcher* (Washington, DC: CQ Press, 2013).

30. Shayla C. Nunnally, *Trust in Black America: Race, Discrimination, and Politics* (New York: New York University Press, 2012).

31. Dawson, *Black Visions: The Roots of Contemporary African-American Political Ideologies,* 61–62; Melissa Harris Lacewell, *Barbershops, Bibles, and Bet: Everyday Talk and Black Political Thought* (Princeton, NJ: Princeton University Press, 2004). The quotation from Kinder and Sanders is found in Kinder and Sanders, *Divided by Color: Racial Politics and Democratic Ideals,* 14.

32. Due to the small samples of minorities included in various surveys/polls, it has been difficult to discern if there has been actual movement in Black and Hispanic attitudes on same-sex marriage/marriage equality despite President Obama's announced support. But news stories and research reports conveyed the possibility of changes. See Scott Clement and Sandhya Somashekhar, "After President Obama's Announcement, Opposition to Same-Sex Marriage Hits Record Low," *Washington Post,* May 23, 2102; and "Two-Thirds of Democrats Now Support Gay Marriage," Pew Research Religion and Public Life Project, July 31, 2012.

33. Todd C. Shaw, *Now Is the Time! Detroit Black Politics and Grassroots Activism* (Durham, NC: Duke University Press, 2009), 15. Two good overviews of community-based grassroots activism are W. Dennis Keating, Norman Krumholz, and Philip Star, eds., *Revitalizing Urban Neighborhoods* (Lawrence, KS: University Press of Kansas, 1996); and Marion Orr, ed., *Transforming the City: Community Organizing and the Challenges of Political Change* (Lawrence: University Press of Kansas, 2007).

34. Sidney Verba, Kay Lehman Scholzman, and Henry E. Brady, *Voice and Equality: Civic Voluntarism in American Politics* (Cambridge, MA: Harvard University Press, 1995), 38–39.

35. Fredrick C. Harris, *Something Within: Religion in African-American Political Activism* (New York and Oxford: Oxford University Press, 1999); Michael Jones-Correa and David L. Leal, "Political Participation: Does Religion Matter?," *Political Research Quarterly* 54 (2001); Cary Funk and Greg Smith, "'Nones' on the Rise: One-in-Five Adults Have No Religious Affiliation," Pew Research Religion and Public Life Project, October 9, 2012.

36. A. Reynaldo Contreras and Leonard A. Valverde, "The Impact of *Brown* on the Education of Latinos," *Journal of Negro Education* 63, no. 3 (1994); Louis DeSipio, *Counting on the Latino Vote: Latinos as a New Electorate* (Charlottesville and London: University of Virginia Press, 1996), 45–46; Luis R. Fraga et al., *Latinos in the New Millenium: An Almanac of Opinion, Behavior, and Policy Preferences* (Cambridge and New York: Cambridge University Press, 2012), 386–405.

37. Janelle Wong, et al., *Asian American Political Participation* (New York: Russell Sage Foundation, 2011), 182–209.

38. Ari Berman, "North Carolina's Moral Mondays: An Inspiring Grassroots Movement Is Fighting Back against the GOP's Outrageous Budget Cuts and Attacks on Democracy," *The Nation,* July 18, 2013; Lizette Alvarez. "Florida Sit-in against 'Stand Your Ground'." The New York Times, 2013.

39. Shaw, *Now Is the Time! Detroit Black Politics and Grassroots Activism.*

40. Fredrick C. Harris, Valeria Sinclair-Chapman, and Brian D. McKenzie, *Countervailing Forces in African-American Civic Activism, 1973–1994* (Cambridge: Cambridge University Press, 2006), 21–22. Social capital is a construct that has been widely examined with regards to its impact on political participation and civic engagement. For examples of its impact in minority communities, especially the African American community, see R. Khari Brown and Ronald E. Brown, "Faith and Works: Church-Based Social Capital Resources and African American Political Activism," *Social Forces* 82, no. 2 (2003); Shawn A. Ginwright, "Black Youth Activism and the Role of Critical Social Capital in Black Community Organizations," *American Behavioral Scientist* 51, no. 3 (2007); Orr, *Black Social Capital;* and Shaw, *Now Is the Time! Detroit Black Politics and Grassroots Activism.*

41. Shaw, *Now Is the Time! Detroit Black Politics and Grassroots Activism,* 18–25.

42. Paula D. McClain and Joseph Stewart Jr., *"Can We All Get Along?" Racial and Ethnic Minorities in American Politics,* 5th ed. (Boulder, CO: Westview Press, 2010), 47–50.

43. Rodolfo Acuna, "Early Chicano Activism: Zoot Suits, Sleepy Lagoon, and the Road to Delano," in *The Latino Condition: A Critical Reader*, ed. Richard Delagado and Jean Stefanic (New York and London: New York University Press, 1998), 316–319.

44. McClain and Stewart, *"Can We All Get Along?" Racial and Ethnic Minorities in American Politics,* 54–55.

45. Saul Alinsky, *Rules for Radicals: A Practical Primer for Realistic Radicals* (New York: Vintage Books, 1972); Sanford Horwitt, *Let Them Call Me Rebel: Saul Alinsky, His Life, and Legacy* (New York: Knopf/Random House, 1989); Peg Knoepfle, *After Alinsky: Community Organizing in Illinois* (Springfield, IL: Sangamon State University, 1990). For a firsthand account of Obama's story as a "community organizer," see Barack Obama, *Dreams of My Father: A Story of Race and Inheritance* (New York: Three Rivers Press, 1995), 133–186.

46. Lydia Savage, "Justice for Janitors: Scales of Organzing and Representing Workers," *Antipode,* no. 3 (June 2006): 645–666; Marion Crain and Ken Matheny, "Labor's Identity Crisis," *California Law Review* 89, no. 6 (December 2001): 1767–1846.

47. Shaw, *Now Is the Time! Detroit Black Politics and Grassroots Activism,* 51–52.

48. Avis C. Vidal, "CDCs as Agents of Neighborhood Change: The State of the Art," in *Revitalizing Urban Neighborhoods*, ed. W. Dennis Keating, Norman Krumholz, and Philip Star (Lawrence: University Press of Kansas, 1996), 149–150.

49. Ibid., 150–151; Norman J. Glickman and Lisa J. Servon, "By the Numbers: Measuring Community Development Corporations' Capacity," *Journal of Planning Education and Research* 22 (March 2003).

50. Todd Shaw and Lester K. Spence, "Race and Representation in Detroit's Community Development Coalitions," *The Annals of the American Academy of Political and Social Science* 594 (2004): 129.

51. DSNI, Dudley Street Neighborhood Initiative "History," and "DNSI Historic Timeline," DSNI, http://www.dsni.org/history.

52. Refer to the following as examples of liberal versus conservative publications that make claims about militancy on the other side: David A. Lieb, "Tea Party Leaders Anxious about Extremists," Today News, March 15, 2010; and Aaron Klein, "New Black Panthers: Zimmerman Verdict Means 'War,'" WND, July 14, 2013.

53. Refer to "Latinos for Mitt Romney," https://www.facebook.com/pages/Latinos-For-Romney/101913399902095; and "American Indians for Obama," https://www.facebook.com/AmericanIndiansForObama.

CHAPTER 9

1. Quoted in Thomas Ehrlich, ed., *Civic Responsibility and Higher Education* (New York: Greenwood Publishing, 2000).

2. Alexis de Tocqueville, *Democracy in America*, Isaac Kramnick (ed., Introduction), Gerald Bevan (trans.) (New York: Penguin: 2003); Robert D. Putnam, *Bowling Alone: The Collapse and Revival of American Democracy* (New York: Simon and Shuster, 2003).

3. We rely on the *New York Times* estimates of group voting based on the national exit polls for 2008 and the CNN estimates for 2012. We are cautious about the accuracy of exit poll estimates for minority voting (and particularly for Latino and Asian American voting). The precincts used to collect exit poll data are often unrepresentative of the composition of minority communities. With this caution in mind, however, analysis of exit poll results across elections offer good indications of trends in group voting even if the estimate for a specific election are inaccurate (such as, for example, the estimate of President Bush's share of the Latino vote in 2004).

See David Leal, Matt Barreto, Jongho Lee, and Rodolfo O. de la Garza, "The Latino Vote in the 2004 Election," *PS: Political Science and Politics* 38, no. 1 (January 2005): 41–49.

4. David E. Wilkins, and Heidi K. Stark, *American Indian Politics and the American Political System* (Lanham, MD: Rowman and Littlefield, 2011), Table 7.7.

5. Ibid.

6. Melissa R. Michelson, Lisa García Bedolla, and Donald P. Green, *New Experiments in Minority Voter Mobilization: Third and Final Report of the California Votes Initiative* (San Francisco: The James Irvine Foundation, 2009).

7. Ricardo Ramírez, *Mobilizing Opportunities: The Evolving Latino Electorate and the Future of American Politics* (Charlottesville: University of Virginia Press, 2013).

8. Twenty-third Amendment to the U.S. Constitution, ratified 1961. Puerto Rico and other outlying territories of the United States do not participate in the general election for the U.S. president.

9. Non-U.S. citizens (including unauthorized residents of the United States) may not make campaign contributions to candidates for federal and most state and local offices. Although immigrants to permanent residence (immigrants with green cards) can legally make contributions, there is a great deal of confusion about who can and cannot make contributions both in immigrant communities and in campaigns. Immigrants (and foreign nationals) may volunteer in a campaign as long as they are not paid. As is the case with the limits on financial contributions, the specifics of who can volunteer are often misunderstood by campaigns as well as potential volunteers.

10. Sidney Verba, Kay Lehman Schlozman, and Henry E. Brady, *Voice and Equality: Civic Voluntarism in American Politics* (Cambridge, MA: Harvard University Press, 1995), particularly chap. 8; Shaun Bowler and Gary M. Segura, *The Future Is Ours: Minority Politics, Political Behavior, and the Multiracial Era of American Politics* (Washington, DC: CQ Press, 2012).

11. Nancy Burns, Kay Lehman Schlozman, and Sidney Verba, *The Private Roots of Public Action: Gender, Equality, and Political Participation* (Cambridge, MA: Harvard University Press, 2001), particularly chap. 11.

12. Although there is some scholarly analysis of Native American civic engagement on reservations, there is little research on the civic activities off of the reservations. See David E. Wilkins and Heidi Kiiwetinepinesiik Stark, *American Indian Politics and the American Political System* (Lanham, MD: Rowman and Littlefield, 2011).

13. Robert D. Putnam and David E. Campbell, *American Grace: How Religion Divides and United Us* (New York: Simon and Schuster, 2010), 26.

14. U.S. Bureau of the Census, *Voting and Registration in the Election of November 2012* (Washington, DC: U.S. Bureau of the Census, 2013), Table 4b, http://www.census.gov/hhes/www/socdemo/voting/publications/p20/2008/tables.html.

15. Bowler and Segura, *The Future Is Ours,* chap. 9.

16. Verba, Kay Schlozman, and Brady, *Voice and Equality;* Lisa García Bedolla and Melissa Michelson, *Mobilizing Inclusion: Transforming the Electorate through Get-Out-the-Vote Campaigns* (New Haven, CT: Yale University Press, 2013).

17. Theda Skocpol, *Diminished Democracy: From Membership to Management in American Civic Life* (Norman: University of Oklahoma Press, 2004); Janelle Wong, Democracy's Promise: Immigrants and American Civic Institutions (Ann Arbor: University of Michigan Press, 2004).

18. See references to Table 9.3, this volume.

19. The two major recent surveys of Latinos and Asian Americans have offered answer options in addition to the traditional seven-point scale from "very liberal" to "very conservative." The Asian American survey (the National Asian American Survey—2008) did not offer a midpoint on the scale. The Latino Survey (the Latino National Survey—2006) offered an answer option of "don't think of oneself in these terms".

20. Louis DeSipio, *Counting the Latino Vote: Latinos as a New Electorate.* (Charlottesville, VA: University Press of America, 1996); see particularly chap. 2.

21. David E. Wilkins, and Heidi K. Stark, *American Indian Politics and the American Political System* (Lanham, MD: Rowman and Littlefield, 2011), 179–185.

22. Taeku Lee and Karthick Ramakrishnan, "Asian Americans Turn Democratic," *Los Angeles Times,* November 23, 2012.

23. In the 2012 race for the Republican nomination for the presidency, the field included corporate executive Herman Cain, who is an African American. He predicted that, were he to get the nomination, he would carry one-third of the Black vote. Although he offered no evidence to substantiate this claim, and it seems unlikely that he could do so well, the prediction itself shows that Republicans are at a severe disadvantage among African Americans even under optimal circumstances.

24. Frank Newport, "Democrats Racially Diverse; Republicans Mostly White" (Princeton, NJ: Gallup Inc., 2013).

25. We present voting data for U.S. citizen adults. The gaps between White and minority communities are much larger if all adults, including non-U.S. citizen adults, are considered. We believe that the numbers presented here offer a more accurate picture, however. Media accounts report the data for all adults and offer a somewhat biased representation of nonvoting in minority communities.

26. One of the most successful examples is the Ya Es Hora campaign organized by national and local Latino community organizations in 2006 and 2008. See http://www.yaeshora.info/english.

27. Pew Charitable Trust Election Reform Information Project. 2007. *Election-Day Registration: A Case Study.* Washington, DC: electionline.org; http://www.pewtrusts.org/en/research-and-analysis/reports/0001/01/01/electionday-registration; National Conference of State Legislators, "Same Day Registration" (Denver, CO: National Conference of State Legislatures, 2013).

28. R. Michael Alvarez and Jonathan Nagler, *Election Day Voter Registration in California,* policy brief, Spring 2011, New York: Demos, http://www.demos.org/sites/default/files/publications/CA_EDR_Report-Demos.pdf.

29. Matt Barreto, *Ethnic Cues: The Role of Shared Ethnicity in Latino Political Participation* (Ann Arbor: University of Michigan Press, 2010).

30. Raymond E. Wolfinger and Jonathan Hoffman, "Registering and Voting with Motor Voter," *PS: Political Science and Politics* 34, no. 1 (March 2001): 85–92.

31. National Conference of State Legislatures, "Voter Identification Requirements." Denver, CO: National Conference of State Legislatures, October 17, 2013, http://www.ncsl.org/default.aspx?tabid = 16602.

32. John Fund, *Stealing Elections: How Voter Fraud Threatens Our Democracy* (San Francisco: Encounter Books, 2004).

33. Ari Berman, "The GOP War on Voting: In a Campaign Supported by the Koch Brothers, Republicans Are Working to Prevent Millions of Democrats from Voting Next Year," *Rolling Stone,* September 15, 2011.

34. Matt Barreto, Stephen A. Nuño, and Gabriel Sanchez, 2009. "The Disproportionate Impact of Voter ID Requirements on the Electorate—New Evidence from Indiana" *PS: Political Science and Politics* (January 2009): 111–116.

35. Matt A. Barreto, Ricardo Ramirez, Luis R. Fraga, and Fernando Guerra, "Why California Matters: How California Latinos Influence Presidential Elections," in Rodolfo O. de la Garza, Louis DeSipio, and David L. Leal, eds., *Beyond the Barrio: Latinos in the 2004 Elections* (Notre Dame, IN: University of Notre Dame Press, 2010), 201–220.

36. Ibid.

37. *Shelby County, Alabama v. Holder,* 133 S. Ct. 2612, 186 L. Ed. 2d 651 (2013).

38. *Shaw v. Reno,* 509 U.S. 630 (1993); *Bush v. Vera,* 517 U.S. 952 (1996).

39. The last enumeration of Black officeholders was conducted by the Joint Center for Political and Economic Studies in 2001. It documented 9,101 Black officeholders. The Joint Center estimates that this number increases by an average of 100 each year.

CHAPTER 10

1. American Civil Liberties Union, Racial Justice Program, https://www.aclu.org/racial-justice.

2. Carolina Reid and Elizabeth Laderman, "Constructive Credit: Revisiting the Performance of the Community Reinvestment Act Lending during the Subprime Crisis," in *The American Mortgage System: Crisis and Reform,* ed. Susan M. Wachter and Marvin M. Smith (Philadelphia: University of Pennsylvania Press, 2011), 159–186, chap. 7; Sadye Paez Errickson, Mayra Alvarez, Ralph Forquera, Tony Whitehead, Anthony Fleg, Tracey Hawkins, Dorothy Browne, M. Cookie Newsom, and Victor J. Schoenbach, "What Will Health-Care Reform Mean for Minority Health Disparities?" *Public Health Reports* (2011): 170–176.

3. For a complete and updated discussion of education, see Susan Aud, William Hussar, Grace Kena, Kevin Bianco, Lauren Frohlich, Jana Kemp, and Kim Tahan, "The Condition of Education 2011" (Washington, DC: National Center for Education Statistics and American Institutes for Research, 2011). For a discussion of one of the ongoing problems, see Judith R. Blau, *Race in the Schools: Perpetuating White Dominance?* (Boulder and London: Lynne Rienner, 2003).

4. Gabriel J. Chin, "Race, the War on Drugs, and the Collateral Consequences of Criminal Conviction," *Journal of Gender, Race and Justice* 6 (2002): 257.

5. Meda Chesney-Lind and Marc Mauer, *Invisible Punishment: The Collateral Consequences of Mass Imprisonment* (New York: The New Press, 2013).

6. Eric Grodsky and Michael Kurleander, eds., *Equal Opportunity in Higher Education: The Past and Future of California's Proposition 209* (Cambridge: Harvard Education Press, 2010); Erica Perez, "Despite Diversity Efforts, U.C. Minority Enrollment Down Since Prop. 209," *California Watch,* http://californiawatch.org/print/15031.

7. This definition of *ideology* is adapted from that of Michael Dawson in *Black Visions: The Roots of Contemporary African-American Political Ideologies* (Chicago and London: University of Chicago Press, 2001).

8. Thomas Sowell, *Black Rednecks and White Liberals* (San Francisco: Encounter Books, 2005); Linda Chavez, *Out of the Barrio : Toward a New Politics of Hispanic Assimilation* (New York: Basic Books, 1992); Dinesh D'Souza, *The End of Racism: Principles for a Multiracial Society* (New York: Free Press, 1996); Stephen Thernstrom and Abigail Thernstrom, *America in Black and White: One Nation, Indivisible* (New York: Simon and Shuster, 1997). A summary of their thinking is found in the work of Michael K. Brown et al., *White-Washing Race: The Myth of a Color-Blind Society* (Berkeley: University of California Press, 2003), 9–12.

9. Cornel West, *Race Matters* (New York: Vintage Books, 1994); Claire Kim, "The Racial Triangulation of Asian Americans," *Politics and Society* 27, no. 1 (1999); Rogers M. Smith, *Civic Ideals: Conflicting Visions of Citizenship in U.S. History* (New Haven: Yale University Press, 1997); Audrey Smedley, *Race in North America: Origin and Evolution of a Worldview* (Boulder, CO: Westview Press, 1993); Eduardo Bonilla-Silva, "The New Racism: Racial Structure in the United States, 1960s–1990s," in *Race, Ethnicity, and Nationality in the United States: Toward the Twenty-first Century,* ed. Paul Wong (Boulder, CO: Westview Press, 1999); Eduardo Bonilla-Silva, *Racism without Racists: Color-Blind Racism and the Persistence of Racial Inequality in the United States* (Lanham, MD: Rowman and Littlefield, 2006); Eduardo Bonilla-Silva, "From Bi-racial to Tri-racial: Towards a New System of Stratfication in the United States," *Ethnic and Racial Studies* 27, no. 6 (2004). For a brief discussion of "statistical discrimination," see WIlliam Julius Wilson, *When Work Disappears: The World of the New Urban Poor* (New York: Alfred A. Knopf Press, 1996), 136–137.

10. "Episode 2138," http://www.nofactzone.net/2006/11/02/episode-2138-1122006.

11. Brown et al., *White-Washing Race: The Myth of a Color-Blind Society.*

12. The quote from King can be found in his famous "I Have a Dream" speech in James M. Washington, ed. *A Testament of Hope: The Essential Writings of Martin Luther King, Jr.* (San Francisco, CA: Harper and Row, 1986), 219.

13. Colbert, Nation. "Nell Irvin Painter." http://thecolbertreport.cc.com/videos/wqbtkw/nell-irvin-painter.;

Brown et al., *White-Washing Race: The Myth of a Color-Blind Society;* Terry H. Anderson, *The Pursuit of Fairness: A History of Affirmative Action* (Oxford: Oxford University Press, 2004), 256–257; Grodsky and Kurleander, *Equal Opportunity in Higher Education: The Past and Future of California's Proposition 209.*

14. Charlie Savage, "Retroactive Reductions Sought in Crack Penalties," *New York Times,* June 1, 2011.

15. Ibid.; Anderson, *The Pursuit of Fairness: A History of Affirmative Action,* 67–72, 248–250.

16. Michael Tonry, *Punishing Race: A Continuing American Dilemma* (New York: Oxford University Press, 2011), 90–97; Lawrence D. Bobo and Victor Thompson, "Racialized Mass Incarceration: Poverty, Prejudice, and Punishment," in *Doing Race: 21 Essays for the 21st Century,* ed. Hazel Rose Markus and Paula M. L. Moya (New York and London: W. W. Norton, 2010); Martin Gilens, *Why Americans Hate Welfare: Race, Media, and the Politics of Antipoverty Policy* (Chicago: University of Chicago Press, 2000).

17. Grodsky and Kurleander, *Equal Opportunity in Higher Education: The Past and Future of California's Proposition 209.* The report that was quoted was Student Academic Services, "Undergraduate Access to the University of California after the Elimination of Race-Conscious Policies" (University of California, Office of the President, 2003), 3. Sentencing cases found in Office of the General Counsel, "Selected Supreme Court Cases on Sentencing Issues" (Washington, DC: United States Sentencing Commission, 2012), 20–21.

18. From 1865 to the 1970s, Democrats in the one-party South were in safe seats, which assured reelection and seniority on congressional committees. As committee chairmen they prevented civil rights bills from passing, which effectively kept non-Whites from getting elected to public office.

19. Mendez et al. v. Westminster School District of Orange County et al., 65 F. Supp. 544 (1946).See also Philippa Strum, *Mendez v. Westminister: School Desegregation and Mexican-American Rights* (Topeka: University Press of Kansas, 2010), 13, 27, 35, 111; *Gong Lum et al. v. Rice et al.,* 275 U.S. 78 (1927).

20. Strum, *Mendez v. Westminister: School Desegregation and Mexican-American Rights,* 111, 13, 27, 35; *Gong Lum et al. v. Rice et al.*

21. Strum, *Mendez v. Westminister: School Desegregation and Mexican-American Rights,* 111. For a great discussion of the complexity of *Brown,* see Charles J. Ogletree Jr., *All Deliberate Speed: Reflections of the*

First Half Century of Brown v. Board of Education (New York and London: W. W. Norton, 2004).

22. Tonry, *Punishing Race: A Continuing American Dilemma,* 81.

23. For a discussion of the enduring inequities, see Richard Rothstein, "For Public Schools, Segregation Then, Segregation Since: Education and the Unfinished March" (Washington, DC: Economic Policy Institute, 2013).

24. Linda Darling-Hammond, "Structured for Failure: Race, Resources, and Student Achievement," in *Doing Race: 21 Essays for the 21st Century,* ed. Markus and Moya.

25. Anderson, *The Pursuit of Fairness: A History of Affirmative Action,* 59–66.

26. The 1965 Howard University speech of President Lyndon B. Johnson can be found at Lyndon B. Johnson, "President Lyndon B. Johnson's Commencement Address at Howard University: 'To Fulfill These Rights,'" *Public Papers of the President of the United States* (Washington, DC: Government Printing Office, 1965).

27. Anderson, *The Pursuit of Fairness: A History of Affirmative Action:* 18–19, 82–109; ibid.

28. William G. Bowen and Derek Bok, *The Shape of the River: Long-Term Consequences of Considering Race in College and University Admissions* (Princeton, NJ: Princeton University Press, 1998).

29. Ibid., 4–7.

30. Ibid.

31. Ibid., 8.

32. Anderson, *The Pursuit of Fairness: A History of Affirmative Action,* 15–155; Bowen and Bok, *The Shape of the River: Long-Term Consequences of Considering Race in College and University Admissions,* 8.

33. Anderson, *The Pursuit of Fairness: A History of Affirmative Action,* 258–259.

34. Jeffrey E. Anderson, *Conjure in African American Society* (Baton Rouge: Louisiana State University Press, 2005), 267–273.

35. O'Connor quote from the majority opinion in *Grutter v. Bollinger,* found in *Barbara Grutter, Petitioner v. Lee Bollinger et al.,* 539 U.S., 10–11 (2003).

36. John Schwartz and Richard Perez-Pena, "Lacking Definitive Ruling on Affirmative Action, Both Sides Claim Victory," *New York Times,* June 24, 2013.

37. Miriam Jordan, "Illegal at Princeton: Dan-el Beat Poverty and Homelessness to Become a Star Student. He Still May Have to Leave the Country," *Wall Street Journal,* April 15, 2006.

38. Douglass Massey and Nancy Denton, *American Apartheid: Segregation and the Making of the*

Underclass (Cambridge: Harvard University Press, 1993); Darling-Hammond, "Structured for Failure: Race, Resources, and Student Achievement."

39.   Aud et al., "The Condition of Education 2011."

40.   Richard J. Herrnstein and Charles A. Murray, *The Bell Curve: Intelligence and Class Structure in American Life* (New York: Simon and Schuster, 1996); Joe L. Kincheloe, Shirley R. Steinberg, and Aaron D. Gresson III, eds., *Measured Lies: The Bell Curve Examined* (New York: St. Martins Press, 1996).

41.   Robert L. Linn, Eva L. Baker, and Damian W. Betebenner, "Accountability Systems: Implications of Requirements of the No Child Left Behind Act of 2001," *Educational Researcher* 31, no. 6 (2002): 3–16. The NCLB immediately had its critics because many states already had established standards for performance. While educators and legislators desired to improve education by setting uniform standards that held schools accountable and by requiring appreciable improvements in the performance of disadvantaged groups, this was difficult to achieve when there was no uniformity across the states or adequate federal subsidies to achieve these ends. Thus there were not sufficient incentives and resources to overcome the cumulative disadvantage of groups that lagged behind.

42.   Linda A. Renzulli and Lorraine Evans. "School Choice, Charter Schools, and White Flight," *Social Problems* 52, no. 3 (2005): 398–418. The Evaluation of Charter Schools Impacts, Final Report, June 2010 (U.S. Department of Education, National Center for Education Evaluation and Regional Assistance, 2010), 4029.

43.   Ana Maria Villegas and Tamara F. Lucas, "Diversifying the Teacher Workforce: A Retrospective and Prospective Analysis," *Yearbook of the National Society for the Study of Education* 103, no. 1 (2004).

44.   Aud et al., "The Condition of Education 2011," 29.

45.   John R. Logan, Jacob Stowell, and Deirdre Oakley, "Choosing Segregation: Racial Imbalance in American Public Schools, 1990–2000" (Albany, NY: U.S. Department of Education, Office of Educational Research and Improvement, Education Resources Information Center, 2002).

46.   "The Urgency of Now: The Schott 50 State Report on Public Education and Black Males, 2012" (Cambridge, MA: Schott Foundation for Public Education, 2012), 7.

47.   Judith R. Blau, *Race in the Schools: Perpetuating White Dominance?* (Boulder and London: Lynne Rienner, 2003), 237.

48.   Rosalind S. Chou and Joe R. Feagin, *The Myth of the Model Minority: Asian Americans Facing Racism* (Boulder and London: Paradigm, 2008). The quote is found in Michelle Alexander, *The New Jim Crow: Mass Incarceration in the Age of Colorblindness* (New York and London: The New Press, 2010). 2.

49.   Lawrence D. Bobo and Victor Thompson, "Racialized Mass Incarceration: Poverty, Prejudice, and Punishment," in *Doing Race: 21 Essays for the 21st Century,* ed. Markus and Moya, 324.

50.   Ibid., 326.

51.   This is a point we have and will reiterate throughout this chapter. See Chin, "Race, the War on Drugs, and the Collateral Consequences of Criminal Conviction"; Tonry, *Punishing Race: A Continuing American Dilemma,* 53–76; Alexander, *The New Jim Crow: Mass Incarceration in the Age of Colorblindness,* 95–136.

52.   Tracy L. Snell, "Capital Punishment, 2010—Statistical Tables" (Washington, DC: Bureau of Justice Statistics, Office of Justice Programs, 2011).

53.   *Slavery by Another Name* (documentary, 2012).

54.   The *Ruffin v. Commonwealth* quote is found in Alexander, *The New Jim Crow: Mass Incarceration in the Age of Colorblindness,* 31.

55.   Ibid., 30–35; Douglas A. Blackmon, *Slavery by Another Name: The Re-enslavement of Black America from the Civil War to World War II* (New York: Random House, 2009).

56.   For an excellent and detailed discussion of the cruelty of the criminal justice system under the old "Jim Crow," refer to ibid. For the parallels with the experiences of other groups, see Ronald Takaki, *A Different Mirror: A History of Multicultural America* (Boston: Little, Brown and Company, 1993), 166–84, 191–215.

57.   Joe T. Darden et al., *Detroit: Race and Uneven Development* (Philadelphia, PA: Temple University Press, 1987), 72–73.

58.   Alexander, *The New Jim Crow: Mass Incarceration in the Age of Colorblindness,* 41.

59.   Ibid., 35–50. Ward Churchill and Jim Vander Wall, *Agents of Repression: The FBI's Secret War against the Black Panther Party and the American Indian Movement* (Boston, MA: South End Press, 1990).

60.   Alexander, *The New Jim Crow: Mass Incarceration in the Age of Colorblindness,* 44.

61.   Republican National Committee, Growth and Opportunity Project, 2013, http://growthopp.gop.com/RNC_Growth_Opportunity_Book_2013.pdf.

62.   Alexander, *The New Jim Crow: Mass Incarceration in the Age of Colorblindness,* 45.

63.   Tonry, *Punishing Race: A Continuing American Dilemma,* 156.

64.   The quote is ibid., 21. Chap. 3 of ibid. provides the context

65. Karen Glover, *Racial Profiling: Research, Racism, and Resistance* (Lanham, MD: Rowman and Littlefield, 2009); Tonry, *Punishing Race: A Continuing American Dilemma:* 83–90; Lee Sigelman et al., "Police Brutality and Public Perceptions of Racial Discrimination: A Tale of Two Beatings," *Political Research Quarterly* 50 (1997); Lizette Alvarez, "A Florida Law Gets Scrutiny after a Teenager's Killing," *New York Times,* March 12, 2012.

66. David A. Harris, "Driving While Black: Racial Profiling on Our Nation's Highways," (American Civil Liberties Union, 1999); Tonry, *Punishing Race: A Continuing American Dilemma,* 59–70.

67. Tonry, *Punishing Race: A Continuing American Dilemma:* 47. Marie Doris Provine and Roxanne Lynn Doty, "The Criminalization of Immigrants as a Racial Project," *Journal of Contemporary Criminal Justice* 27, no. 3 (2011).

68. Jennifer Hochschild and Vesla Weaver, "The Skin Color Paradox and the American Racial Order," *Social Forces* 86, no. 2 (2007): 49, 644, as cited in Tonry, *Punishing Race: A Continuing American Dilemma,* 88.

69. Christopher Uggen, Sara Shannon, and Jeff Manza, "State-Level Estimates of Felon Disenfranchisement in the United States, 2010" (Washington, DC: The Sentencing Project, 2012); Ryan S. King, "Expanding the Vote: State Felony Disenfrachisement Reform, 1997–2008" (Washington, DC: The Sentencing Project, 2008), 3.

70. Joseph E. Kennedy, "The Jena Six, Mass Incarceration, and the Remoralizaiton of Civil Rights," *Harvard Civil Rights–Civil Liberties Law Review* 44 (2009); Alexander, *The New Jim Crow: Mass Incarceration in the Age of Colorblindness.*

71. Darren Wheelock, "Collateral Consequences and Racial Inequality: Felon Status Restrictions as a System of Disadvantage," *Journal of Contemporary Criminal Justice* 21 (2005).

72. Patricia Gurin et al., *Defending Diversity: Affirmative Action at the University of Michigan* (Ann Arbor: University of Michigan Press, 2004).

73. Andrew Gelman, Jeffrey Fagan, and Alex Kiss, "An Analysis of the New York City Police Department's 'Stop-and-Frisk' Policy in the Context of Claims of Racial Bias," *Journal of the American Statistical Association* 102, no. 479 (2007).

74. Rothstein, "For Public Schools, Segregation Then, Segregation Since: Education and the Unfinished March."

75. Tonry, *Punishing Race: A Continuing American Dilemma;* Bobo and Thompson, "Racialized Mass Incarceration: Poverty, Prejudice, and Punishment."

CHAPTER 11

1. Emma Lazarus, "The New Colossus," 1883: engraving on the Statue of Liberty National Monument, http://www.libertystatepark.com/emma.htm.

2. Michael LeMay and Elliott Robert Barkan, *U.S. Immigration and Naturalization Laws and Issues: A Documentary History* (Westport, CT: Greenwood Press, 1999), Document 6.

3. Barack Obama, "Remarks by the President on Comprehensive Immigration Reform," American University School of International Service, July 1, 2010, http://blogs.wsj.com/washwire/2010/07/01/transcript-of-obamas-immigration-speech.

4. Ibid.

5. Randall Monger, *Nonimmigrant Admissions to the United States: 2012* (Washington, DC: U.S. Department of Homeland Security, Office of Immigration Statistics, 2013).

6. Jeffrey Passel, D'Vera Cohn, and Ana Gonzalez-Barrera, *Population Decline of Unauthorized Immigrants Stalls, May Have Reversed* (Washington, DC: Pew Research Hispanic Trends Project, 2013).

7. Samuel P. Huntington, *Who Are We? The Challenges to America's National Identity* (New York: Simon and Schuster, 2004).

8. Aristide R. Zolberg, *A Nation by Design: Immigration Policy in the Fashioning of America* (Cambridge, MA, and New York: Harvard University Press and Russell Sage Foundation, 2006).

9. John Torpey, *The Invention of the Passport: Surveillance, Citizenship, and the State* (New York: Cambridge University Press, 2000); Kelly Lytle Hernández, *Migra! A History of the U.S. Border Patrol* (Berkeley: University of California Press, 2010).

10. Candice Lewis Bredbenner, *A Nationality of Her Own: Women, Marriage, and the Law of Citizenship* (Berkeley: University of California Press, 1998).

11. U.S. Department of Homeland Security, *2009 Yearbook of Immigration Statistics* (Washington, DC: Office of Immigration Statistics, 2010), http://www.dhs.gov/xlibrary/assets/statistics/yearbook/2009/ois_yb_2009.pdf, Table 2.

12. Daniel J. Tichenor, *Dividing Lines: The Politics of Immigration Control in the United States* (Princeton, NJ: Princeton University Press, 2002), chaps. 4, 5, and 6.

13. Andrew Gyory, *Closing the Gate: Race, Politics, and the Chinese Exclusion Act* (Chapel Hill: University of North Carolina Press, 1998); Zolberg, *A Nation by Design: Immigration Policy in the Fashioning of America.*

14. Tichenor, *Dividing Lines: The Politics of Immigration Control in the United States.*

15. Kitty Calavita, *Inside the State: The Bracero Program, Immigration, and the I.N.S.* (New York: Routledge, 1992).

16. Peter Schrag, *Not Fit for Our Society: Immigration and Nativism in America* (Berkeley: University of California Press, 2010); Peter Schrag, "Unwanted: Immigration and Nativism in America," Immigration Policy Center, *Perspectives* (September 2010).

17. Peter Slevin, "Deportation of Illegal Immigrants Increases under Obama Administration," *Washington Post,* July 26, 2010; U.S. Department of Homeland Security, *Immigration Enforcement Actions: 2012* (Washington, DC: U.S. Department of Homeland Security, Office of Immigration Statistics, 2013).

18. U.S. Department of State, n.d., "Diversity Visa (DV) Program," http://travel.state.gov/content/visas/english/immigrate/diversity-visa.html.

19. Peter H. Schuck and Rogers Smith, *Citizenship without Consent: Illegal Aliens in the American Polity* (New Haven: Yale University Press, 1985).

20. Audrey Singer, "Welfare Reform and Immigrants: A Policy Review," in Philip Kretsedemans and Ana Aparicio, eds., *Immigrants, Welfare Reform, and the Poverty of Policy* (Westport, CT: Praeger, 2004), 21–34.

21. Janelle Wong, *Democracy's Promise: Immigrants and American Civil Institutions* (Ann Arbor: University of Michigan Press, 2006); Irene Bloemraad, *Becoming a Citizen: Incorporating Immigrants and Refugees in the United States and Canada* (Berkeley: University of California Press, 2006).

22. Bryan C. Baker, *Naturalization Rates among IRCA Immigrants: A 2009 Update,* Office of Immigration Statistics Fact Sheet (Washington, DC: U.S. Department of Homeland Security, Office of Immigration Statistics, October 2010).

23. Nancy Rytina, *Estimates of the Legal Permanent Resident Population in 2009,* Office of Immigration Statistics Population Estimates (Washington, DC: U.S. Department of Homeland Security, Office of Immigration Statistics, 2010).

24. Harry Pachon and Louis DeSipio, *New Americans by Choice: Political Perspectives of Latino Immigrants* (Boulder, CO: Westview Press, 1994); Louis DeSipio, Natalie Masuoka, and Christopher Stout, "Asian American Immigrants as the New Electorate: Exploring Turnout and Registration of a Growing Community," *Asian American Policy Review* XVII (2008): 51–71.

25. Authors' analysis of Luis R. Fraga, John A. García, Rodney Hero, Michael Jones-Correa, Valerie Martinez-Ebers, and Gary M. Segura, *Latino National Survey* (LNS), 2006 [Computer file]. ICPSR20862-v1.

Miami, FL: Geoscape International [producer], 2006. Ann Arbor, MI: Inter-university Consortium for Political and Social Research [distributor].

26. Bloemraad, *Becoming a Citizen: Incorporating Immigrants and Refugees in the United States and Canada.*

27. Louis DeSipio, Harry P. Pachon, and W. Andrew Moellmer, *Reinventing the Naturalization Process at INS: For Better or Worse* (Claremont, CA: The Tomás Rivera Policy Institute, 2001).

28. Louis DeSipio, "Immigrant Incorporation in an Era of Weak Civic Institutions: Immigrant Civic and Political Participation in the United States," *American Behavioral Scientist* 55, no. 9 (September 2011); Bloemraad, *Becoming a Citizen: Incorporating Immigrants and Refugees in the United States and Canada,* 215–232.

29. Woodrow Wilson Center for Scholars, "Immigrants' Rights Marches, Spring 2006," http://www.wilsoncenter.org/index.cfm?topic_id=5949& fuseaction=topics.item&news_id=150685; Kim Voss and Irene Bloemraad, eds., *Rallying for Immigrant Rights: The Fight for Inclusion in 21st Century America* (Berkeley: University of California Press, 2011).

30. Louis DeSipio, "Drawing New Lines in the Sand: A Retrospective Evaluation of Immigration Reform's Failure in 2006 and 2007," in *Rallying for Immigrant Rights,* ed. Voss and Bloemraad.

31. Zolberg, *A Nation by Design: Immigration Policy in the Fashioning of America.*

32. The importance of immigrant/ethnic communities to national immigration reform debates is not unique to the current era; see Tichenor, *Dividing Lines: The Politics of Immigration Control in the United States.*

33. Frank D. Bean and Gillian Stevens, *America's Newcomers and the Dynamics of Diversity* (New York: Russell Sage Foundation, 2003); Alejandro Portes and Rubén Rumbaut, *Legacies: The Story of the Immigrant Second Generation* (Berkeley and New York: University of California Press and Russell Sage Foundation, 2001).

34. Samuel Huntington, *Who Are We? The Challenges to America's National Identity* (New York: Simon and Schuster, 2004); Stanley Renshon, *The 50% American: Immigration and National Identity in an Age of Terror* (Washington, DC: Georgetown University Press); Peter Spiro, *Beyond Citizenship: American Identity after Globalization* (New York: Oxford University Press, 2008).

35. Bean and Stevens, *America's Newcomers and the Dynamics of Diversity;* Portes and Rumbaut, *Legacies:*

The Story of the Immigrant Second Generation; Richard, Alba and Victor Nee, *Remaking the American Mainstream: Assimilation and Contemporary Immigration* (Cambridge, MA: Harvard University Press, 2003); Louis DeSipio and Carole Jean Uhlaner, "Immigrant and Native: Mexican American 2004 Presidential Vote Choice across Immigrant Generations," *American Politics Research* 35, no. 2 (March 2007): 176–201; Luis Ricardo Fraga, John A. Garcia, Rodney E. Hero, Michael Jones-Correa, Valerie Martinez-Ebers, and Gary M. Segura, *Latino Lives in America: Making It Home* (Philadelphia: Temple University Press, 2010); Philip Kasinitz, John H. Mollenkopf, Mary C. Waters, and Jennifer Holdaway, *Inheriting the City: The Children of Immigrants Come of Age* (Cambridge, MA, and New York: Harvard University Press and Russell Sage Foundation, 2008). For a more cautionary evaluation, see Edward E. Telles and Vilma Ortiz, *Generations of Exclusion: Mexican Americans, Assimilation, and Race* (New York: Russell Sage Foundation, 2008).

36. See PollingReport.com. 2010. *Immigration.* http://www.pollingreport.com/immigration.htm, for a compendium of polls on U.S. attitudes toward aspects of U.S. immigration policy; Jeffrey M. Jones, "Slim Majority of Americans Would Vote for DREAM Act Law," *Gallup,* December 10, 2010.

37. *Pew Research Center/National Journal Congressional Connection Poll* (Washington, DC: Pew Research Center and National Journal, September 9–12, 2010).

38. Louis DeSipio, "Transnational Politics and Civic Engagement: Do Home-Country Political Ties Limit Latino Immigrant Pursuit of U.S. Civic Engagement and Citizenship?" In Taeku Lee, S. Karthick Ramakrishnan, and Ricardo Ramírez, eds., *Transforming Politics, Transforming America: The Political and Civic Incorporation of Immigrants in the United States* (Charlottesville: University of Virginia Press, 2006), 106–126.

39. U.S. Department of Homeland Security, *2009 Yearbook of Immigration Statistics.*

CHAPTER 12

1. Manmohan Singh, "Prime Minister Dr. Manmohan Singh's Speech to the Ina Community in Washington," Embassy of India, November 25, 2009, http://www.indianembassy.org/prdetai11649/prime-minister-dr.-manmohan-singhandrsquo%3Bs-speech-to-the-indian-community-in-washington.

2. Mark Wyman, *Round-trip to America: The Immigrants Return to Europe, 1880–1930* (Ithaca, NY: Cornell University Press, 1993), 11.

3. Sophie Quinn-Judge, *Ho Chi Minh: The Missing Years* (Berkeley: University of California Press, 2002).

4. World Bank, *Migration and Remittance Flows: Recent Trends and Outlook 2013–2016* (Washington, DC: World Bank, 2013); World Bank, *Migrant Remittance Outflows,* 2014,http://siteresources.worldbank.org/INTPROSPECTS/Resources/334934–1288990760745/RemittanceData_Outflows_Oct2013.xls.

5. Rodolfo de la Garza and Briant Lindsay Lowell, eds., *Sending Money Home: Hispanic Remittances and Community Development* (Lanham, MD: Rowman and Littlefield, 2002).

6. The World Bank defines migrant remittances as the sum of workers' remittances, compensation of employees, and migrants' transfers. Workers' remittances are current private transfers from migrant workers who are considered "residents" of the host country to recipients in the workers' country of origin. The World Bank considers migrants as "residents" if they live in the host country for one year or longer, regardless of their immigration status. If the migrants have lived in the host country for less than one year, their entire income in the host country is classified as compensation of employees and counted in these figures. Migrants' transfers are the net worth of migrants' assets that are transferred from one country to another at the time of migration (for a period of at least one year). These figures do not include what we have defined as "collective remittances" and rely on statistical estimates of informal transfers (such as monies carried across the border and not transferred through the banking system). Other estimates find considerably higher estimates of U.S. remittances to Mexico, as high as $21.5 billion in 2009.

7. Authors' analysis of Luis R. Fraga, John A. García, Rodney Hero, Michael Jones-Correa, Valerie Martinez-Ebers, and Gary M. Segura, Latino National Survey (LNS), 2006 [Computer file]. ICPSR20862-v1. Miami, FL: Geoscape International [producer], 2006. Ann Arbor, MI: Inter-university Consortium for Political and Social Research [distributor].

8. Michael Peter Smith and Matt Bakker, *Citizenship across Borders: The Political Transnationalism of El Migrante* (Ithaca, NY: Cornell University Press, 2008).

9. Josefina Vázquez Mota, "El Programa Iniciativa Ciudadana 3X1," *Foreign Affairs en Español* 5, no. 3 (July–September 2005).

10. Louis DeSipio, "Sending Money Home . . . for Now: Remittances and Immigrant Adaptation in the

United States," in de la Garza and Lindsay Lowell, eds., *Sending Money Home: Hispanic Remittances and Community Development,* 157–188.

11. Michael Smith and Luis Guarnizo, *Transnationalism from Below* (Piscataway, NJ: Transaction Publishers, 1988).

12. Kim Voss and Irene Bloemraad, eds., *Rallying for Immigrant Rights: The Fight for Inclusion in 21st Century America* (Berkeley: University of California Press, 2011).

13. Manuel Orozco and Rebecca Rouse, "Migrant Hometown Associations and Opportunities for Development: A Global Perspective" (Washington, DC: Migration Policy Institute, 2007), http://www.migra tioninformation.org/feature/print.cfm?ID = 579.

14. S. Karthick Ramakrishnan and Celia Viramontes, "Civic Spaces: Mexican Hometown Associations and Immigrant Participation," *Journal of Social Issues* 66, no. 1 (2010): 155–173.

15. Louis DeSipio, "Drawing New Lines in the Sand: Evaluating the Failure of Immigration Reforms from 2006 to the Beginning of the Obama Administration," in Voss and Bloemraad, eds., *Rallying for Immigrant Rights: The Fight for Inclusion in 21st Century America,* 215–232; Ricardo Ramírez, *Mobilizing Opportunities: The Evolving Latino Electorate and the Future of American Politics* (Charlottesville: University of Virginia Press, 2014).

16. Authors' analysis of Luis R. Fraga, John A. García, Rodney Hero, Michael Jones-Correa, Valerie Martinez-Ebers, and Gary M. Segura, Latino National Survey (LNS), 2006 [Computer file]. ICPSR20862-v1. Miami, FL: Geoscape International [producer], 2006. Ann Arbor, MI: Inter-university Consortium for Political and Social Research [distributor].

17. Louis DeSipio, with Harry Pachon, Rodolfo O. de la Garza, and Jongho Lee, *Immigrant Politics at Home and Abroad: How Latino Immigrants Engage the Politics of Their Home Communities and the United States* (Claremont, CA: Tomás Rivera Policy Institute, 2003).

18. Jean-Michel Lafleur and Leticia Calderón Chelius, "Assessing Emigrant Participation in Home Country Elections: The Case of Mexico's 2006 Presidential Election," *International Migration* 49, no. 3 (2011): 99–124.

19. Institute for Democracy and Electoral Assistance, *Voting from Abroad: The International IDEA Handbook* (Stockholm, Sweden: International IDEA, 2007), http://www.idea.int/publications/voting_ from_abroad/index.cfm.

20. Authors' analysis of Luis R. Fraga, John A. García, Rodney Hero, Michael Jones-Correa, Valerie Martinez-Ebers, and Gary M. Segura, Latino National Survey (LNS), 2006 [Computer file]. ICPSR20862-v1. Miami, FL: Geoscape International [producer], 2006. Ann Arbor, MI: Inter-university Consortium for Political and Social Research [distributor].

21. Ibid.

22. Michael Jones Correa, "Under Two Flags: Dual Nationality in Latin America and Its Consequences for Naturalization in the United States," *International Migration Review* 35, no. 4 (Winter 2001): 997–1029.

23. David Fitzgerald, "Nationality and Migration in Modern Mexico," *Journal of Ethnic and Migration Studies* 31, no. 1 (January 2005): 171–191; David Fitzgerald, *A Nation of Emigrants: How Mexico Manages Its Migration* (Berkeley: University of California Press, 2009).

24. U.S. law establishes different standards for the children of married couples in which both are U.S. citizens or in which one is a U.S. citizen, and for the children of nonmarried couples in which the father is a U.S. citizen or the mother is a U.S. citizen. The consistent characteristic of each of these possible parentages is that the U.S. citizen parent(s) have had a legal residence in the United States prior to the child's birth. This ensures that U.S. citizenship cannot become an ancestral legacy for the children of citizens who have never lived in the United States. For specifics, see "Acquisition of U.S. Citizenship by a Child Born Abroad," U.S. Department of State, 2011, http://travel.state.gov/law/citizenship/citizen-ship_5199.html.

25. Peter Spiro, *Beyond Citizenship* (New York: Oxford University Press, 2008).

26. George W. Bush, "Detention, Treatment, and Trial of Certain Non-Citizens in the War against Terrorism," Military Order, November 13, 2001, 66 FR 57833.

27. *Hamdan v. Rumsfeld,* 548 U.S. 557 (2006); *Boumediene v. Bush,* 553 U.S. 723 (2008).

28. Marc Jayson Climaco, "Why Federal Court Is the Right Way to Try Dzhokhar Tsarnaev" (Washington, DC: Human Rights First, 2013).

29. Gilbert González, *Mexican Consuls and Labor Organizing: Imperial Politics in the American Southwest* (Austin: University of Texas Press, 1999).

30. See *Korematsu v. United States,* 323 U.S. 214 (1944).

31. Approximately 110,000 Japanese immigrants and Japanese American residents of the West Coast of the United States were interned during World War II. Approximately 11,000 Germans and 1,000 Italians were interned.

32. Center for Humans Rights and Global Justice and the Asian American Defense and Education Fund, *Under the Radar: Muslims Deported, Detained, and Denied on Unsubstantiated Terrorism Allegations* (New York:

NYU School of Law, 2011), http://www.chrgj.org/projects/docs/undertheradar.pdf.

33. Rodolfo de la Garza and Jesus Velasco, *Bridging the Border: Transforming U.S.-Mexico Relations* (Lanham, MD: Rowman and Littlefield, 1997); Carlos González-Gutierrez, "Fostering Identities: Mexico's Relationship with Its Diaspora," *Journal of American History* 86, no. 2 (1999): 545–567.

34. David Ayón, "Mexican Policy and Émigré Communities in the U.S." Background paper presented at the seminar "Mexican Migrant Social and Civic Participation in the United States," Woodrow Wilson Center for Scholars, Washington DC, November 4–5, 2005, http://www.wilsoncenter.org/news/docs/Ayon-MexPolicy1.pdf. Also see http://www.ime.gob.mx, for information on the current activities of Instituto de los Mexicanos en el Exterior (the Institute for Mexicans Abroad, IME).

35. United States Department of State, *Foreign Consular Offices in the United States* (Washington, DC: U.S. Department of State, 2013).

36. Stanley A. Renshon, *The 50% American: Immigration and National Identity in an Age of Terror* (Washington, DC: Georgetown University Press, 2005).

37. Samuel P. Huntington, *Who Are We? The Challenges to America's National Identity* (New York: Simon and Schuster, 2004), chaps. 8 and 9.

38. Ibid., 221.

39. Quoted in Edward S. Morgan, *Not Your Usual Founding Father: Selected Readings from Benjamin Franklin* (New Haven: Yale University Press, 2006), 149–150.

40. Madison Grant, *The Passing of the Great Race; or, The Racial Basis of European History* (New York: Charles Scribner's and Sons, 1918), 89–90.

41. Luis Ricardo Fraga, John A. García, Rodney E. Hero, Michael Jones-Correa, Valerie Martínez-Ebers, and Gary M. Segura, *Latino Lives in America: Making It Home* (Philadelphia, PA: Temple University Press, 2010), 124.

42. Pei-te Lien, M. Margaret Conway, and Janelle Wong, *The Politics of Asian Americans: Diversity and Community* (New York: Routledge, 2004), chap. 2; Pei-te Lien and Janelle Wong, "Like Latinos? Explaining the Transnational Political Behaviors of Asian Americans," in Christian Collet and Pei-te Lien, eds., *The Transnational Politics of Asian Americans* (Philadelphia, PA: Temple University Press, 2009), 137–152.

43. Louis DeSipio, "Transnational Politics and Civic Engagement: Do Home-Country Political Ties Limit Latino Immigrant Pursuit of U.S. Civic Engagement and Citizenship?" In Taeku Lee, S. Karthick Ramakrishnan, and Ricardo Ramírez, eds., *Transforming Politics, Transforming America: The Political and Civic Incorporation of Immigrants in the United States* (Charlottesville: University of Virginia Press, 2006), 106–126.

44. Francis Njubi Nesbitt, *Race for Sanctions: African Americans against Apartheid, 1946–1994* (Bloomington: Indiana University Press, 2004).

45. National Association for the Advancement of Colored People, "Advocacy and Issues," 2011, http://www.naacp.org/programs.

46. National Council of La Raza, "Issues and Programs," 2011, http://www.nclr.org/index.php/issues_and_programs.

47. Asian American Legal Defense and Education Fund, "Program Overview," 2011, http://aaldef.org/programs.

48. See, for example, TransAfrica, http://transafrica.org.

CHAPTER 13

1. Patricia Hill Collins, "It's All in the Family: Intersections of Gender, Race, and Nation," *Hypatia* 13, no. 3 (Summer 1998): 63; Uma Narayan and Sandra Harding. "Introduction, Border Crossings: Multicultural and Postcoloinal Feminist Challenges to Philsophy (Part I)," *Hypatia: A Journal of Feminist Philosophy* 13, no. 2 (May 2009): 1–6.

2. Nell Irvin Painter, *The History of White People* (New York: W. W. Norton, 2010).

3. Cindy Boren, "President Obama: Donald Sterling's Alleged Comments 'Incredibly Offensive,'" *Washington Post,* April 27, 2014.

4. Peter Kolchin, "Whiteness Studies: The New History of Race in America," *Journal of American History* 89, no. 1 (2002).

5. Matt A. Barreto, Stephen A. Nuno, and Gabriel R. Sanchez, "Voter ID Requirements and the Disenfranchisements of Latino, Black, and Asian Voters" (paper presented at the Annual Meeting of the American Political Science Association, Chicago, Illinois, 2007); Spencer Overton, "Voter Identification," *Michigan Law Review* (2007); David Eugene Wilkins and K. Tsianina Lomawaima, *Uneven Ground: American Indian Sovereignty and Federal Law* (Norman: University of Oklahoma Press, 2001).

6. Painter, *The History of White People,* 359–373.

7. Ronald Takaki, *A Different Mirror: A History of Multicultural America,* rev. ed. (eBookIt.com, 2012).

8. Eduardo Bonilla-Silva, "From Bi-Racial to Tri-Racial: Towards a New System of Racial Stratification in the USA," *Ethnic and Racial Studies* 27, no. 6 (2004).

9. Vijay Sekhon. "The Civil Rights of 'Others': Antiterrorism, the Patriot Act, and Arab and South Asian American Rights in Post-9/11 American Society." *Texas Journal on Civil Liberties and Civil Rights* 8, no. 1 (Spring 2003): 117–148.

10. Paula S. Rothenberg, *White Privilege* (New York: Macmillan, 2008).

11. Ira Berlin, *Many Thousands Gone: The First Two Centuries of Slavery in North America* (Cambridge, MA: Harvard University Press, 1998); Robert Wooster, *The Military and United States Indian Policy 1865–1903* (Lincoln: University of Nebraska Press, 1995).

12. Bill Plaschke, "Magic Johnson Blasts Sterling," *Los Angeles Times,* April 28, 2014; Nathan Fenno, "Clippers Owner Donald Sterling Is No Stranger to Race Lawsuits," *Los Angeles Times,* April 26, 2014.

13. Angelique C. Harris, "Marginalization by the Marginalized: Race, Homophobia, Heterosexism, and 'the Problem of the 21st Century,'" *Journal of Gay and Lesbian Social Services* 21, no. 4 (2009).

14. Mary Bernstein and Verta Taylor, "Identity Politics," in *The Wiley-Blackwell Encyclopedia of Social and Political Movements* (Wiley Online Library, 2005).

15. Iris Marion Young, *Justice and the Politics of Difference.* (Princeton, NJ: Princeton University Press, 1990). In *Stanford Encyclopedia of Philosophy Online,* s.v. "Identity Politics," http://plato.stanford.edu/entries/identity-politics.

16. Ben L. Martin, "From Negro to Black to African American: The Power of Names and Naming," *Political Science Quarterly* (1991); Barbara Ryan, *Feminism and the Women's Movement: Dynamics of Change in Social Movement Ideology and Activism* (New York: Routledge, 2013); Lillian Comas-Diaz, "Hispanics, Latinos, or Americanos: The Evolution of Identity," *Cultural Diversity and Ethnic Minority Psychology* 7, no. 2 (2001); Didi Khayatt, "Toward a Queer Identity," *Sexualities* 5, no. 4 (2002).

17. For one of the classic anthologies regarding the Gay Rights Movement and Queer Theory, see David Halperin and Henry Abelove, *The Lesbian and Gay Studies Reader* (New York and London: Routledge, 1993).

18. Linda Napikoski, About.com, "What Is the Problem That Has No Name?" s.v. "Women's History," http://womenshistory.about.com/od/bettyfriedan/a/Problem-That-Has-No-Name.htm.

19. *Encyclopaedia Britannica Online,* s.v. "Women's Movement," http://www.britannica.com/EBchecked/topic/647122/womens-movement.

20. Cynthia Deitch, "Gender, Race, and Class Politics and the Inclusion of Women in Title VII of the 1964 Civil Rights Act," *Gender and Society* 7, no. 2 (1993).

21. Jone Johnson Lewis, About.com, "Coverture," s.v. "Women's History," http://womenshistory.about.com/od/laws/g/coverture.htm.

22. Rosalyn Baxandall and Linda Gordon, "Second Wave Feminism," *A Companion to American Women's History* (2002).

23. "But Some of Us Are Brave: A History of Black Feminism in the United States," *Thistle* 9, no. 1 (n.d.), http://www.mit.edu/~thistle/v9/9.01/6blackf.html.

24. Equal Credit Opportunity Act of 1974, 15 U.S.C. § 1691.

25. Leslie W. Gladstone, "The Long Road to Equality: What Women Won from the ERA Ratification Effort," Library of Congress, *American Women,* http://memory.loc.gov/ammem/awhhtml/aw03e/aw03e.html.

26. "The Gender Wage Gap: 2013 Differences by Race and Ethnicity, No Growth in Real Wages for Women," in *Fact Sheet* (Washington, DC: Institute for Women's Policy Research, 2014).

27. "Union Members Summary," in *Economic News Release* (Washington, DC: Bureau of Labor Statistics, 2014).

28. Estelle Sommeiller and Mark Price, "The Increasingly Unequal States of America: Income Inequality of State, 1917 to 2011," in *Economic Analysis and Research Network Report* (Washington, DC: Economic Analysis and Research Network, 2014), 3. DC: Economic Analysis and Research Network, 2014.

29. Costas Panagopoulos, "Occupy Wall Street Survey: Initial Report, October 2011," Elections and Campaign Management Research, http://www.fordham.edu/academics/programs_at_fordham_/elections_campaign_/research_31711.asp.

30. Guida West, *The National Welfare Rights Movement: The Social Protest of Poor Women* (New York: Praeger, 1981); Robert Pollin and Stephanie Luce, *The Living Wage* (New Press, 2000).

31. "Timeline: Milestones in the American Gay Rights Movement," http://www.pbs.org/wgbh/americanexperience/features/timeline/stonewall.

32. Ibid.; David Carter, *Stonewall: The Riots That Sparked the Gay Revolution* (Macmillan, 2010).

33. Marc Stein, *Rethinking the Gay and Lesbian Movement* (New York: Routledge, 2012), 41–78.

34. Ibid.

35. Trevor G. Gates and Colleen G. Rodgers, "Repeal of Don't Ask Don't Tell as 'Policy Window': A Case for Passage of the Employment Non-Discrimination Act," *International Journal of Discrimination and the Law* 14, no. 1 (2013).

36. R. Albelda and Williams Institute, *Poverty in the Lesbian, Gay, and Bisexual Community* (Los Angeles: Williams Institute, UCLA School of Law, 2009); K. Boykin, *One More River to Cross: Black and Gay in America* (New York: Knopf Doubleday, 1997).

37. Kimberle Crenshaw, "Demarginalizing the Intersection of Race and Sex: A Black Feminist Critique of Antidiscrimination Doctrine, Feminist Theory and Antiracist Politics," *University of Chicago Legal Forum* 19 (1989): 140.

38. T. Wise, *Colorblind: The Rise of Post-Racial Politics and the Retreat from Racial Equity* (San Francisco: City Lights Books, 2013), 21.

39. M. L. Oliver and T. M. Shapiro, *Black Wealth, White Wealth: A New Perspective on Racial Inequality* (New York: Routledge, 2006); "The Gender Wage Gap: 2013 Differences by Race and Ethnicity, No Growth in Real Wages for Women," 2.

40. *San Antonio School District v. Rodriquez*, 411 U.S. 1 (1973).

41. Karen E. Rosenblum and Toni-Michelle C. Travis, eds., *The Meaning of Difference: American Constructs of Race, Sex and Gender, Social Class, Sexual Orientation, and Disability*, 6th ed. (New York: McGraw-Hill, 2012), 403.

42. *San Antonio School District v. Rodriquez*, 411 U.S. 1 (1973)

43. Rosenblum and Travis, eds., *The Meaning of Difference: American Constructs of Race, Sex and Gender, Social Class, Sexual Orientation, and Disability*, 6th ed., 405.

44. Sam Roberts, "Identity Politics, in a Brand-New Form," *New York Times,* September 14, 2013, http://www.nytimes.com/2013/09/15/sunday-review/identity-politics-in-a-brand-new-form.html.

45. Krissah Thompson and Lonnae O'Neal Parker, "New York's Incoming First Family Says It All with Their Hair," *Washington Post,* November 6, 2013, http://www.washingtonpost.com/lifestyle/style/new-yorks-incoming-first-family-says-it-all-with-their-hair/2013/11/06e01ab558–4702–11e-a196–3544a03c2351 story.html.

46. Kristen A. Lee, "Mayoral Candidate Bill de Blasio's wife Chirlane McCray, a Former Lesbian, Opens Up about Falling in Love with a Man," *New York Daily News,* May 9, 2013, http://www.nydailynews.com/news/election/de-blasio-wife-chirlane-mccray-talks-lesbian-article-1.1339398.

47. *Stanford Encyclopedia of Philosophy Online,* s.v. "Identity Politics," http://plato.stanford.edu/entries/identity-politics.

48. Wise, *Colorblind: The Rise of Post-Racial Politics and the Retreat from Racial Equity,* 21.

49. Ibid., 153–194.

50. C. J. Kim, *Bitter Fruit: The Politics of Black-Korean Conflict in New York City* (New Haven: Yale University Press, 2003); Sallie A Marston, "Making Difference: Conflict over Irish Identity in the New York City St. Patrick's Day Parade," *Political Geography* 21, no. 3 (2002).

51. S. Bowler and G. Segura, *The Future Is Ours: Minority Politics, Political Behavior, and the Multiracial Era of American Politics* (Washington, DC: CQ Press, 2012), 65–68.

52. J. Kotkin, *The Next Hundred Million: America in 2050* (New York: Penguin, 2010).

53. Ethan Bronner, "Asian Americans in the Argument," *New York Times,* November 1, 2012, http://www.nytimes.com/2012/11/04/education/edlife/affirmative-action-a-complicated-issue-for-asian-americans.html?pagewanted = all&_r = 0.

54. Nadra Kareem Nittle, About.com, "Affirmative Action Bans in Universities: Who Gains?" s.v. "Race Relations."

55. Sally Kohn, "Affirmative Action Has Helped White Women More Than Anyone," *Idea Times,* June 17, 2013, http://ideas.time.com/2013/06/17/affirmative-action-has-helped-white-women-more-than-anyone.

56. Ibid.

57. Nelson D. Schwartz, "The Middle Class Is Steadily Eroding: Just Ask the Business World," *New York Times,* February 2, 2014, http://www.nytimes.com/2014/02/03/business/the-middle-class-is-steadily-eroding-just-ask-the-business-world.html.

58. Ibid.

59. Amy Wilkins and Frederick Hess, interview by Neal Conan, *Talk of the Nation,* "Income, More Than Race, Is Driving Achievement Gap," February 13, 2012, http://www.npr.org/2012/02/13/146816813/income-more-than-race-is-driving-achievement-gap.

60. Christopher S. Elmendorf and Douglas M. Spencer, "After *Shelby County:* Getting Section 2 of the VRA to Do the Work of Section 5," *UC Davis Legal Studies Research Paper,* no. 372 (2014); Michael Parkin and Frances Zlotnick, "The Voting Rights Act and Latino Voter Registration Symbolic Assistance for English-Speaking Latinos," *Hispanic Journal of Behavioral Sciences* 36, no. 1 (2014).

Index

Barretto, Matt, 250 (fig.)
Bates, Ruby, 105
Baton Rouge, LA, 257–258
Battle of Little Big Horn (1876), 46
Bayonet Constitution (1898, Hawaii), 148
Becker, David, 229
Bennett, Nathaniel, 152
Berkeley, William, 77
Berthold Indian Tribal Business Council,
    60 (photo)
Bethune, Mary McLeod, 95, 98
BIA. *See* Bureau of Indian Affairs (BIA)
Bigler, John, 152
Birmingham, AL
    African American voting in, 213 (photo)
    African Americans migration to, 97
    Freedom Rides and, 105
    labor activism in, 100
    "Letter from a Birmingham Jail" (King) and, 105
    school integration in, 209
    voting rights in, 221
The Birth of a Nation film (1915), 88, 97
Birthright citizenship, 341–342, 352–353
Black Belt region (South), 82
Black Civil Rights Movement, 207–209
Black Hills, SD
    Battle of Little Big Horn (1876) and, 46
    Treaty of Fort Laramie (1868) and, 46, 64
Black nationalism, 106, 362
Black Nationalist groups, 418–419 (n33)
Black Panthers, 106, 238, 319, 419 (n33)
Black politics
    all-Black national conventions and, 85–86
    antislavery resistance and, 85–86
    Black community-building and,
        84–85, 350, 442 (n32)
    Black nationalism *vs.* liberal intergeneration's
        and, 86
    Black popular culture factor in, 240
    Black WW II service members and, 101
    civil society and, 84–85, 95–96,
        108–109, 424 (n43)
    Fair Employment Practices
        Committee (FEPC), 101
    grassroots activism and, 100, 101–102,
        237, 256–261
    from Great Depression to World War II,
        98–101, 99 (fig.)
    labor movement and, 100
    NAACP Civil Rights legal victories and,
        99 (fig.), 155
    National Negro Congress and, 100
    New Deal programs discrimination and, 100
    F. D. Roosevelt's economic reform and, 100–101
    Scottsboro Boys case and, 100
    Social Security discrimination and, 100
    Underground Railroad and, 86
    votes by party across racial/ethnic groups,
        1972–2012, 3–4, 3 (table)
    See also African Americans; Civil Rights
        Movement (1950s-1970s)
Black Power (Carmichael and Hamilton), 13
Black Power Movement (1966), 102, 106, 387
Black Reconstruction in America, 1860–1880
    (Du Bois), 88
*Black Space: Imagining Race in Science Fiction
    Film* (Nama), 14
Black term, 387
*Black Visions: The Roots of Contemporary
    African-American Political Ideologies*
    (Dawson), 235 (quote)
Black Women Organized for Action (BWAO), 390
Black Women's Club Movement, 98
Blackmon, Douglas A., 317
Blackmun, Harry, 1 (quote)
Blalock, Hubert, 146
Blood quantum concept
    Native Americans and, 54–56, 66, 66 (table)
Blumenbach, Johann Friedrich, 16
Blumer, Herbert, 244
Bobo, Lawrence, 238, 243–244, 246, 298
Boehner, John, 385
Bolden, Wiley, 218
Bonilla-Silva, Eduardo, 10, 13, 15, 296, 386
Boston, MA
    Boston Marathon Bomber trial and, 373–374
    Boston Tea Party and, 147
    busing in, 303
    Dudley Street Neighborhood Initiative
        (DSNI) in, 261
    ethnic-White immigrants in, 175, 186
    free Blacks in, 83
    Native Americans relocated to, 60–61
    Robert Gould Shaw Memorial in, 87 (photo)
Boston Globe, 210
Boston Tea Party (1773), 147

⑤SAGE. research**methods**

The essential online tool for researchers from the world's leading methods publisher

Find exactly what you are looking for, from basic explanations to advanced discussion

More content and new features added this year!

"I have never really seen anything like this product before, and I think it is really valuable."

John Creswell, University of Nebraska–Lincoln

Discover **Methods Lists**— methods readings suggested by other users

Watch video interviews with leading methodologists

Explore the **Methods Map** to discover links between methods

Search a custom-designed taxonomy with more than 1,400 qualitative, quantitative, and mixed methods terms

Uncover more than 120,000 pages of book, journal, and reference content to support your learning

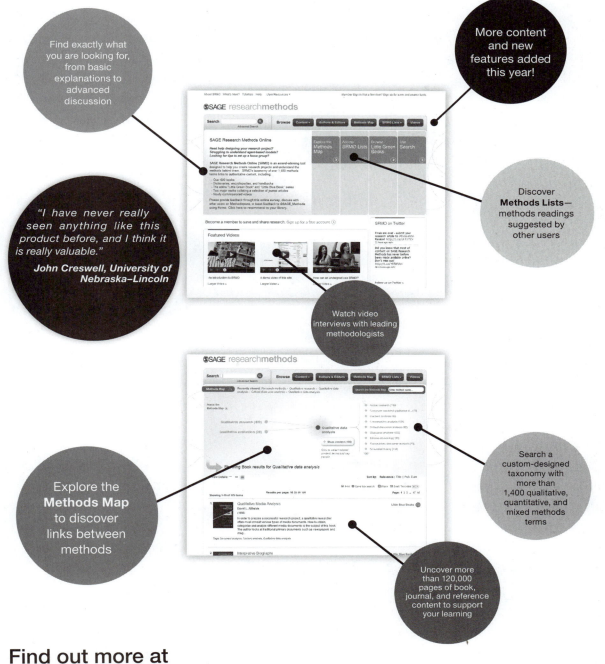

Find out more at
www.sageresearchmethods.com